I could not have made this journey without the support of my family and loving wife, Michelle.

This book is dedicated to the newest member of my family, Emily Diane White.

— Kevin White

Much appreciation to my amazing wife, Berit Benson, and her uncanny ability to sense when I needed coffee the most.

—Gordon Davisson

Acknowledgments In addition to the amazing Peachpit staff members who were instrumental in completing this work, we would like to thank the development team for their hard work: Adam Karneboge and Shane Ross. Additional thanks go out to those involved with Apple Training & Communications including Eugene Evon, Judy Lawrence, John Signa, Cindy Waller, Anne Renehan, Margaret Bethel, Arek Dreyer, Ben Greisler, and Benjamin Levy. Also, the accuracy of this guide is greatly enhanced from my experience at camps held by the Apple Professional Services team, which includes Schoun Regan, David Starr, Patrick Gallagher, H Göck, Tim O'Boyle, John Poynor, Ben Harper, and Jeff Walling.

Apple Pro Training Series

OS X Support Essentials

Kevin M. White and Gordon Davisson

Apple Pro Training Series: OS X Support Essentials
Kevin M. White and Gordon Davisson
Copyright © 2013 by Peachpit Press

Published by Peachpit Press. For information on Peachpit Press books, go to:
www.peachpit.com

To report errors, please send a note to errata@peachpit.com.
Peachpit Press is a division of Pearson Education.

Apple Series Editor: Lisa McClain
Production Coordinator: Kim Elmore, Happenstance Type-O-Rama
Technical Editor: Adam Karneboge
Apple Reviewers: Shane Ross, Anne Renehan, Margaret Bethel
Apple Project Manager: Shane Ross
Copy Editors: Darren Meiss, Jessica Grogan
Proofreader: Darren Meiss
Compositor: James D. Kramer, Craig Johnson; Happenstance Type-O-Rama
Indexer: Jack Lewis
Cover Illustration: Kent Oberheu
Cover Production: Cody Gates, Happenstance Type-O-Rama

Notice of Rights
All rights reserved. No part of this book may be reproduced or transmitted in any form by any means, electronic, mechanical, photocopying, recording, or otherwise, without the prior written permission of the publisher. For information on getting permission for reprints and excerpts, contact permissions@peachpit.com.

Notice of Liability
The information in this book is distributed on an "As Is" basis, without warranty. While every precaution has been taken in the preparation of the book, neither the author nor Peachpit Press shall have any liability to any person or entity with respect to any loss or damage caused or alleged to be caused directly or indirectly by the instructions contained in this book or by the computer software and hardware products described in it.
IMPORTANT: Some of the exercises contained in this guide can be temporarily disruptive, and some exercises, if performed incorrectly, could result in data loss or damage to system files. As such, it's recommended that you perform these exercises on a Mac computer that is not critical to your daily productivity.

Trademarks
Many of the designations used by manufacturers and sellers to distinguish their products are claimed as trademarks. Where those designations appear in this book, and Peachpit was aware of a trademark claim, the designations appear as requested by the owner of the trademark. All other product names and services identified throughout this book are used in editorial fashion only and for the benefit of such companies with no intention of infringement of the trademark. No such use, or the use of any trade name, is intended to convey endorsement or other affiliation with this book.

ISBN 13: 978-0-321-88719-1 ISBN 10: 0-321-88719-0
9 8 7 6 5 4 3 2 1 Printed and bound in the United States of America

Contents at a Glance

Applications and Processes

Network Configuration

Network Services

Peripherals and Printing

System Startup

Table of Contents

Installation and Configuration

Applications and Processes

Network Configuration

Network Services

Installation and Configuration

Lesson **1**

About This Guide

GOALS

- Understand how this guide is organized to facilitate learning
- Set up an environment for self-paced exercises
- Introduce Apple Authorized Training and Certification

This guide serves as a tour of the breadth of functionality of OS X and the best methods for effectively supporting users of OS X systems. In addition, this guide is the curriculum for the Apple official training course, Mountain Lion 101: OS X Support Essentials 10.8, a three-day, hands-on course that provides an intense and in-depth exploration of how to troubleshoot on OS X Mountain Lion. This course is facilitated by an Apple Certified Trainer and is organized into multiple lessons, each containing instructor presentations followed by related student exercises. In other words, this guide is for both self-paced learners and those participating in an instructor-led course.

The primary goal of this guide is to prepare help desk specialists, technical coordinators, service technicians, system administrators, and others who support Mac users to knowledgeably address customer concerns and questions. This includes the ability to return a Mac computer running OS X back to normal operation using the proper utilities, resources, and troubleshooting techniques.

Whether you are an experienced system administrator or just want to dig deeper into OS X, you'll learn in-depth technical information and procedures used by Apple-certified technicians to install, configure, maintain, and diagnose Mac computers running OS X.

NOTE ► Unless otherwise specified, all references in this guide to OS X or OS X Mountain Lion refer to version 10.8.2, which was the most current version available at the time of writing. Due to subsequent updates, some screens, features, and procedures may be slightly different from those presented on these pages.

Learning Methodology

Each lesson in this guide is designed to help experienced users become experts who are able to support other OS X users by:

- Providing knowledge of how OS X works
- Showing how to use diagnostic and repair tools
- Explaining troubleshooting and repair procedures

For example, in Lesson 22, "Network Essentials," you'll learn basic networking concepts (knowledge). You'll acquire network configuration and troubleshooting techniques using the Network preferences (tools). And you'll explore methods for identifying network issues (procedures). In addition, each lesson includes troubleshooting techniques for dealing with common issues related to the topic at hand.

This guide assumes a basic level of familiarity with OS X at the user level. This guide does not cover basic usage of the system, but a good place to start is the Apple Mac 101 support site, www.apple.com/support/mac101/. If you are familiar with Microsoft Windows, another good reference is the Apple Switch 101 site, www.apple.com/support/switch101/switcher/. Again, it's strongly suggested that you are comfortable using a Mac before you begin the exercises in this guide.

Lesson Structure

Each lesson in this guide contains a reference section followed by an exercise section.

> **NOTE ▸** "Note" resources, like this one, offer important information to help clarify a subject. For example, to avoid confusion you should know that this first lesson is the only one in the guide without a specific exercise section.

The reference sections contain initial explanatory material teaching essential concepts. The exercise sections augment your understanding of concepts and develop your skills through step-by-step instruction for both self-paced learners and the hands-on portions of an instructor-led course.

> **TIP** "Tip" resources, like this one, provide helpful hints, tricks, or shortcuts. For example, each lesson begins with an opening page that lists the learning goals for the lesson.

We refer to Apple Knowledge Base documents throughout the lessons. The Knowledge Base is a free online resource (www.apple.com/support) containing the very latest technical information on all the Apple hardware and software products. We strongly encourage you to read the suggested documents and search the Knowledge Base for answers to any problems you encounter.

> **MORE INFO ▶** The "More Info" resources, like this one, provide ancillary information. These resources are merely for your edification, and are not considered essential for the coursework.

Bonus Materials are available online when you register your guide at www.peachpit.com/apts.osxmountainlion. The "Lesson Review Questions & Answers" appendix recaps each lesson through a series of questions that reinforce the material you learned in the guide. You can refer to the lessons and various Apple resources, such as the Knowledge Base and documentation, mentioned in the guide. Answers are also provided to confirm your understanding of the concepts. The "Additional Resources" appendix contains a list of relevant Apple Knowledge Base articles and recommended documents related to the topic of each lesson. The "Updates & Errata" document contains updates and corrections to the guide.

Exercise Requirements

This guide is written so that an Apple Authorized Training Center (AATC) attendee, a student at an educational institution, or a self-paced learner can complete most of the exercises using the same techniques. Those attending at an AATC will have the appropriate exercise setup provided as part of the training experience. On the other hand, self-paced learners attempting these exercises will have to set up an appropriate environment using their own equipment.

> **NOTE ▶** Some of these exercises can be disruptive—for example, they may turn off network services temporarily—and some exercises, if performed incorrectly, could result in data loss or damage to system files. As such, it's recommended that you perform these exercises on a Mac computer that is not critical to your daily productivity. Apple, Inc., and Peachpit Press are not responsible for any data loss or any damage to any equipment that occurs as a direct or indirect result of following the procedures described in this guide.

Mandatory Requirements

In order to perform the exercises in this guide, you must have some basic necessities:

- Mac computer meeting the requirements to run OS X Mountain Lion.
- OS X Mountain Lion (Exercise 2.2 includes instructions for purchasing Mountain Lion if you do not already own it).
- A broadband Internet connection.
- Student Materials demonstration files, which can be downloaded after registering your book at www.peachpit.comapts.osxmountainlion. Instructions for registration and download are included in Exercise 3.5.

Optional Add-ons

A significant portion of these exercises assume access to one or more of the following additional resources. The specific resources needed for each exercise will be listed as a prerequisite at the beginning of the exercise.

- An iCloud account. You can use an existing iCloud account or set up a new free account during the exercises.
- An Apple ID that can purchase from the Mac App Store. You can use an existing account or set up a new free account during the exercises.
- An erasable external USB or FireWire disk, with a capacity of at least 1 GB (or 8 GB for Exercise 4.3).
- An isolated network or subnet with an exercise-specific configuration. This can be facilitated with something as simple as a small network Wi-Fi router with multiple Ethernet ports. For example, the Apple AirPort Extreme would be a good choice (www.apple.com/airportextreme/). Instructions for the general setup of an exercise network and specific instructions for the configuration of AirPort Extreme are available in the Bonus Materials at www.peachpit.com/apts.osxmountainlion after you register your guide.
- A Wi-Fi interface in your computer, and access to at least two Wi-Fi networks (at least one of which is visible).
- An additional Mac system running OS X Mountain Lion.
- A FireWire or Thunderbolt cable (as appropriate) to connect the two computers.

- Optionally, the additional Mac system can have OS X Server installed and set up with an exercise-specific configuration. Any Mac that can run OS X v10.8 can be upgraded to run OS X Server for an additional $19.99 purchase from the Mac App Store. Specific instructions for configuring an OS X Server for exercise use are available in the Bonus Materials at www.peachpit.com/apts.osxmountainlion after you register your guide.

If you lack the equipment necessary to complete a given exercise, you are still encouraged to read the step-by-step instructions and examine the screen shots to understand the procedures demonstrated.

Exercise Order

The exercises in this guide are designed to be relatively independent of each other, so that you can perform them out of order or skip exercises you are not interested in. However, there are some exercises you must perform in the correct order:

- If your computer is not running OS X Mountain Lion yet, you must perform the appropriate exercises in Lesson 2 to upgrade or reinstall it.
- You must perform the appropriate exercises in Lesson 3 to set up your computer for any of the later exercises.
- Exercises 6.1 and 7.1 create user accounts that many later exercises depend on.

Some exercises also have specific dependencies on other exercises; these will be listed as prerequisites at the beginning of the exercise.

Apple Certification

After following this guide, you may want to take the OS X Support Essentials 10.8 Exam to earn the Apple Certified Support Professional 10.8 status. This is the first level of the Apple certification programs for Mac professionals:

- Apple Certified Support Professional 10.8 (ACSP)—Ideal for help desk personnel, service technicians, technical coordinators, and others who support OS X Mountain Lion customers over the phone or who perform Mac troubleshooting and support in schools and businesses. This certification verifies an understanding of OS X core functionality and an ability to configure key services, perform basic troubleshooting, and assist end users with essential Mac capabilities. To receive this certification, you must pass the OS X Support Essentials 10.8 Exam. This guide is designed to provide you with the knowledge and skills to pass that exam.

- Apple Certified Technical Coordinator 10.8 (ACTC)—This certification is intended for OS X technical coordinators and entry-level system administrators tasked with maintaining a modest network of computers using OS X Server. Since the ACTC certification addresses both the support of Mac clients and the core functionality and use of OS X Server, the learning process is correspondingly longer and more intensive than that for the ACSP certification, which addresses solely Mac client support. This certification requires passing both the OS X Support Essentials 10.8 Exam and the OS X Server Essentials 10.8 Exam.

  MORE INFO ▶ To learn more about Apple Certification, visit http://training.apple.com/certification/macosx.

Apple hardware service technician certifications are ideal for people interested in becoming Mac repair technicians, but also worthwhile for help desk personnel at schools and businesses, and for Mac consultants and others needing an in-depth understanding of how Apple systems operate:

- Apple Certified Macintosh Technician (ACMT)—This certification verifies the ability to perform basic troubleshooting and repair of both desktop and portable Mac systems, such as iMac and MacBook Pro. ACMT certification requires passing the Apple Macintosh Service Exam and the OS X Troubleshooting Exam. To learn more about hardware certification, visit http://training.apple.com/certification/acmt.

  NOTE ▶ Although all the questions in the OS X Support Essentials 10.8 Exam are based on material in this guide, simply reading it will not adequately prepare you for the exam. Apple recommends that before taking the exam, you spend time actually setting up, configuring, and troubleshooting OS X Mountain Lion systems.

Lesson **2**

Install OS X Mountain Lion

Every Mac computer has some version of OS X preinstalled when built. The version of OS X that ships with a computer is usually the latest available at the time. Thus, every Mac will at some time need a later version of the operating system to have the latest features and updates. This lesson guides you through both upgrading an existing system and performing a new installation. This lesson also includes troubleshooting issues that may arise during these processes.

> **NOTE** ► Several of the operations you will learn about in this lesson involve significant changes to your Mac computer's setup. Many of them are difficult to reverse, if not irreversible. If you plan to follow the exercises in this lesson, you should do so on a spare computer or an external disk that does not contain critical data.

GOALS

- ► Prepare a computer for an upgrade to OS X
- ► Prepare a computer for a new installation of OS X
- ► Successfully upgrade or install OS X
- ► Troubleshoot potential installation problems

Reference 2.1
About OS X Mountain Lion

Those unfamiliar with Mac computers may look upon their design and assume that beauty is only skin deep. After all, it's true that today's Macs use much of the same technology found in other Intel-based computers. So it could seem that elegant design is all that sets Apple computers apart from the competition. Yet, for the Mac, what's on the inside makes it special as well. Seasoned Mac users know the true differentiator is the software that transforms hardware into a functional computer: the operating system, the true soul of a computer.

What's New in OS X

OS X Mountain Lion is the latest version of the Apple desktop and portable computer operating system. Since its introduction in 2001, OS X has become an increasingly attractive alternative to other operating systems because of its combination of innovative technologies. OS X is the only operating system that combines a powerful open-source UNIX foundation with a state-of-the-art user interface, offering all the ease of use for which Apple is known. Furthermore, Apple provides an exceptional development platform, as evidenced by the large selection of high-quality third-party software titles available for it.

In addition to the features found in previous versions, OS X Mountain Lion includes over 200 new features. The central theme of this upgrade is the marriage of the best features in iOS with the flexibility of the Mac operating system. Those familiar with iOS will immediately recognize its influence in OS X Mountain Lion. Many of the upgrades in OS X provide feature parity for applications and services also found in iOS. Examples include Mail, Contacts, Calendar, Messages, Reminders, Notes, Dictation, Notification Center, Game Center, and systemwide support for iCloud.

OS X Mountain Lion also features deeper integration with social network services, including Facebook, Twitter, Flickr, and Vimeo. Improvements to OS X security are also present via automatic security updates, downloaded application quarantine with Gatekeeper, process sandboxing, and user privacy controls. Finally, newer OS X systems support Power

Nap, which allows Mac systems to automatically update software, update iCloud services, or back up to Time Machine while the system is asleep.

MORE INFO ▶ A full list of the new OS X features can be found at www.apple.com/osx/whats-new/features.html.

Integration Through Standards

Much of the success of OS X can be attributed to Apple embracing industry-standard formats and open-source software. The historic perception of the Mac platform being closed or proprietary is far from today's reality. Nearly every technology in OS X is based on well-known standards. Adoption of common standards saves engineering time and allows for much smoother integration with other platforms. Even when Apple developers must engineer a technology for a new feature, Apple often releases the specs to the developer community, fostering a new standard. An example of this is the Bonjour network discovery protocol, which Apple pioneered and has maintained as an open standard, commonly known as Multicast DNS (mDNS), for others to develop and use.

Some examples of common standards supported by OS X are:

- Connectivity standards—Universal Serial Bus (USB), IEEE 1394 (FireWire), Thunderbolt, Bluetooth wireless, and the IEEE 802 family of Ethernet standards
- File system standards—File Allocation Table (FAT), New Technology File System (NTFS), ISO 9660 optical disc standard, and Universal Disk Format (UDF)
- Network standards—Dynamic Host Configuration Protocol (DHCP), Domain Name System (DNS), Hypertext Transfer Protocol (HTTP), Internet Message Access Protocol (IMAP), Simple Mail Transfer Protocol (SMTP), File Transfer Protocol (FTP), Web Distributed Access and Versioning (WebDAV), and Server Message Block/Common Internet File System (SMB/CIFS)
- Application and development standards—Single UNIX Specification v3 (SUSv3), Portable Operating System Interface (POSIX), C and C++, Objective C, Ruby, Python, and Perl
- Document standards—ZIP file archives, Rich Text Format (RTF), Portable Document Format (PDF), Tagged Image File Format (TIFF), Portable Network Graphics (PNG), Advanced Audio Coding (AAC), and the Moving Picture Experts Group (MPEG) family of media standards

Reference 2.2
Installation Choices

Depending on the state of your Mac, not all of this lesson will be appropriate for you. Of course, you could simply read through the entire lesson, but it might not be the best idea to attempt all the techniques described here on your working Mac.

> **TIP** If you don't know what version of OS X your Mac is running, simply choose About This Mac from the Apple menu.

Odds are, your Mac falls into one of the following general categories:

Your Mac is already running OS X Mountain Lion and is not experiencing any significant problems

If this is the case, upgrading isn't necessary and you probably don't want to reinstall the operating system. You may still wish to read through this lesson, but you should avoid performing any of the exercises in this lesson.

Your Mac is running OS X Mountain Lion but is experiencing significant problems

If this is the case, back up important data, erase the system disk, and perform a "clean" installation. Fortunately, you should have access to Time Machine and OS X Recovery. You will be best served by first familiarizing yourself with Lesson 18, "Time Machine," and Lesson 4, "OS X Recovery," and then returning to this lesson to learn about reinstallation options.

When ready for reinstallation, read Reference sections 2.4, "Preparing the System Disk," and 2.5, "Upgrading and Installing." Then perform the steps outlined in Exercise 2.3, "Erase a Mac System and Install OS X Mountain Lion."

Your Mac is running OS X v10.6.x or OS X Lion and is not experiencing any significant problems

If this is the case, you will be able to perform a standard upgrade in-place installation to OS X Mountain Lion.

To perform a standard upgrade installation, read Reference sections 2.3, "Before Upgrading a Previous System," and 2.5, "Upgrading and Installing." Then perform the steps outlined in Exercises 2.1, "Prepare a Mac for Upgrade," and 2.2, "Upgrade to OS X Mountain Lion."

Your Mac is running OS X v10.6.x or OS X Lion but is experiencing significant problems

If this is the case, back up important data, erase the system disk, and perform a "clean" installation. While you do have access to Time Machine, you don't yet have access to the Mountain Lion version of OS X Recovery. You will be best served by first familiarizing yourself with Lesson 18, "Time Machine." You will also need to create an external OS X Recovery disk as covered in Exercise 4.3, "Create a Full OS X Recovery Disk." Once you have access to the Mountain Lion version of OS X Recovery you can return to this lesson to learn about reinstallation options.

When ready for reinstallation, read Reference sections 2.4, "Preparing the System Disk," and 2.5, "Upgrading and Installing." Then perform the steps outlined in Exercise 2.3, "Erase a Mac System and Install OS X Mountain Lion."

Your Mac is running a version of OS X prior to v10.6 and you want to upgrade

Apple doesn't officially support upgrading to OS X Mountain Lion from any version of OS X prior to v10.6.8. If you have access to the OS X v10.6 installation media, perform the necessary updates to get the Mac to OS X v10.6.8 and then follow the standard recommendations for upgrading to OS X Mountain Lion as covered previously.

However, if you don't have access to the OS X v10.6 installer, you will have to create your own on another Mac running OS X 10.6.8 or later, as covered in Exercise 4.3, "Create a Full OS X Recovery Disk." Once you have access to the Mountain Lion version of OS X Recovery, you can follow the recommendations for upgrading an OS X v10.6.x or OS X Lion system experiencing problems as covered previously.

Reference 2.3
Before Upgrading a Previous System

Because every Mac ships with OS X preinstalled, the majority of installations of OS X Mountain Lion are upgrades. This implies there is an existing operating system that the Installer will be upgrading to a later version. There will probably also be important user data on this system. The OS X installation process is designed to retain nonsystem data, like user accounts and additional applications, during an upgrade installation.

Upgrading an operating system is a complicated process that isn't entirely free from issues. Apple has worked hard to improve the OS X upgrade experience through the years, but other variables involved could still lead to issues. For instance, a hardware failure issue could prevent a successful upgrade installation. For these reasons, you should take some preparatory steps to prevent Installer issues and data loss.

Verifying Installation Requirements

It's important to understand the installation requirements for the copy of OS X you plan to use and also the requirements of the particular Mac you intend to install it on. If you're not sure what the intended Mac computer's specifications are, use the System Profiler application to view the computer's status. On OS X Lion and Mountain Lion systems, this application was renamed System Information, but provides identical functionality.

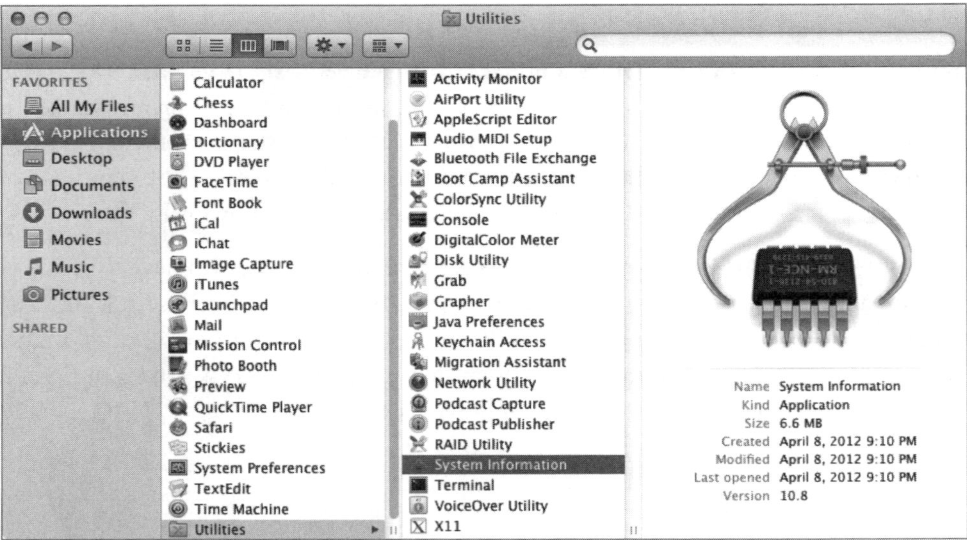

You can find System Profiler or System Information in the /Applications/Utilities folder. Within System Profiler or System Information, verify the computers' specifications by selecting and viewing the various content areas in the Hardware section. Specifically, you should note the computer's Memory and Serial Number information. You should also check the Serial-ATA section for the amount of free space on the system disk, often named Macintosh HD.

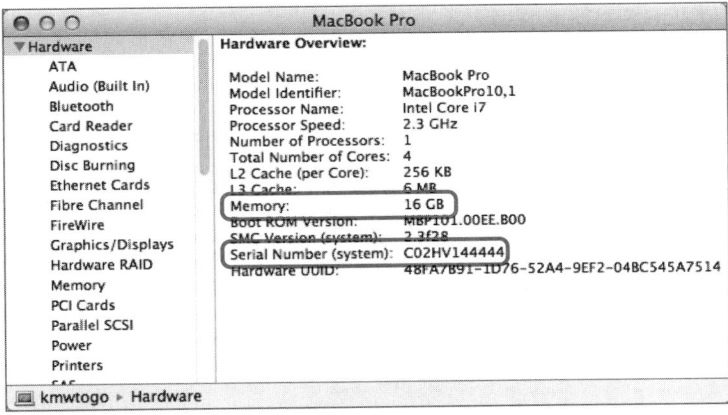

Upgrading to OS X Mountain Lion has the following general requirements:

- OS X v10.6.8 or later
- 2 GB of memory
- 8 GB of available space
- Some features require an Apple ID.
- Some features require a compatible Internet service provider.

Beyond this, you need to find out if your specific Mac model is supported. Once you have the Mac computer's serial number, you can check it against the Apple Support Tech Spec website (http://support.apple.com/specs/). Simply enter the Mac computer's serial number on that site and it will return the specific model name for the Mac. For example, the preceding screenshot shows a Mac identified as a MacBookPro10,1. While that is a specific identifier, it's not the name Apple has defined for technical specifications. Entering this Mac computer's serial number in the Apple Support Tech Spec website returns the official name of MacBook Pro (Retina).

TIP If a Mac is running OS X Lion, you can find out its full model name by selecting the Apple menu, then About This Mac, and then finally clicking the More Info button. This will open System Information and display the full model name.

Knowing the full model name of your Mac is important as OS X Mountain Lion supports only the following Mac models:

- MacBook (Late 2008 Aluminum, or Early 2009 or newer)
- MacBook Air (Late 2008 or newer)

- MacBook Pro (Mid/Late 2007 or newer)
- Mac mini (Early 2009 or newer)
- iMac (Mid 2007 or newer)
- Mac Pro (Early 2008 or newer)
- Xserve (Early 2009)

MORE INFO ▶ This seemingly arbitrary selection of Mac models actually shares a specific new feature for their respective model lines. Each Mac model is the first in their line to support 64-bit EFI firmware.

MORE INFO ▶ Some OS X Mountain Lion features have additional requirements beyond these minimum system requirements. You can learn more about feature-specific requirements at the OS X technical specifications website: www.apple.com/osx/specs/.

Preparing for an Upgrade Installation

While you could jump right into the OS X upgrade installation without any preparation, completing some preliminary steps will reduce the chances of upgrade problems or losing important data. There are four crucial steps you should take before any system upgrade installation:

- Check for Apple software and firmware updates.
- Verify application compatibility.
- Back up important files and folders.
- Back up critical settings.

NOTE ▶ This may seem like a no-brainer, but obviously you don't want to lose power halfway through an upgrade installation. Plug any portable Mac into AC power for the duration of the installation process to ensure its completion.

Apple Software and Firmware Updates

As mentioned previously, OS X v10.6.8 or later is the recommended version to upgrade to OS X Mountain Lion. Furthermore, there have been numerous updates to other Apple software in preparation for this release. For example, both iLife and iWork have received updates. Additionally, older Macs may require a firmware update to properly access all the OS X Mountain Lion features. You should ensure that the Mac you're going to upgrade has all available Apple software updates.

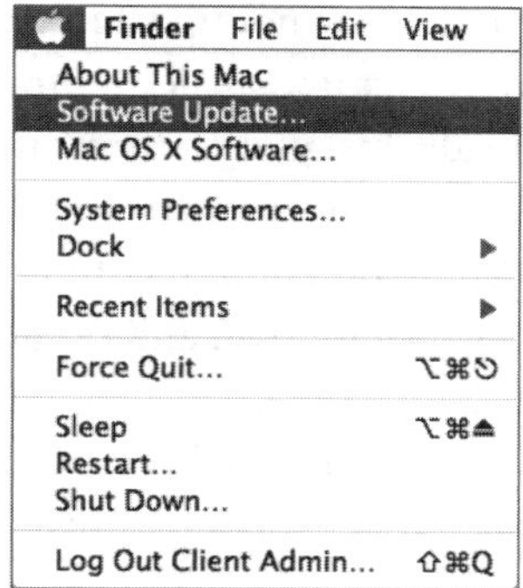

Assuming the Mac is connected to the Internet, choose Software Update from the Apple menu. You should install all available updates. If no updates are found, your Mac is running the latest software, which will ensure a smooth OS X upgrade.

Firmware is low-level software that facilitates the startup and management of system hardware. Though rare, Apple may release firmware updates that older Mac computers need to operate properly with new system software. Often these updates are caught by the Apple Software Update mechanism. However, some Macs may require manual firmware updates. It's always best to check for firmware updates prior to installing a later version of OS X.

The default view for System Profiler or System Information (again found in the /Applications/Utilities folder) will identify the versions of the two types of firmware on Intel-based Macs. The first, listed as Boot ROM Version, is for the Extensible Firmware Interface (EFI), which is responsible for general hardware management and system startup. The second, listed as SMC Version, is the System Management Controller (SMC) firmware responsible for managing hardware power and cooling. Once you have located your computer's firmware versions, you can determine if you have the latest updates by accessing Knowledge Base document HT1237, "EFI and SMC firmware updates for Intel-based Macs."

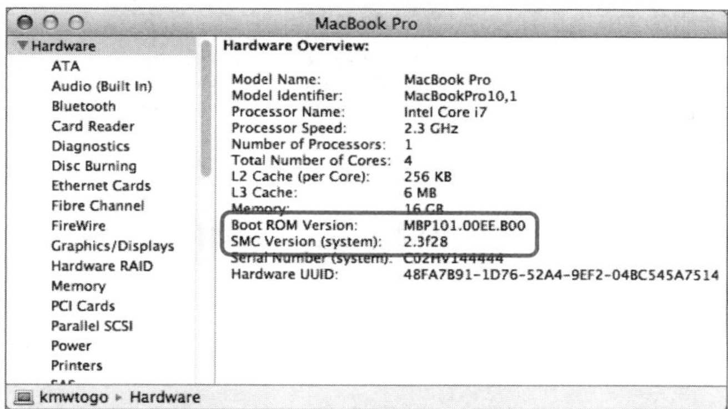

If you determine that your Mac requires a firmware update, and it was not updated via the automatic Software Update process, you need to find the correct update at the Apple Support Download website, http://support.apple.com/downloads. Installing a firmware update is similar to other system software updates in that it requires administrative user authorization and a restart. However, some older Macs have an extra requirement for firmware updates: After the initial installation process, you must shut down and restart the computer, holding down the power button until you hear a long tone. This will initiate the remainder of the firmware update process. Be sure to carefully read any instructions that come with a firmware updater! Failure to properly update a Mac computer's firmware could lead to hardware failure.

NOTE ► If you experience an unsuccessful update, you can restore your Mac computer's firmware with a Firmware Restoration CD. You can find out more about acquiring and using this CD from Knowledge Base document HT2213, "About the Firmware Restoration CD (Intel-based Macs)."

Verify Application Compatibility

When moving to a new operating system, third-party applications may require updates to function properly. Once again, you can use System Profiler or System Information to easily collect a list of installed applications. If you're using the older System Profiler application, you will need to verify that View > Full Profile is selected, to reveal the Applications section in the Contents list. Selecting Applications from the Contents list prompts the system to scan common locations on the local disk for available applications.

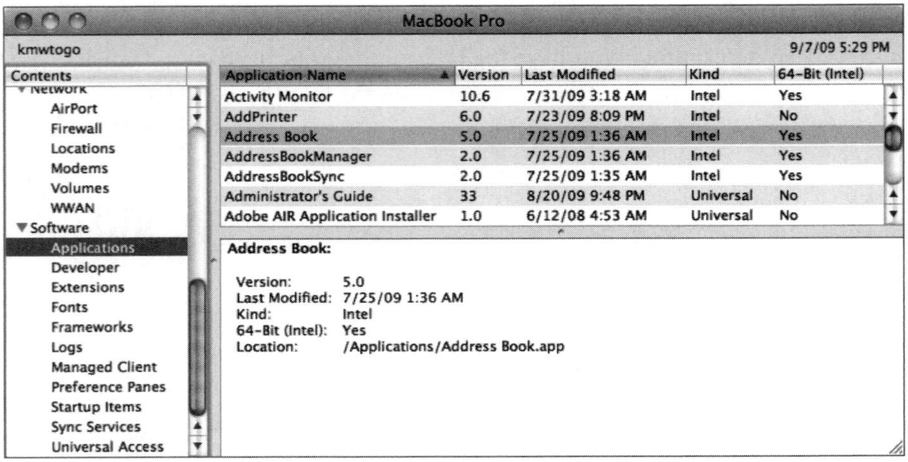

You don't have to worry about the applications installed as part of the operating system. Those will be replaced when you install the new system. However, you may have to do your own research to determine if third-party applications require updates.

OS X also includes a list of known incompatible software. If the OS X Installer detects known incompatible software during an upgrade installation, it will move incompatible software to a folder named Incompatible Software. In some cases the incompatible software isn't moved, but the operating system prevents you from opening the software. Instead, it displays a warning dialog stating that the software is known to be incompatible. You can find out more about this feature in Knowledge Base document HT3258, "About incompatible software (Mac OS X v10.6, OS X Lion, OS X Mountain Lion)."

Back Up Important Files and Folders

Experienced computer users already know to keep backups of their important files and folders. Having a current backup is important before making significant changes to the computer. Installing a new operating system is a significant change that if done improperly could result in complete data loss.

If the system is already running OS X v10.5 or later, you can use the built-in Time Machine software to easily create a backup before you start your installation. Using Time Machine is covered in Lesson 18, "Time Machine."

Document Critical Settings

Apple has designed Migration Assistant and the OS X Installer to help ensure that previous settings are not lost when you are upgrading OS X. Nonetheless, some settings are so critical to your computer's function that you need to document them in case something should go wrong.

Specifically, network settings are critical and should be documented before a system upgrade is attempted. Network settings for all previous versions of OS X can be located in the Network pane of System Preferences, accessed from the Apple menu. Avoid missing settings by navigating through all the available network interface and configuration tabs.

> **TIP** You can quickly document your settings by using the screen capture keyboard shortcut, Command-Shift-3, to create picture files of the dialogs onscreen.

Keeping Up-to-Date

For the most recent information regarding the installation process, your best source is the Apple Support page and Knowledge Base. A good place to start is the OS X Mountain Lion page at www.apple.com/support/osx/. Anytime you intend to install OS X, visit these resources to catch any recently discovered issues. The Apple Knowledge Base documents are sprinkled throughout this guide for a reason: They are the best source for official, up-to-date support information.

Reference 2.4
Preparing the System Disk

If you need to perform an erase and install for a "clean" system or you are planning on repartitioning the disk, you have to prepare the system disk prior to installing OS X. Specifically, OS X only supports installation on disks that are partitioned via the GUID Partition Table (GPT) scheme and contain at least one Mac OS Extended (Journaled) formatted volume.

> **NOTE** ► Any disk containing OS X v10.6 or later is already properly formatted for OS X Mountain Lion. In other words, if you only need to upgrade a working OS X system, you don't need to make any system disk changes and can simply follow the steps in Exercise 2.2, "Upgrade to OS X Mountain Lion."

Erasing the system disk before a system installation may be necessary for various reasons. Obviously erasing the system disk will erase any existing data, but sometimes this may be necessary. For example, if you are upgrading the Mac computer's internal disk to a bigger or faster disk, it must be properly formatted for OS X. Another instance is when the operating system has serious issues; in this case, erasing and installing a "clean" copy of OS X may resolve the situation.

The reasons to repartition your system disk are a bit more complex, so they are covered in the next section. Nevertheless, the process of repartitioning may require erasing data on the disk, and thus is often done prior to installing OS X. You will use Disk Utility for both erasing and repartitioning the disk. Disk Utility can be found on any Mac in the /Applications/Utilities folder or, as covered later in Lesson 4, from OS X Recovery. If you're going to make changes to the system disk before you install OS X, you must do so while started up from a system on another physically different disk.

MORE INFO ▶ This lesson does not include details about erasing or repartitioning disk drives; these procedures are covered extensively in Lesson 10, "File Systems and Storage."

Understanding Partitioning Options

Before selecting a destination disk, you may want to pause and consider the various partition methodologies that are available as installable OS X destinations. Most Macs have a single disk formatted as a single partition that defines the entire space on that disk. This is the Apple default partition setup. However, by repartitioning the disk, you can choose to break up that single large partition into separate smaller partitions. This allows you to treat a single physical storage device as multiple separate storage destinations.

Just as installing a new operating system will have long-lasting ramifications on how you use your computer, so does your choice of partition options. Thus, before you install a new operating system you should consider your partition philosophy. The following lists present the pros and cons of various partition options. Again, many of these concepts will be further discussed in Lesson 10, "File Systems and Storage."

Single Partition

- Pros—Most drives are formatted with a single partition by default, so no changes are necessary and no data will be lost. Also, a single partition is the most efficient use of space on your disk, as you won't have wasted space due to having separate partitions.
- Cons—Having only a single partition severely limits administrative flexibility. Many maintenance and administrative tasks require multiple partitions, so you will have to use an additional physical storage device to accommodate those needs. Further, because system and user data are combined on a single disk, administration can be more difficult.

Multiple Partitions

- Pros—Multiple partitions allow you to have multiple operating systems and multiple storage locations on a single device. Having multiple operating systems allows you to run different versions of OS X from one disk or create utility systems that can be used to repair the primary system. With multiple storage locations, replacing a damaged operating system is much easier because all the user's data resides on another partition.
- Cons—Most drives need to be repartitioned to use multiple partitions. While Mountain Lion supports dynamic partitioning without losing data, it can only do so when working within the free space of a disk. Therefore certain partition configurations may require you to completely erase the disk. Any future partition changes may require you to sacrifice data on the disk as well. Additionally, Boot Camp Assistant, used to configure a partition for Windows or another non-Apple operating system, does not support multiple-partition drives. Finally, multiple partitions can be very space inefficient if you don't plan carefully, as you may end up with underused partitions that run out of space too soon.

Reference 2.5
Upgrading and Installing

Apple is well known for designing every operation to be as easy as possible, and the OS X installation process is an example of this. It's so well-engineered that most users can easily complete it with no training. However, anyone tasked with supporting OS X computers should be more familiar with all the necessary procedures to ensure a smooth installation.

Acquiring the OS X Installer

OS X Mountain Lion is only available for download from the Mac App Store. That said, once you have downloaded the OS X Installer, you can also create your own OS X

Recovery media by following the instructions in Exercise 4.3, "Create a Full OS X Recovery Disk."

If you are acquiring OS X Mountain Lion for the first time, the process is as simple as buying a song in iTunes or a new game from the Mac App Store. Using the Mac App Store does have a few prerequisites, though:

- You must be running OS X v10.6.6 or later.
- You must be connected to the Internet, ideally at broadband speeds. The OS X Installer is around 4.5 GB, so it can take a while to download even on "fast" connections.
- You must have an Apple ID associated with valid credit card information. If you have purchased items from Apple via iTunes or the Mac App Store previously, you are already set. If you have yet to purchase products online from the App Store or iTunes, you can set up your information within the Mac App Store.

MORE INFO ▶ Details regarding the Mac App Store are covered in Lesson 19, "Application Installation."

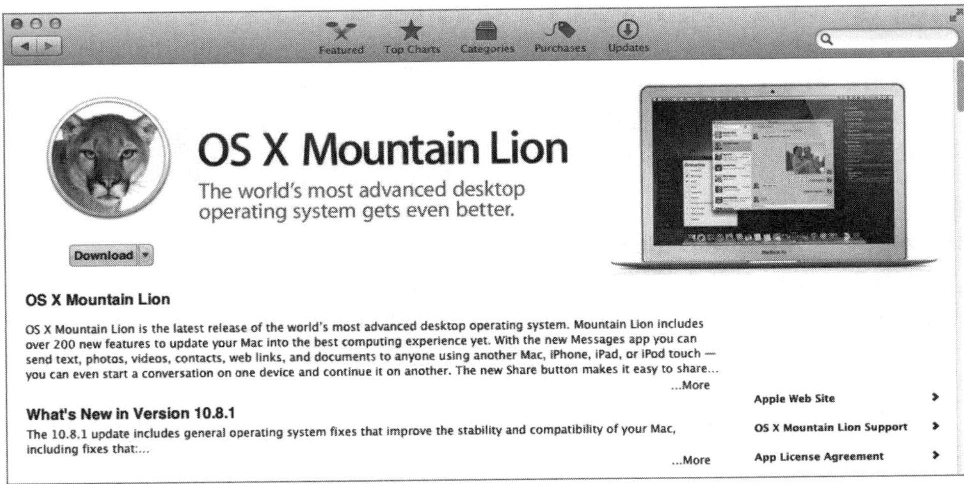

Assuming you meet this criteria, simply open the App Store from the Apple menu. OS X Mountain Lion will likely remain as one of the featured items on the store, so it should be easy to find. Complete the purchase and it will automatically download the Install OS X Mountain Lion application to your Mac. Once the download is complete, the installer will automatically open and run.

NOTE ▸ If you already have OS X Mountain Lion installed on your Mac, the Mac App Store may show that it's already "Installed" or "Downloaded." Thus, the OS X Mountain Lion Installer may still be in the /Applications folder. If not, you also have access to the installer via the steps covered in Lesson 4, "OS X Recovery."

Newer Mac Systems

New Macs usually ship with a computer-specific release of OS X that was engineered for that model and may include additional bundled software. This guide assumes that you will be using a standard copy of OS X Mountain Lion, so you may find that some details vary if you are using a computer-specific install. You may also find that if your Mac is brand new, the current Mac App Store version of the OS X Installer is not compatible with your system.

While OS X Mountain Lion supports hardware from several years prior to its release, a specific version of OS X does not support hardware that is newer than the operating system's release. In other words, you may come across a Mac that's newer than the OS X Mountain Lion installer you're trying to use. In this case, the installation will fail to start up the Mac or simply refuse to install in the first place, whereupon you should use the original OS X Recovery system that came with the Mac.

MORE INFO ▸ See Knowledge Base document HT1159, "Mac OS X versions (builds) for computers" and document HT2186, "Don't install a version of Mac OS X earlier than what came with your Mac."

Install OS X Mountain Lion

The installation process itself involves just a few simple choices up front, followed by the actual installation. This allows the user to spend only a few moments choosing the installation destination, and then leave the computer unattended while the installation completes.

TIP The installation process can be safely restarted after a power loss or disk disconnection. If this occurs, simply restart the installation.

Upgrade vs. Install

There are two primary types of installations: upgrade installs take an existing OS X system and upgrade it to a later version, and new installs that place a new copy of OS X on a disk without a system. The Installer will automatically choose the appropriate installation type based on your selected destination. As far as installation destinations go, the OS X Installer can upgrade the system from which your Mac is currently running, or you can install to another disk attached to your Mac.

NOTE ▸ You cannot upgrade OS X if any other users are currently logged into the Mac via Fast User Switching. You will either need to have those users log out of their sessions or restart the computer to forcibly end the other user sessions.

Performing a "Clean" Install

If you want to perform an erase and install, also known as a "clean" install, you must manually erase the destination system disk using Disk Utility before running the OS X Installer. If the destination is another system disk, like an external drive, you can erase and install from your currently running Mac. However, if you want to erase the system disk your Mac is currently running from, you need to start up from another system, as covered by Lesson 4, "OS X Recovery."

The Installation Destination

During installation of OS X Mountain Lion, the only choice you will be prompted with is to select the installation destination. You are simply selecting the disk volume where OS X will be installed. This can be an internal or an external disk as long as it's properly formatted. The default selection is the current startup disk; you will have to click the Show All Disks button to choose an alternate destination.

You may notice that the installer will not let you select certain drives or partitions. This is because the installer has determined that your Mac cannot start from that item. Possible reasons include:

- The disk does not use the proper partition scheme for your Mac. Intel Macs use the GUID partition scheme (GPT). You can resolve this issue by repartitioning the disk using Disk Utility.
- The specific partition is not formatted properly. OS X requires a partition formatted as a Mac OS Extended (Journaled) volume. You can resolve this issue by erasing the partition using Disk Utility.
- The OS X Installer can't create the OS X Recovery HD. This issue can be resolved by adjusting the destination partition size. For more information, see Knowledge Base document TS3926, "OS X Lion: Installer reports 'This disk cannot be used to start up your computer.'"
- The OS X Installer does not support installing to a disk containing Time Machine backups. For more information, see Knowledge Base document TS2986, "OS X: Cannot install on a volume used by Time Machine for backups."

Again, the system automatically determines if there is an existing version of OS X on the selected destination. If there is an existing system, the installer will upgrade the system to the version of OS X Mountain Lion included with the installer.

Reference 2.6
Installer Troubleshooting

Apple has worked hard to make the OS X installation as painless and reliable as possible. Yet, as with any complicated technology, problems may arise. The good news is that the OS X Installer has the ability to "back out" of an installation and restart to the previous system. If this is the result, obviously the installation did not complete, but at least you still have a functioning Mac.

Thoroughly verifying that your computer meets the requirements for OS X Mountain Lion and completing the installation preparation steps as outlined in this lesson will go a long way toward preventing or resolving any serious problems.

Beyond the appropriate preparation steps covered earlier in this lesson, the most common installation failures arise from problems with the destination disk. Here are a few specific issues regarding this:

- ▶ The installer was unable to verify the selected disk or partition. This indicates serious disk problems. You should refer to the troubleshooting steps in Lesson 10, "File Systems and Storage," to resolve this issue.
- ▶ The installer may give you an error message saying that some features of OS X are not supported on the selected disk. You will see this message if your system disk is a software RAID set or uses nonstandard Boot Camp partitioning. If this is the case, the installer will not be able to create an OS X Recovery HD, but you will still be able to install OS X Mountain Lion.

  MORE INFO ▶ See Knowledge Base document HT4649, "OS X: 'Some features of Mac OS X are not supported for the disk (volume name)' appears during installation."

- ▶ In some cases, even when a disk is partitioned and formatted properly, the installer will not let you select that disk. This error most often occurs when there is also a Boot Camp partition on the disk. The resolution in this case involves slightly decreasing the size of the Mac partition to make room for the OS X Recovery HD.

  MORE INFO ▶ See Knowledge Base document TS3926, "OS X Lion: Installer reports 'This disk cannot be used to start up your computer.'"

The Installer Log

The granddaddy of all troubleshooting resources for OS X is the log file. Nearly every process writes entries in a log file, and the installer is no different. The installer log contains progress and error entries for nearly every step of the installation process, including steps not shown by the standard interface.

During the installation process, you can access the installer log by simply selecting Installer Log from the Window menu. Information in the installer log will allow you to more precisely pinpoint problems or verify installation.

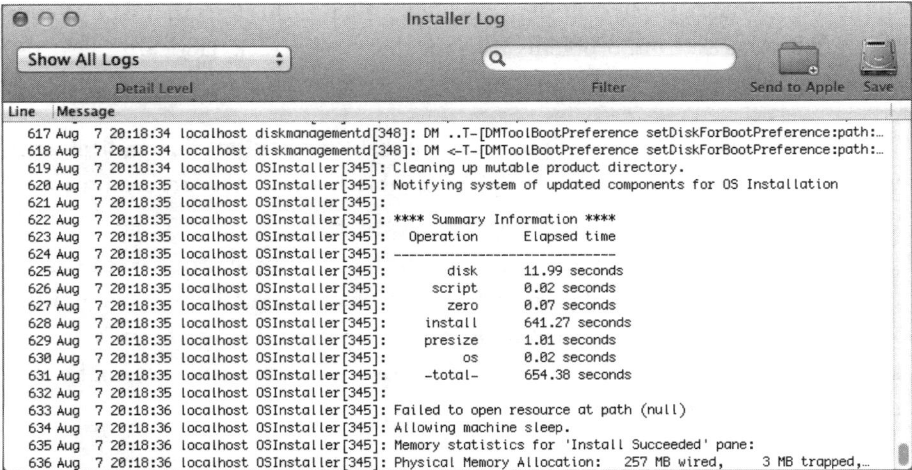

TIP You can also use this technique to check on the progress of any general software installation via the Installer application.

TIP After installation you can access the Installer log on a normally running Mac from the /Applications/Utilities/Console application. Once Console is open, expand the /var/log folder and then select the install.log.

You can leave the Installer Log window open during the entire installation process to monitor progress. You may find that, even during a successful installation, the Installer reports many warnings and errors. Many of these reported issues are benign, and you should only concern yourself with them if you are trying to isolate a show-stopping problem. When the installation successfully completes, the summary entries in the Installer log will look similar to those in the preceding screenshot.

Exercise 2.1
Prepare a Mac for Upgrade

Prerequisites

This exercise is necessary only if you are upgrading your computer from an older version of OS X to Mountain Lion.

In this exercise, you will verify that your computer's hardware and firmware support OS X Mountain Lion, as well as check for old software and record important settings.

Use System Information (/System Profiler) to Check Hardware, Firmware, and Application Compatibility

1. If necessary, log in to your existing administrator account on your computer.
2. In the Finder, navigate to the /Applications/Utilities folder (you can use the Finder keyboard shortcut Command-Shift-U).
3. Open the System Information or System Profiler utility (its name depends on which version of OS X you are using).

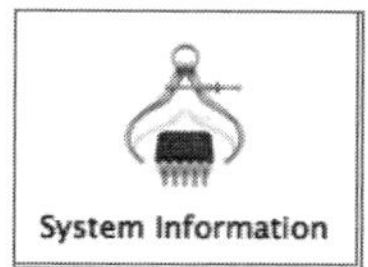

4. If necessary, select the Hardware entry in the sidebar.

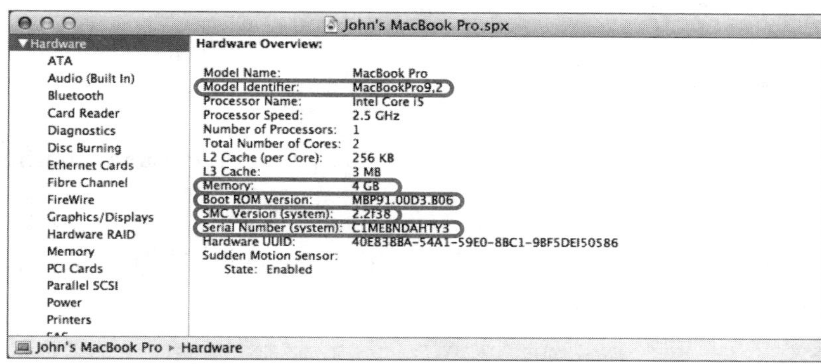

5. Verify that the Memory listed is at least 2 GB. If it is less than that, you cannot use Mountain Lion on this computer.

6 Make notes of the Model Identifier, Boot ROM Version, SMC Version, and Serial Number:

Model Identifier: ____________________

Boot ROM Version: ____________________

SMC Version: ____________________

Serial Number: ____________________

7 Select the sidebar entry for the bus your computer's startup disk is attached to (for most models, this is the Serial-ATA bus).

8 Find your startup volume in the listing on the bottom right, and verify that it has at least 8 GB of available space. Ideally, there should be a lot more than 8 GB available, but 8 GB is the bare minimum for installing OS X Mountain Lion.

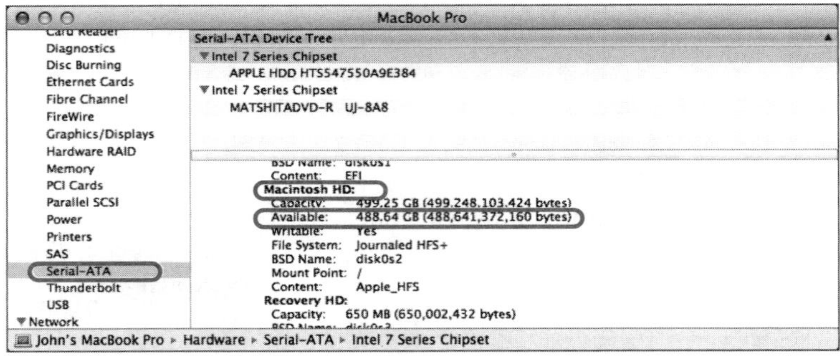

9 In the sidebar under Software, select Applications and wait for it to gather information on the applications installed on your computer.

10 Click the heading for the Last Modified column. If the column's triangle is pointing down, click again so that it points up.

Your applications are listed with the oldest ones at the top. In general, your oldest applications are the most likely to be incompatible with newer versions of OS X. You may want to research the older applications to see if they are compatible with OS X Mountain Lion or if updates are available for them.

11 Click the heading for the Kind column.

12 Scroll through the list to see if you have any PowerPC or Classic applications. These kinds of applications are not supported by OS X Mountain Lion. Some applications may have a blank in this column; this does not indicate a problem.

13 Quit System Information/System Profiler.

14 Open Safari, and navigate to the Apple Mountain Lion support page (www.apple.com/support/osx/).

This page has links to support information on OS X Mountain Lion.

15 Click the link for Installation and Recovery.

This page has information and links specifically about installing OS X Mountain Lion, including requirements for installing Mountain Lion.

16 Navigate to the Apple Tech Specs web page (http://support.apple.com/specs/).

17 Enter your computer's serial number (recorded in step 6) in the Search Tech Specs field and press Return.

A link to your computer's technical specs listed by its model name appears. Verify that the model name is on the list of supported models in the Reference section 2.3, "Before Upgrading a Previous System."

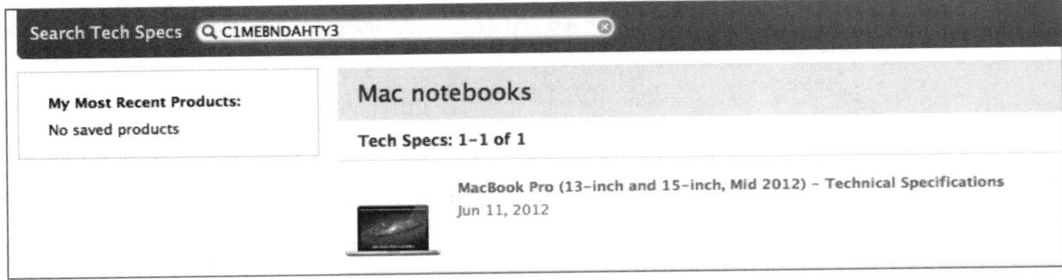

18 If you wish, click the link to view your computer's detailed specifications.

19 In the search field near the upper-right corner of the Apple webpage (*not* the field in the Safari toolbar), enter **HT1237** and press Return.

This takes you to the Apple Knowledge Base document HT1237, "EFI and SMC firmware updates for Intel-based Macs."

20 Find your model in the list. Note that you can find it either by model name (which you found in step 17) or its model identifier (which you found in step 6).

21 Verify that the Boot ROM and SMC versions listed match what you found in step 6. If they do not, update your computer's firmware before upgrading OS X. The easiest way to do this is with Software Update (and it checks other things, so you should run it even if your firmware is up to date).

NOTE ► You can find more information about Software Update in Lesson 5, "OS X Software Updates."

22 From the Apple menu, choose Software Update and wait while your software and firmware is checked for updates.

23 If a dialog appears informing you that your computer is up to date, proceed to the "Document Network Settings" section of this exercise.

24 If a dialog appears informing you that updates are available for your computer, click Show Details to view the updates it found.

25 Look through the available updates, and deselect any that you do not want to perform at this time.

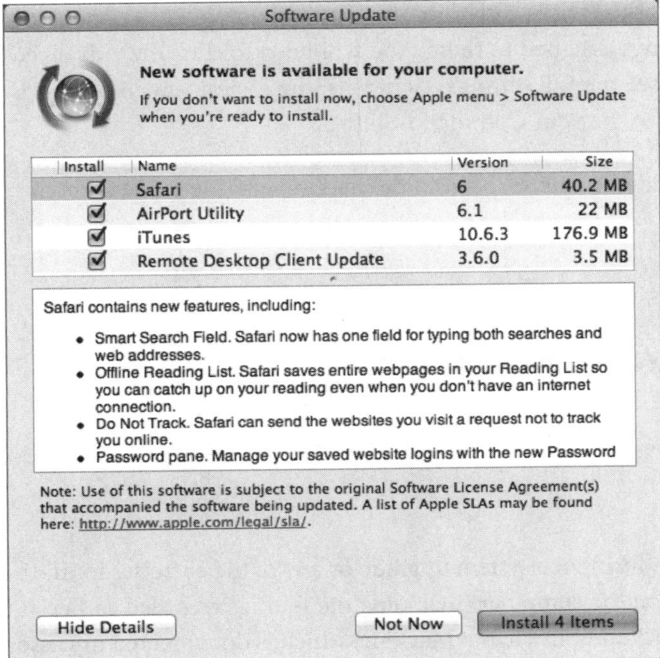

26 Click Install *x* Items, where *x* is the number of items you have chosen to install, and follow any prompts and instructions to complete the updates. Note that the process for updating firmware can vary from model to model.

27 After the updates have finished, repeat starting at step 22 to verify that all updates installed successfully, and no more updates have become available.

Document Network Settings

1 From the Apple menu, choose System Preferences.

2 In System Preferences, click the Network icon.

3 Select each of the network services (listed on the left of the preference pane), and record any special settings assigned to them. You will need to click the Advanced button for each service to see the full settings. Generally, the easiest way to do this is to take screenshots with the shortcut Command-Shift-3.

4 If your computer has more than one location defined, repeat this process for each location.

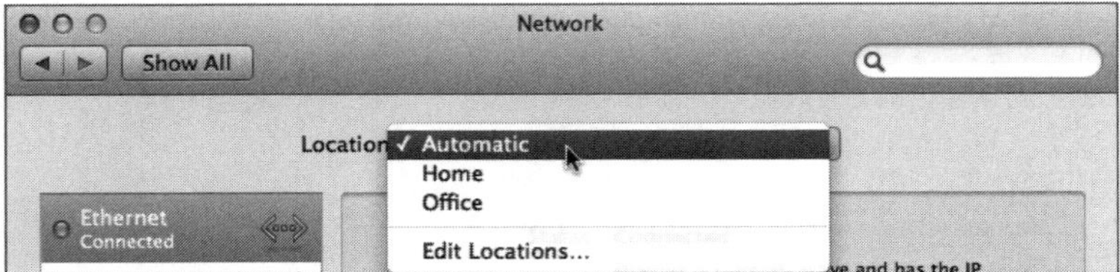

Back Up Your Data

In case anything goes wrong during the system upgrade or any of the exercises in this book, back up any important data on the computer (including the settings recorded earlier in this exercise). OS X includes a backup utility, Time Machine, which is documented in Lesson 18 of this guide. There are also many third-party options for backing up OS X computers.

Whichever backup option you choose, make sure your backup is up to date and includes all important data before proceeding any further. The process will depend on your chosen backup solution, but usually the best test is to try restoring critical data from the backup.

Exercise 2.2
Upgrade to OS X Mountain Lion

Prerequisites

This exercise is necessary only if you are upgrading your computer from an older version of OS X to Mountain Lion.

- Your computer must be running OS X version 10.6.6 or later to perform this exercise.
- Perform Exercise 2.1 before beginning this exercise.

In this exercise, you will purchase OS X Mountain Lion from the Mac App Store, and install it as an upgrade on your computer.

Use the App Store to Download the Installer

1 Log in to your existing administrator account on your computer.

2 From the Apple menu, choose App Store. If App Store is not one of the choices under the Apple menu, you may be running a version of OS X earlier than 10.6.6, in which case you cannot use this method to upgrade to OS X Mountain Lion.

3 If you are not already signed in but have an Apple ID set up, choose Store > Sign In and sign into your Apple ID account.

4 If you do not have an Apple ID set up, choose Store > Create Account, and follow the prompts to create an Apple ID to use for your App Store purchases.

5 In the search field of the App Store window, enter **Mountain Lion** and press Return.

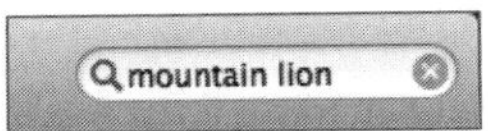

6 Find OS X Mountain Lion in the search results, and check the label on the button underneath its star rating.

▶ If the button gives a price, you have not purchased OS X Mountain Lion under this Apple ID. This is the price that will be charged to your Apple ID's payment method to buy OS X Mountain Lion from the App Store.

▶ If the button says Purchased or Download, you have already purchased OS X Mountain Lion under this Apple ID, and you can download it without further charge.

▶ If the button says Downloaded or Installed, you have already downloaded and/or installed OS X Mountain Lion on this computer. In this case, you do not need to perform this exercise, and you can proceed to the next lesson.

7 If necessary, click the price listing under OS X Mountain Lion; it changes to Buy App.

8 Click Buy App or Download, as appropriate.

9 If the App Store requests any additional information, supply it as requested.

10 Wait for the Install OS X Mountain Lion app to download.

When the download is complete, the app opens automatically.

NOTE ► The installation process will delete the installer application. If you want to upgrade several computers or create a full OS X recovery disk, quit the installer and make a copy of it before proceeding. The process for creating a full OS X recovery disk is given in Exercise 4.3.

Upgrade Your Computer to OS X Mountain Lion

1 If necessary, open the /Applications/Install OS X Mountain Lion application.

2 At the Welcome screen, click Continue.

3 Read the license agreement, and if its terms are acceptable to you, click Agree.

4 In the confirmation dialog that appears, click Agree.

5 At this point, you can select the install destination.

The default selection is the current startup volume; if other volumes are available, you can click the Show All Disks button to select a different destination.

6 Enter the name and password of your administrator account to authorize the installation.

7 Click Install to start the installation. If you are warned about not being connected to a power source, connect your power adapter before continuing.

To see the details of the installation process, follow the instructions in Exercise 2.4 as soon as the installation has started.

The installation will normally complete automatically without further interaction. First, the Installer will create or update an OS X Recovery system on the destination disk. This step will take only a few minutes, as the OS X Recovery system is only around 700 MB. When this first stage is complete, the Mac will restart to the freshly minted OS X Recovery system.

If your startup volume is encrypted with FileVault 2, you will be prompted to authenticate to allow the installation to continue.

Once started from the OS X Recovery system, the Installer will automatically continue with the remainder of the install process. This second stage, when the "real" copy of OS X is installed to the destination disk, will take quite a while, as it must install over 4 GB of data. When this stage is complete, the Mac will restart once more, into the installed copy of OS X. If you are using FileVault 2, you will need to authenticate again.

The first time you log into your account after upgrading, you will be prompted to link your computer account with an Apple ID. You can skip this step, as you will explore the Apple ID and iCloud features of OS X Mountain Lion in later exercises.

Now that your computer is running OS X Mountain Lion, follow the instructions in Exercise 3.2 to set up your computer for the rest of the exercises in this book.

Exercise 2.3
Erase a Mac System and Install OS X Mountain Lion

▶ **Prerequisites**

This exercise is necessary only if your computer needs to be erased before installing OS X Mountain Lion, as covered in Reference section 2.2, "Installation Choices."

- You need an OS X Mountain Lion Recovery partition or disk (see Lesson 4, "OS X Recovery" for details). Note that you can use the procedure in Exercise 4.3 to create a recovery disk in OS X version 10.6.6 or later.

WARNING ▶ This exercise will erase all existing data on your computer. If you want to keep any of this data, you **must** ensure that it is safely backed up to some other computer or disk.

If your computer is having trouble, it may be best to erase the existing data and start over with a completely clean installation of OS X Mountain Lion. In order to do this, you must start up from another disk, erase your computer's internal disk, and then install a new operating system.

Start Up from a Recovery Disk or Partition

1 Before proceeding with this exercise, make sure all the files you want to preserve from this computer are safely backed up elsewhere.

2 If your computer is running, shut it down.

3 If you are using a USB recovery disk, insert the recovery disk into one of your computer's USB slots.

4 Press the power button on your computer to turn it on, and then immediately press and hold the Option key until you see a row of icons appear on the screen.

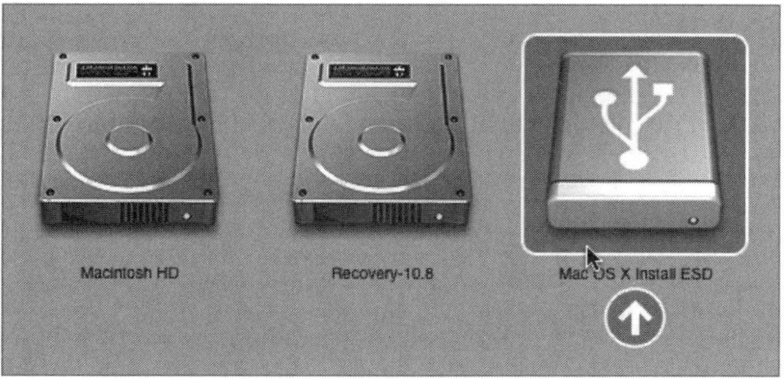

5 Click the recovery disk or partition's icon. Depending on the type and version of recovery disk you are using, it may be labeled Recovery HD (if it is a 10.7 recovery partition), Recovery-10.8 (if it is a 10.8 recovery partition), or Mac OS X Install ESD (if it is a full recovery disk).

6 Click the arrow that appears under the icon.

The computer boots into the installer/recovery environment. Lesson 4 of this guide has more information about using recovery mode.

Erase Your Computer's Disk Drive

1 In the OS X Utilities window, select Disk Utility and click Continue.

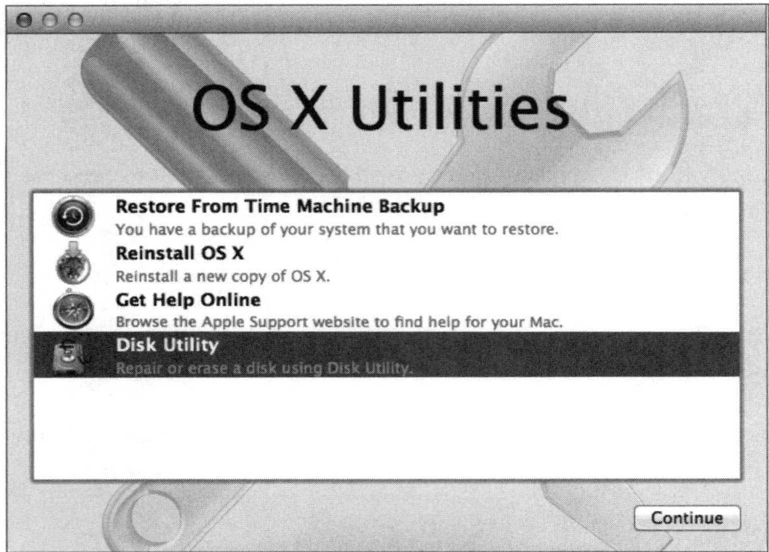

Disk Utility opens. Lesson 10, "File Systems and Storage" has more information about using Disk Utility.

2 From the sidebar, select your computer's internal disk drive.

3 Click the Erase tab near the top of the Disk Utility window.

4 Choose Mac OS Extended (Journaled) from the Format pop-up menu.

5 If you wish, enter a new name for your computer's disk. The rest of this guide will assume that it is named Macintosh HD.

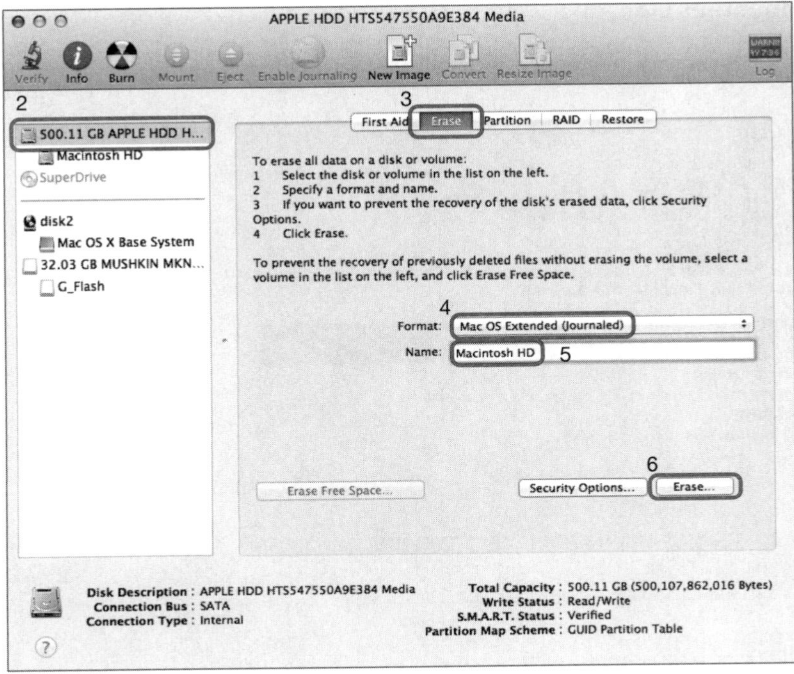

6 Click the Erase button near the bottom right of the Disk Utility window.

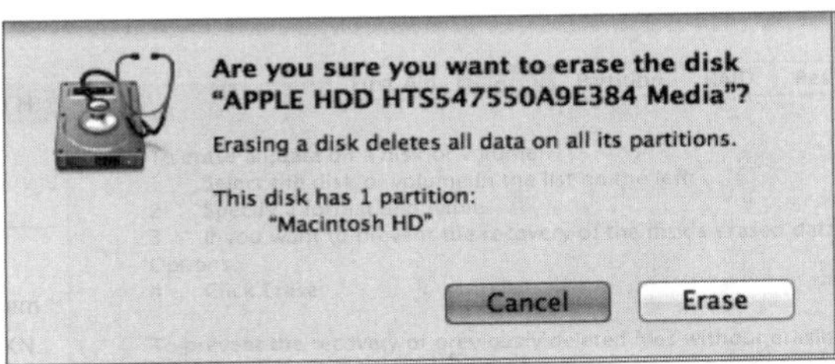

7 In the confirmation dialog that appears, click Erase.

8 From the menu bar, choose Disk Utility > Quit Disk Utility.

Install OS X Mountain Lion

1 In the OS X Utilities window, select Reinstall OS X and click Continue.

2 In the Install OS X window, click Continue.

3 Read the license agreement, and if its terms are acceptable to you, click Agree.

4 In the confirmation dialog that appears, click Agree.

5 Select your computer's disk drive from the list of available volumes, and click Install.

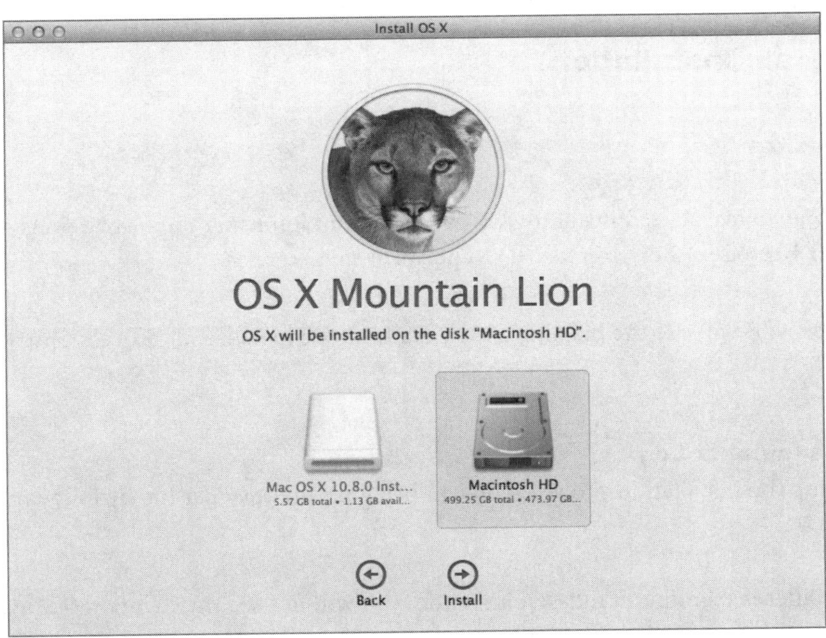

To see the details of the installation process, follow the instructions in Exercise 2.4 as soon as the installation begins.

The installation will complete automatically without further interaction. First, the Installer will create an OS X Recovery HD system on the destination disk. This step will only take a few minutes, as the OS X Recovery system is only around 700 MB. When this first stage is complete, the Mac will restart to the freshly minted OS X Recovery system.

Once started from the OS X Recovery system, the Installer will automatically continue with the remainder of the install process. This second stage, when the "real" copy of OS X is installed to the destination disk, will take quite a while, as it must install over 4 GB of data. When this stage is complete, the Mac will restart once more, into the installed copy of OS X.

Upon restart you will be greeted by the full Setup Assistant experience, as covered in Lesson 3, "Setup and Configuration." Follow the instructions in Exercise 3.1 to set up your computer for the rest of the exercises in this book.

Exercise 2.4
Verify System Installation

Prerequisites

- You must have started installing OS X Mountain Lion using the instructions in either Exercise 2.2 or Exercise 2.3 to perform this exercise.

In this exercise, you will use the installer log to examine the installation process as it happens.

Examine the Installer Log

Anytime during the installation process, you can bring up the Installer log by following these steps:

1. If the Installer is running in full-screen mode, you will not see the menu bar. Move your mouse to the top of the screen to reveal the menu bar.

2. Choose Window > Installer Log (or press Command-L).

3. Choose Show All Logs from the Detail Level pop-up menu to view the entire contents of the Installer log.

4. Use the Spotlight search field in the toolbar to isolate specific entries in the Installer log.

5 To save the Installer log, click the Save button in the toolbar.

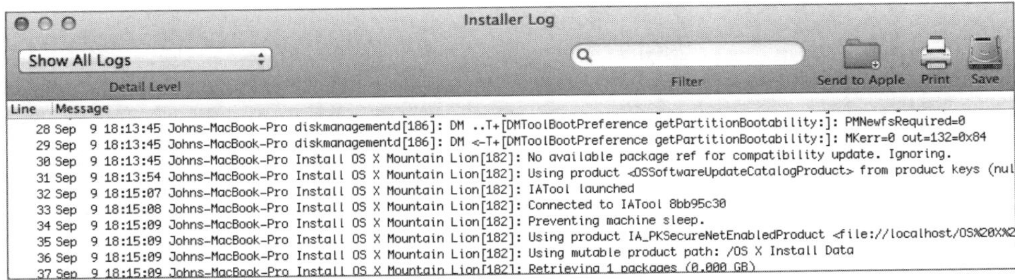

NOTE ▶ The installer will restart the computer partway through the installation process. When the computer restarts for the second phase, the log window will not be automatically reopened.

TIP ▶ The Mac will not automatically restart after the second phase as long as the Installer Log window is the foremost window.

Lesson 3

Setup and Configuration

Providing competent system configuration is a primary concern of technical support personnel. This lesson focuses on both initial setup and ongoing system configuration. Preliminary OS X configuration is handled via Setup Assistant, while subsequent configuration is almost entirely handled via System Preferences and configuration profiles. Finally, this lesson introduces the tools used to gather and verify system information.

GOALS

- Complete the initial configuration of an OS X system
- Adjust common system settings
- Identify and install a configuration profile
- Examine and verify system information

Reference 3.1 Setup Assistant

If you are using a brand-new Mac for the first time or you have just completed a new install of OS X on a disk or partition with no previous system, you will be presented with the Setup Assistant. The Setup Assistant will guide you through the preliminary configuration required to use a new system. Several of the steps in Setup Assistant are optional and can be skipped, but the required steps are necessary for good reason. Any of the configurations made while using the Setup Assistant can be easily changed later by accessing the appropriate system preferences, as covered later in this lesson.

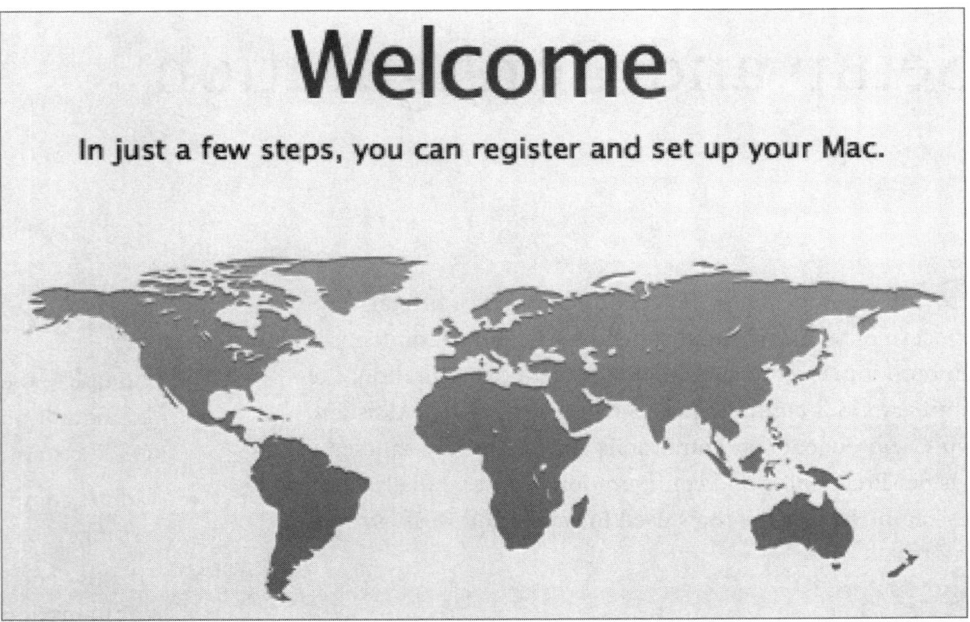

NOTE ▸ Attempting to use the Command-Q keyboard shortcut to skip optional screens in the Setup Assistant will not allow you to skip those screens. Instead, you will be forced to shut down or continue.

The Setup Assistant will guide you through several steps:

Setup Assistant: Language and Keyboard

First you will choose the primary language, which ensures that the applications on your system use appropriate language and dialect. This information is also used to complete the registration process. At this point you will also select the primary keyboard layout. Both language and keyboard layout settings can be changed later from the Language & Text preferences.

Setup Assistant: Network Settings (Optional)

The Setup Assistant will attempt to establish a connection to the Internet by automatically configuring the Mac computer's network settings. It will first attempt to automatically configure via DHCP on a wired Ethernet network or open Wi-Fi network. If successful via either connection, you won't be prompted to set up networking.

Otherwise, the assistant will try to figure out which type of network connection you need to set up and present you with the appropriate configuration screen. On most Macs this will be the Wi-Fi network setup screen, where you can select and authenticate to a wireless network. Alternatively, you don't have to set up networking at this point, and you can do so at any time from the Network preferences. Lesson 22, "Network Essentials," covers this topic in greater detail.

Setup Assistant: Migration Assistant (Optional)

This optional utility allows you to migrate computer and user information from another computer or backup to the new system. Completing the Migration Assistant will allow you to skip most of the remaining steps of the Setup Assistant, as the configuration will be gathered from the migrated system. Otherwise, if you do not have a previous system to migrate from, simply leave the default choice and click Continue to proceed with the Setup Assistant. The next reference section in this lesson covers Migration Assistant in greater detail.

Setup Assistant: Enable Location Services (Optional)

Enabling this service allows applications to locate your Mac based on the Apple Wi-Fi based geo-location technology. You can further adjust Location Services in the Security & Privacy preferences. Lesson 8, "System Security," covers this topic in greater detail.

Setup Assistant: Apple ID (Optional)

The registration process, though not required, is an important part of system setup. If you're connected to the Internet at this point, you can enter an existing Apple ID, recover a lost Apple ID password, or create a new Apple ID. An Apple ID is free to set up and provides login access for all Apple online and store services. Thus, if you have ever purchased anything from an Apple online store, like the iTunes Store, you already have an Apple ID.

Once entered, your Apple ID will be automatically configured for several services, including the Mac App Store, the iTunes Store, and Game Center. Also, in subsequent Setup Assistant steps this Apple ID will be pre-entered for optional configuration of iCloud services, local user account setup, and system registration.

> **MORE INFO ▸** For more information about Apple ID, visit the Apple ID website at https://appleid.apple.com/.

Setup Assistant: Terms and Conditions

Accepting the Apple terms and conditions is the only registration event you are required to complete in order to use OS X. The content of the Terms and Conditions page will vary depending on whether or not you entered an Apple ID in the previous step. Accepting the terms and conditions does not send any personal or technical information to Apple. In fact, you can accept these terms and conditions even if the Mac is offline and will never access the Internet.

MORE INFO ▶ For more information about Apple terms and conditions, visit the Apple Legal Information website at www.apple.com/legal/.

Setup Assistant: iCloud (Optional)

If you previously entered an Apple ID, you will be prompted to set up iCloud, the Apple free cloud storage and communication service. Though not required for setup, iCloud is the easiest way to share information between OS X, iOS, and even Windows devices. Perhaps the most significant new feature of OS X Mountain Lion is deeper integration with iCloud throughout the operating system.

Enabling a single checkbox here in Setup Assistant will automatically configure your Mac to use iCloud for Mail, Contacts, Calendars & Reminders, Notes, Safari, Photo Stream, and any other applications that support iCloud integration. You will also be prompted to set up the iCloud Find My Mac service, which helps you to locate a lost or stolen Mac system. Much like how iCloud features are spread throughout OS X, iCloud coverage is spread throughout this guide where appropriate. Specifically Lesson 8, "System Security," Lesson 20, "Document Management," and Lesson 25, "Network Services" include additional iCloud service details.

MORE INFO ▶ For more information about iCloud, visit the iCloud web portal at www.icloud.com.

Setup Assistant: Create Computer Account

After making a choice about iCloud, you will be presented with one of the most important steps of the setup process, the Create Your Computer Account screen. From this screen you must create the initial administrative user account for the system. If you previously entered an Apple ID, that information will be used to pre-populate the fields. However, you don't have to associate this account with an Apple ID and can define any account name and password you like.

The account you create here will be the only administrative user account initially allowed to modify system settings, including the creation of additional user accounts. Therefore, until you create additional administrative user accounts, you must remember the authentication information for this first account. Lesson 6, "User Accounts" and Lesson 8, "System Security" cover these topics in greater detail.

Setup Assistant: Time Zone

You're almost done; at this point in the Setup Assistant process you must configure the time zone settings on your Mac. OS X features automatic time zone selection if your Mac includes a Wi-Fi card and is connected to the Internet.

If your Mac isn't connected to the Internet at this point, you will have to manually select a time zone. Even when not connected to the Internet, OS X features a time zone selector with a large database of locations. You can either approximate your location by clicking the map, or you can enter a city name in the field. Try your closest city first, as even small cities are part of the database. If your first choice isn't found, try a larger city in your time zone but still try to stay as local as possible.

> **TIP** Time zone, date, and time settings can all be reconfigured via the Date & Time preferences.

Setup: Registration Process (Optional)

Finally, the registration process will allow you to optionally send system registration information to Apple. This information is used to associate your contact information with the system. This information is primarily used to facilitate AppleCare support.

Again, if you previously entered an Apple ID, Setup Assistant will optionally submit the registration based on your Apple ID account. Conversely, if you didn't enter an Apple ID, you can manually enter your contact information. However, if you do not want to complete the registration process during the initial setup, you can skip it now by clicking the Skip button. You can always complete system registration later by visiting www.apple.com/register.

Reference 3.2
Migration Assistant

If you are migrating from a previous system, the Migration Assistant is a huge time-saver. It enables you to easily transfer all the settings, user accounts, and data from another OS X or Windows system to your new Mac system. During initial system setup, you will be presented with the Migration Assistant. However, you can also use the Migration Assistant at any time after the initial setup by opening /Applications/Utilities/Migration Assistant.

NOTE ▸ When using the Migration Assistant after setup, you cannot migrate Legacy FileVault-protected home folders; to migrate them with Migration Assistant, you must do it during the initial system setup.

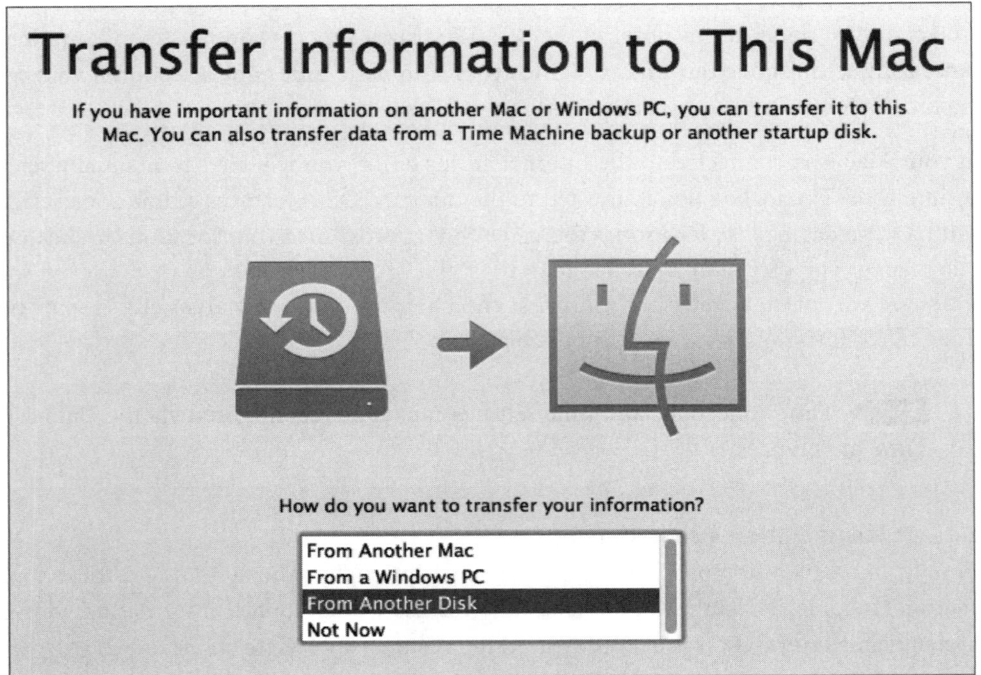

If you choose to use Migration Assistant, you can migrate:

- From another Mac—This option will scan the local network looking for other Macs running Migration Assistant and ready to transfer their information. If you don't have a local network, you can directly connect two running Macs via Ethernet or FireWire, and they will create a local network with each other. You will find Migration Assistant in the /Applications/Utilities/ folder on Macs running Mac OS X v10.4 or later. To migrate from any previous version of Mac OS X, you should always install all available Apple software updates to ensure they include the latest version of Migration Assistant.

MORE INFO ▸ See Knowledge Base document HT4889, "How to use Migration Assistant to transfer files from another Mac."

- From a Windows PC—This option will scan the local network looking for other Windows PCs running Migration Assistant and ready to transfer their information. OS X can migrate from Windows XP SP3 or later, assuming those systems have Windows Migration Assistant installed; it can be downloaded from the Apple support website.

  MORE INFO ▸ See Knowledge Base document HT4796, "About Windows Migration Assistant."

- From Time Machine or another disk—This option will scan all locally mounted disks and the local network looking for Time Machine backups. It will also scan all locally mounted disks for a previous system. This includes any external disks or other Macs in target disk mode connected via FireWire or Thunderbolt.

  MORE INFO ▸ To engage target disk mode on your previous Mac, start up the Mac while holding the T key. Using target disk mode is further detailed in Lesson 13, "File System Troubleshooting."

When the Migration Assistant finds another system or Time Machine backup, it scans the contents and presents you with a list of available items to migrate. If the Migration Assistant discovers multiple system disks or archives, you must select the specific system you wish to migrate from the Information pop-up menu.

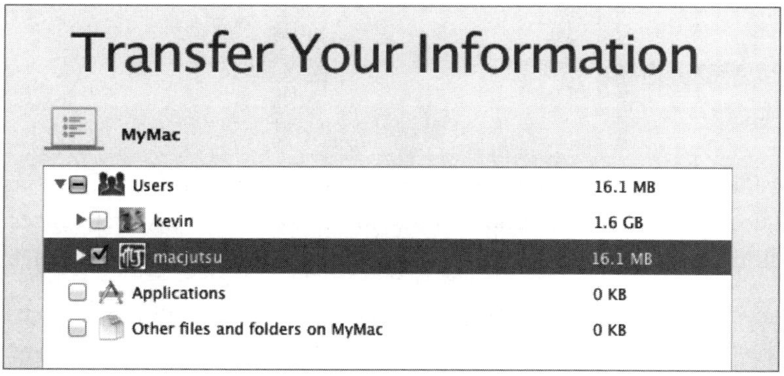

NOTE ▶ If multiple disks are available on a system, you can choose to migrate that data as well. However, the migration process does not create new partitions on the new system; instead, it creates folders on the new system with the contents of the migrated disks.

Once you make your selections, you can begin the transfer process. The more data you have selected to transfer, the longer the process will take. Mature systems with lots of data can take several hours to migrate. After completing the migration, you will be presented with the Setup Assistant Registration and Finishing Up screens.

Reference 3.3
System Preferences

Once your Mac has completed its initial configuration via Setup Assistant, you will rely on various system tools for administration and troubleshooting. The System Preferences application is the primary interface for adjusting user and system settings. (In other operating systems, these settings may be referenced as "control panels.")

You will use System Preferences throughout this guide and any time you are setting up a new Mac. The quickest access to System Preferences is via the Apple menu, because it's always available from any application that shows the menu bar.

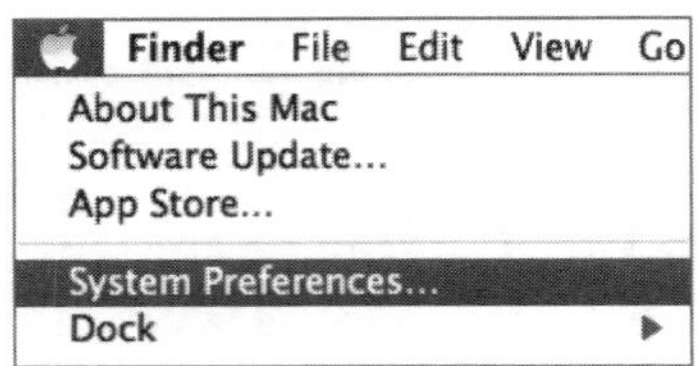

TIP ▶ The System Preferences application can also be found in the /Applications folder. You can use any shortcut method you like to access the System Preferences application, including using its icon in the Dock and placing it in the Finder sidebar.

The first time you access System Preferences, you'll notice it is divided into four separate rows representing the four main categories of System Preferences: Personal, Hardware, Internet & Wireless, and System. Any third-party preference panes you install will appear automatically in a fifth row categorized as simply "Other."

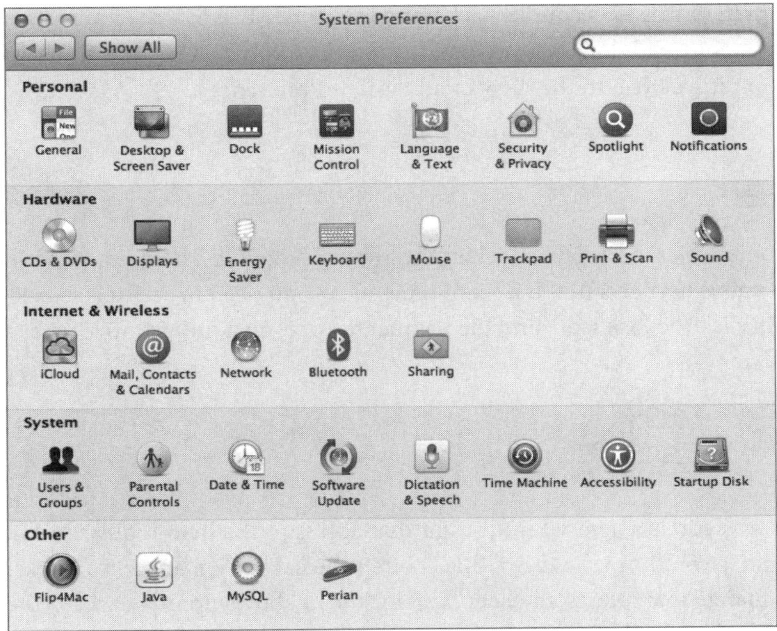

The categorization of the individual System Preferences is deliberate:

- Personal—These preference panes will generally affect only settings for the active user account. In other words, for most of the System Preferences in this category, each user has his or her own discrete settings.
- Hardware—These preference panes are specific to hardware settings. For example, the Energy Saver and Print & Scan preferences in this category can affect every user on the Mac, and thus they require administrator user access to make changes.
- Internet & Wireless—These preference panes are used to configure various Internet and network-related services. The Network preferences pane is the primary interface for managing the network and Internet configuration on your Mac. The iCloud and "Mail, Contacts, & Calendars" preferences are unique to every user, while the Network and Sharing preferences in this category can affect every user on the Mac, and thus require administrative access to make changes.
- System—These preference panes have a systemwide effect when changed. Consequently, all the preferences in this category require administrative access.
- Other (optional)—These preference panes are not part of the standard OS X installation. The developers of third-party preferences decide whether their preferences require administrative access.

Accessing a set of preferences is as simple as clicking the icon. Most System Preferences changes are instantaneous and don't require you to click an Apply or OK button. Clicking the Show All button returns you to the view of all System Preferences.

You'll notice that some preferences have a lock in the lower-left corner. These can be accessed only by an administrative user account. If a set of preferences you need to access is locked from editing, simply click the lock icon, and then authenticate as an administrative user to unlock it.

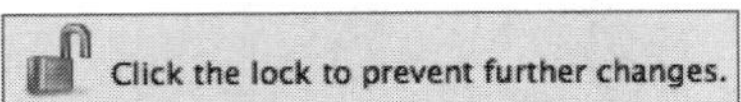

NOTE ▶ The lock icon is a general indication that access to the item requires administrative authentication. In many cases, this is often the case when an item represents a systemwide change that affects all users. The lock icon shows up in a variety of places, not just in System Preferences.

Reference 3.4
Configuration Profiles

An alternative method for system setup is to install configuration profiles. These files were originally created to provide easy setup for iOS devices, but have since made their way to OS X. A configuration profile is a document that includes instructions for specific system settings. For example, configuration profiles can define settings for Mail, Contacts, & Calendars or Network preferences. An administrator can create a configuration profile that contains a variety of settings that would otherwise be difficult for a user to configure. Configuration profiles can be identified by their icon and the filename extension of .mobileconfig.

Trust Profile for Pretendco.mobileconfig

Both Apple and third-party developers provide software for creating configuration profiles. Apple alone is responsible for several tools that can create configuration profiles, including the iPhone Configuration Utility, the Apple Configurator application, and the Profile Manager service of OS X Server.

Administrators can provide configuration profiles through any means that one would share any other document. For example, an administrator could send a configuration profile via email or make it available as a downloadable link on a website. Alternatively, administrators can automatically push configuration profiles to an OS X system that is enrolled in a management server like that provided by the OS X Server Profile Manager. Details regarding the creation of configuration profiles are beyond the scope of this guide, but every Mac administrator should be familiar with how to identify and verify these profiles.

> **MORE INFO ▶** For more information about configuration profiles, see the Apple Technical White Paper: Managing OS X with Configuration Profiles (http://training.apple.com/pdf/wp_osx_configuration_profiles.pdf).

If you are presented with a configuration profile that needs to be installed, simply double-click the file to install it. This will automatically open the configuration profile in the Profiles preference. The Profiles preference appears only when configuration profiles are installed.

From the Profiles preference, any user with administrative privileges can install, verify, or delete a configuration profile. The prior screenshot shows an installed configuration profile that contains a digital certificate, which is used to validate and secure server connections. Delivering this type of information via a configuration profile is ideal because it simplifies a process that would take several more complicated steps using a traditional method.

Verifying the results of an installed configuration profile is a bit more difficult, as the profile could contain multiple settings that affect a variety of different services and applications. However, inspecting the details section of an installed configuration profile in the Profiles preference is a good starting point. Again, in the previous example the Details section shows that this profile contains a digital certificate. As covered in Lesson 9, "Keychain Management," you can open the Keychain Access application to verify the installation of this certificate.

Reference 3.5
System Information

Knowledge of your Mac computer's specifications is always important when installing new software, updating installed software, performing maintenance, or troubleshooting a problem. In this section you will learn how to gather essential system information with the About This Mac dialog and the System Information application.

About Your Mac

Your first stop to discovering a Mac computer's specifications is the About This Mac dialog. You can open this dialog at any point by choosing About This Mac from the Apple menu.

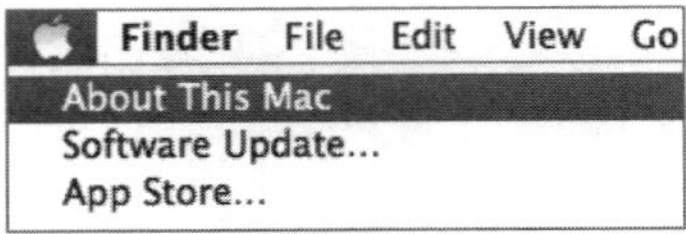

Initially, the About This Mac dialog will show you the system software version, processor type and speed, total system memory, and current startup disk. You can also find the system build identifier and hardware serial number by repeatedly clicking the system version number directly below the bold "OS X" text:

- System version number—This number represents the specific system software version currently installed on the Mac. The first part, 10, obviously represents the tenth generation of the Mac operating system. The second digit, 8, represents the eighth major release of OS X. The final digit, if any, represents an incremental update to the operating system. Incremental updates generally offer very few feature changes but often include a number of bug fixes.
- System build number—This is an even more granular representation of the specific system software version currently installed on the Mac. Apple engineers create hundreds of versions of each system software release as they refine the product. The build number is used to track this process. Also, you may find that the computer-specific builds of OS X that come preinstalled on new Mac hardware will differ from the standard installation builds. This is an important detail to note if you are creating system images for mass distribution, as computer-specific builds of OS X may not work on other types of Mac hardware.
- Hardware serial number—The hardware serial number is also located somewhere on the Mac case. However, Apple has a tendency to choose form over function, so the serial number may be quite difficult to find. As with many other complicated products, the Mac serial number is a unique number used to identify that particular Mac for maintenance and service issues.

NOTE ▶ Macs that have had their logic boards replaced may not properly display the serial number in the About This Mac dialog.

System Information

The information in the About This Mac dialog is only the tip of the iceberg compared with what can be found via the System Information (formerly System Profiler) application. From the About This Mac dialog, click the More Info button to open System Information. If you open System Information via this method, you will be presented with a more informative About This Mac window.

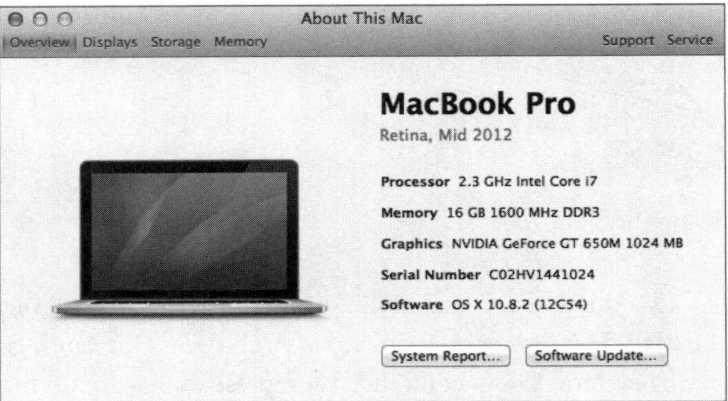

From this window you can view a bit more detail about your Mac, including its primary specifications, display configuration, storage allocation, and installed memory. Note the light grey text below the Mac model shows the model's specific full name. For example, the previous screenshot was taken from a MacBook Pro (Retina, Mid 2012). Quite possibly the best feature of this window is the Support and Service tabs to the far right that link directly to specifically useful areas of the Apple support and service websites.

To examine the full gamut of what System Information offers, return to the Overview section of the About This Mac window and click the System Report button. This will open a new System Information window revealing all available reporting options.

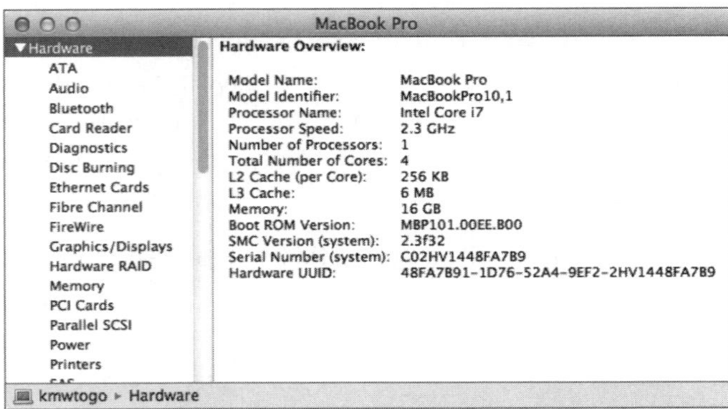

You will use System Information to locate critical system details in nearly every lesson of this guide. Additionally, one of the most important uses of System Information is as a documentation tool. Anytime you need to document the current state of a Mac, you can use System Information to create a detailed system report. To create this report while in System Information, simply choose File > Export As Text.

Exercise 3.1
Configure a New OS X System for Exercises

Prerequisites

This exercise is only necessary if your computer has not already been set up. If you are using a Mac with existing accounts, perform Exercise 3.2 instead.

- Your computer must have a new installation of OS X Mountain Lion, and not have been set up yet.

The initial OS X configuration is made very simple thanks to the Setup Assistant. However, in this lesson you will learn how a few of these initial configurations have a fundamental and widespread effect on the system.

In this exercise you will configure a clean installation of OS X on your class computer. Configuring OS X for this class entails answering a few basic questions and setting up the initial administrator user account. Completing these tasks will acquaint you with the Setup Assistant application.

Configure OS X with Setup Assistant

The following steps will walk you through the basic setup of OS X using the Setup Assistant:

1 At the Welcome screen, select the appropriate region and click Continue.

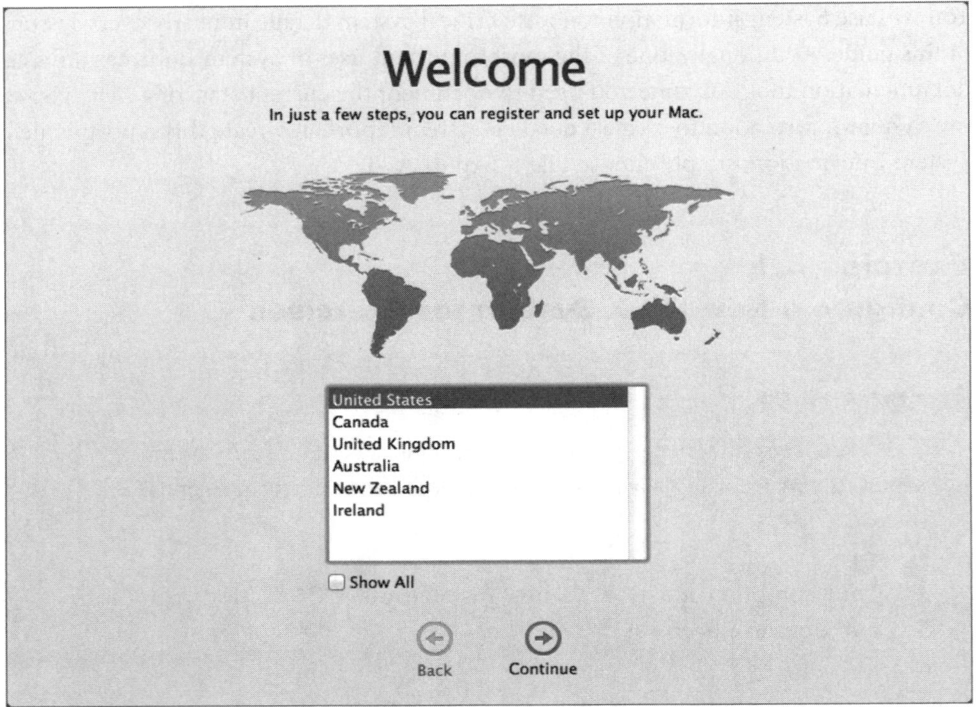

NOTE ► If you pause for a few moments at the Setup Assistant Welcome screen, the VoiceOver tutorial will begin. This is an optional tutorial that explains how to use the VoiceOver assistance technology designed for visually impaired people. VoiceOver will be further discussed in Lesson 21, "Application Management and Troubleshooting"

2 In the Select Your Keyboard screen, select the appropriate keyboard layout and click Continue.

   The Setup Assistant will evaluate your network environment and try to determine if you are connected to the Internet. This can take a few moments.

3 If asked to Select Your Wi-Fi Network or How Do You Connect to the Internet, configure it appropriately for your Internet connection. If you are performing this exercise in a class, please ask your instructor how you should configure your computer.

If you are not asked about your Internet connection, your computer's network settings have already been configured via DHCP and you may move on to step 4.

4. In the "Transfer Information to this Mac" screen, select "Not Now," and click Continue.

   If you were replacing a computer, the other options would assist you in migrating user data and system information from the old computer to the new one.

5. In the "Enable Location Services" screen, select "Enable Location Services on this Mac," and click Continue.

   Location Services will attempt to infer your location from nearby wireless networks, and allows you to grant applications access to this information.

6. In the "Apple ID" screen, click Skip.

   You will set up an Apple ID account in a later exercise.

7. When asked if you are sure you want to skip signing in, click Skip.

8. In the "Terms and Conditions" screen, you may use the right-arrow buttons to read the OS X Software License Agreement. When you have finished reading, click Continue.

9. In the dialog that appears, click Agree.

10. In the Create Your Computer Account screen, enter the following information:

    NOTE ▶ It is important that you create this account as specified here. If you do not, future exercises may not work as written. **This bold blue text** is used throughout this guide to indicate text that you should enter exactly as shown.

    - Full Name: **Local Admin**
    - Account Name: **ladmin**

    If you are performing this exercise in a class, enter **ladminpw** in the Password and Verify fields. If you are performing this exercise on your own, select a more secure password for the Local Admin account. Be sure to remember the password you have chosen, as you will need to reenter it periodically as you use this computer.

    Leave "Require password when logging in" selected.

    You may provide a password hint if you want to.

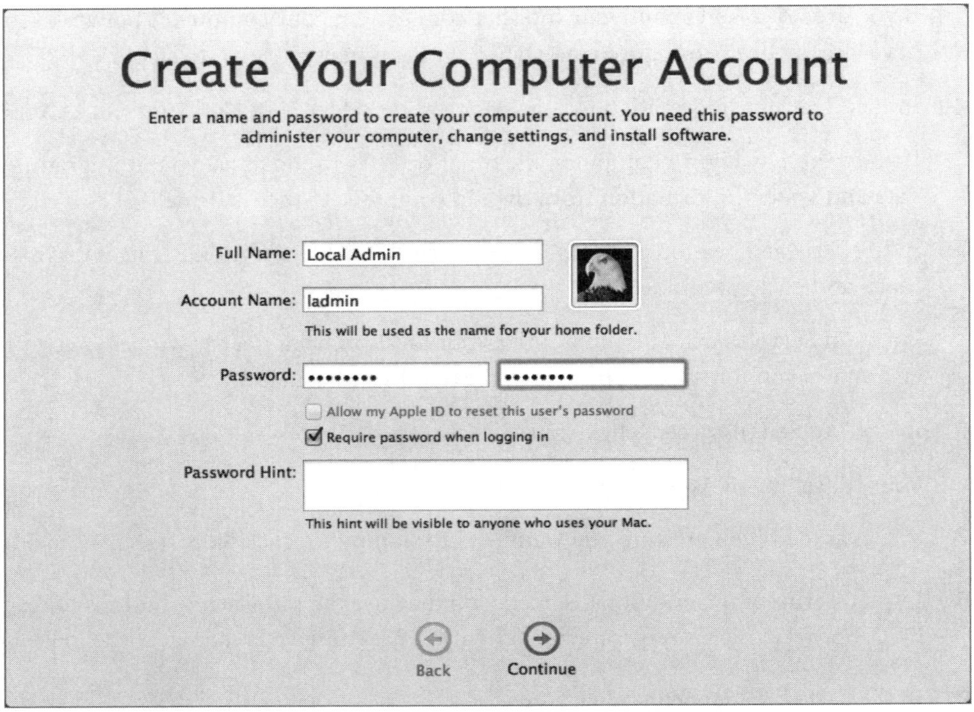

11 Click Continue.

12 If you did not enter a password hint, you will be given another chance to enter one. Click Continue again to skip entering a hint.

13 In the “Select Time Zone” screen, choose your correct time zone. Choose the nearest location from the pop-up menu.

14 Click Continue.

15 If you are presented with a “Register” screen, click Skip.

16 When asked if you are sure you don’t want to register, click Skip.

17 If you are presented with a "Finishing Up" screen with information about using multi-touch scrolling, follow the instructions to complete the introduction.

18 If you are presented with the Thank You screen, click Start Using Your Mac.

Skip Exercise 3.2 and proceed to Exercise 3.3 to configure your preference settings.

Exercise 3.2
Configure an Existing OS X System for Exercises

Prerequisites

- Your computer must be running OS X Mountain Lion.
- Your computer must already have been set up, and you must have an existing administrator account on it. If your computer has not been set up (that is, if the initial administrator account has not been created), perform Exercise 3.1 instead.

In order to provide a consistent environment for the rest of the exercises in this guide, you will use System Preferences to create a new administrator account.

Create a New Administrator Account in System Preferences

1 If necessary, log into your existing administrator account.

2 From the Apple menu, choose System Preferences.

3 In System Preferences, click Users & Groups.

4 In the lower-left corner, click the lock icon.

5 In the dialog that appears, enter the password for your existing administrator account and click Unlock.

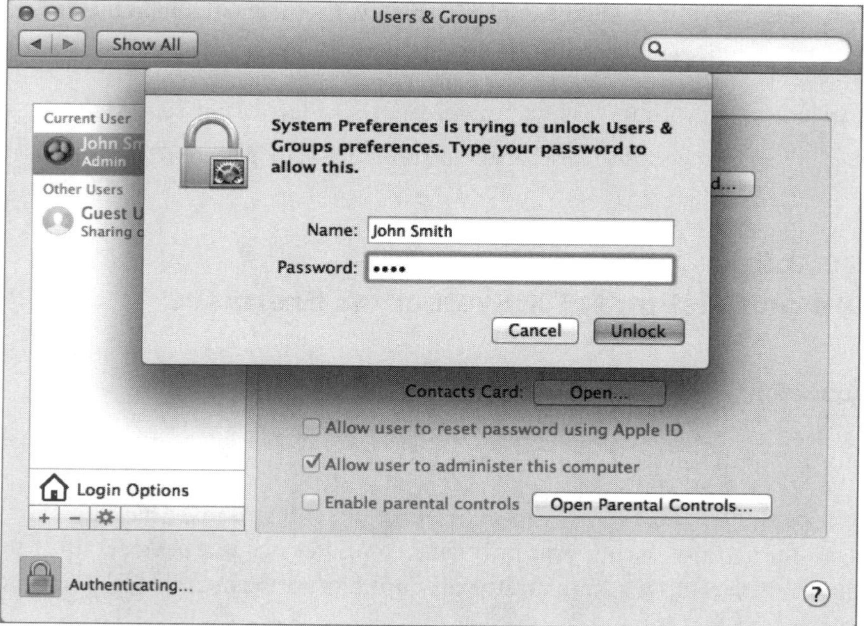

6 Click the Add (+) button under the user list.

7 In the dialog that appears, enter the following information:

NOTE ► It is important that you create this account as specified here. If you do not, future exercises may not work as written. If you already have an account named "Local Admin" or "ladmin", you will have to use a different name here and then remember to use your substitute name throughout the rest of the exercises. **This bold blue text** is used throughout this guide to indicate text that you should enter exactly as shown.

- New Account: choose Administrator
- Full Name: **Local Admin**
- Account Name: **ladmin**

If you are performing this exercise in a class, enter **ladminpw** in the Password and Verify fields. If you are performing this exercise on your own, select a more secure password for the Local Admin account. Be sure to remember the password you have chosen, as you will need to reenter it periodically as you use this computer.

You may provide a password hint if you want to.

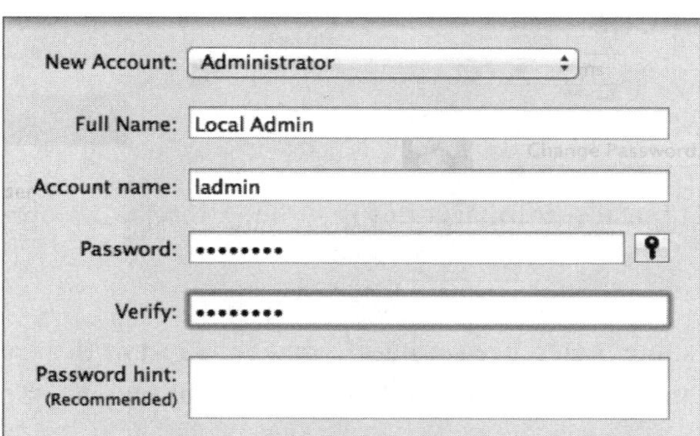

8 Click Create User.

9 At the bottom of the user list, click Login Options.

10 If an account is selected for Automatic Login, use the pop-up menu to switch it to Off.

11 Close System Preferences and log out.

12 At the login screen, select the Local Admin account and enter its password (**ladminpw**, or whatever you chose earlier).

13 Press Return.

14 When you are prompted to enter an Apple ID, click Skip, and then click Skip in the confirmation dialog.

You will set up an Apple ID account in a later exercise.

15 If a Thank You screen appears, click Start Using Your Mac.

Proceed to Exercise 3.3 to configure your preference settings.

Exercise 3.3
Examine System Preferences

> **Prerequisites**
>
> - You must have created the Local Admin account in either Exercise 3.1 or Exercise 3.2.

In this exercise, you will configure some preference settings to make the rest of the exercises easier. This will also give you an introduction to configuring application and system preferences in OS X.

Adjust Finder Preferences

The OS X default Finder settings make it very easy for users to find and work with their own files, but are not optimal for system administrators who frequently access files outside their Home folder. Since you will be exploring the OS X system more than working with your own files, some customization is in order.

1 If a notification opens, informing you that software updates are available for your computer, ignore it for the moment (or dismiss it by clicking it and swiping to the right).

2 If any dialogs open asking, "Do you want to use <*some volume*> to back up with Time Machine?", click Don't Use in each dialog.

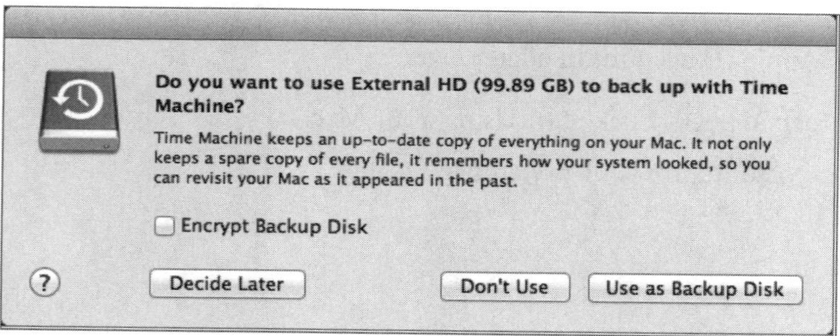

3 From the menu bar, choose Finder > Preferences. If you prefer, you can use the keyboard shortcut Command-Comma instead.

The Finder is actually an application, and its preferences can be configured in much the same way as any other OS X application.

4 Select the options to show Hard disks, External disks, and Connected servers on the desktop.

5 From the "New Finder windows show" pop-up menu, choose your startup volume (typically Macintosh HD).

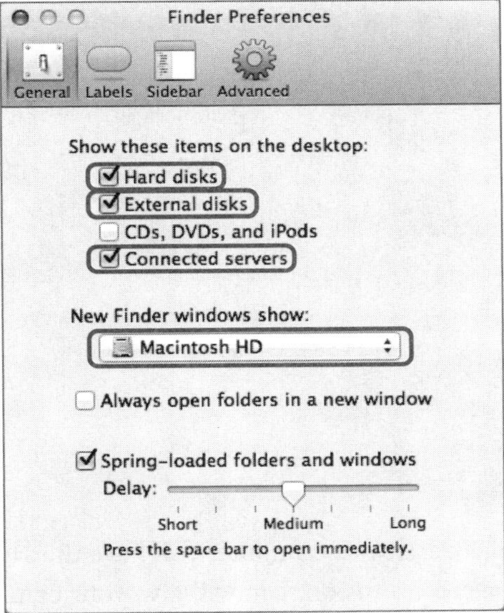

6 At the top of the Finder Preferences window, select the Sidebar button.

7 Enable ladmin in the Favorites section of the sidebar, and Hard disks in the Devices section. Note that Hard disks should be fully enabled (check mark in the checkbox), not just partially enabled (dash in the checkbox).

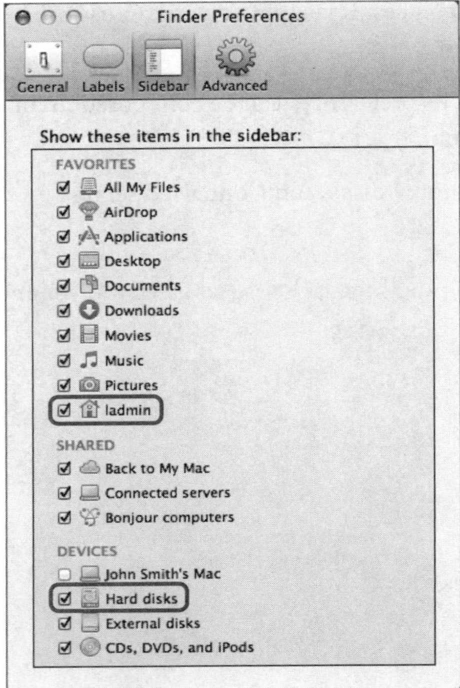

8 Close the Finder Preferences window.

Set the Computer Name

If you are performing these exercises as part of a class, your computer will have the same name as all the other students' computers. To avoid confusion, you will give your computer a unique name.

1 From the Apple menu, choose System Preferences.

2 In System Preferences, click Sharing.

Note that if you aren't sure where to find something in System Preferences, you can use the Spotlight search field in the top right of the window. It will search for matching or related settings and highlight the preference panes they can be found in.

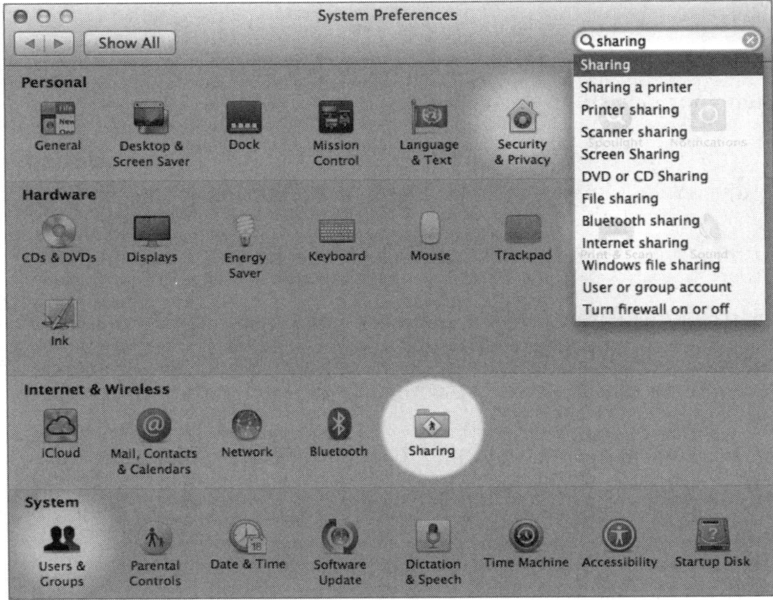

3 Enter a unique name for your computer in the Computer Name field. If you are performing these exercises in a class, using your full name is recommended.

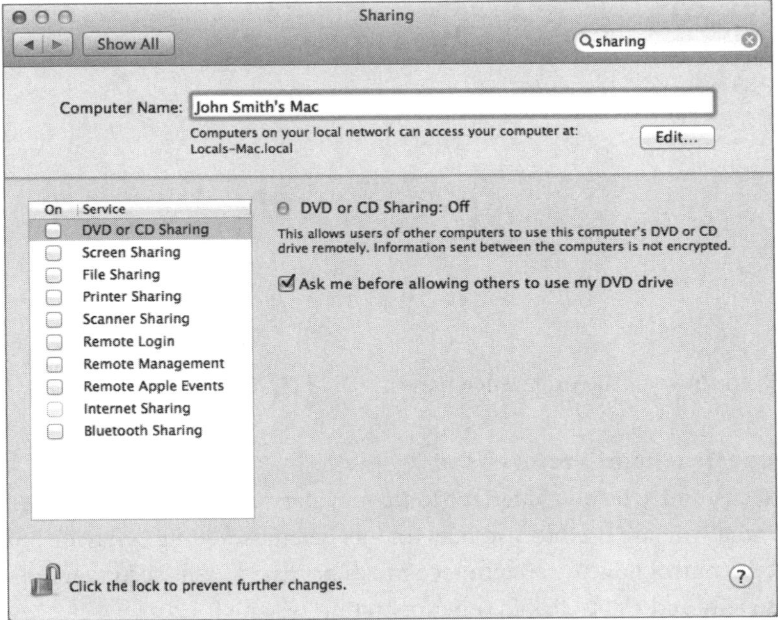

4 Press Return.

Notice that your local host name (.local name) displayed under your computer name updates to match your new computer name.

5 If you are performing these exercises on your own, click Show All, and then skip ahead to the "Adjust Your Mouse/Trackpad Preferences" section of this exercise.

6 If you are performing these exercises in a class, select the Remote Management checkbox.

NOTE ▶ In a classroom situation, remote management will allow your instructor to control the keyboard and mouse, gather information, and update your Mac throughout this course, enabling him to assist you with steps and exercises if necessary.

A dialog asks what you want users to be able to do using remote management.

7 Hold down the Option key while clicking one of the checkboxes to select all the options in the dialog.

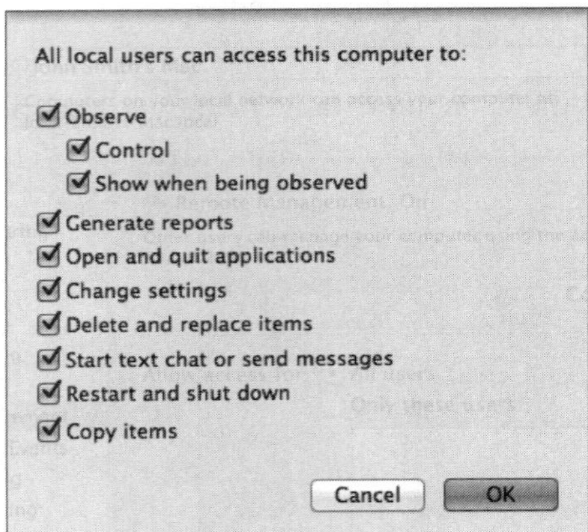

8 Click OK.

9 Click Show All to show all the preference panes.

Adjust Your Mouse/Trackpad Preferences

OS X allows you to customize its user interface to fit your personal preferences. For example, depending on what you are used to you may find its default scrolling behavior unintuitive. Also, you can control how the system recognizes primary versus secondary mouse clicks (analogous to left- and right-click in other operating systems).

Note that since Control-click always works as a secondary click, these instructions will describe it as Control-click.

1 If you are using a mouse, select the Mouse preference pane.

- If your mouse has a scroll wheel (or equivalent), use the "Scroll direction: natural" option to adjust which direction it works. The default is that pushing the wheel up moves the window's contents up.
- If your mouse has multiple buttons, use the "Primary mouse button" option to control which button is the "primary" (used for selecting, normally the left button), and which button is the "secondary" (used for opening shortcut menus, normally the right button or Control-click).

2 If you are using a Trackpad, select the Trackpad preference pane.

- Adjust the "Tap to Click" and "Secondary click" to your liking (used for opening shortcut menus, normally the right mouse button or Control-click).
- Click "Scroll & Zoom," and use the "Scroll direction: natural" option to adjust which direction it works. The default is that moving two fingers up moves the window's contents up.
- Check the other options under "Scroll & Zoom" and "More Gestures" and make any appropriate changes.

3 Quit System Preferences.

You should now proceed to either Exercise 3.4 or 3.5, depending on whether you are performing these exercises in a classroom or independently.

Exercise 3.4
Download the Student Materials in a Classroom

Prerequisites

- You must have performed Exercise 3.3.
- You must be performing these exercises in a class, or have set up your own server configured as in the Mainserver Setup Instructions. If you are following these exercises on your own and have not set up a server to support the exercises, perform Exercise 3.5 instead.

NOTE ▶ This exercise is written for students performing these exercises in a classroom environment. You can also use this exercise if you have set up your own server configured as in the Mainserver Setup Instructions (available in the Bonus Materials for this guide after you register at www.peachpit.com/apts.osxmountainlion). If you are following these exercises on your own and have not set up a server to support the exercises, perform Exercise 3.5 instead.

In this exercise you will download the student materials required for the rest of the exercises in the course.

Connect to Mainserver

You will now connect to the file server (called Mainserver) to download the student materials. The details of networking, connecting to, and providing network services will be covered in later lessons.

1. If necessary, open a new Finder window by choosing File > New Finder Window or using the shortcut Command-N.

   Look for the server named Mainserver in the shared section of the sidebar (under Shared). If Mainserver is not shown, click All to view all the shared items.

2. Select Mainserver. If you had to click All in the previous step, you will have to double-click the Mainserver icon.

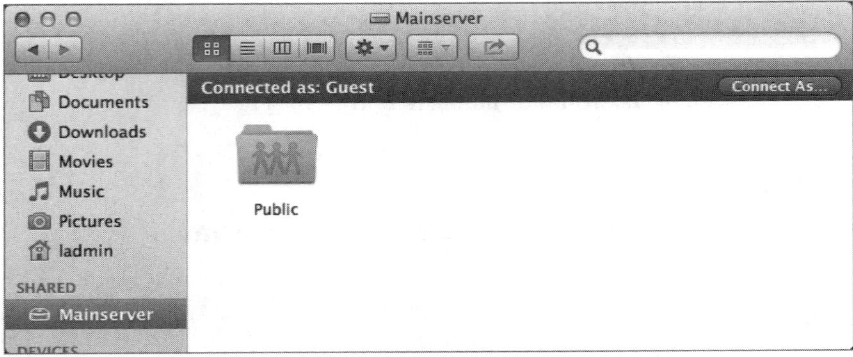

3. Double-click the Public folder to open it.

Copy the StudentMaterials Folder to your Computer

1 Inside the Public folder, select (single-click) the StudentMaterials folder.

2 Copy the folder by choosing Edit > Copy "StudentMaterials", by pressing Command-C, or by Control-clicking the folder and choosing Copy "StudentMaterials" from the shortcut menu.

3 Open the Macintosh HD (either from your desktop, or the Finder window's sidebar).

4 Open the Users folder.

5 Open the Shared folder.

6 Paste the StudentMaterials folder into the Shared folder by choosing Edit > Paste Item, by pressing Command-V, or by Control-clicking in the Shared folder and choosing Paste Item from the shortcut menu.

   This creates a copy of the student materials on your computer. If your instructor has included software updates in the student materials, it may take several minutes to download them. You do not need to wait for it to finish.

7 Drag your copy of the StudentMaterials folder to the right side of the Dock. You will be accessing the StudentMaterials folder frequently, and this gives you an easy shortcut to it. Be sure to place it between other entries (so it is added to the Dock) rather than over another entry (which would move it to that folder).

8 Optionally, you can also drag the StudentMaterials folder to the Finder's sidebar in the Favorites section to give yourself another shortcut to access it. As in the Dock, be sure to place it between other entries.

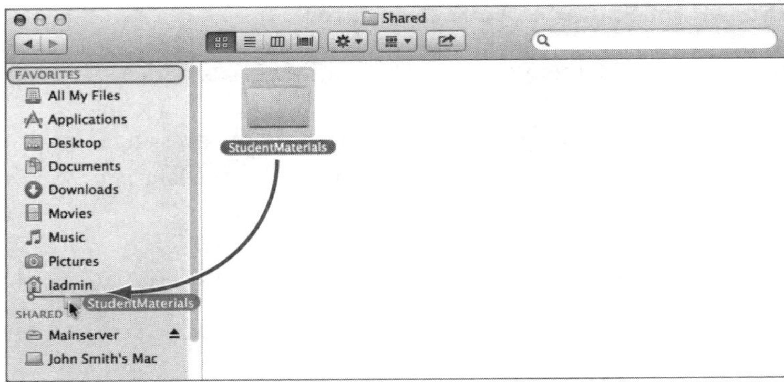

9 Choose Go > Applications (or use the shortcut Command-Shift-A).

10 Drag the TextEdit application into the left side of your Dock, so that you will always have an easy way to launch it.

11 If necessary, wait for the StudentMaterials folder to finish downloading to your computer.

12 Unmount Mainserver by clicking the eject icon next to it in the Finder sidebar.

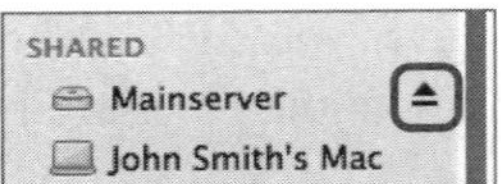

You should now skip Exercise 3.5 and proceed to Exercise 3.6.

Exercise 3.5
Download the Student Materials Independently

Prerequisites

- You must have performed Exercise 3.3.
- Do not perform this exercise if you are in a class, or have set up your own server configured as in the Mainserver Setup instructions. If you have access to a server configured to support these exercises, perform Exercise 3.4 instead.

In this exercise you will download the student materials required for the rest of the exercises in the course.

Download the StudentMaterials Folder from the Web

You will now connect to the Pearson Education web server to download the student materials.

1. Open Safari.
2. Navigate to **www.peachpit.com/apts.osxmountainlion.**
3. Click the "Register your product" link.
4. Enter the guide's 13-digit ISBN and click Submit.
5. If you do not already have a Peachpit account, follow the prompts to create one.

   You will be taken to the Registered Products page of your account.
6. Click the "Access Bonus Content" link to access the bonus material.

   NOTE ▸ If you have access to another computer running OS X Mountain Lion and want to configure it as a server to support these exercises, do not download the Student Materials here. Instead, download the Mainserver Setup file onto the computer you will use as a server, and follow the enclosed Mainserver Setup Instructions.
7. Click the link to download the Student Materials.

   The student materials for these exercises will be downloaded as a Zip archive and automatically expanded into the StudentMaterials folder.
8. Click the downloads button (down-arrow icon) near the top right of the window.
9. Click the view (magnifying glass icon) next to StudentMaterials.

Your Downloads folder opens in the Finder, showing the StudentMaterials folder inside it.

10 On your desktop, find the icon for your startup disk (generally Macintosh HD), and double-click it.

This opens a new Finder window showing the contents of the startup disk.

11 Open the Users folder.

12 Open the Shared folder.

13 Drag the StudentMaterials icon from the Downloads folder into the Shared folder.

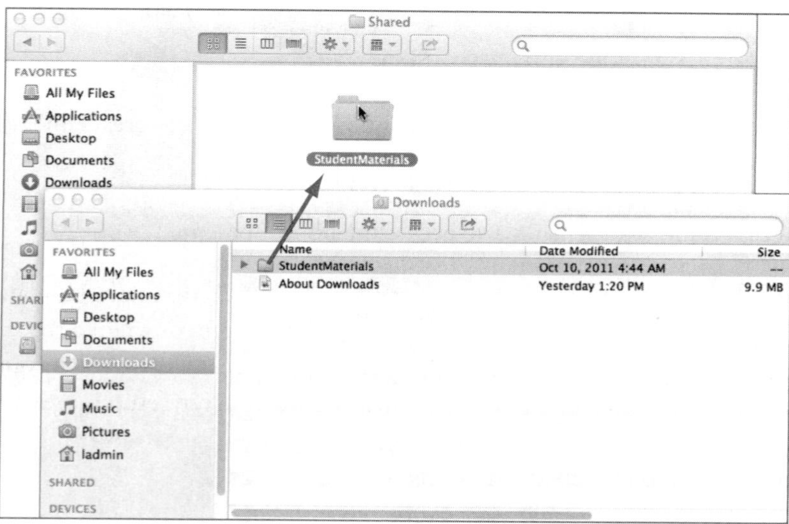

14 Close the Downloads folder.

15 Drag the StudentMaterials icon from the Shared folder to the right side of the Dock. You will be accessing the StudentMaterials folder frequently, and this will give you an easy shortcut to it. Be sure to place it between other entries (so it is added to the Dock) rather than over another entry (which would move it to that folder).

16 Optionally, you can also drag the StudentMaterials folder to the Finder sidebar in the Favorites section to give yourself another shortcut to access it. As in the Dock, be sure to place it between other entries.

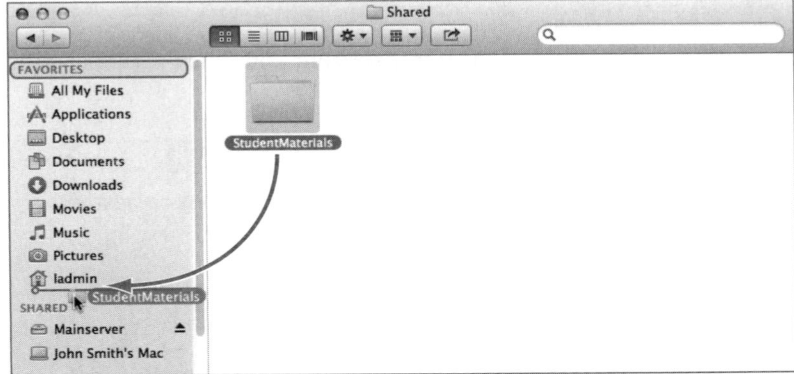

17 Choose Go > Applications (or use the shortcut Command-Shift-A).

18 Drag the TextEdit application into the left side of your Dock, so that you will always have an easy way to launch it.

Exercise 3.6
Install a Configuration Profile

Prerequisites

- You must have downloaded the StudentMaterials folder, using the instructions in either Exercise 3.4 or Exercise 3.5.

In addition to manually configuring settings on OS X computers, you can also control a computer's settings by installing configuration profiles. This capability allows you to easily standardize configuration across multiple computers.

In this exercise, you will demonstrate this by setting your Energy Saver settings with a configuration profile.

Change Your Energy Saver Settings with a Configuration Profile

1 If necessary, open System Preferences by choosing Apple menu > System Preferences.

2 Select the Energy Saver preference pane.

3 Note your computer's sleep settings. Depending on your computer, they may differ from those shown below.

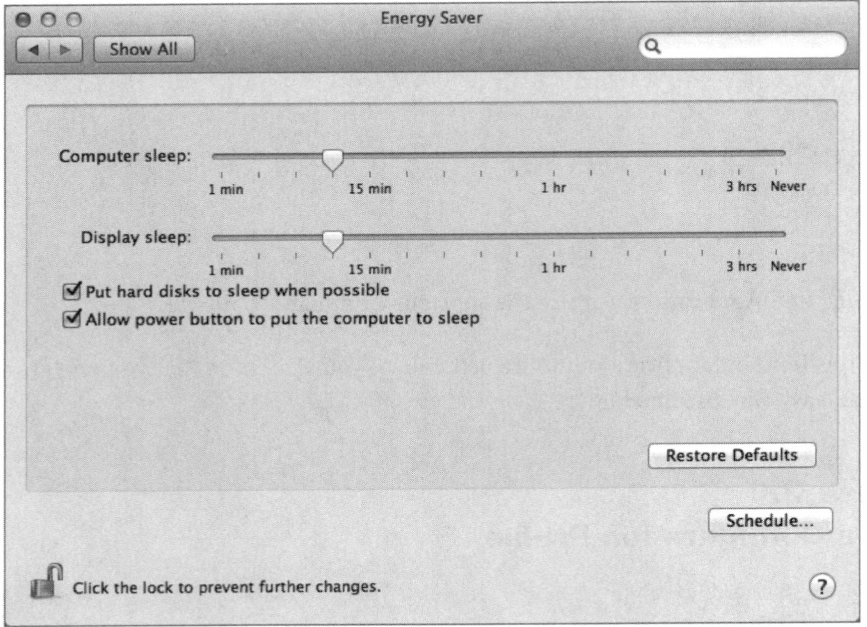

4 Open the StudentMaterials folder. Remember that you put a shortcut to it in your Dock.

5 Open the Lesson3 folder.

6 Open Energy_Saver.mobileconfig.

The profile automatically opens in the Profiles pane of System Preferences.

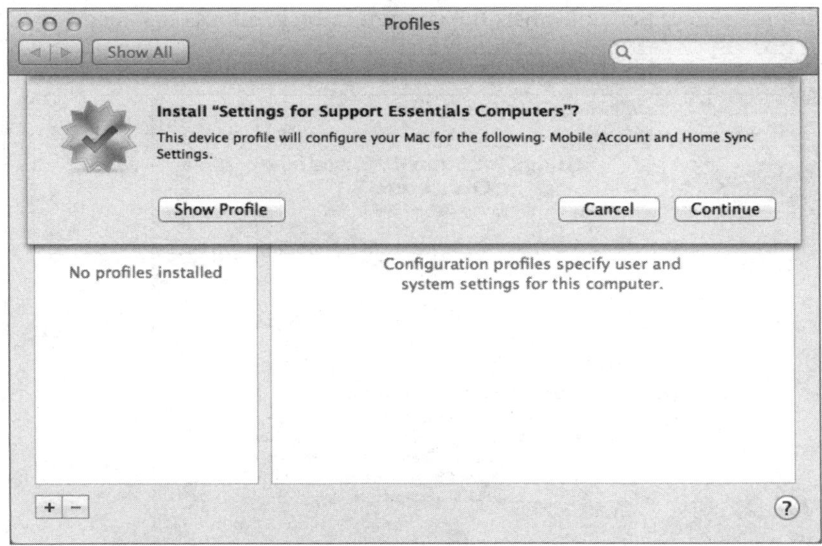

7 Click Show Profile to display the details of the profile and its payload (contained settings). You will need to scroll down to see its full contents.

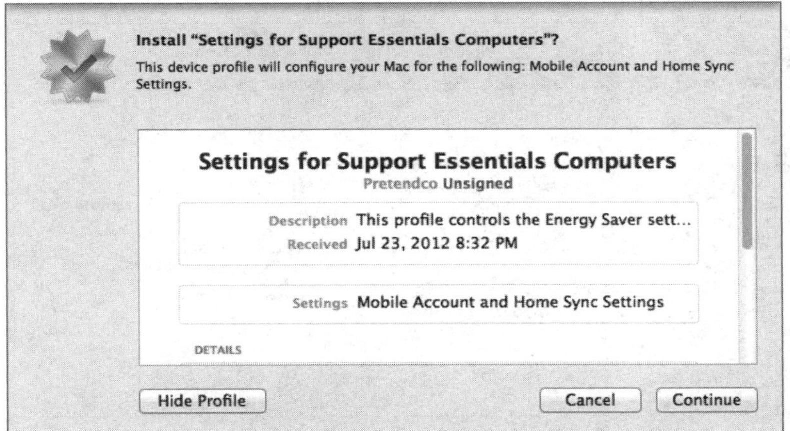

8 Click Continue.

9 Click Install.

10 Enter the Local Admin account's password (ladminpw, or whatever you chose earlier) when prompted.

The Profile preferences pane now lists the configuration profile as installed.

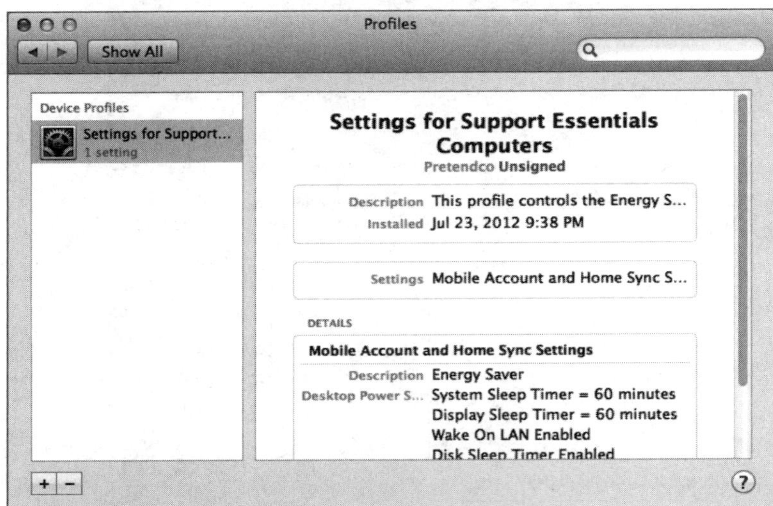

11 Click Show All, and then select the Energy Saver preferences pane.

The Energy Saver settings have changed to match those in the profile.

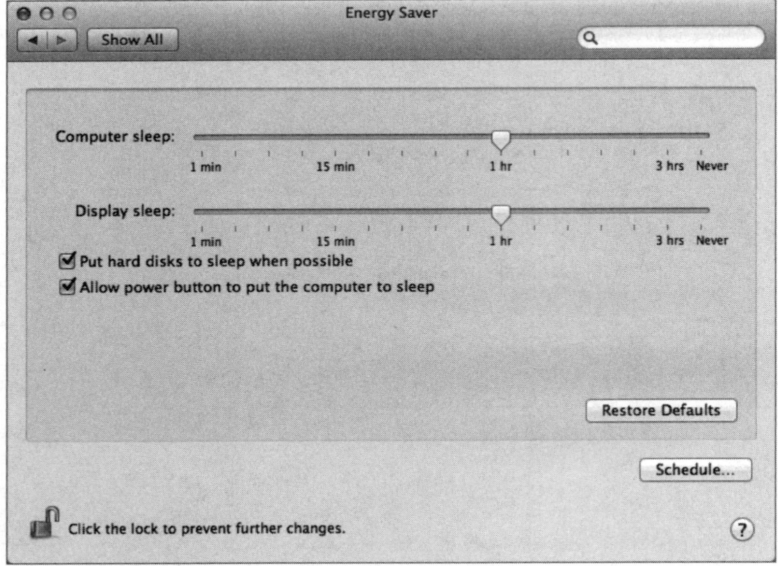

12 Close System Preferences.

Exercise 3.7
Examine System Information

System Information is the primary tool for gathering configuration information in OS X. In this exercise, you will explore its features.

Use About This Mac

1 From the Apple menu, choose About This Mac.

A dialog opens showing basic information about your computer.

2 Click the OS X version number (below the large "OS X"). The version number will be replaced by the system's build number (a more specific identifier for the version of OS X you are using).

3 Click the build number, and it will be replaced by your computer's hardware serial number.

Use System Information

1 In the About This Mac dialog, click the More Info button.

The System Information utility opens, and displays most of the same information that was in the About This Mac dialog.

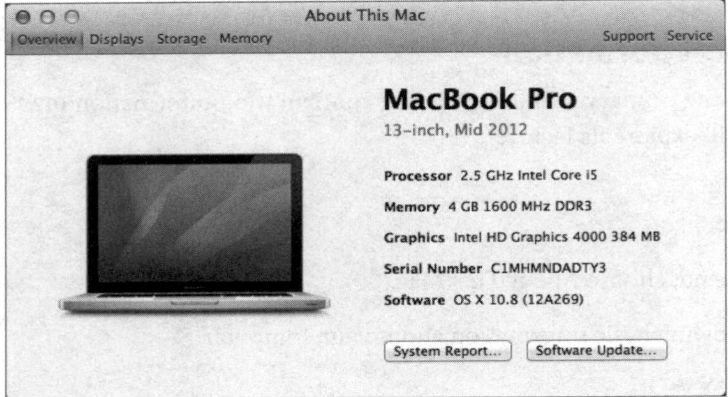

TIP The System Information application can also be found in the /Applications/Utilities folder, or in the Other section of Launchpad. You can use any shortcut method you like to access the System Information application, including placing it in the Dock and the Finder sidebar.

TIP You can also directly access System Information from the Apple menu by holding the Option key. This changes the About This Mac Apple menu choice to System Information. When opening System Information directly, you will skip the summary About This Mac window and instead be presented with the full system report.

2 Click through the Displays, Storage, and Memory tabs in System Information's toolbar to view more information about your computer's hardware configuration.

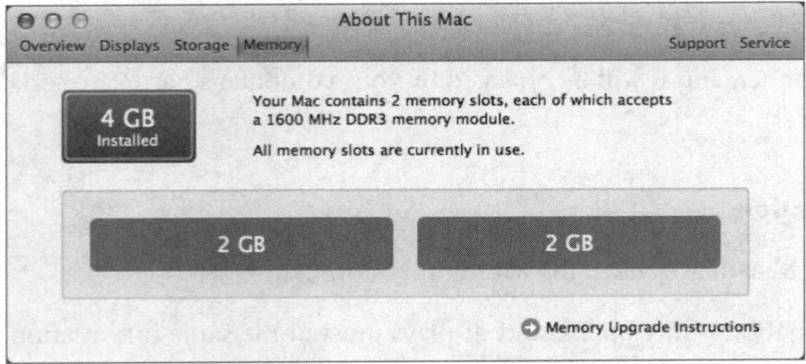

3 Click the Service tab.

System Information displays information and options for repair and warranty coverage of your computer.

4 Click "Check my service and support coverage status."

5 In the confirmation dialog that appears, click Allow.

Safari opens, and shows your computer's model name and warranty status.

6 Quit Safari

7 In System Information, choose File > Show System Report.

System Information displays a more detailed report of the hardware, network, and software configuration of your computer.

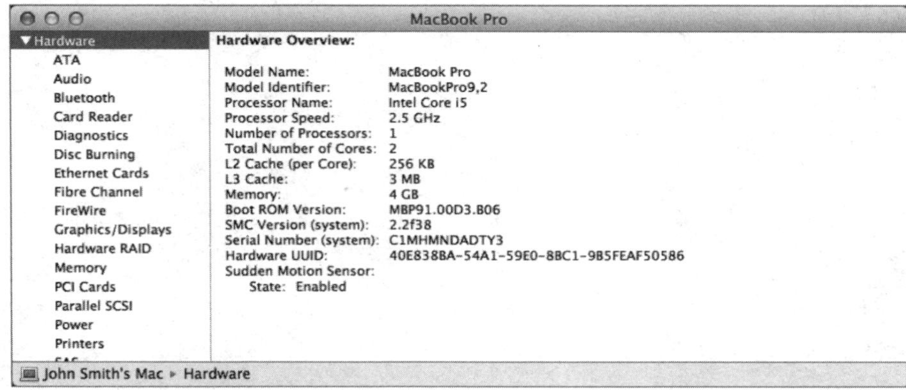

8. Explore the system report by clicking various categories of information in the report's sidebar. Note that some categories may take a while to load.

9. From the menu bar, choose File > Save, enter a name for your system's report, and then click Save.

   When saving reports like this, it is usually best to choose a naming convention that includes the computer name (or other identifier) and the date.

   This finishes gathering information on your computer, and saves it in a report that documents your computer's current status.

10. Quit System Information.

Lesson **4**

OS X Recovery

From a troubleshooting viewpoint, one of the most useful OS X features is the OS X Recovery system. OS X Recovery replaces functionality previously accessed via an OS X installation DVD. This enables you to not only reinstall OS X but also to access a variety of administration and troubleshooting utilities. The primary difference is that the OS X Recovery system is, by default, located on the primary system disk. This allows easy "anytime" access to recovery utilities without the need for additional media.

GOALS

- ▶ Access the utilities available in OS X Recovery
- ▶ Reinstall OS X from OS X Recovery
- ▶ Create an external OS X Recovery disk

> **TIP** The OS X Recovery system partition, dubbed Recovery HD, is a hidden partition that will never appear in the graphical interface when running OS X. The Recovery HD partition is automatically created out of the last 700 MB or so of the installation destination.

In this lesson you will learn how to access OS X Recovery on both new Macs that came with OS X preinstalled and on systems that were upgraded to OS X. You will also briefly explore the utilities available from OS X Recovery. As long as you don't make any permanent changes using the utilities in OS X Recovery, you can safely explore without damaging your primary OS X system.

Reference 4.1
Startup from OS X Recovery

Mac systems running OS X Mountain Lion, including both systems that shipped with OS X Mountain Lion and upgraded systems, include a hidden OS X Recovery system on the local system disk. To access this copy of OS X Recovery, simply restart the Mac while holding the Command-R keyboard shortcut. Once the OS X Recovery system fully starts, the OS X Utilities window appears. From there you can install (or reinstall) OS X and choose from a variety of maintenance applications.

If for some reason OS X Recovery doesn't start or isn't installed on the local system disk, there are two alternatives for accessing it:

- If you have a Mac model released in mid-2010 or later—Assuming your Mac has the latest firmware updates, it's capable of accessing OS X Internet Recovery. As the name implies, your late-model Mac can attempt to redownload the OS X Recovery system from Apple servers. If the local OS X Recovery system is missing, late-model Macs should automatically attempt to access OS X Internet Recovery. You can also force a system to start up to OS X Internet Recovery by holding the Command-Option-R keyboard shortcut.

  MORE INFO ▸ For more about using OS X Internet Recovery, see Knowledge Base document HT4718, "OS X: About OS X Recovery," and document HT4904, "Computers that can be upgraded to use OS X Internet Recovery."

- If you have an external OS X Recovery disk—Connect the OS X Recovery disk to your Mac and restart the Mac while holding the Option key. This opens the Mac computer's Startup Manager, where you can use the arrow and Return keys or the mouse and trackpad to select the OS X Recovery HD. Reference section 4.3, "External OS X Recovery Disks," covers this topic in greater detail.

Reference 4.2
OS X Recovery Utilities

OS X Recovery is a useful administrative and troubleshooting resource. When you start up from this system, you will have access to several system administration and maintenance tools. This system even has a few utilities you cannot find anywhere else in OS X. Again, when you first start the OS X Recovery system, you are greeted with the OS X Utilities window.

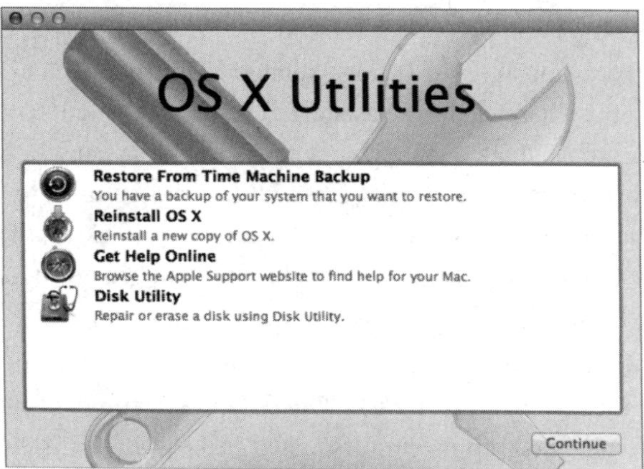

NOTE ▸ When a Mac is started up from OS X Recovery, Ethernet and Wi-Fi networking is available if the network provides DHCP services. While Ethernet is automatically enabled if physically connected, you can connect to a wireless network from the Wi-Fi menu item.

NOTE ▸ While running from OS X Recovery, if the Mac computer's system disk is protected by FileVault 2, any access to this disk will first require unlocking of the disk. In most cases, any local user's password on the system should be allowed to unlock the system FileVault 2 drive. Lesson 11, "FileVault 2," covers this topic in greater detail.

From the OS X Utilities window in OS X Recovery, you can access:

- Restore From Time Machine Backup—You can use this to restore a full-system Time Machine backup from either a network or a locally connected disk. Lesson 18, "Time Machine," covers this topic in greater detail.
- Reinstall OS X—As the name implies, this will open the OS X Installer. If you are running from a full OS X Restore system, like the OS X Mountain Lion Recovery Disk purchased from Apple, the disk contains all the OS X installation assets. However, the local hidden OS X Recovery HD and disks created with OS X Recovery Disk Assistant do not contain the installation assets and thus require Internet access to reinstall OS X. Further, the OS X Installer must verify that the user is allowed access to the OS X Mountain Lion assets. On older Macs that were upgraded to OS X Mountain Loin, you will have to verify the installation by providing the Apple ID used to purchase OS X. For Macs that shipped with OS X Mountain Lion, this verification is automatic. Lesson 2, "Install OS X Mountain Lion," covers this topic in greater detail.

- Get Help Online—This will open Safari, directed to the Apple support website.
- Disk Utility—This application is responsible for storage-related administration and maintenance. It is especially useful when the Mac has started up from OS X Recovery, because Disk Utility can be used to manage a system disk that otherwise can't be managed when in use as the startup disk. Specifically, Disk Utility can be used to prepare a disk for a new installation of OS X or to attempt repairs on a disk that fails installation. Lesson 10, "File Systems and Storage," covers this topic in greater detail.
- Startup Disk (by clicking the close button or quitting)—If you attempt to quit the OS X Utilities window, it will prompt you to start the Startup Disk utility. This utility will allow you to select the default system startup disk. The default startup disk can be overridden using any of the alternate startup modes discussed in Lesson 30, "System Troubleshooting."

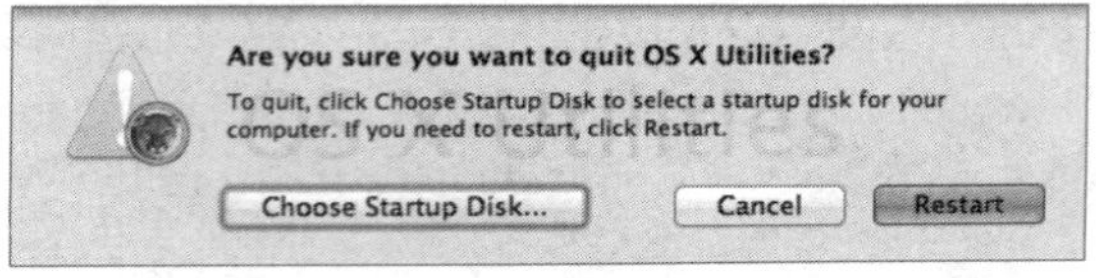

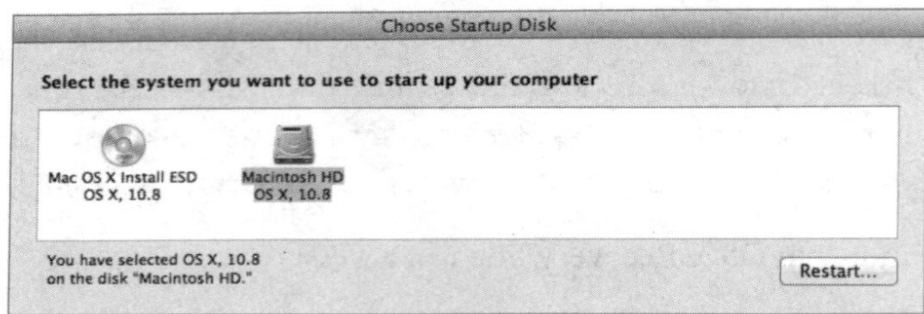

Wait, there's more. OS X Recovery has a few extra utilities hidden in the Utilities menu at the top of the screen:

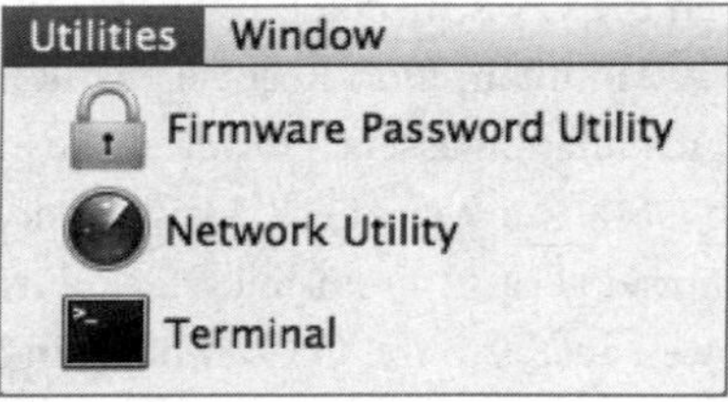

- Firmware Password Utility—This utility will allow you to secure the Mac computer's startup process by disabling all alternate startup modes without a password. You can disable or enable this feature and define the required password. You can find out more about Firmware Password in Lesson 8, "System Security."

- Network Utility—This is the primary network and Internet troubleshooting utility in OS X. The primary use of this utility in OS X Recovery is to troubleshoot any network issues that could prevent the download of OS X installation assets. The Network utility is further discussed in Lesson 24, "Network Troubleshooting."
- Terminal—This is your primary interface to the UNIX command-line environment of OS X. The most useful command you can enter from here is simply `resetpassword` followed by the Return key.
- Reset Password opened via Terminal—This utility will allow you to reset the password of any local user account, including the root user, on the selected system disk. Obviously, this is a dangerous utility that can pose a serious security threat. Because of this, the Reset Password utility will only run from OS X Recovery. You can find out more about Reset Password in Lesson 8, "System Security."

  NOTE ▶ The utilities available from OS X Recovery can certainly be used to compromise system security. Then again, any system whose default startup disk can be overridden during startup is wide open to compromise. Therefore, in secured environments it's often necessary to use the Firmware Password utility to help protect your systems.

Reference 4.3
External OS X Recovery Disks

In some cases, a Mac with OS X installed does not have a local OS X Recovery HD. For example, if you just replaced the internal disk with a new disk, nothing will be on the new disk. Also, OS X systems on RAID sets and disks with nonstandard Boot Camp partitioning will not have a local OS X Recovery HD. In these cases, you would need to start up from an external OS X Recovery disk. Also, having an external OS X Recovery disk handy can be a real lifesaver should you come across a Mac with a dysfunctional system disk.

Alternatively, two do-it-yourself solutions exist to convert a standard disk into an OS X Recovery disk. The first involves creating a minimal OS X Recovery disk using OS X Recovery Disk Assistant. The second solution creates a full OS X Recovery disk using the contents inside the Install Mac OS X application.

- Create a minimal OS X Recovery disk—The advantage to creating an OS X Recovery disk with this method is that it only requires a 1 GB USB flash disk. This method is fully supported by Apple as it's initiated through the OS X Recovery Disk Assistant, available on the Apple support downloads website. The downside to this method is that the resulting OS X Recovery disk will not contain the OS X installation assets.

Thus, when running OS X Recovery from this disk, if you need to reinstall OS X, the system will have to download the OS X installation assets from the Internet. Exercise 4.2, "Create a Minimal OS X Recovery Disk," outlines the steps necessary to create this type of disk.

- Create a full OS X Recovery disk—The advantage to creating an OS X Recovery disk with this method is that it will include the full OS X installation assets on the disk. This method involves using Disk Utility to copy the Install OS X Mountain Lion application assets to an external drive. However, the downside to this method is that it requires an 8 GB disk. Exercise 4.3, "Create a Full OS X Recovery Disk," outlines the steps necessary to create this type of disk.

NOTE ▶ When creating your own OS X Recovery disks, make sure to keep track of the specific version of OS X you are using. As covered in Lesson 2, "Install OS X Mountain Lion," newer Mac systems do not support older versions of OS X and may require computer-specific builds of OS X. As such, you should always keep your OS X Recovery disks updated to the latest versions of OS X available from the Mac App Store.

Exercise 4.1
Use OS X Recovery

Prerequisites

- Your computer must have a local hidden Recovery HD partition. This partition normally is created by the OS X Mountain Lion installation process.

In this exercise you will start up your computer in OS X Recovery. OS X Recovery is stored on a hidden partition named Recovery HD that is created automatically when OS X is installed on the hard disk. You will review the included utilities as well as how OS X Recovery can reinstall the system itself.

NOTE ▶ You will not perform an installation, but you will get an opportunity to look at the steps leading up to the installation.

Start Up Using OS X Recovery

To access the Installer and other utilities in OS X Recovery, you need to start up from the hidden Recovery HD partition.

1 If your computer is on, shut it down by choosing Apple menu > Shut Down.

2 Press the power button on your computer, and then hold down Command-R until the gray Apple appears on the screen.

When you hold down Command-R during startup, the computer attempts to start up using a recovery partition on the hard disk.

If no recovery partition is available, Macs with newer firmware can actually start up from an Apple server over the Internet and get access to the OS X Recovery features.

If your computer starts up to the login screen instead of OS X Recovery, you may not have held Command-R long enough. If this happens, click the Shut Down button and try again.

If your computer displays a globe icon with the text "Starting Internet Recovery. This may take a while," your computer was unable to find a local Recovery partition. If the Recovery partition exists, you can shut down your computer by holding the power button for 10 seconds, and then select the Recovery partition using the Startup Manager (see the instructions in Exercise 4.2, in the "Test the OS X Recovery Disk" section). If your computer does not have a Recovery partition, you can let it finish starting into Internet Recovery, and then proceed with this exercise.

3 If a language selection screen appears, select your preferred language and click the right-arrow button.

4 After OS X Recovery starts up, you will see a Mac OS X Utilities window. This window is the primary interface for OS X Recovery.

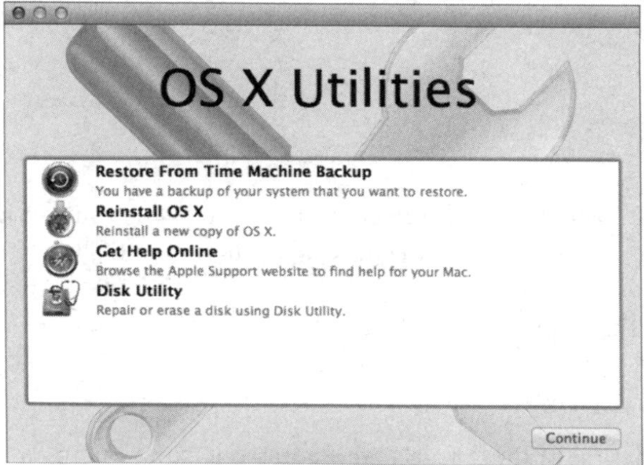

If you see a Welcome screen instead, you probably pressed Command-R too late or did not hold it down long enough. You can start over by pressing Command-Q, and then clicking the Shut Down button.

Examine the Utilities Available in OS X Recovery

While running OS X Recovery, you have access to some utilities for recovering, repairing, and reinstalling OS X. In this part of the exercise you will look at some of these utilities in order to become more familiar with them.

NOTE ▸ While running from OS X Recovery, if the Mac computer's system disk is protected by FileVault 2, any access to this disk will first require unlocking of the disk. In most cases, any local user's password on the system should be allowed to unlock the system FileVault 2 drive. Lesson 11, "FileVault 2," covers this topic in greater detail.

View Help for OS X Recovery

You will use Safari to view the built-in instructions of OS X Recovery and to browse the web.

1. Select Get Help Online, and then click Continue.

   Safari opens and displays a document with information about how to use OS X Recovery. Take a moment to skim the document.

   This document is stored on the Recovery HD partition, but as long as you have an Internet connection available, you can also use Safari to view online documentation such as the Apple Knowledge Base.

2. Click the Apple bookmark.

   Safari now displays the Apple website.

3. If Safari displays a message that "You are not connected to the Internet," you can join a wireless network using the Wi-Fi icon near the right side of the menu bar.

4. If you are prompted to unlock the Login keychain, click OK.

5. Click the Support link near the top right of the page.

   You are taken to the support section of the Apple site. If you were experiencing a problem with your computer, this would be a good place to look for solutions and information. You will use some of the Apple support resources later in this guide.

6. From the menu bar, choose Safari > Quit Safari to return to the main utilities screen.

Note that closing the Safari window does not actually quit Safari. This is common among Mac applications, but if you are accustomed to using Microsoft Windows it may be contrary to your expectations. Generally, the best way to quit a Mac application is to choose Quit <*Application Name*> from the application menu (the menu next to the Apple menu, named for the current application); you can use the keyboard shortcut Command-Q.

Examine Disk Utility

Disk Utility is provided in OS X Recovery to allow you to repair, image, reformat, or repartition your computer's disk.

1 Select Disk Utility, and then click Continue.

In the Device List on the left, you will see your disk device and Mac OS X Base System disk image. Note the primary entry for each physical disk device and an indented list of volumes on each device (discussed in more detail in Lesson 10, "File Systems and Storage").

2 Select the entry that represents your startup volume. It will typically be named Macintosh HD.

Notice the options available to perform on the volume: First Aid, Erase, RAID, and Restore. Among the reasons Disk Utility is provided in OS X Recovery is to allow you to verify or repair the startup volume's file structure, or if necessary to erase the volume before reinstalling OS X.

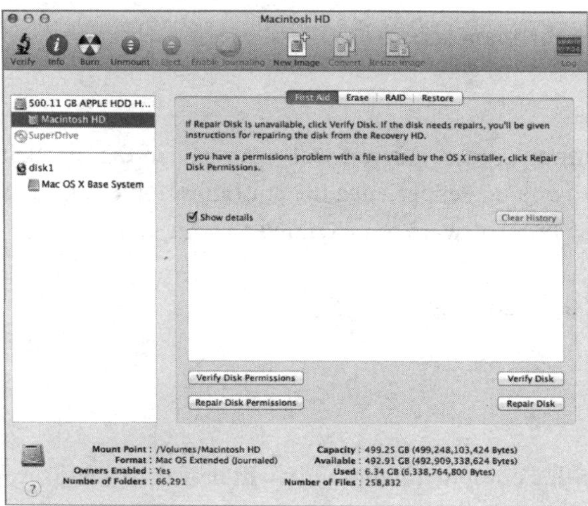

3 Select the entry that represents your disk (just above the startup volume).

Notice that the Partition option is now available.

4 Quit Disk Utility by choosing Disk Utility > Quit Disk Utility (or by pressing Command-Q).

You are returned to the main screen.

Examine Time Machine Restoration

If you backed up your computer with Time Machine, OS X Recovery has the capability to do a full system restoration from that backup. Setting up Time Machine is covered in Lesson 17, "File Archives."

1 Select Restore From Time Machine Backup, and then click Continue.

A page of notes on the restoration process appears. It is important to note that this restoration interface will erase all current data and replace it from the backup; other restoration interfaces that let you control which files or folders are restored are examined later.

2 Click Continue.

The "Select a Backup Source" screen appears. If you had configured a Time Machine backup target, it would be available here as a source for restoring your system.

3 Click Go Back to return to the Restore Your System screen.

4 Click Go Back again to return to the main screen.

Examine the OS X Installer

Now you will examine the reinstallation process, but you will not perform the installation. By going through the following steps, you can experience the configuration of an installation without actually waiting for the OS X software to be copied to your system.

1 Select Reinstall OS X, and then click Continue.

The OS X Mountain Lion installer opens.

2 Click Continue.

A dialog appears indicating that this computer's eligibility will be verified with Apple.

3 Click Continue.

4 At the license agreement, click Agree.

5 In the license confirmation dialog, click Agree again.

The OS X installer displays a list of partitions where you could install or reinstall OS X.

NOTE ▶ Do not click the Install button; otherwise the Installer will reinstall OS X, which you do not want to do at this time.

6 Quit the Installer.

Verify Your Startup Disk and Restart

The Startup Disk utility allows you to select the volume from which to start up. If you are having problems during system startup from your computer's internal disk, you could connect a second disk with OS X installed and use Startup Disk to configure the computer to start up from the new disk.

1 From the Apple menu, choose Startup Disk. Notice that Startup Disk shows you a list of all startup volumes. One of the options may be Network Startup or one or more NetBoot images, depending on what it finds on your network.

2 Verify that your computer's normal startup volume (typically named Macintosh HD) is selected; if necessary, select it.

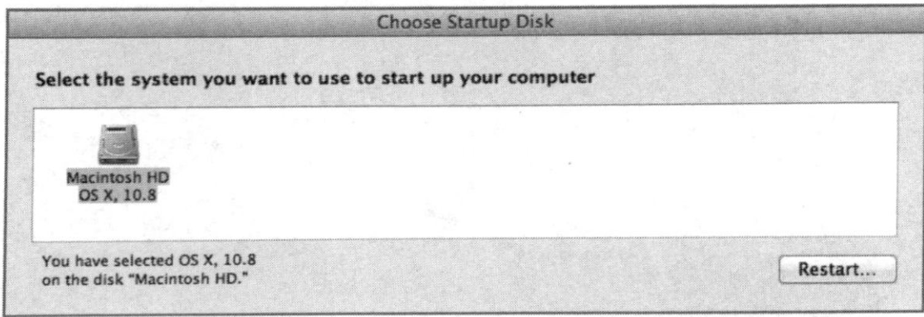

3 Click Restart.

4 In the confirmation dialog, click Restart.

You could also restart without using the Startup Disk utility by choosing Apple menu > Restart.

Exercise 4.2
Create a Minimal OS X Recovery Disk

Prerequisites

- Your computer must have a local hidden Recovery HD partition.
- You need an erasable external disk with a capacity of at least 1 GB.
- You must have created the Local Admin account (Exercise 3.1 or 3.2).

The OS X Recovery partition can help you recover from many problems that might otherwise render your computer unusable, but there are a few issues it cannot help with. For instance, anything that renders the computer's startup disk unreadable, such as a damaged partition table or even complete disk failure, will also prevent the Recovery HD partition from being used. This exercise will explore another option: You can copy OS X Recovery onto an external disk, such as a USB flash disk, for use in case of emergency.

NOTE ▶ You must run the Recovery Disk Assistant from a Mac system that contains a local hidden OS X Recovery HD.

Download the Recovery Disk Assistant

The following steps walk you through searching the Apple support resources for the OS X Recovery Disk Assistant, and downloading it.

1 Open Safari. Note the shortcut for it in your Dock.

2 If you are not automatically taken to the Apple website, click the Apple shortcut in the Safari bookmark bar.

3 Click the Support link near the top right of the Apple web page.

The support section of the Apple website includes a wide variety of resources, including software downloads, manuals and specifications, the Apple Knowledge Base, and links to warranty and repair information.

4 In the search field to the right of the Support link (not the search field in the Safari toolbar), enter **recovery disk assistant**, and press Return.

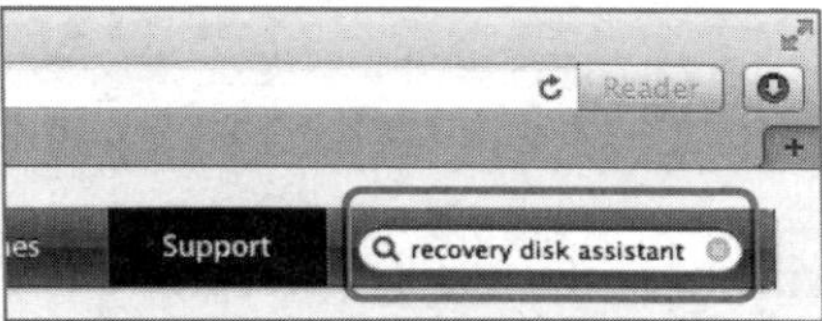

The search results page has a number of options to change and refine your search, but you should not need these here; one of the first search results should be a download page (indicated by a green down-arrow icon) for OS X Recovery Disk Assistant.

OS X Recovery Disk Assistant v1.0
Built right into OS X, OS X Recovery lets you repair disks or reinstall OS X without the need for a physical disc. The OS X **Recovery Disk Assistant** lets you create OS X Recovery on an external drive that has all of the same capabilities as the built-in OS X Recovery: reinstall Lion or Mountain Lion, repair the disk using Disk Utility, restore from a Time Machine backup, or browse the web with Safari. Note
http://support.apple.com/kb/DL1433

5 Click the link for the OS X Recovery Disk Assistant.

6 Click the Download button.

While it downloads, take a moment to skim the information in the download page. Note that it includes a summary of what the program is and how to use it, as well as its version, system requirements, and a list of supported languages.

7 When the download is complete, quit Safari.

Reformat the External Disk

Most external disks come preformatted with the MBR partition scheme; in order to allow an Intel Mac to start up from it, you must reformat this disk with the GUID Partition Table (GPT) partition scheme. Disk formats are discussed in more detail in Lesson 10 "File Systems and Storage."

WARNING ▸ This operation will erase all information on the external disk. *Do not* perform this exercise with a disk that contains any files you want to keep.

1 Open Disk Utility. It is located in the Utilities folder, which is inside the Applications folder. You can navigate to this folder in the Finder, use the Finder shortcut Command-Shift-U, or open Launchpad from the Dock and then select the Other icon in Launchpad.

2 Plug the external disk into your computer.

3 If you are prompted for a password to unlock the disk, the disk is encrypted and cannot be used for this exercise. If this happens, eject the disk and use a different disk for the exercise.

4 Select the external disk device entry in the Disk Utility sidebar. Be sure to select the device entry, not the volume entry indented beneath it.

5 Check the Partition Map Scheme listed at the bottom of the window.

Depending on what this disk was used for most recently, the partition scheme could be anything. In order to convert it to the GPT scheme, you will erase the disk. If it is already using the GPT scheme, this is not strictly necessary, but you should erase it just to be sure.

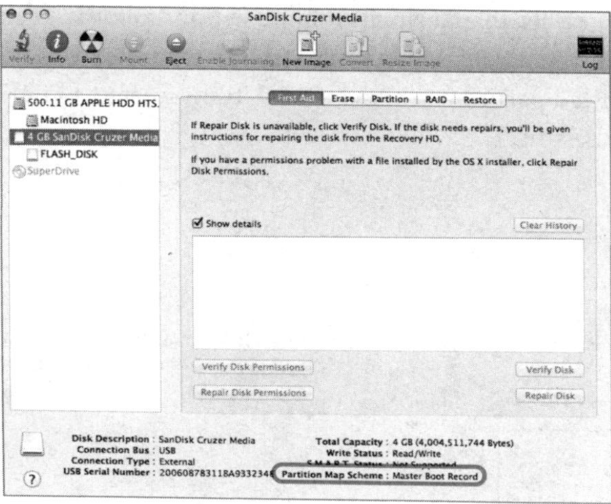

It is also possible to partition the disk, and use only part of it for OS X Recovery. The download page has a link to more information about OS X Recovery Disk Assistant, including the partitioning procedure.

6 Click the Erase tab.

7 Choose Mac OS Extended (Journaled) from the Format pop-up menu.

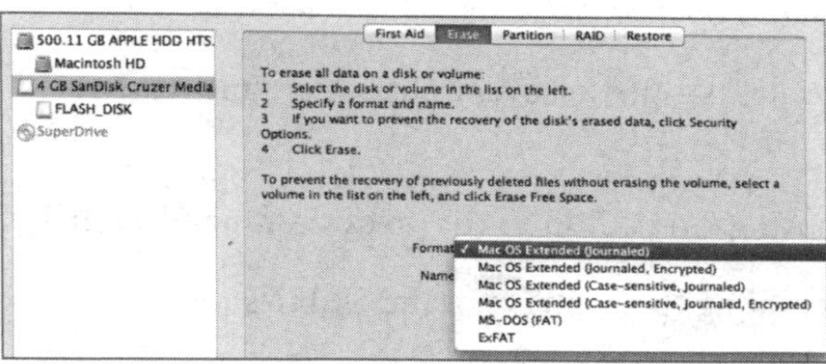

8 Click the Erase button near the bottom right of the window.

9 In the confirmation dialog, click Erase.

10 Verify that the Partition Map Scheme is now listed as GUID Partition Table.

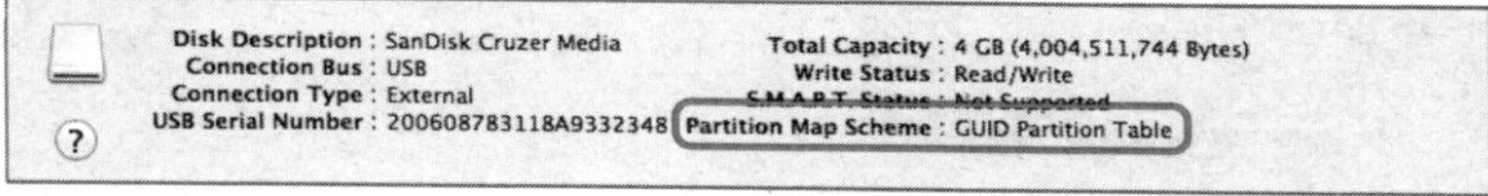

Since you erased the entire disk, rather than a single volume within the disk, Disk Utility has rebuilt the partition map as well. Although a Mac OS Extended volume can be created under any supported partition scheme, Disk Utility created a GUID Partition Table because it is the best fit.

11 Quit Disk Utility.

Create an OS X Recovery Disk

1 Near the right of the Dock is a shortcut for your Downloads folder. Click it once to show its contents.

2 Click RecoveryDiskAssistant.dmg to open it.

The disk image opens, and its contents—the Recovery Disk Assistant application—appear.

3 Open the Utilities folder by choosing Go > Utilities (or press Command-Shift-U).

A new Finder window opens, revealing the contents of the Utilities folder.

4 Drag the Recovery Disk Assistant application to the Utilities folder.

5 A warning dialog appears. Click Authenticate and then enter the password for the Local Admin (**ladminpw**, or whatever you chose when you created the account).

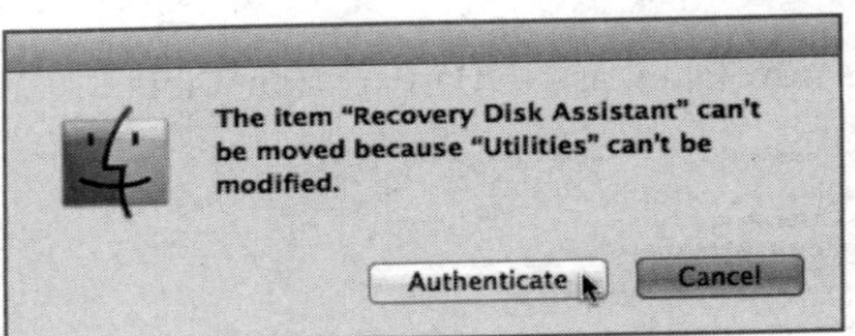

6 Once the copy is complete, double-click the Recovery Disk Assistant in the Utilities folder.

Since this application was downloaded from the Internet, a warning dialog opens providing information about where the application came from. Since malware is sometimes distributed via web download, this warning gives you a chance to decide if you can really trust this software before running it. This feature is discussed in more detail in Lesson 19, "Application Installation." As this application was downloaded directly from the Apple website, you can go ahead and trust it.

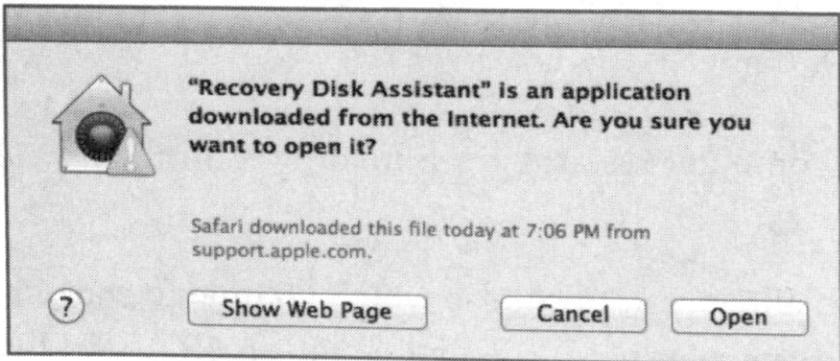

7 Click Open.

8 In the license agreement, click Agree.

9 Select the icon for your external disk and click Continue.

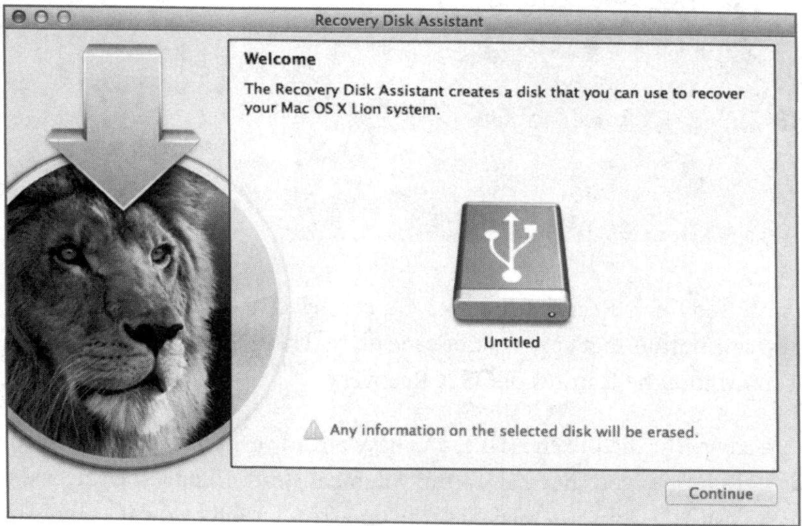

10 Authenticate as Local Admin when prompted.

The creation process takes a few minutes.

11 When the process completes, click Quit.

Test the OS X Recovery Disk

1 From the Apple menu, choose Restart.

2 In the confirmation dialog, click Restart.

3 Hold down the Option key as the computer restarts. Keep holding it until a row of icons appears across the screen.

This is the Startup Manager, which allows you to choose which volume to start up from. You will see your regular startup volume (normally Macintosh HD), and two volumes named Recovery-10.8, one with a disk icon and one with a USB, FireWire, or Thunderbolt icon. Since both your external disk and your computer's internal disk now have valid, up-to-date Recovery-10.8 volumes, you could access OS X Recovery with either one of them.

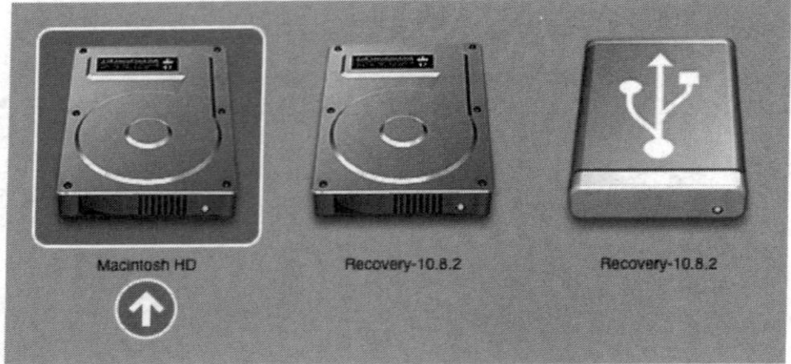

4 If you have not used OS X Recovery before, you can select the Recovery drive, then click the up-arrow button that appears underneath it. Then, follow the instructions in Exercise 4.1 to explore the features of OS X Recovery.

5 If you have already performed Exercise 4.1, you have already experienced OS X Recovery, and you can start up from your normal startup volume instead. Unplug the external disk, select the Macintosh HD icon, and then click the up-arrow button below it.

Exercise 4.3
Create a Full OS X Recovery Disk

Prerequisites

- You need an erasable external disk with a capacity of at least 8 GB.
- You must have created the Local Admin account (Exercise 3.1 or 3.2).

In this exercise, you will create a "Full" OS X Recovery disk, which not only includes the OS X Recovery environment and tools, but also a full set of installation assets. With a disk created by this method, you can reinstall OS X Mountain Lion without needing to redownload the installer application from the Internet.

NOTE ▸ When creating your own OS X Recovery disks, make sure to keep track of the specific version of OS X you are using. As covered in Lesson 2, "Install OS X Mountain Lion," newer Mac systems do not support older versions of OS X and may require computer-specific builds of OS X. As such, you should always keep your OS X Recovery disks updated to the latest versions of OS X available from the Mac App Store.

Acquire a Copy of the Install OS X Mountain Lion Application

If you upgraded to OS X Mountain Lion following the instructions in Exercise 2.2 and saved a copy of the installer application, you may use it and skip this section. If you are performing these exercises as part of a class, the instructor may have provided a copy in the StudentMaterials folder. Otherwise, if you have already purchased OS X Mountain Lion from the Mac App Store you can redownload the installer with the following procedure:

1. From the Apple menu, choose App Store. Note that the Mac App Store is discussed in more detail in Lesson 19, "Application Installation."

2. From the menu bar, choose Store > Sign In.

3 Enter the Apple ID and password you used to purchase OS X Mountain Lion. Click Sign In.

4 Hold the Option key as you click the Purchases icon in the toolbar.

Holding the Option key makes OS X Mountain Lion appear in your purchases list with a Download button, even though you have already installed it.

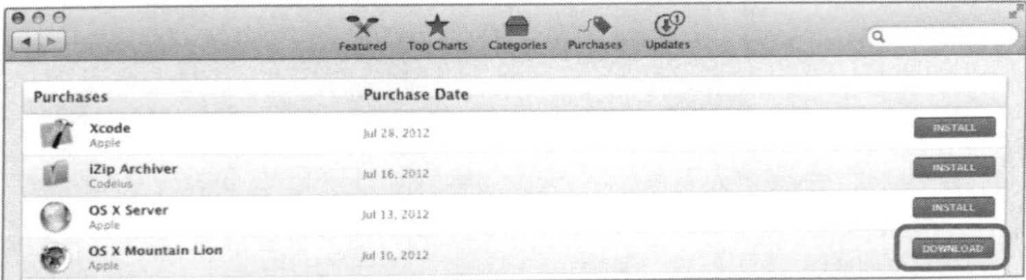

5 Click the Download button for OS X Mountain Lion and wait for it to download.

Reformat the External Disk

Follow the instructions in the "Reformat the External Disk" section of Exercise 4.2, but do not quit Disk Utility at the end.

Create a Full OS X Recovery Disk

1 In Disk Utility, click the Restore tab near the top right.

2 Drag the volume from your external disk (generally named Untitled since it was just erased) from the sidebar into the Destination field.

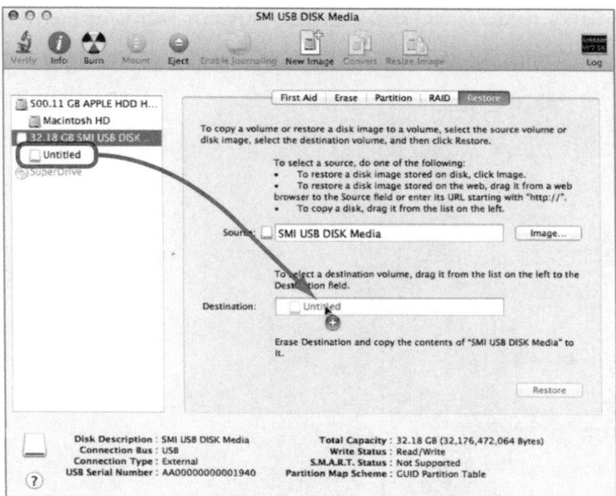

The image you need to use as a source is concealed inside the Install OS X Mountain Lion package, so you will need to use a special trick to find it. Packages are discussed in Lesson 14, "Hidden Items and Shortcuts."

3 Switch to the Finder, and find the installer app, in either the Applications folder or StudentMaterials/Lesson4.

4 Control-click the installer app, and choose Show Package Contents from the shortcut menu.

5 Inside the package, navigate to Contents/SharedSupport.

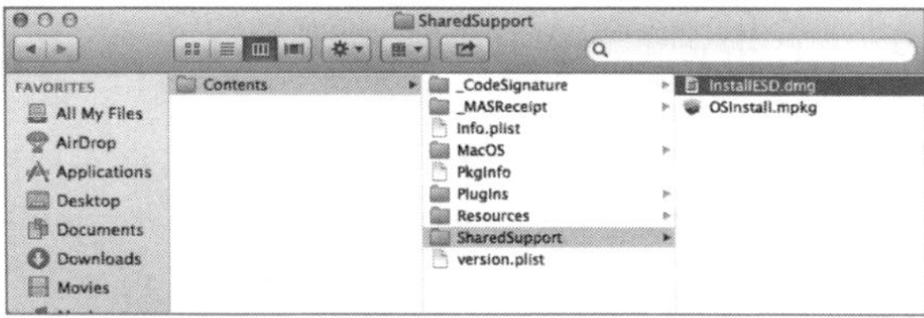

6 In the SharedSupport folder, select the file InstallESD.dmg, and drag it into the Source field in the Disk Utility window.

The Disk Utility window now shows InstallESD.dmg in the Source field and Untitled in the Destination field.

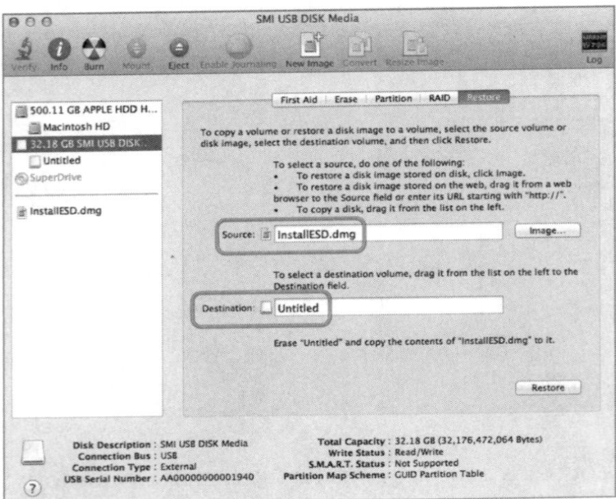

7 Click the Restore button near the bottom right of the window.

8 In the confirmation dialog, click Erase.

9 When you are prompted, authenticate as Local Admin (password: ladminpw, or whatever you chose when you created the account).

It will take anywhere from a few minutes to a half hour to copy the full installer to the external disk.

10 When the copy is complete, quit Disk Utility.

11 If you like, you can use the Finder to change the disk's name from "Mac OS X Install ESD" to something more descriptive. Adding the specific version number is a good idea.

Test the OS X Recovery Disk

Follow the instructions in the "Test the OS X Recovery Disk" section of Exercise 4.2, but note that the disk will be named either "Mac OS X Install ESD" or whatever you renamed it to in the previous section.

Lesson 5

OS X Software Updates

Adding new capabilities is the very reason "software" exists. It's expected that you will add new applications to increase the capabilities of your Mac and, as products are refined, new software updates as well. In this lesson you will configure and use the OS X software update technology, which is an automatic method to keep all your Apple-sourced software up to date. You will also explore an alternative method to automatic software updates: manually downloading and installing software update packages.

GOALS

- Configure automatic software update settings
- Automatically update Apple-sourced software
- Manually update Apple software

Reference 5.1
Apple Software Update

Keeping current with software updates is an important part of maintaining a healthy Mac. Fortunately, OS X includes an easy-to-use software update mechanism that automatically checks the Apple servers via the Internet to make sure you're running the latest Apple-sourced software. Automatic software update checking is enabled by default the first moment you start using your Mac.

> **NOTE ►** An Internet connection is required to use software update for both automatic and manual updates. Also software update checks only for updates of currently installed Apple-sourced software. Finally, some software updates require that you also agree to a new Apple Software License Agreement.

Automatic Software Updates

Previous versions of OS X included a separate dedicated application just for OS X software updates. OS X Mountain Lion now features unified software updates via integration with the Mac App Store, meaning that all software you have installed from the Mac App Store, including OS X itself and applications created by both Apple and third parties, are updated from a single location. Further, software update is integrated with the new OS X Mountain Lion Notification Center to let you know as soon as new updates are available for installation.

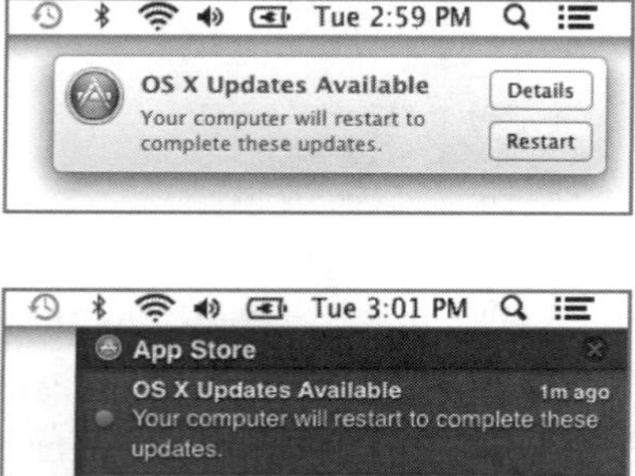

MORE INFO ▶ Though covered briefly here, using the Mac App Store is discussed further in Lesson 19, "Application Installation."

Assuming the default settings, all updates will be automatically downloaded in the background. When updates are ready to be installed, you will be presented with an App Store notification stating, "New Updates Available." From the notification you can open the Mac App Store or ignore the update. If you choose to ignore important system and security updates, after some time the system will automatically install those updates for you without any further action. Non-essential system updates and application updates will never automatically install.

TIP When updates are available, the Mac App Store Dock icon and the Mac App Store toolbar Updates button will display a small number that represents the number of available updates.

If you're ready to install deferred updates, or you want to manually check for new updates, you can do so at any time via the following methods:

- From the Apple menu, choose Software Update.
- In the About This Mac dialog, click the Software Update button.
- In the Software Update preferences, click the Check Now button.
- In the toolbar of the Mac App Store, click the Updates button.

NOTE ▶ Only administrative user accounts are allowed to initiate the installation of any software, new or updated, from the Mac App Store. In other words, standard user accounts are not allowed to install updates from the Mac App Store. Lesson 6, "User Accounts," covers administrative user accounts in greater detail.

App Store Update Details

When the Mac App Store opens to show you new updates, each update is listed with detailed information, which allows you to individually inspect all the available software updates. The information provided includes the update name, version, and a detailed description. Note that some updates require a system restart, which will be noted below the update's name.

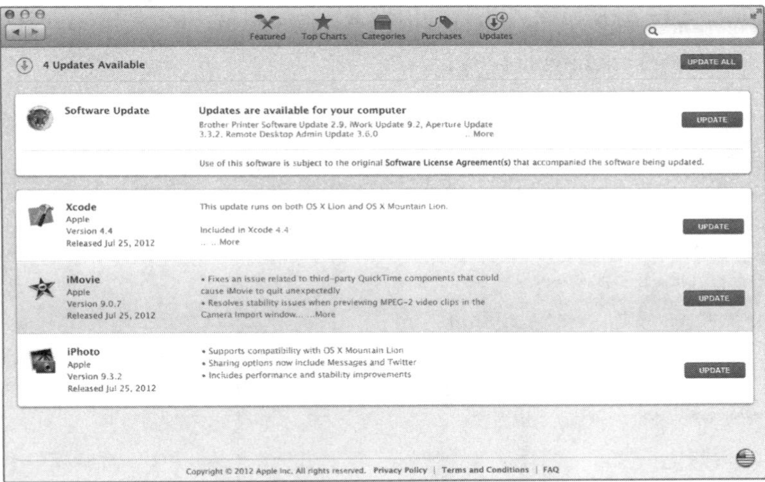

Note in the screenshot showing Mac App Store updates that the available updates are split in two, with a top Software Update section and individual application updates in a lower section. The Software Update section shows updates for OS X itself or updates for Apple software installed outside of the Mac App Store. This is similar to the software update mechanism available in previous versions of OS X. On the other hand, the lower individual updates are for applications installed only via the Mac App Store.

Simply click an individual Update button to install that update, or click the Update All button to install all available updates. If none of the updates require a restart for installation, the software will automatically install without any further user interaction. But if any of the updates requires a restart after the install process, you will be presented with a dialog featuring a Restart and Not Now button. Clicking Restart will log out the current user, install the updates, and then restart the system. You can, of course, choose to install these updates later, but you will eventually have to restart to take advantage of the new software.

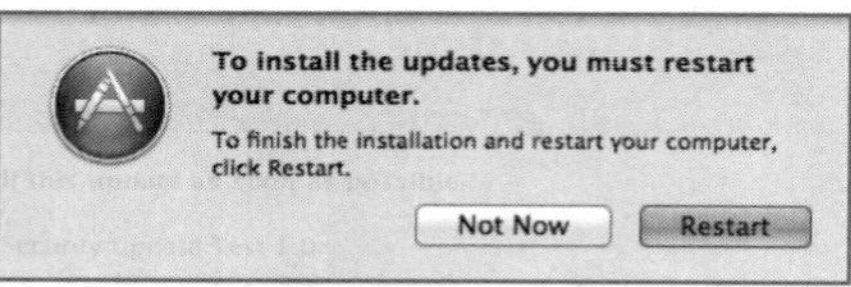

Software Update Preferences

The Software Update preferences, accessed via System Preferences, allow you control the software update automation. Unlike previous versions of OS X, changes made in the Software Update preferences will apply to all users of the system. In other words, Software Update preferences are now systemwide settings.

From the Software Update preferences you can:

- Enable or disable automatic checking for software updates. When enabled the system will check for updates once a day. Note that "check" implies only a small amount of Internet bandwidth is used in order to determine if updates are needed.
- Enable or disable the automatic download of updates. In this case, the update system has the potential to use a large amount of Internet bandwidth to download updates. It's not uncommon for OS X system updates to weigh in at over 1 GB. Also, because this option will automatically download updates for applications purchased from the Mac App Store, systems with more applications will likely use more Internet bandwidth.
- Enable or disable the automatic installation of important system files and security updates. Security updates of this type tend to be smaller than other updates, so Internet bandwidth

is less of an issue. Further, if Apple deems these updates are important enough that they should be always installed, it's considered best practice to leave this option enabled.

- Enable or disable the automatic installation of new applications purchased on other Macs. This feature requires that an Apple ID is signed into the Mac App Store, but even then it's disabled by default. When this is enabled, new installations made from another Mac system using the same Apple ID will automatically install on this Mac system as well. This is obviously useful for those who use multiple Mac systems.
- Click the Check Now button to manually open the Updates section of the Mac App Store.

Reference 5.2
Manual Software Updates

Before the Mac App Store, all software was acquired and installed manually. Fortunately, OS X has always featured relatively simple software installation. In fact, many applications require only that the user copy a single application file to the local Applications folder. At the same time, more complicated software may require multiple resources placed at a variety of specific locations on your Mac.

A prime example of a complicated software installation is any system software update. In some cases it may be more convenient to manually install an update as opposed to using software update via the Mac App Store. For example, perhaps you need to install a particularly large software update for a system with limited Internet bandwidth. It may be better to manually download the update to a portable flash drive at a location with more bandwidth, and then physically deliver the flash drive to the Mac requiring the update. An experienced OS X support specialist will always have an external drive with the most common large updates handy for just such an occasion.

TIP You have the option of manually downloading and installing Apple software updates. You can find all Apple updates at http://support.apple.com/downloads/. After you download the updates, you will use the Installer application to apply them.

Installer Application

The Installer application makes complicated application installations simple. Often, software developers will create an "installer package" with all the instructions necessary for the Installer application to set up the new software on your system.

MORE INFO ▸ Though covered briefly here, installing new applications will be further discussed in Lesson 19, "Application Installation."

Double-clicking one of these software installer packages will open the Installer application and begin the installation process. Much like the OS X installation process, the Installer application will guide you through the steps necessary to install or update software. This may include agreeing to software licenses, selecting a destination, selecting package options, and authenticating as an administrative user.

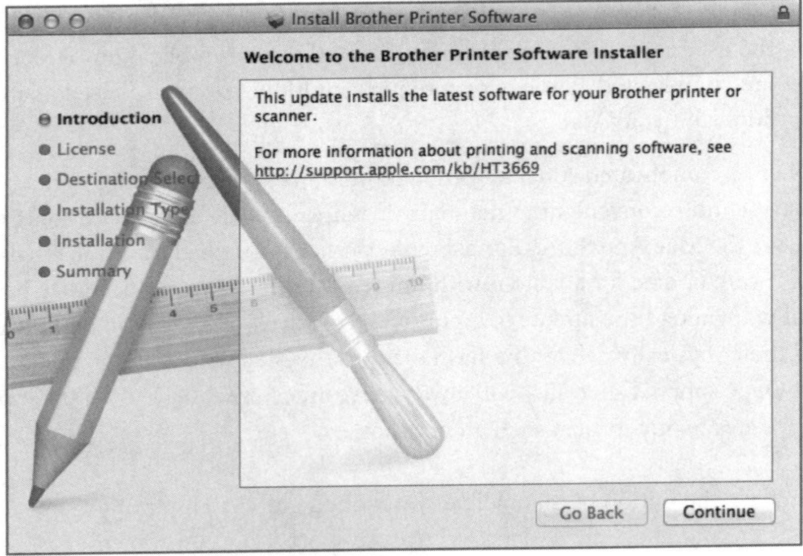

NOTE ▸ Third-party software developers may choose to use a proprietary non-Apple installer for their product. These installers will behave differently than the Apple Installer.

NOTE ▸ Proceed with caution if an installer requires you to authenticate as an administrative user. These installers need administrative access so they can make changes that modify parts of the system that may affect all users.

Advanced Installer Features

If you're curious about what an installation package is actually doing to your Mac, you have two ways to find out. First, you can view the Installer log at any time while using the Installer application by choosing Window > Installer Log or pressing Command-L. The Installer log is a live view of any progress or errors reported during the installation process.

TIP After installation you can access the Installer log from the /Applications/Utilities/Console application. Once Console is open, select /private/var/log/install.log.

If you want to inspect an installer package before installing the application, you can do so, but not using the Installer log. After passing the initial installation welcome screens and agreeing to any software license agreements while using the Installer application, you can preview the list of files to be installed by choosing File > Show Files or pressing Command-I.

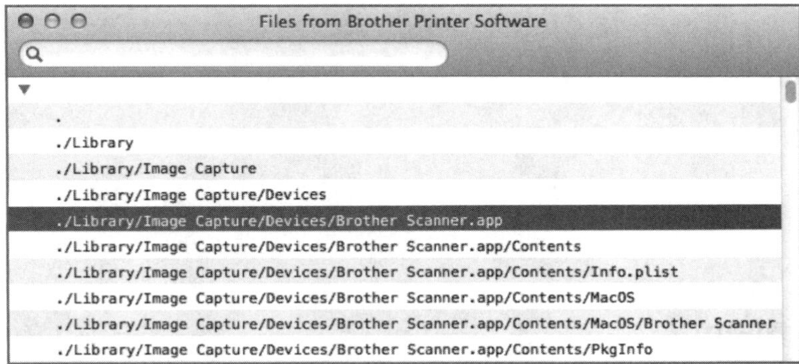

TIP Save time looking for what you need by using the search field in the toolbar when examining the Installer log or file list.

With OS X v10.5, Apple introduced a few new significant Installer application features. For starters, users may specify their home folder as the installation destination for applications that allow it. Apple also introduced a dynamic installation package that remains up-to-date as long as the Mac has Internet access. Network-based installation packages automatically download the latest software from a vendor's servers during the installation process.

Finally, Apple increased the security and reliability of software installation packages by supporting signed packages. These packages contain special code used to validate the authenticity and completeness of the software during installation. This makes it nearly impossible for nefarious hackers to insert illegitimate files in trusted installation packages. You can identify a signed installer package by a small certificate icon in the far right of the installer window title bar. Clicking this icon reveals details about the signed package, including its certificate status.

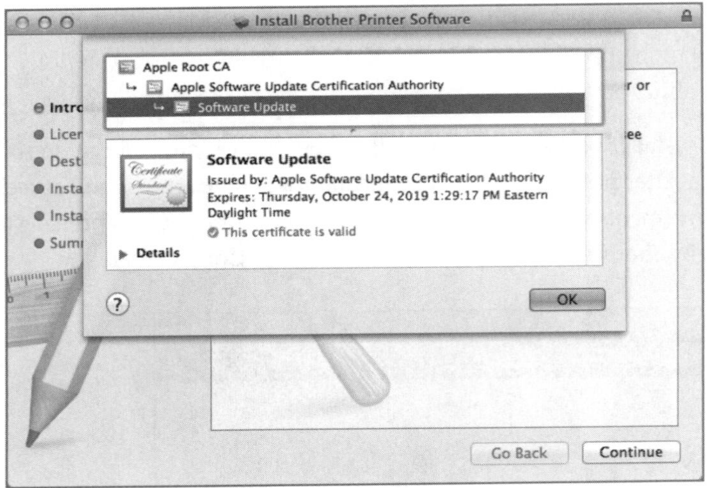

Reference 5.3
Installations History

The automatic software update mechanism in OS X Mountain Lion has made it incredibly easy for the average user to maintain an up-to-date system. So much so, the user probably isn't even aware of how many updates or installations have taken place. Yet, from a support perspective, it's important to know exactly which installations have taken place.

The System Information application in OS X Mountain Lion features a consolidated installations history view. To view this history, open /Applications/Utilities/System Information, and then select the Installations item in the left column. This interface shows all software that was installed via the Mac App Store or the OS X Installer. This includes both new and update installations, from both Apple and third parties. You will be able to view the name, version, acquisition source, and date installed.

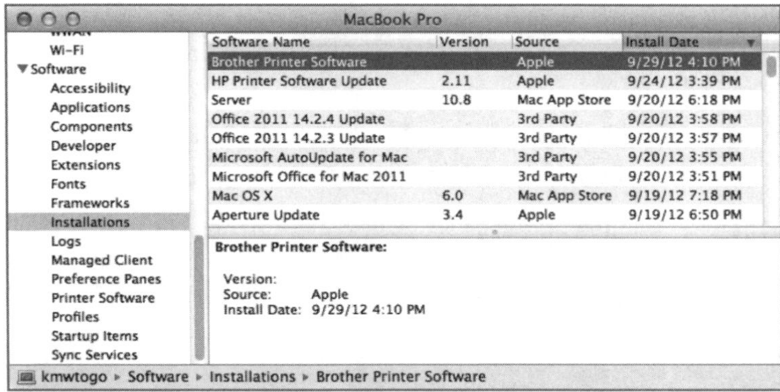

Exercise 5.1
Use Apple Software Update

Prerequisites

- You must have created the Local Admin account (Exercise 3.1 or 3.2).

In this exercise, you will use Software Update to check for, download, and install updates for OS X. You will also see how to view installed software and updates.

Check Your Software Update Preferences

1. From the Apple menu, choose System Preferences.

2. Select the Software Update preference pane.

   Notice that by default, Software Update will automatically download new updates in the background, and then notify you when they are ready.

3. Close System Preferences.

Configure Your Computer's Software Update Server (Classroom Only)

If you are performing these exercises in a classroom environment, you need to configure your computer to use the classroom software update server instead of the general Apple servers. Since no user-accessible interface exists to change this setting, you will install a profile to control it.

If you are performing these exercises on your own, skip ahead to the "Update Your Software" section of this exercise.

1 Open the StudentMaterials folder, and then the Lesson5 folder inside it. Remember that you created a shortcut to the StudentMaterials folder in your Dock.

2 Open Classroom Software Update Server.mobileconfig.

The profile opens in the Profiles pane of System Preferences.

3 Click Show Profile, and then examine the payload of the profile.

This configures your computer to pull updates from the classroom server, instead of directly from the Apple servers on the Internet.

4 Click Continue, and then click Install.

5 When prompted, authenticate as Local Admin (password: **ladminpw**, or whatever you chose when you created the account).

6 Close System Preferences.

Update Your Software

1 From the Apple menu, choose Software Update.

The App Store opens and checks for new software.

2 If it says "No Updates Available," your computer is up to date. Proceed to the "Check Installed Updates" section.

3 Decide which updates you wish to install on your computer. You may want to avoid installing an update so you have something to install manually in Exercise 5.3.

4 If there is more than one update, you can click More to see a detailed list. Click the Update button(s) for the updates you want to install.

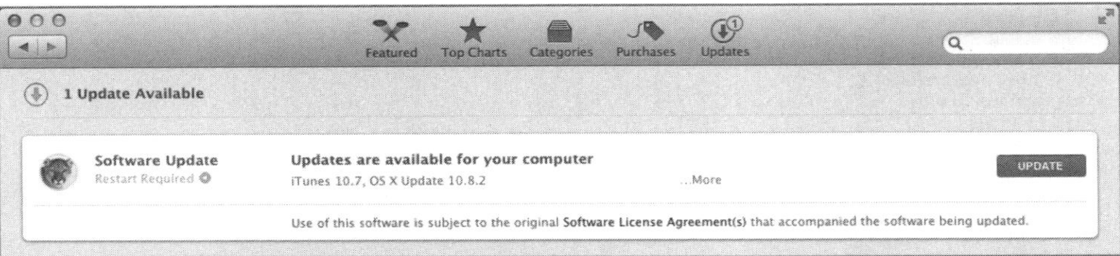

The update(s) now download and install. Depending on the size of the update(s), the download may take a while.

5 If any of the updates are subject to license agreements, you will be prompted to agree to them. Read the agreement(s), and if they are acceptable click Agree.

6 If you are prompted to restart your computer, click Restart. Then, log back into the Local Admin account and check for more updates by repeating step 1.

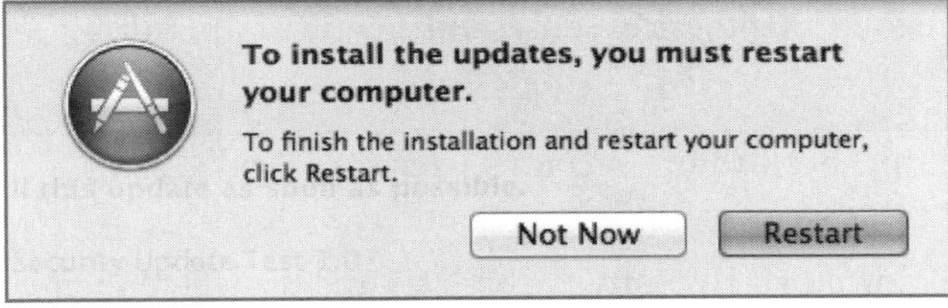

7 When all updates have been installed, quit the App Store.

Check Installed Updates

1 Hold the Option key down while you choose Apple menu > System Information.

System Information opens directly in its full report.

2 In the sidebar, select Installations.

A list of installed software and updates appears, including the updates you just installed. You can click specific updates to get more information about them.

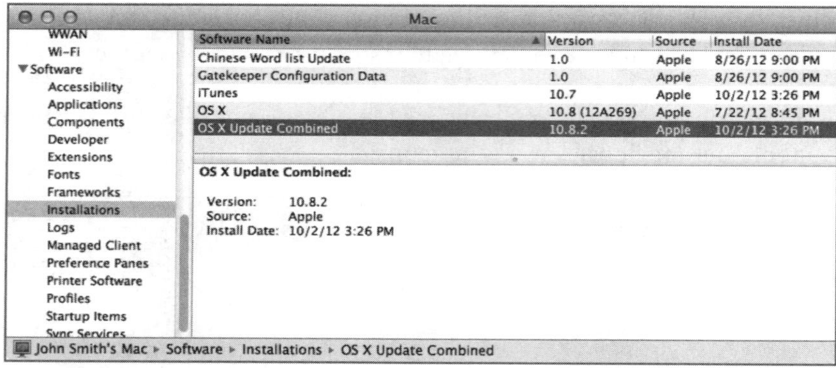

3 Quit System Information.

Exercise 5.2
Manually Install Software Updates in a Classroom

Prerequisites

- This exercise is written for students performing these exercises in a classroom environment. If you are following these exercises independently, perform Exercise 5.3 instead.
- You must have created the Local Admin account (Exercise 3.1 or 3.2).

If your instructor has chosen to download any software updates and distribute them as part of the student materials, you can to follow these steps to install them. Your instructor will tell you if you need to do this.

Install Updates from StudentMaterials

1 In the Finder, open the Software Updates folder inside the StudentMaterials folder. Remember that you created a shortcut to the StudentMaterials folder in your Dock.

2 For each software update your instructor says should be installed (your instructor may additionally specify an order in which they should be installed), do the following:

- Open the disk image file. After a short while a new volume mounts. It contains the update package.

- Open the update package. Installer opens and walks you through the installation process.
- Continue through the installer prompts, and agree to the license agreement if required.
- When prompted, authenticate as Local Admin again (password: ladminpw, or whatever you chose when you created the account). Software updates require administrative privileges to install.
- When each update has installed, click Close or Restart as appropriate.

3 Repeat these steps until all the updates have been installed.

4 If you did not restart, eject the disk image(s) before proceeding. You can do this by Control-clicking in the background of the image's window and choosing Eject from the shortcut menu.

Exercise 5.3
Manually Install Software Updates Independently

Prerequisites

- This exercise is written for students performing these exercises independently. If you are performing these exercises in a classroom environment, perform Exercise 5.2 instead.
- You must have created the Local Admin account (Exercise 3.1 or 3.2).

If you skipped any available updates with Software Update or would like to install additional software (such as printer drivers) available for download from the Apple support site, this exercise shows you how to download and install them manually.

Download an Update from the Internet

1 Open Safari.

2 Navigate to http://support.apple.com/downloads/.

As an alternative to entering the URL directly, you can reach this page starting from the Apple main website by clicking the links for Support and then Downloads.

This page includes a list of the 10 most recent updates Apple has made available for download. If you do not see the update you want, you can enter its name in the Search Downloads field.

The following screenshots use the Infotec Printer Drivers package as an example, but you can choose any update for which your computer is eligible.

3 When you find the update you want to install, click its Download button.

4 Wait for the download to complete (note that its progress is indicated by a progress bar in the Safari download button, near the top right of the window.

5 Click the downloads button (down-arrow icon) near the top right of the window.

6 Click the view (magnifying glass icon) next to the update you downloaded.

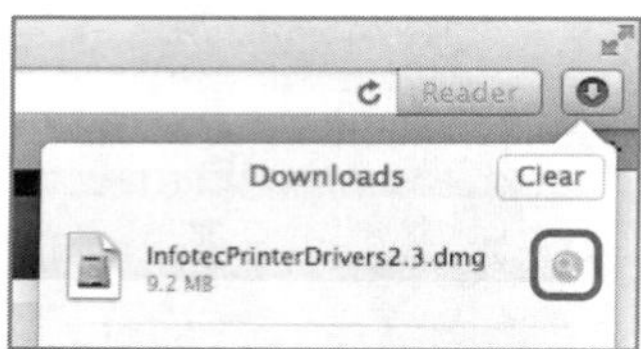

Your Downloads folder opens in the Finder, and the disk image containing the update is selected.

Install the Update

1 Open the disk image file.

The disk image mounts, and you will see the installer package it contains.

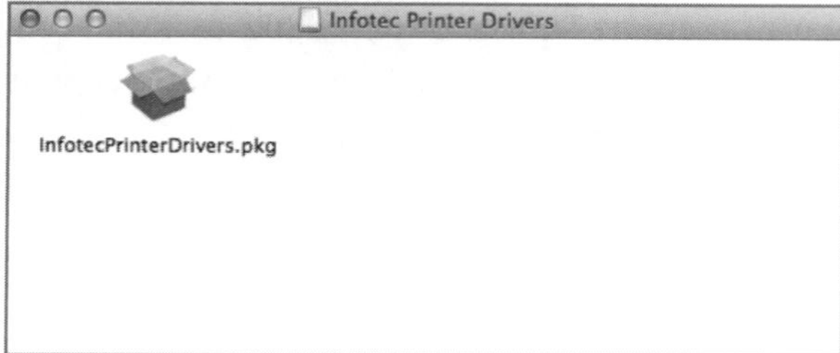

2 Open the installer package.

The Installer opens and walks you through the installation process.

3 Continue through the Installer prompts, and agree to the license agreement if required.

4 When prompted, authenticate as Local Admin (password: ladminpw, or whatever you chose when you created the account).

   Software updates usually require administrative privileges to install.

5 After the update installs, click Close or Restart as appropriate.

6 If you did not restart, eject the disk image before proceeding. You can do this by Control-clicking in the background of the image's window and choosing Eject from the shortcut menu, or by using the Eject button next to the disk image's name in the Finder sidebar.

User Accounts

Lesson 6

User Accounts

One of the hallmarks of a modern operating system is support for multiple user accounts. OS X delivers this in spades with a robust, secure, and highly polished multiuser environment. The UNIX foundation of OS X is the source of this sophisticated multiple-user environment. UNIX operating systems have a long history of providing such services. Apple has made many improvements to the UNIX functionality by providing advanced user management features and streamlined administration tools, all with traditional Apple ease of use.

In this lesson, you will explore the technologies that allow individuals to log in and use the Mac. You will also learn how to create and manage multiple user accounts in OS X.

GOALS

- Recognize various user account types and user attributes
- Create and manage user accounts
- Adjust login and fast user switching settings

Reference 6.1
User Account Management

Mac users have been known to identify their beloved computers with a pet name; nevertheless, your Mac absolutely identifies you via a user account. With the exception of the rarely used single-user mode, you are required to log in with a user account to perform any task on the Mac. Even if the Mac is sitting at the login window and you haven't yet authenticated, the system is still using a handful of system user accounts to maintain background services. Every single file and folder on a Mac computer's hard disk, every item and process, belongs to some type of user account. Consequently, a thorough understanding of user accounts is necessary to effectively administer and troubleshoot OS X.

NOTE ▶ OS X Mountain Lion defaults to requiring a user login even if only a single user account is created for the system. This setting enhances security, as it requires every user to log in. Further, training the user to log in every time the computer restarts is important if the user is to enable FileVault 2, which requires the user to log in on startup.

NOTE ▶ This lesson focuses on user accounts that are available only to a single local Mac. Network user accounts, on the other hand, are available to multiple Macs and are hosted from shared directory servers. You can find out more about this from *Apple Pro Training Series: OS X Server Essentials*.

User Account Types

The majority of home Mac users are only aware of, and therefore only use, the account created when the Mac was initially set up with the Setup Assistant. Apple has engineered OS X to mimic a single-user operating system by default. However, OS X supports multiple simultaneous user accounts. The system also supports several types of user accounts to facilitate different levels of access. Essentially, you choose a specific account type to grant a defined level of access that best meets the user's requirements. User accounts are categorized into one of five types: standard users, administrative users, the guest user, sharing only users, and the root user.

Standard Users

Ideally, standard is the account type most should use on a daily basis. Because standard accounts strike the best balance between usability and security, they are also commonly used when multiple people share a computer. Standard users are members of the "staff" group and have read access to most items, preferences, applications, the /Users/Shared folder, and other users' shared items, including Public folders. Yet they are only allowed to make changes to personal preferences and items inside their own home folders. Standard users are not allowed to make changes to systemwide preferences, system files, or anything that might affect another user's account, which also means that standard users are not allowed to install most applications.

NOTE ▶ Standard users can be further restricted using parental controls. The account type known as managed is a standard account with parental controls enabled, as covered later in this lesson.

Administrative Users

Administrative users aren't much different from regular users, save for one important distinction: Administrative users are part of the "admin" group and are allowed full access to almost all applications, preferences, and most system files. By default, administrative users do not have access to protected system files or other users' items outside of shared items like the Public folders. Despite this, administrative users can bypass these restrictions in both the graphical environment and using Terminal if needed. For example, administrative users are allowed to update system software as long as they successfully authenticate when the installer application asks for authorization.

Because administrative access is required to make changes to the system, this is the default account type for the initial account created when OS X is first set up with the Setup Assistant. Additional standard user accounts can be created for daily use, but the Mac should have access to at least one administrative account.

Guest User

By default OS X only uses the guest account to facilitate file sharing by allowing nonauthenticated access to shared folders. However, you can optionally enable support for a full guest user account. Once enabled, the guest user is similar to a nonadministrative user but without a password. Anyone with access to the Mac can use it to log in. However, when the guest user logs out, the guest user's home folder is deleted. This includes the deletion of any home folder items that would be normally saved, like preference files or web browser history. The next time someone logs in as a guest, a brand-new home folder is created for that user. Keep in mind, though, a guest user could place files in other shared folders, like /Users/Shared or users' Public folders, that will not be purged when the guest user logs out.

Sharing Only Users

OS X allows for the creation of special user accounts that have access only to shared files and folders. Sharing only users have no home folder and cannot log in to the Mac computer's user interface or Terminal. Administrative users can create multiple shared users with unique names and passwords. Sharing users start out with access similar to that of the guest user, with access only to shared folders. Administrative users can, however, define specific shared user access to any folder via Sharing preferences or the Get Info window in Finder.

Root User

The root user account, also known as System Administrator, has unlimited access to everything on the Mac. The root user can read, write, and delete any file; can modify any setting; and can install any software. To help prevent abuse of this account, by default no one is allowed to log in as root, as a password hasn't been set for the root user. Since many system processes run as the root user, it needs to exist on the system; otherwise, OS X wouldn't be able to start up. The root user is covered in greater detail in Lesson 8, "System Security."

Local Group Accounts

Essentially, a group account is nothing more than a list of user accounts. Groups are primarily used to allow greater control over file and folder access. OS X uses several dozen built-in groups to facilitate secure system processes and sharing. For instance, all users are members of the staff group; administrative users are also members of the admin group; and the root user has its own group, known as wheel. Using groups to manage sharing is discussed in Lesson 12, "Permissions and Sharing."

NOTE ▶ Standard accounts are always members of the staff group, and administrative accounts are always members of the staff and admin groups.

Users & Groups Preferences

In OS X the Users & Groups preferences in the System Preferences is the primary interface for managing local user accounts, local group accounts, and login settings. From this preference pane, any local user can manage basic settings for his or her own account, and any user with administrative privileges can unlock this preference pane and manage attributes for all local accounts.

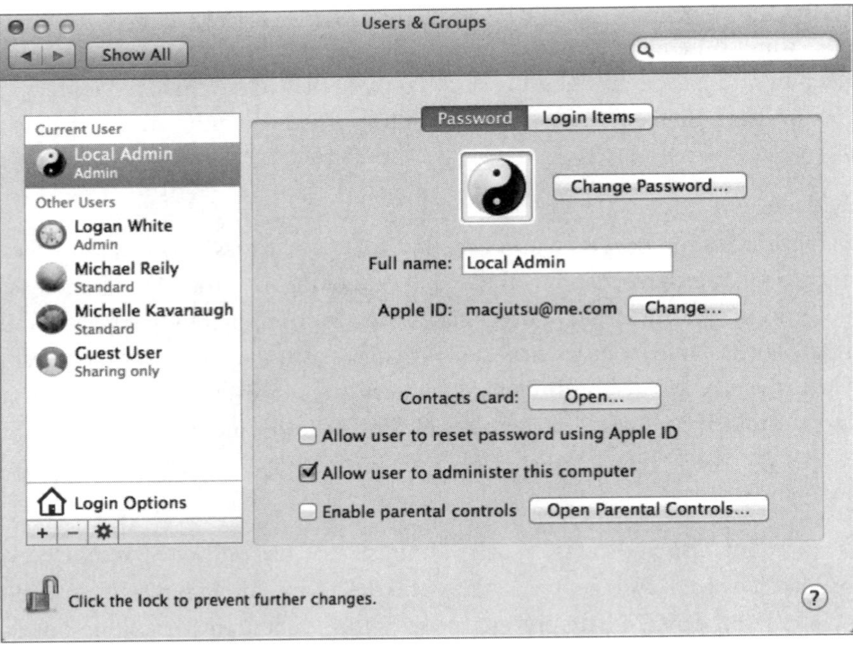

From the Users & Groups preferences, after authenticating as an administrator, you can also access normally hidden user account attributes by using secondary (or Control) click on a user account to reveal the Advanced Options dialog. Although you are allowed to manually edit these attributes to make a desired change or fix a problem, you can just as easily break the account by entering improper information. For example, you can restore access to a user's home folder by correcting the Home Directory information, or you can accidentally prevent a user from accessing his or her home folder by mistyping this information.

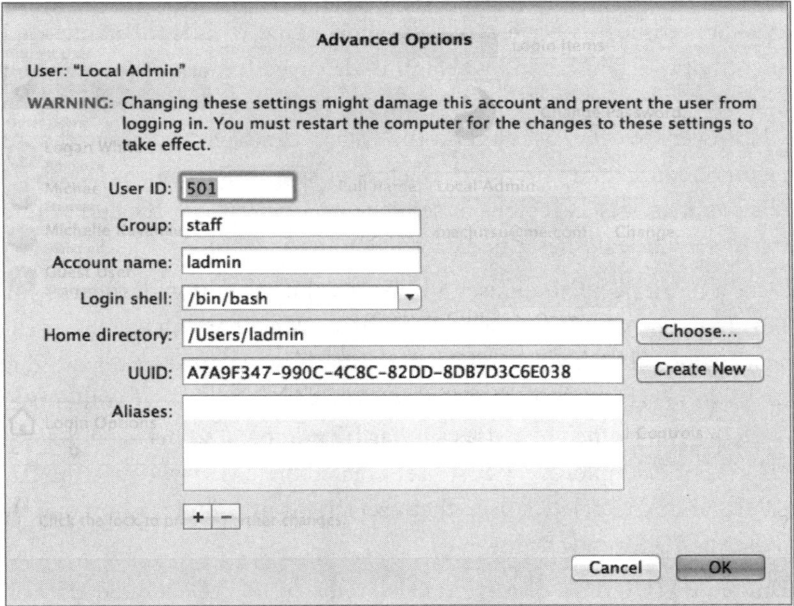

User Account Attributes

Although the login window enables you to log in to the Mac environment, the Open Directory system is responsible for maintaining the account information. Open Directory stores local user account information in a series of XML-encoded text files located in the /var/db/dslocal/nodes/Default/users folder. This folder is only readable by the System Administrator (root) account, but if you were to inspect these files, you would discover that they are organized into lists of user attributes and their associated values.

Each user has a variety of attributes that define the account details. All the attributes are important, but for the scope of this lesson you need only be familiar with the primary user account attributes. These attributes can also be accessed from the Users & Groups preferences.

User account attributes include:

- Full name—This is the full name of the user. It can be quite long and contain nearly any character. However, no other account on the system can have the same full name. You can easily change the full name later at any point.
- Alias names—These names are used to associate the local Mac user account with other service accounts. For example, a user's Apple ID can be associated with a local account. This attribute is optional for OS X, but it is required for integration with Apple Internet services like iCloud and Back to My Mac.
- Account name—Sometimes also referred to as "short name," this is the name used to uniquely identify the account and by default is also used to name the user's home folder. A user can use either the full name or the account name interchangeably to authenticate. However, no other account on the system can have the same account name, and it cannot contain any special characters or spaces. Special characters not allowed include commas, slashes, colons or semicolons, brackets, quotes, and symbols. Allowed characters include dashes, underscores, and periods.
- User ID—This is a numeric attribute used to identify the account with file and folder ownership. This number is almost always unique to each account on a single system, though overlaps are possible. User accounts start at 501, while most system accounts are below 100. It's important to note that the user ID is only "unique" to other users on the local system. Every other Mac uses similar ID numbers, so between Macs this uniqueness is lost. For example, every first user created on a Mac will have the ID number 501. Further, if you delete a user, that user's ID is now up for grabs and the system will reuse the ID for new users.
- Universally Unique ID (UUID)—Sometimes also referred to as Generated UID or GUID, this alphanumeric attribute is generated by the computer during account creation and is unique in both space and time: Once created, no system anywhere will ever create an account with the same UUID. It is used to reference the user's password and for group membership and file permissions. It's important to note that while UUIDs may be truly unique, a Mac won't be able to identify another Mac computer's UUIDs. In other words, UUIDs created on one Mac are not known by another Mac. Thus, locally created UUIDs cannot be used between Macs for mutual identification.
- Group—This is the user's primary group. As covered previously, the default primary group for all local users is the staff group. This means that when you create a new file, it belongs to your user account and to the staff group.
- Login shell—This file path defines the default command-line shell used in Terminal by the account. Any user who is allowed to use the command line in Terminal has

this set to /bin/bash by default. Both administrative and standard users are given this access by default.

- Home directory—This file path defines the location of the user's home folder. All users except for sharing users, who do not have home folders, have this set to /Users/<name>, where <name> is the account name.

NOTE ▸ Account passwords are stored as an encrypted attribute to enhance security. Password management is covered in greater detail in Lesson 8, "System Security."

Reference 6.2
Parental Controls

OS X includes an extensive collection of managed preferences that enable you to further restrict what users can and cannot do. Apple puts these managed preferences under the parental controls moniker, but they are also applicable in a business or institutional setting. As parental controls are designed to further limit standard user accounts, they cannot be applied to an administrative user.

MORE INFO ▸ Parental controls is a limited subset of a much more extensive managed preferences system available when using OS X Server. You can find out more about this from *Apple Pro Training Series: OS X Server Essentials*.

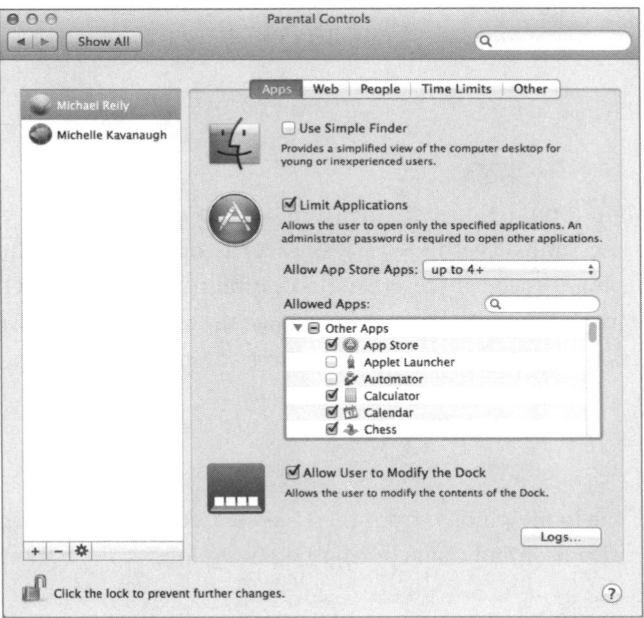

Management options available via parental controls include the following:

- Use Simple Finder to simplify the Finder to show only the items most important to your managed user.
- Create a list that defines which applications or widgets a user is allowed to open. Users will not be allowed to open any application or widget not specified in the list. You can also limit applications available from the Mac App Store based on minimum age recommendation.
- Enable automatic Safari website content filtering, or manually manage a list of permitted websites or a combination of both automatically and manually permitted websites.
- Limit Game Center, Mail, and Messages to allow exchanges only with approved addresses.
- Set weekday and weekend time usage limits.
- Hide profanity in the built-in Dictionary.
- Restrict access to dictation services, printers, password changes, optical media, and the Dock.
- Maintain Safari, Messages, and application usage logs. Doing this logs both allowed and attempted but denied access.

NOTE ▶ Most third-party applications will not honor parental controls' content filters and account limit settings. Examples of unsupported applications include the Firefox browser and Outlook email client. This is, however, easily remedied using the aforementioned parental controls application restriction list.

Reference 6.3
Login and Fast User Switching

The login window may look simple, but because it's the front door to each system, as an administrator you should become familiar with a variety of security options here. Primarily, these options either provide higher security or greater accessibility. Additionally, OS X allows for multiple users to be logged in at the same time via fast user switching. However, this feature is not without issues unique to having multiple users attempting to access resources simultaneously.

Login Window Options

You can adjust the behavior of the login window from the Users & Groups preferences by authenticating as an administrative user and then clicking Login Options at the bottom of the user accounts list.

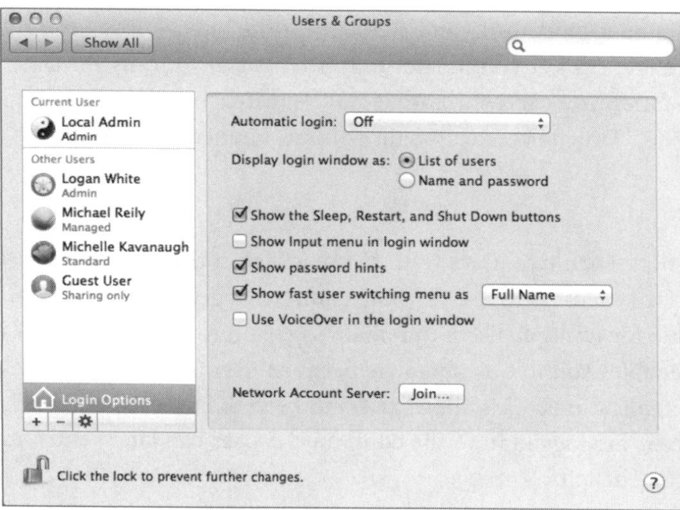

Login window options include:

- Enable or disable automatic login as the Mac starts up. This option is disabled in OS X by default. Obviously, you can only define one account for automatic login.
- Choose whether the login window shows a list of available users, the default setting, or blank name and password fields. Choosing to have name and password fields is more secure.
- Determine the availability of Restart, Sleep, and Shut Down buttons at the login window. Macs in environments that require more stringent security should not have these buttons available at the login window.
- Specify whether users can use the input menu. This allows users easy access to non-roman characters, like Cyrillic or Kanji, at the login window.
- Determine whether the login window will show password hints after three bad password attempts. This may seem to be an insecure selection, but remember that password hints are optional for each user account.
- Disable fast user switching and adjust the look of the associated menu item.
- Enable users to take advantage of VoiceOver audible assistant technology at the login window.
- Configure the Mac to use accounts hosted from a shared network directory. You can find out more about this from *Apple Pro Training Series: OS X Server Essentials*.

TIP You can configure a short three-line message for the login window from the Security & Privacy preferences as covered later in this lesson. If your organization requires a full login banner, you can configure it via the instructions in Knowledge Base document HT4788, "How to create a Login window banner in OS X Lion."

Fast User Switching

It's easy to imagine a situation when two users want to use a Mac at the same time. Although it's not possible for two users to use the Mac computer's graphical interface simultaneously, it is possible for multiple users to remain logged into the Mac at the same time. Fast user switching enables you to quickly move between user accounts without logging out or quitting open applications. This allows users to keep their work open in the background while other users are logged in to the computer. A user can later return to his account instantly, right where he left off.

NOTE ▸ Fast user switching is not recommended or supported for network accounts.

Fast user switching is enabled by default in OS X. The fast user switching menu item appears on the far right next to the Spotlight search menu. By default this menu will appear as your user account full name. If you don't see this menu item, you need to enable fast user switching from the Login options pane of the Users & Groups preferences. Initiate the switch to another user by simply selecting her name from the fast user switching menu, and then entering her password.

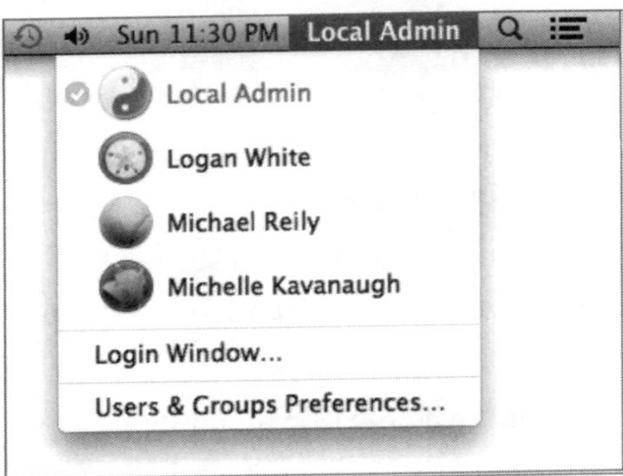

TIP You can move the fast user switching menu item, or any other menu item on the right side of the menu bar, by dragging the menu item while holding down the Command key.

Fast User Switching Contention Issues

Apple has worked hard to make fast user switching a reliable feature. Many of the built-in OS X applications are fast user switching savvy. For instance, when you switch between accounts, iTunes will automatically mute or unmute your music, Messages will toggle between available and away chat status, and Mail will continue to check for new messages in the background. However, in some circumstances you will experience resource contention when more than one user attempts to access an item.

Examples of fast user switching resource contention are:

- Application contention—Some applications are designed in such a way that only one user can use the application at a time. If other users attempt to open these applications, they are met with an error dialog or the application simply doesn't open. Most of the applications that fall into this category are professional applications, which tend to be resource intensive, so it's advantageous to keep only one instance running at a time.
- Document contention—These are cases where one user has a document open and remains logged in with fast user switching, often preventing other users from fully accessing the document. As an example, Microsoft Office applications such as Word and Excel will allow other users to open the document as read-only and will display an error dialog if the user tries to save changes. In a more extreme example, some applications will not allow other users to open the document at all. In the worst-case scenario, an application will allow two people to edit the file simultaneously, but it will only save changes made by the user who saved last. In this case, the application's developers simply didn't account for the possibility that two users might edit the same document at the same time, so you often won't even see an error message.
- Peripheral contention—Many peripherals can be accessed by only one user at a time. This becomes a fast user switching issue if a user leaves an application running that has attached itself to a peripheral. The peripheral will not become available to other applications until the original application is quit. Examples of this include video cameras, scanners, and audio equipment.

Fast User Switching Storage Issues

Fast user switching also has interesting ramifications for nonsystem disks. For example, if one user attaches an external storage device, the disk is available to all other users on the system, even if they weren't logged in when the storage was attached. Mounted disk images are handled a bit more securely. Only the user who mounted the disk image will have full read/write access to it. However, other users may still have read access to the mounted disk image.

Network shares are the only volumes that remain secure in a fast user switching environment. By default, only the user who originally connected to the share can access it. Even if multiple users attempt to access the same network share, the system will automatically generate multiple mounts with different access for each user. The exception to this rule is network home folder shares used by network accounts. While one network user can successfully log in, additional network users from the same server will not be able to access their network home folders. For this reason, fast user switching does not support network accounts.

Resolving Fast User Switching Issues

Unfortunately, because each resource and application can act differently, fast user switching issues are not always consistently reported or readily apparent. OS X doesn't have a "fast user switching is causing a problem" dialog. Still, if you are experiencing access errors for files, applications, or peripherals, your first step should be to check if any other users are still logged in. If so, have them log out and then reattempt access to the previously inaccessible items.

If you cannot log out the other users—perhaps because they are currently unavailable and you don't know their passwords—your options are to force the other users' suspect applications to quit or to force the other users to log out by restarting the Mac. Changing a logged-in user's password isn't an option at this point because administrators cannot manage user accounts that are currently logged in to the Mac. These accounts will be dimmed and not available in the Users & Groups preferences.

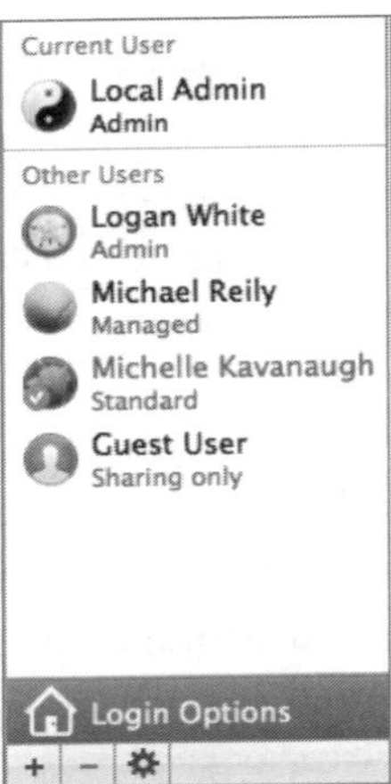

Thus, an administrator will have to force the other users' applications to quit or restart the Mac to free up any contested items or make any changes to the logged-in users. Neither option is ideal because forcing an application to quit with open files can result in data loss. Forcing an open application to quit is covered in Lesson 21, "Application Management and Troubleshooting."

> **TIP** If you have already set the master password, you can reset a currently logged-in user's password from the login window using the master password. Setting the master password and resetting a user's password is covered in Lesson 8, "System Security."

Attempting to restart, though, will reveal another fast user switching issue: If any other users are still logged in, an administrator will have to force those users' open applications to quit in order to restart. The system makes it easy for an administrator to force these applications to quit via an authenticated restart dialog, but once again this may cause data loss to any open files.

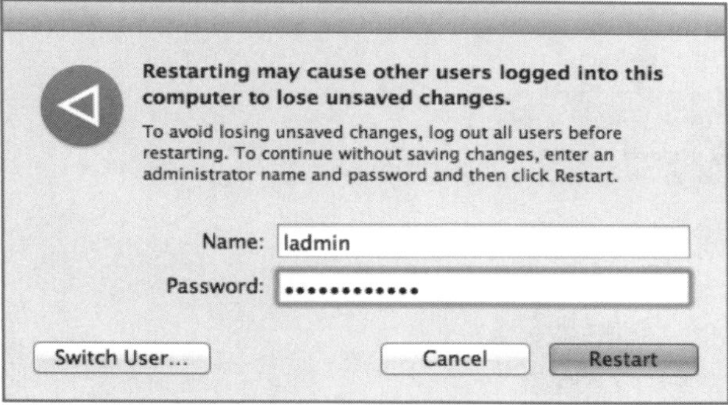

Exercise 6.1
Manage User Accounts

Prerequisites

- You must have created the Local Admin account (Exercise 3.1 or 3.2).
- This exercise is required for most of the remaining exercises, so do not skip this exercise.

You already created an administrator account during the initial configuration of your computer. You will now create additional accounts to gain a better understanding of the user experience. The next user account will be a standard user. It is a best practice to use a standard user account for your day-to-day use. The Local Admin account should be used only for system administration tasks such as software installation and system configuration, and you can perform most of these tasks while logged in as a standard user, simply by providing the administrator account's name and password.

Create a Standard User Account

These steps guide you through account creation.

1. If necessary, log in as Local Admin (password: ladminpw, or whatever you chose when you created the account).

2. Open System Preferences and click Users & Groups.

3. Unlock the Users & Groups preference pane by clicking the Lock button and authenticating as the admin user.

   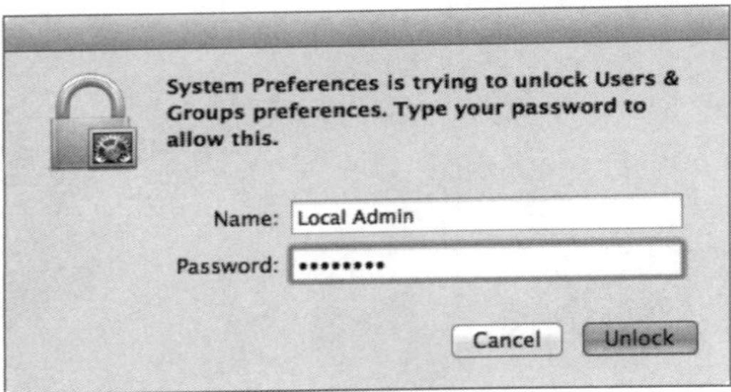

4. Click the New User button (+) beneath the accounts list and enter the following information:

   New Account: Standard

   Full Name: Chris Johnson

   Account Name: chris

   If you are performing this exercise in a class, enter chris in the Password and Verify fields. If you are performing this exercise on your own, select a more secure password for the Chris Johnson account. Be sure to remember the password you have chosen, as you will need to reenter it periodically as you use this computer.

   You may provide a password hint if you want to.

NOTE ► If you already have an account named "Chris Johnson" or "chris," you will have to use a different name here and then remember to use your substitute name throughout the rest of the exercises.

5 Click Create User.

6 Verify that Chris's account is selected in the account list.

7 Click the Picture button (the "image well" next to the Reset Password button), select a picture from the menu that pops up, and click Done.

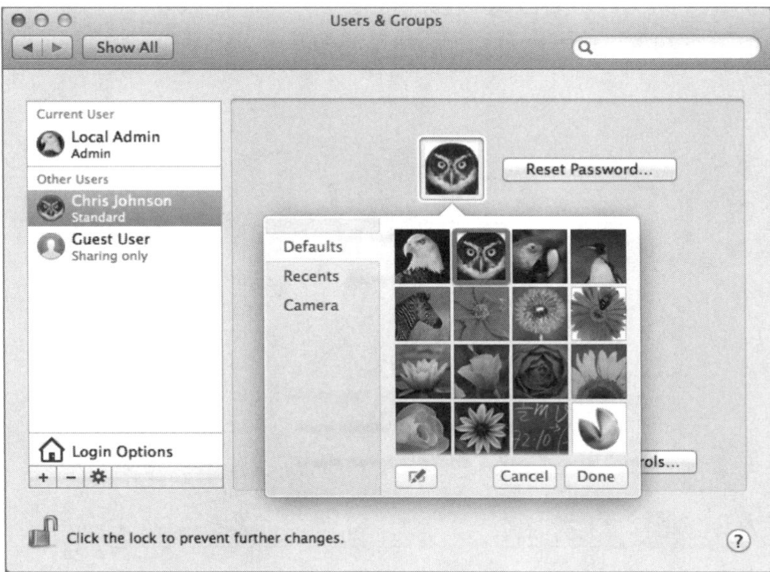

Note that you could configure a number of other account properties here, including tying the account to an Apple ID and using parental controls to limit the account.

Log In to the New User Account

You will now log in to Chris's user account to verify that it was created correctly.

1. Choose Apple menu > Log Out Local Admin.

2. In the dialog asking if you are sure, leave "Reopen windows when logging back in" selected and click Log Out.

3. At the login screen, select Chris Johnson and enter the password.

4. Press Return.

   You are now logged in as Chris Johnson. Since this account is not yet tied to an Apple ID account, a screen opens to allow you to configure an Apple ID.

   If you are performing these exercises in a classroom environment, the instructor will provide you with an Apple ID to use. If you are performing them on your own, creating a new one for these exercises is a good idea. You could use your own Apple ID for these exercises, but the data already in your iCloud account may interfere with or slow down the exercises, and you may want to remove the data from your account afterward.

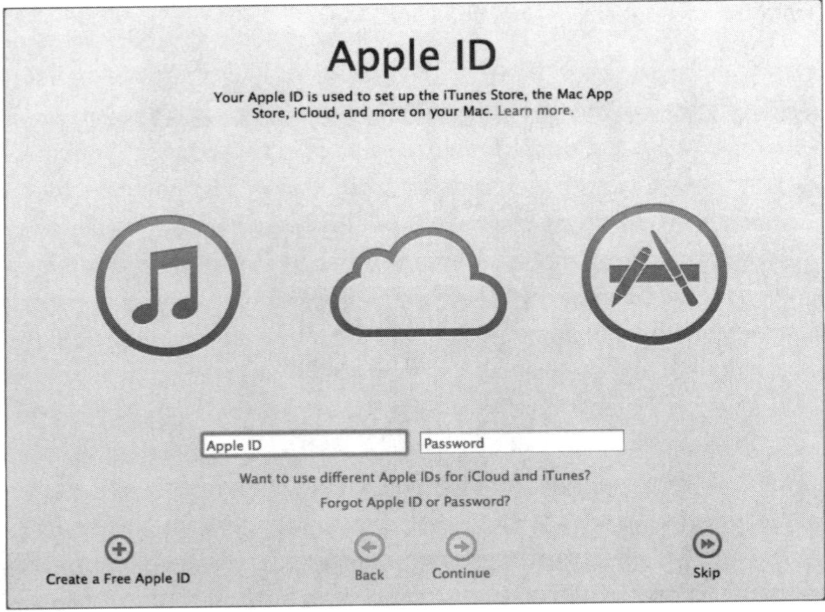

Option 1: Use an Existing iCloud Account

If you are performing these exercises in a classroom environment, or wish to use your existing iCloud account for these exercises, follow these instructions to link the Chris Johnson account to the Apple ID:

1. Enter the Apple ID and password your instructor provided (or for your own Apple ID account), and click Continue.
2. In the "Terms and Conditions" screen, you may use the right-arrows to read the various agreements that apply to OS X and Apple cloud services. When you finish reading, click Agree.
3. In the dialog that appears, click Agree.
4. In the "Set Up iCloud" screen, make sure that "Set up iCloud on this Mac" is selected, and click Continue.
5. In the confirmation dialog that appears, click Continue.
6. If a "Use iCloud for Find My Mac" screen appears, ensure that "Set up Find My Mac on this Mac" is deselected and click Continue.
7. If a Thank You screen appears, click Start Using Your Mac.

Option 2: Create a New iCloud Account

> **NOTE** ► Do not use this option in a classroom environment. Apple limits the number of Apple ID/iCloud accounts that can be created using this method on a particular computer, so doing this on a classroom computer may interfere with future classes. If you are using your own computer for these exercises and already have an Apple ID/iCloud account, you might also want to use it (with the Option 1 instructions) to avoid using up one of your computer's quota.

If you are performing these exercises independently and wish to create a new Apple ID to use in these exercises, follow these instructions to link the Chris Johnson account to a new Apple ID:

1. In the Apple ID window, click Create a Free Apple ID.

   If you are notified that you cannot create an Apple ID because "This Mac is no longer eligible to create Apple ID accounts," your computer has reached the number of Apple

IDs it is allowed to create. In this case, you need to create an Apple ID on another computer or device, and then follow Option 1 (the preceding section) to use it.

2 In the first "New Apple ID" screen, use the pop-up menus to enter your birthday, and then click Continue.

3 Enter your name, select "Get a free iCloud email address," and then enter an email name you'd like to use for the class.

   If you see a warning that the "Email address is already being used," you need to choose a different name.

4 When you see a green check mark next to the email address, you have entered an allowable name and can click Continue.

5 Choose a password and enter it in the Password and Verify Password fields. Then choose a security question from the pop-up menu and enter its answer below. Click Continue.

   NOTE ► Especially if you are performing these exercises in a class, do not use the same password you use for anything else. Reused passwords are a common security problem, and in this case your Apple ID password may be left on the computer after class is over. In this case, a better option is to choose a random password, write it down, and store the note in a secure location (that is, *not* on a sticky note on your monitor or even under the keyboard).

6 In the "Terms and Conditions" screen, you may use the right-arrows to read the various agreements that apply to OS X and Apple cloud services. When you finish reading, click Agree.

7 In the dialog that appears, click Agree.

8 In the "Set Up iCloud" screen, make sure that "Set up iCloud on this Mac" is selected, and click Continue.

9 In the confirmation dialog that appears, click Continue.

10 If a Thank You screen appears, click "Start Using Your Mac."

Adjust Chris Johnson's Preferences

Just as you did in the Local Admin account, you will adjust Chris Johnson's preferences to allow easy access to system files.

1 In the Finder, choose Finder > Preferences.

2 Select the options to show Hard disks, External disks, and Connected servers on the desktop.

3 From the "New Finder windows show" pop-up menu, choose your system disk (typically Macintosh HD).

4 Select the Sidebar button at the top of the Finder Preferences window.

5 Select "chris" in the Favorites section of the sidebar, and Hard disks in the Devices section. Note that Hard disks should be fully enabled (check mark in the checkbox), not just partially enabled (dash in the checkbox).

6 Close the Finder Preferences window.

7 Navigate to /Applications (use Go > Applications or Command-Shift-A).

8 Just as you did in the Local Admin account, drag the TextEdit application into the left side of Chris's Dock.

9 Navigate to /Users/Shared. Since Chris's Finder preferences are set to show the hard disks on the desktop, you can open Macintosh HD from the desktop, then open Users, then open Shared.

10 Drag the StudentMaterials folder into the right side of Chris's Dock.

11 Open System Preferences and then click the Desktop & Screen Saver icon to open that preference pane.

12 Select a different desktop picture.

13 If you like, adjust the Mouse and/or Trackpad preferences to your personal taste just as you did in the Local Admin account.

Examine Chris Johnson's Account

1 In System preferences, click the Show All button and then open the Users & Groups preferences.

Notice that you have different options than you had logged in as Local Admin. For instance, you cannot allow yourself to administer the computer, or enable parental controls for yourself. You can, however, configure a Contacts card or add login items (which will be opened every time you log in). Also, you cannot select any account other than your own.

2 In the lower-left corner, click the Lock button and then authenticate as Local Admin (you can use either the Full Name **Local Admin** or the Account Name **ladmin**). This unlocks the Users & Groups preferences and allows you to make changes to other user and group accounts while remaining logged in as Chris.

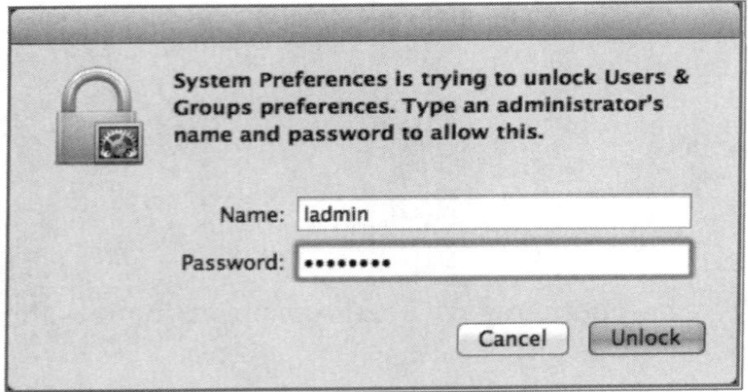

3 Control-click Chris's account and choose Advanced Options from the shortcut menu.

The Advanced Options dialog appears, and displays the hidden attributes of the Chris Johnson account.

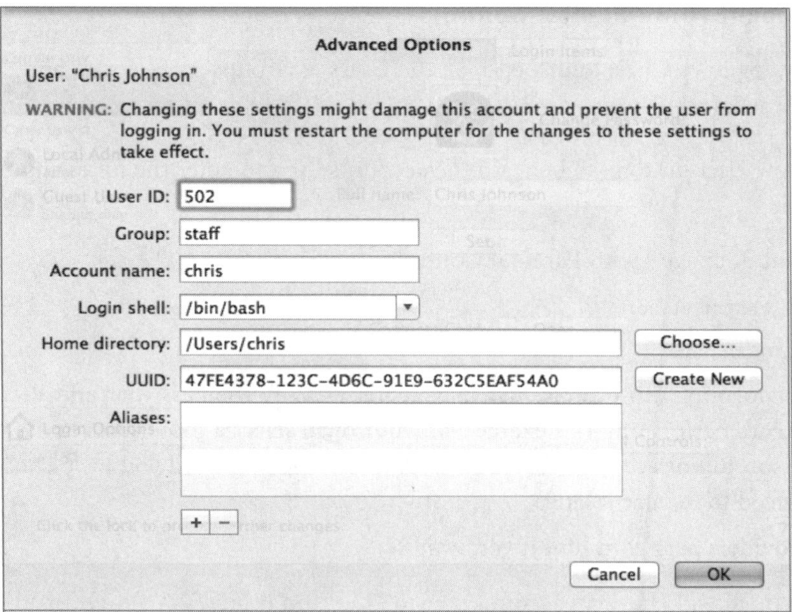

4 Click Cancel (or press Command-period) to dismiss the dialog. It is always a good idea to cancel a settings dialog when you have not made changes to it.

5 Leave System Preferences open for the next exercise.

Exercise 6.2
Create a Managed User Account

Prerequisites

- You must have created the Local Admin (Exercise 3.1 or 3.2) and Chris Johnson (Exercise 6.1) accounts.

In this exercise, you will create a managed account with parental controls applied and observe the resulting restrictions on that account.

Create an Account with Parental Controls

1. If necessary, log in as Chris Johnson, open the Users & Groups preferences, and authenticate as Local Admin.

2. Click the New User button (+) beneath the accounts list and enter the following information:

   New Account: Managed with Parental Controls

   Full Name: **Johnson Junior**

   Account Name: **junior**

   If you are performing this exercise in a class, enter **junior** in the Password and Verify fields. If you are performing this exercise on your own, select a more secure password for the Johnson Junior account. Be sure to remember the password you have chosen, as you will need to reenter it later.

   You may provide a password hint if you want to.

   NOTE ▶ If you already have an account named "Johnson Junior" or "junior," you will have to use a different name here and then remember to use your substitute name throughout the rest of the exercises.

3. Click Create User.

4. Verify that Junior's account is selected in the account list.

   Since you created the account as managed, the "Enable parental controls" checkbox is selected.

5. Click the Open Parental Controls button.

   This takes you to Parental Controls, which is actually a separate pane in System Preferences.

6. Select the options for "Use Simple Finder" and "Limit Applications."

7. Click the Other Apps disclosure triangle to see what applications are allowed by default.

8 Click the Web tab to configure Junior's web restrictions.

9 Select "Allow access to only these websites," and leave the default site list.

10 Click through the People, Time Limits and Other tabs of Parental Controls to see what other restrictions are available.

TIP Your Mac computer's Parental Controls preferences can be managed remotely by another Mac running OS X. To enable this feature in the Parental Controls preferences, click the Action menu (the small gear icon) at the bottom of the user list and choose Allow Remote Setup. From another Mac on the local network, open the Parental Controls preferences, and any Mac allowing this remote control will automatically appear in the user list. You will have to authenticate using an administrator account on the selected Mac to be granted Parental Controls preferences access.

11 Quit System Preferences and log out of the Chris Johnson account.

Test the Managed User Account

You will now log in to Johnson Junior's user account to see the effects of the parental controls you have configured.

1 At the login screen, select Johnson Junior, enter the password (junior, or whatever you chose), and press Return.

2 Click Skip to skip setting up an Apple ID, and then confirm by clicking Skip again.

3 If a Thank You screen appears, click Start Using Your Mac.

   Because you restricted Junior's account to the Simple Finder, the interface looks a bit different than normal.

4 Look at the options available under the Apple, Finder, File, and Help menus. Notice that most of the usual Finder capabilities are missing.

5 In the Dock, click the leftmost of the folder icons (it has a stylized "A" for Applications).

   The Simple Finder application launcher opens, and shows icons for the apps Junior is allowed to open.

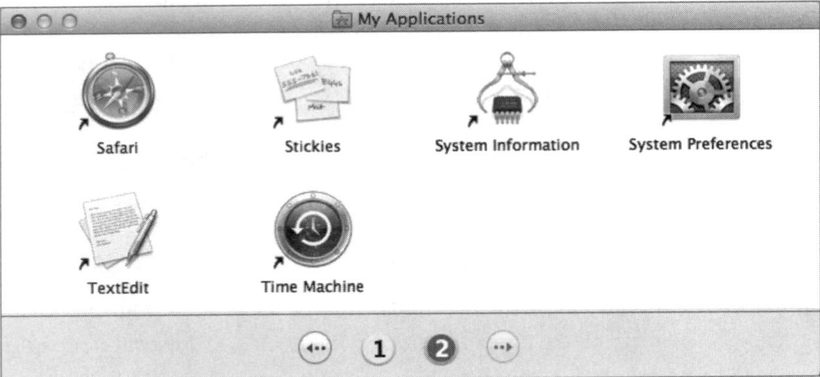

6 Open Safari. If it is not shown on the first screen of apps, click the right-arrow to show more apps.

Safari automatically takes you to the Apple website. Note that bookmarks are shown for the other allowed websites.

7 Use the Safari address bar to navigate to www.wikipedia.org.

Since this is not on the list of allowed sites, an error message appears.

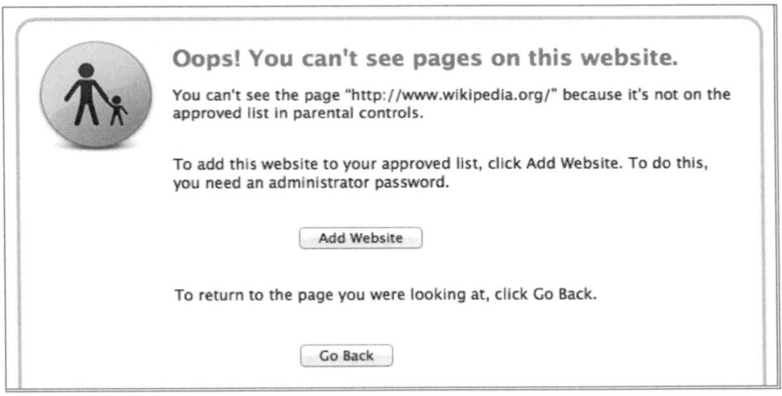

8 Click Add Website, and authenticate as Local Admin.

This action overrides the restriction, and the Wikipedia front page loads.

9 Quit Safari and log out as Johnson Junior.

Lesson **7**

User Home Folders

If you think of a user's account information as his mailing address, you can think of his home folder as his house and its contents. The directions to his house are certainly important, but it's the stuff inside the house that's really valuable to the owner. The same is true on the Mac. Aside from the initial account attributes, every other item the user is likely to create or need is stored in that user's home folder. As mentioned earlier, the default location for a locally stored user home folder is /Users/<name>, where <name> is the user's account name.

GOALS

- Understand user home folder layout and contents
- Delete users and archive home folder content
- Migrate and restore a user's home folder

Reference 7.1
Home Folder Contents

Traditional Mac users are notorious for putting personal files anywhere they like with little regard for order. Yet, with every revision of OS X and its included applications, Apple has been coaxing users into a tidier home folder arrangement. Though users can still create additional folders to store their items, most applications will suggest an appropriate default folder, while other applications won't even ask users and simply use the assigned default folder.

All the contents of the default folders inside a user's home folder are only viewable by the user, with the exception of the Public folder. Other users are allowed to view the contents of the Public folder, but they are not allowed to add items or make changes. There is a Drop Box folder inside the Public folder that others are allowed to put files in, but they still cannot see inside this folder. It's important to note that if a user puts other files and folders at the root level of her home folder, by default, other users will be able to view those items. Of course, you can change all these defaults by adjusting file and folder access permissions as outlined in Lesson 12, "Permissions and Sharing."

The default items in an OS X user's home folder are:

- Desktop—Many an old-school Mac user's files end up right here. This has been the traditional dumping ground for many users' files. Although this practice may be aesthetically unpleasing, there is no reason to stop users from keeping their items here, as it does not slow down or in any way harm the system.
- Documents—This is the default storage location for any document type that does not have a dedicated folder. Most famously, Microsoft Office prefers this folder as the default location for all its user documents and Entourage/Outlook profiles. Certainly putting items here is the best alternative to cluttering up the desktop.
- Downloads—This folder is the default location for Internet applications to store downloaded files. Sequestering all Internet downloads to this folder also enables virus and malware protection utilities to more easily identify potentially harmful files.
- Library—Whether a user knows it or not, this folder has become a collection for many user resources. Previous versions of OS X did not hide this folder. Starting with OS X Lion, Apple has chosen to hide this folder. While you may not see this folder from the Finder, currently many non-document-type resources end up in the user's Library folder. This includes, but isn't limited to, user-specific preference files, fonts,

contacts, keychains, mailboxes, favorites, screen savers, widgets, and countless other application resources.

TIP The quickest method to reveal the user's Library folder is to manually go to the folder in the Finder. While holding the Option key, choose Go > Library to reveal the hidden user's Library folder. You can learn more about hidden items in Lesson 14, "Hidden Items and Shortcuts."

- Movies—This is obviously the default location for movie files, and therefore it is often preferred by applications such as iMovie and iDVD.
- Music—This is, naturally, the default location for music files, and therefore it is often preferred by applications such as GarageBand, Logic, and iTunes. It is also the default location for synced iOS application resources and backups, which are managed by iTunes. Further, any movies that are part of an iTunes library will end up in this folder as opposed to the default Movies folder.
- Pictures—This is the default location for picture files, and therefore it is often preferred by applications such as iPhoto and Aperture
- Public—This is the default location for users to share files with others. Everyone who has access to a computer locally can view the contents of this folder. Inside this folder is a Drop Box folder where others can place files that only the owner of the home folder can see.

Optional items commonly found in a Mac user's home folder are:

- Applications—This optional folder must be created manually, but as you can see by its custom icon, the system recognizes this as a special folder. As the name implies, this is the preferred location for users to install their own applications.
- Sites—This is a legacy folder that might appear for home folders that have been upgraded or migrated from previous versions of OS X. This folder was the default location for personal websites when Web Sharing was enabled. OS X Mountain Lion no longer supports enabling Web Sharing via the Sharing preferences; however, other local users can actually view the contents inside this folder.

MORE INFO ▶ To find out more about alternatives to Web Sharing, see Knowledge Base document, HT5230, "OS X Mountain Lion: Options for web sharing."

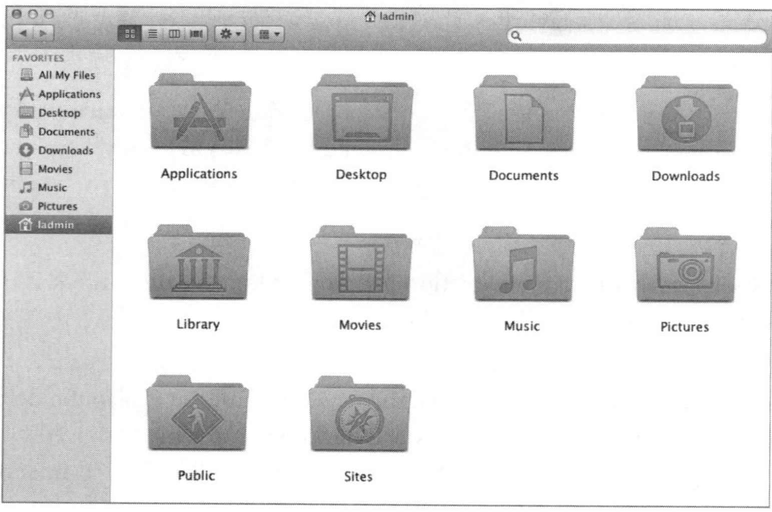

Reference 7.2
Deleting User Accounts

Deleting a user account in OS X is even easier than creating one. To delete a user account, simply select it from the list of users in the Users & Groups preferences, and then click the Delete (–) button at the bottom of the list. An administrator need only make one choice when deleting a user account: what to do with the user's home folder contents.

NOTE ▶ If a user has a particularly large home folder, the delete options dialog may take several minutes to appear.

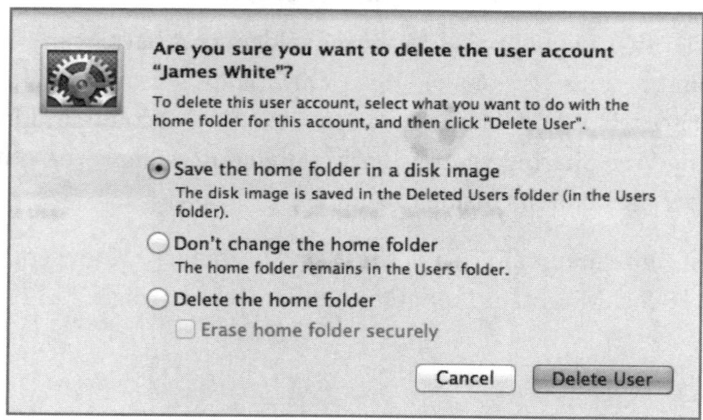

The administrator deleting the user account can choose one of three options:

- Save the home folder in a disk image—This option creates an archive of the user's home folder as a disk image file. The disk image file is saved in the /Users/Deleted Users folder with the account name as the name of the disk image file. Retaining the home folder as a disk image makes it easy to transport to other systems or import archived items to another user's home folder.

  Keep in mind you must have sufficient free disk space available on the local system disk, essentially enough to duplicate the original home folder, to create the archive disk image. This process can take quite a bit of time, depending on the size of the user's home folder.
- Don't change the home folder—This option leaves the user's folder unchanged save for its name. It simply appends "(Deleted)" to the home folder's name, letting you know the user account no longer exists. The deleted user's home folder maintains the same access restrictions as a normal user home folder. Subsequently, even though this is a much quicker and more space-efficient method when compared to the archival option, you have to manually adjust file ownership and permissions to access the items, as covered in Lesson 12, "Permissions and Sharing."
- Delete the home folder—This option deletes the home folder contents immediately. The items are not stored in a Trash folder before they are deleted, so they are not easily recoverable using this method.

  MORE INFO ▶ The default method used to delete a user's home folder is equivalent to a quick erase. Thus, the contents are potentially recoverable using third-party data forensics tools. Select the "Erase home folder securely" option to make the system perform a secure erase of the user's home folder items. You can learn more about securely erasing items in Lesson 10, "File Systems and Storage."

Reference 7.3
Migrating and Restoring Home Folders

The best method to move or restore a user's account and home folder is with the Apple Migration Assistant. Sometimes though, it's not the best solution, and you may have to manually restore a user's account. In this section you will explore both Migration Assistant and the manual steps for restoring a home folder.

Migration Assistant

This handy application does all the hard work for you when it comes to properly moving a user account and home folder from one Mac to another. As covered in Lesson 3, "Setup and Configuration," the Migration Assistant runs as part of the OS X Setup Assistant on new or newly installed Mac systems. However, you can also run this application at any point by opening /Applications/Utilities/Migration Assistant. Once open, the Migration Assistant walks you through a few easy steps to migrate the data.

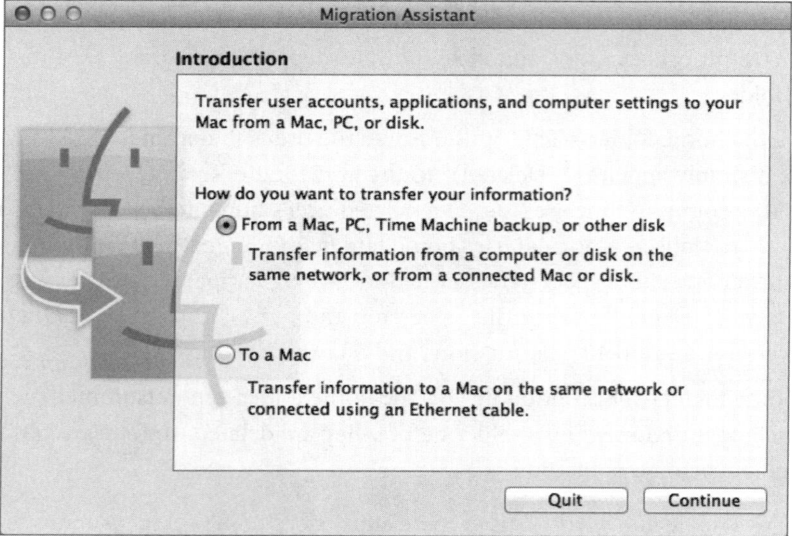

In a nutshell, Migration Assistant automates all the steps necessary to migrate individual user accounts, nonsystem applications, and other nonsystem resources to a Mac. The migration can occur between two Macs on the same network or directly connected via a Thunderbolt or FireWire cable. Migration Assistant can also restore user accounts from Time Machine backups, either directly connected or via the network or any other disk containing an OS X system. This is useful when problematic hardware prevents a Mac from starting up but the system disk itself remains functional. In this case you could physically remove the system disk and connect it to another Mac for migration. Lastly, Migration Assistant can copy information from another Windows PC via a local network.

NOTE ▶ Migration Assistant can only migrate a Legacy FileVault–protected user account to a Mac during the initial Setup Assistant process.

NOTE ▶ Always run Apple Software Update on computers you are about to migrate from. This process ensures that they have the latest copy of the Migration Assistant application.

Manually Restore a User's Home Folder

In certain situations you may need to erase and install a new system to repair or update a Mac. Unfortunately, you can't always count on the user having a recent Time Machine backup of the system. Thus, erasing the system disk would also destroy any user accounts on the Mac. In this case, because you're only working with a single Mac, as opposed to moving from one Mac to another, and you don't have a Time Machine backup, Migration Assistant isn't going to work for you.

If you find yourself in a situation where Migration Assistant won't fit your needs, you can manually move the user's home folder data. While this doesn't require another Mac, it does require that you temporarily copy the user's home folder to another "backup" storage disk. Once you have additional backup storage available, log into the user's account and, in the Finder, simply drag his home folder to the backup disk. As long as you copy the root of the user's home, the folder with the user's account name, then the Finder copies the entirety of the user's home folder in one move.

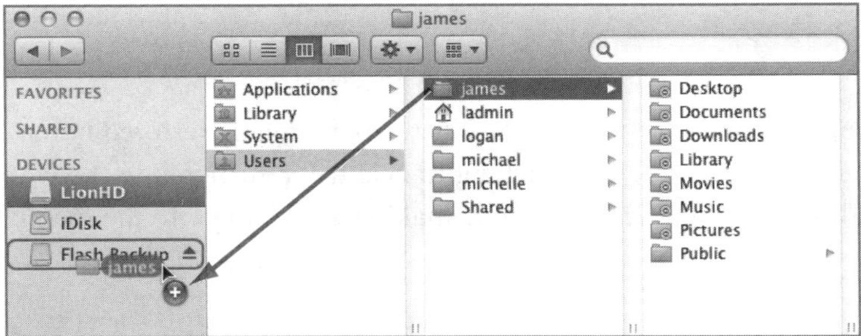

NOTE ▶ If you are creating a copy of another user's home folder contents, you will be prompted to authenticate as an administrative user to continue.

Once you are sure you have a complete copy of the user's home folder on the backup storage, you can erase the system disk and repair it. With the new system working in place, first start by creating an administrator account with a different name than the user account to be restored. You must set up this other administrator account because the proper method to manually restore a user's home folder requires that the user account not yet exist on the system.

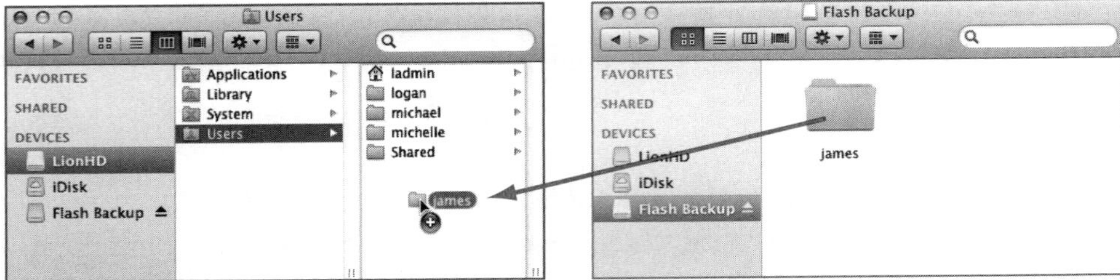

To complete the home folder restore, in the Finder simply copy the backup of the user's home folder into the /Users folder, making sure the home folder's name is titled appropriately. Finally, in the Users & Groups preference, create the user's account making sure to use the same account name. Upon creation of the new user account, if the names match, the system prompts you to associate a manually restored home folder in the /Users folder with a newly created user account.

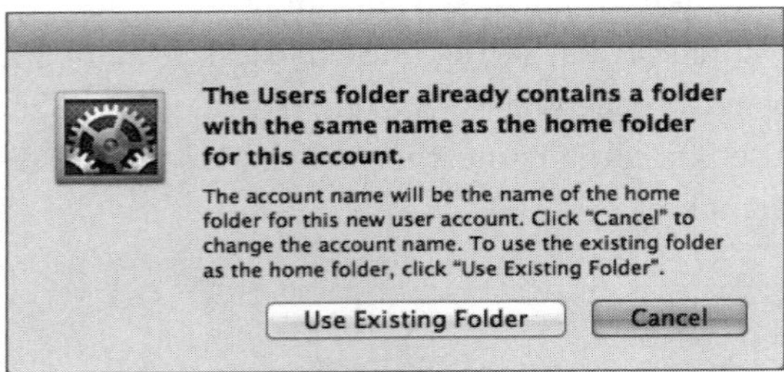

By clicking Use Existing Folder, the system will associate the manually restored home folder with the newly created user account. Clicking Cancel will return you to the Users & Groups preference without creating the new user or making any changes to the manually restored home folder.

Exercise 7.1
Restore a Deleted User Account

Prerequisites

- You must have created the Local Admin account (Exercise 3.1 or 3.2).

In this exercise, you will create a user account and populate the home folder for the user. Then you will delete the account, preserving the contents of the home folder. Finally, you will create a new account, ensuring that the new user gets the old user's home folder contents. Besides illustrating how to restore a deleted user account, this technique can also be used for changing a user's short name. It also provides an alternative to the Migration Assistant for moving user accounts between computers.

The scenario is that HR asked you to create an account for Marta Mishtuk. Her real name is Mayta Mishtuk, so you'll need to fix the error.

Create Marta Mishtuk's Home Folder

1 If necessary, log in as the Local Admin (password: **ladminpw**, or whatever you chose when you created the account).

2 Open System Preferences and select the Users & Groups pane.

3 Click the lock icon and authenticate as Local Admin.

4 Create a new user account for Marta Mishtuk:

   New Account: Standard

   Full Name: **Marta Mishtuk**

   Account Name: **marta**

   Password: **marta**

   Verify: **marta**

   Do not provide a password hint.

5 Click Create User.

6 Control-click Marta's account and choose Advanced Options from the shortcut menu.

   You will now take a screenshot to record Marta's account attributes for later reference. You could record the entire screen by pressing Command-Shift-3, but you will use another method to selectively record just the System Preferences window.

7 Press Command-Shift-4.

   The arrow pointer changes to a crosshair; you could use this to drag a rectangle around the region you wanted to record, but again you will use another method.

8 Press the Spacebar.

The crosshair changes into a camera icon, and the region of the screen it is over is highlighted in blue.

9 Move the camera pointer over the System Preferences window, and then click to record its contents.

The image is saved to your desktop, named "Screen Shot" followed by the date and time it was taken.

10 In the Advanced Options dialog, click Cancel.

11 Log out as Local Admin.

12 Log in as Marta Mishtuk.

13 At the Apple ID screen, click Skip, and then click Skip in the confirmation dialog.

14 If a Thank You screen appears, click Start Using Your Mac.

15 In the Dock, click the Launchpad icon.

Launchpad is a feature in OS X that gives users an easy way to launch applications that aren't in their Dock, without having to navigate to the Applications folder in the Finder.

16 Click the TextEdit icon to open TextEdit.

17 In the Untitled document, enter the text **This is Mayta's project document**. ("Mayta" is not a typo.)

18 From the menu bar, choose File > Save (or press Command-S) to save the file.

19 Name the file **Project**, and save it to Marta's desktop.

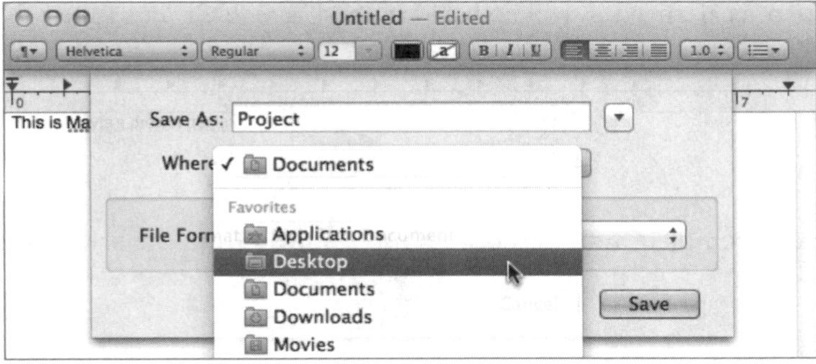

20 Quit TextEdit and log out of the Marta Mishtuk account.

Delete Marta's Account

You will delete Marta's account, preserving her home folder in a disk image file. A disk image is a file that contains a file system.

1 Log in as Local Admin.

2 Open Users & Groups preferences in System Preferences, if necessary. Unlock the preference pane.

3 Delete Marta's account by selecting her name and then clicking the Delete (–) button.

4 In the dialog that appears, select "Save the home folder in a disk image" and click Delete User.

While Marta's account is archived, it will be listed in the Users & Groups list as "Deleting Account."

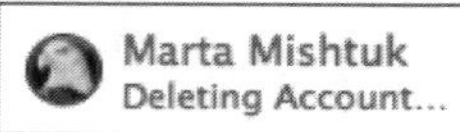

5 Wait for the archive to complete and Marta's account to vanish from the list, and then quit System Preferences.

Restore Marta's Account for Mayta

Marta's files (actually Mayta's) have been preserved in a disk image. Now you need to copy them to Mayta's new home folder so that when the new account is created she gets her old (the Marta account's) files.

Note that since disk images are portable and easy to store, you could use this technique to recreate the account on another computer, even long after it had been deleted.

1 Navigate to the folder /Users/Deleted Users.

   You can reach this folder by opening Macintosh HD from your desktop, opening the Users folder inside of that, and then opening Deleted Users inside of that.

   If you don't have permissions to open the Deleted Users folder, you may be logged in as a standard user. Log out, and log back in as Local Admin.

2 Open marta.dmg.

   The disk image opens and displays the contents of the marta account's home folder. However, as Lesson 14 discusses, an invisible subfolder named Library contains account settings and preferences for the marta account; in order to fully restore this account, you need to restore the entire home folder, not just its visible contents.

3 Close the "marta" window (but do not eject the disk image). The disk's icon is still visible on your desktop.

4 In the remaining Finder window, navigate back to the /Users folder. You can do this by clicking the left arrow in the window's toolbar, by pressing Command-[(left bracket), or by Control-clicking the folder name in the window's title bar and choosing Users from the shortcut menu.

5 Hold down the Option key as you drag the marta icon from your desktop to the Users folder. Make sure the pointer changes to show a green plus sign, indicating that

the item will be copied, and that you keep holding Option until after you release the mouse button.

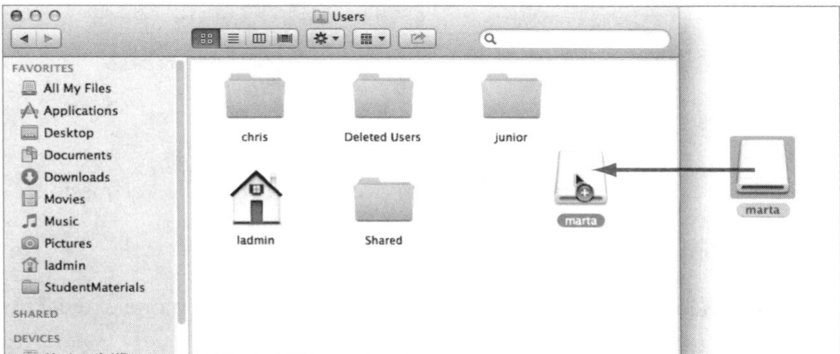

When you drag a mounted disk image icon without holding any modifier keys, the Finder creates an alias (indicated by a curved arrow on the pointer). Holding down the Option key forces it to create a copy instead.

The file permissions on /Users do not allow you to add items to it. The Finder asks you to authenticate as an administrator in order to override this.

6 Enter Local Admin's password and click OK.

7 Verify that there is now a folder called marta in the Users folder. If there is an alias instead (indicated by a curved arrow in the lower-left corner of the icon), delete it and retry starting at step 5.

8 In the Users folder, select the marta folder and press Return.

This allows you to edit the folder's name.

9 Change the folder's name to mayta and press Return.

10 Again, authenticate as Local Admin in order to override normal file permissions.

11 Open the mayta folder, and the Desktop folder inside of that.

You will be able to see Mayta's Project document (Project.rtf if filename extensions are visible).

12 After verifying that Mayta's document is in place, unmount the marta volume by clicking the eject icon next to its entry in the sidebar. Note that you may need to scroll to view more of the sidebar to see the icon.

Create and Verify Mayta Mishtuk's Account

You will now create the Mayta Mishtuk user account, using the restored home folder as the new account's home folder.

1 Open System Preferences and select Users & Groups.

2 Click the lock icon and authenticate as Local Admin.

3 Click the Add (+) button to create another account:

New Account: Standard

Full Name: **Mayta Mishtuk**

Account Name: **mayta**

If you are performing this exercise in a class, enter **mayta** in the Password and Verify fields. If you are performing this exercise on your own, select a more secure password for the Mayta Mishtuk account. Be sure to remember the password you have chosen, as you will need to reenter it periodically as you use this computer.

You may provide a password hint if you want to.

4 Click Create User.

A dialog appears that asks if you would like to use "mayta" as the home folder for this user account.

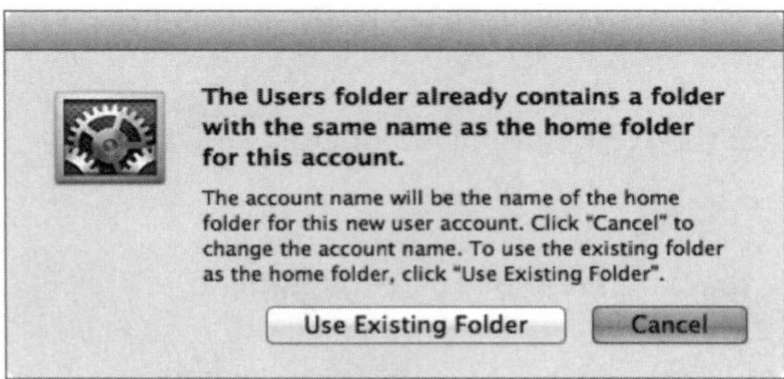

5 Click Use Existing Folder.

6 Control-click Mayta's account and choose Advanced Options from the shortcut menu.

7 Open the Screen Shot file on your desktop, and compare the account attributes of Mayta's new account with her original account. The User ID of the old account may have been reused for the new account, but their UUIDs will be different. Each account is assigned a completely new UUID when it is created.

8 Quit Preview.

9 In the Advanced Options dialog, click Cancel, and then quit System Preferences.

10 Try to open the Desktop folder in Mayta's home folder now. If your Finder window is still displaying the Desktop folder, click the back button and then double-click the Desktop folder again. You no longer have permission because the files are now owned by Mayta's new account.

11 Close the Finder window.

Verify Mayta Mishtuk's Home Folder

To make sure Mayta's files are all here, you will explore her restored home folder.

1 Log out as Local Admin and log in as Mayta.

2 If you are alerted that the system could not unlock Mayta's keychain, click "Update Keychain Password," and enter marta (the original password for the Marta Mishtuk account).

3. Verify that the Project file is on the desktop.
4. In the Finder, open Mayta's home folder by choosing Go > Home (or by pressing Command-Shift-H).
5. Make sure all the usual subfolders are there: Desktop, Documents, Downloads, Movies, Music, Pictures, and Public.
6. Open the Desktop folder and verify that you see the Project document.
7. Navigate back to the home folder, and then open the Public folder, where you will see a Drop Box folder. These folders are discussed more in Lesson 12, "Permissions and Sharing."

   In addition to the visible folders inside Mayta's home folder, it should also contain an invisible Library folder.
8. Hold down the Option key, and choose Go > Library. Note that the Library choice is hidden except when you are holding the Option key.

   Mayta's Library folder contains a large number of subfolders. This folder and its contents are discussed in more detail in Lessons 14 and 15.
9. Close the Library folder and log out as Mayta Mishtuk.

Lesson 8

System Security

The primary purpose of a multiple-user operating system is to provide all users with a secure work environment. OS X provides a relatively secure out-of-the-box experience for most situations. Yet some situations call for greater security than the defaults afford. This lesson focuses on the built-in advanced security features of OS X and how best to manage and troubleshoot these features.

GOALS

- Understand password types and their usage
- Use a variety of methods to reset lost user passwords
- Manage user and system security settings

Reference 8.1
User Account Security

As was discussed previously in this guide, OS X uses a variety of user account types: standard users, administrative users, the guest user, sharing users, and the root user. Apple has made these different account types available to allow greater flexibility for managing user access. Because each account type is designed to allow different levels of access, you should be aware of each account type's potential security risk.

Standard Users

This account type is very secure, assuming an appropriate password is set. This user is allowed to use nearly all the resources and features of the Mac, but he can't change anything that might affect the system software. You can further restrict this account by using managed parental control settings.

Administrative Users

Because this is the initial account created when the Mac is set up for the first time using the Setup Assistant, many use this as their primary account type. This is advantageous because it allows the user to literally change anything on the computer, as is required for system management. The downside is that she will be allowed to make changes or install software that can render the system insecure or unstable.

Additional administrative accounts can be used for daily use, but this isn't always the best idea, as all administrative accounts are created equal. In other words, all administrative accounts have the ability to make changes to anything on the system, including deleting or changing the passwords to other administrative accounts. Administrative users can also change the administrative rights for any other user account, either disabling current administrators or changing standard users into administrators. Further, opening poorly written or intentionally malicious software as an administrative user could seriously harm the system software.

Most significantly, though, any administrative user can enable the root account or change the root account password using the Directory Utility application located in the /System/Library/CoreServices folder. For these reasons, you should seriously consider limiting the number of administrative user accounts on your Mac systems.

Guest Users

Guest users are allowed, by default, to access your Mac via network file sharing without a password. Additionally, you can allow guests to log in to your Mac computer's graphical user interface without a password. Even though the guest home folder is deleted every time the guest logs out, the obvious security risk here is that literally anyone has access equivalent to that of a standard user account, including access to the /Users/Shared folder and users' Public folders. This means he could execute some potentially nasty applications or fill your disk with unwanted files. The guest user can also restart or shut down your Mac, potentially allowing him to compromise the system during startup.

Fortunately, you can restrict the guest account using parental controls to prevent that account from running unapproved applications or restarting the Mac. Additionally, you can change the access permissions on shared folders so the guest account is not allowed to copy any items to your disk. Changing file and folder permissions is covered in Lesson 12, "Permissions and Sharing."

Sharing Only Users

Sharing users are by default allowed file sharing access to users' Public and Drop Box folders, so, like the guest user, they can potentially fill your disk with unwanted files. On the other hand, shared users cannot log in to the Mac otherwise and they can be required to use a password, so designating sharing users is generally much safer than using the guest account for file sharing. You can further control sharing users' access to your files by adjusting file and folder permissions. Changing permissions is a two-way street, though, and you could accidentally give a sharing user too much access.

Root User

The root user account, also known as the System Administrator, is disabled by default on OS X clients, and for good reason: The root account has unlimited access to everything on the Mac, and root users can do anything they want with the system. The potential for nefarious activity is literally unlimited with root account access. Remember, though, it only takes an administrative account to initially access the root account, so strictly limiting administrative usage is the key to safeguarding the root account.

> **NOTE ▶** Anyone with access to OS X Recovery can also reset the password for the root account. If security is a concern in your environment, it's highly recommended that you set a firmware password to prevent OS X Recovery access. Setting a firmware password is covered in the "Firmware Password" section later in this lesson.

Reference 8.2
Account Passwords

OS X relies on passwords as its primary method of verifying a user's authenticity. There are other more elaborate systems for proving a user's identity, such as biometric sensors and two-factor random key authentication, but these require special hardware. It's a pretty safe bet that every Mac is attached to an alphanumeric input device such as a keyboard, so passwords are still the most relevant security authentication method.

Understanding Password Types

If you look closer at the security systems used by OS X, you will discover that it uses a variety of passwords at different levels to secure the computer. Most users are only familiar with their account password, but the Mac can also have a firmware password, a master password, many resource passwords, and several keychain passwords.

Each password type serves a specific purpose:

- Account password—Each user account has a variety of attributes that define the account. The account password is the attribute used to authenticate the user so he can log in. For security reasons, a user's account password is stored as encrypted data in the user's record. Only the root user can access and view the encrypted data in the user's record.

- Apple ID and password—This is a user name and password combination that can be used to authorize many Apple and OS X services. The creation and use of an Apple ID requires an Internet connection, as Apple uses your Apple ID to keep record of a multitude of services. An Apple ID provides access to all the Apple online services, including iCloud and various stores. In the context of system security an Apple ID can be used to reset the password of a lost local account and used to find a lost Mac using the iCloud Find My Mac feature. Both features are covered later in this lesson.
- Legacy FileVault password—Versions of OS X prior to OS X Lion supported home folder–based encryption. If an older system is upgraded or migrated with Legacy FileVault accounts, they will remain encrypted. The password for a Legacy FileVault account can only be reset using a known master password. Resetting and disabling Legacy FileVault accounts is covered in greater detail later in this lesson.
- Master password—The master password is used to reset standard, administrative, and Legacy FileVault user accounts if the user has forgotten his account password. Configuring and troubleshooting with the master password is covered in greater detail later in this lesson.
- Keychain password—OS X protects the user's important authentication assets, outside of the account password, in encrypted keychain files. Each keychain file is encrypted with a keychain password. The system will attempt to keep keychain passwords synchronized with the user's account password. However, you can maintain unique keychain passwords separate from an account password as well. Maintaining synchronization between a user's keychain password and account password is covered later in this lesson. Details regarding advanced keychain features are covered in Lesson 9, "Keychain Management."
- Resource password—This is a generic term that describes a password used by nearly any service that requires you to authenticate. Resource passwords include email, website, file server, application, and encrypted disk image passwords. Many resource passwords are automatically saved for the user by the keychain system.
- Firmware password—The firmware password protects the Mac during startup. By default, anyone can subvert system security settings by simply using one of the commonly known startup-interrupt keyboard shortcuts. For example, anyone can hold down the Option key during startup to select an alternate operating system, thus bypassing your secure system. Setting the firmware password will prevent unauthorized users from using any startup-interrupt keyboard shortcuts. Setting a firmware password is covered in the "Firmware Password" section later in this lesson.

Password Changes

If a user already knows her own password, but she wants to change it, she can do so at any time from the Users & Groups preferences. She simply selects her account, and then clicks Change Password to access a dialog allowing her to change her password. Further, if her account password matches her keychain password this technique will also synchronize the two passwords.

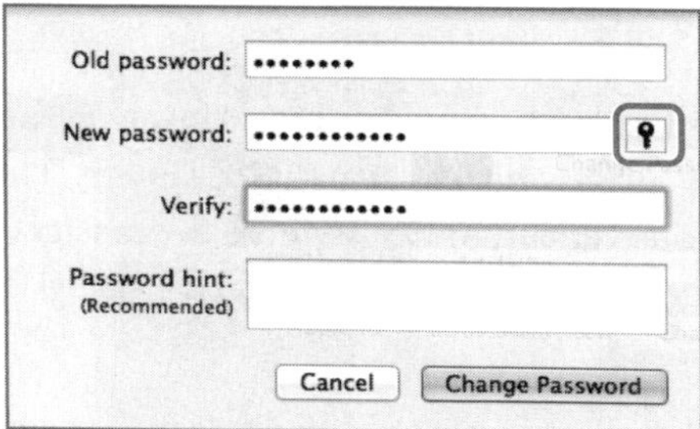

It's important to recognize that a password *change* is distinct from a password *reset*. A known password can be "changed," but an unknown password needs to be "reset" by some other authorization mechanism. The following section discusses various tools and methods for resetting lost passwords.

Password Assistant

Regardless of how sophisticated a security system is, the protection it affords is only as strong as the password you choose. For this reason, OS X includes a handy Password Assistant utility that will gauge the strength of your passwords or automatically create strong passwords for you. Anytime you are creating or modifying a password that will grant access to a substantial resource, like an account or keychain password, you can use the Password Assistant. The Password Assistant is available anytime you see the small key icon next to a password field, as you can see in the previous screenshot of the Users & Groups preferences.

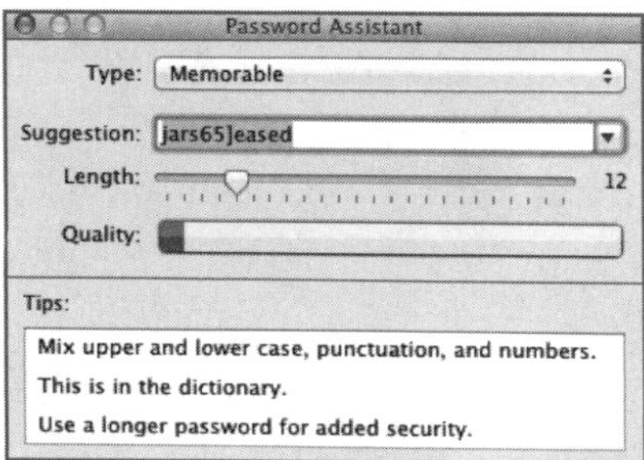

Master Password

As mentioned previously, the master password can be used to reset regular account passwords and is required to reset Legacy FileVault user account passwords. The master password isn't tied to any local user account, so it's an effective method of providing a password reset mechanism that does not require the creation of an additional administrator account. If you are maintaining a large deployment of Macs that are using local accounts, setting a uniform master password is an easy method to ensure you always have a back door in without having your own local account.

New installations of OS X do not normally have the master password set. However, there are two cases in which the master password may already be set on an OS X system. The first is if you have upgraded a Mac from a previous version of OS X where the master password was set. The second is if you used Migration Assistant to transfer a Legacy FileVault account to the OS X system.

If you think you know the current master password, or you would like to set a new master password, you can do so in the Users & Groups preferences. Once you have opened the Users & Groups preferences, and authenticated as an administrator, click the Action menu (the small gear icon) at the bottom of the users list to reveal a menu with Set Master Password or Change Master Password options. As expected, changing the password requires knowledge of the current master password.

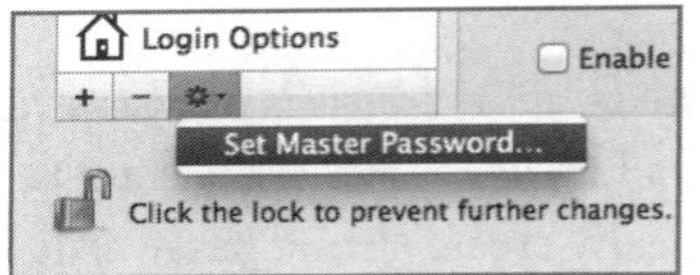

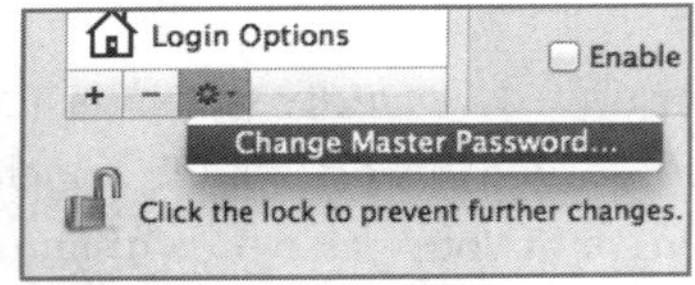

TIP If you are logged into a Legacy FileVault account, you can also change the master password from the Legacy FileVault pane of the Security & Privacy preferences.

Reference 8.3
Resetting Passwords

A user mistyping or forgetting her password is the primary cause of most login and access issues on any platform. The second most common issue, specific to OS X, is when a user's keychain passwords become out of sync with that user's account password. Fortunately, with a few rare exceptions, OS X provides ways to easily resolve these types of password issues.

Password Reset Methods

OS X offers several methods for resetting a local user account password:

- Administrator Account in Users & Groups—If you have access to an administrator account on the system, you can easily reset other user account passwords from the Users & Groups preferences. Simply authenticate as an administrator, select another user account and click Reset Password. If the selected user account is configured for Legacy FileVault, you will have to enter the master password to reset her account password. However, in all other cases, by virtue of previously authenticating as an administrator, you will be allowed to enter a new password for the user.

- Master Password at Login—If a user enters an incorrect password three times at the login window, and the master password is set, he will be prompted to reset the password. Authenticating with the current master password will allow you to enter a new password for the local user account. Note this is the only method for resetting a Legacy FileVault user account at login. Details regarding the master password are covered later in this section.
- Apple ID at Login—If a non-Legacy FileVault user enters an incorrect password three times at the login window, and the account is associated with an Apple ID, she will be prompted to reset the password. Authenticating with the user's Apple ID will allow you to enter a new password for the local user account. Details regarding setup of a user's Apple ID are covered in Lesson 3, "Setup and Configuration."

NOTE ▶ User accounts on Mac systems protected by FileVault 2 cannot have passwords reset using an Apple ID.

- FileVault 2 Recovery Key at Startup—If a user enters an incorrect password three times at startup on a Mac with FileVault 2 enabled, he will be prompted to reset the password using a Recovery Key. Lesson 11, "FileVault 2," covers this topic in greater detail.
- Reset Password in OS X Recovery—Anyone with access to OS X Recovery can use the Reset Password application to reset any local user password without any other authorization. While this last resort option is useful, it's also a significant security risk, as it requires no knowledge of any other passwords by default. Enabling FileVault 2 or a firmware password can mitigate this risk by requiring authentication to access the system disk from OS X Recovery. Both OS X Recovery Reset Password and firmware passwords are covered later in this lesson.

Login Keychain After Reset

OS X user accounts are given a login keychain encrypted with a password that is normally synchronized with their account password. Resetting an account password with any of the methods just discussed will not reset the user's login keychain password. However, by default in OS X, the next time the user logs in, he will be prompted to fix his login keychain. Lesson 9, "Keychain Management," covers this topic in greater detail.

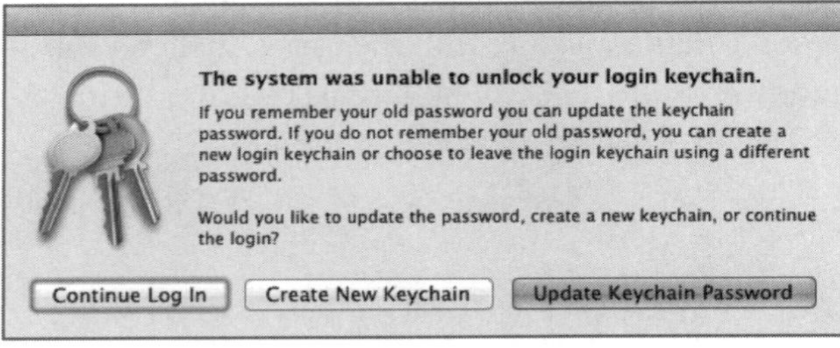

Reset Legacy FileVault Passwords

Legacy FileVault accounts are unique because the user's home folder is saved inside an encrypted disk image protected by that user's account password. Consequently, it is extremely important for an administrator to have the ability to reset a Legacy FileVault user's account password if the user ever wants to access her home folder files again.

A normal administrative user account is not enough to reset a lost Legacy FileVault password. Frankly, Legacy FileVault wouldn't be very secure if just any old administrative user could come along and break in. Therefore, if a Legacy FileVault user has forgotten her account password, the master password is required to reset the account.

As covered previously, if you do know the master password, OS X provides two methods for easily resetting Legacy FileVault user passwords. The first method allows you to reset a Legacy FileVault user at the login window, and the second method involves resetting a Legacy FileVault account password from the Users & Groups preferences.

If you lost the master password along with the user's Legacy FileVault password, you are completely out of luck. You must have at least one of these two passwords to recover a Legacy FileVault account. Otherwise, you are never, ever going to be able to recover the user's data. Not even Apple can help you—it designed Legacy FileVault to be as secure as possible and thus created only one method to reset a Legacy FileVault account: the master password. For this reason alone, you should abandon using Legacy FileVault accounts in favor of OS X FileVault 2 full disk encryption.

> **MORE INFO ▸** Turning off Legacy FileVault encryption is covered in the "Legacy FileVault Settings" section later in this lesson. OS X full disk encryption technology is covered in Lesson 11, "FileVault 2."

Reset the Master Password

If Legacy FileVault accounts are still being used, it's vital that the master password be properly configured and known by an administrator. If the master password is lost, an administrative user should reset it immediately for the benefit of being able to reset normal user passwords. Resetting the Master Password involves simply deleting the /Library/Keychains/FileVaultMaster.cer and /Library/Keychains/FilevaultMaster.keychain files.

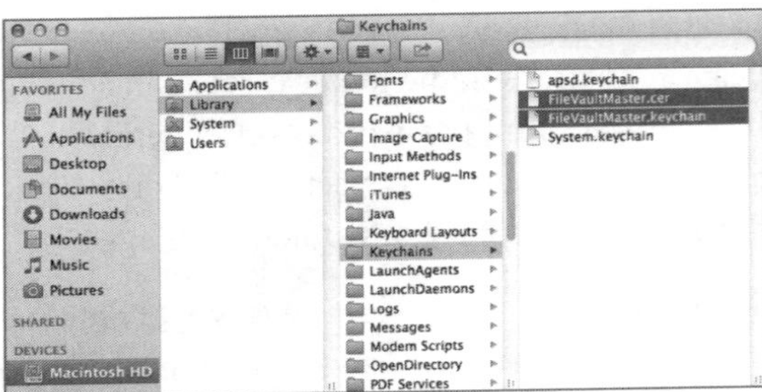

Once these files are deleted, an administrative user can return to the Users & Groups preferences and set a new master password using the techniques covered previously in this lesson. However, just because you can set a new master password for your Mac doesn't mean you can recover a Legacy FileVault account that was created with the old master password. Only the master password created when the Legacy FileVault user was enabled can unlock an inaccessible account.

Even if a new master password is set, this new master password will not have the ability to reset Legacy FileVault account passwords. This is because OS X Mountain Lion does not support re-encrypting Legacy FileVault accounts, which is a necessary step for lost master password resets. Thus, if you lost the master password used to create a Legacy FileVault user, there is no recovery method should the user also lose his password. This is yet another reason to abandon the use of Legacy FileVault accounts in favor of FileVault 2 full disk encryption.

OS X Recovery Password Reset

Many Macs intended for personal use have only the single primary administrator user account that was created when the Mac was initially set up with the Setup Assistant. Even if more than one person uses this Mac, quite often its owner is not very concerned about security. Thankfully, OS X now defaults to requiring a password at login so users are forced to enter their password at login.

However, if the computer was upgraded to OS X, it's very common for the primary user account to automatically log in during startup and to not have a master password set. This results in a high likelihood of Mac owners forgetting their primary administrator account password and not having any way to reset this password because they never enabled the master password or created another administrator account. Fortunately, Apple has prepared for these occasions by including the Reset Password application in OS X Recovery.

NOTE ► If the system disk is protected with FileVault 2 full disk encryption, you have to first unlock the system disk via Disk Utility. However, if there is only one account on the Mac and its password is lost, odds are you don't know the FileVault 2 password either. In this case the Reset Password application can't help you. Thus, your best bet to regain access to a FileVault 2 system is to use a recovery key as outlined in Lesson 11, "FileVault 2."

The Reset Password application is only available from an OS X Recovery system. Once running from OS X Recovery, you must open the Terminal application (via the Utilities menu), type `resetpassword`, and then press Return. Once Reset Password opens, simply select the system volume and the user account you wish to reset. You do not have to enter anything but the new password you wish to set for the selected user account.

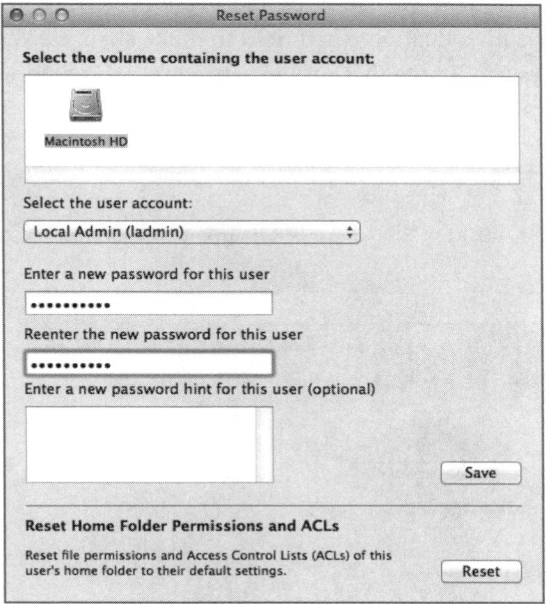

Obviously, the Reset Password utility is a dangerous application that can completely eliminate any of the security settings you've configured to protect your Mac. Because of this, the Reset Password utility will not run if copied off the original media, but this still doesn't prevent any user with access to OS X Recovery from using this utility. Once again, Apple prepared for this situation by providing another utility on OS X Recovery: Firmware Password Utility. As covered later in this lesson, setting a firmware password will prevent any nonauthorized user from circumventing normal system startup.

Reference 8.4
System Security Settings

In addition to specific user security settings, such as account passwords and keychain items, there are systemwide security preferences that affect all users on the Mac. Many of these options are disabled by default because the average Mac user would probably consider them inconveniences. However, if your environment requires greater security, these additional security features are indispensable.

Security & Privacy Settings

The Security & Privacy preferences have undergone significant changes in OS X Mountain Lion. These changes bring increased security for both the system and for the individual user. As such, there is a combination of both system settings and personal settings. Like all other system settings, administrator authentication is required to make changes. When using the Security & Privacy preferences you'll note that system settings are dimmed when the lock is present, but personal settings are always available.

General Settings

First this pane provides another location, besides the Users & Groups preferences, for any user to change her password.

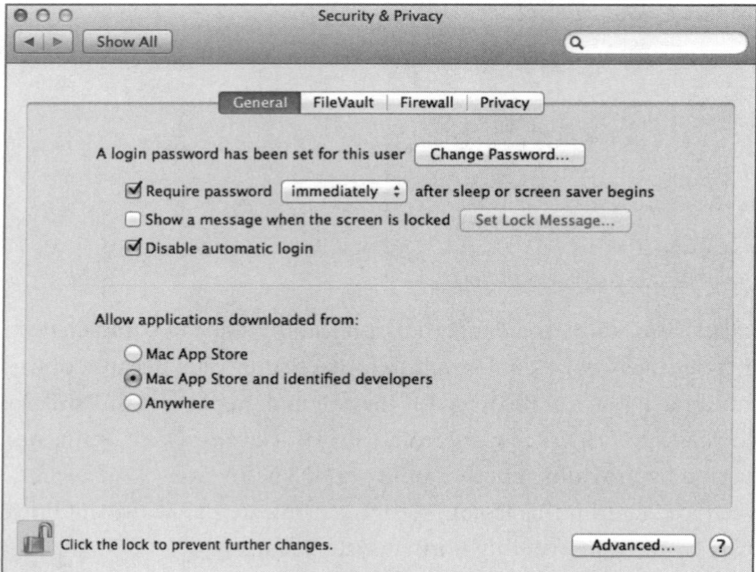

You can also choose to require a password to wake the computer from sleep or screen saver mode, and define a grace period before this requirement sets in. Both standard and administrative users can set this for their account, but an administrator cannot set this for every account from the Security & Privacy preferences. The exception to this is that systems with FileVault 2 enabled always require a password on wake. Such systems do not show the checkbox to disable password on wake.

Other login options include the ability to disable automatic login for all accounts. This system setting is also always required on systems with FileVault 2 enabled. Such systems do not show the choice to disable automatic login.

Administrators can also configure a custom message to show at the login window or when the screen is locked. When setting the message, you can use press Option-Return to force a new line. However, the system will only allow for three lines of text.

Finally, at the bottom of the General pane, you'll find settings for a significant new safety feature of OS X Mountain Lion, dubbed Gatekeeper. This allows administrators to restrict applications downloaded from the Internet based on the trustworthiness of the source. Lesson 19, "Application Installation," covers this topic in greater detail.

Advanced Settings

Additional security settings are available to an administrator who unlocks the Security & Privacy preferences and then clicks the Advanced button in the lower-right corner.

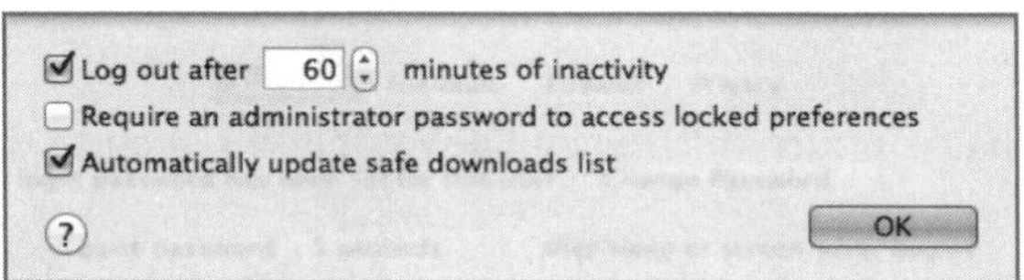

Administrators can choose to require that users automatically log out accounts after a certain amount of inactivity, and that all system preferences with locking access require an administrator password every time. For example, the default setting allows an administrative user to change Date & Time preferences without actually authenticating. Enabling this option will require an administrator to enter his password to use the Date & Time preferences.

Lastly, you can choose to disable the automatic update of a list of known unsafe downloads. Despite this option's description of maintaining a "safe downloads list," the system actually maintains a list of unsafe items such as known malware applications.

FileVault Settings

This is where you enable and configure OS X FileVault 2 full disk encryption. Lesson 11, "FileVault 2," covers this topic in greater detail.

Legacy FileVault Settings

Prior to OS X Lion, FileVault existed as a technology that secured user data by encrypting the user's home folder content. This technique, while effective, has a variety of drawbacks. For one, it did not protect data outside the user's home folder. More problematic, though, was that many system management and backup utilities simply didn't work properly with FileVault home folders. With OS X now featuring FileVault 2 full disk encryption, FileVault home folder encryption has been deprecated.

The previous version of FileVault, now dubbed Legacy FileVault, is still supported by OS X Mountain Lion for existing or migrated user accounts, but you can no longer enable it for new user accounts. If you are currently using a Legacy FileVault account on an OS X system, the Security & Privacy preferences will present a window prompting you to turn off Legacy FileVault.

NOTE ▶ It is strongly suggested that you turn off Legacy FileVault and switch to the much more robust FileVault 2.

NOTE ▶ You must disable all Legacy FileVault users to enable FileVault 2.

NOTE ▶ Turning off Legacy FileVault will require a logout and a potentially lengthy copy process as the system migrates the encrypted data back to "regular" data.

NOTE ▶ Turning off Legacy FileVault requires enough free space on the system disk to duplicate an entire decrypted copy your home folder data. If there is not enough free space, you will not be able to turn off Legacy FileVault. You may want to consider manually migrating a copy of your home folder as covered in Lesson 7, "User Home Folders."

If you dismiss this dialog, you can always decide later to turn off Legacy FileVault. Simply return to the Legacy FileVault pane of the Security & Privacy preferences. Note that you can reset the master password from this location as well.

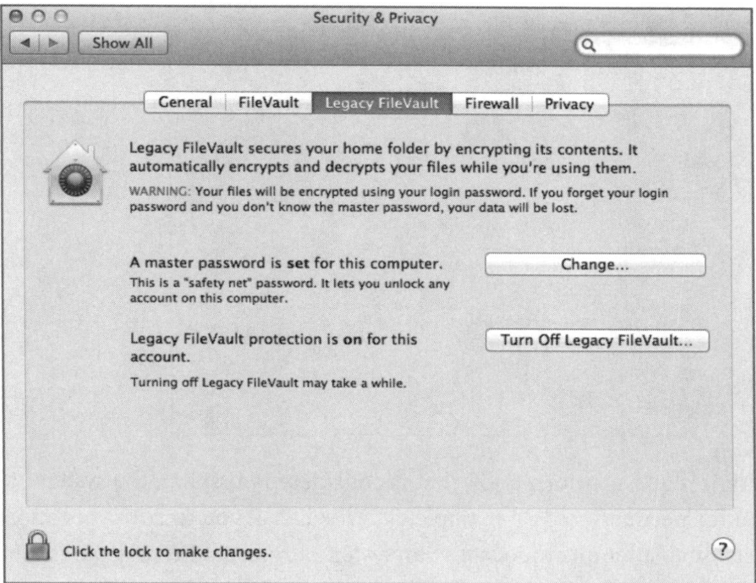

If you decide to stick with Legacy FileVault home folders, they will behave as they did in OS X v10.6. Other sections in this lesson cover techniques for managing passwords. Be sure to look for techniques pertaining to Legacy FileVault, as these accounts must be handled differently than standard user accounts.

Firewall Settings

This pane is where you enable and configure the personal network firewall settings. Lesson 26, "Host Sharing and Personal Firewall" covers this topic in greater detail.

Privacy Settings

This pane gives both administrators and standard users the ability to adjust services' access to personal information.

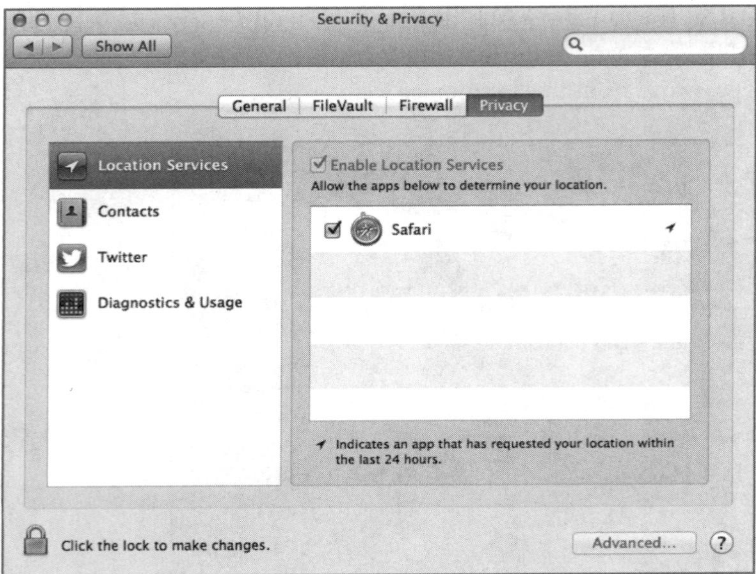

When a new application requests information that is considered personal, the system will automatically ask you for permission. For example, Safari will ask you to allow Location Services if a web-based map attempts to locate your system. From the Privacy pane, a user can view all the applications that have asked for this information and choose to allow or disallow further attempts to collect information. Examples of the types of services an application may request include Location Services, Contacts, Twitter, and Facebook information.

NOTE ▶ Any Mac with Wi-Fi capabilities can use Location Services; Wi-Fi must be enabled to use Location Services.

NOTE ▶ Anytime an application takes advantage of Location Services, the Location Services status menu will appear near the upper-right corner of the screen. The menu item appears as a north-east compass arrow, similar to that seen in the Privacy tab of Security & Privacy preferences.

NOTE ▶ The list of items in the Privacy pane will vary based on configured services. For example, the Twitter service will only appear once the user has configured Twitter in the Mail, Contacts, and Calendars preferences.

The last privacy setting allows administrators to disable the reporting of diagnostic information to Apple. The primary source of information sent with this option is application hangs or crashes. This information helps Apple resolve reoccurring issues faster.

Safari Privacy

In regards to privacy, another growing area of concern is the ever-expanding reach of website tracking systems. As social networking sites blossom across the Internet, those looking to take advantage of personal information invent more sophisticated techniques of gathering this information. While the OS X default web browser, Safari, can't prevent you from giving away your personal information, it can try to block the "hidden" methods used to gather information about your web usage.

You can find additional Privacy settings in the Safari preferences window. From here you can manage existing website cookies or adjust automatic blocking of cookies. Website *cookies* are bits of information about your web history that can be used to track your presence on the Internet. Other options include the ability to further limit website tracking, location services, and search engine suggestions.

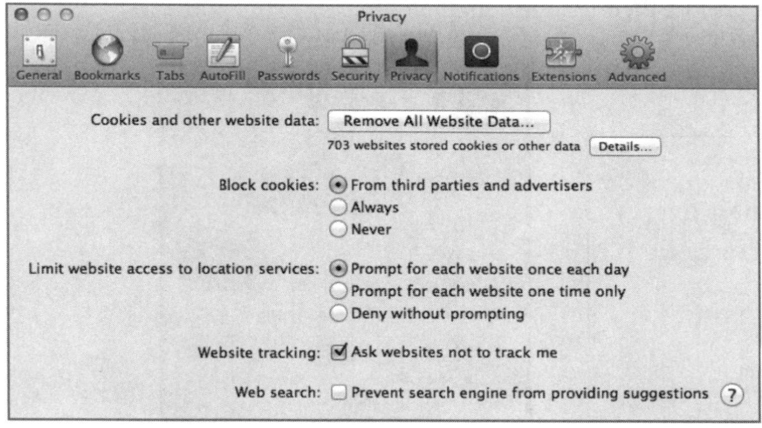

MORE INFO ▶ For more information about the Safari security features, visit www.apple.com/safari/features.html#security.

Find My Mac

From a security standpoint, one of the most significant features of iCloud is Find My Mac. This service helps you locate a lost Mac system by allowing you to remotely access the Location Services of the lost Mac. In addition to locating a lost Mac, the service also allows you to remotely lock, erase (or wipe), and display a message on the Mac.

TIP ▶ iCloud can also be used to locate a lost iPhone, iPod touch, or iPad. Though a misnomer, this is collectively known as Find My iPhone, which also happens to be the name of a free iOS application that can be used to find both Macs and iOS devices.

Several prerequisites must be met to use Find My Mac:

- The Mac system must have Wi-Fi enabled, and an active connection to the Internet.
- The Mac system must have a local OS X Recovery partition.
- The Mac system must be configured for iCloud with Find My Mac enabled. As covered in Lesson 3, "Setup and Configuration," the initial system setup will prompt to enable Find My Mac. You can also configure or disable Find My Mac at any time from the iCloud preferences.

Once you configure Find My Mac, you can use it from another PC by accessing the iCloud website at www.icloud.com. Simply log in with the appropriate iCloud account and then select Find My iPhone on the iCloud home page. As you can tell by the name, the "Find" services use the same Location Services technology for both iOS and OS X devices, but it would seem more users lose their iPhone than their Mac.

If successful, the Find My iPhone site will display a map with the relative location of all the devices configured for this iCloud account. Selecting a located device on the map will allow you to play a sound, send a message, lock, or wipe a device. Both remote lock and wipe will immediately restart the selected Mac system. The remote lock will let you set a new four-digit pin number for the Mac, and upon restart the Mac will prompt for the new pin number. If a remote wipe is issued, upon restart a FileVault 2–protected Mac will erase the encryption keys necessary to decrypt the system disk, while other Mac computers will simply delete the system partition.

TIP Systems with Find My Mac enabled also feature a "Guest" mode when the system is restarted. However, it's a trap. The intent is that a stolen Mac will be locked and likely restarted. Upon startup the suspect can choose Guest as a login option, which allows them to select a Wi-Fi network and use Safari. This is actually an attempt to get the stolen Mac back online so the owner can use Find My Mac.

Reference 8.5
Firmware Password

As covered previously, setting the firmware password prevents unauthorized users from using any startup-interrupt keyboard shortcuts. This protects your system from someone trying to circumvent an otherwise secure installation of OS X. Firmware passwords are not in any way tied to a user account. Instead, the password is saved to the Mac computer's firmware chip, so this password remains separate from the installed software.

TIP ▶ Even without setting a firmware password, enabling OS X FileVault 2 full disk encryption will prevent unauthorized access to the encrypted system disk.

With a firmware password set, all startup-interrupt keyboard shortcuts are disabled except for one. When you start up the Mac holding the Option key, an authentication window appears, where you can enter the firmware password. If you enter the correct password, you can pick a different startup disk from the Startup Manager. This gives the administrator the flexibility to start up from another system should the need arise, but otherwise prevents users from affecting the standard OS X startup process.

MORE INFO ▶ All the available startup keyboard shortcuts are covered in Lesson 30, "System Troubleshooting."

If you require the highest level of security for your Mac, you must set the firmware password, as any user with access to OS X Restore can set the password if it hasn't already been set. You set the firmware password using the Firmware Password Utility, available when the Mac is started up from OS X Recovery, as covered in Lesson 4.

Once the Mac is started into OS X Recovery, the Firmware Password Utility is available in the Utilities menu. If the firmware password isn't currently set, simply click Turn On Firmware Password and enter the desired password.

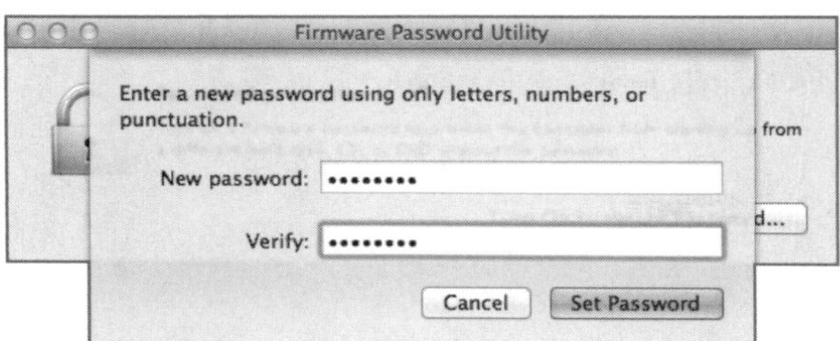

If a firmware password is already set for the system, you can change it or turn it off using the appropriate buttons. However, you must know the current firmware password to change or disable it.

If for some reason the Mac computer's firmware password is lost, it can be reset. For many Mac models made before 2010, you can reset the firmware password by first removing some of the system memory from the Mac. This "proves" that you have access to the internals of the Mac. Then when you restart the Mac, hold the Command-Option-P-R keys. Continue holding until you hear the Mac restart; then you can let go of the keys. At this point the firmware password has been cleared.

Unfortunately, most Mac models from 2010 or later don't support this method of resetting the firmware password. If this is the case, you need to visit an Apple Authorized Service Provider to clear the firmware password.

Exercise 8.1
Reset Account Passwords in OS X Recovery

Prerequisites

- You must have created the Local Admin (Exercise 3.1 or 3.2) and Chris Johnson (Exercise 6.1) accounts.
- Your computer must have a local hidden Recovery HD partition. This partition is normally created by the OS X Mountain Lion installation process.

OS X provides a number of ways of resetting lost account passwords. In this exercise, you will use OS X Recovery mode to reset Chris Johnson's password.

Reset a User Password in OS X Recovery

1 Shut down your computer.

2 Start your computer, and hold down Command-R until the gray Apple appears on the screen.

3 From the menu bar, choose Utilities > Terminal.

The Terminal utility provides access to a command-line (text-based) interface in OS X. We don't cover the command-line interface in this book, but it is necessary to reach the reset password utility in OS X Recovery.

4 Type the command resetpassword and press Return.

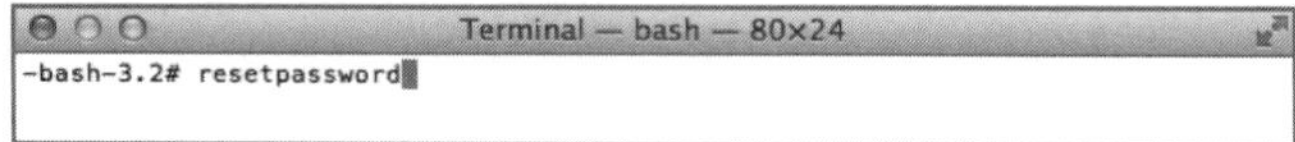

The Reset Password utility opens.

5 In the volume list, select Macintosh HD, and then choose Chris Johnson (chris) from the user account pop-up menu.

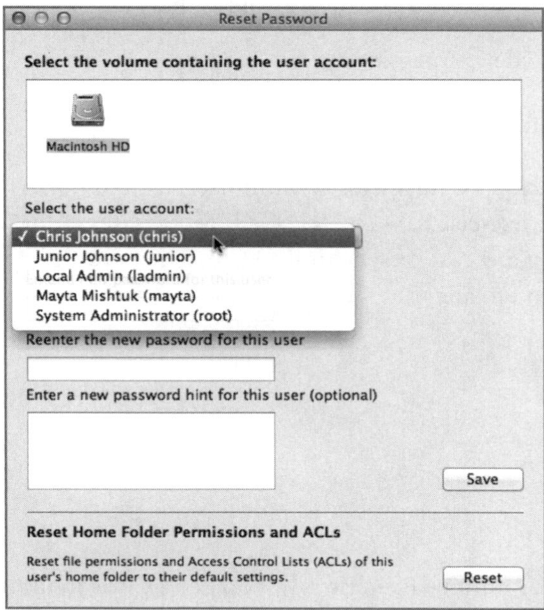

6 Enter password1 in both password fields. Leave the hint field blank.

7 Click Save.

A warning appears, stating that the user's default keychain password wasn't changed (more on the implications of this in Exercise 8.3, "Synchronize Keychain Passwords").

8 Click OK.

In addition to resetting user passwords, the Reset Password utility can also repair some permissions issues with user home folders. In this case, nothing is wrong with Chris Johnson's home folder permissions, resetting them anyway doesn't hurt anything.

9 Click Reset to reset Chris's home folder permissions.

10 From the Apple menu, choose Restart.

NOTE ▸ Chris Johnson's login keychain is no longer synchronized with his login password. You may either perform Exercise 8.2 next, followed by Exercise 8.3; or you may skip directly to Exercise 8.3. In any case, resynchronize Chris's passwords by performing Exercise 8.3 before going on to any other lesson.

Exercise 8.2
Reset Account Passwords

Prerequisites

- You must have created the Local Admin (Exercise 3.1 or 3.2) and Chris Johnson (Exercise 6.1) accounts.

OS X provides a number of ways of resetting lost account passwords. In this exercise, you will reset Chris Johnson's password as an administrator, and then again using Chris's Apple ID account.

Reset a User Password as an Administrator

1. If necessary, log in as Local Admin (password: **ladminpw**, or whatever you chose when you created the account).
2. Open the Users & Groups preference pane.
3. Click the padlock and authenticate as Local Admin.
4. Select the Chris Johnson account.
5. Select "Allow user to reset password using Apple ID." You will use this capability later in the exercise.
6. Click Reset Password.
7. In the dialog that appears, enter **password** in the New password field.
8. Click the small key icon next to the "New password" field.

   The Password Assistant opens to help you choose a better password. It rates the quality of this proposed password (red, to indicate it's very bad), suggests a better password (in the Suggestion field), and lists Tips on how to avoid such bad passwords.

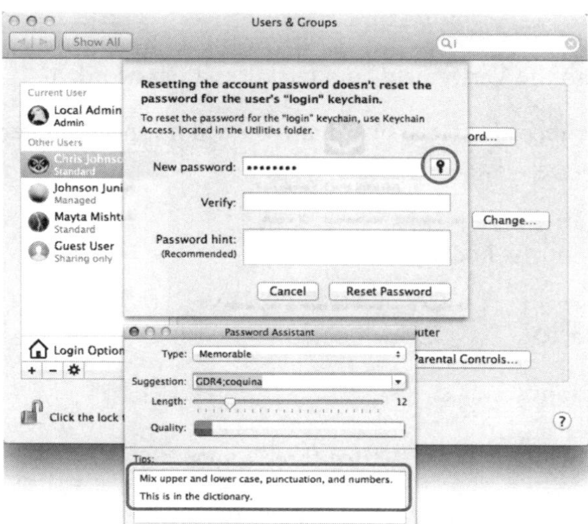

9. Click the triangle next to the Suggestion field to show more suggested passwords.

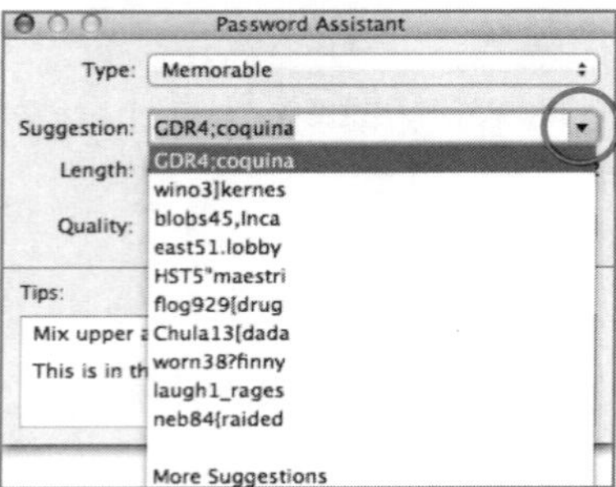

10 Click one of the suggested passwords. The selected password copies into the New Password and Suggestion fields, and the Quality bar expands and turns green to indicate this is a much better option.

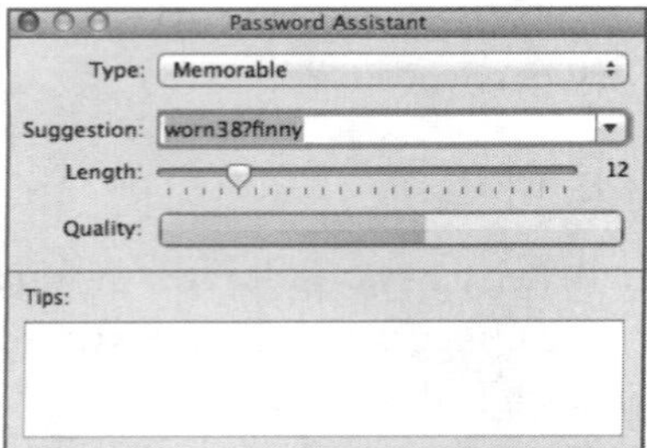

11 Type the password you chose into the Verify field, and click Reset Password.

You do not need to memorize or record this password, as you will not need it later.

12 Close the Password Assistant.

13 Quit System Preferences and log out as Local Admin.

Reset a Password with an Apple ID

1 At the login screen, select Chris Johnson.

2 Enter the wrong password for Chris, and press Return three times.

A popover appears, listing options for resetting Chris' password.

3 Click the arrow next to "reset it using your Apple ID."

4 Enter your Apple ID and its password, and click Reset Password. Note that you may need to enter your Apple ID in lowercase.

A dialog warns that you will create a new keychain.

5 Click OK.

6 In the Reset Password popover, enter the following:

New password: **password2**

Verify password: **password2**

Do not provide a password hint.

7 Click Reset Password.

A dialog warns that the system was unable to unlock your login keychain. Leave this dialog open for the next exercise.

NOTE ► Chris Johnson's login keychain is no longer synchronized with his login password. You need to resynchronize his passwords by performing Exercise 8.3 before going on to any other exercise.

Exercise 8.3
Synchronize Keychain Passwords

► Prerequisites

- You must have created the Local Admin (Exercise 3.1 or 3.2) and Chris Johnson (Exercise 6.1) accounts.
- You must perform Exercise 8.1 and/or 8.2 before this exercise.

Update the Login Keychain Password

After the last exercise(s), Chris Johnson's account password has been reset, but his login keychain is still encrypted with his old password. Fortunately, the login process provides an easy way to resynchronize the login keychain's password.

1 If you aren't already logged in (or logging in) as Chris Johnson, log in now (after the last exercises, his password is either **password1** or **password2**).

Because Chris's account password no longer matches his keychain password, the system cannot use this password to unlock his keychain, and you receive a warning to this effect.

If you did not remember Chris's old password, there would be no way to recover the contents of his old keychain, and you could click Create New Keychain to delete it and create a new one. In this case, however, because you do remember the old password, you can use it to recover the contents and update the keychain password.

2 Click Update Keychain Password.

3 When prompted, enter Chris's old login password from before his account was reset (chris, or whatever you chose as Chris's original password in Lesson 6) and click OK.

Verify the Synchronization

1 From the Utilities folder, open Keychain Access.

Keychain Access displays the status and contents of your login keychain. Note that the keychain appears as unlocked, which means that the correct password has been supplied and its contents are available.

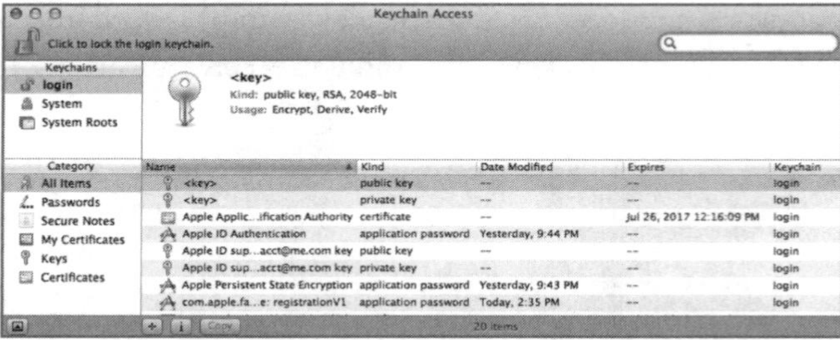

2 From the menu bar, choose Keychain Access > Preferences (or press Command-comma).

Command-comma is a shortcut for application preferences that works in most applications.

3 Click the First Aid tab.

4 Ensure that the "Synchronize login keychain password with account" option is selected.

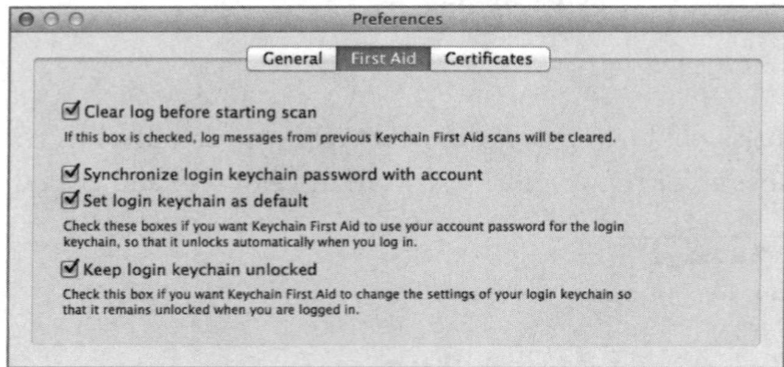

5 Close the Preferences window.

6 Choose Keychain Access > Keychain First Aid.

7 In the Keychain First Aid window's Password field, enter Chris's current account password (**password1** or **password2**).

8 Click Start.

Keychain Access checks the login keychain for a variety of problems, including synchronization with the account password. Its report shows "No problems found." If it does find any problems, select the Repair option and click Start again.

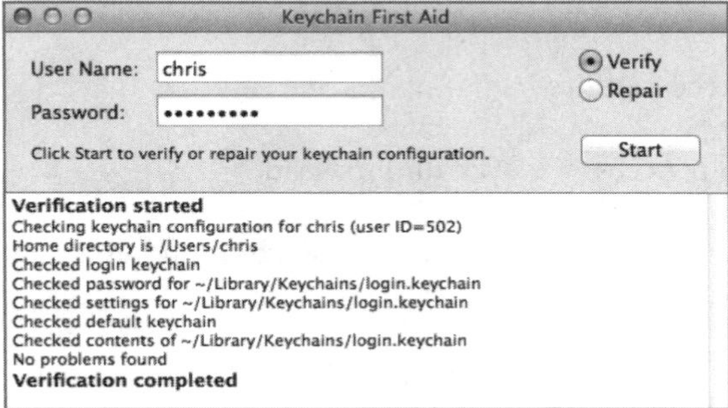

9 Close the Keychain First Aid window, but leave Keychain Access open.

Change Chris's Password

Resetting Chris's account password desynchronized it from his login password. Changing his password normally does not cause this problem. To test this, you will change Chris's password the normal way.

1 Open the Users & Groups pane in System Preferences.

2 Make sure that the Chris Johnson account is selected.

3 Click Change Password.

Note that unlike the Reset Password options you used earlier, this has a field for the Old password. It uses this old password to decrypt the login keychain, and then reencrypt it with the new password.

4 Enter the following:

Old password: **password1** or **password2**

New password: **chris** (or whatever you chose in Lesson 6)

Verify: **chris** (or whatever you chose in Lesson 6)

You may enter a password hint if you want to.

5 Click Change Password.

6 Quit System Preferences.

Re-verify the Synchronization

1 If necessary, open the Keychain Access utility.

2 As you did before, choose Keychain Access > Keychain First Aid.

3 Enter Chris's current account password (chris, or whatever you chose in Lesson 6) in the Password field, and click Start.

   As before, it reports "No problems found," which indicates that the keychain password has stayed synchronized with the account password.

4 Quit Keychain Access.

Exercise 8.4
Use a Firmware Password

In this exercise, you will set a firmware password to control the startup process of your computer.

> **WARNING** ► If you forget the firmware password, you might have to take your computer to an Apple Authorized Service Provider to unlock it. If you do not want to risk this, please skip ahead to the next lesson.

Set a Firmware Password

1 Shut down your computer.

2 Start your computer, and hold down Command-R until the gray Apple appears on the screen.

3 From the menu bar, choose Utilities > Firmware Password Utility.

4 Click Turn On Firmware Password.

5 Enter the password apple in both the “New password” and “Verify” fields.

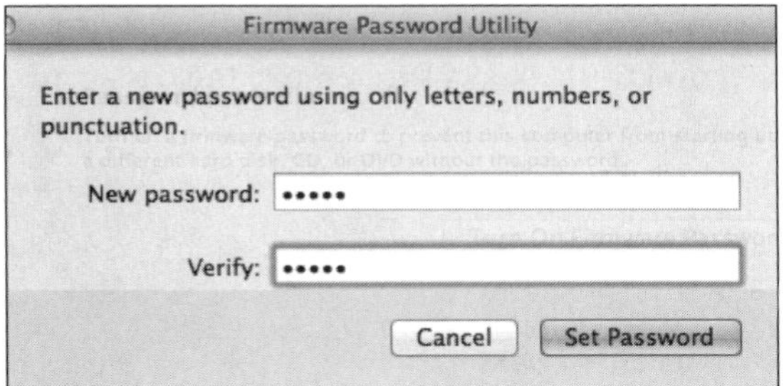

6 Click Set Password.

The utility indicates that password protection is enabled.

Test the Firmware Password

1 From the Apple Menu, choose Restart.

Your computer restarts normally. The firmware password does not interfere with a normal startup.

2 At the login screen, click Restart, and then hold Command-R until a padlock icon appears onscreen.

Alternative boot modes, including OS X Recovery, are not available without entering the firmware password.

3 Enter the password (apple) and press Return.

Remove the Firmware Password (Optional)

If you are performing these exercises on your own and want to leave the firmware password enabled, restart your computer normally and skip this section.

If you are performing these exercises in a classroom, or you do not want to leave the firmware password set on your own computer, follow these steps to remove the password:

1. Choose Utilities > Firmware Password Utility.
2. Click Turn Off Firmware Password.
3. When prompted, enter the firmware password (**apple**).

   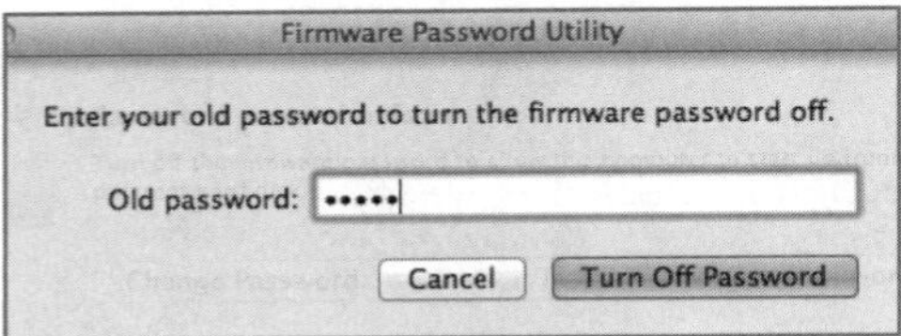

   WARNING ▸ There is no general way to remove or reset a forgotten firmware password.

   The Firmware Password Utility shows that password protection is disabled.

4. From the Apple menu, choose Restart.

   Your computer restarts normally.

Lesson 9

Keychain Management

OS X features a sophisticated system that automatically protects all your authentication assets in encrypted keychain files. Much as service workers might keep a keychain containing all the keys needed during their workday, OS X will keep all your resource passwords, certificates, keys, website forms, and even secure notes in a single secure location. Every time you allow OS X to remember a password or any other potentially sensitive item, it will save it to a keychain file. Only your account password remains separate from all the other items saved to your keychains.

GOALS

- Understand the keychain system
- View and edit items saved inside a keychain
- Create, manage, and repair keychain files

In this lesson you first will identify where the keychain system stores various keychain files. Then, the majority of this lesson shows you how to manage the keychain system, including the use of multiple keychains and advanced keychain settings.

Reference 9.1
Keychain System

Because so many important items end up in keychain files, the keychain files themselves are encrypted with a very strong algorithm: They are impenetrable unless you know the keychain's password. In fact, if you forget a keychain's password, its contents are lost forever. Not even the software engineers at Apple can help you—the keychain system is *that* secure. Yet, probably the single best feature of the keychain system is that it's entirely automatic using the default settings. Most users will never know just how secure their saved passwords are because the system is so transparent.

Understanding Keychain Files

Keychain files are stored throughout the system for different users and resources. Here are a few of note:

- /Users/<username>/Library/Keychain/login.keychain—Every standard or administrative user is created with a single login keychain. As a default, the password for this keychain matches the user's account password, so this keychain is automatically unlocked and available when the user logs in. If the user's account password does not match the keychain's password, it will not automatically unlock during login.

  Users can create additional keychains if they wish to segregate their authentication assets. For example, you can keep your default login keychain for trivial items, and then create a more secure keychain that does not automatically unlock for more important items.
- /Library/Keychain/System.keychain—This keychain maintains authentication assets that are not user specific. Examples of items stored here include Wi-Fi wireless network passwords, 802.1X network passwords, and local Kerberos support items. Although all users benefit from this keychain, only administrative users can make changes to this keychain. You'll also find additional keychains in this folder for use by Legacy FileVault and the Apple Push Service.
- /Library/Keychain/FileVaultMaster.keychain—This keychain is encrypted with the FileVault master password. Configuring and troubleshooting FileVault and the master password is covered in Lesson 8, "System Security."
- /System/Library/Keychains/—You will find several keychain files in this folder that store root certificates used to help identify trusted network services. Once again, all users benefit from these keychains, but only administrative users can make changes to them.

  NOTE ▶ Some websites will remember your authentication inside a web cookie, so you might not see an entry in a keychain file for every website that automatically remembers your account.

Reference 9.2
Keychain Management

The primary tool you will use to manage keychains is the Keychain Access application found in the /Applications/Utilities folder. With this application you can view and modify any keychain item, including saved resource passwords, certificates, keys, website forms, and secure notes. You can also create and delete keychain files, change keychain settings and passwords, and repair corrupted keychains.

Manage Items in a Keychain

To manage keychain items, including saved passwords, start by opening /Applications/Utilities/Keychain Access. The default selection shows the contents of the user's login keychain, but you can select another keychain from the list to view its items.

NOTE ▸ The iCloud authentication mechanisms create many keychain items that may seem unfamiliar to you. Many of these are in the form of certificates or keys, the contents of which should not be tampered with. In short, refrain from "cleaning out" keychain secrets that may appear unfamiliar to you.

Simply double-click a keychain item to view its attributes. If the item is a password, you can reveal the saved password by selecting the "Show password" checkbox. You'll find that this, and other changes, will often prompt for the keychain's password. This is a safety measure to ensure that only the keychain's owner can make changes. Once you have authenticated, you can change any attribute in the keychain item dialog, including any saved passwords. You can also click the Access Control tab to adjust application access for the selected item.

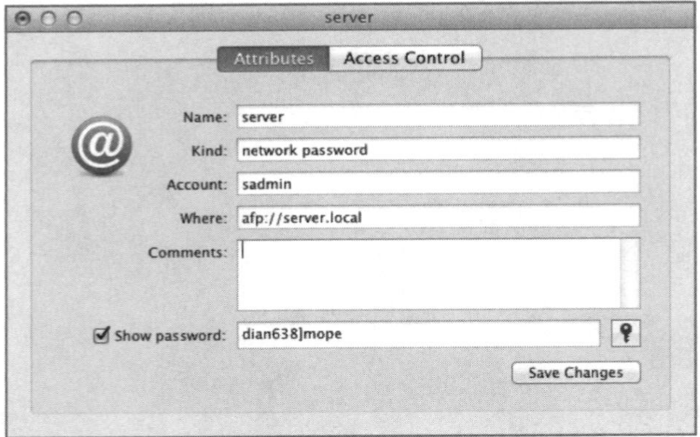

TIP To easily search through all the keychain items, use the Category views to the left or the Spotlight search in the upper-right corner of the toolbar.

TIP The safest place to store secure text on your Mac is in keychains. In Keychain Access, you can create a new secure note by choosing File > New Secure Note Item.

Resetting Keychain Passwords

Only if a user knows her current account password and then decides to change her password will the system also change the user's login keychain password. So that they remain as secure as possible, keychain passwords cannot be changed by any outside password-resetting process. Apple did not design the keychain system with a back door, as doing so would render the system less secure.

Consequently, whenever an administrative user resets a user's account or FileVault password, the keychain password will remain unchanged and will not automatically open as the user logs into her account. However, by default in OS X, when a user with a recently reset password logs in, she will be prompted with a dialog to update or reset her login keychain.

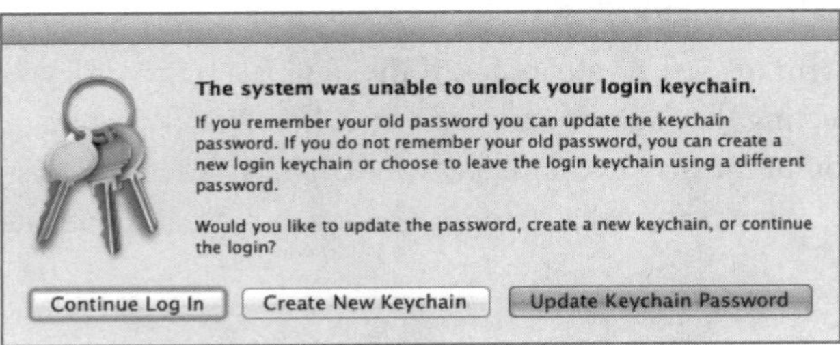

TIP ▶ The keychain synchronization dialog can be disabled from the First Aid tab of the Keychain Access application preferences.

The default selection, Update Keychain Password, works only if the user knows his previous keychain password, which is probably not the case if you just had to reset the password. If so, the user should click the Create New Keychain button to create a new login keychain. The system renames his old login keychain and leaves it in the user's ~/Library/Keychains folder in case he ever remembers his old password. Finally, though it's not recommended, the user can simply choose to ignore the warning by clicking Continue Log In.

NOTE ▶ Creating a new login keychain resets all saved authentication secrets. This includes resetting authentication for network accounts configured via the Mail, Contacts, and Calendars preferences and iCloud services.

If the automatic keychain synchronization dialog does not appear, you can still reset the user's login keychain password from the Keychain Access application, assuming the previous keychain password is known. As you'd expect, if you do not know the user's previous keychain password, the contents of that keychain are lost forever. Using Keychain Access to manage a user's keychain is covered in the following section.

Manage Keychain Files

To manage keychain files, including resetting a keychain's password, open /Applications/Utilities/Keychain Access. You can create a new keychain by choosing File > New Keychain, and then entering a password, six characters or longer, for the keychain. The default location for new keychains is the Keychains folder inside your home folder.

You can further adjust a keychain's settings by selecting it from the list, and then choosing Edit > Change Settings for Keychain. A dialog sheet appears, allowing you to change automatic keychain locking settings for the selected keychain file.

To change a keychain's password, first select it from the list, and then choose Edit > Change Password for Keychain. You have to enter the keychain's current password first, followed by a new password and verification.

Finally, to delete a keychain, select it from the list and choose File > Delete Keychain. When the Delete Keychain dialog appears, click Delete References to simply ignore the keychain or click Delete References & Files to completely erase the keychain file.

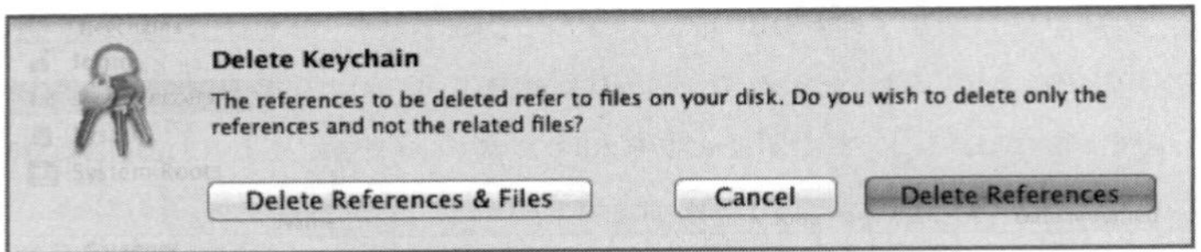

TIP You can move keychain items between keychains by dragging and dropping an item from one keychain to another.

TIP For quick access to your keychains and other security features, you can enable the Keychain menu item by choosing Keychain Access > Preferences. Then select the "Show keychain status in menu bar" checkbox to reveal the Keychain menu item, as indicated by a small key icon.

Repair Keychain Files

If the system is unable to open a keychain file or retrieve secrets from it, the keychain file may have become corrupted. Fortunately, the Keychain Access application can verify and repair keychain files, provided that you know the keychain's password.

To verify or repair a keychain file, start by opening /Applications/Utilities/Keychain Access. If the troublesome keychain is not already in your keychain list, choose File > Add Keychain to browse for it. When you are ready to attempt the repair, choose Keychain Access > Keychain First Aid.

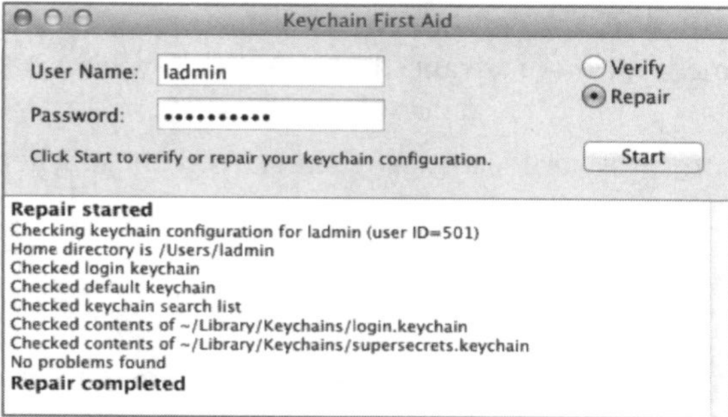

In the Keychain First Aid window, select the Repair option and then enter a user name and password to start the repair. Note that you will only be allowed to repair keychains that you can unlock with the entered password. Also note that if you enter an administrator account, Keychain First Aid attempts to repair keychains stored in /Library/Keychains. A log shows the keychain verification or repair process. More than one pass may be necessary to fully repair all keychain issues.

TIP Find additional Keychain First Aid preferences by choosing Keychain Access > Preferences.

Exercise 9.1
Manage Keychains

Prerequisites

- You must have created the Chris Johnson account (Exercise 6.1).

As you've seen, in most cases a user's keychain password and account password are the same. When you create a user account, the login keychain file is created to store the user's passwords and is secured with his account password. However, in environments where more security is desired, a user can decouple his keychain password from his account password by using the Keychain Access application to change the login keychain's password. In this case, the user will have to enter the login keychain's password before applications such as Mail and Safari can access stored passwords. The system provides various features to help users keep their account and keychain passwords synchronized.

In this exercise, you will explore various keychain management techniques.

Show Keychain Status in the Menu Bar

You will prepare the keychain environment for more advanced users using Keychain Access.

1. If necessary, log in as Chris Johnson (password: **chris**, or whatever you chose when you created the account).

2. Open Keychain Access from the Utilities folder.

3. From the menu bar, choose Keychain Access > Preferences (or press Command-comma).

4. Enable "Show keychain status in menu bar."

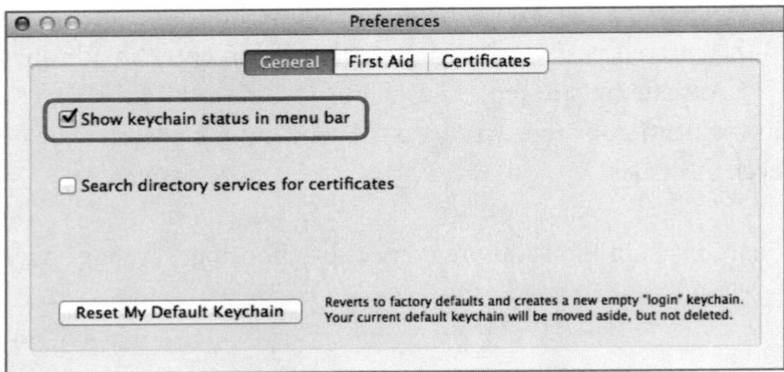

This places a lock icon in the menu bar, making it more convenient to perform various security-related functions.

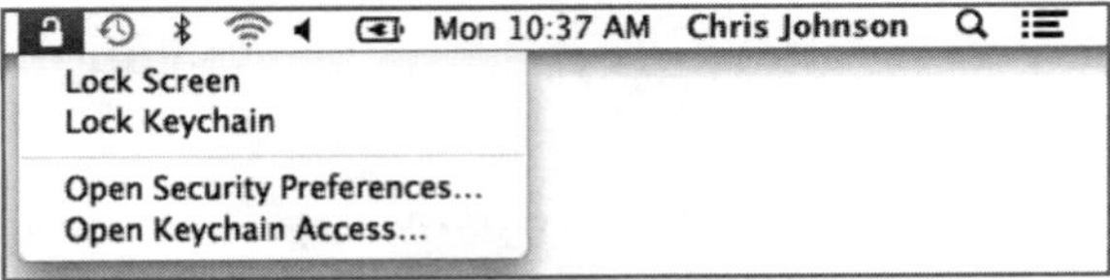

5. Close Keychain Access preferences.

6. Choose Edit > Change Password for Keychain "login."

7. Enter the current password (**chris**, or whatever you chose when you created the account), a new password (**keychain**), and verify the new password.

   This desynchronizes the keychain password from Chris's account password.

   NOTE ► Normally you would want to test the strength of your passwords by clicking the key icon to invoke the Password Assistant. However, this exercise uses simple passwords for academic purposes only.

8 Click OK, and then log out and log back in.

Notice that the "The system was unable to unlock your login keychain" dialog did not appear this time. Because you desynchronized the keychain password using Keychain Access, it assumed this was intentional and disabled the warning message.

9 If you receive any requests for the keychain password, click Cancel (or use the shortcut Command-period) to dismiss them. You may be prompted a number of times.

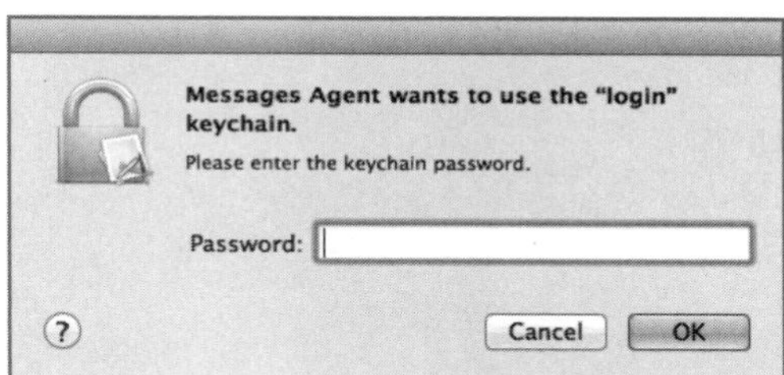

This happens because various parts of OS X want to use passwords from the keychain to access services such as iCloud.

10 Look at the Keychain menu bar icon.

Notice that the lock icon appears locked, not open, which means that although you logged in successfully to your account, your keychain did not automatically unlock. If Keychain Access reopened automatically, it will also show the keychain status as locked.

When the keychain and login passwords are the same, the login keychain unlocks when the user logs in to allow applications to access the passwords stored on it. Because the account and login passwords don't match, Chris will have to enter his login keychain password in order for applications to access stored passwords.

Store a Password in a Keychain

Your keychain already has a number of automatically created entries. In this section you will create an entry manually.

1 Open the StudentMaterials/Lesson9 folder. Remember that you created a shortcut to StudentMaterials in your Dock.

2 Open the file "Chris's private files.dmg".

This disk image is encrypted, so the system prompts you for the password to open it.

3 Enter the password **private**.

4 Select "Remember password in my keychain."

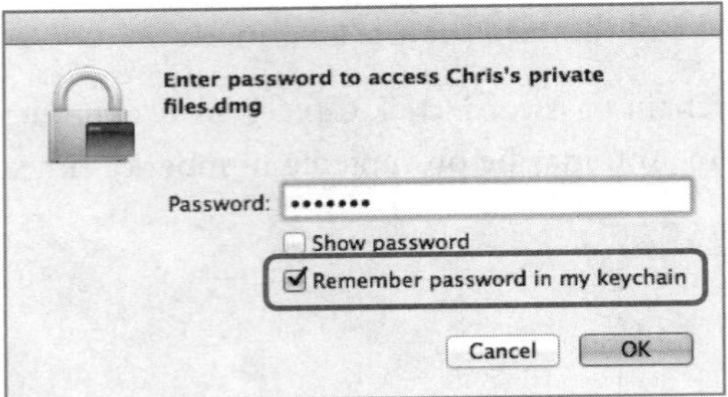

5 Click OK.

The system again prompts you for the keychain password. The keychain must be unlocked to store passwords in the keychain, as well as to access them.

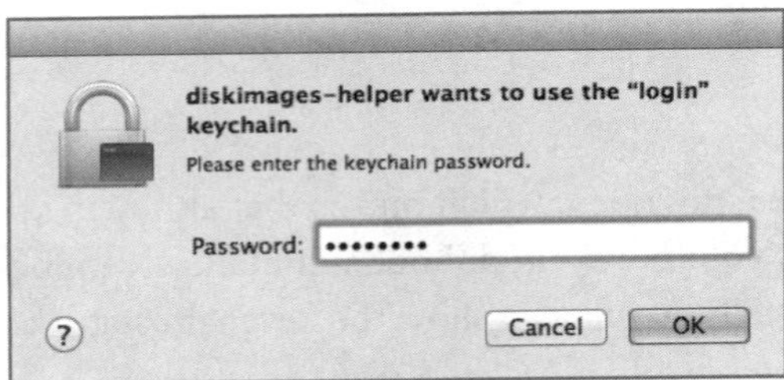

6 Enter the keychain password (**keychain**), and click OK.

The Keychain menu item now shows that the keychain is unlocked.

7 Select the disk image on your desktop, and press Command-E to eject it.

8 Open the disk image again.

Since the password is now stored in your keychain and the keychain is unlocked, the image opens without asking you for the password.

9 Eject the disk image again.

Retrieve a Password in a Keychain

Even though passwords are stored to make them conveniently available for applications, there may be times when a user needs to retrieve a stored password. For example, a user who wants to use webmail on a different computer may want to retrieve her email password in order to do so. You will use the keychain to retrieve a forgotten password.

1 If necessary, open Keychain Access from the Utilities folder.

2 Find the password entry named "Chris's private files.dmg", and double-click it. Use the search filter at the upper-right corner of Keychain Access if you need to.

   A window opens displaying information about this password entry.

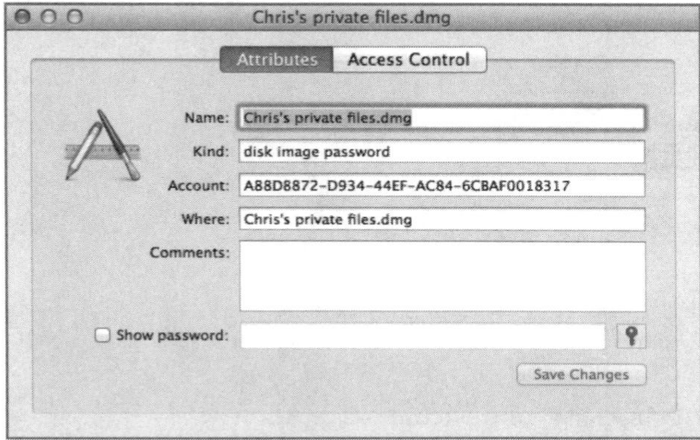

3 Click the Access Control button.

   The Access Control pane displays information about what applications or system components are allowed access to the keychain entry. In this case, diskimages-helper can automatically access the password, but if any other application requests access the system asks the user for confirmation first.

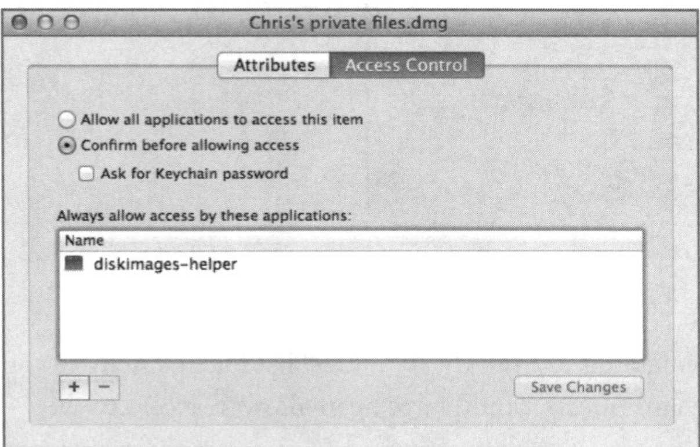

Normally, the application that created a keychain entry is the only one that is allowed automatic access to it, but you can change this policy as needed.

4 Click the Attributes tab.

5 In the Attributes pane, select Show Password.

A dialog informs you that Keychain Access wants to use your confidential information stored in "Chris's private files.dmg" in your keychain. Even though your keychain is unlocked, this item's access policy requires confirmation before anything other than diskimages-helper is allowed to read the password.

6 Enter your keychain password (**keychain**) and click Always Allow.

The disk image password becomes visible.

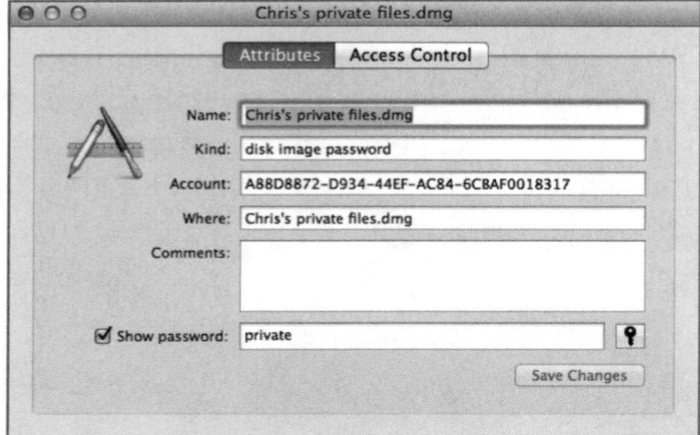

7 Click the Access Control tab.

Keychain Access has now been added to the "Always allow" list for this item. If you clicked "Allow" instead, Keychain Access would have been allowed access to the password, but would not have been added to this access control list. Since it has been added to the list, Keychain Access can now display the password without asking for confirmation.

8 Close the "Chris's private files.dmg" window.

Sync Keychain Password with Account

If you want to resynchronize the login keychain password with the login password, you can use Keychain First Aid to synchronize the two. In addition to the synchronization feature, Keychain First Aid can repair certain application issues with stored passwords, such as when an application erroneously asks for a password that has previously been stored.

1 Still logged in as Chris Johnson, open Keychain Access preferences, and then click First Aid.

2 Select "Synchronize login keychain password with account."

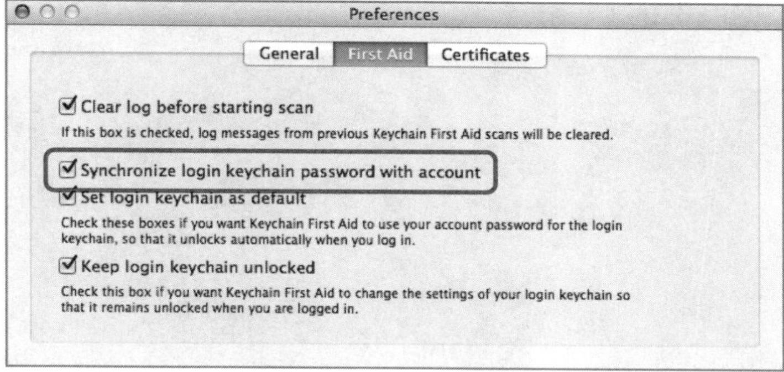

This preference setting controls whether the system warns you at login if your keychain password is out of sync with your account password. It is normally enabled by default, but was disabled when you desynchronized Chris's keychain password by changing it in Keychain Access earlier.

3 Close the Preferences window.

4 Choose Keychain Access > Keychain First Aid.

5 Enter Chris's account password (**chris**, or whatever you chose when you created the account), select Repair, and click Start.

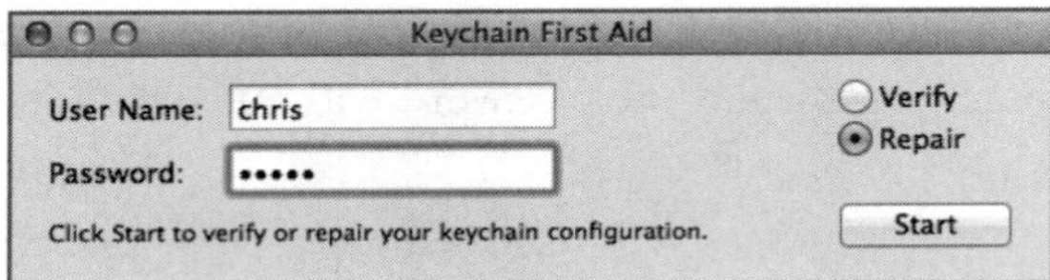

6 If asked to provide the keychain password for the login keychain, enter it (**keychain**) and click OK.

The bottom section of the Keychain First Aid window displays a log of the repair process.

7 If the log indicates that the repair failed, repeat the repair process.

8 After repair completes successfully, log out.

9 Log back in as Chris Johnson, and check the Keychain menu item in the menu bar. Note that the keychain is automatically unlocked as the login password and the keychain password are synchronized.

File Systems

Lesson **10**

File Systems and Storage

Although personal computer processor speed has increased around a thousandfold since the first Mac was introduced in 1984, storage capacity has easily increased a million times over. Compare 1984's 400 KB floppy to today's average desktop disk at 1 TB, which is roughly equivalent to 1,000,000,000 KB, or 2.5 million 400 KB floppies. Users have responded by moving thousands of pictures and hundreds of hours of music and video, historically stored in analog form, to digital storage. Even though the Internet has recently changed our perception of what a computer is used for, it's clear that the computer's primary role continues to be a tool to organize, access, and store our stuff.

GOALS

- Recognize the various file systems supported by OS X
- Manage disks, partitions, and volumes
- Properly unmount and eject disks and volumes

In this lesson, you will examine the storage technology used by OS X. Storage hardware, like flash disks, will be covered alongside logical storage concepts like partitions and volumes. Naturally, you will learn how to properly manage and troubleshoot these storage assets as well.

Reference 10.1
File System Components

Before you begin managing storage in OS X, it is important to understand the distinction between storage, partitions, and volumes. Traditionally, computer storage has been defined by spinning disk hardware. After all these years, spinning disk hardware still maintains the storage lead, as it has moved from removable floppy disks to enclosed hard disks. However, alternative formats have become extremely popular as they have increased in capacity and performance. This primarily includes internal solid-state disks (SSDs) or flash storage, USB "key" or "thumb" drives, and removable storage like CompactFlash cards. All are equally viable storage destinations for OS X.

Storage Concepts

Without proper formatting, though, any storage technology is nothing more than a big empty bucket of ones and zeros, and consequently not very useful to the Mac. Formatting is the process of applying logic to storage in the form of partitions and volumes. Partitions are used to define boundaries on a storage device. You can define multiple partitions if you want the physical storage to appear as multiple separate storage destinations. Even if you want to use the entire space available on a device as a single contiguous storage location, the area must still be defined by a partition.

Once partitions have been established, the system can create usable volumes inside the partition areas. Volumes define how the files and folders are actually stored on the hardware. In fact, it's the volume that is ultimately mounted by the file system and then represented as a usable storage icon in the Finder. Obviously, a storage device with several partitions, each containing a separate volume, will appear as several storage location icons in the Finder.

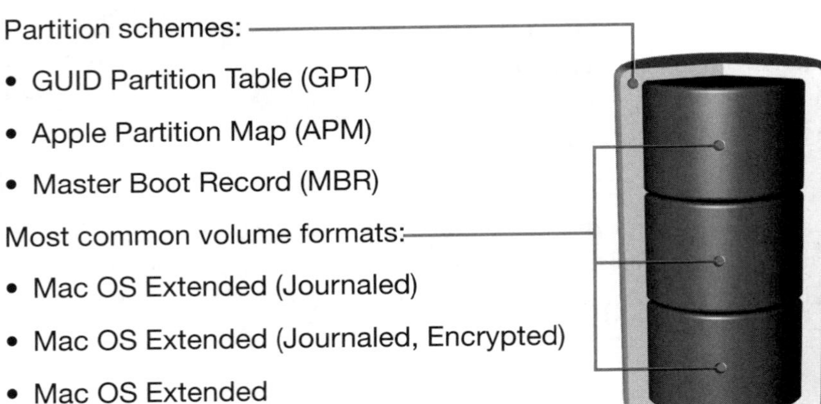
Partition schemes:
• GUID Partition Table (GPT)
• Apple Partition Map (APM)
• Master Boot Record (MBR)
Most common volume formats:
• Mac OS Extended (Journaled)
• Mac OS Extended (Journaled, Encrypted)
• Mac OS Extended
• MS DOS File System (FAT32, ExFAT)
• NT File System (NTFS) *
* read only

Partition Schemes

As mentioned earlier, disks must be partitioned in order to define and possibly segregate the disk's usable space. Every disk requires at least one partition, but OS X can support up to 16 partitions per disk. You learned the advantages and disadvantages of using single or multiple partitions in Lesson 2, "Install OS X Mountain Lion."

OS X supports three types of partition schemes. This may seem excessive, but it's necessary for Macs to support multiple partition schemes in order to start up computers using modern Intel processors, support older Mac disks, and use standard PC-compatible volumes.

The three partition schemes supported by OS X are:

- GUID Partition Table (GPT)—This is the default partition scheme used by Intel-based Macs. It is also the only partition scheme supported for Intel-based Macs to start up using disk-based storage. However, PowerPC-based Macs running OS X v10.4.6 or later can also access this type of partitioning, but they will not be able to start up from it.
- Apple Partition Map (APM)—This is the default partition scheme used by previous PowerPC-based Macs. It is also the only partition scheme that PowerPC-based Macs can start up from. However, all Intel-based Macs can also access this type of partitioning.
- Master Boot Record (MBR)—This is the default partition scheme used by most non-Mac computers, including Windows-compatible PCs. Consequently, this is the default partition scheme you will find on most new preformatted storage disks. This partition scheme is also commonly used by peripherals that store to flash disks, such as digital cameras or smart phones. Even though no Mac can start up from this type of partitioning, all Macs can fully use MBR partitioned disks.

Obviously, if you have any additional disks formatted with APM or MBR, you will have to repartition those disks in order for them to act as a startup disk for an Intel-based Mac. But if you don't plan on ever using the additional disks as a system disk, there is no advantage to repartitioning. Also, you should keep MBR disks unmodified if you intend to keep them backward compatible with generic PCs or peripherals.

> **TIP** Intel-based Macs can start up from USB, FireWire, and Thunderbolt external disks.

Volume Formats

The volume format defines how the files and folders are saved to the disk. To maintain compatibility with other operating systems and provide advanced features for later Mac systems, OS X supports a variety of storage volume formats.

Volume formats supported as read/write in OS X:

- Mac OS Standard—This is the legacy volume format used by the classic Mac OS. This format, though a precursor to Mac OS Extended, is not supported as a startup volume for OS X.
- Mac OS Extended—Mac OS Extended is the legacy volume format designed and supported by Apple for Mac computers. This format is itself an update from the earlier Mac OS Standard format. Mac OS Extended supports all the advanced features required by OS X, including Unicode filenames, rich metadata, POSIX permissions, access control lists (ACLs), UNIX-style links, and aliases.
- Mac OS Extended (Case-Sensitive)—This Mac OS Extended format adds case sensitivity to the file system. Normally Mac OS Extended is case-preserving but case-insensitive, which means that a normally formatted Mac volume will remember what case you chose for the characters of a file's name, but it cannot differentiate between similar filenames where the only difference is the case. In other words, it would not recognize "MYfile" and "myfile" as different filenames. By adding support for case sensitivity, Apple resolved this issue. However, this is generally an issue only for volumes that need to support traditional UNIX clients, like those shared from Mac systems running OS X Server. Further, many third-party applications exhibit significant issues when running from a case-sensitive file system. Thus, the case-sensitive option is not supported as a default for OS X client systems.
- Mac OS Extended (Journaled) or Mac OS Extended (Case-Sensitive, Journaled)—This feature is an option for the Mac OS Extended format that adds advanced file system journaling to help preserve volume structure integrity. The journal records what file operations (creation, expansion, deletion, and so on) are in progress at any given moment. If the system crashes or loses power, the journal can be "replayed" to make sure operations that were previously in progress are completed, rather than left in a half-completed, inconsistent state. This helps avoid the possibility of file corruption and greatly reduces the amount of time it takes to complete the check-and-repair process on the volume after a crash. Because of these enhancements the default format for an OS X system volume is Mac OS Extended (Journaled).

  NOTE ► While journaling protects the file structure, it cannot protect the contents of files themselves against corruption. If a large file was half-written when the system crashed, the journal will make sure that half-file is consistently entered in the volume's file-tracking databases, but it's still only half a file.

- Mac OS Extended (Journaled, Encrypted) or Mac OS Extended (Case-Sensitive, Journaled, Encrypted)—This feature is an option to the Mac OS Extended format that adds full disk, XTS-AES 128 encryption. This is the technology behind FileVault 2 full disk encryption. Lesson 11, "FileVault 2," covers this topic in greater detail.

NOTE ▶ Encrypted Mac OS Extended volumes are not compatible with versions of OS X prior to OS X Lion.

- File Allocation Table (FAT)—FAT is the legacy volume format used by Windows PCs and by many peripherals. This format has evolved over the years, with each progressive version supporting larger volumes: FAT12, FAT16, FAT32. Apple Boot Camp supports running Windows XP from a FAT32 volume, but OS X itself cannot start up from such a volume.
- Extended File Allocation Table (ExFAT)—Created specifically for large flash storage disks, ExFAT basically extends the legacy FAT architecture to support disks larger than 32 GB. Many flash-based digital camcorders use ExFAT to support the large storage volumes required for high-definition video.
- UNIX File System (UFS)—UFS is the legacy native volume format supported by UNIX systems. UFS served as the default UNIX file system for decades. Beginning with OS X v10.5, though, UFS volumes are no longer supported as startup volumes. Further, Disk Utility does not support the creation of UFS volumes.

Volume formats supported as read-only in OS X:

- NT File System (NTFS)—Windows 7, Windows Vista, Windows XP, and Windows Server all use this as their default native volume format. Once again, Boot Camp supports running Windows from an NTFS volume, but OS X itself cannot write to or start up from such a volume. Further, Disk Utility does not support the creation of NTFS volumes.

TIP You can add NTFS volume write support to OS X by installing the free and open source NTFS-3G + Ntfsprogs software available at www.tuxera.com/community/ntfs-3g-download/.

- ISO 9660 or Compact Disk File System (CDFS)—This is a common standard for read-only CD media. Note, however, that "Mac formatted" CD media can also contain Mac OS Standard formatted volumes.
- Universal Disk Format (UDF)—This is a common standard for read-only DVD media. Again, note that "Mac formatted" DVD media can also contain Mac OS Standard volumes.

MORE INFO ▶ Wikipedia has a great comparison of the wide variety file systems: http://en.wikipedia.org/wiki/Comparison_of_file_systems.

Reference 10.2
Managing File Systems

The internal storage originally included with your Mac is probably the only new storage device you will ever come across that is already properly formatted for full Mac compatibility. Most new storage devices are either completely blank or formatted for Windows. For the most part, you can still use Windows-formatted disks on the Mac without reformatting. Conversely, if you want to install the Mac operating system on a disk or you have a new disk that is completely blank, you have to reformat the disk.

The primary storage management tool included in OS X is /Applications/Utilities/Disk Utility. You may have already used this utility from OS X Recovery to reformat the system disk before you installed the operating system. Here you are going to explore all the aspects of this tool for managing disks.

Formatting or Reformatting a Disk

Despite all the choices OS X gives you for configuring storage, actually formatting a disk is quite easy. If you attach an unformatted device, the Mac automatically prompts you to open Disk Utility. On the other hand, if you have an already-formatted disk and you want to change the partition scheme or the volume structure, you can just as easily reformat the disk using the same steps.

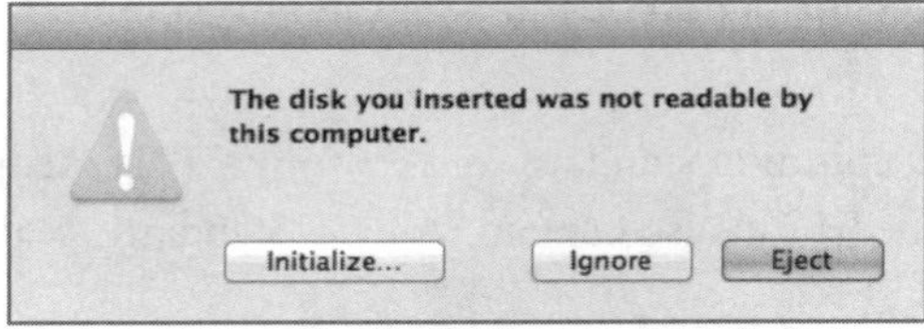

Remember that reformatting a disk will destroy any existing formatting; a reformatted disk is effectively losing its contents. The disk is not technically erased by default—all the bits are still stored on the device. Reformatting simply replaces the previously populated partition and volume structure with new partitioning and empty volume structures. Truly erasing the contents of a disk is covered in the "Securely Erasing Files" section later in this lesson.

Opening Disk Utility reveals a list of connected storage devices and volumes. Storage devices are identified by the size, manufacturer, and model number of the device. Select the storage device you want to format, and then click the Partition tab. To reformat a disk, you must select the Partition Layout pop-up menu and define the number of desired partitions. Once you have selected the number of partitions, you can define the remaining parameters for the storage device, including partition scheme, volume formats, and names.

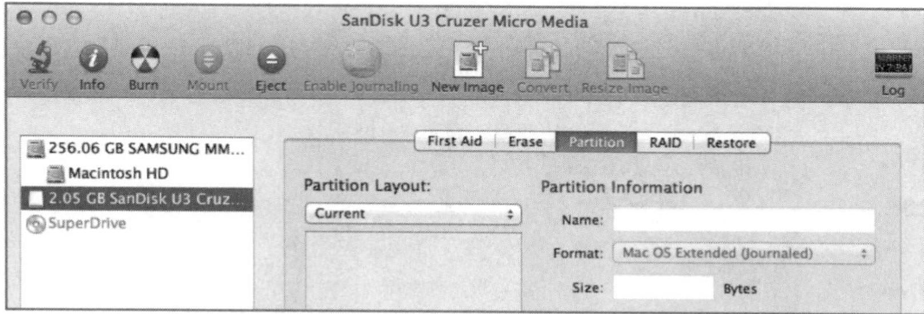

NOTE ▶ You cannot select any disk encryption options from the Disk Utility Partition interface. You can, however, select encryption options from the Erase interface, as covered in the "Erasing a Disk or Volume" section later in this lesson.

Repartitioning a Disk

Disk Utility also allows you to dynamically repartition a disk without destroying any currently stored data on the disk. This functionality was introduced in OS X v10.5 primarily to facilitate the Boot Camp setup process. OS X upgrade installations also benefit from this functionality to create the hidden OS X Recovery HD on an existing system disk.

The only downside to dynamic repartitioning is that some disks may not support the partition changes you want to make. For instance, some disks may be too full for you to repartition. Also, Disk Utility is less flexible in its ability to modify a disk containing encrypted volumes, and does not support dynamically repartitioning disks formatted with the Master Boot Record partition scheme. If you come across any of these issues, you can resort to using the previous method for repartitioning a disk, which does erase any previous formatting, as outlined in the prior section of this lesson.

NOTE ▶ Always back up important data before making changes to a disk's file system.

NOTE ▶ Modifying an OS X system disk may also require relocating the hidden OS X Recovery HD. Fortunately, Disk Utility in OS X handles this automatically for you.

Again, opening Disk Utility reveals a list of connected storage devices and volumes. Storage devices are identified by the size, manufacturer, and model number of the device. Select the storage device you want to format, and then click the Partition tab. Any data currently on the disk appears as a light blue area in the partition layout diagram. White areas indicate free space.

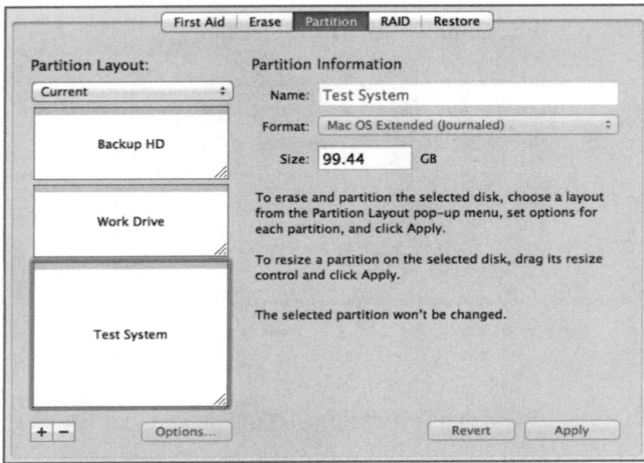

The partition layout area in Disk Utility allows you to:

- Resize a volume—Click and drag from the lower-right corner until you reach the desired new size. You cannot shrink a volume past the light blue that represents data on the disk. You may choose to leave parts of the disk empty if you plan on formatting those parts later using another operating system.
- Add a new volume—Click the Add (+) button below the partition diagram. Remember, you can have as many as 16 partitions per disk. Be sure to choose an appropriate name and volume format from the pop-up menu for each new volume.
- Delete a volume—Select it from the partition diagram and click the Delete (–) button below the partition diagram. If you are deleting a preexisting partition, you're presented with a verification dialog. If you are certain that you want to delete the selected partition, click Remove to finish the process. The volume is deleted immediately, leaving free space where you can resize other volumes or create new volumes.

Erasing a Disk or Volume

You have seen earlier in this lesson how Disk Utility can be used to quickly erase an entire disk or volume by reformatting it. Yet the default reformatting process does not actually erase any files from the disk; Disk Utility simply creates new blank volumes by only replacing the file and folder structure data of any volume. The old data files still remain on the disk and can be recovered using third-party recovery tools.

In fact, there is no such thing as erasing data from a disk—all you can do is write new data on top of the old data. Therefore, if you want to truly "erase" a disk or volume, you must somehow write new nonsensitive data on top of it. Disk Utility includes a variety of options that let you securely erase old data. You can securely erase an entire disk or volume, or just a volume's remaining free space.

> **NOTE ▶** Erasing a disk automatically sets the partition scheme based on the new volume format. To select a different partition scheme, you must repartition the disk, as detailed previously in this lesson.

Again, opening Disk Utility reveals a list of connected storage devices and volumes. Storage devices are identified by the size, manufacturer, and model number of the device. Volume names vary, but always appear indented below the storage device. Select the storage device or volume you want to format, and then click the Erase tab.

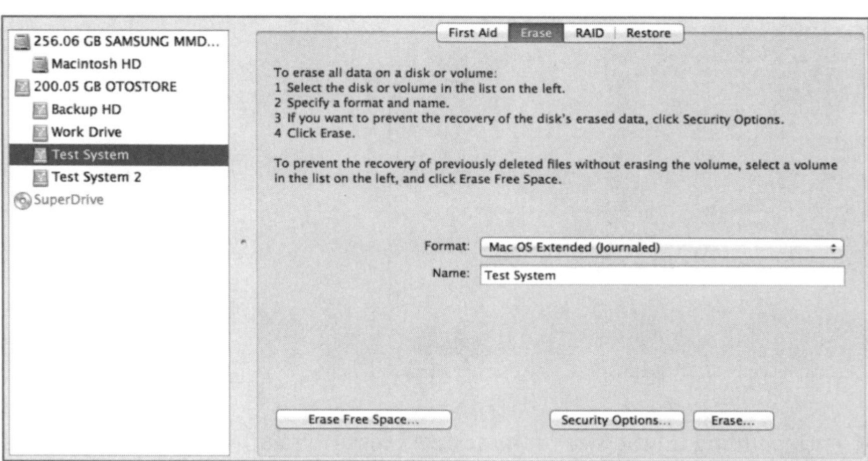

To quickly erase the selected item, simply click Erase. You also have the option of selecting a different volume format or name for the erased volume. If you require a secure erase, click Security Options to reveal a dialog with four options along a slider:

- Fastest: Don't Erase Data—This is the default action that occurs when you erase or reformat a disk or volume. Obviously, this does not provide any security from disk-recovery utilities. On the other hand, this choice provides a nearly instantaneous erase option.
- Second Choice: Single-Pass Erase—This option writes zeros over all the data once. This is the quickest of the secure erase options, and for most users provides an adequate level of security.

NOTE ▶ When erasing solid-state disks, only a single-pass erase is recommended. In fact, multipass erasing of solid-state disks can lead to degraded disk performance over time.

- Third Choice: 3-Pass Erase—This is a very secure option that writes two passes of random data followed by a single pass of known data to the disk. According to Apple, this option meets U.S. Department of Energy standards for securely erasing data. The downside is that this method will take three times longer than the standard single-pass method.
- Most Secure: 7-Pass Erase—This is the most secure option, which according to Apple meets U.S. Department of Defense standards for securely erasing data. The Mac writes seven different passes of random and patterned data to the disk. Obviously, this method takes seven times longer than the standard single-pass method.

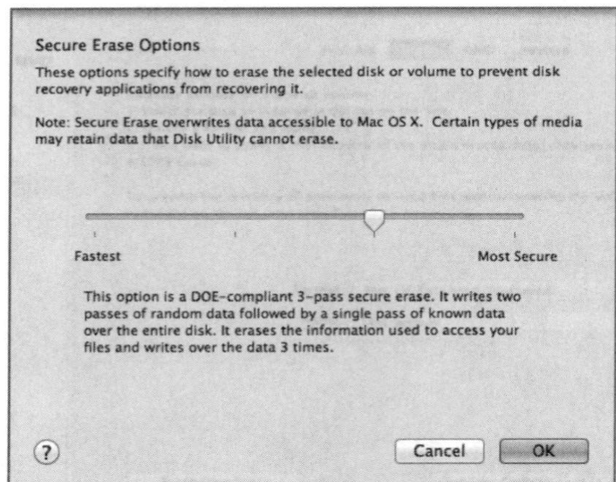

NOTE ▶ Depending on the size of the selected disk or volume and the secure erase option you chose, this process can take anywhere from seconds to days.

NOTE ▶ If you have selected an encrypted volume type, a dialog appears, allowing you to set the encrypted volume's password. Note that as the dialog states, you will not be able to recover data from the encrypted volume if you lose the password. Choose the password wisely.

Securely Erasing Files

Because securely erasing an entire disk or volume can take quite a bit of time, you may find it's much quicker to use a more subtle secure erase method. Also, you may not want to erase the entire contents of a volume or disk—you may just want to securely erase a few specific files or only the free space on your disk. Fortunately, OS X provides targeted secure erase options from the Finder and Disk Utility.

Finder Secure Erase

From the Finder you can securely erase any item in the Trash by choosing Finder > Secure Empty Trash. The Secure Empty Trash feature in Finder is a secure erase method, which writes seven different passes of random and patterned data on top of the erased files. According to Apple, this feature even meets U.S. Department of Defense standards for securely erasing data. Depending on the number and size of the files to be erased, this process can take anywhere from seconds to days. The Finder will show you a progress indicator, but it will not show an estimated time.

Disk Utility Secure Erase

If, however, past users have neglected to securely erase their files, you can cover their tracks by securely erasing a volume's free space. In Disk Utility select the volume with the free space you want to securely erase from the column on the left. Make sure not to select the storage device, only a volume of the disk. Next, click the Erase tab, and then click Erase Free Space.

The dialog that appears allows you to choose one of the three available secure erase options, similar to those for erasing an entire volume or disk: Fastest is a single-pass erase, the second choice is a 3-pass erase, and Most Secure is a 7-pass erase. Again, depending on the amount of free space to erase and the erase option you choose, this process can take anywhere from seconds to days.

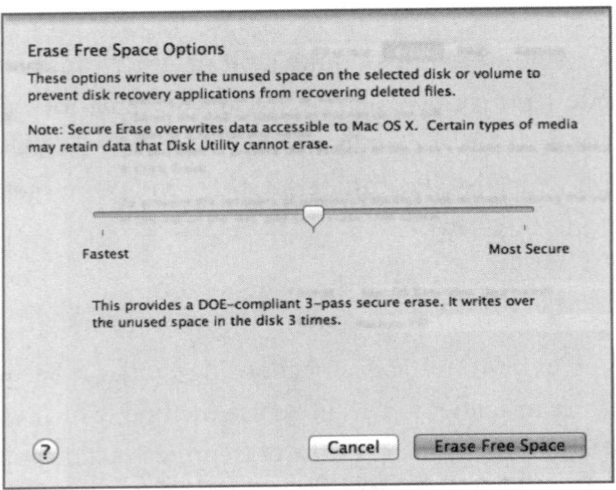

NOTE ▶ Again, when erasing solid-state disks, only a single-pass erase is recommended. In fact, multipass erasing of solid-state disks can lead to degraded disk performance over time.

Encrypting a Disk

Disk Utility cannot convert an existing Mac OS Extended volume to an encrypted volume. Instead, as covered earlier, it can only erase and reformat the volume as encrypted. This is obviously inconvenient if you want to encrypt the contents of an existing disk. Fortunately, in OS X Mountain Lion you can easily convert an existing disk into an encrypted disk via the Finder.

NOTE ▶ Encrypted Mac OS Extended volumes are not compatible with versions of OS X prior to OS X Lion.

NOTE ▶ To encrypt the system volume, you need to enable FileVault 2. Lesson 11, "FileVault 2," covers this topic in greater detail.

NOTE ▶ The Finder can only convert volumes on disks formatted with the GPT partition scheme. Attempting to encrypt a volume on a disk with another partition scheme will result in either the "Encrypt disk" menu option not appearing or an error message upon attempted encryption. If this is the case, you will have to resort to erasing and reformatting the disk with Disk Utility.

To encrypt a disk in the Finder, use secondary (or Control) click the on disk you want to encrypt and from the shortcut menu choose Encrypt <diskname>, where <diskname> is the name of the disk you've selected.

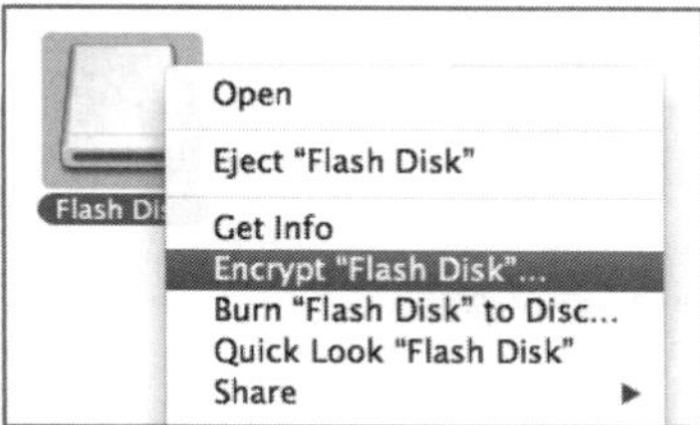

The Finder prompts you to set a password and a password hint for the encrypted disk. You must set a password hint, as it's the only thing that will help you recover a lost password. Should you lose the password there is no method to recover the drive's data. Once you enter these items and then click Encrypt Disk, the system begins encrypting the contents of the disk.

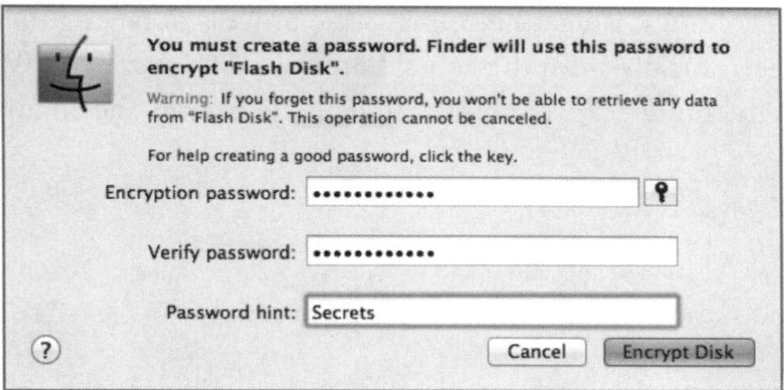

Amazingly, you can continue to use the disk as normal while the system encrypts the disk's contents in the background, though you might notice some performance degradation. From this point forward, any time you attempt to mount the encrypted disk, you will be prompted for the disk's password.

Once the encryption is complete, you may notice the disk quickly unmounts and then remounts in the Finder. You can also verify if the encryption is complete in the Finder by using secondary (or Control) click on the disk. In the shortcut menu, a fully encrypted disk will show an option to Decrypt <diskname>, where <diskname> is the name of the disk you've selected.

Reference 10.3
Mounting, Unmounting, and Ejecting

Mounting a volume is the process by which the system establishes a logical connection to a storage volume. This is not something users normally concern themselves with on the Mac, because the system automatically mounts any volume connected to the Mac. Simply plug a disk in and the disk's volumes automatically appear in the Finder and Disk Utility. The only exception to this rule is for Mac OS Extended (Journaled, Encrypted) volumes, which require that you enter a password to unlock the disk's contents.

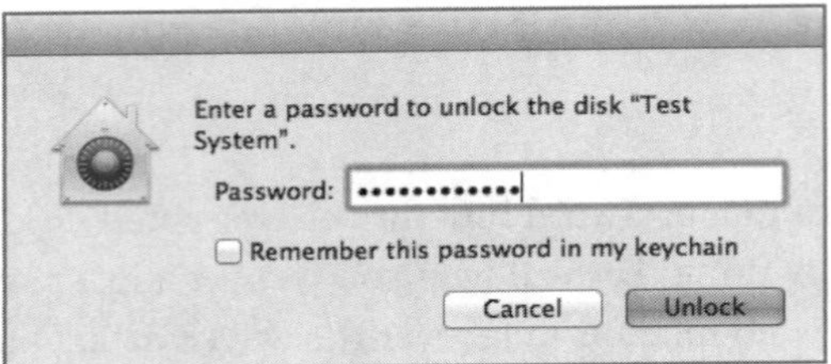

On the other hand, ensuring that users properly unmount and eject volumes is very important to maintaining data integrity. Unmounting is the process of having the Mac cleanly disconnect from a disk's volumes, whereas ejecting is the process of having the Mac additionally disconnect electronically from the actual hardware disk or media. When you choose to eject a disk from the Finder, the computer actually unmounts the volumes first and then ejects the disk.

Ejecting Disks

There are four methods to unmount and eject a disk from the Finder:

- In the Finder, drag the disk icon to the Trash icon in the Dock. You'll note the Trash icon changes to an Eject icon, indicating the appropriate action.
- Pressing and holding the Eject key, the farthest top-right key on a Mac keyboard, for a few moments will only unmount and eject optical media. If you have more than one optical disk, press Option-Eject to unmount and eject the second optical disk.
- In the Finder sidebar, select the volume you want to unmount and eject, and then choose File > Eject.
- In the Finder sidebar, click the small Eject button next to the volume you want to unmount and eject.

When you use the Finder to unmount and eject a single volume that is part of a disk with several mounted volumes, you are presented with a warning dialog giving you the choice to unmount and eject all the volumes on the disk or just the one you originally selected. You shouldn't experience any problems with a disk by having some volumes mounted while others are unmounted. Just remember to properly unmount the remaining volumes before you disconnect the disk.

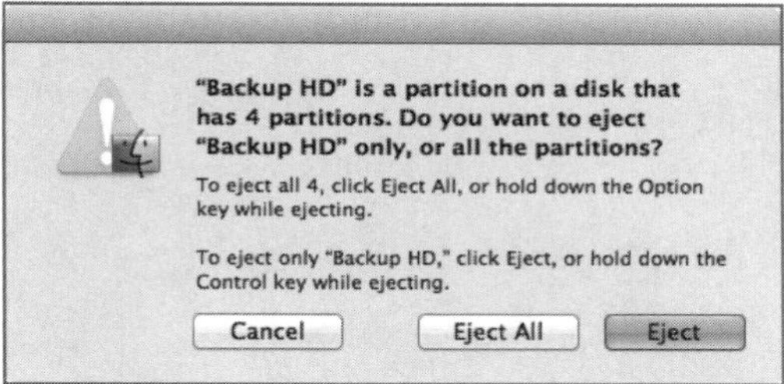

TIP In the Finder, you can eject all the volumes of a disk by holding down the Option key while you click the Eject button.

Disk Utility Mount Management

When using the Finder, remounting volumes on a connected disk is a bit of a hassle. You must first unmount and eject any remaining volumes, and then physically disconnect and reconnect the disk. Alternatively, you can use Disk Utility to manually mount, unmount, and eject items without physically disconnecting and reconnecting the disk.

In the following example screenshot from Disk Utility, a variety of volumes are shown. Notice that the volume names from the second disk appear in dimmed text; those volumes are physically connected to the Mac but are not mounted.

In Disk Utility, select the disk or volume you want to manage. To mount an unmounted volume on a connected disk, click the volume's dimmed name, and then click the Mount button in the toolbar. The volume immediately mounts and appears in the Finder and as normal text in Disk Utility.

If you select an unmounted Mac OS Extended (Journaled, Encrypted) volume, the Mount button is replaced by an Unlock button. Clicking the Unlock button presents a dialog where you enter a password to unlock the disk's contents. Once authenticated, the volume immediately mounts.

If you have selected a volume to unmount, simply click the Unmount button in the toolbar. If you have selected an entire disk to unmount all its volumes and eject, click the Eject button in the toolbar. All the disk's volumes unmount, and then the disk disconnects from the system, disappearing from the Finder and Disk Utility. In this case, you have to physically disconnect and reconnect the disk for its volumes to be remounted.

Ejecting In-Use Volumes

Any volume that contains files currently in use by an application or system process cannot be unmounted or ejected. The obvious reason for this is to avoid data corruption when a process attempts to write to files on that volume. If you attempt to eject a volume with in-use files, the Finder does not allow you to eject the volume, but, depending on the situation, it does try to help you eject the volume. If the application or process using the volume belongs to your account, it lets you know via the following dialog. In this case the resolution is as simple as quitting the suspect application and attempting to eject the volume again.

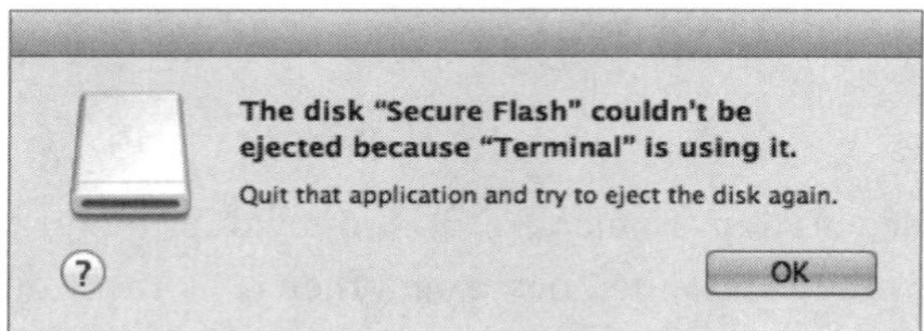

NOTE ▸ As the example screenshot shows, using Terminal can prevent you from ejecting a volume. Even if there is no active process, just having Terminal open with the volume as the current working directory prevents unmounting.

If you don't own the application or process using the volume, the Finder asks if you want to attempt to forcibly eject the volume. To take this path, you have to click the Force Eject button twice, but the Finder then tries to quit the offending application or process to release the volume you're attempting to eject. If the volume was successfully ejected, you are notified by the dialog.

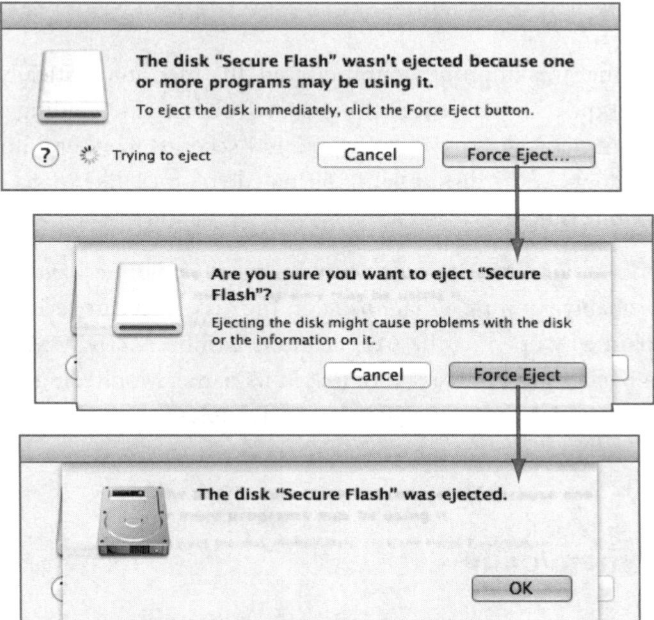

If this doesn't work or the Finder doesn't tell you which application is suspect, you can always log out the current user to quit all her processes and log in again, or fully restart the Mac to clear the issue. While this may seem excessive, it is not advisable to physically disconnect a volume without first unmounting it, as covered in the next section.

Improperly Unmounting or Ejecting

Disconnecting a volume from the Mac that you did not first unmount can lead to data corruption. If you forcibly eject a disk by physically disconnecting it before you unmount it, or if the system loses contact with the disk due to power failure, the Mac warns you with a device removal dialog. You should immediately reconnect the device so the Mac can attempt to verify or repair its contents.

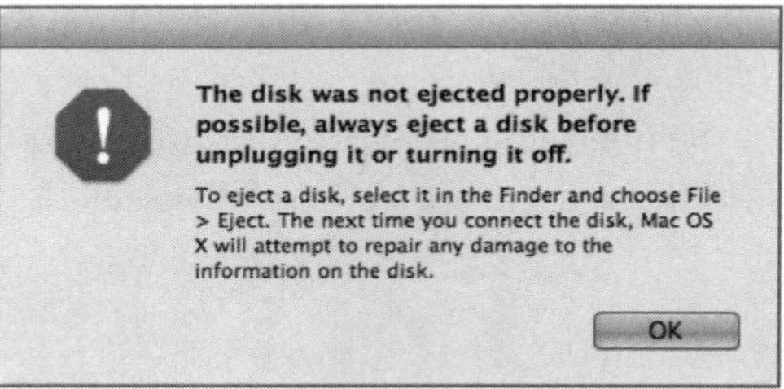

Anytime you reconnect a disk that was improperly unmounted, the Mac automatically runs a file system diagnostic on the disk before it remounts any volumes. Depending on the format and size of the disk, it may take anywhere from a few seconds to several hours for the system to verify the contents of the disk. Again, journaled volumes, like Mac OS Extended (Journaled), verify quite quickly.

If you connect a disk and notice a fair amount of disk activity but the volumes have not mounted yet, the system is probably running a diagnostic on the disk. You can verify that the system is diagnosing a volume by opening the /Applications/Utilities/Activity Monitor application and looking for a background process with `fsck` in its name. Monitoring processes is covered in Lesson 21, "Application Management and Troubleshooting."

Exercise 10.1
Repartition a Disk Dynamically

Prerequisites

- You must have created the Local Admin account (Exercise 3.1 or 3.2).
- Your startup volume must be less than half full.

In early versions of OS X, using Disk Utility to partition a disk meant erasing the disk first. Since OS X v10.5, Disk Utility has been able to live-partition GPT-formatted disks without destroying the data. As always, backing up your data before partitioning is a good idea.

In this exercise section, you will partition your computer's internal disk. If you do not want to repartition your internal disk, you can skip this exercise; however, if you choose to skip this exercise, you will need an external disk to use as a Time Machine backup volume in Lesson 18. It is also possible to partition your disk now, and then remove the additional partition after you have finished testing Time Machine.

Repartition Your Startup Disk Without Erasing

1 Log in as Local Admin (password: **ladminpw**, or whatever you chose when you created the account).

2 If any applications other than Disk Utility are running, quit them.

Do not use any other applications while Disk Utility is working to repartition the disk.

3 Select the disk device entry for your hard disk in Disk Utility, and then click the Partition tab.

NOTE ▶ If you have enabled FileVault 2 encryption on your startup volume, the Disk Utility sidebar shows your startup volume indented under a Logical Volume Group instead of under the disk device. In this case, select the Logical Volume Group (generally the top entry in the sidebar) to make the Partition tab appear.

4 If necessary, select your startup volume in the graphical depiction of the Partition Layout.

5 Click the Add (+) button below the Partition Layout.

The disk's layout appears divided into two equally sized partitions.

6 Select the second partition and change its name to **Backup**.

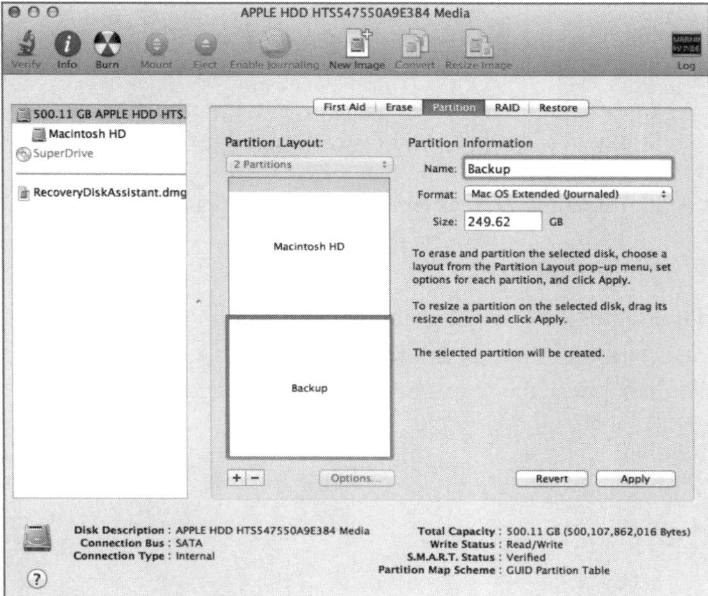

7 Click Apply.

Disk Utility opens a dialog asking you to confirm partitioning the disk. Note that the dialog indicates that no partitions will be erased.

8 Click Partition.

Disk Utility now partitions the disk, which can take a few minutes. Disk Utility has to move any data that resides in the space allocated to the second partition. It also verifies the file system before beginning its work.

9 Wait for Disk Utility to finish repartitioning before going on to the next exercise.

Exercise 10.2
Erase and Partition a Disk

Prerequisites

- You must have created the Local Admin account (Exercise 3.1 or 3.2).
- This exercise is best performed with an erasable external disk, such as a flash drive.

In this exercise, you will use Disk Utility to erase and partition a disk using a new partition scheme. The exercise is written to use an external disk, such as a USB flash drive, but if no erasable external disk is available it can be performed on a disk image in the StudentMaterials folder.

Use Disk Utility to Create a New Partition Scheme

Most external storage systems (USB flash drives, USB and FireWire hard disks, and so on) come preformatted, most of those for Windows. Many of them are partitioned using Master Boot Record (MBR). If you would like to start up your computer from one of these devices, you need to erase all existing partitions in order to switch to the GUID partition scheme (GPT).

1. If necessary, log in as Local Admin (password: `ladminpw`, or whatever you chose when you created the account).

2. Plug in the external disk you're using for this exercise. If you do not have an external disk that can be erased for this exercise, open the disk image StudentMaterials/Lesson10/Partitionable_Image.dmg. Remember that you have a shortcut to the StudentMaterials folder in your Dock.

   Note that the screenshots in this exercise were taken using an external disk; if you are using the disk image, things will look slightly different.

   NOTE ▸ This exercise erases all information on the external disk. Do not perform this exercise with a disk that contains any files you want to keep.

3. If necessary, open Disk Utility from the Utilities folder.

4. In the source list, select the external disk device (or Partitionable_Image.dmg). Be sure to select the device, not the volume(s) it contains.

   Note that the Partition Layout field displays a diagram of the disk's current partition(s), and at the bottom of the Disk Utility window, the disk's current Partition Map Scheme is listed. Both of these depend on what this disk has been used for in the past.

5. Click Partition and view the partitioning options available.

   If the Partition tab is not shown, make sure you have the disk device selected, not the volume(s) it contains.

   If all the controls in the Partition pane are disabled, you may not be logged in as Local Admin. In this case, eject the disk (or Partitionable_Image.dmg), and then log out and return to step 1.

6 Choose 2 Partitions from the Partition Layout pop-up menu.

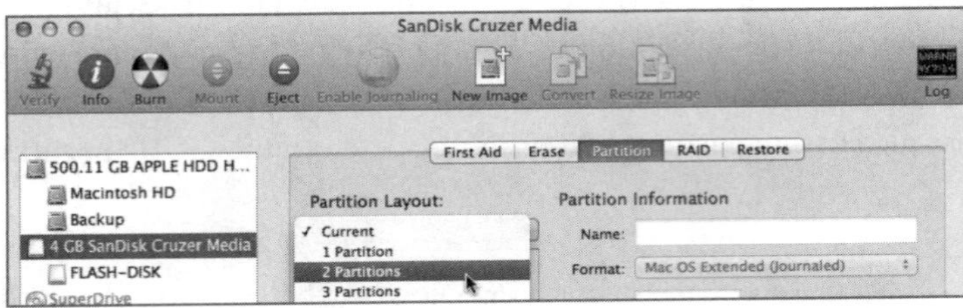

This option gives you two equally sized partitions.

7 Click Options to choose a partition scheme.

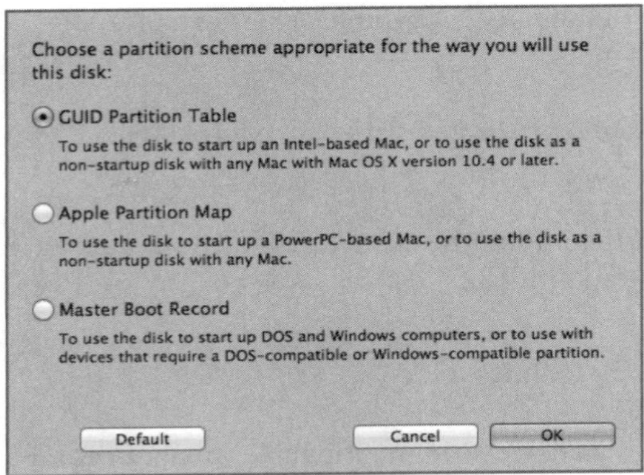

8 If it is not already selected, select GUID Partition Table and then click OK. This is generally the best partition scheme for disks that will be used only in OS X.

9 Select the first partition, and then choose Mac OS Extended (Journaled) from the Format pop-up menu.

10 In the Name field, change the partition's name to **Partition 1**.

Note that if you try to change the Name first, you may not be able to use lowercase letters. This is because lowercase volume names are not supported by some volume formats.

11 Repeat for the second partition, choosing Mac OS Extended (Journaled) from the Format menu and renaming the partition to **Partition 2**.

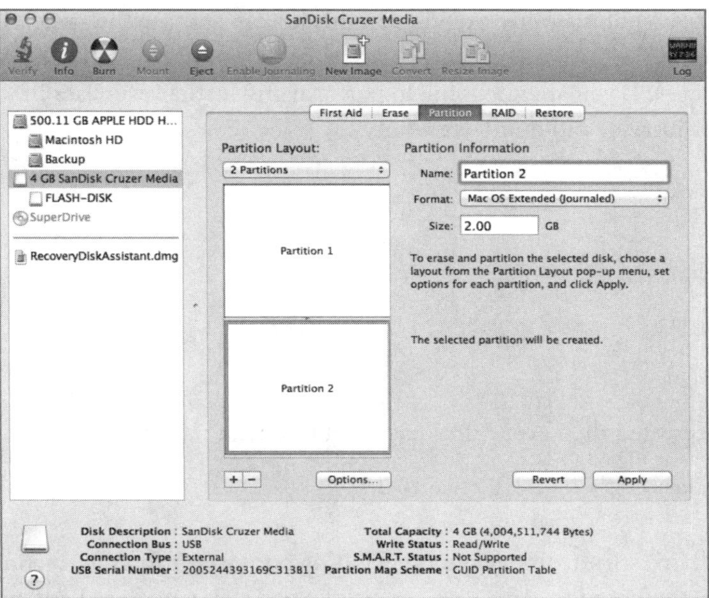

12 When you have finished, click Apply.

A confirmation dialog appears.

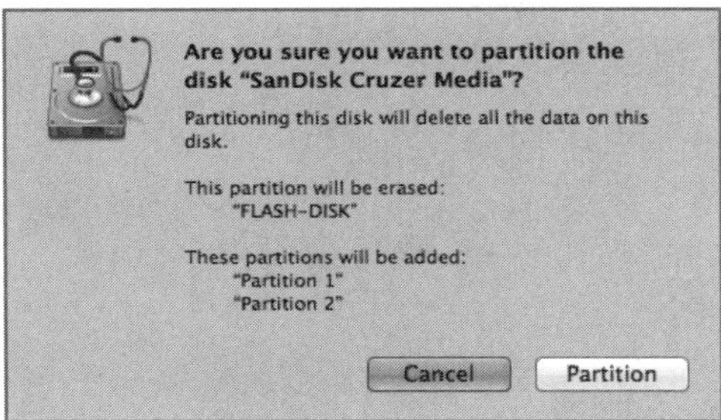

Note that the dialog may differ from the screenshot shown here. If the disk contains only a Recovery partition, the dialog will say "No partitions will be erased."

13 Click Partition to confirm that you want to destructively repartition this disk image.

Disk Utility then unmounts the disk volume(s), repartitions it as two volumes using GUID Partition Table, formats those volumes, and mounts those volumes.

You may now proceed to any of the other exercises in this lesson, and use the same disk to explore other features of OS X (although note that you cannot perform Exercise 10.5 if you are using a disk image). If you are not going to perform any further exercises in this lesson, eject the disk (or image), and quit Disk Utility.

Exercise 10.3
Examine Disk Ejection

Prerequisites

- You must have created the Local Admin account (Exercise 3.1 or 3.2).
- You must have just performed Exercise 10.2.

In this exercise, you will investigate disk ejection, including options for forcing ejection of disks that are in use. You will use the same disk (or disk image) that you erased and partitioned in the previous exercise.

Create a Text Document

In order to support this exercise you need to create a document on the disk.

1. If necessary, log in as Local Admin, and mount the disk (or disk image) you partitioned in Exercise 10.2.
2. Open TextEdit.

   TextEdit opens a new Untitled document.
3. Type some text into the TextEdit document.
4. Choose Format > Make Plain Text.
5. Choose File > Save.
6. Name the document **Example document** and choose Partition 1 from the Where pop-up menu (or from the sidebar if you have expanded the Save dialog).

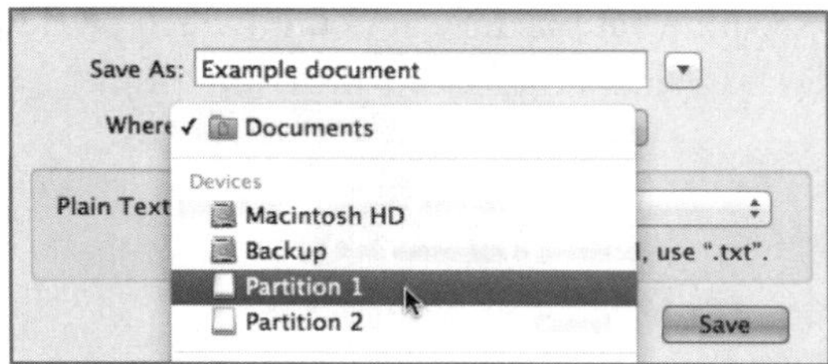

7 Click Save.

8 Close the document and quit TextEdit.

9 Open the Partition 1 volume in Finder.

10 Control-click the Example document, and choose Open With > Console from the shortcut menu.

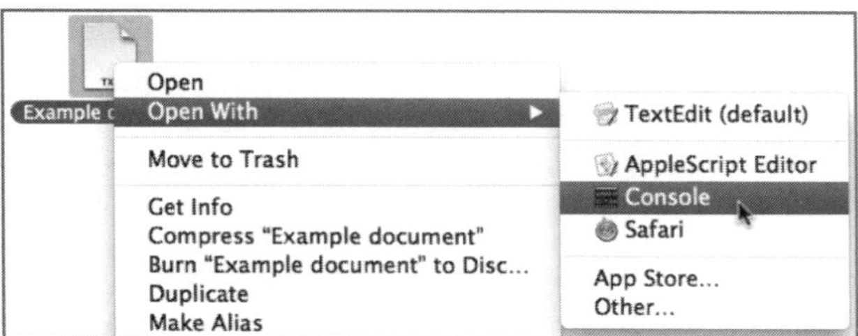

The Example document opens in the Console utility. Console is primarily used for viewing system logs, but it can also display the contents of plain text documents. In this exercise, you are using it because it keeps the file continuously open to monitor it for changes (such as new log entries).

Leave the document open in Console for use in the next section.

Eject Volumes as Local Admin

1 If necessary, open Disk Utility. Since you used it in the last exercise, you can open it from the Apple menu's Recent Items submenu.

2 In Disk Utility, select Partition 1 in the sidebar.

Note that the Disk Utility toolbar has separate buttons for Unmount (which unmounts only this partition, not the entire disk) and Eject (which ejects the entire disk).

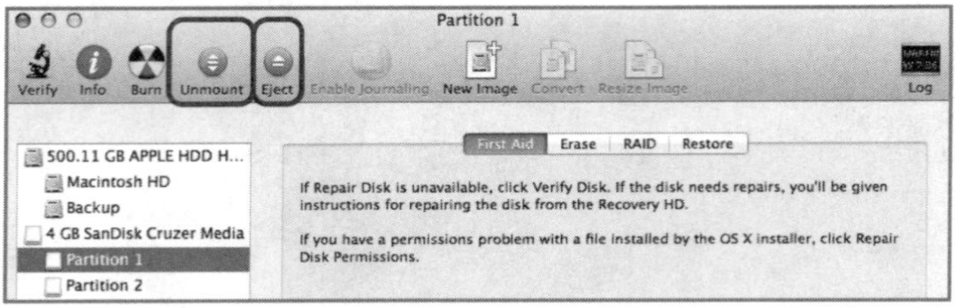

3 Click the Unmount button.

Since Console is using a file on the Partition 1 volume, the unmount operation fails.

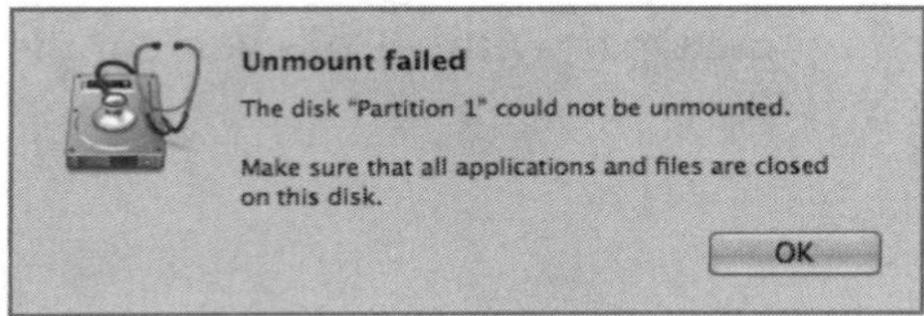

4 Click OK.

5 In the Finder desktop, drag the Partition 1 icon to the Trash. The Trash icon turns into an Eject symbol.

A dialog asks if you want to eject one or both partitions.

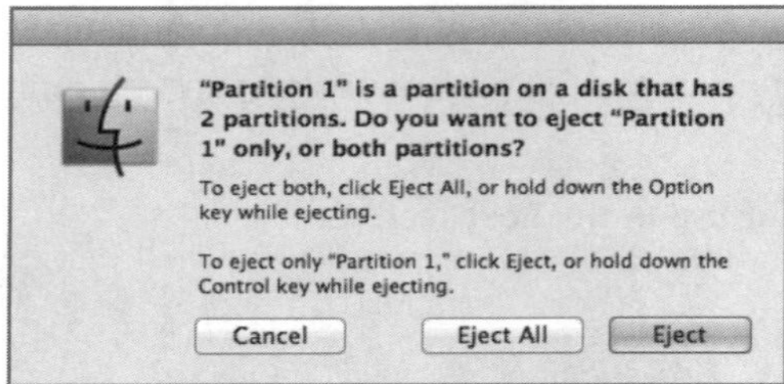

6 Click Eject All.

Partition 2 is ejected successfully, but again Partition 1 cannot be ejected. The Finder identifies that Console is the app using Partition 1.

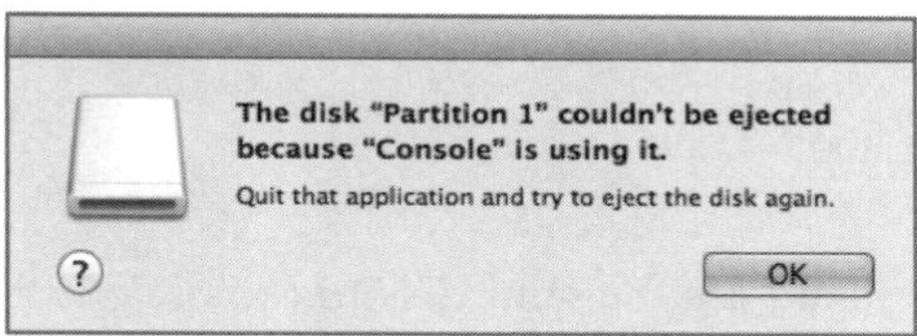

7 Click OK.

Eject Volumes as Chris Johnson

1 Use fast user switching to switch to Chris Johnson (password: chris, or whatever you chose when you created the account).

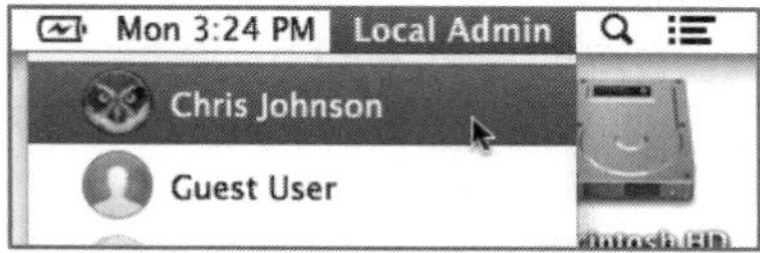

2 In the Finder desktop, drag the Partition 1 icon to the Trash.

Since the volume is in use by another user, the Finder does not display what app is using it. Instead, it gives you the option to Force Eject the volume.

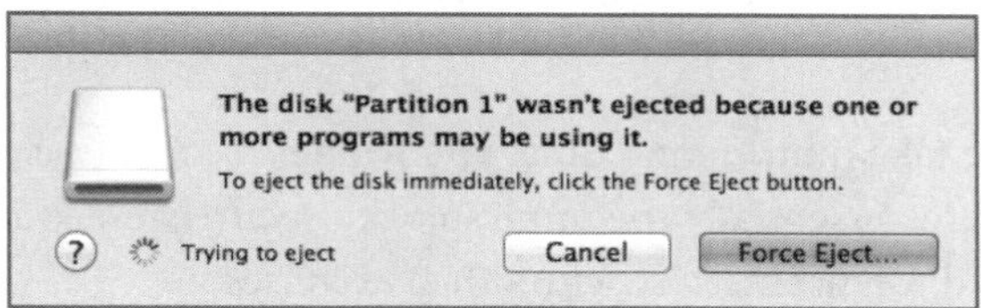

3 Click Force Eject.

4 In the confirmation dialog that appears, click Force Eject.

This time, the disk ejects successfully.

5 If necessary, click OK to dismiss the success dialog.

6 If you are using an external disk (not a disk image), unplug it from your computer.

7 Log out as Chris Johnson.

8 Log back in as Local Admin.

9 Quit Console.

You may now proceed to Exercise 10.4 or 10.5, and use the same disk to explore other features of OS X (although note that you cannot perform Exercise 10.5 if you are using a disk image). If you are not going to perform any further exercises in this lesson, eject the disk (or image), and quit Disk Utility.

Exercise 10.4
Securely Erase Disk Data

Prerequisites

- You must have created the Local Admin account (Exercise 3.1 or 3.2).

The Finder has an option to securely empty the Trash to make sure the data from deleted files is not left on a disk. However, if a file is deleted insecurely, it may be necessary to overwrite all free space on the volume to make sure none of the file's data remains. In this exercise, you will explore Disk Utility's options to erase either just the free space on a volume, or an entire volume.

Since secure erasure on a real disk can take quite a long time, you will test secure erasure on a disk image instead. You could follow essentially the same steps to securely erase a real disk, but it could take quite a while and might interfere with other exercises.

Securely Erase Free Space on a Volume

1 If necessary, log in as Local Admin.

2 Open StudentMaterials/Lesson10/Pretendco Documents.dmg. Remember that you have a shortcut to the StudentMaterials folder in your Dock.

   The Pretendco SSED Plans volume mounts.

3 Open the Pretendco SSED Plans volume in the Finder.

   The only thing visible in the volume is a file named Note.rtf. However, it used to contain Pretendco's secret plans to develop a next-generation solid-state encabulation device (SSED), and they were not deleted securely.

4 If necessary, open Disk Utility.

5 In Disk Utility, select the Pretendco SSED Plans volume in the sidebar.

6 Click the Erase tab.

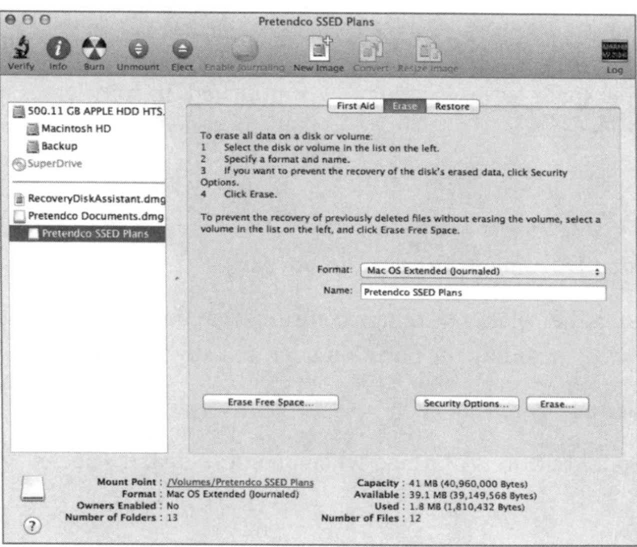

7 Click Erase Free Space.

A dialog appears with a slider that lets you choose the level of speed versus security you would like. The Fastest option is good enough for almost all purposes.

8 Leave the slider at Fastest, and click Erase Free Space.

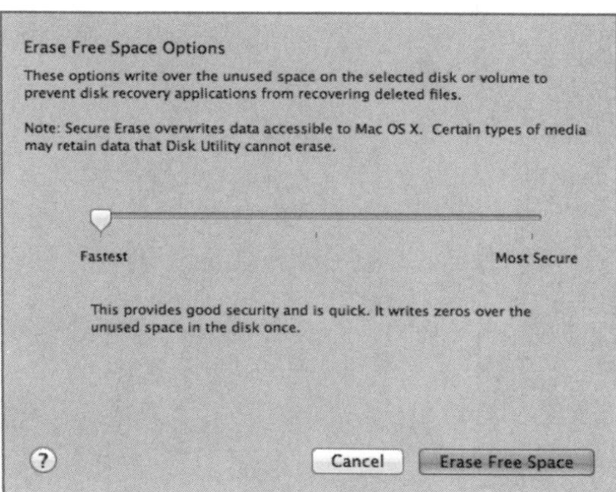

Since this is a small disk image, the erasure finishes quickly. An actual disk might take minutes or even hours depending on its size, speed, and the amount of free space.

9 Open Pretendco SSED Plans in the Finder.

Notice that Note.rtf is still there.

Securely Erase an Entire Volume

The option to securely erase free space leaves existing files untouched. In some cases, you may want to erase the existing files as well.

1 Switch back to Disk Utility.

2 If necessary, select Pretendco Documents.dmg in the sidebar.

Selecting the disk (rather than the volume it contains) ensures that the entire contents of the disk will be securely erased, including the partition table and any hidden partitions.

3 If necessary, select the Erase tab.

Note that the Erase Free Space button is dimmed when an entire disk is selected.

4 Click Security Options.

A dialog appears with a slider that looks very similar to the one in the last section. In this case, however, the Fastest option provides no real security.

5 Drag the slider one tick to the right.

The description under the slider says that it writes a single pass of zeros over the entire disk. This is equivalent to the Fastest option of Erase Free Space.

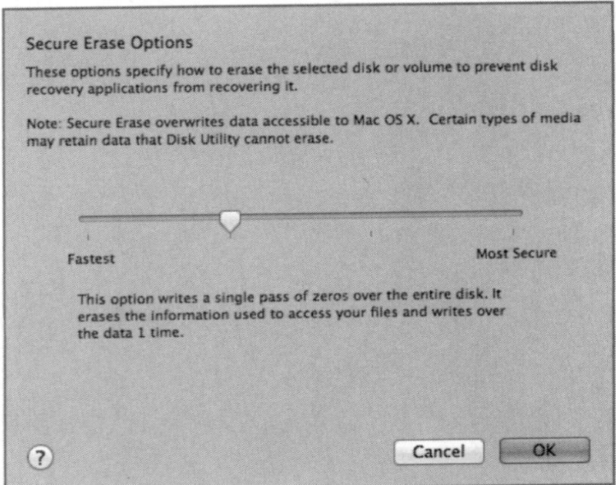

6 Click OK.

7 Click Erase.

8 In the confirmation dialog that appears, click Erase.

   If you receive a message that the disk could not be unmounted, make sure that TextEdit is not running and try again.

   As before, the operation completes quickly.

9 Open the volume (now named Untitled) in the Finder.

   This time, notice that Note.rtf is not present because it was erased.

10 Click the Eject button to eject the disk image.

Exercise 10.5
Encrypt a Volume

Prerequisites

- You must have created the Local Admin account (Exercise 3.1 or 3.2).
- This exercise requires that you have just performed Exercise 10.2 (and optionally 10.3) using an external disk (not disk image).

The Finder in OS X Mountain Lion has an option to encrypt an existing volume, preserving all existing files. In this exercise, you will test this feature using the same disk that you used for Exercise 10.2.

Note that if you performed Exercise 10.2 with a disk image, you will not be able to use it for this exercise; disk images can be encrypted, but use a different encryption mechanism.

Encrypt a Volume in the Finder

1 If necessary, log in as Local Admin.

2 If necessary, plug the disk you used for Exercise 10.2 back into your computer.

3 Click in the desktop to bring the Finder to the foreground.

4 In the Finder, Control-click the Partition 1 volume and choose Encrypt "Partition 1" from the shortcut menu.

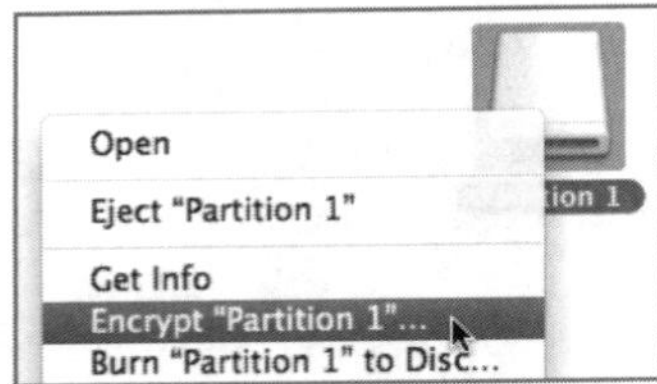

5 In the dialog that appears, enter **encryptPW** in the "Encryption password" and "Verify password" fields, and enter an appropriate hint.

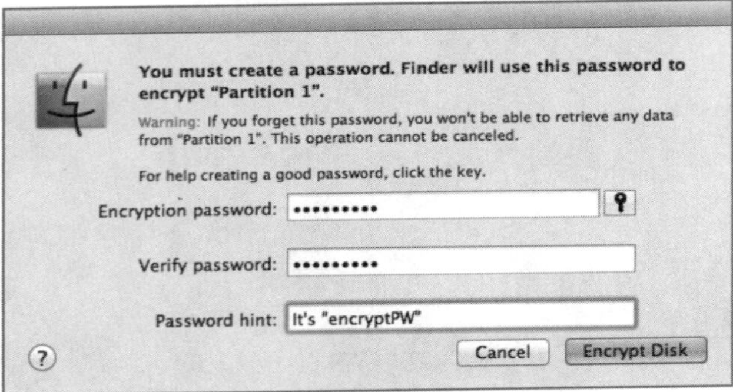

6 Click Encrypt Disk.

After a short delay, the Partition 1 icon vanishes from your desktop and then reappears.

7 Switch to Disk Utility, and note that your disk's entry in the sidebar changed. There is now a main entry named Partition 1, with Partition 1 and Partition 2 listed as the volumes under it.

8 Select the main (upper) Partition 1 entry.

The information at the bottom of the window now lists this as a Logical Volume Group. In order to support encryption, the disk has been converted to the new Core Storage format.

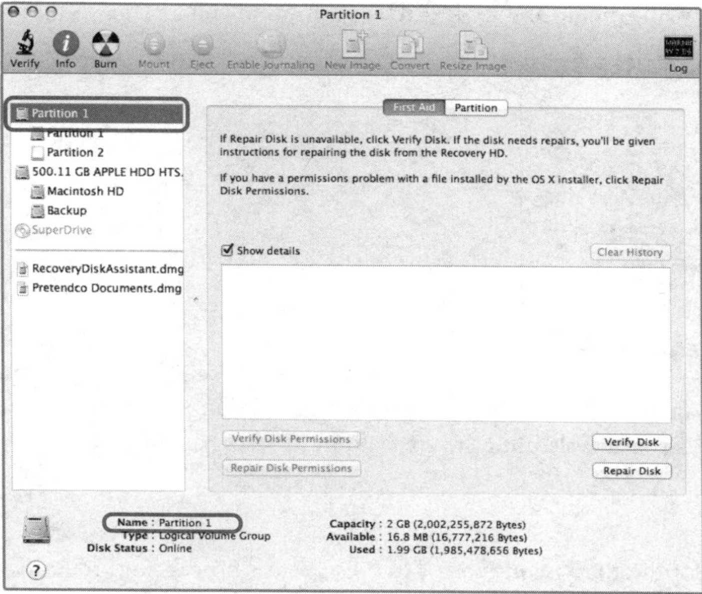

9 Select the Partition 1 volume (lower) entry.

Its format is listed as Encrypted Logical Partition. The volume is actually being encrypted in the background, so the data it contains is not completely secure until the encryption has time to complete.

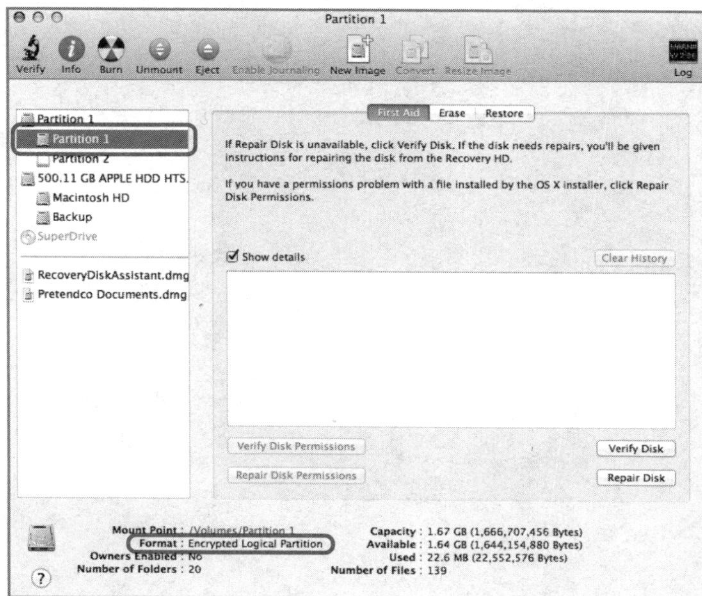

10 Click the Disk Utility File menu, and look at the options available.

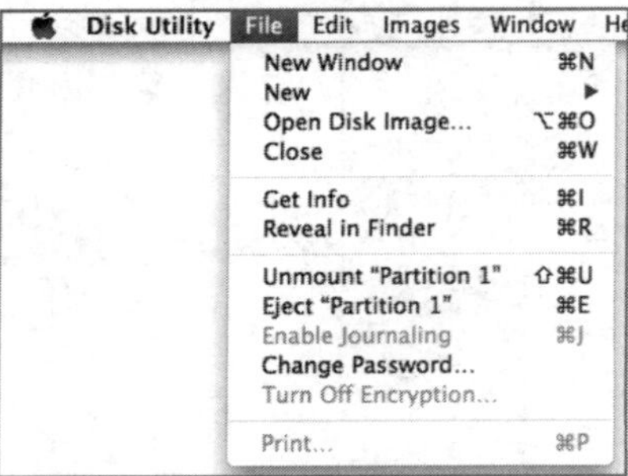

The menu contains an option to change the volume's encryption password, but the option to decrypt it isn't available until the encryption process has finished.

11 Quit Disk Utility.

You do not need to wait for the encryption process to finish before proceeding. You can even eject it before it has finished encrypting, although its contents will not be fully secure yet.

NOTE ► Disk Utility cannot erase disks that contain encrypted volumes. If you want to erase or repartition the disk, you must first either erase the encrypted volume in Disk Utility, or decrypt it in the Finder.

Lesson **11**

FileVault 2

Prior to OS X Lion, the Apple solution for protecting user data involved encrypting just the user's home folder content. This system, now dubbed Legacy FileVault, came with a list of caveats that prevented many system features and third-party software from behaving as expected. Further, it did not meet the security requirements of many organizations that require full-disk encryption.

While third-party solutions for full-disk encryption did emerge for previous versions of OS X, they often exhibited issues whenever Apple updated hardware or software. If Apple elected to make certain updates to the system, many third-party full-disk encryption schemes would simply stop working, leaving the user literally stranded with no way to reach his encrypted data.

GOALS

- Understand how FileVault 2 helps protect your data
- Enable FileVault 2 protection
- Recover a FileVault 2 system when all passwords are lost

Apple engineers finally decided to take this problem into their own hands and introduced FileVault 2. In this lesson you will learn how FileVault 2 protects the system volume, and how to enable this protection. You will also learn how to recover a FileVault 2 protected system when all local users' passwords are lost.

Reference 11.1
FileVault 2 Technology

FileVault 2 protects the entire system volume by converting it to Mac OS Extended (Journaled, Encrypted) format, which uses XTS-AES 128 encryption. This move to a full disk encryption scheme resolves all the limitations of Legacy FileVault by performing the encryption at the file system driver level of the operating system. In other words, most processes and applications don't even know the disk is encrypted, so they simply behave as normal.

This was not the case with Legacy FileVault, as the system and applications were unable to access an encrypted user's home folder contents when the user was logged out of the system. Also, obviously, FileVault 2, by encrypting the entire system volume, provides better protection than Legacy FileVault. Further, because FileVault 2 is fully supported by Apple, changes to Apple hardware and software should no longer cause compatibility issues.

> **NOTE ▸** You cannot enable FileVault 2 if any local user is still configured to use Legacy FileVault. Details regarding Legacy FileVault, including how to disable it for a user account, are covered in Lesson 8, "System Security."

The Apple FileVault 2 solution is more than just a new disk format; it's a system of new technologies that enables your Mac to transition from a standard system disk to a protected system disk. Full details of all the changes required for FileVault 2 are beyond the scope of this text, but the primary new technologies instrumental in FileVault 2 include seamless volume format conversion, user account password synchronization, secure key storage on Apple servers for lost password recovery, OS X Recovery for initial system startup, and a new firmware login window.

You can see many of these new pieces at work during startup to an encrypted system disk. What was traditionally a straightforward task, starting up the system, takes on a new level of complexity when you can't read the system disk to start with. Thus, Apple had to devise a method to authenticate and decrypt the protected system disk during startup.

When starting up from an encrypted system, the Mac actually starts from the hidden OS X Recovery HD volume first in order to present the user with a login window. The user enters her account password, which is then used to access the decryption key that ultimately unlocks and decrypts the protected system volume. Once the Mac has access to the system volume, startup continues normally, with one exception: The user, having already authenticated to unlock encryption, will be automatically logged into her account.

NOTE ► If the system disk is missing the hidden OS X Recovery HD volume, you cannot enable FileVault 2. Fortunately, OS X makes it impossible to accidentally engage FileVault 2 without meeting this requirement. Lesson 4, "OS X Recovery," covers this topic in greater detail.

Reference 11.2
Enabling FileVault 2

In typical Apple style, despite the underlying complexity of transitioning an existing system to a secure encrypted system, turning on FileVault 2 requires only a few simple steps. An administrative user can enable FileVault 2 from the Security & Privacy preferences. Note the appropriate tab is labeled as simply "FileVault." Clicking the Turn On FileVault button will initiate the FileVault 2 setup process.

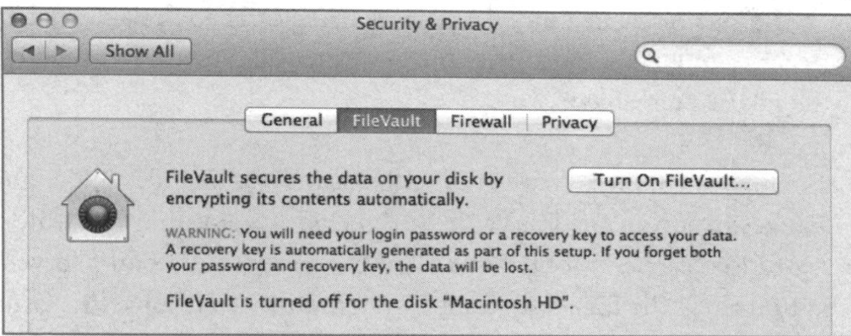

FileVault-Enabled Users

If more than one local user is on the system, a dialog appears, allowing you to enable existing local users to unlock and decrypt the protected system disk. This grants these other users the ability to start up the system. Click the Enable User button next to each user you want to make unlock-capable for FileVault system disk access. Each user must then enter his account password to enable this ability. An administrator cannot override this step, as each user must each enter his (supposedly) unique password.

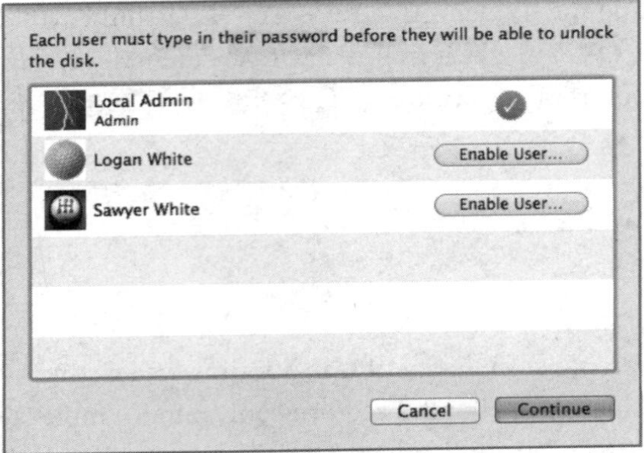

NOTE ► Any user not initially enabled to unlock FileVault 2 can be enabled at a later point by clicking the Enable Users button in the FileVault pane of the Security & Privacy preferences. Only local users or cached mobile network users can be FileVault enabled. New local users or cached mobile network users created after FileVault 2 is turned on will automatically be FileVault enabled.

NOTE ► Any user password changes that occur will continue to be FileVault enabled as long as those changes occur on the FileVault 2 protected system. In other words, if you reset the password to a cached mobile user from the network directory server, he will not be allowed to unlock the local FileVault 2 system disk. To resolve this issue, re-enable his account by clicking the Enable Users button in the FileVault pane of the Security & Privacy preferences.

Saving the FileVault 2 Recovery Key

During the setup for FileVault 2, a dialog appears, presenting you with an automatically generated encryption recovery key. You can use this key later if all FileVault-enabled user passwords are lost. As the dialog insists, you should copy this key and store it someplace safe besides the computer on which you are currently enabling FileVault. Once you have copied the recovery key, click Continue.

Another dialog appears, giving you the choice to have Apple securely store your recovery key. If you choose to save the recovery key with Apple, you have to pick and answer three randomly selected self-identifying questions. Only by answering these questions will Apple be able to recover the key. Once you have created the questions to your satisfaction, click Continue to securely send the information to Apple servers for safekeeping.

NOTE ► An Internet connection is, obviously, required to save the recovery key with Apple.

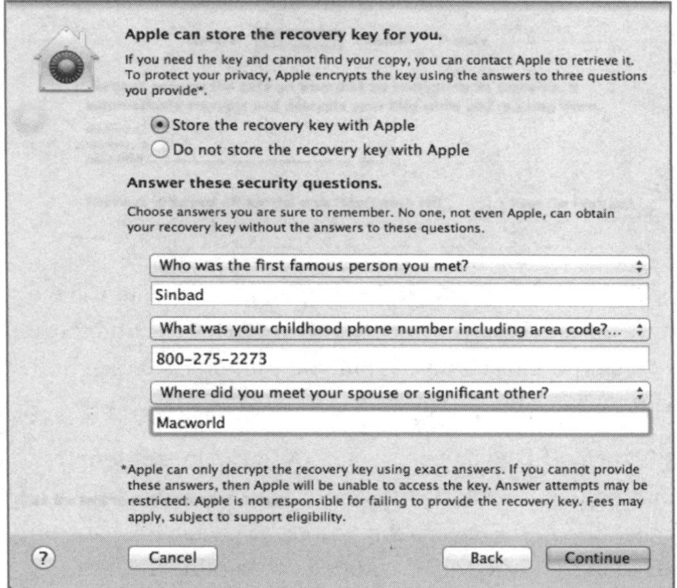

Restart and Encrypt

The system needs to restart to begin the system volume encryption. Upon restart, notice that a login window appears much quicker than normal. This is the new FileVault login window hosted from the hidden OS X Recovery HD volume. Authenticate as any FileVault-enabled user, and system startup continues until the user is automatically logged into his account.

From the FileVault tab of the Security & Privacy preferences, you can view the progress of the system disk encryption as well as an estimated completion time. It may take several hours to completely encrypt a system disk. Obviously, the length of time varies greatly based on the amount of data that must be encrypted.

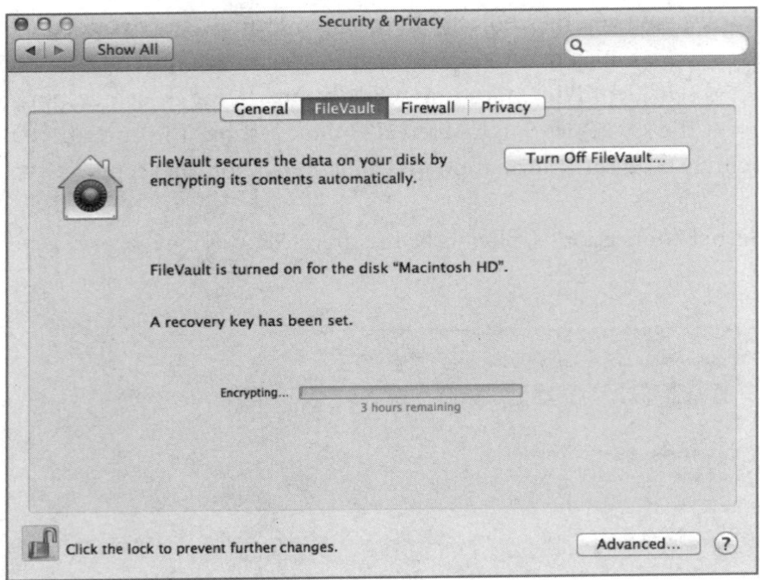

Amazingly, you can close the Security & Privacy preferences and continue to use the Mac as normal even though the system is slowly encrypting the disk it's running from. No notification appears once encryption is complete, but you can always return to the Security & Privacy preferences to check the progress.

If for some reason you want to turn off FileVault encryption, you can do so from this same Security & Privacy pane. Doing so requires another system restart and a potentially lengthy decryption process. However, similar to the encryption process to enable FileVault, the decryption process can continue in the background without interrupting the user.

Reference 11.3
FileVault 2 Recovery

While highly unlikely on multiuser systems, it's probably more common than you think for a single-user Mac computer's human to lose the login password. If by some means all FileVault-enabled account passwords are lost on a FileVault-protected system, you may still be able to unlock the system. The ability to unlock a FileVault protected system lies with the recovery key. Hopefully, the user dutifully copied and saved his recovery key someplace safe.

If you do have access to the FileVault 2 recovery key, at the FileVault login window, select a user and enter a bad password three times. A popover appears, suggesting you reset the user's password with the recovery key.

Click the triangle next to the words Recovery Key to enter the recovery key. After you successfully enter the recovery key, the system unlocks and decrypts the system disk and continues the startup process. The traditional Mac login window eventually appears, prompting you to set a new password for the user. Enter a new password twice, then an optional password hint, and then click Reset Password to log in the user.

Apple Saved Recovery Key

If the user has also lost his recovery key, all is not lost providing he chose to have Apple store his key in case of a situation just like this. At this point you must contact AppleCare directly. You have to provide the Mac computer's serial number, and they ask you to answer the three security questions that were configured when FileVault was enabled to access the recovery key. You must successfully answer all three questions to retrieve the recovery key. Obviously, AppleCare does not make exceptions if you are unable to answer the questions, as that would seriously undermine the intended security of the FileVault solution.

> **MORE INFO ▶** You can find out more about Apple policies regarding access to a saved recovery key from Knowledge Base document HT4790, "OS X: About FileVault 2." You can find out how to directly contact AppleCare from Knowledge Base document HE57, "Contacting Apple for support and service."

If, in a worst-case scenario, you have lost all FileVault-enabled account passwords and the recovery key, there is no way to recover the data on the system disk. You might as well start up to OS X Recovery (covered in Lesson 4) and then repartition the system disk (covered in Lesson 10). At that point, you could then reinstall OS X (covered in Lesson 2) or restore from a Time Machine backup (covered in Lesson 18).

Exercise 11.1
Enable FileVault 2

Prerequisites

- You must have created the Local Admin (Exercise 3.1 or 3.2) and Chris Johnson (Exercise 6.1) accounts.

WARNING ▶ If you lose all the passwords and the recovery key for a FileVault 2–encrypted volume, you will not be able to regain access to the data stored in it. If you are performing this exercise on your own computer and have any files you do not want to risk losing, you must back up your computer before starting this exercise.

FileVault 2 allows you to encrypt your startup volume and control which users can gain access to the volume. In this exercise, you will enable FileVault protection for your startup volume. If you do not want to protect your computer with FileVault 2, you can turn it off again in Exercise 11.4.

Using System Preferences to Enable FileVault

1. If necessary, log in as Local Admin.
2. Open the Security & Privacy pane in System Preferences.
3. Click the FileVault tab.

   If a dialog appears indicating that "You're using an old version of FileVault," it means that you have old user accounts set up using Legacy FileVault encryption. You can either click Turn Off Legacy FileVault and follow the prompts to disable it, or click Keep Using Legacy FileVault and skip this lesson's exercises. You cannot use both Legacy FileVault and FileVault 2 at the same time.

4 Unlock the preference pane by authenticating as Local Admin.

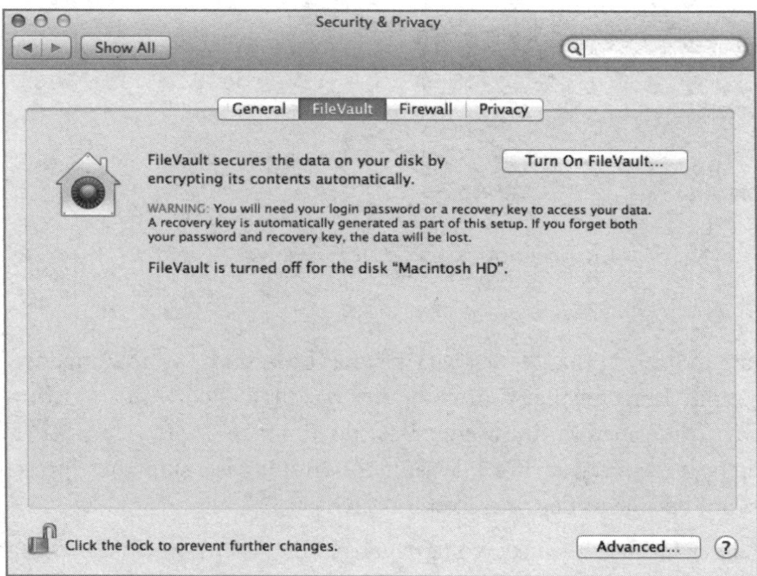

5 Click Turn On FileVault.

A dialog appears allowing you to select which users can unlock the disk.

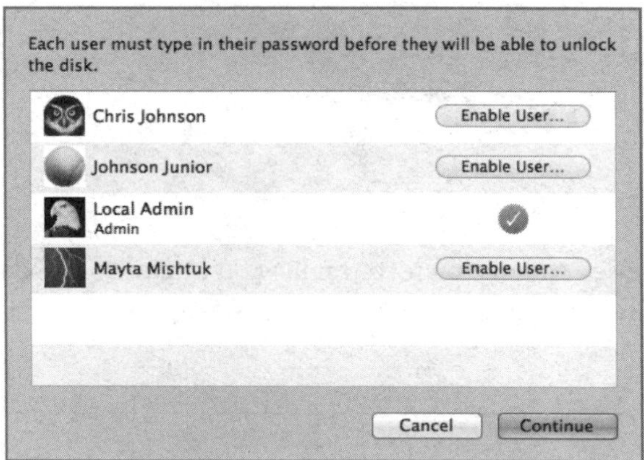

6 Click the Enable User button for Chris Johnson.

7 Enter Chris's password (chris, or whatever you chose when you created the account) and click OK.

Do not enable Mayta's or Johnson Junior's accounts.

8 Click Continue.

If a dialog appears indicating that "A recovery key has been set by your company, school, or institution," it means that your computer was preloaded with an institutional recovery key (described in Knowledge Base document #HT5077, "OS X: How to create and deploy a recovery key for FileVault 2"). In this case, skip ahead to step 10. You will also not be able to perform Exercise 11.3.

If an institutional key has not been set, you are given a recovery key, which you can use to unlock the disk if you forget all users' passwords.

9 Record your recovery key.

If you are performing these exercises on your own computer and intend to leave FileVault enabled at the end of these exercises, store the recorded recovery key in a physically secure location.

Recovery key: ______________________________

10 Click Continue.

You are given an option to store the recovery key with Apple.

11 Select "Store the recovery key with Apple" and click Continue.

The dialog expands to allow you to choose three security questions and corresponding answers.

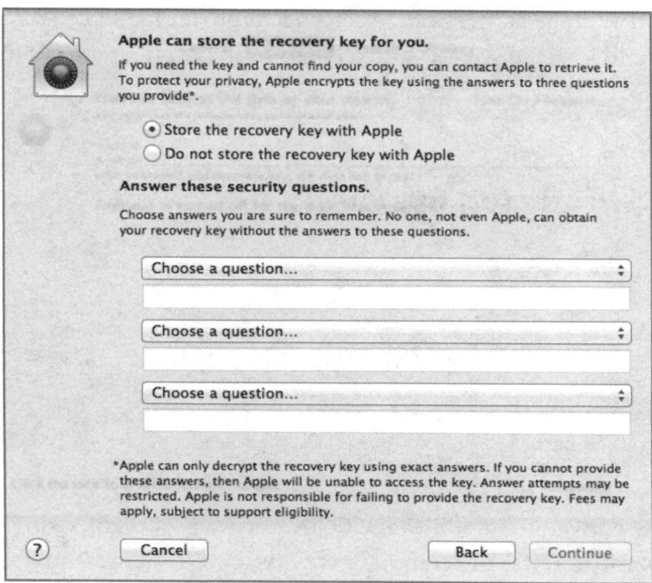

12 If you are performing these exercises on your own computer and intend to leave FileVault enabled at the end of these exercises, choose security questions and enter your answers to them. If you ever need to use the stored key, you need to type in all three answers *exactly* as you enter them here.

13 If you are performing these exercises in a class or intend to turn off FileVault at the end of the lesson, do not choose questions or enter answers. Instead, select "Do not store the recovery key with Apple".

14 Click Continue.

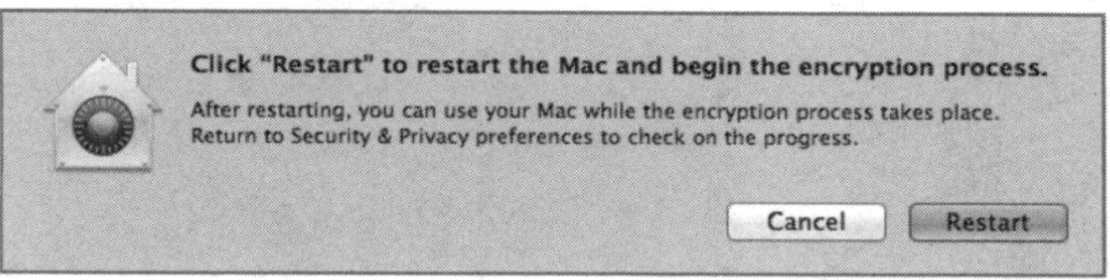

15 Click Restart to begin the encryption process.

Your computer restarts. Encrypting the entire partition takes awhile, but you can use the computer normally during the encryption process.

You can now leave your computer at the authentication screen and proceed to Exercises 11.2 and/or 11.3; if you do not want to leave FileVault 2 enabled, use Exercise 11.4 to turn it off.

Exercise 11.2
Restart a FileVault 2–Protected System

Prerequisites

- You must have created the Local Admin (Exercise 3.1 or 3.2) and Chris Johnson (Exercise 6.1) accounts.
- You must have performed Exercise 11.1.

In this exercise, you'll see how FileVault 2 modifies the OS X startup process by requiring one of the selected user's passwords. Once the computer is fully started, all users may use the computer normally.

Your computer restarts and displays a FileVault 2 access screen. This looks similar to the login screen, but you will notice only Chris Johnson and Local Admin. The operating system itself has not started yet, as you need to unlock the disk before the system files can be read.

If Find My Mac were enabled, you would also see a Guest account listed here. Selecting Guest starts the computer in a Safari-only mode with no access to the startup volume. This exists primarily to tempt computer thieves into connecting the computer to the Internet so that it can be located, locked, or wiped.

Log Into an Enabled Account

1 Click Chris Johnson.

2 Enter Chris's password, and press Return.

If you lose all the selected users' passwords, you could enter an incorrect password three times to be prompted for the recovery key.

At this point, the normal OS X startup process proceeds, and you are logged in as Chris Johnson.

3 Open the Security & Privacy preferences, and click the FileVault tab.

A progress indicator shows the encryption status. As you have just seen, FileVault 2 provides some protection immediately, but your data is not fully secured until the encryption process finishes.

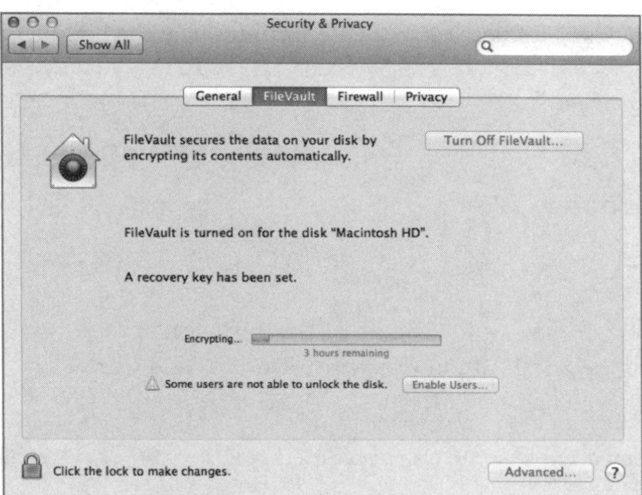

4 Quit System Preferences.

5 Open Disk Utility.

Note that the disks and volumes list displays your internal disk differently. The top entry is now labeled "Macintosh HD" rather than named for the physical disk type.

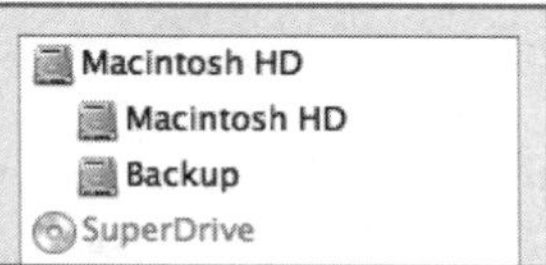

6 Select the top Macintosh HD entry.

The information at the bottom of the window now lists this as a Logical Volume Group, which indicates that the disk has been converted to the new Core Storage format. If you encrypted an external disk in Exercise 10.5, this is using exactly the same format.

7 Select the lower (indented) Macintosh HD entry.

At the bottom of the window, the volume Format is shown as Encrypted Logical Partition.

8 Quit Disk Utility and log out as Chris Johnson.

Notice that even though Chris's account was used to gain access to Macintosh HD, all users can now log in normally.

9 If you plan to perform Exercise 11.3 next, click the Restart button at the bottom of the screen.

Exercise 11.3
Use a FileVault 2 Recovery Key

Prerequisites

- You must have created the Local Admin (Exercise 3.1 or 3.2) and Chris Johnson (Exercise 6.1) accounts.
- You must have performed Exercise 11.1 and recorded your recovery key.

The FileVault recovery key can be used to reset user passwords at startup. In this exercise you will use this capability to reset Chris Johnson's password.

Reset Chris Johnson's Password

1 If your computer is not at the FileVault authentication screen, restart it.

2 At the FileVault authentication screen, click Chris Johnson.

3 Click the Help (question mark) button at the right of the Password field.

A popover appears, offering to let you reset the password with the recovery key.

4 Click the arrow to start the reset process.

The Password field is replaced by a Recovery Key field.

5 Enter the recovery key you recorded earlier, and press Return.

If the Recovery Key field shakes and resets, you have not entered the recovery key correctly. If reentering it does not correct the problem, you may have recorded it incorrectly. In this case, you can't perform the password reset portion of this exercise; instead, cancel the password reset by clicking the left-arrow button, log in normally using Chris's current password (chris, or whatever you chose when you created the account), and skip ahead to Exercise 11.4.

The operating system starts up. Once the startup process finishes, a password reset popover for Chris Johnson appears.

6 Enter **chrisvault** in the New Password and Verify Password fields, and then click Reset Password.

You are now logged in to Chris's account. Since his password has been reset, you receive the warning that the system was unable to unlock his login keychain.

7 Click Continue Log In.

8 If you are prompted, enter the password for Chris's login keychain (**chris**, or whatever you chose when you created the account).

Restore Chris Johnson's Original Password

To avoid confusion for the rest of the exercises, you will now change Chris Johnson's password back to "chris".

1 Open the Users & Groups pane in System Preferences.

2 Click Change Password, and change Chris's password from **chrisvault** back to **chris**, or whatever you chose when you created the account.

Note that this also brings Chris's account password back in sync with his keychain password.

Exercise 11.4
Turn Off FileVault 2

Prerequisites

- You must have created the Local Admin (Exercise 3.1 or 3.2) and Chris Johnson (Exercise 6.1) accounts.
- You must have performed Exercise 11.1.

FileVault encryption can be disabled as easily as it is enabled. If you are performing these exercises on your own and want to leave FileVault 2 protection enabled on your computer, you can skip this exercise.

If you are performing these exercises in a class, you should not skip this exercise.

Disable Encryption on the Macintosh HD Volume

1 If necessary, log in as Chris Johnson.

2 Open the Security & Privacy preferences.

3 Click the FileVault tab.

The encryption process may not have finished yet. This is OK, since FileVault allows you to reverse the encryption process at any point.

4 Click the Lock icon and authenticate as Local Admin.

5 Click Turn Off FileVault.

You are asked to confirm that you want to turn off FileVault.

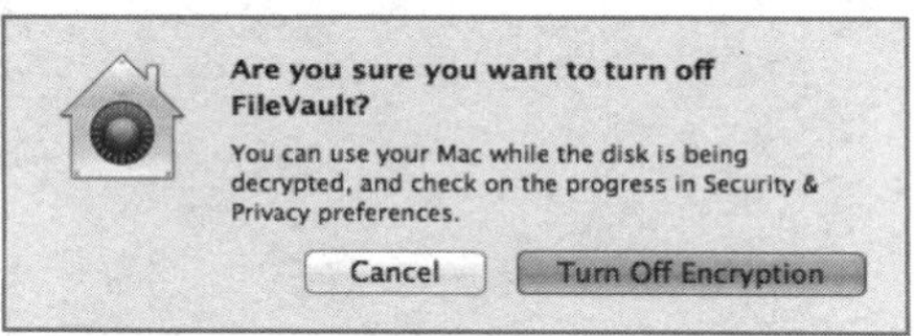

6 Click Turn Off Encryption.

The decryption process begins. Note that since you authenticated to FileVault when you started up the computer, no special FileVault password is required at this point.

As with the encryption process, you can continue to use the computer normally during the decryption process. Unlike encryption, decryption does not require restarting your computer.

7 Quit System Preferences.

Lesson **12**

Permissions and Sharing

The technologies collectively known as file system permissions are used to control file and folder authorization for OS X. File system permissions work alongside the user account technologies, which control user identification and authentication, to provide the secure multiuser environment of the Mac. File system permissions—just like user accounts—permeate every level of the operating system, so a thorough investigation of this system is required to fully understand OS X.

In this lesson, you will learn how file system ownership and permissions allows you protect local files and folders. You will also explore the default permissions used by OS X to provide secure access to shared files. Finally, you will use the Finder to make ownership and permissions changes.

GOALS

- ► Understand file ownership and permissions
- ► Explore the default shared folders in OS X
- ► Securely manage file and folder access

Reference 12.1
File System Permissions

In short, every single item on the system volume has permissions rules applied to it by the operating system. Only users and processes with root account access can ignore file system permissions rules. Thus, these rules are used to define file and folder access for every standard, administrative, guest, and sharing user. Any user can easily identify the permissions of a file or folder with the Finder Get Info window.

> **NOTE** ► The OS X interface sometimes uses the word "privileges" in place of permissions. In general, the meaning of these two terms is similar.

Viewing File System Permissions

There are several methods for opening the Finder Get Info window. First, select the file or folder for which you want to identify the permissions. You can select multiple items to open multiple Get Info windows.

There are several ways to access the Finder Get Info window:

- Press Command-I.
- Choose File > Get Info.
- Use secondary (or Control) click on the selected item, and then choose Get Info from the shortcut menu.
- In a Finder window toolbar, click the Action (gear icon) button, and then choose Get Info from the pop-up menu.

Once you open a Get Info window, click the Sharing & Permissions disclosure triangle to reveal the item's permissions. Note that the permissions list is broken into two columns. To the left is a list of users or groups with access to this item, and to the right is the associated privilege assigned per user or group. Modifying these settings is covered in the "Managing Permissions" sections later in this lesson.

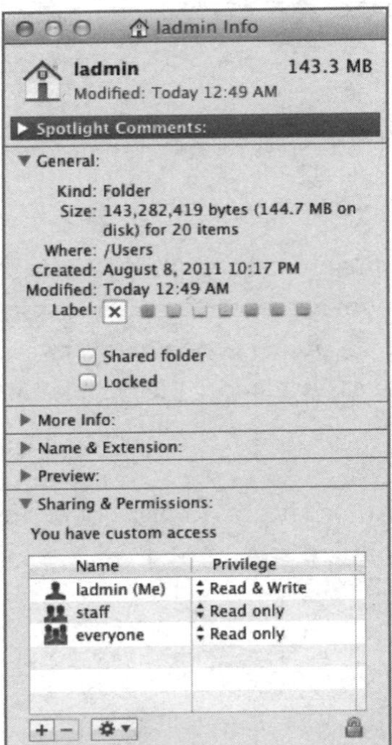

TIP You can also identify ownership and permissions from the Finder dynamic Inspector window. This is a single floating window that automatically refreshes as you select different items in the Finder. To open the Inspector window in the Finder, press Command-Option-I.

Ownership for Permissions

Every file and folder belongs to at least one owner and one group and also has an ownership setting for everyone else. This three-tiered ownership structure provides the basis for file system permissions:

- Owner—By default, the owner of an item is the user who created or copied the item to the Mac. For example, the user owns most of the items in her home folder. The system or root user almost always owns system software items, including system resources and applications. Traditionally, only the owner can change the item's ownership or permissions. Despite this, OS X makes management easier by giving every administrative user the ability to change ownership and permissions regardless of who the item's owner is.
- Group—By default, the group of an item is inherited from the folder it was created in. Thus, most items belong to the staff (the primary group for local users), wheel (the primary group for the root system account), or admin groups. Group ownership is designated to allow users other than the owner to have access to an item. For instance, even though root owns the /Applications folder, the group is set to admin so administrative users can make changes to the contents of this folder.
- Everyone—The Everyone setting is used to define access for anyone who isn't the owner and isn't part of the item's group. In other words, this means everyone *else*. This includes local, sharing, and guest users.

The simple three-tiered ownership structure presented here has been part of traditional UNIX operating systems for decades. However, with only three levels of permissions to choose from, it is quite difficult to define appropriate access settings for a computer with many user accounts and shared files, as is the case with many servers. Fortunately, as you'll see later, access control lists (ACLs) were developed to allow for nearly limitless ownership and permissions configurations.

Standard UNIX Permissions

The standard file system permissions structure of OS X is based on decades-old UNIX-style permissions. This system is also sometimes referred to as POSIX-style permissions.

The system may be old, but for most Mac users it is quite adequate because you can define privilege rules separately at each ownership tier. In other words, the owner, the group, and everyone else has individually specified access to each file or folder. Further, because of the inherent hierarchy built into the file system, where folders can reside inside other folders, you can easily create a complex file structure that allows varying levels of sharing and security.

Apple has streamlined the Finder to allow for the most common permissions options. Alternatively, the full range of UNIX privilege combinations are available from Terminal, but this topic is beyond the scope of this guide.

MORE INFO ▶ Wikipedia has an excellent overview of UNIX-style permissions: http://en.wikipedia.org/wiki/Filesystem_permissions.

Permissions that you can assign to a file using the Finder are:

- Read & Write—The user or group members can open the file and save changes.
- Read Only—The user or group members can open the file but cannot save any changes.
- No Access—The user or group members have no access to the file at all.

Permissions that you can assign to a folder using the Finder are:

- Read & Write—The user or group members can browse and make changes to the contents of the folder.
- Read Only—The user or group members can browse the contents of the folder but cannot make changes to the contents of the folder.
- Write Only (Drop Box)—The user or group members cannot browse the folder but can copy or move items into it.
- No Access—The user or group members have no access to the contents of the folder.

NOTE ▶ The Finder assumes that the UNIX "execute" permission goes along with "read" access for folders.

Access Control Lists (ACLs)

Access control lists (ACLs) were developed to expand the standard UNIX permissions architecture to allow more control of file and folder access. OS X has adopted a style of

ACLs similar to that available on Windows-based NTFS file systems and UNIX systems that support NFSv4. This ACL implementation is extremely flexible but increases complexity by adding more than a dozen unique privilege and inheritance attribute types.

Further, the OS X implementation of ACLs supports an essentially unlimited number of access control entries (ACEs). An ACE is a set of permissions defined for a specific user or group. In other words, ACLs provide a near unlimited list of permission rules or ACEs for every file or folder. Hence the "list" in access control list.

Finally, it's important to note that if an ACL rule applies to a user or group, this rule trumps standard UNIX permissions. However, any users or groups that don't apply to a specific ACL are still bound by the standard permissions currently in place.

Apple does not expect average users to navigate through all the options available using ACLs, so once again the Finder has been streamlined to allow only the most common ACL configurations. In fact, the Finder only allows you to assign ACL attributes that match the most common permissions configurations that were previously listed in this lesson. The only feature of ACLs that the Finder actually implements is the ability to have an unlimited number of user or group privilege rules. In other words, the Finder uses the ACL architecture to let you configure unique privileges for an essentially unlimited number of users or groups.

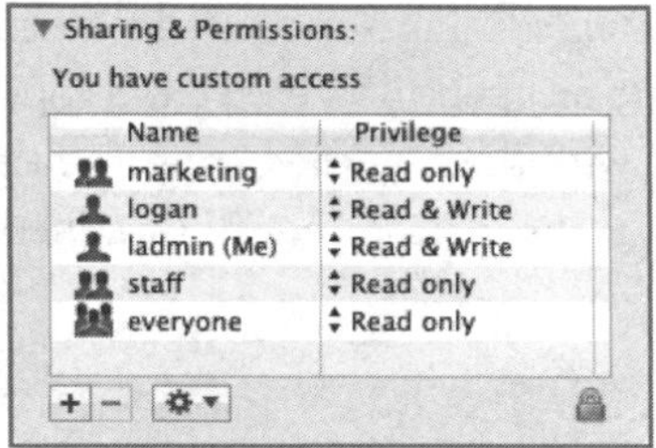

Permissions in a Hierarchical Context

It is important to remember that permissions do not exist in isolation; rather, permissions are applied in the context of folder hierarchy. In other words, your access to an item is based on an item's permissions in combination with the permissions of the folder in which it resides. If you're still confused, it's easiest to think of permissions as defining access to an item's content, not the item itself. Remember the word "content" as you consider the following three simplified examples.

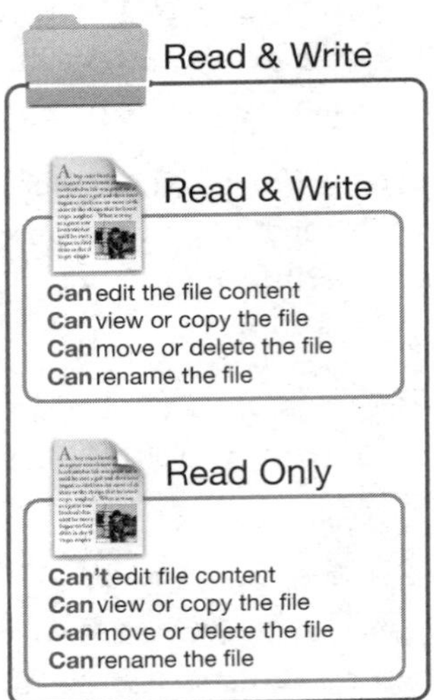

Example 1: Your permissions to the folder are read and write. It's obvious that you should have full access to the first file, as your permissions here are read and write as well. You can also view and copy the second file, but you can't make changes to the file's content because your permissions are read only. Yet you can still move, delete, or rename the second file because you have read and write access to the folder's contents. Thus, the second file isn't secure in this example because you can make a copy of the original file, change the copied file's content, delete the original file, and finally replace it with the modified copy. In fact, this is how many applications save document changes; thus the file can indeed be edited.

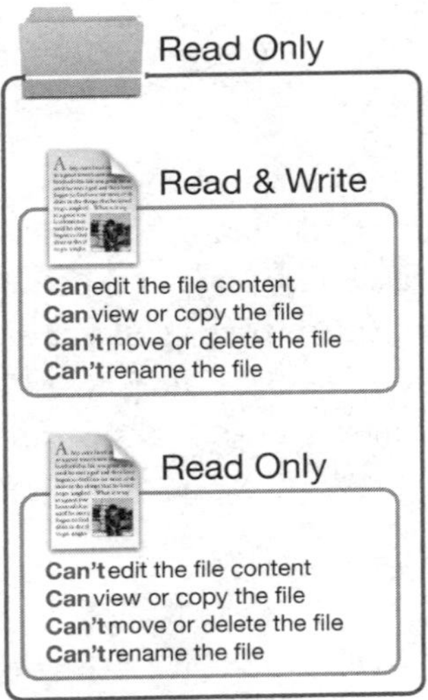

Example 2: You have read-only permission to the folder. You can edit the content of the first file because you have read and write access to it, but you can't move, delete, or rename it because you have read-only access to the folder's contents. On the other hand, you can effectively delete the file by erasing its contents. The bottom file here is the only truly secure file, as you're only allowed to view or copy the file. Granted, you can make changes to the contents of a copied file, but you still can't replace the original.

NOTE ► Many applications cannot save changes to files inside read-only folders, because these applications attempt to replace the original file during the save process, instead of revising the file's content. In other words, you may need read and write access to both the file and the folder it's inside to save changes to the file.

Example 3: Your permissions are identical to the first folder in the first example, with one significant change. The owner of this file has enabled the locked attribute, perhaps through the new OS X Versions document control feature. Even though you have read and write access to the example folder and file, the locked attribute prevents all users who aren't the file's owner from modifying, moving, deleting, or renaming the file. From most applications, only the owner is allowed to change the file's content or delete it, but the owner can also disable the locked attribute to return the file to normal. You can still make a copy of the locked file, but the copy will be locked as well. However, you will own the copy, so you can disable the locked attribute on the copy, but you still can't delete the original locked file unless you're the owner.

MORE INFO ► Managing the locked file attribute is detailed in Lesson 20, "Document Management."

Reference 12.2
Permissions for Sharing

Once you have an understanding of the available permissions options in OS X, you should explore how the local file system is set up by default to provide a secure environment that still allows users to share files.

If you don't have fast user switching enabled, as outlined in Lesson 6, "User Accounts," enable it now to make it easy to test file system permissions as different users. Further, to aid in your exploration of the file system, use the Finder Inspector window. This single floating window, which automatically refreshes as you select different items in the Finder, allows you to quickly explore the default permissions settings without having to open multiple Finder Get Info windows. Open the Inspector from the Finder by pressing Command-Option-I, and then click the disclosure triangle to reveal the Sharing & Permissions section.

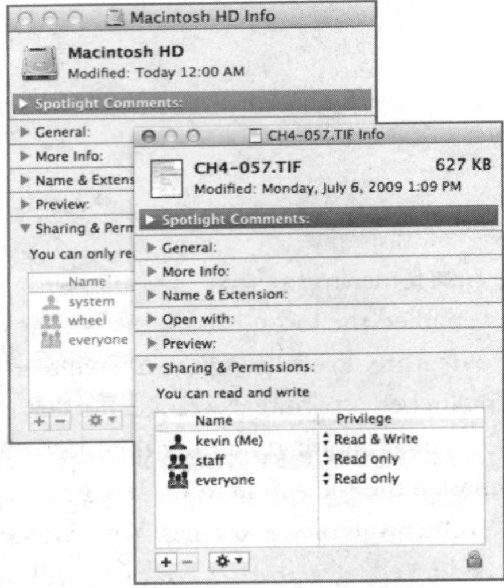

NOTE ▸ The Inspector window sports a different title bar than the Get Info window. Also, the Inspector window always floats on top of all other windows in the Finder.

Home Folder Sharing

OS X protects the user's files by default and allows them to be shared easily when needed. This starts with the user's home folder. Notice that users are allowed read and write access to their home folder, while the staff group and everyone are allowed only read access.

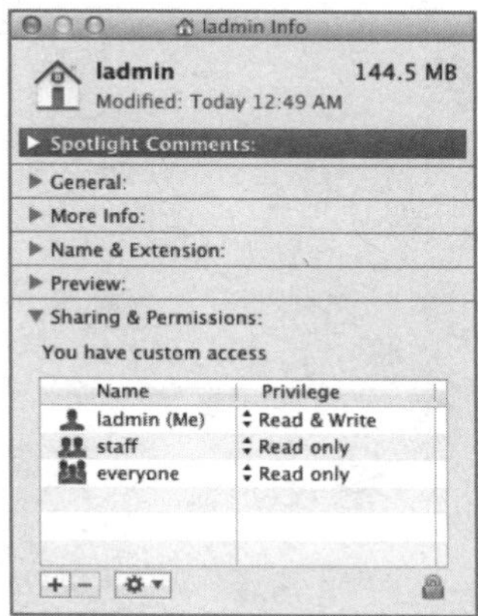

This means that every local user or guest can view the first level of every other user's home folder. (As a reminder, guests are allowed access to your computer without a password. This is why you can disable guest access in the Users & Groups preferences.) The default home folder permissions may seem insecure until you look at the permissions in context. Most user data is actually stored inside a subfolder in the user's home folder, and if you inspect those subfolders, you'll notice that other users are not allowed to access most of them.

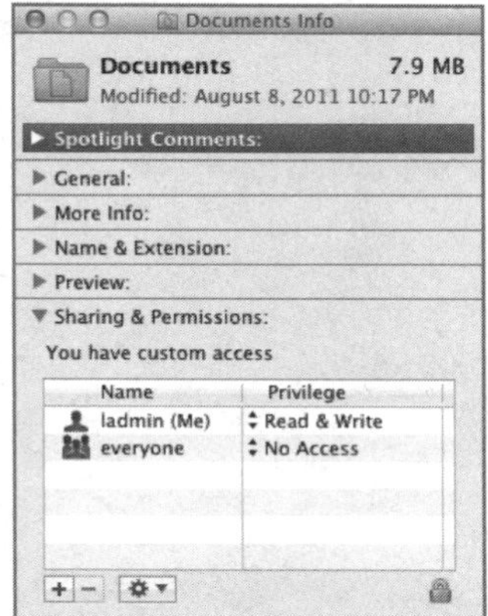

A few subfolders in a user's home folder, however, are specifically designed for sharing. The Public folder and legacy Sites folder remain readable to everyone. A user can easily share files without having to mess with permissions by simply moving the files into those two folders. Others will be able to read those files, but they still cannot make any changes to them.

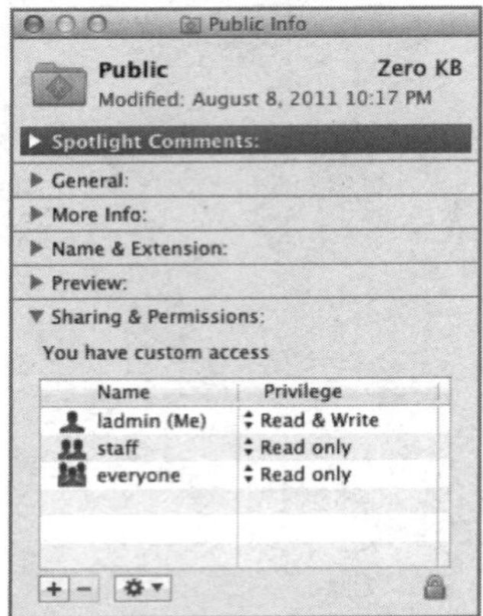

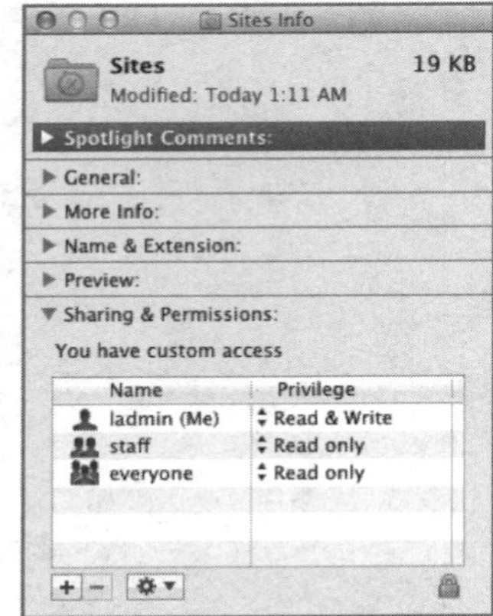

NOTE ▶ User-created files and folders at the root of the home folder will, by default, have permissions like the Public folder's. To secure new items at the root of the home folder, simply change the permissions as outlined in the "Managing Permissions" section later in this lesson.

Looking deeper, you'll notice that a subfolder of the Public folder is the Drop Box. This folder's permissions allow all other users to copy files into the folder even though they cannot actually see other files in the Drop Box folder. This allows other users to discreetly transfer files without others knowing.

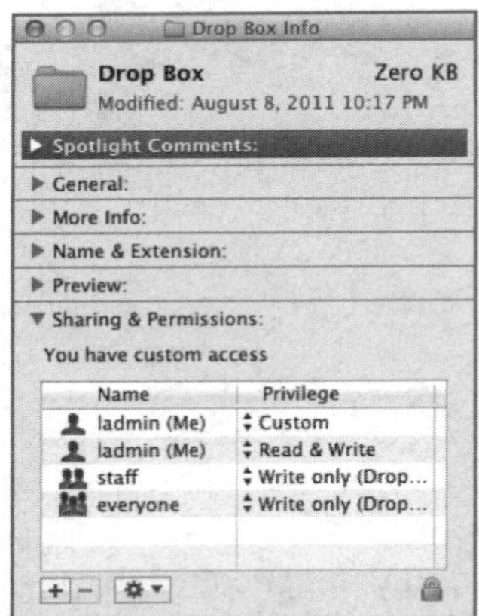

The Shared Folder

An additional folder set aside for sharing is the /Users/Shared folder. Notice that this is a general sharing location that allows all users to read and write items to the folder.

Normally this permissions setting would also allow any user to delete another user's item in this folder.

Yet the Finder Inspector window is not showing you the full permissions picture here. A unique permissions setting on the Shared folder prevents other users from being able to delete items they don't own. This permission setting, known as the "sticky bit," can only be viewed and managed via the Terminal.

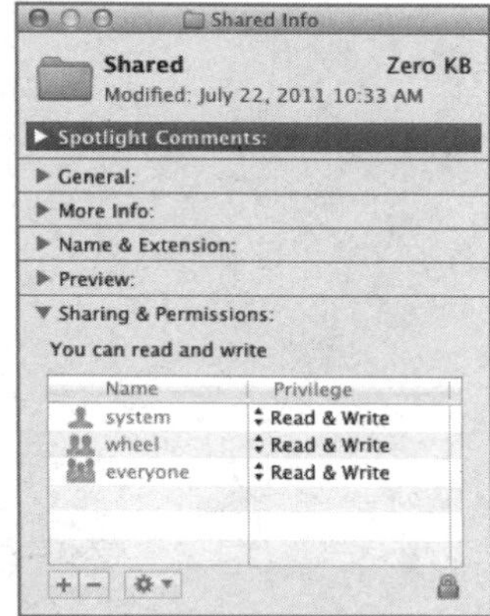

Securing New Items

Once you understand how the OS X file system security architecture works with the folder hierarchy, it's time to consider how this technology is used to secure new items. You've learned previously in this lesson that OS X is preconfigured for secure file and folder sharing, but you will find that new items are created with unrestricted read access.

For example, when a user creates a new file or folder at the root of her home folder, by default all other users, including guest users, are allowed to view this item's contents. The same is true for new items created by administrators in local areas such as the root of the system volume and the local Library and Applications folders.

New items are created this way to facilitate sharing, so you do not have to change any permissions to share a new item. All that is required of you is to place the new item in a folder that other users can access, like the predefined sharing folders covered in the previous section. It's assumed that if you want to secure a new item, you will place it inside a folder that no one else has access to, like your home Desktop or Documents folders.

On the other hand, this default behavior is inconvenient if you want to safely store your items in an otherwise public area, like the root of the system volume. To store items in a public area so they are only accessible to the owner requires you to change the item's permissions using either the Finder or Terminal, as outlined later in this lesson.

Specifically, from the Finder Sharing & Permissions section of the Get Info window, you must remove all other users and all group accounts from the permissions list. You cannot remove the Everyone permission, so you have to set it to No Access. Once you have made these permissions changes, only the owner has access to the item.

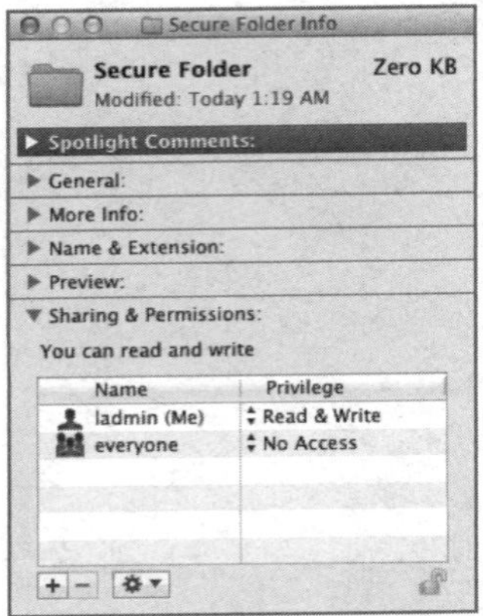

Reference 12.3
Managing Permissions

You may find that while the Finder makes permissions management simple, it does so through a form of obfuscation. In other words, the Finder hides the complexity of permissions by intentionally misrepresenting the full permissions of an item.

Thus, if you're more comfortable with standard UNIX permissions, or you simply require full access to an item's permissions, you're best served by managing permissions via Terminal. This however, is beyond the scope of this guide. Yet, for the most common permissions settings, the simplified Finder permissions interface is still the quickest and easiest solution.

Permissions Management via Finder

As covered previously in the "Viewing File System Permissions" section of this lesson, you can view and manage permissions in the Sharing & Permissions section of the Finder Get Info window. If you aren't the owner of the item, you must click the small lock icon in the bottom-right corner of the Get Info window and authenticate as an administrative user.

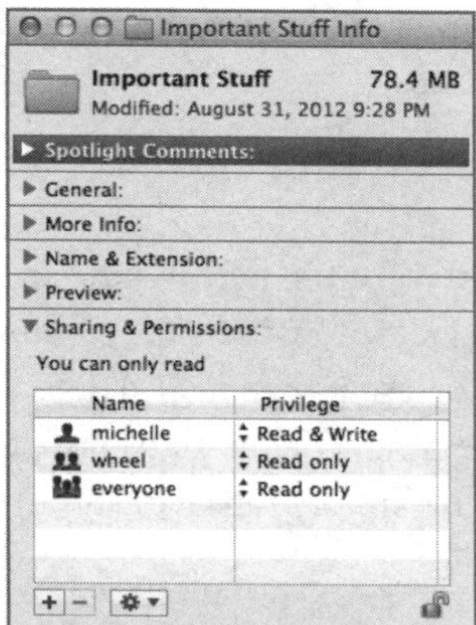

It's important to note that changes made using the Get Info window are applied immediately. However, as long as you keep the Get Info window open, the Finder also remembers the original permissions setting for the item. This is useful for testing different permissions configurations, as you can always revert to the original permissions setting. To do so, click the Action button (gear icon) at the bottom of the Get Info window to reveal the Action pop-up menu, and then choose "Revert changes."

Add a Permission Entry

To add new permissions entry for a user or group, click the Add (+) button in the bottom-left corner of the Get Info window. A dialog appears, allowing you to search for and select a user or group. Alternatively, you can create a new Sharing user account by clicking the New Person button or selecting a contact from your Address Book. Creating a new Sharing account requires that you also enter a new password for the account.

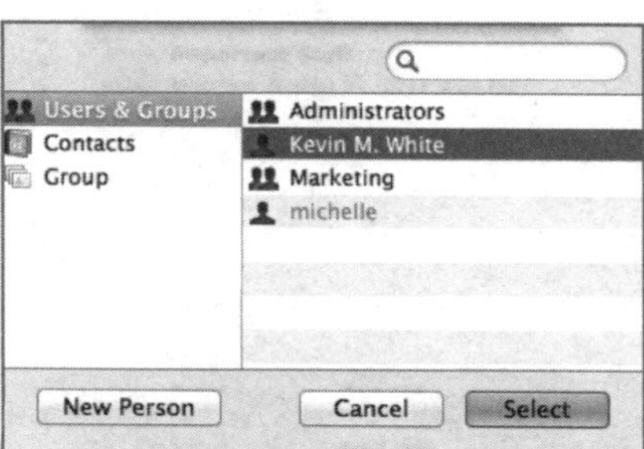

MORE INFO ▸ Details about creating Sharing user accounts and how to create additional groups are covered in Lesson 6, "User Accounts."

Delete a Permissions Entry

To delete a user or group permissions entry, select the account from the permissions list and click the Delete (–) button in the lower-left corner of the Get Info window. The Finder Get Info window doesn't allow you to delete or change the original owner or delete the Everyone privilege of an item. You can use this window to seemingly delete all group privileges, but this isn't truly deleting the group privilege. Instead, it's simply removing all the privileges for the item's original group.

Change Ownership

Even though ACLs allows you to define multiple user permissions for an item, only the user closest to the bottom in the permissions list is the owner of the item. Again, an item's owner is allowed to change the privileges of an item even if they are not an administrative user. However, only administrative users can change both the ownership and privileges of an item.

To assign a new owner using the Finder Get Info window you must first add that user as an additional permissions entry. Once the user is added, select them from the permissions list and then choose the "Make 'user name' the owner" option from the Action pop-up menu.

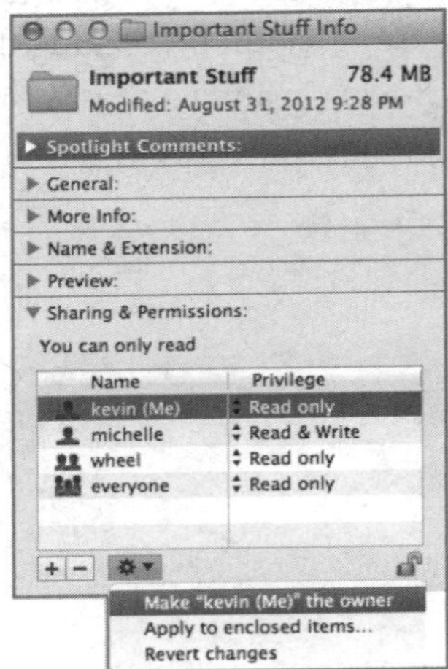

Modify a Permissions Entry

To assign different permissions to an entry, simply click any privilege, and then choose another access option for that user or group from the pop-up menu that appears.

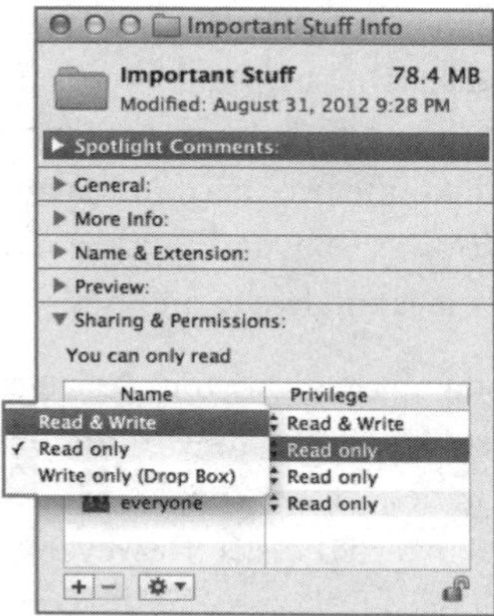

Propagate Folder Permissions

If you are changing the permissions of a folder, by default the Finder does not change the permissions of any items inside the folder. In many cases, you may want to apply the same permissions to the items inside the folder. This task is sometimes known as "propagating permissions." You can accomplish this quickly by choosing the "Apply to enclosed items" option from the Action pop-up menu.

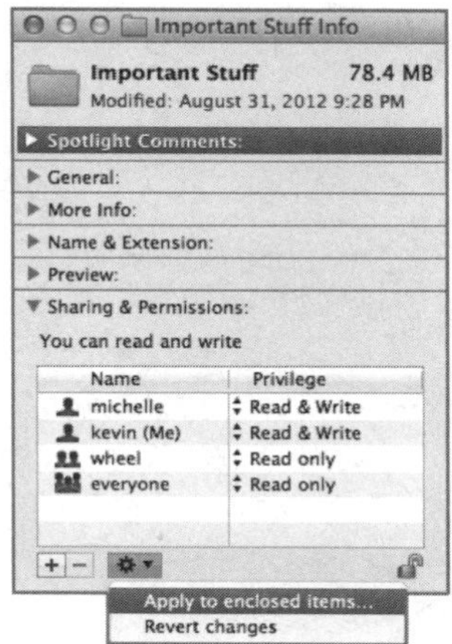

NOTE ▶ Even if you are the owner of a folder, applying permissions to the enclosed folder items may require administrator authentication.

NOTE ▶ Applying permissions to the enclosed folder items applies all permissions settings to all enclosed items, not just the changes you recently made. Further, these changes cannot be easily reverted. The exception to this is that any locked items inside the folder remain in their original state.

Permissions for Nonsystem Volumes

Portable external disk and flash drives are useful tools for transferring files and folders from one computer to another. A downside to this technology, though, is that computers can't properly interpret file ownership because they don't share the same user account database. In other words, most Macs don't have the exact same user accounts, so when a disk is moved from one Mac to another, the file ownership from one Mac is meaningless to another.

Unless you plan to implement a centralized network user database so all your Macs do share the same user account database, ownership on nonsystem volumes, like those found on external disks, will have to be ignored to prevent access issues. This is the default behavior in OS X for all nonsystem volumes on both internal and external disks. However, this approach introduces the security risk that all local users will have full access to the contents of any nonsystem volumes, including other partitions of a system disk. If you find this an unacceptable risk, you can disable the default behavior and force OS X to honor ownership on nonsystem volumes.

To do this in the Finder, select the nonsystem volume for which you want the system to honor the ownership, and then open the Get Info window. In the Sharing & Permissions section, click the small lock icon in the lower-right corner and authenticate as an administrative user to unlock the Sharing & Permissions section. Finally, deselect the "Ignore ownership on this volume" checkbox.

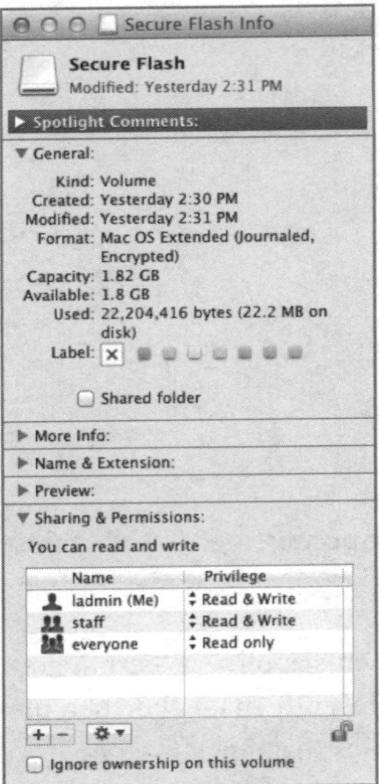

Exercise 12.1
Create Items with Default Permissions

Prerequisites

- You must have created the Local Admin (Exercise 3.1 or 3.2), Chris Johnson (Exercise 6.1), and Mayta Mishtuk (Exercise 7.1) accounts.

A thorough understanding of ownership and permissions is essential to supporting and troubleshooting OS X. Permissions control the access to files and folders by users and system services such as the printing system. The following exercise gives you a brief introduction to permissions in a user's home folder.

Store Files and Folders in Chris Johnson's Home Folder

To see the effects of the OS X default permissions, you will create some items with which to experiment.

1. If necessary, log in as Chris Johnson.
2. Navigate to your home folder in the Finder by pressing Command-Shift-H.
3. Choose File > New Folder.
4. Name the new folder **Payroll Reports**, and be sure it is located in your home folder, along with the default user folders.

   As you will see shortly, this is not a good place to store confidential documents.
5. Open TextEdit.
6. In the TextEdit opening window, click New Document (near the lower-left corner).
7. In TextEdit, choose File > Save, name the new file **Secret Bonus List** and save it to the desktop. (Note that in a save dialog, you can use the shortcut Command-Shift-D to select the desktop.)

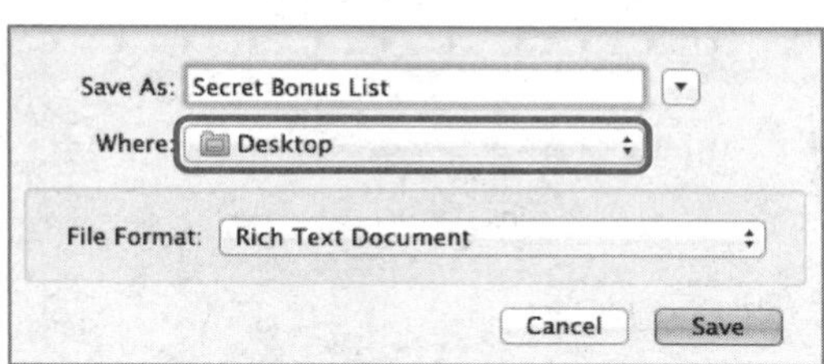

8 Quit TextEdit.

9 Drag the Secret Bonus List.rtf file inside the Payroll Reports folder.

Examine Permissions as Another User

Now that Chris Johnson has created some test files, experiment to see what Mayta Mishtuk can do with them.

1 Use fast user switching to log in as Mayta Mishtuk (password: mayta, or whatever you chose when you created the account).

2 In the Finder, navigate to Chris Johnson's home folder.

Mayta's Finder preferences have not been customized to allow easy access outside her home folder; however, you can reach Chris's home folder by choosing Go > Computer, and then opening the Macintosh HD > Users > chris folder.

3 Click the Desktop folder, and then choose File > Get Info. Expand Sharing & Permissions if necessary.

With the exception of Public, the folders that OS X creates by default in the home folder are protected from access by other users (the No Access permission).

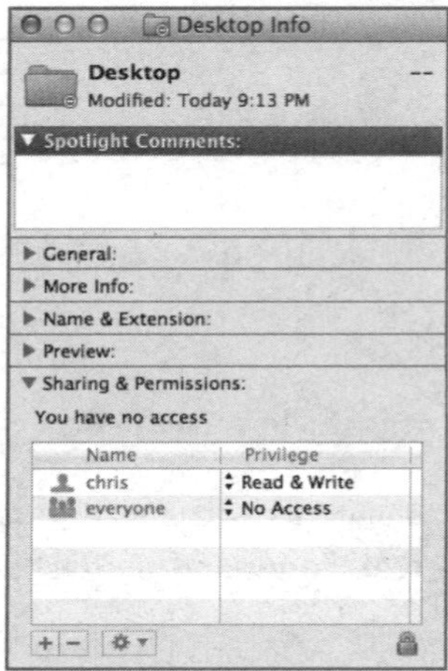

4 Close the Info window.

5 Open the Payroll Reports folder.

The folder opens, and the Secret Bonus List is visible.

This behavior may be contrary to what is expected by users. Be sure to guide your users to store their folders in the right place, based on the type of access they want to allow for other users. While others cannot add or remove items stored in the Payroll Reports folder, they can open and read the contents. You can see the permissions explicitly when you select the folder, and choose File > Get Info.

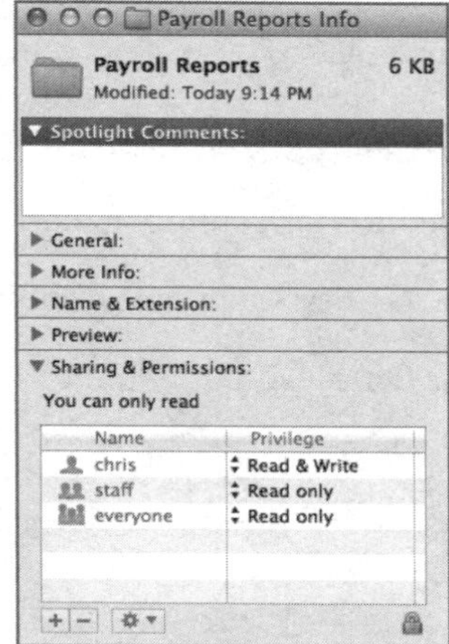

6 Open the Secret Bonus List file.

Since the file is readable by everyone but only writable by its owner, Chris Johnson, TextEdit shows that it is locked.

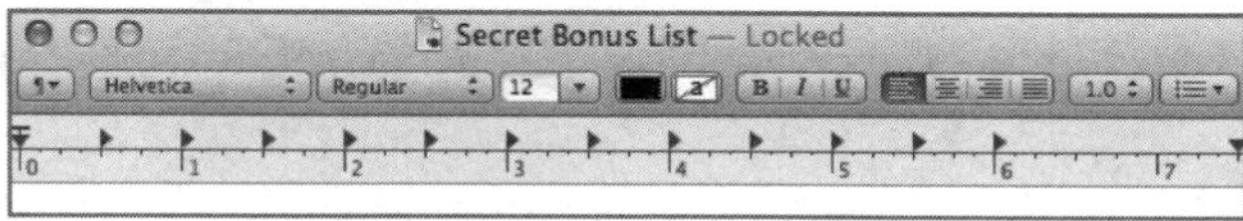

7 Try to enter some text into the file.

TextEdit asks if you would like to create a duplicate, so that you can save your changes.

8 Click Duplicate.

A duplicate document named Untitled (Secret Bonus List copy) opens and allows you to enter text.

9 Save the duplicate document to your desktop.

10 Quit TextEdit

11 In the Finder, navigate back to Chris's home folder and open Chris's Public folder.

12 Try to open Chris's Drop Box folder.

The default permissions do not allow you to open another user's Drop Box folder.

13 Try to copy the Secret Bonus List copy from your desktop to Chris Johnson's Drop Box.

The Finder warns you that you will not be able to see the items you put into the Drop Box.

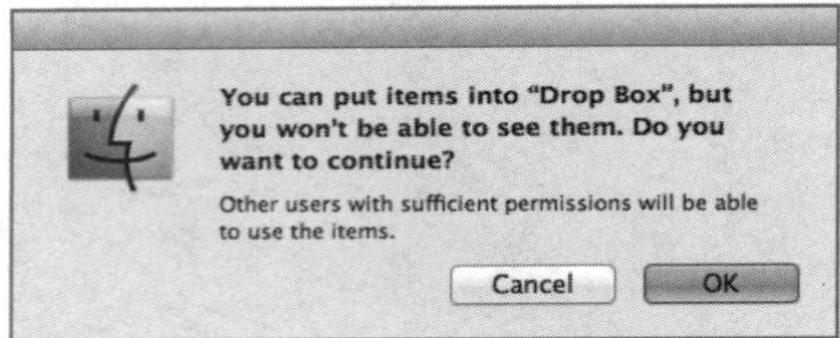

14 Click OK.

Proceed to Exercise 12.2 to see how to adjust the permissions on the Payroll Reports folder.

Exercise 12.2
Test Permissions Changes

Prerequisites

- You must have performed Exercise 12.1.

Chris Johnson will now change the permissions on the Payroll Reports folder, and test the results from Mayta Mishtuk's account.

Change Permissions as Chris Johnson

1. Use fast user switching to switch back to Chris Johnson's account.
2. Select the Payroll Reports folder that resides in Chris's home folder, and then choose File > Get Info. Open Sharing & Permissions if necessary.
3. If necessary, expand Sharing & Permissions. Click the small lock in the Info window, and then authenticate as Local Admin.
4. Select the group (Staff), and click the Delete (–) button below the permissions list.
5. Change the Privilege level for everyone to No Access.

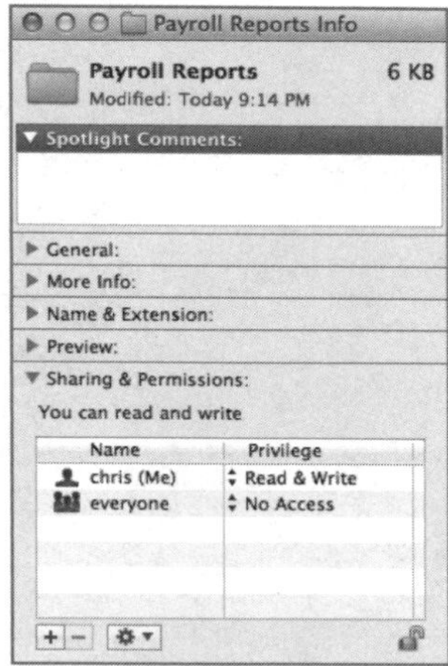

6. Close the Info window.

Test the New Permissions as Mayta Mishtuk

1. Use fast user switching to switch back to Mayta's account.
2. Try to open the Payroll Reports folder.

   This time you cannot open the folder, because the new permissions do not grant you read access.

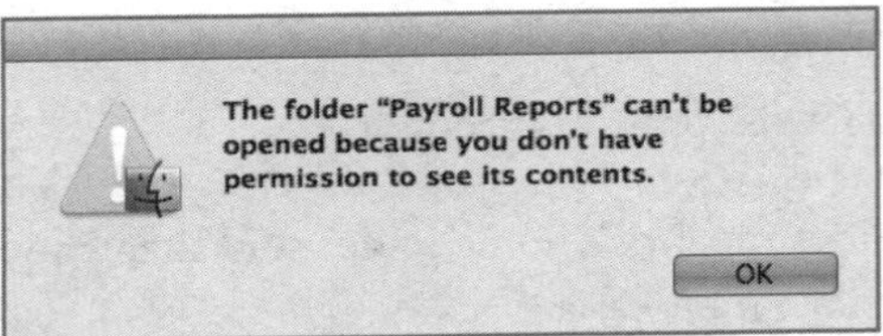

The default permissions did not protect the Payroll Reports folder as Chris intended, but by changing the permissions the folder is now protected from access by other users.

3 Log out of Mayta's account.

4 At the login window, switch to Chris Johnson.

5 Drag the Payroll Reports folder file to the Trash.

Lesson **13**

File System Troubleshooting

Because the operating system requires a functional file system, the software that drives the file system is very reliable. In fact, most file system failures are due to bad hardware or media. It doesn't matter how good the software is, though; if the hardware is no longer reading or writing bits, it's pretty much useless to the file system.

If, during troubleshooting, you determine that catastrophic hardware failure is the problem, there really isn't anything you can do from a software perspective to repair the device. Only a data recovery service, such as DriveSavers, might have a chance at recovering your data.

GOALS

- Examine file system elements
- Troubleshoot and repair partition and volume issues
- Troubleshoot and repair file system permission issues

MORE INFO ▸ When storage hardware suffers from catastrophic failure, DriveSavers is the most popular hard disk recovery service for Macs. You can find out more about its product at www.drivesaversdatarecovery.com.

Conversely, if you're experiencing file system issues but the storage hardware still appears to function, you may be experiencing partial hardware failure or file system corruption. In these cases, you can try some steps using the built-in utilities in OS X to repair the volumes or at least recover data. This lesson focuses on inspecting, verifying, and potentially repairing file system elements.

Reference 13.1
File System Inspection

Before attempting any fixes, you should become fully familiar with the file system configuration you're dealing with. The availability and status of storage hardware in the Disk Utility and System Information applications will help determine if you are indeed experiencing hardware failure.

Examine Storage via Disk Utility

The /Applications/Utilities/Disk Utility application is your main tool for gathering file system information. When you open Disk Utility, it scans the file system for all attached devices and volumes. To gather detailed information about a specific disk or volume in Disk Utility, simply select the item from the column on the left and then click the Info button in the toolbar. Remember, the disk's name is its size and manufacturer information, whereas a disk's volumes appear directly below the disk name in the list.

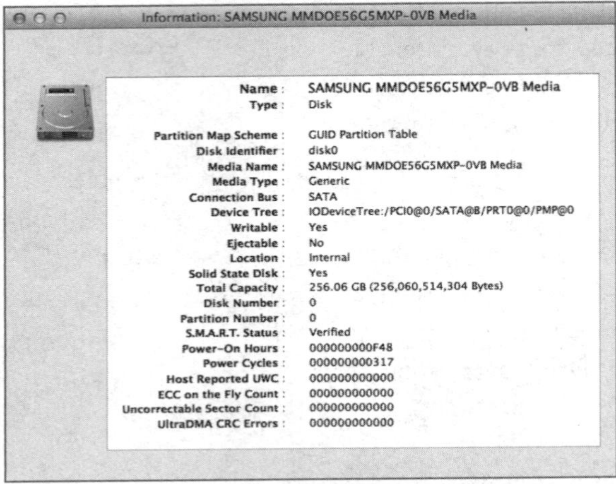

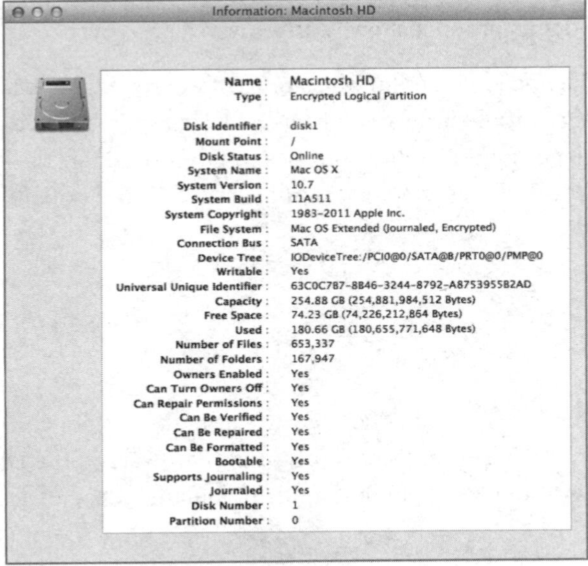

The information gathered from these dialogs reveals a great deal about the status of a disk or volume. Of most importance for determining hardware failure is a disk's S.M.A.R.T. (Self-Monitoring, Analysis, and Reporting Technology) status. A disk that features S.M.A.R.T. technology can automatically determine if the disk is suffering from some sort of internal hardware failure.

Examine Storage via System Information

If a connected disk doesn't even appear in the Disk Utility list, it is possible that the disk has suffered a catastrophic failure. Double-check the disk's status using /Applications/Utilities/System Information to verify that the disk is unreachable. When you open System Information, the disk's information should appear when you select the bus that the disk is connected to, such as Serial-ATA or FireWire.

If a disk does not appear in System Information either, it is not available to the Mac in its current state. At this point you should focus your efforts on troubleshooting the disk hardware. This includes simple fixes, such as looking for loose connections or replacing bad cables, as well as more complex fixes, such as having to replace bad hardware such as the disk enclosure.

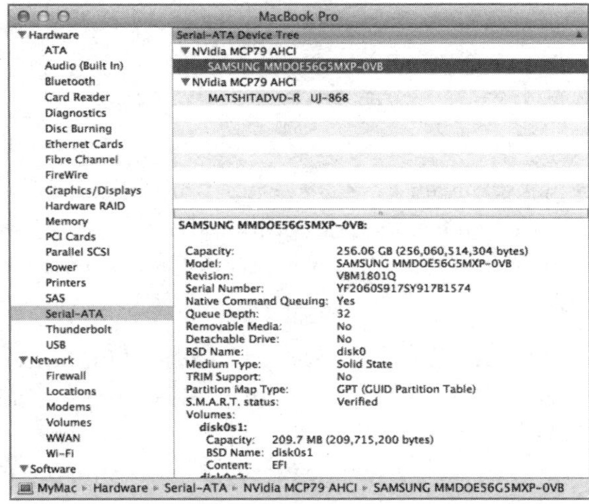

Reference 13.2
Troubleshoot Partitions and Volumes

Disk Utility can be used to examine and attempt to repair a partition scheme or volume directory structure. The partition scheme is used to define the space where volumes exist.

The volume directory structure is used by the file system to catalog where files and folders exist on the disk. To access data on the disk, the file system must first check with the partition scheme and volume directory structure in order to locate the appropriate bits on the disk that make up the requested file. Obviously, any damage to this information can lead to serious problems, including data loss.

Before any disk is mounted, the Mac will automatically perform a quick consistency check to verify the disk's partition scheme and volume directory structure. The system will also quickly scan the startup disk during the startup process. However, if the system is unable to mount a disk or its volumes, or you are experiencing issues accessing a disk's content, you can use Disk Utility to verify and repair the partition scheme or volume directory structures.

> **NOTE ►** If you're attempting to repair the system disk, first start up from OS X Recovery by holding Command-R at startup, and then choose Disk Utility from the OS X Utilities window. If the default OS X Recovery system doesn't work, you can use any of the alternative methods detailed in Lesson 4, "OS X Recovery."

Disk Utility Verify and Repair

To use the verify and repair features in Disk Utility, first double-check that the disk you want to verify or repair is attached to the computer, and then open /Applications/Utilities/Disk Utility. Select the disk or volume you want to verify or repair from the column on the left, and then click the First Aid tab.

By selecting a disk, you are indicating that you want to verify or repair the selected disk's partition scheme. However, by selecting a volume, you are indicating that you want to verify or repair the selected volume's directory structure. As a best practice, you should verify or repair all components of a single disk.

First verify the selected item by clicking the Verify Disk button. The verification process may take a few minutes to complete. During this time Disk Utility shows a progress indicator and log entries in the history area. Click the "Show details" checkbox to view more detail in the history log. You can stop the process at any time by clicking the Stop button.

If no problems are found, an entry with green text appears in the history log. If problems are uncovered, they appear in bright red text. If the disk has problems, and you haven't already started the repair process, do so now. The system continues to run the repair process until no more problems are found. This may take a while because the system may run through the repair process several times.

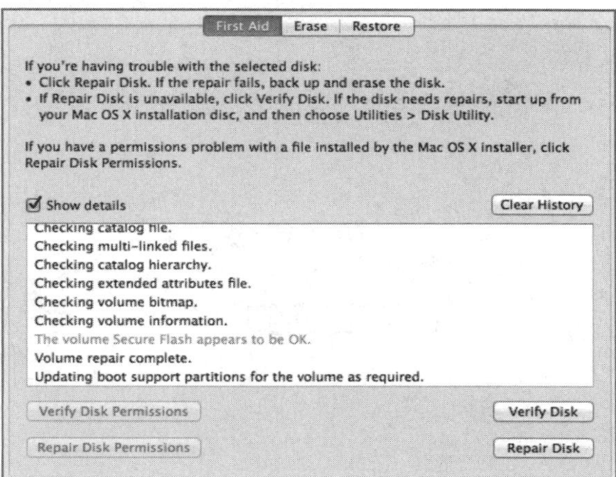

Target Disk Mode

Mac hardware has a unique ability to share its internal disks via a feature called target disk mode. Basically, when target disk mode is engaged, instead of starting up normally from the system disk, the Mac will bridge any internal disks to the FireWire or Thunderbolt ports.

Because target disk mode is a function built into the Mac computer's hardware, even if the installed operating system volume is corrupted, you can still use this feature. An administrative user can enable target disk mode on a currently running Mac by clicking the Target Disk Mode button in the Startup Disk preferences. Alternatively, you can engage target disk mode during system startup by holding down the T key while you turn on the Mac.

NOTE ▸ Certain forms of hardware failure can prevent a Mac from entering target disk mode. If you suspect this is the case, try using Apple Hardware Test as covered in Lesson 30, "System Troubleshooting."

NOTE ▸ Target disk mode is not supported on any Mac that lacks FireWire or Thunderbolt ports or that uses third-party storage interfaces like those found on PCI Express expansion cards.

NOTE ▸ Target disk mode cannot be engaged during system startup when using a Bluetooth wireless keyboard.

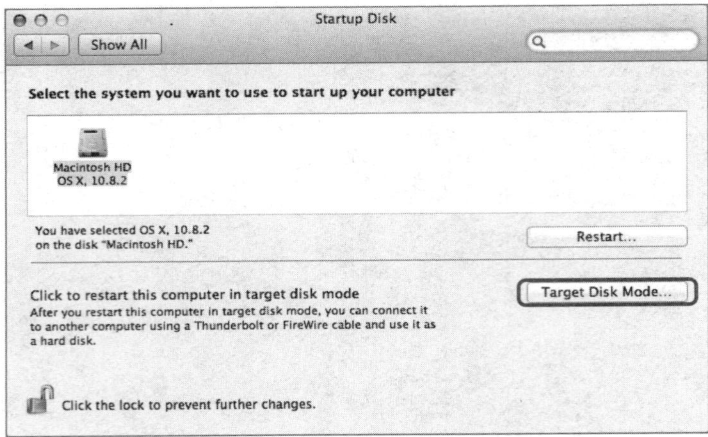

Once target disk mode is engaged, large FireWire and/or Thunderbolt symbols appear on the screen, and then you can simply plug the targeted Mac into another fully functioning Mac via a FireWire or Thunderbolt cable. The targeted Mac computer's internal volumes will mount normally on the other Mac as if you had plugged in a normal external disk. At this point, you can do anything to the targeted Mac computer's internal disk that you could do to any local disk, including installations, repairs, and data migration.

Recovering Data from a Nonstarting System

If you are still stuck with a Mac that refuses to fully start up from its internal system disk, you might be able to recover important data off the disk as long as it's functional. You can use the Mac computer's built-in target disk mode to easily access the internal system disk and recover important data from another fully functional Mac.

> **NOTE ►** If your Mac doesn't support, or is unable to engage, target disk mode, your best bet is to visit an Apple Authorized Service Provider. An alternate solution would be to remove the disk from the troubled computer and attach it to another fully functional Mac.

First, turn on or restart the troublesome Mac while holding down the T key to engage target disk mode, and connect the computer to another fully functioning Mac using a standard FireWire or Thunderbolt cable. If the targeted Mac computer's volume appears in the Finder, first attempt to repair the volume using Disk Utility, as detailed previously in this lesson.

Once repairs have been completed, you have a variety of data recovery options:

- Use the Finder to manually copy data from the targeted Mac to storage attached to the functioning Mac.

- Use Disk Utility on the functioning Mac to create a disk image archive of the targeted Mac computer's system volume. Creating disk images is covered in Lesson 17, "File Archives."
- Migrate the user's data to the other system either manually or using Migration Assistant. Migrating user data is detailed in Lesson 7, "User Home Folders."
- After you have migrated the data, use Disk Utility to reformat the targeted Mac computer's disk, and then attempt to reinstall the operating system. Lesson 2, "Install OS X Mountain Lion," covers this topic in greater detail.

Depending on the amount of corruption present on the targeted Mac computer's system disk, you may not be able to use Disk Utility or the Migration Assistant. The disk may simply be too corrupted to recover all that data. In this case, you will have to resort to manually copying data.

In general, the items most important to users are stored in their home folder, so you should start there. This can be a time-consuming process; as the Finder discovers damaged files, you will have to manually restart the copy process and omit the damaged files.

TIP Use the ample spare time between manual file copies to remind the Mac computer's owner (or yourself) that you wouldn't have to labor over a broken disk if there was a good backup! Lesson 18, "Time Machine," covers this topic in greater detail.

TIP Several third-party disk recovery utilities are available for OS X. This text doesn't recommend one over another—contact an Apple Authorized Service Provider for recommendations.

Reference 13.3
Troubleshoot File System Permissions

Permissions issues can be caused by a variety of situations. Many are due to user error, but others can be the result of an unintentional failure elsewhere in the system. For instance, some software installers may improperly change permissions during the installation process. You may also experience permissions issues after restarting from a power loss or system freeze.

System and application errors, such as applications that will not open or an inability to empty the Trash, may occur due to incorrect permissions. Many of these permissions issues can be resolved by utilities that are part of OS X. If you are having trouble accessing an application, attempt to resolve the issue using the Disk Utility Repair Disk Permissions feature. Also, if you are experiencing problems trying to access home folders, you can use the Reset Password utility in OS X Recovery to reset home folder permissions. The use of these two utilities for resolving permissions issues is covered later in this section.

Most general permissions issues are revealed in obvious ways. A user attempting to access a file or folder is immediately stopped and presented with a dialog stating that he doesn't have the appropriate permissions. In this case, a permissions change on the item, or the folder it's inside, is usually all that's needed to resolve the issue. If you are going to attempt to repair the item's permissions manually, you should be familiar with the methods for managing permissions previously outlined in this lesson.

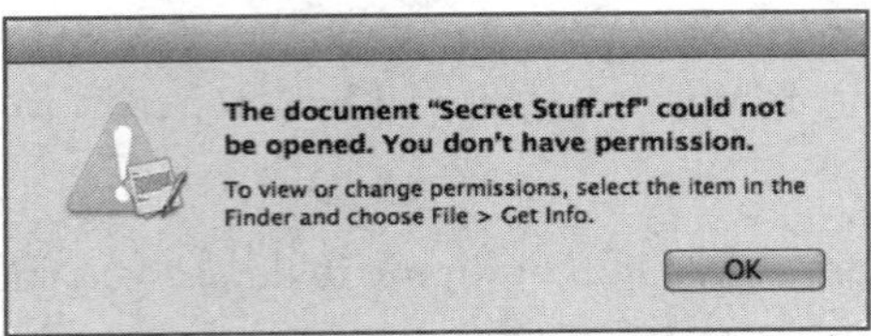

MORE INFO ▸ For further guidance on general permissions troubleshooting, you can also refer to Apple Knowledge Base document HT2963, "Troubleshooting permissions issues in Mac OS X."

Disk Utility Repair Permissions

One of the most common troubleshooting techniques for OS X is to use the Disk Utility Repair Disk Permissions feature. Many novice Mac administrators use this technique every time they encounter any problem.

The reality, however, is that this process fixes only file permissions issues specific to certain installed Apple software. Further, this process doesn't touch any incorrect permission settings on personal or user data. In other words, this process, though a good starting point for addressing system and application issues, doesn't fix every incorrect permissions issue on a problematic Mac.

MORE INFO ▸ For more information, you can also reference Apple Knowledge Base document HT1452, "About Disk Utility's Repair Disk Permissions feature."

The upside is that the repair permissions process is an easy troubleshooting step that could resolve many permissions issues. Keep in mind that many default folders were also installed as part of the operating system. Thus, the repair permissions process not only repairs system items but also important folders like /Applications and /Library.

To verify or repair disk permissions, open Disk Utility on a currently running Mac, or on a Mac started up from OS X Recovery. In Disk Utility select a volume containing an OS X system you want to repair from the column on the left, and then click the First Aid tab. Click the Verify Disk Permissions button to view a log of any potential problems, or click the Repair Disk Permissions button to view and fix any permission problems.

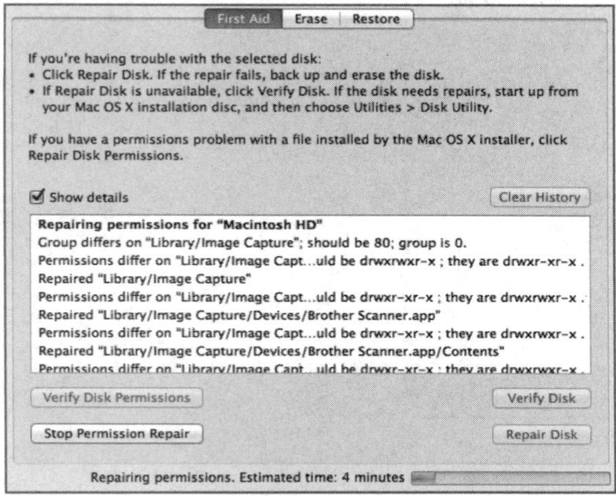

Reset Home Folder Permissions

If a user's home folder becomes inaccessible due to improper permissions, you can attempt to fix the issue by manually adjusting the permissions yourself, or you can try the Reset Password application found in OS X Recovery.

> **TIP** You can, obviously, also use the Reset Password utility to change a user's lost password.

This utility was primarily designed to reset user passwords; nonetheless, this tool also has the ability to reset a user's home folder permissions and ACLs. Keep in mind that this process resets all home folder permissions, including intentionally changed permissions that may have benefited the user.

Again, the Reset Password application is only available from an OS X Recovery system. Once running from OS X Recovery, you must open the Terminal application (via the Utilities menu), type `resetpassword`, and press Return. Once Reset Password opens, simply select the system volume and the user account you want to reset and click Reset. Note that you do not have to enter a new user password.

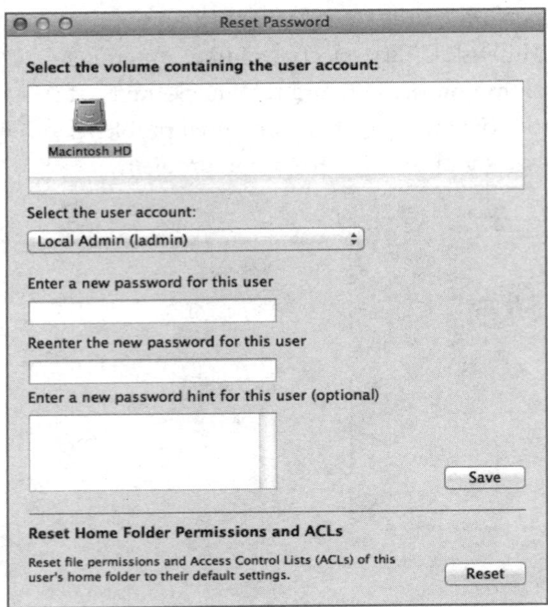

Exercise 13.1
Examine Local Storage

Prerequisites

- You must have created the Chris Johnson account (Exercise 6.1).

OS X provides multiple ways to gather information about disks. In this exercise, you will use System Information and Disk Utility to gather certain information about your computer's disk.

View Disk Information with System Information

System Information provides information about devices that are connected to your computer. In this exercise, you will view disk information with System Information.

1 If necessary, log in as Chris Johnson.

2 Choose Apple menu > About This Mac and then click the More Info button.

The System Information window opens with the Hardware Overview displayed.

3 In the System Information toolbar, click the Storage tab.

System Information displays a summary of the storage devices and volumes on your computer.

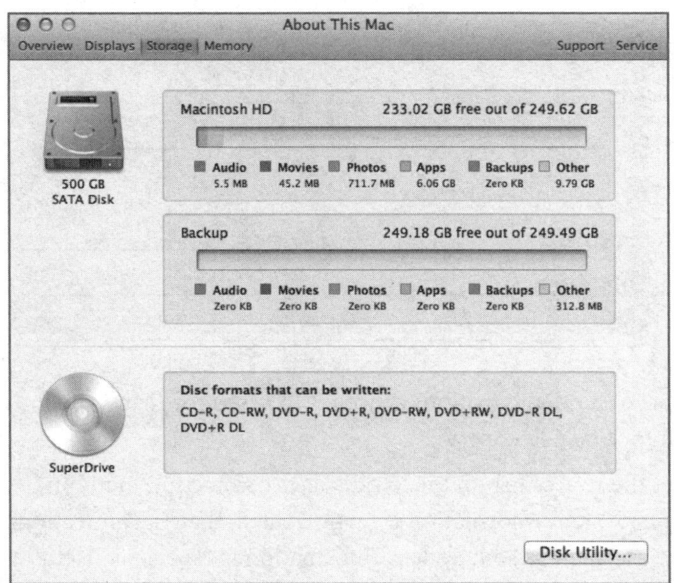

4 Choose File > Show System Report.

System Information displays a more detailed report of the hardware, network, and software configuration of your computer.

5 On the left click Serial-ATA to display internal disks connected to your computer.

NOTE ▶ If you are using a first-generation MacBook Air, select ATA. These computers use an ATA hard disk instead of a Serial ATA hard disk.

6 If necessary, select your computer's internal disk and make a note of the following information:

NOTE ▶ If your startup disk is encrypted with FileVault 2 (or you have not restarted it since turning off FileVault 2), some information will not be available here. Specifically, your startup disk will appear with a generic identifier (like disk0s2) instead of a name, and most of its other properties will not be listed.

Disk Device

- Partition Map Type: ____________________

Volume Macintosh HD

- File System (Volume Format): ____________________
- Capacity (Volume Size): ____________________
- Available (Free Space): ____________________

Volume Backup

- File System (Volume Format): ____________________
- Capacity (Volume Size): ____________________
- Available (Free Space): ____________________

You may also see a couple of hidden partitions as well: EFI (used for firmware updates) and Recovery HD (used for OS X Recovery).

The Hardware section of the source list on the left displays connection methods. The information shown in System Information is bus-oriented, that is, connection-oriented. As you will see in a later lesson, System Information is especially useful when you are troubleshooting a suspected connection issue.

7 Quit System Information.

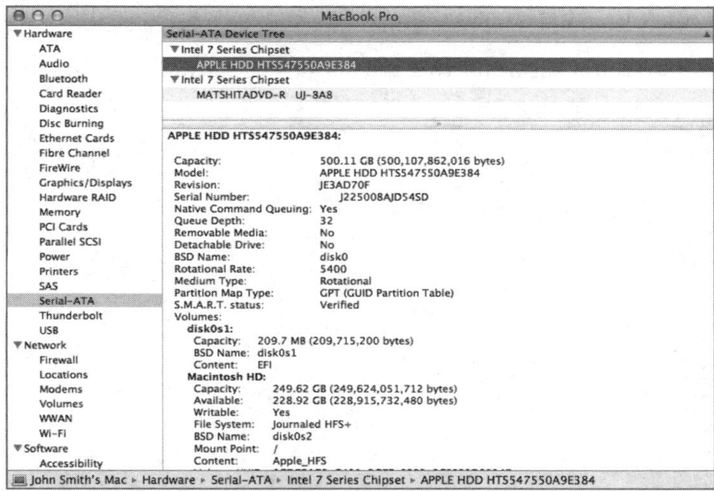

View Disk Information with Disk Utility

Disk Utility is storage device–oriented, in that it provides both information on disks connected to your computer and management tools for those disks. In this exercise, you will gather information about your computer's disk using Disk Utility.

1 Open Disk Utility.

2 Click the entry for your internal disk device (generally the top item) in the source list on the left.

NOTE ► As before, if you are using FileVault, the display will be different. The disk device will not be shown; instead, you will see a Logical Volume Group with the same name as your startup volume, with the volumes listed under it. Since you cannot see the device, skip ahead to step 5.

3 In the toolbar, click the Info button to view information about your hard disk.

Note that this window does not show information about space available or space used.

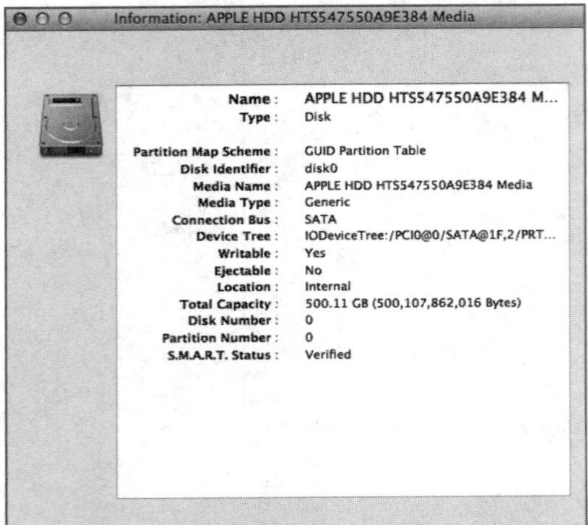

Depending on your disk, you may also see detailed S.M.A.R.T. statistics listed.

4 Close this information window.

5 In the source list, click the indented entry for your startup volume (generally Macintosh HD), and then click the Info button.

This window displays information for the volume, including capacity, free space, and used space.

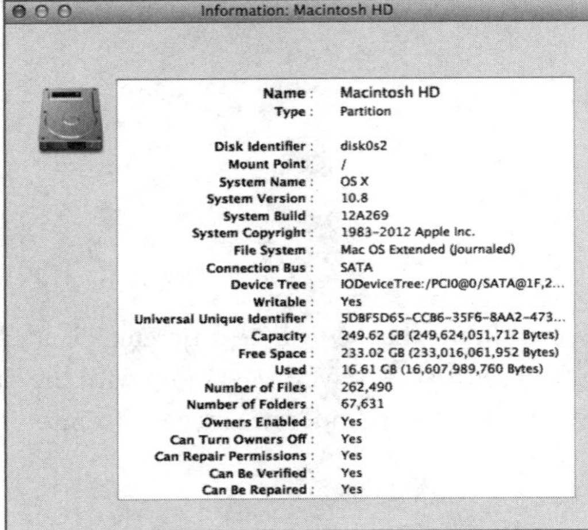

6 Get info on the Backup volume as well, and then use these three windows in Disk Utility to make a note of the following information:

NOTE ▶ Again, if you are using FileVault 2, some information will not be available. While System Information showed full disk-level information but left out information on the encrypted volume, Disk Utility shows full volume information but not disk-level information.

Disk Device

- Partition Map Scheme: ______________________________

Volume Macintosh HD

- File System (Volume Format): ______________________________
- Capacity (Volume Size): ______________________________
- Available (Free Space): ______________________________

Volume Backup

- File System (Volume Format): ______________________________
- Capacity (Volume Size): ______________________________
- Available (Free Space): ______________________________

The details for your computer are likely to be different from what you see pictured. Disk Utility refers to the Partition Map Scheme, whereas System Information refers to the Partition Map Type. These are interchangeable terms.

7 If you are not going to perform the next exercise, quit Disk Utility.

Exercise 13.2
Repair Partitions and Volumes in Target Disk Mode

Prerequisites

- You must have created the Mayta Mishtuk account (Exercise 7.1).
- You need another computer running OS X Mountain Lion.
- Both computers must have FireWire or Thunderbolt interfaces, and you need the appropriate cable to connect them.

In this exercise, you will start your computer in target disk mode, and use another computer to check its file structure, system file permissions, and examine its files directly in the Finder. These are techniques that could be used to repair and/or recover files from a computer that could not start up normally due to file system damage.

> **NOTE ▶** This exercise and Exercise 13.3 cover many of the same operations, but using different modes to run the disk repair tools. You do not need to perform both. Generally, if you have access to another Mac running Mountain Lion, and both Macs have FireWire or Thunderbolt (and you have the appropriate cable), Exercise 13.2 is the preferred exercise. If you are participating in a classroom setting, you can perform this exercise with a partner, using one of your computers as the host and the other as the target.

Start Your "Target" Computer in Target Disk Mode

Choose one of your computers to act as a "host" (the computer that will run the disk repair tools), and one to act as a "target" (the computer that will have its disk repaired).

1. Shut down the target computer.
2. Hold down the T key on the target computer while you press the power button. Keep holding the T key until you see a FireWire and/or Thunderbolt logo on the screen.
3. When you see the logo on the screen, release the T key.
4. If necessary, log in to the host computer.
5. Connect the two computers with a FireWire or Thunderbolt cable.
6. If the target computer's startup disk is encrypted with FileVault 2, you are prompted for a password to unlock the disk; you can enter the password of any FileVault-enabled account (**ladminpw** or **chris**, or whatever passwords you chose).
7. If a dialog appears asking if you want to use this disk as a Time Machine device, click Don't Use.
8. On the host computer, open Disk Utility.

9 Select your computer's internal disk device, or if you are using FileVault 2 the Logical Volume Group that appears instead.

10 In the toolbar, click Info.

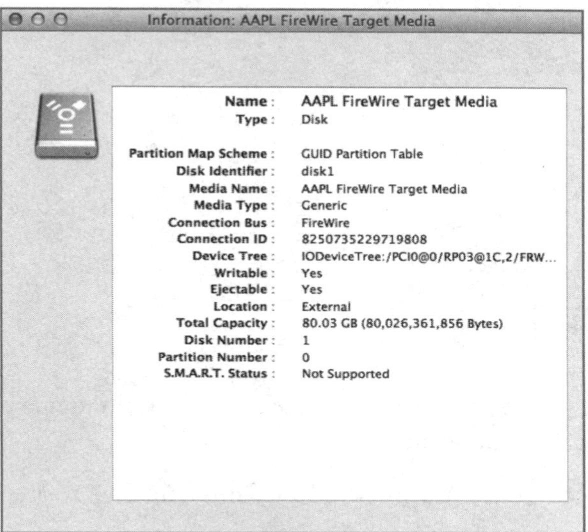

Note that the Connection Bus is listed as FireWire or Thunderbolt. If the target computer is using FileVault 2, the Logical Volume Group is shown instead, which does not list the Connection Bus.

11 Close the Information window.

Repair the Partition Table and Volume

1 If necessary, click the First Aid tab.

2 Click Repair Disk.

Disk Utility checks (and if necessary, repairs) the partition table as well as certain hidden disk contents such as the EFI system partition. If you are using FileVault 2, checking the Logical Volume Group actually checks the volumes as well, so you can skip ahead to the next section of this exercise ("Examine Files Manually in Target Disk Mode").

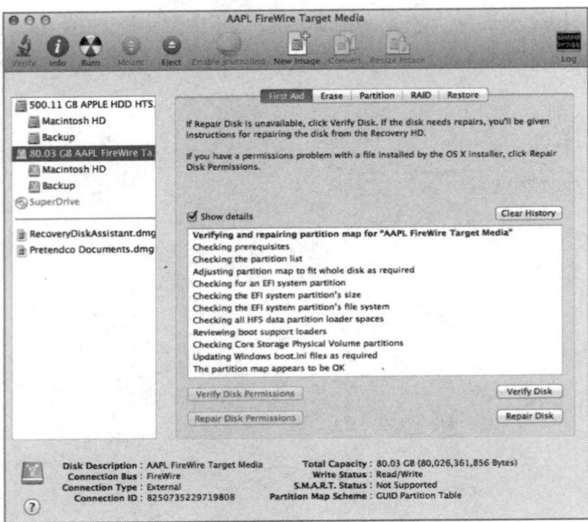

Disk Utility shouldn't find any problems; if it does, use Repair Disk again to make sure that all problems were repaired successfully.

3 Select the entry for the target computer's Macintosh HD volume, and then click Repair Disk again.

This time, Disk Utility checks (and if necessary, repairs) the file structure within the Macintosh HD volume. Since there are a large number of files in the volume, this process may take a few minutes.

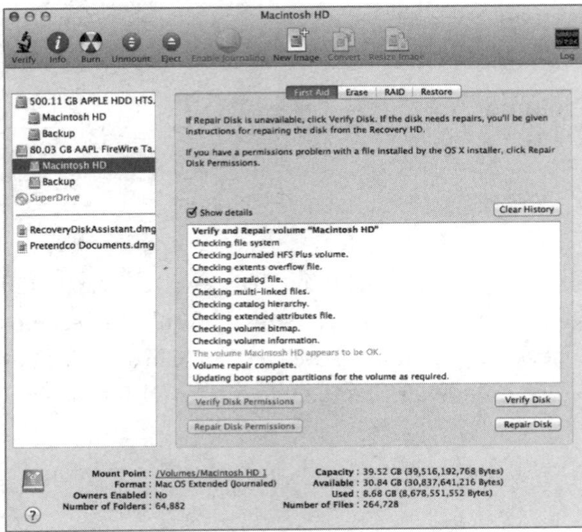

As before, it should not find any problems; if it does, use Repair Disk again to make sure that all problems are repaired successfully. You can also verify and/or repair the Backup volume.

Note that the Verify and Repair Disk Permissions buttons are dimmed, because the volume is external, and your computer is ignoring file ownership on it. You will change this shortly.

4 Select the host computer's startup volume.

The Repair Disk button is dimmed, because you cannot repair a volume that is in use. You can verify it, but even that may not work if the volume is too active.

Examine Files Manually in Target Disk Mode

1 In the host computer's Finder, open the Computer view by pressing Command-Shift-C.

Both computer's volumes appear. Generally, you can distinguish them by the target computer's orange volume icons (and FireWire symbols if appropriate).

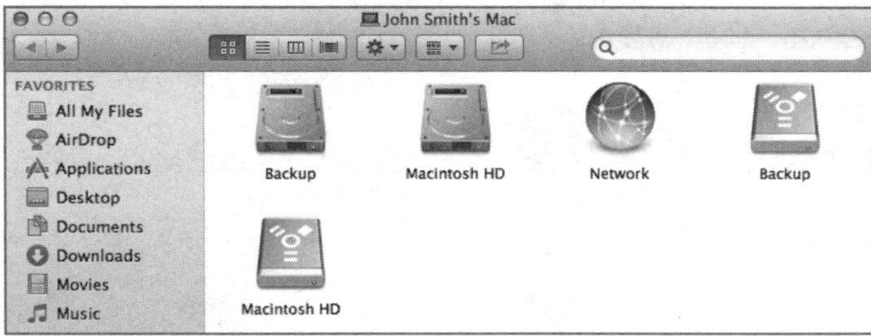

2 Select the target computer's Macintosh HD volume, and choose File > Get Info (Command-I).

The bottom of the Sharing & Permissions section shows that "Ignore ownership on this volume" is enabled. Because the host computer sees this as an external disk, it assumes file ownership and permissions relate to user accounts from some other computer, and it shouldn't attempt to apply them to users on this computer. This was discussed in Reference 12.3.

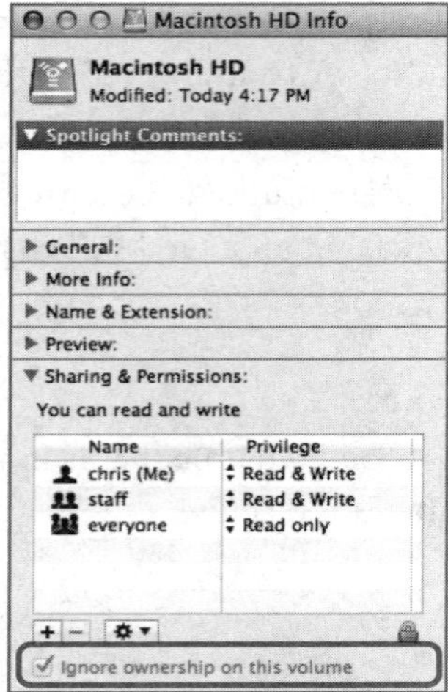

3 Open the target computer's Macintosh HD volume, and then navigate into Users/mayta/Desktop.

Because ownership is being ignored, you can access Mayta's files directly. If necessary, you could recover files from a computer this way even if the computer could not start up normally.

4 In the volume's Info window, click the small lock icon, and authenticate as Local Admin.

5 Deselect the "Ignore ownership on this volume" checkbox.

6 Close the Info window.

Repair System File Permissions

1 Switch back to Disk Utility.

2 Select the entry for the target computer's Macintosh HD volume.

Since ownership is now enabled, the Verify and Repair Disk Permissions buttons are available.

3 Click Repair Disk Permissions.

Disk Utility checks the system files against their installation records, and repairs any discrepancies. Again, since there are a large number of files to check, this process may take a few minutes.

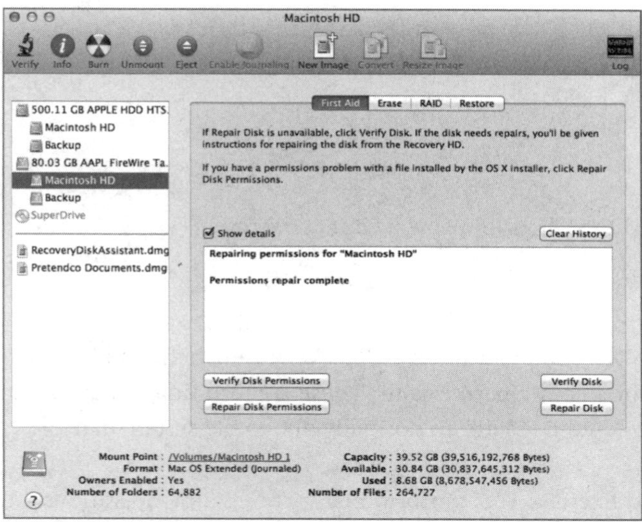

It is normal for a few errors to be listed here; usually they do not represent a real problem, just Disk Utility being picky. See the Apple Knowledge Base document TS1448, "Mac OS X: Disk Utility's Repair Disk Permissions messages that you can safely ignore" for more info.

Note that the Disk Utility permissions repair does not fix user files. If you need to repair user home directories, you need to use the Reset Password utility in OS X Recovery mode (shown in the next exercise).

4 In the Disk Utility toolbar, click the Eject button.

   Note that the Eject button will eject the entire disk (including all volumes on it), while the Unmount button will only operate on the selected volume. There is an exception, however: encrypted volumes are treated separately, so ejecting them does not eject the rest of the disk.

5 If any of the target computer's volumes remain undimmed in the list, select them and click Eject again.

6 Quit Disk Utility.

7 Press and hold the power button to shut down the target computer, and then unplug the cable when it is turned off.

8 If you are not going to perform the next exercise, restart the target computer normally.

Exercise 13.3
Repair Partitions and Volumes in OS X Recovery Mode

▶ Prerequisites

- ▶ You must have created the Chris Johnson account (Exercise 6.1).
- ▶ Your computer must have a local hidden Recovery HD partition.

In this exercise, you will start your computer in OS X Recovery and check its file structure, system file permissions, and home folder permissions. These are techniques that could be used to repair a computer that could not start up normally due to file system damage.

NOTE ▶ This exercise and Exercise 13.2 perform many of the same operations, but using different modes to run the disk repair tools. You do not need to perform both.

Repair the Partition Table and Volume

1. Restart your computer, and then hold down Command-R until the gray Apple appears on the screen.
2. At the Utilities screen, select Disk Utility and click Continue.
3. If your startup volume is encrypted with FileVault 2, it appears dimmed in the disks and volumes list; select it and click the Unlock button in the toolbar, and then enter the password of any FileVault-enabled account (`ladminpw` or `chris`, or whatever passwords you chose).
4. Select your computer's internal disk device, or if you are using FileVault 2 the Logical Volume Group appears instead. In either case, it is generally the top entry in the sidebar.
5. If necessary, click the First Aid tab.
6. Click Repair Disk.

   Disk Utility checks the partition table as well as certain hidden disk contents such as the EFI system partition, and attempts to repair any problems it finds. If you are using FileVault 2, checking the Logical Volume Group actually checks the volumes as well, so you can skip ahead to the "Repair System File Permissions" section of this exercise.

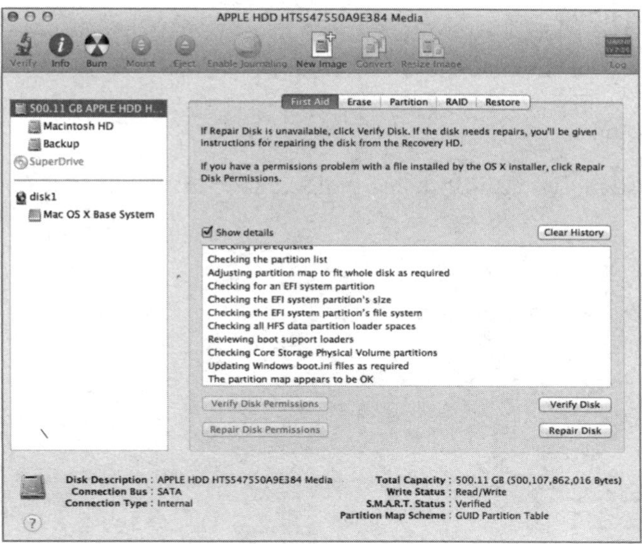

7 Select the entry for the Macintosh HD volume, and then click Repair Disk again.

This time, Disk Utility checks the file structure within the Macintosh HD volume and repairs it if necessary.

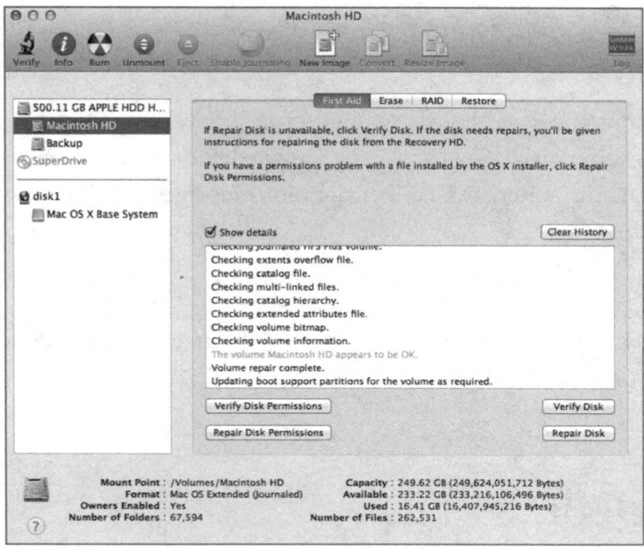

You can also verify and/or repair the Backup volume.

Repair System File Permissions

1 If necessary, select the entry for the Macintosh HD volume.

2 Click Repair Disk Permissions.

Disk Utility checks the system files against their installation records, and repairs any discrepancies.

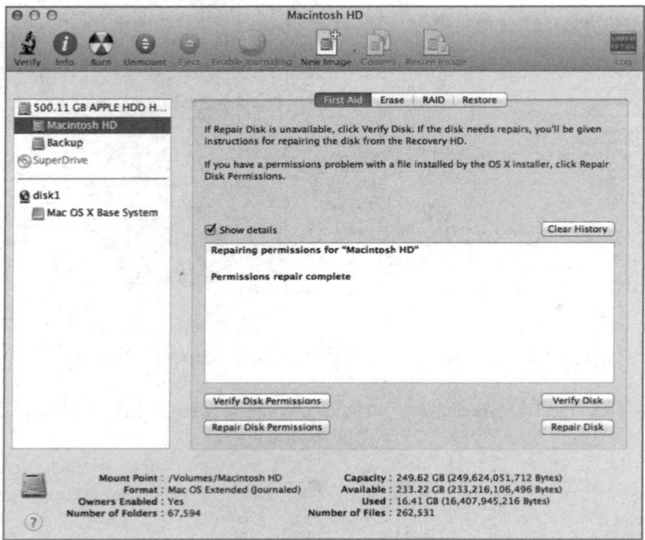

It is normal for a few errors to be listed here; usually they do not represent a real problem, just Disk Utility being picky. See the Apple Knowledge Base document TS1448, "Mac OS X: Disk Utility's Repair Disk Permissions messages that you can safely ignore" for more info.

3 Select the entry for the Backup volume.

The Verify and Repair Disk Permissions buttons are dimmed, since this volume does not have OS X Mountain Lion installed on it.

4 Quit Disk Utility.

Repair Home Folder Permissions

1 From the Utilities menu, choose Terminal.

The Terminal utility provides access to a command-line (text-based) interface in OS X. We do not cover the command-line interface in this book, but it is necessary to reach the reset password utility in OS X Recovery.

2 Type the command **resetpassword**, and press Return.

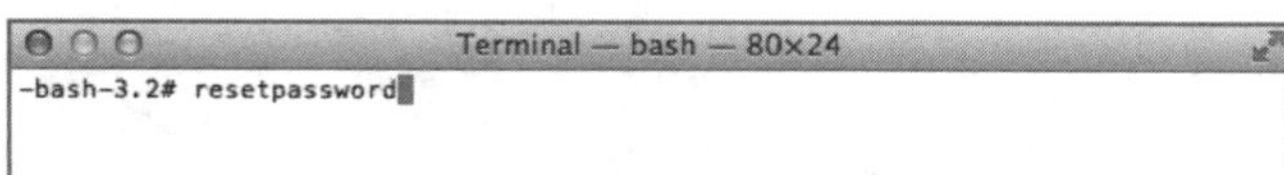

The Reset Password utility opens.

3 Select Macintosh HD in the volume list, and then choose Chris Johnson (chris) from the user account pop-up menu.

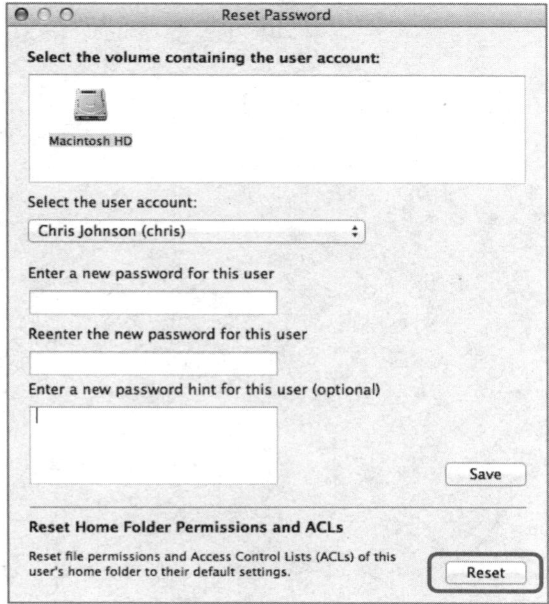

4 Click Reset.

The Reset Password utility checks (and if necessary, repairs) the ownership for Chris Johnson's home folder and its contents.

This tool does not report whether it found any problems.

5 Choose Apple menu > Restart to restart your computer normally.

Data Management

Lesson **14**

Hidden Items and Shortcuts

Apple is known for making complex things appear simple. An excellent example of this is how the Finder displays the OS X file system to the user. By default the Finder hides much of the complexity of OS X from the user, and reveals only four folders at the root (or beginning) level of the system volume. Applications also appear to be single icons, despite containing all the resources necessary for a modern application. Also, many items appear in a more convenient location, but are actually stored elsewhere.

GOALS

- Navigate to hidden files and folders
- Examine packages and bundles
- Manage aliases and links

In this lesson you will explore the file system technologies that assist in either hiding or redirecting items. This includes an exploration of the hidden items in OS X, including bundles and packages. You will also learn how to manage file system aliases and links.

Reference 14.1
Hidden Items

OS X is a fully UNIX-compliant operating system, and as such requires a number of files that the average user will never touch. The root level of the Mac system volume is littered with resources that UNIX processes require and UNIX administrators expect. Apple made the wise choice of configuring the Finder to hide these items from the average user. On a daily basis, the average user—and even most administrative users—does not need to access any of these items from the graphical interface.

Realistically, the only people who even care about these normally hidden resources are going to be using Terminal to do their work anyway. In other words, keeping these system items hidden in the Finder not only provides a tidier work environment but also prevents average users from poking around in places they don't need to go.

As a hybrid of UNIX and Mac OS technologies, OS X uses two methods to hide files and folders. The first is a UNIX tradition: simply using a period at the beginning of the item's name will hide the item in the Finder and while using the default options to list items in the Terminal. The second method is a Mac OS tradition: enable an item's hidden file flag. This method, however, will only hide the item in the Finder.

NOTE ▶ To prevent user confusion, OS X does not let you hide items using the Finder or any of the default applications. Only from the Terminal can a user name items beginning with a period or manage the hidden file flag. Use of the Terminal is beyond the scope of this guide.

Finder Hidden Folder Navigation

Should you want or need to open normally hidden items in the Finder, there are two methods. The first method is a shortcut to the most commonly accessed hidden folder, the user's Library folder. The second involves use of the Go menu in the Finder to open any folder.

The User's Hidden Library Folder

As detailed in Lesson 15, "System Resources," the user's Library folder is full of important resources, but is hidden in the Finder. Fortunately, the Go menu provides a quick shortcut to this oft-visited location. Simply hold the Option key while clicking the Go menu to reveal the Library menu item.

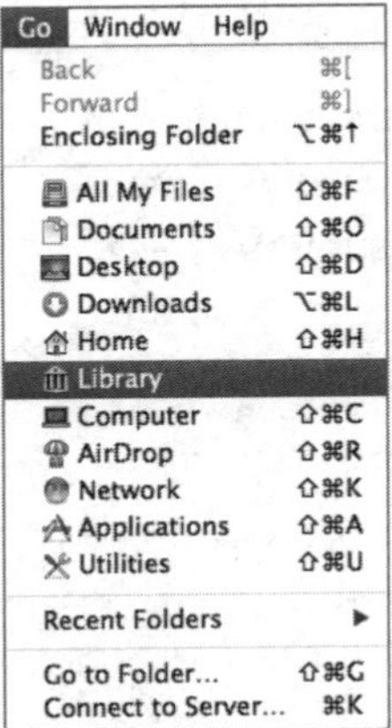

Go to Folder

To reveal any hidden folder in the Finder, choose Go > Go to Folder, or press Command-Shift-G. This reveals a dialog allowing you to enter an absolute path to any folder on the Mac. A good starting place is the /private folder; as this folder contains many common UNIX system resources.

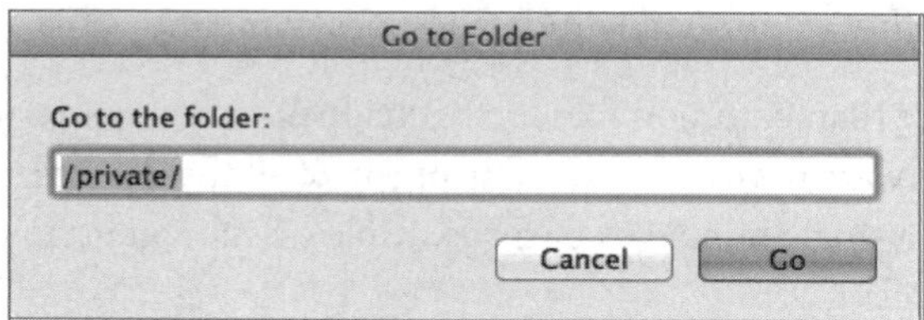

TIP ▶ An incredibly useful shortcut is to use Tab key completion when entering file system paths. Simply press Tab once you have started a path name, and the system attempts to automatically fill in the rest of the name. For example, navigating to the /private folder requires that you only enter "/p" and then press Tab.

Click the Go button once you have entered a path. The Finder reveals the hidden folder in a window. Note the dimmed folder icon representing the normally hidden folder. To save time for when you return to the Go dialog, the previous path you entered is there.

NOTE ▶ Some folders, both visible and invisible, have permissions that do not allow standard or administrative users to view the contents.

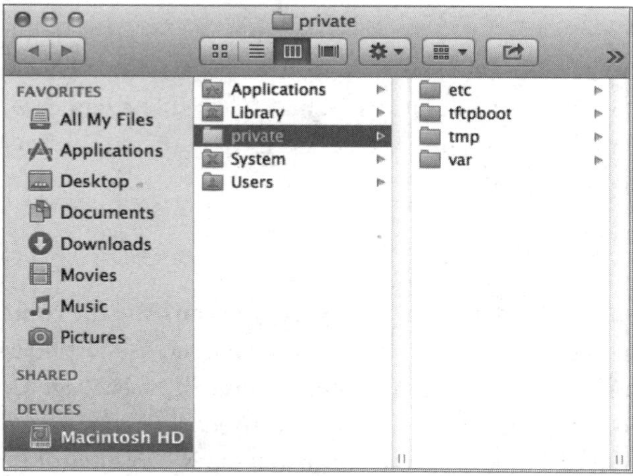

Reference 14.2
Bundles and Packages

Sometimes hiding individual items isn't the most efficient solution for hiding data, especially if you have a lot of related files you need to hide. Conveniently there is already a method for combining files: the common folder. Apple simply modified this existing file system container by adding the capability to optionally hide a folder's content.

Bundles and packages are nothing more than common folders that happen to contain related software and resources. This allows software developers to easily organize all the resources needed for a complicated product into a single bundle or package, while discouraging normal users from interfering with the resources.

Bundles and packages use the same technique of combining resources inside special folders. The difference is that the Finder treats packages as opaque objects that, by default, users cannot navigate into. For example, where a user sees only a single icon in the Finder representing an application, in reality it is a folder potentially filled with thousands of resources.

The word "package" is also used to describe the archive files used by the installer application to install software—that is, installer packages. This is appropriate, though, as users cannot, by default, navigate into the contents of an installer package because the Finder again displays it as a single opaque object. Starting with OS X v10.5, Apple allowed the creation of fully opaque installation packages wherein the entire contents are inside a single file, further preventing users from accidentally revealing installation content.

> **NOTE ▶** Because bundles and packages are really just special folders, these items simply copy over to non–Mac OS Extended volumes as regular folders. The Finder will continue to recognize the items as bundles or packages even when they reside on a third-party volume.

Reveal Package Content

Although the Finder default is to hide the contents of a package, you can view the contents of a package from the Finder. To access a package's contents in the Finder, use secondary (or Control) click on the item you want to explore, and then choose Show Package Contents from the shortcut menu. You may recall this technique is used in Lesson 4, "OS X Recovery," to reveal the installation disk image inside the Install OS X Mountain Lion application.

Nevertheless, be very careful when exploring this content. Modifying the content of a bundle or package can easily leave the item unstable or unusable. If you can't resist the desire to tinker with a bundle or package, always do so from a copy and leave the original safely intact.

MORE INFO ▸ Tools for creating and modifying bundles and packages are available for those who have Mac Dev Center access. You can find out more about the Apple developer programs at https://developer.apple.com.

Package Resources

The anatomy of an installer package is quite simple; it usually contains only a compressed archive of the software to be installed and a few configuration files used by the installer application. Other software bundles and packages, on the other hand, are often much more complex as they contain all the resources necessary for the application or software.

Software bundles or packages often include:

- Executable code for multiple platforms
- Document description files
- Media resources such as images and sounds
- User interface description files
- Text resources
- Resources localized for specific languages
- Private software libraries and frameworks
- Plugins or other software to expand capability

Reference 14.3
File System Shortcuts

Another example of OS X being a hybrid of both UNIX and the classic Mac OS is the multiple methods used for file system pointers or shortcuts. Generally speaking, file system shortcuts are files that reference other files or folders, which allows you to have a single item appear in multiple locations or with multiple names without having to create multiple copies of the item. Both the system and users take advantage of file system shortcuts to access items in more convenient locations without having to duplicate those items.

> **NOTE ▶** Do not confuse the shortcuts found in the Dock or the Finder sidebar with true file system shortcuts. Both the Dock and Finder save their references to original items as part of their configuration files, whereas file system shortcuts appear as individual files that can be located anywhere on a volume.

File System Shortcut Comparison

OS X uses three primary file system shortcut types: aliases, symbolic links, and hard links. For this comparison a 100 MB disk image file named BigFile was created. This file will be referenced using each shortcut type, and you will see the difference illustrated by the Finder Get Info window.

Aliases

Aliases are a holdover from the classic Mac OS but have been updated for OS X duties. Aliases can be created with the Finder but are useless in Terminal. Command-line tools think that aliases are nothing more than data files and do not know how to follow their references back to the original items.

Aliases, however, are more resilient than other shortcut types in that if the original item is replaced or moved, the alias will almost never lose the original item. An example of how aliases are used by the operating system is the Finder Burn Folder feature, which allows you to organize files before you burn them to an optical disc. The Finder populates the burn folder with aliases instead of copies of the original items in order to save space.

The following screenshot shows the Finder Get Info window inspecting an alias pointing to BigFile. Note that the Kind is reported as Alias and the file is smaller than the original, but it's still not exactly small weighing in at roughly 1.2 MB. The extra information in the alias is what allows the system to keep track of the original item if it should ever change locations.

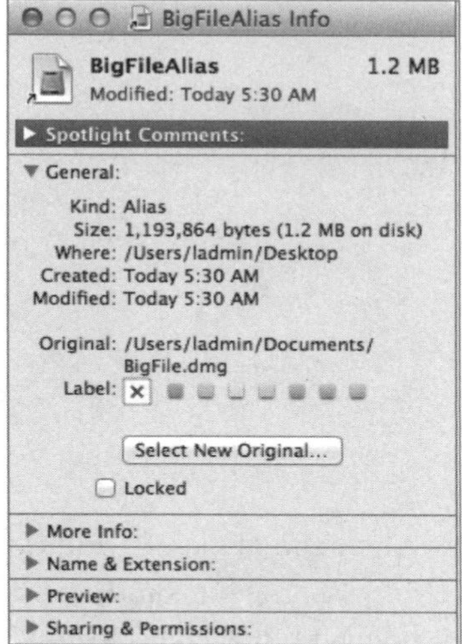

Symbolic Links

These shortcuts are part of the traditional UNIX file system and are simple pointers to the file system path of the original item. Thus, if you move the original item, the symbolic link will be broken. However, replacing the original item works because the path remains the same.

You can only create symbolic links in the Terminal. The Finder cannot create symbolic links, but it can follow them to the original item. An example use of symbolic links in OS X is the way the system layout stores several fundamental UNIX folders in the /private folder but also makes those items available at the root of the file system using symbolic links.

The following screenshot shows the Finder Get Info window inspecting a symbolic link pointing to BigFile. Note that the Kind is also reported as an Alias but the file itself is tiny at only 35 bytes. This illustrates that a symbolic link is merely saving a path to the original item. Also note the lack of a Select New Original button, indicating that the Finder is incapable of repairing a symbolic link.

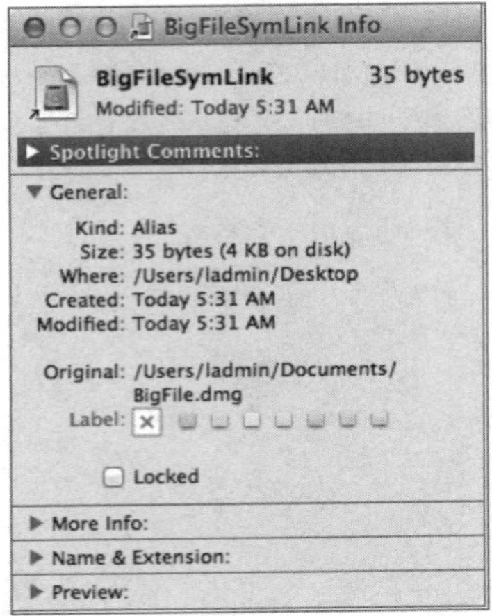

Hard Links

These shortcuts are also part of the traditional UNIX file system and are actual additional references to the original item. Think of a normal file as two parts: the bits on the physical disk that make up the file's actual content, and a name that points to those bits. Technically, every file always uses at least one hard link. Creating an additional hard link is like creating another name that points to the same bits on the physical disk.

As such, removing additional hard links does not delete the original item. Furthermore, deleting the "original" item does not delete the additional hard links. This is because the other hard links still point to the same bits on the disk, which won't be freed until there are no links left to them. This is unlike aliases and symbolic links, where deleting the original item leaves the shortcut pointing at nothing.

You can only create hard links in the Terminal. The Finder cannot create hard links, but it can follow them. An example use of hard links in OS X is for Time Machine backups. Time Machine uses hard links to reference items that have not changed since the previous backup, thus saving a tremendous amount of space. Finally, OS X is unique in its ability to use hard links of both files and folders; again, this is to support Time Machine backups.

The following screenshot shows the Finder Get Info window inspecting a hard link pointing to BigFile. Notice that the hard link is reporting the exact same information as the original item, indicating that they share the same bits on the physical disk.

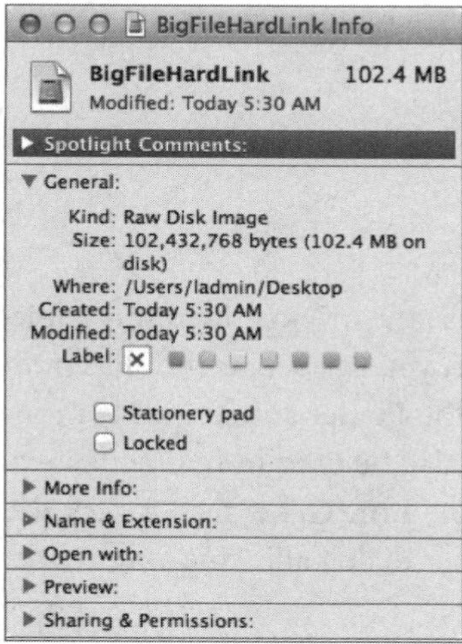

Managing Aliases

To create an alias in the Finder, simply select the item you want to create an alias for, and then choose one of the following methods:

- Choose File > Make Alias.
- Press Command-L.
- In a Finder window, choose Make Alias from the Action (small gear) pop-up menu.
- In the Finder use secondary (or Control) click on the item and then choose Make Alias from the shortcut menu.
- Click and drag the original item while holding down the Option and Command keys to drop the alias in another location. This is the only method that doesn't append the word "alias" to the new alias filename.

Once you have created the alias, you can rename it or move it anywhere you like. As long as the original item remains somewhere on the original volume, even if it's replaced or its name changes, the Finder will be able to locate the alias. An alias file is easy to recognize by the small curved arrow that appears at the lower-left corner of the icon. From the Finder, you can locate the alias's target by Control-clicking the alias and then choosing Show Original from the shortcut menu, or by pressing Command-R.

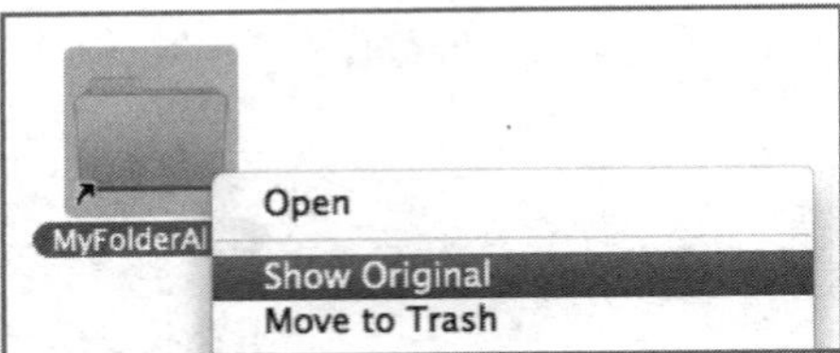

In the rare case that an alias is broken, most likely because the original item was copied to another volume and then deleted off the original volume, you can repair the alias in the Finder. One method is to double-click the broken alias; the Finder automatically prompts you to select a new original. Another option, which can also be used to redirect an existing alias, is to open the Finder Get Info window and then in the General area click the Select New Original button. Both methods open a browser dialog allowing you to select a new original for the alias.

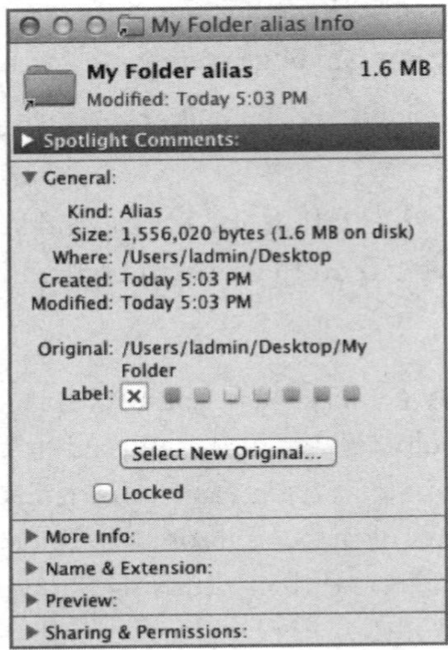

Exercise 14.1
Navigate Hidden Items

Prerequisites

- You must have created the Chris Johnson account (Exercise 6.1).

OS X hides certain portions of its folder structure, both to simplify the user experience and to prevent users from accidentally damaging the workings of the operating system. As an administrator, however, it is sometimes useful to know what these hidden folders are and how to reach them. In this exercise you will explore some of the hidden folders in OS X.

Examine Your User Library Folder

1 If necessary, log in as Chris Johnson.

2 In the Finder, open your home folder.

Note that no folder named Library is visible.

3 Hold down the Option key, and choose Go > Library. Note that the Library option is only available while the Option key is held down.

This opens the hidden Library folder in Chris's home folder.

4 If necessary, change to column view by choosing View > as Columns, or by clicking the Column View button in the Finder toolbar.

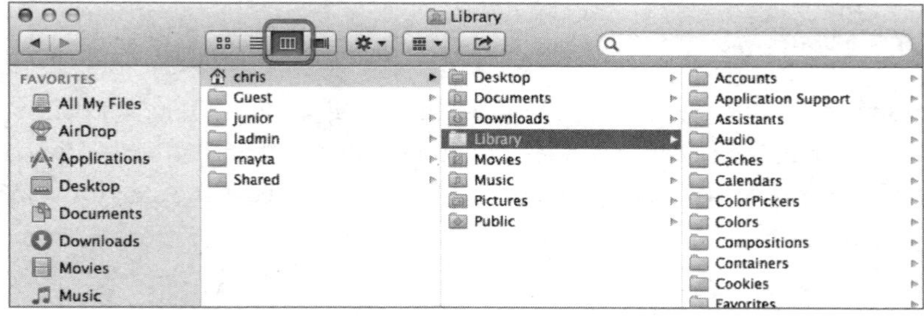

Chris's user Library folder is now shown inside Chris's home folder, but is dimmed to indicate that it's normally invisible.

5 Explore some of the subfolders under Chris's user Library folder. Note that you can navigate into them normally.

6 Close the Finder window showing Chris's user Library.

7 Press Command-Shift-H to open Chris's home folder in a new Finder window.

The Library folder is not shown.

8 Choose Go > Go to Folder, or press Command-Shift-G.

9 In the "Go to the folder" dialog, enter ~/Li and press Tab.

The field automatically completes the path to ~/Library/.

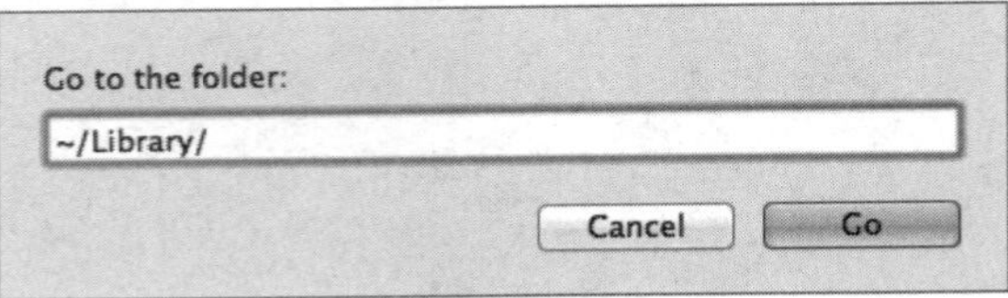

This is an example of specifying a folder by the path to reach it. In this case, the "~" means "start at my home folder," and "/Library" means "then go into the Library folder." This is another way to reach your user Library folder.

10 Click Go.

As before, Chris's user Library is shown in the Finder.

Examine Hidden System Folders

1 Press Command-Shift-G to reopen the Go to Folder dialog.

2 This time, enter /L and press Tab.

The field automatically completes the path to /Library/. This path looks very similar to the previous one, but because it does not start with "~" it actually specifies a completely different folder. When a path starts with "/", it starts at the startup volume (sometimes called the "root" of the file system).

3 Click Go.

This time the Finder opens the Library folder at the top of the startup volume. The various Library folders are discussed in the next lesson.

This Library folder is not hidden, but you can use the same technique to reach any folder you know the path to, whether it is hidden or not.

4 Use Go to Folder to reach the **/private/var/log/** folder (again, you can type part of a name and then press Tab to complete it).

The /private folder holds some of the OS X "private" system files. /private/var/log holds some of the system log files (there are more in /Library/Logs and ~/Library/Logs). Normally, you do not need to access these in the Finder, so they are hidden from view unless you specifically navigate to them.

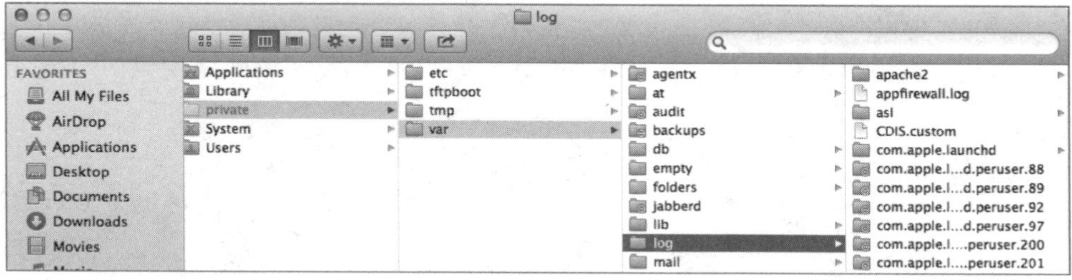

5 Use Go to Folder to reach the **/var/log/** folder.

This also takes you to /private/var/log, because /var is a symbolic link to /private/var.

Lesson 15
System Resources

It is not unusual for an OS X system volume to contain well over 100,000 folders and 500,000 files just to support the operating system and its applications. As you can imagine, the number of items in a user's home folder varies widely, depending on the user, but even the most frugal of users will have thousands of items in his home folder. With this many files on hand, attempting to explore and fully comprehend the OS X file layout may seem like a monumental task. To the contrary: the OS X system files have been streamlined and reorganized into an easy-to-understand layout that is both easier for the Mac administrator to manage and provides enhanced security.

GOALS

- Explore and understand the OS X file layout
- Discover common system files, their location, and their purpose
- Manage font resources

This lesson focuses more specifically on the composition and organization of the files and folders that make up OS X. In this lesson you, acting as an administrator, will use the file layout to strategically allocate resources. The exercises in this lesson specifically discuss management of font resources, as they are one of the most commonly modified by users. However, many of the same management techniques can be used for other system resources.

Reference 15.1
OS X File Structure

The OS X system layout is designed to strike a balance between ease of use and advanced functionality. For the basic user, looking at the root, or beginning, of the file system from the Finder reveals only four default folders: Applications, Library, Users, and System.

The contents of these four folders represent all that most users, and many administrators, will ever need to access. Yet when advanced users look at the system root from Terminal, they see many more items that the Finder would normally hide. Thus, the complexity and flexibility of a UNIX operating system remains for those users who require it.

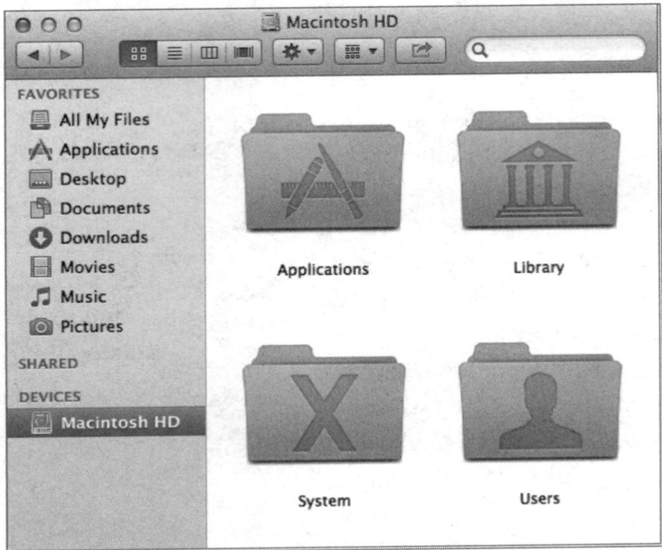

The following describes the default system root folders you see from the Finder:

- Applications—Often called the local Applications folder, this is the default location for applications available to all local users. Only administrative users can make changes to the contents of this folder.
- Library—Often called the local Library folder, this is the default location for ancillary system and application resources available to all users of the system. Once again, only administrative users can make changes to the contents of this folder.
- System—This folder contains resources required by the operating system for primary functionality. Users very rarely have to make changes to the contents of this folder. Even administrative users are unable to make changes to items in the System folder without re-authenticating. Further, it is not recommended to make any changes to the System folder as a system update may negate any changes you have made.
- Users—This is the default location for local user home folders. Lesson 7, "User Home Folders," covers this topic in greater detail.

System Resource Types

All OS X–specific system resources can be found in the various Library folders throughout the system volume. System resources can be generally categorized as any resource that is not a general-use application or user file. That's not to say that applications and user data can't be found in the Library folders. On the contrary, the Library folder is designed to keep both user and system resources organized and separated from the items you use every day. This keeps the Applications folder and user home folders free from system resource clutter.

Opening any of the Library folders reveals several dozen categories of items. It is not necessary to explore every possible Library item, but there are a few system resources you should be familiar with:

- Application Support—This folder can be found in both the user and local Library folders. Any ancillary data needed by an application may end up in this folder. For example, it often contains help files or templates for an application. Once again, application resources are placed here to keep the Applications folders tidy.
- Extensions—Also called kernel extensions, these items are found only in the system and local Library folders. Extensions are low-level drivers that attach themselves to the kernel, or core, of the operating system. Extensions provide driver support for hardware, networking, and peripherals. Extensions load and unload automatically, so there is little need to manage them, as is common in other operating systems. Extensions are covered in greater detail in Lesson 27, "Peripherals and Drivers."
- Fonts—Found in every Library folder, fonts are files that describe typefaces used for both screen display and printing. Font management is covered in the "Manage Font Resources" section later in this lesson.
- Frameworks—Found in every Library folder, frameworks are repositories of shared code used among different parts of the operating system or applications. Frameworks are similar to extensions in that they load and unload automatically, so again, there is little need to manage these shared code resources. You can view your Mac computer's currently loaded frameworks from the /Applications/Utilities/System Information application.
- Keychains—Found in every Library folder, keychains are used to securely store sensitive information, including passwords, certificates, keys, website forms, and notes. Keychain technology was covered previously in Lesson 9, "Keychain Management."

- LaunchDaemons and LaunchAgents—These items can both be found in the local and system Library folders, and LaunchAgents can also be found in the user's Library folder. These Launch items are used to define processes that start automatically via the launchd process. OS X uses many background processes, which are all started by launchd. Furthermore, every single process is a child of the launchd process. LaunchAgents are for processes that need to start up only when a user is logged in, whereas LaunchDaemons are used to start processes that will always run in the background even when there are no users logged in. More about launchd can be found in Lesson 29, "Startup, Shutdown, and Sleep Modes."
- Logs—Many system processes and applications archive progress or error messages to log files. Log files can be found in every local Library folder. Log files are viewed using the /Applications/Utilities/Console application.
- PreferencePanes—PreferencePanes can be found in any Library folder. These items are used by the System Preferences application to provide interfaces for system configuration. System Preferences usage is covered in Lesson 3, "Setup and Configuration."
- Preferences—Preferences, found in both local and user libraries, are used to store system and application configuration settings. In other words, every time you configure a setting for any application or system function, it is saved to a preference file. Because preferences play such a critical role in system functionality, they are often the cause of software problems. Troubleshooting preference files is covered in Lesson 21, "Application Management and Troubleshooting."
- Startup Items—Found in only the local and system Library folders, these are precursors to LaunchAgents and LaunchDaemons. Starting with OS X v10.5, Apple is officially discouraging the use of Startup Items. In fact, you will have Startup Items only if you've installed third-party software that hasn't been updated. In OS X the launchd process still supports many Startup Items, but this may not be true for future versions.

System Resource Hierarchy

Library folders, and thus system resources, are located in each of the four domain areas: user, local, network, and system. Segregating resources into four domains provides increased administrative flexibility, resource security, and system reliability. Resource domains are more flexible because administrators can choose to allocate certain resources to all users or just specific users. Using resource domains is more secure because standard users can add resources only to their own home folder and cannot access other users' resources. In addition, it's more reliable because, in most cases, you don't have to make changes to the core system functionality in order to provide more services.

TIP The quickest method to reveal the user's Library folder is to manually go to the folder in the Finder. While holding the Option key, choose Go > Library to reveal the hidden folder. You can learn more about hidden items in Lesson 14, "Hidden Items and Shortcuts."

The four system resource domains are, in order:

- User—Each user has his own Library folder in his home folder for resources. When resources are placed here, only the user has access to them. Also, a user can have his own Applications folder in his home folder. This folder is hidden in OS X as it's now deprecated and thus may not appear in future versions of OS X. However, you can still find many thousands of items in this folder as developers continue to rely on this location for resources.
- Local—Both the root Applications and root Library folders are part of the local resource domain. This is why they are known as the local Applications and local Library folders. Any resources placed in these two folders are available to all local user accounts. By default, only administrative users can make changes to local resources.
- Network—OS X can access system resources and applications from a network file share. Administrators must configure an automounted share in order to enable the Network resource domain. Configuring automounted shares goes beyond the scope of this guide.
- System—Finally, the system domain encompasses all the items necessary to provide core system functionality. Many hidden items at the root of the system volume make up the system resource domain, but the only one you will see in the Finder is the root System folder. In many cases, you do not need to add or manage any resources here.

With four different domains containing resources, a strong likelihood exists for overlap in resources, meaning there may be multiple copies of similar resources available to the system and user at any given time. The system is designed to handle this by searching for resources from the most specific, those in the user domain, to the least specific, those in the system domain. If multiple similar resources are discovered, the system uses the resource most specific to the user. For example, if multiple versions of the font Times New Roman are found, one in the local Library and one in the user's Library, the copy of the font in the user's Library is the one used.

/
/Applications
/Library ← Second: Local Library
/Network
/Network/Library ← Third: Network Library
/System
/System/Library ← Fourth: System Library
/Users
/Users/cadmin
/Users/logan
/Users/michelle
/Users/michelle/Desktop
/Users/michelle/Documents
/Users/michelle/Downloads
/Users/michelle/Library ← First: User Library
/Users/michelle/Movies
/Users/michelle/Music
/Users/michelle/Pictures
/Users/michelle/Public
/Users/michelle/Sites

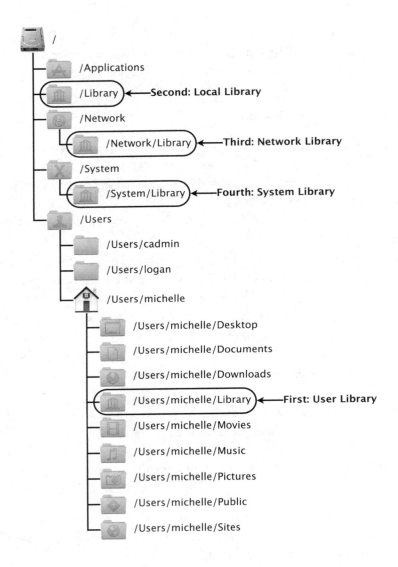

System Resource Troubleshooting

System resource issues are rare, and they are generally easy to identify. You will occasionally see an error message calling out an issue with a specific item, but you may also experience a situation where the item appears to be missing. In some cases, the system resource in question may be missing, but many times the system simply ignores a system resource if it determines that the resource is in some way corrupted. The solution for both of these situations is to simply replace the missing or suspect item with a known working copy.

When troubleshooting system resources, you must also remember to heed the resource domain hierarchy. Using fonts as an example, you may have loaded a specific version of a font in the local Library that is required by your workflow to operate properly. In spite of this, a user may have loaded another version of the same font in her home folder. In this case, the system loads the user's font and ignores the font you installed. Therefore, this user may experience workflow problems even though it appears that she is using the correct font.

> **TIP** If fonts are missing from within applications but appear to be properly installed, remember to check Font Book as the font may be temporarily disabled. Font Book is covered in the next section of this lesson.

Logging in with another account on the Mac is always a quick way to determine if the problem is in the user's home folder. You can also use /Applications/Utilities/System Information to list active system resources. System Information always shows the file path of the loaded system resources, so it's easy to spot resources that are loading from the user's Library.

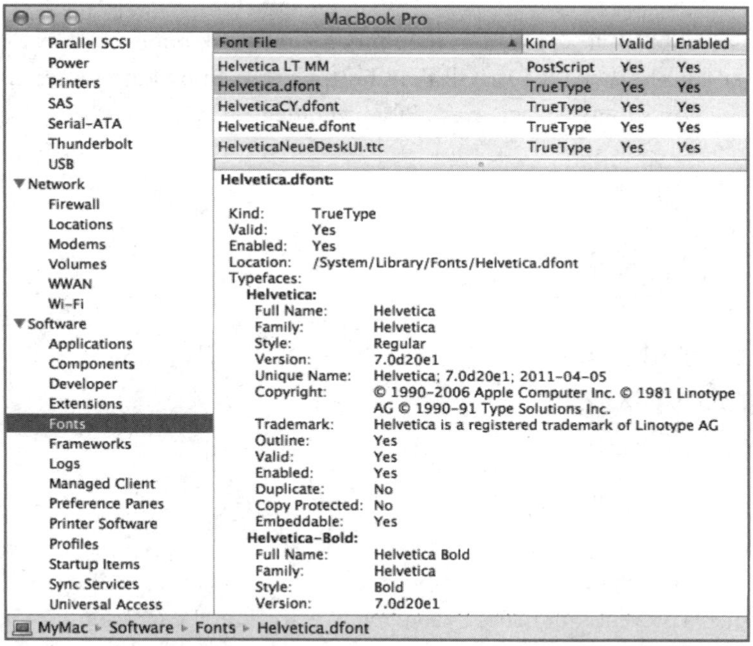

Reference 15.2
Font Resources and Font Book

An excellent way to experience the system resource domain hierarchy is by managing fonts. OS X has advanced font-management technology that enables an unlimited number of fonts using nearly any font type, including bitmap, TrueType, OpenType, and all PostScript Type fonts. As mentioned previously, fonts are installed in the various Font folders located in the Library folders throughout the system. A user can manually install fonts simply by dragging them into a Fonts folder.

Install Fonts via Font Book

On the other hand, OS X includes a rather nice font-management tool, /Applications/Font Book, which automatically installs fonts for you. Font Book can also be used to organize fonts into more manageable collections, enable or disable fonts to simplify font lists, and resolve duplicate fonts.

NOTE ▸ Third-party font-management tools, such as Extensis Suitcase Fusion or Universal Type Server, interrupt Font Book and take over font management for the system.

By default, when a user double-clicks a font in the Finder, Font Book opens and previews the font. When a user simply clicks the Install Font button, Font Book automatically copies the font into the Fonts folder in the user's Library folder.

NOTE ▸ Font Book, by default, automatically validates a font before installing and enabling it. This helps prevent font issues by making sure the font file isn't compromised. Thus, installing fonts via Font Book is favored over manual installation via the Finder.

NOTE ▶ Some applications may need to be restarted to take advantage of recently added fonts.

Upon the installation of a new font, the Foot Book main window appears, previewing the new font. Manually opening Font Book also opens the main window. To preview any currently installed font, simply click it in the Font list.

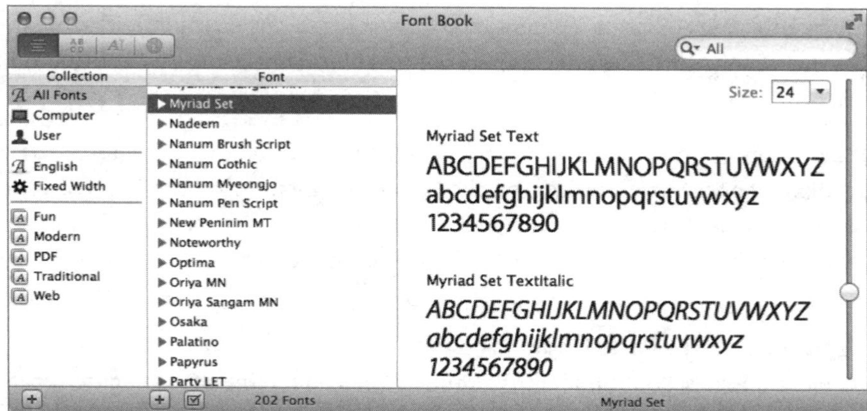

With Font Book open, you can adjust the default install location for fonts by choosing Font Book > Preferences. If you are an administrative user, you can choose to install fonts to the local Library folder by choosing Computer from the pop-up menu. Close the Font Book Preferences dialog once you have made your selections.

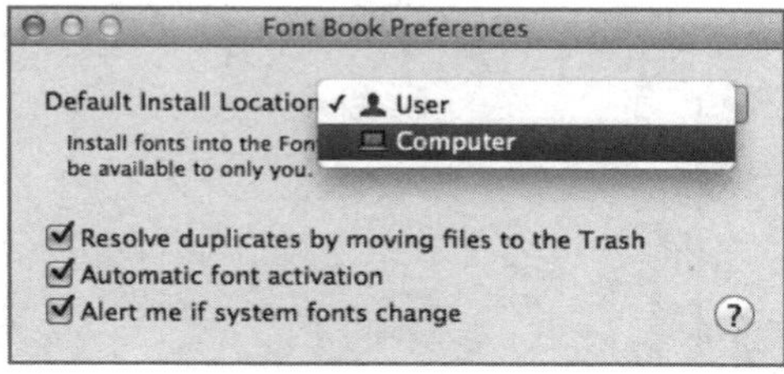

Disable Fonts via Font Book

If you, or the application you're using, have difficulties choosing fonts from a large list, you can temporarily disable fonts within Font Book by selecting the font and then clicking the small checkbox button at the bottom of the font list. Disabled fonts appear dimmed in the font list with the word "Off" next to their name. To enable the font, simply select it again and select the same checkbox button at the bottom of the font list.

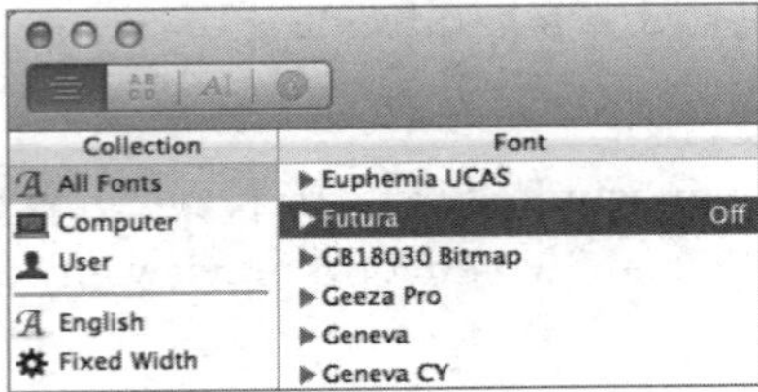

Fonts that have multiple copies on your system show a small dot next to their name in the font list. You can automatically disable duplicate fonts with Font Book by choosing Edit > Look for Enabled Duplicates.

If you feel the need to remove a font, simply select it from the font list and press Delete. A summary dialog appears, reminding you that continuing will move the selected fonts to the Trash folder. If you are sure this is what you want to do, click Remove. Remember, however, you can always disable a font instead of deleting it entirely.

Resolve Font Issues via Font Book

If you're having font issues, you can identify problem fonts by forcing the system to revalidate all the fonts on your system. To do this, select a single font in the Font list, and then press Command-A to select all the fonts. Choose File > Validate Fonts to start the validation process.

The Font Validation window opens and scans all the selected fonts. This window clearly shows any problem font with a status indicator (exclamation mark icon) next to the font's name. To remove a problem font, simply select the checkbox next to its name and then click the Remove Checked button.

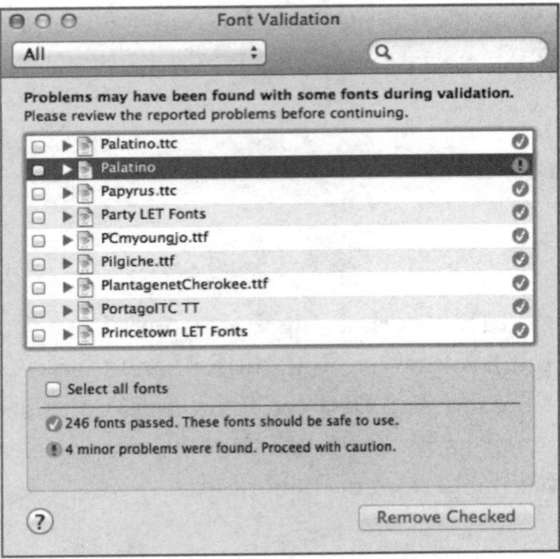

If you're still having problems with fonts, a final option in Font Book is to restore all the system fonts back to the defaults for OS X. To do this, choose File > Restore Standard Fonts. A dialog appears, verifying your choice. Click Proceed to remove third-party fonts from the system.

Exercise 15.1
Manage Font Resources

▶ Prerequisites

- You must have created the Local Admin (Exercise 3.1 or 3.2), Chris Johnson (Exercise 6.1), and Mayta Mishtuk (Exercise 7.1) accounts.

In this exercise, you will remove a font from /Library/Fonts, where it was available to all users, and install it in a single user's Fonts folder.

Remove a Font

You can use Font Book to watch what happens when you move a font to the Trash.

1. Verify that no users have fast user switching sessions active. If any users other than Chris are logged in, log them out.

2. If necessary, log in as Chris Johnson.

3. Open the Font Book application, which is located in the Applications folder.

4. Locate Andale Mono in the Font column.

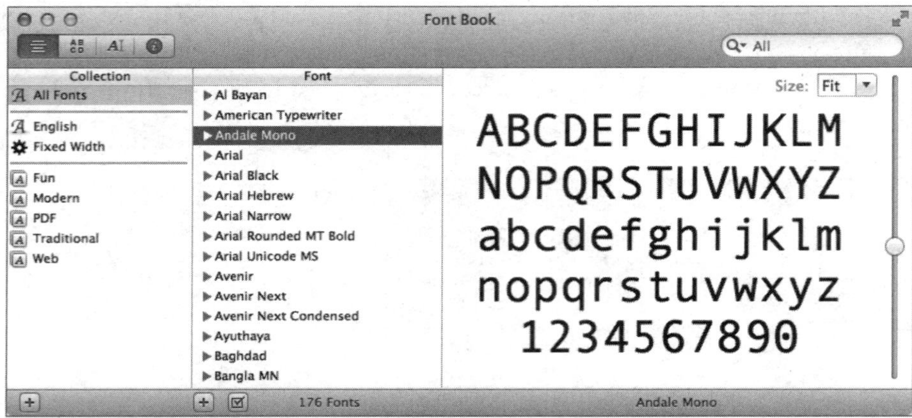

5 In the Finder, navigate to the folder /Library/Fonts. If Macintosh HD is not displayed on Chris's desktop, you can find it in the Computer view, available by choosing Go > Computer (or pressing Command-Shift-C).

6 To verify your location, choose View > Show Path Bar.

Make sure the path bar at the bottom of the window matches this screenshot (although the rest may not match unless you are in list view):

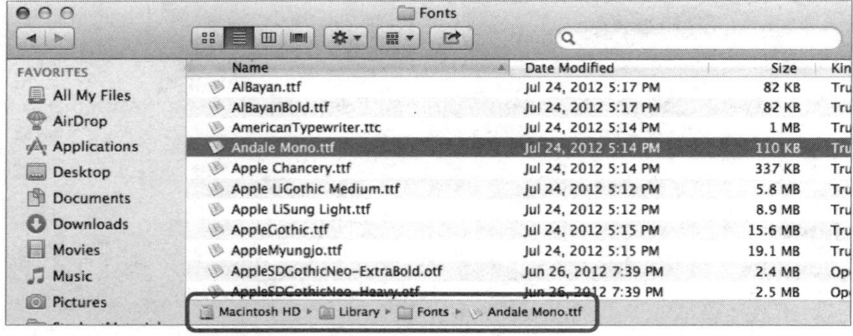

These fonts are available to all users on the system.

7 Locate the file Andale Mono.ttf.

8 Drag Andale Mono.ttf to the desktop. As you drag, a cursor with a green badge with a plus sign on it appears attached to the pointer. This will be your backup copy of the Andale Mono font.

9 Move the Andale Mono.ttf file from /Library/Fonts to the Trash. To do so, you have to authenticate as Local Admin.

10 Click the Font Book window to make it the active application.

The Andale Mono font is no longer listed in the Font Book window. Font Book shows a real-time display of all the fonts in the system search path.

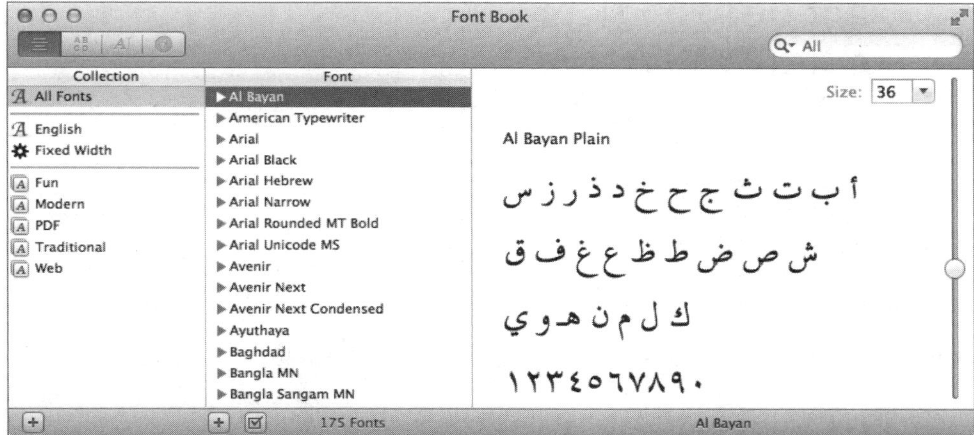

Add a Font for Only One User

You can use Font Book to install a font that only one user of the computer can use.

1 In Font Book, choose Font Book > Preferences.

2 Ensure that the Default Install Location is set to User.

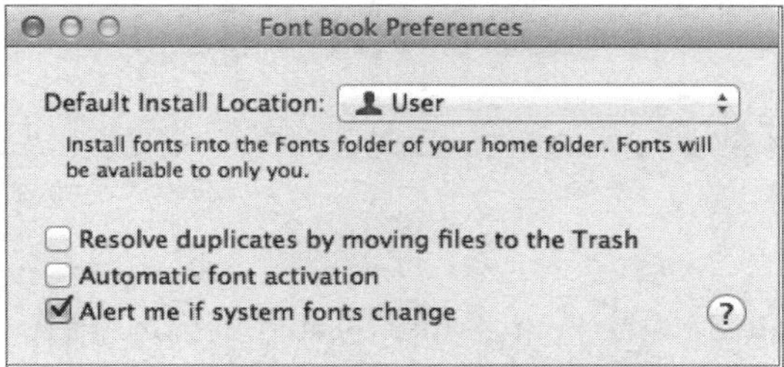

3 Close Font Book Preferences.

4 Switch to the Finder and double-click Andale Mono.ttf on the desktop.

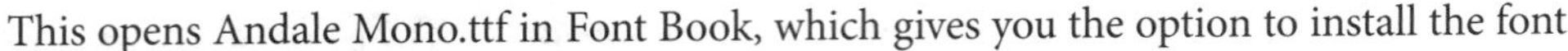

This opens Andale Mono.ttf in Font Book, which gives you the option to install the font.

5 Click Install Font.

Andale Mono reappears in the Font column of Font Book.

6 In the Collection list, select User. Andale Mono is the only font listed there.

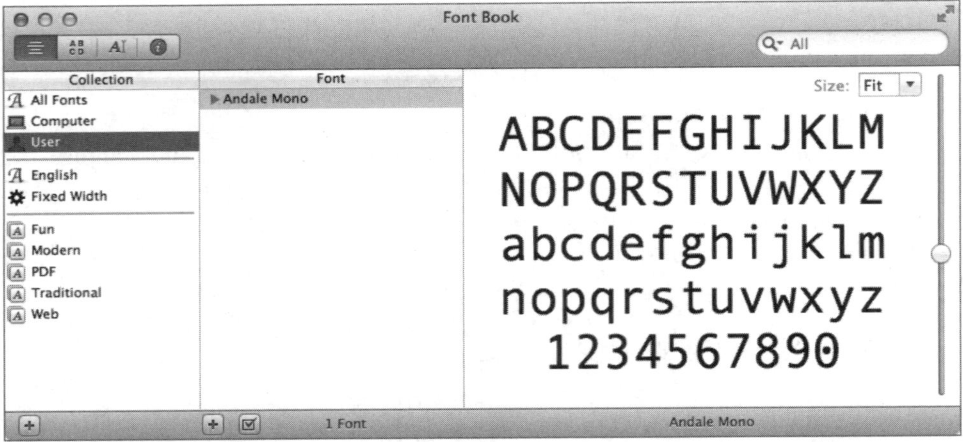

7 Quit Font Book.

The Andale Mono font is now installed in the Fonts folder located in Chris's Library folder. The user Library folder is hidden, but the Finder has a hidden menu option to open it.

8 In the Finder, hold down the Option key and choose Go > Library. This menu selection appears only when you hold down the Option key.

9 Open the Fonts folder.

Andale Mono.ttf is the only font installed in Chris's Fonts folder.

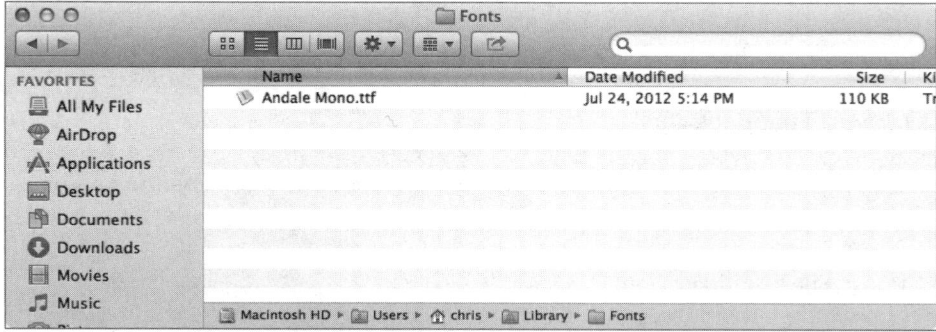

Confirm the Font Is Unavailable to Other Users

If you log in as a different user, you don't have access to the fonts in Chris's Fonts folder.

1 Use fast user switching to switch to Mayta Mishtuk's account (password: **mayta**, or whatever you chose when you created the account).

2 Open Font Book and look for the Andale Mono font.

Notice that Andale Mono is not visible in Font Book for Mayta's account. At this time, you could add Andale Mono to Mayta's user account, just as you added it to Chris's account earlier. You would have to copy the font file to a location that Mayta can access.

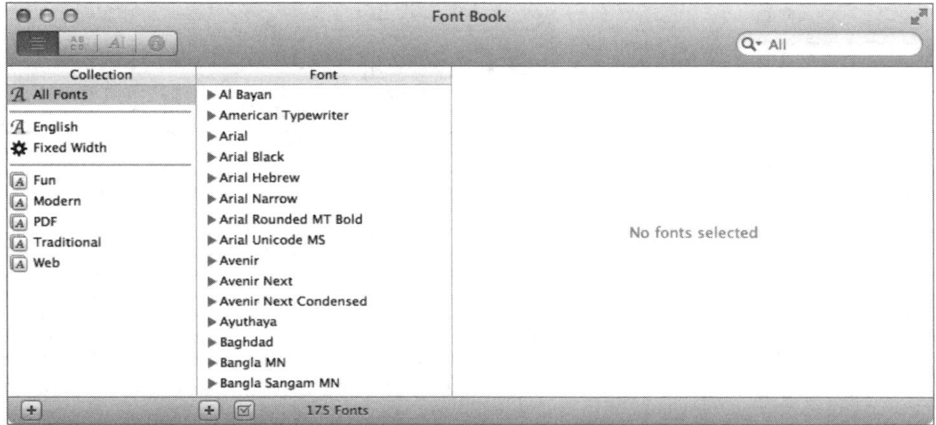

3 Quit Font Book and log out of Mayta's account.

Validate Fonts

Since you have changed your font configuration, you will use Font Book to check your new setup.

1. Log back in to the Chris Johnson account.

2. Open the Font Book application.

3. Select the All Fonts collection, and then click a font in the Font column and press Command-A to select all the fonts.

4. Choose File > Validate Fonts.

   This causes Font Book to read and validate all the font files, checking for any corruption.

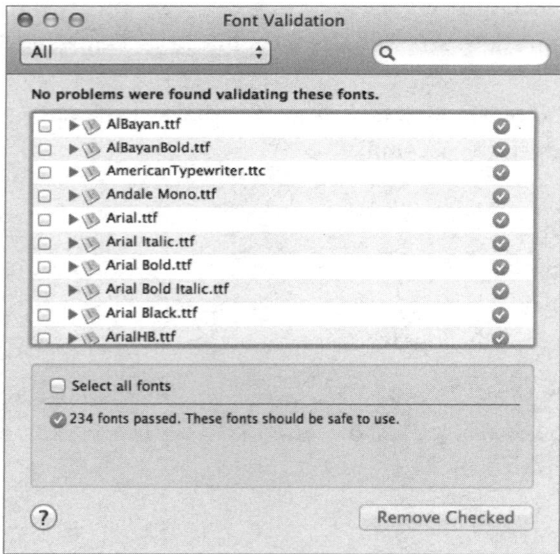

5. Quit Font Book

Lesson **16**

Metadata and Spotlight

Metadata is data about data. More specifically, metadata is information used to describe content. The most basic forms of file and folder metadata employed by nearly every operating system are names, paths, modification dates, and permissions. These metadata objects are not part of the item's content, yet they are necessary to describe the item in the file system. OS X uses several types of additional file system metadata for a variety of technologies that ultimately lead to a richer user experience.

This lesson details how OS X makes use of file metadata, and how this metadata is stored on various file systems. You will also learn how to take advantage of all this metadata by using the OS X advanced Spotlight search technology.

GOALS

- Understand how OS X stores and uses file metadata
- Leverage file metadata by using Spotlight for advanced searching

Reference 16.1
File System Metadata

Resource forks, dating back to the original Mac OS, are the legacy metadata technology in the Mac operating system. To simplify the user experience, Apple created a forked file system to make complex items, such as applications, appear as a single icon. Forked file systems, like Mac OS Extended, allow multiple pieces of data to appear as a single item in the file system. In this case, a file appears as a single item, but it is actually composed of two separate pieces: a data fork and a resource fork. This also allows the Mac OS to support standard file types in the data fork, while the extra Mac-specific information resides in the resource fork. For many years the Mac OS has relied on forked files for storing both data and associated metadata.

OS X not only continues but also expands the use of metadata, even going so far as to allow developers to take advantage of an arbitrary number of additional metadata items. This enables Apple, and other developers, to implement unique file system solutions without having to modify the existing file system. For instance, OS X v10.6 introduced compressed application code, wherein the actual executable program files are all compressed to save space and then when needed automatically decompressed on the fly. To prevent previous versions of OS X or older applications from improper handling of these compressed executables, Apple chose to hide the compressed bits in additional metadata locations.

The downside to legacy resource forks, and other types of additional file system metadata, is that some third-party file systems, like FAT, do not know how to properly store this additional data. The solution to this issue is addressed with the AppleDouble file format covered later in this lesson.

File Flags and Extended Attributes

OS X also uses file system flags and extended attributes to implement a variety of file system features. In general, file system flags are holdovers from the original Mac OS and are primarily used to control user access. Examples of file system flags include the hidden flag covered in Lesson 14, "Hidden Items and Shortcuts," and the locked flag covered in Lesson 20, "Document Management."

With OS X, Apple needed to expand the range of possible attributes associated with any file or folder, which is where so-called extended attributes come into play. Any process or application can add an arbitrary number of custom attributes to a file or folder. Again, this allows developers to create new forms of metadata without having to modify the existing file system. The Mac OS Extended file system stores any additional attributes as another fork associated with the file.

The Finder uses extended attributes for several general file features, including setting an item's color label, stationery pad option, hide extension option, and Spotlight comments. All of these items can be accessed from the Get Info window in the Finder.

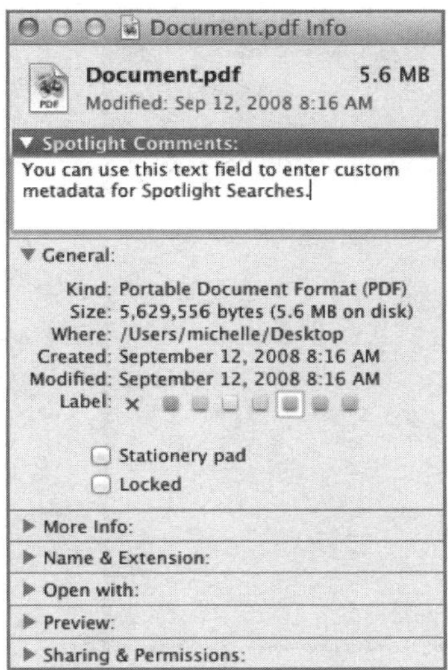

AppleDouble File Format

While file system metadata helps make the user's experience on OS X richer, compatibility with third-party file systems can be an issue. Only volumes formatted with the Mac OS Extended file system fully support OS X style resource forks, data forks, file flags, and extended attributes. Third-party software has been developed for Windows-based operating systems to allow them to access the extended metadata features of Mac OS Extended. More often, though, users use the compatibility software built into OS X to help other file systems cope with these metadata items.

For most non-Mac OS Extended volumes, OS X stores the file system metadata in a separate hidden data file. This technique is commonly referred to as AppleDouble. For example, if you copy a file containing metadata named My Document.docx to a FAT32 volume, OS X automatically splits the file and writes it as two discrete pieces on the FAT32 volume. The file's internal data would be written with the same name as the original, but the metadata would end up in a file named ._My Document.docx that would remain hidden from the Finder. This works out pretty well for most files because Windows applications only care about the contents of the data fork. But, some files do not take well to being split up, and all the extra dot-underscore files create a bit of a mess on other file systems.

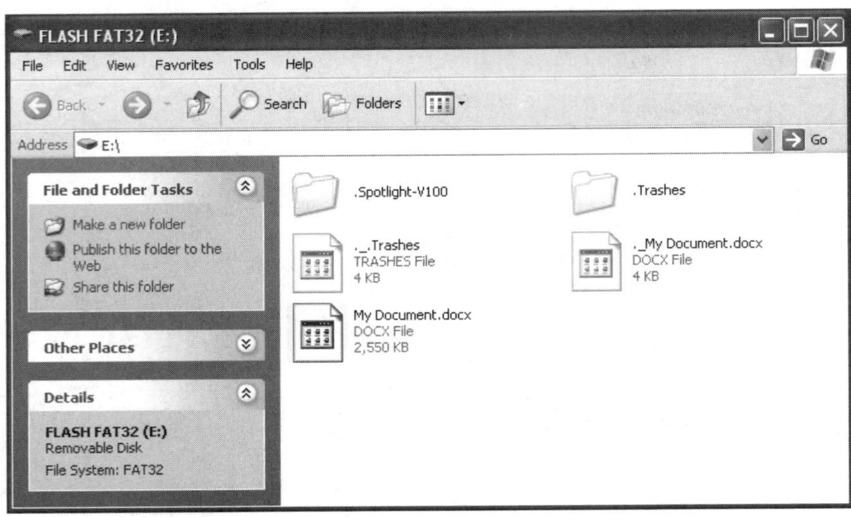

NOTE ▶ Window systems default to automatically hiding these dot-underscore files. In fact, to acquire the Windows XP screenshot shown here, showing hidden files had to be manually enabled.

OS X includes a method for handling metadata on SMB network shares from NTFS volumes that doesn't require the AppleDouble format. The native file system for modern Windows-based computers, NTFS, supports something similar to file forking known as alternative data streams. The Mac file system writes the metadata to the alternative data stream so the file will appear as a single item on both Windows and Mac systems.

NOTE ▶ OS X always reverts to using dot-underscore files when writing to FAT volumes, some Xsan volumes, and older NFS shares.

Reference 16.2
Spotlight Search

Spotlight was a significant new feature in OS X v10.4 that revolutionized the way users searched for files on their Macs. Spotlight enables you to perform nearly instantaneous searches that go wider and deeper than previous Mac desktop search technology. Spotlight can go beyond simple file system searches and actually search for relevant metadata inside application files and databases. For example, an application like Contacts stores user contact information in a database that appears opaque to the file system. Nevertheless, Spotlight can return search results from the Contacts application along with results from other databases and the entire file system hierarchy nearly instantly.

In addition to the file system metadata that was covered previously in this lesson, many files also contain internal metadata used to describe the file's content. For example, many digital camera image files contain additional camera setting information embedded as metadata inside the file. Spotlight can search through both file system and internal metadata information.

Though Spotlight was pretty amazing when it debuted, Apple added a few more tricks to Spotlight over the years. These included the ability to search through the contents of shared files from other Mac clients, servers, AirDisk volumes over the network, and Time Machine backups. OS X Lion introduced the ability for Spotlight searches to automatically return results from your default web search engine and Wikipedia.

Apple has also incorporated the ability to use advanced search operations while performing Spotlight searches from the Finder or menu bar. Advanced Spotlight search operations include:

- The use of multiple search criteria types in a single search
- The use of Boolean logic by using AND, OR, or NOT
- The use of exact phrases and dates by using quotation marks
- The use of search ranges by using greater-than and less-than symbols

Another feature, dubbed Quick Look, augments Spotlight by allowing you to quickly preview the content of most files even if you don't have the application that created the file installed on your Mac. The combination of Spotlight and Quick Look allows you to locate and preview items with unmatched ease and speed.

> **MORE INFO ▸** Though briefly covered here, Quick Look details can also be found in Lesson 20, "Document Management."

Searching with Spotlight

You can initiate a Spotlight search any time by clicking the Spotlight icon on the far right of the menu bar or using the Command-Spacebar keyboard shortcut. The Spotlight search is so fast that the results actually change in real time as you type in your search query. In the results list, moving your mouse over an object (but not clicking) or using the arrow keys opens a Quick Look preview of the content. Clicking an item or pressing Return with a result selected opens it immediately.

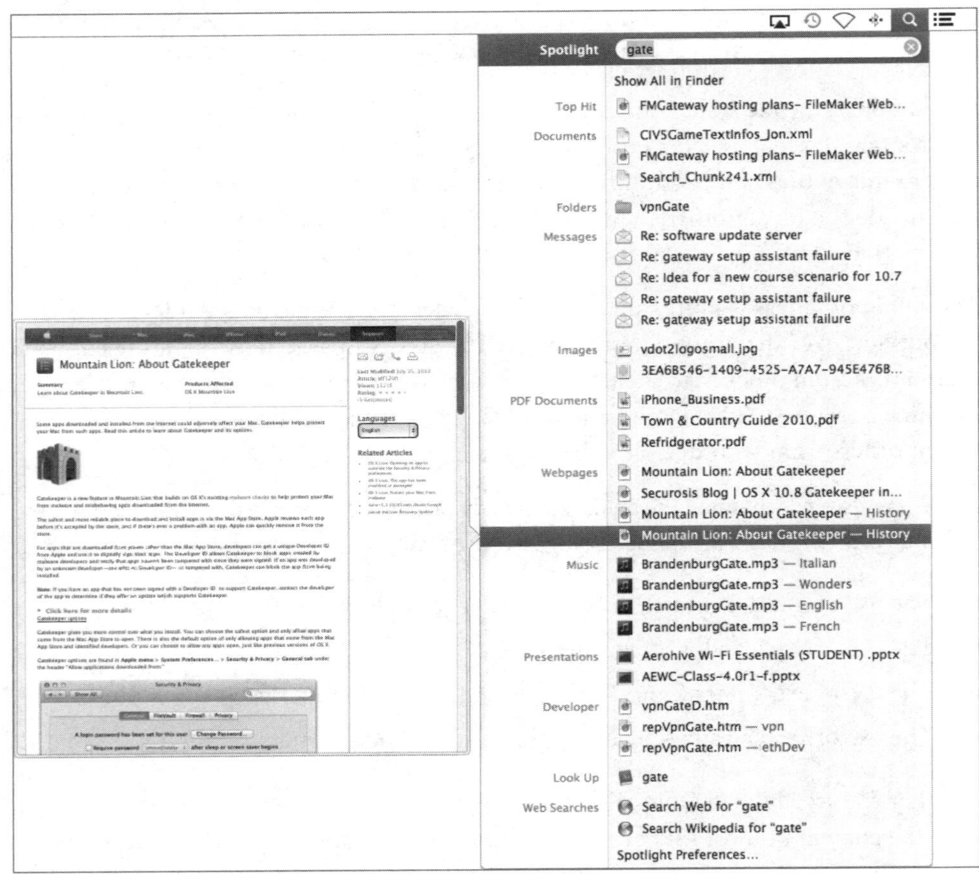

TIP When previewing with Quick Look from the Spotlight search, hold the Command key to reveal location information at the bottom of the Quick Look window.

Selecting "Show All in Finder" from the Spotlight search results menu opens a new Finder window with the results. You could also arrive at this same window by opening a new Finder window and entering your search in the Spotlight field, or by choosing File > Find, or by pressing Command-F. Selecting an item from the search results shows you the path to the selected item at the bottom of the Finder window. Selecting an item and then tapping the Spacebar opens a Quick Look preview of the selected item.

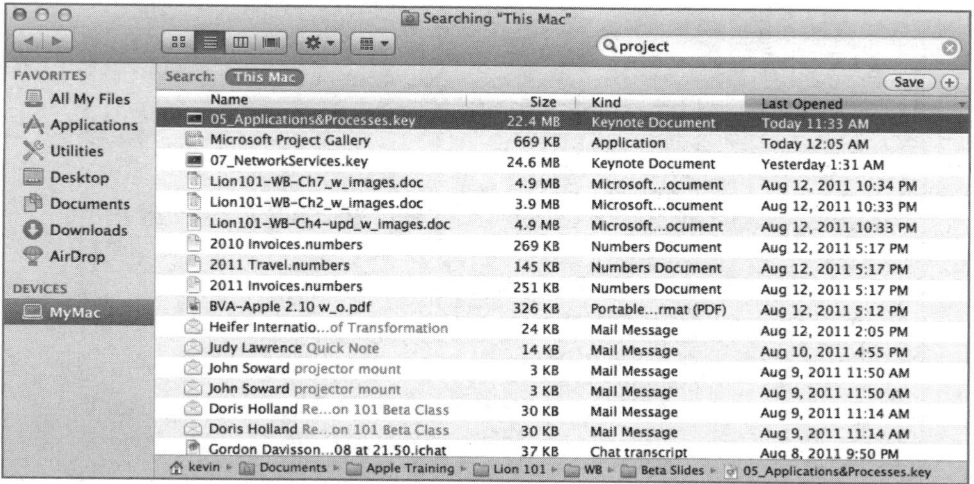

You can refine your Spotlight search from a Finder search window by clicking the small plus buttons below the search field, which allow you to add as many specific search attributes as you need. After you add a new search attribute, click the first word in the search attribute to choose another type from the pop-up menu.

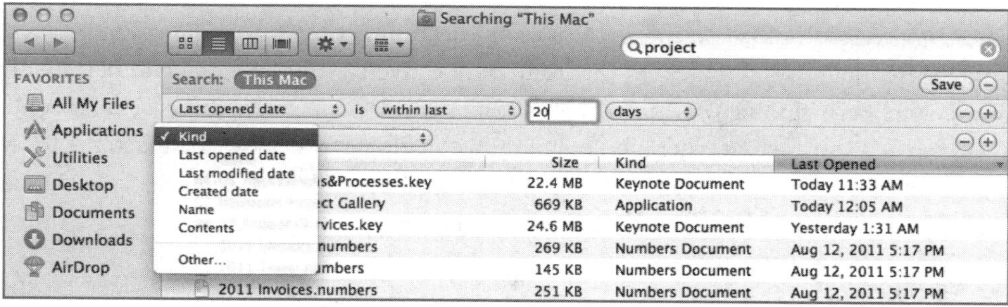

If you don't see the search attribute you're looking for, you can add literally dozens of other attributes that aren't enabled by default. To enable additional search attributes, select any attribute, and from the pop-up menu choose Other. In the dialog that appears, you can add search attributes to the pop-up menu. Two especially useful search attributes for administrators are "File visibility" and "System files," neither of which is shown by default in any Spotlight search.

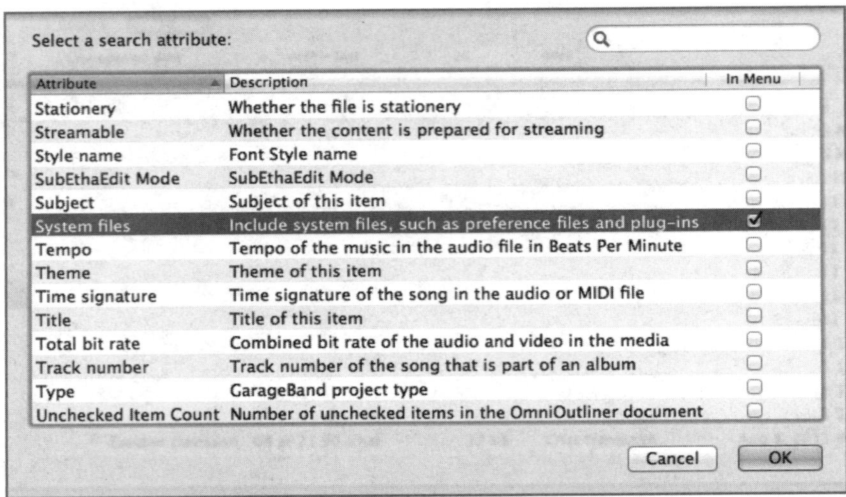

TIP Take some time to explore the additional search attributes; you may be surprised at the depth of the Spotlight search capabilities. Search attributes include specifying audio file tags, digital camera metadata, authorship information, contact information, and many other metadata types.

Clicking the Save button on the right saves these search criteria as a Smart Folder. Smart Folders are like normal folders in that they can be given a unique name and placed anywhere you like, including the Finder sidebar. Smart Folders are special because their contents always match your search criteria no matter how the file system changes. In fact, the All My Files item in the Finder sidebar is simply a predefined Smart Folder searching for the most recently opened documents in the user's home folder.

Spotlight Indexing

Spotlight is able to perform wide and deep searches quickly because it works in the background to maintain highly optimized databases of indexed metadata for each local volume. When you first set up OS X, it creates these databases by indexing all the available local volumes. The system also indexes new local volumes when they are first attached.

On OS X, a background process automatically updates the index databases on the fly as changes are made throughout the file system. Because these indexes are kept current, the Spotlight process need only search through the databases to return thorough results. Essentially, Spotlight preemptively searches everything for you in the background so you don't have to wait for the results when you need them.

> **NOTE ▸** Spotlight does not create index databases on read-only volumes or write-once media such as optical discs.

> **NOTE ▸** Your Mac computer's Spotlight service indexes Time Machine and AirDisk volumes directly, but it does not index shared volumes from other computers. However, Spotlight can connect to indexes on AFP shares hosted from OS X Server systems.

You can find the Spotlight general index databases at the root level of every volume in a folder named .Spotlight-V100. A few applications maintain their own databases separate from these general index databases. One example is the built-in email application Mail. It maintains its own optimized email database in each user's folder at ~/Library/Mail/Envelope Index.

Also, the Spotlight index database for a Legacy FileVault user is stored at the root level inside his encrypted home folder for enhanced security. If you are experiencing problems with Spotlight, you can force it to rebuild the index databases by deleting them and restarting your Mac or by managing the Spotlight settings as covered later in this lesson.

Spotlight Security

In order to provide security on par with the rest of the file system, Spotlight also indexes every item's permissions. Even though Spotlight indexes every item on a volume, it automatically filters search results to show only items that the current user has permissions to access.

There is still a security concern, though, when users search through locally attached non-system volumes because they can choose to ignore ownership on these volumes. In other words, all users can search through locally attached nonsystem volumes, including mounted disk images, even if another user attached the device.

Spotlight Plug-Ins

Spotlight is able to create indexes, and thus search, from an ever-growing variety of metadata using a plug-in technology. Each Spotlight plug-in is designed to examine specific types of files or databases. Many Spotlight plug-ins are included by default, but Apple and third-party developers can create additional plug-ins to expand the Spotlight search capabilities.

Included Spotlight plug-ins enable you to:

- Search via basic file metadata, including name, file size, creation date, and modification date
- Search via media-specific metadata from picture, music, and video files, including time code, creator information, and hardware capture information
- Search through the contents of a variety of file types, including text files, iLife-related files and databases, Photoshop files, PDF files, iWork files, and Microsoft Office files
- Search through personal information like that found in the Contacts and Calendar applications
- Search for correspondence information like the contents of Mail emails and Messages chat transcripts
- Search for highly relevant information like your favorites or web browser bookmarks and history

Spotlight plug-ins, like any other system resource, are stored inside the various Library folders. The Apple built-in Spotlight plug-ins can be found in both the /System/Library/Spotlight folder and the /Library/Spotlight folder. Third-party plug-ins should always be installed in either the /Library/Spotlight or the ~/Library/Spotlight folder, depending on who needs access to it.

TIP You can create custom metadata for Spotlight by entering Spotlight comments in the Get Info and Inspector windows from the Finder.

Spotlight Settings

From the Spotlight preferences, any user can choose to disable specific categories from appearing in Spotlight searches. A user can also prevent volumes from being indexed by specifying those volumes in the privacy list. However, by default all new volumes are automatically indexed, so a user must manually configure Spotlight to ignore a volume.

The Spotlight privacy list is a computer-level setting that remains the same across all user accounts, but it's not protected by administrative access, which means any user can change the privacy list. In this case, the Spotlight privacy list isn't any less secure than the rest of the file system, as any user can still have full access to locally connected nonsystem volumes because the system defaults to ignoring ownership on those volumes.

Opening the Spotlight preferences defaults to the Search Results tab, allowing you to disable specific categories from the search results. Simply deselect the checkboxes next to the categories you want to ignore. You can also drag categories to change their order in the search results. Each user has her own separate Search Results settings.

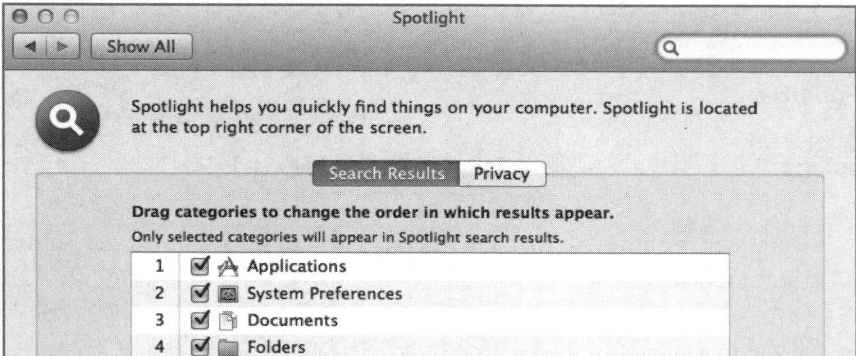

To prevent Spotlight from indexing specific items, click the Privacy tab to reveal the list of items for Spotlight to ignore. To add new items, click the Add (+) button at the bottom of the privacy list and choose the items from a browser dialog, or simply drag and drop items into the privacy list. You can delete an item from the privacy list by selecting it and then clicking the Delete (–) button at the bottom of the list.

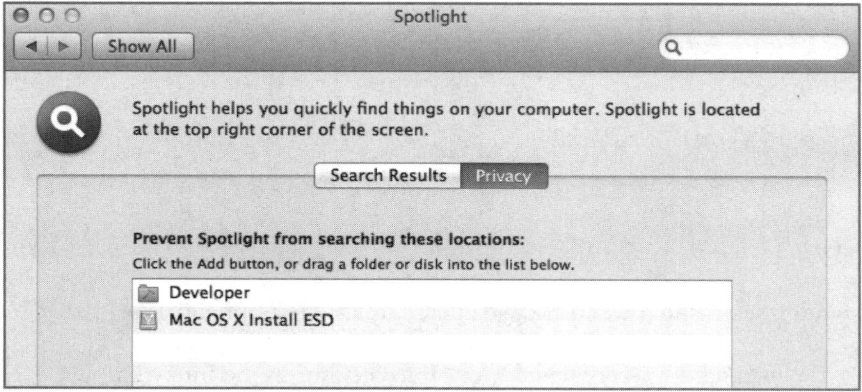

aaAll Spotlight settings are applied immediately. If you add an entire volume to the privacy list, the system deletes the Spotlight index database from that volume. In turn, removing a volume from the privacy list rebuilds the Spotlight index database on that volume. This technique, to rebuild the Spotlight index databases by adding, then removing, a volume from the privacy list, is the most common method to resolve problematic Spotlight performance.

Exercise 16.1
Examine File Metadata

Prerequisites

- You must have created the Chris Johnson account (Exercise 6.1).

In this exercise, you will examine some file metadata in the Info window in the Finder, and also add custom metadata.

1 If necessary, log in as Chris Johnson.

2 Open Safari, and navigate to www.apple.com.

3 Choose File > Save As (Command-S), and save the Apple homepage on the desktop, in the Web Archive format.

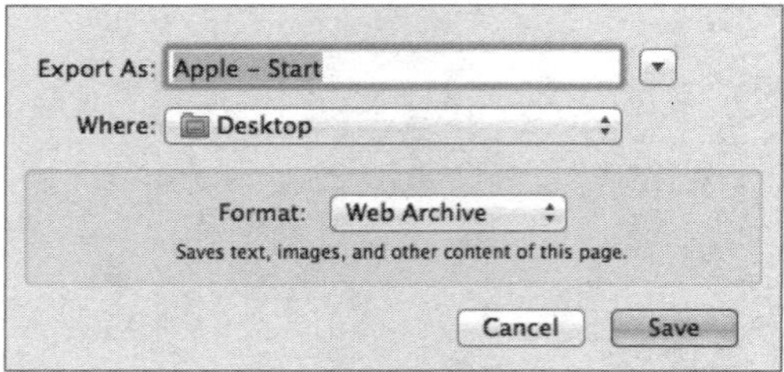

4 Quit Safari.

5 In the Finder, select the file and choose File > Get Info (Command-I).

6 If necessary, expand the General and More Info sections of the Info window.

The Info window in the Finder displays a variety of information about the file, from basic metadata like its size to information about where on the web it came from.

7 In the Spotlight Comments field, type **The Apple orchard**.

This field adds custom metadata to the file, allowing you attach searchable comments and keywords. You will see how to use this comment in the next exercise.

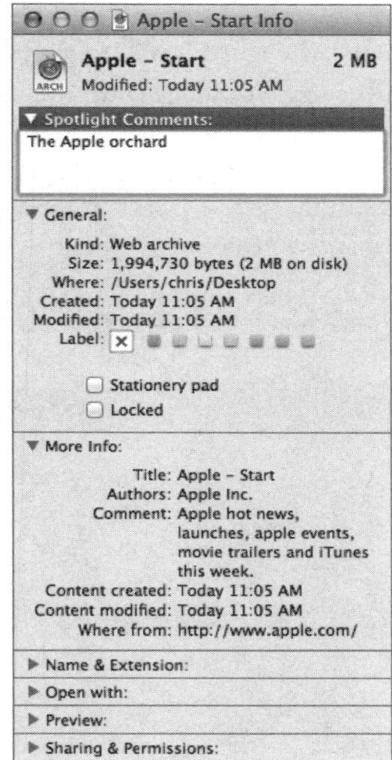

8 Close the Info window.

You should now perform Exercise 16.2 to see how to use the Spotlight comment.

Exercise 16.2
Search Using Spotlight

Prerequisites

- You must have performed Exercise 16.1.

In this exercise, you will use Spotlight to search for user documents, and also learn how to extend its search to system files.

Search for User Documents

1 In the Finder, choose File > Find (Command-F).

2 In the search field of the window that opens, type **orchard**.

The search finds the web archive you saved earlier, because the word "orchard" appears in its Spotlight comment. Note that you can also restrict the search to files with "orchard" in the name.

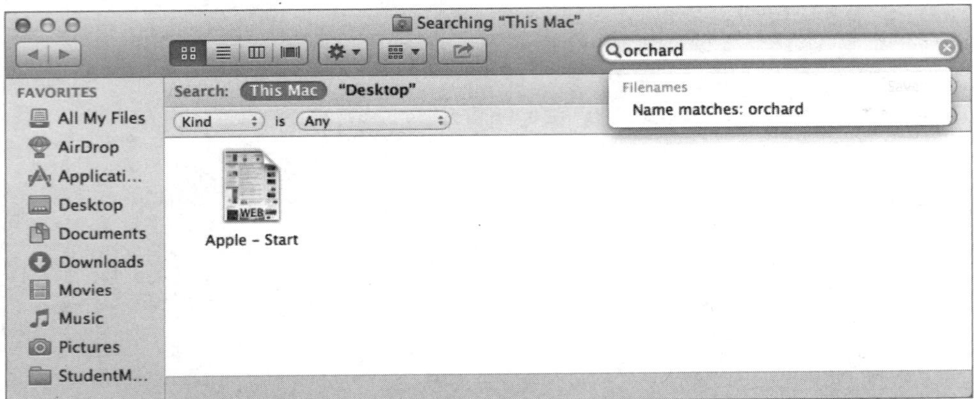

3 Change the search to **www.apple.com**.

Again, the web archive is found, this time because your search matches the site it was downloaded from. It also finds several .mobileconfig files in the StudentMaterials folder, because each of them contains a document type descriptor that says they conform to a format defined at http://www.apple.com/DTDs/PropertyList-1.0.dtd. If you had any text files or PDFs that mentioned www.apple.com, they would be listed as well.

Spotlight can search a wide variety of file metadata as well as the contents of files. It generally displays all possible matches, and then suggests ways to narrow the search (for example, only Filename matches, or Downloaded From matches).

Search for System Files

1 Change the search to **.log**, and then choose Log File from the search results menu.

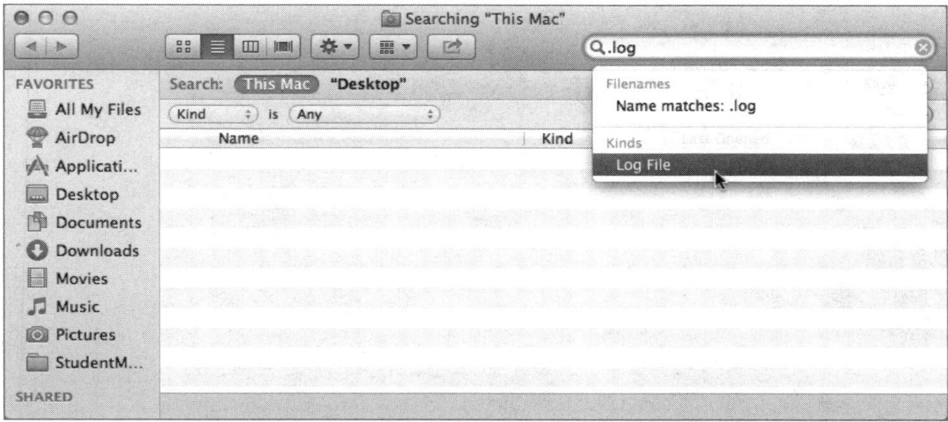

2 If necessary, select This Mac from the Search bar.

The search does not find any matching files, because, by default, Spotlight omits system files from its search results.

3 From the left pop-up menu, choose Other.

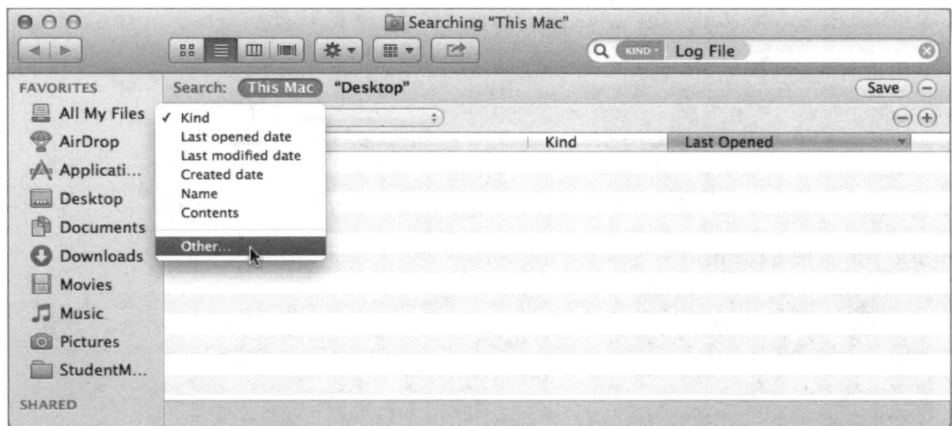

A dialog appears with a wide array of search criteria.

4 Find or use the search box to find "File invisible" and "System files" and select the In Menu checkboxes for both. This places those options in the pop-up menu you just used.

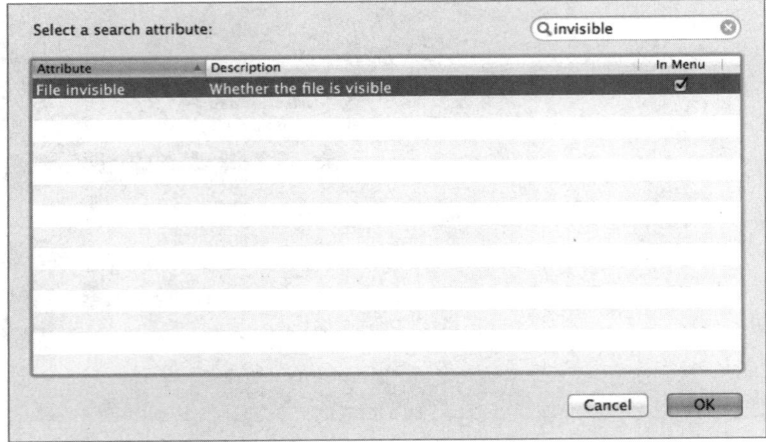

5 Click OK.

6 From the left pop-up menu, ensure that "System files" is chosen.

7 From the right pop-up menu, choose "are included."

Although you may not see any results yet, Spotlight has already begun searching.

8 Click the Add (+) button on the same row as the System Files settings.

9 From the left pop-up menu of the new row, choose "File visibility."

10 From the right pop-up menu on that row, choose "Visible or Invisible."

You now see a number of system log files listed.

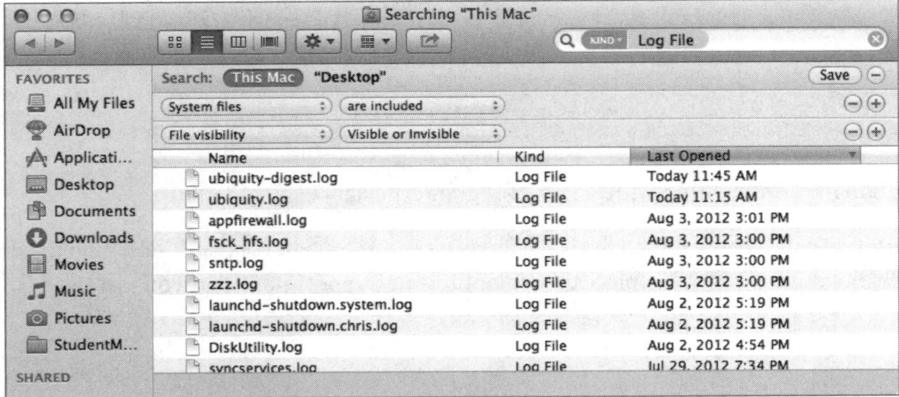

11 Click the Save button near the top right of the window.

12 Save the search as **All Logs** in Saved Searches, and make sure that Add To Sidebar is selected.

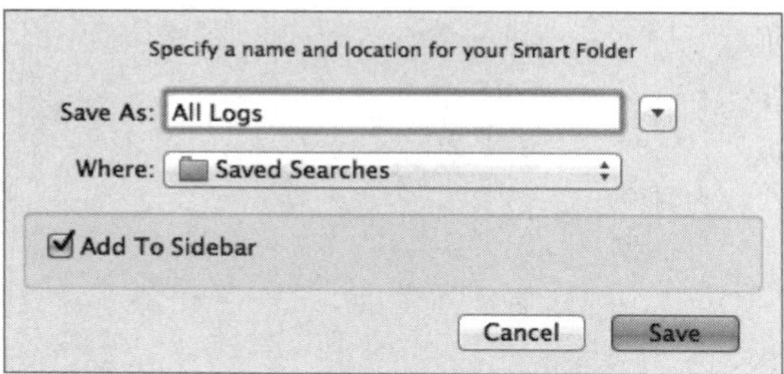

13 Close the search window.

Lesson **17**

File Archives

Archiving and backup are both synonymous with copying data to another location for safekeeping, yet in the context of this guide, they are different processes serving different purposes. In OS X, archiving is typically a manual process that involves creating compressed copies of selected data. Archive formats are efficient from a storage and data transfer perspective, but they generally require user interaction.

GOALS

- Create and open archive files via Finder
- Create and manage disk images

While backup is detailed in Lesson 18, "Time Machine," this lesson focuses on the archive technologies in OS X: zip archives and disk images. This lesson compares the benefits of each archive technology and then guides you through the creation and management of these archives.

Reference 17.1
File Archive Comparison

At its essence, archiving is the practice of saving copies of important information to another location or format better suited for long-term storage or network transfer. Large amounts of hard disk storage have become much less expensive in the last few years, but this type of storage is still not as reliable as tape or optical media in terms of longevity. This type of archival media has not kept up with the tremendous growth of hard disks, so storing archival data in a more efficient form by compressing it is still relevant. Also, no matter how robust your Internet connection is, there never seems to be enough bandwidth, so compressing items in preparation for data transfer is almost always a time-saver.

OS X includes two archival technologies, archives and disk images, which allow you to combine multiple files and compress the data into a more efficient file suited for long-term storage or network data transfer.

Zip Archives

First, the Finder allows you to create zip archives from a selection of files or folders. This is an efficient method for archiving relatively small amounts of data quickly. The zip archive format is also widely compatible, as many operating systems include software to decompress zip archives back to their original items. However, zip archives in OS X do not offer the flexibility provided by disk images.

Disk Images

Disk images, created using Disk Utility, are more widely used in OS X for archival purposes because they offer many features not available from zip archives. Primarily, disk images allow you to archive the contents of an entire file system into a single file that can be compressed, encrypted, or both. Disk images can also be created as read/write so you can easily make changes to them over time. The only downside to disk images created using Disk Utility is that, by default, only Macs can access the content—other systems require third-party software to access Mac disk image content.

Reference 17.2
Zip Archives

The Finder allows you to quickly create a compressed zip archive from any number of selected items, or expand a zip archive to its original number of items. By default, creating a zip archive in the Finder doesn't delete the original items, and expanding a zip archive doesn't delete the original archive.

Create Zip Archives

To create a zip archive in the Finder, select the items you want to archive and compress in the Finder. You can hold down the Shift key to quickly select contiguous lists of items, or hold down the Command key to quickly select noncontiguous items. Then simply choose File > Compress "Items," or use secondary (or Control) click on the items and choose Compress "Items" from the shortcut menu. The word "Items" in the menu will be replaced by the name of a single item you have selected or the number of items you have selected.

If the archival process is going to take more than a few seconds, the Finder shows a progress dialog with the estimated time required to complete the compression task. You can also choose to cancel the archive by clicking the small X button on the far right. When the process finishes, you are left with a zip archive named either Archive.zip or Item.zip, where Item is the name of the single item you chose to archive and compress.

Once the archive process is complete, it's always interesting to compare the original items' size with the archive's size using the Get Info or Inspector windows in the Finder. In many cases, you can expect at least a 50 percent decrease in file size. On the other hand, many media formats are already quite compressed in their original form, so you may not experience very good results when compressing these types of files.

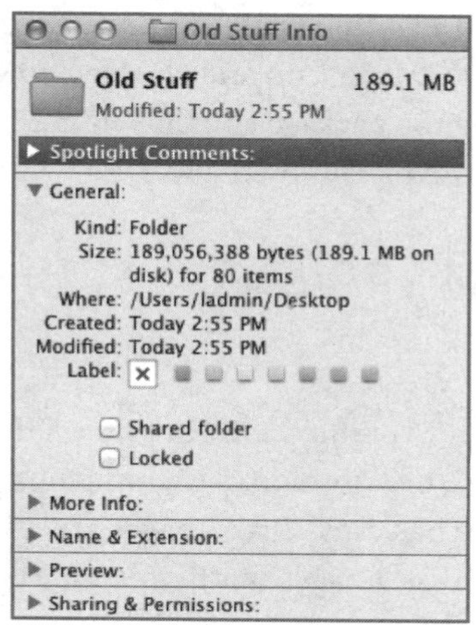

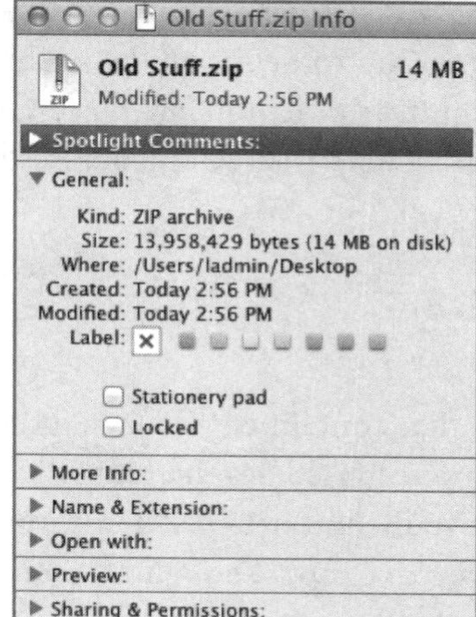

Expand Zip Archives

Expanding a zip archive in the Finder is as simple as double-clicking the zip archive file. The Finder, by default, decompresses the entire archive file and places the resulting files and folders in the same folder as the original zip archive. The Finder cannot list or extract individual items from a zip archive. Also by default, the Finder does not delete the original zip archive.

If you need more control over how zip archives are expanded, open /System/Library/CoreServices/Archive Utility.app, and then choose Archive Utility > Preferences. These preferences allow you to adjust how zip archives are both expanded and compressed. Specifically, this includes options about how original items are handled after an archive transition.

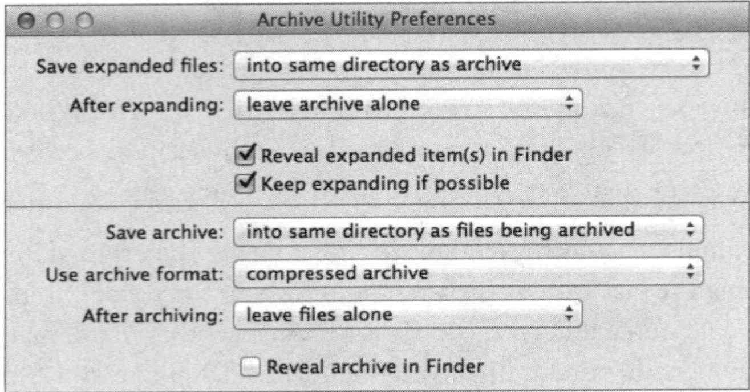

Alternatively, the Archive Utility contains a system preference pane that can be installed if you find yourself making frequent changes to these settings. To install this preference pane, use secondary (or Control) click on the Archive Utility.app icon and choose Show Package Contents from the shortcut menu. Once viewing the package contents in the Finder, navigate to and double-click /Contents/Resources/Archives.prefPane.

Reference 17.3
Disk Images

Disk images are files that contain entire virtual disks and volumes. OS X relies on disk images for several core technologies, including software distribution, system imaging, NetBoot, Legacy FileVault, and network Time Machine backups. Disk images are also useful as a personal archive tool. Though Mac-created disk images work only on Mac computers by default, they are much more flexible to use than zip archives. Disk images provide advanced compression and encryption, but their greatest benefit is that they can be treated like a removable volume.

Mounting Disk Images

If in the past you have manually installed any Apple or third-party software downloaded from the Internet, you have already used a mounted disk image. By default the Safari web browser automatically mounts any downloaded disk image, but you can also manually mount disk images at any time from the Finder. To access the contents of a disk image, you simply double-click the disk image file in the Finder.

This mounts the volume inside the disk image file as if you had just connected a normal storage device. Even if the disk image file is located on a remote file server, you can still mount it as if it were a local disk. You can treat the mounted disk image volume as you would any other storage device by navigating through its hierarchy and selecting files and folders as you need them. Further, if the disk image is read/write, you can add to the contents of the disk image by simply dragging items to the volume.

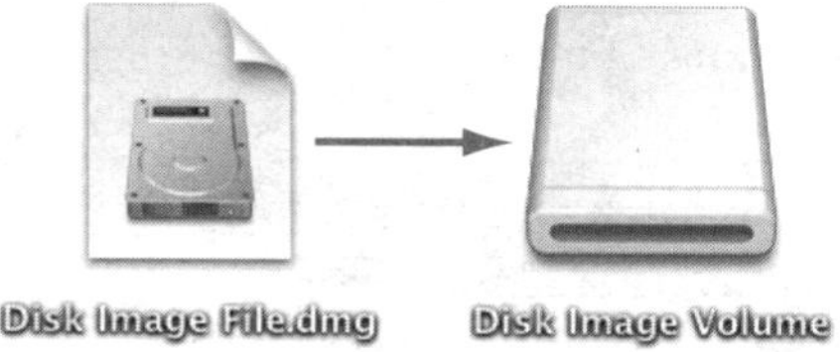

NOTE ► When you are done with a disk image volume, be sure to properly unmount and eject it as you would any other removable volume.

Disk Image Options

Using /Applications/Utilities/Disk Utility to make disk images allows you to create blank images, or images containing copies of selected folders or even entire file systems. OS X supports disk images up to 2 terabytes. Disk images also feature a number of configuration options, including:

- Image format—Disk images can be read-only or read/write. They can also be a set size or expandable as a sparse disk image. Sparse disk images take up only as much space as necessary and automatically grow as you add items to them.

- Compression—Read-only disk images can be compressed to save space. With a compressed disk image, any free space becomes negligible in size, and most other files average a 50 percent reduction in size.
- Encryption—Any disk image can be protected with a password and encrypted with strong 128-bit or 256-bit AES encryption. Choosing a higher bit rate is more secure but degrades performance. This feature is useful for securing data stored on otherwise unsecure volumes like removable disks and network shares. The encryption always happens on the local computer, so even if the disk image file is physically stored externally, as on a network file share, the data is always encrypted as it travels across the connection.
- File system—Disk images can contain any partition scheme or volume format that OS X supports, including optical media formats. Details regarding the differences between file system options are covered in Lesson 10, "File Systems and Storage."

Create Empty Disk Images

You can create an empty disk image, which you can fill with content over time by opening Disk Utility and then choosing File > New > Blank Disk Image. Alternatively, with nothing selected in the disks list, you can click the New Image button.

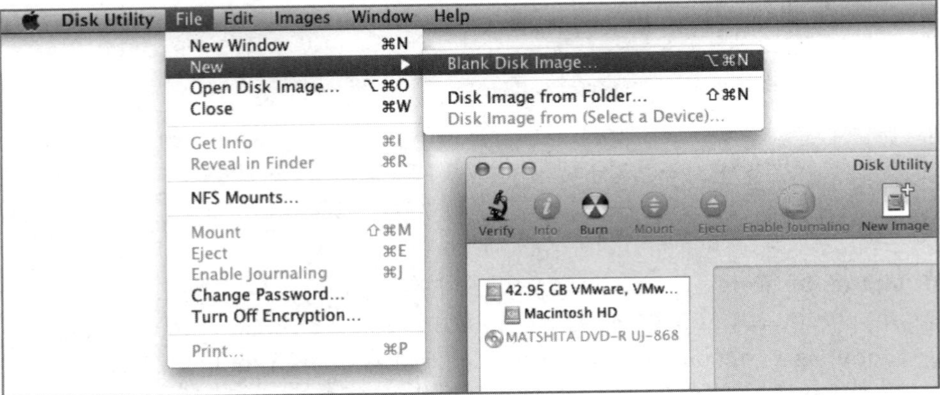

The New Blank Image dialog allows you to define the parameters for the new disk image. At minimum you need to select a name and destination for the resulting disk image file. You should also enter a name for the volume inside the disk image. Note that the disk image file and volume names do not have to match but should be similar so that you can recognize their relationship.

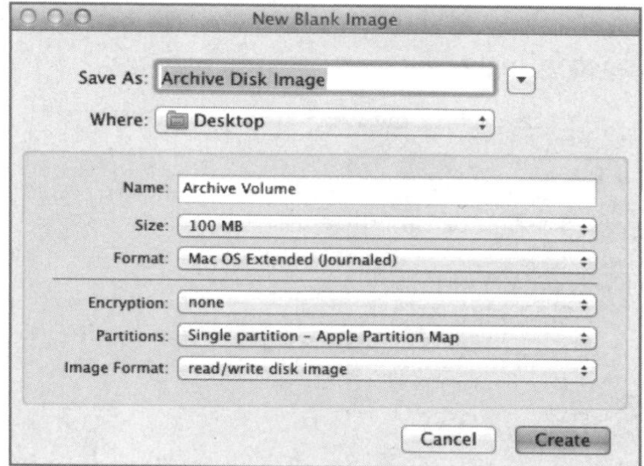

The remaining options can remain as default, but they likely won't serve your needs. The options include:

- Size—Selecting the right disk image size is key, as this disk image will occupy only as much space as the files you copy inside it. Obviously if you're going to save it on an external volume of limited size, that should define your maximum size.
- Format—You can select a different volume format from this pop-up menu, but in most cases you will want to stick with the default Mac OS Extended (Journaled) selection.
- Encryption—You can optionally select an encryption at this point from the pop-up menu. For most uses, 128-bit AES is secure enough and still provides good performance. If you chose to have an encrypted disk image, you will be prompted to enter a password for the disk image upon creation.
- Partitions—You can select a different partition scheme from this pop-up menu, but in most cases you will want to stick with the default Apple Partition Map selection.
- Image Format—Choosing "sparse disk image" from this pop-up menu will create an automatically resizable disk image. This provides the most flexible option as the disk image will remain writable and always occupy the least amount of space. Thus, selecting this format of disk image allows you to define a very large disk image size without actually using that much free space to start with.

Once you have defined your disk image options, click Create to create the disk image. After the system has created the new blank disk image, it automatically mounts it. From the Finder, you can open Get Info windows on both the disk image file and the disk image volume to verify that the volume size is much larger than the image size. As you copy files to the volume, the disk image file grows accordingly.

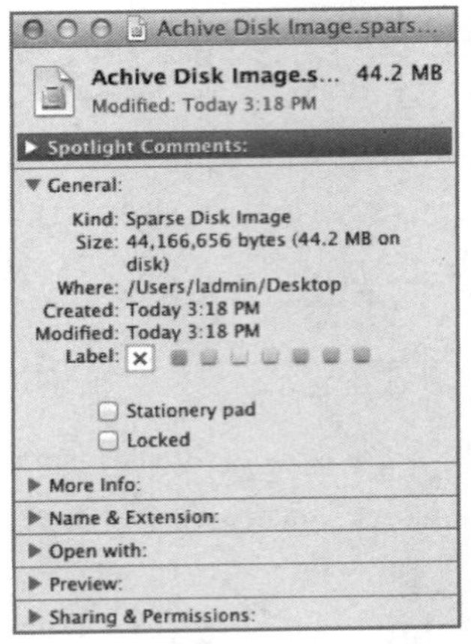

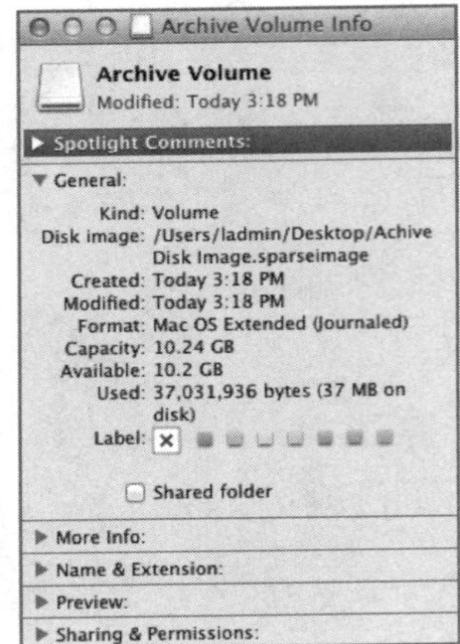

TIP You can change the format of a disk image at any time in Disk Utility by choosing Images > Convert. This opens a dialog allowing you to select the image you want to change and save a copy of the image with new options.

Create Disk Image Archives

To create a disk image that contains copies of selected items, open Disk Utility and choose File > New > Disk Image from Folder. This opens a file browser window allowing you to select the folder you want to copy into a new disk image.

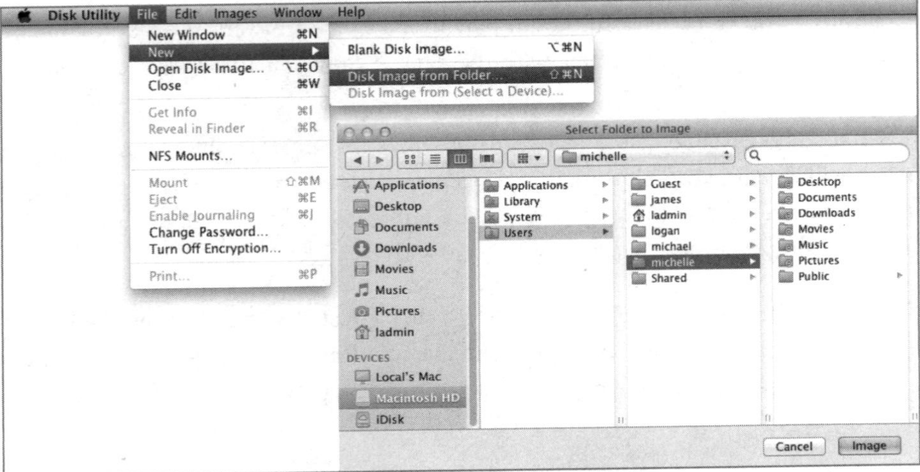

To create a disk image from the contents of an entire volume, use the same menu option, Disk Image from Folder, and then simply select the volume. It may be tempting to choose Disk Image from (Select a Device), but this option copies the empty space on the volume as well, making the resulting disk image artificially large. The only time you should create an image of a device is when creating images of optical media.

NOTE ► Disk Utility can only make disk images of volumes that it can temporarily unmount. Thus, you cannot make a disk image of the currently running system volume.

Upon selection of the disk image source the "New Image from Folder" dialog appears. At minimum you need to select a name and destination for the resulting disk image file. Note that the name of the volume inside disk image is automatically set to the name of selected source.

NOTE ► Make sure you have enough free space on the destination volume where you plan to save your disk image file.

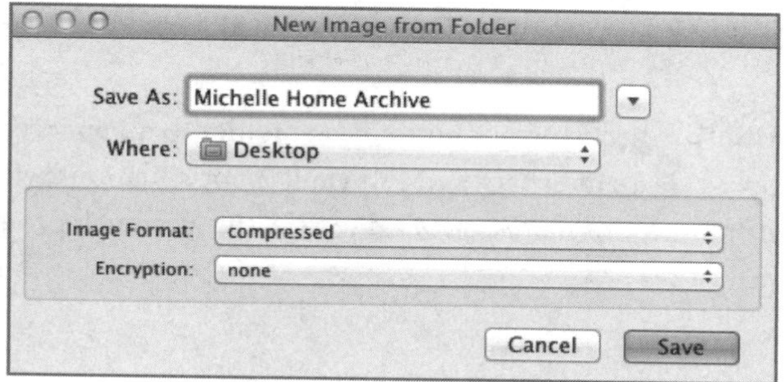

The remaining options in the "New Image from Folder" dialog can remain as default, but they may not serve your needs. The options include:

- Image Format—The default selection of "compressed" is probably the best choice for archive purposes as the resulting disk image file will use the least amount of space. However, it takes nearly twice as much free space to *create* a compressed disk image. This is because the system must create a noncompressed image first, and then convert the first image into a compressed image.
- Encryption—You can optionally select an encryption at this point from the pop-up menu. For most uses, 128-bit AES is secure enough and still provides good performance. If you choose to have an encrypted disk image, you will be prompted to enter a password for the disk image upon creation. Note that the choice to save the password to the login keychain is enabled by default.

Once you have defined your disk image options, click Save to create the disk image. Depending on the amount of data that has to be copied and the image format you chose, it can take anywhere from minutes to hours for the disk image copy process to complete. Disk Utility opens a small progress dialog that also allows you to cancel the disk image copy by clicking Cancel.

NOTE ▶ You have to authenticate as an administrator in order to create an image containing items for which you don't have read permissions.

Exercise 17.1
Create Disk Images

▶ Prerequisites

- ▸ You must have created the Local Admin (Exercise 3.1 or 3.2) and Chris Johnson (Exercise 6.1) accounts.

In this exercise, you will use Disk Utility to archive your entire home folder to an encrypted disk image. Encrypted disk images provide an alternative to FileVault 2, for situations where you don't need to protect the entire volume, or where you want to selectively unlock groups of files only when they're needed.

Create a Disk Image with Disk Utility

1. If necessary, log in as Chris Johnson.
2. Open Disk Utility from the Utilities folder.
3. Choose File > New > Disk Image from Folder.

   An Open dialog appears.
4. Select your home folder.

5 Click Image.

The New Image from Folder dialog appears.

6 Set the image settings as follows:

Save As: **ChrisHome**

Where: /Users/Shared (you have to click the disclosure button in order to select this location)

Image Format: compressed

Encryption: 128-bit AES encryption (recommended)

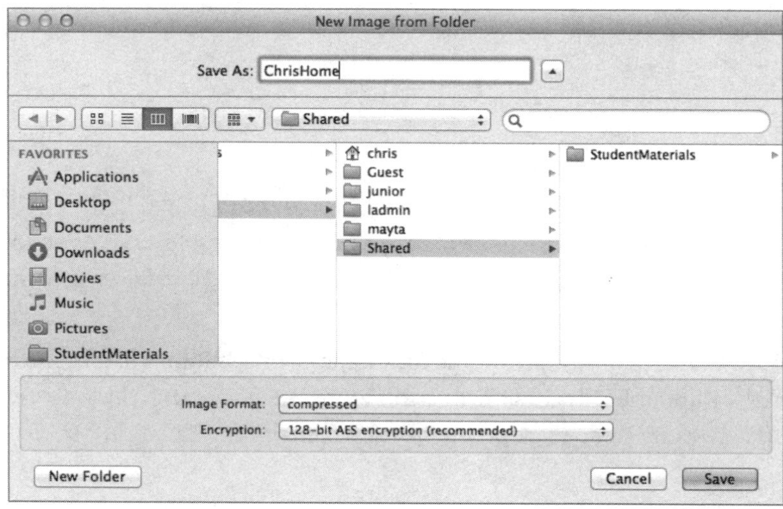

7 Click Save.

8 If prompted, authenticate as Local Admin.

9 When asked to provide a password to secure ChrisHome.dmg, type **chris**, and then click OK.

Normally you would want to use a much more secure password. Notice that the Password Assistant is available.

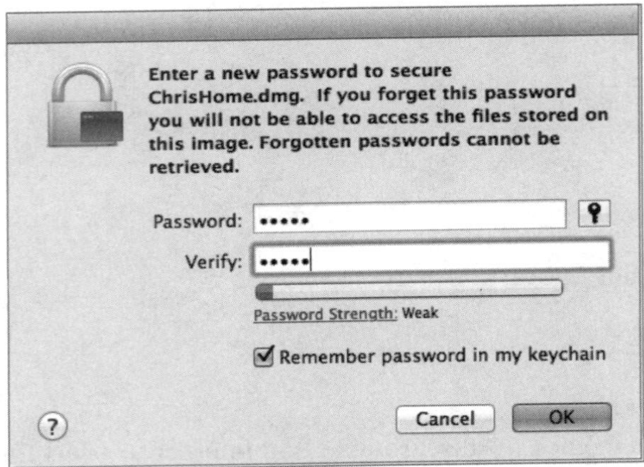

A Disk Utility Progress window appears.

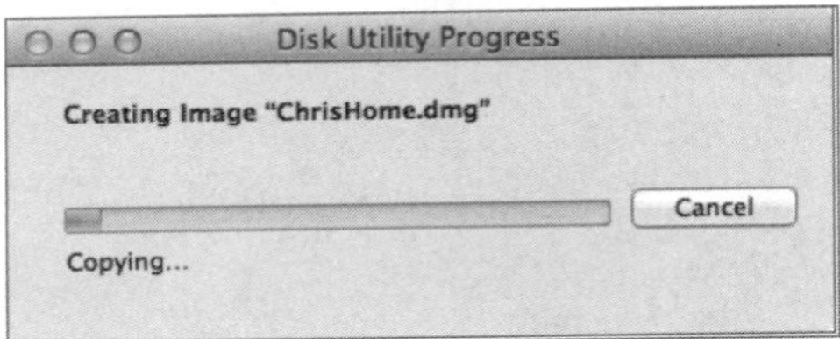

When Disk Utility is finished, the image file ChrisHome.dmg appears in Disk Utility.

You can use this method to quickly create backups of important folders. As you saw, you do not need to encrypt every disk image. You can also use the read/write format if you want to be able to modify the contents.

Note that Disk Utility keeps the name of the disk image in its volumes list, in the bottom section. You can double-click that icon and mount the image later, as long as the disk image remains in the same place where it was originally saved.

10 Quit Disk Utility.

11 Navigate to /Users/Shared, and open ChrisHome.dmg.

   The disk image opens without you having to provide the password because the password was stored in your keychain for you by default. You can change this behavior by deselecting the "Remember password in my keychain" checkbox when asked to set the password for the image.

   The chris volume mounts, and a Finder window opens to show you the contents of the image. This is the volume contained within the ChrisHome.dmg disk image. The filename does not have to reflect any volume name inside it.

12 Eject the disk image.

Lesson **18**

Time Machine

Several mature and relatively easy-to-use backup solutions are available for OS X, so you may be wondering why Apple chose to invent a new backup architecture when they introduced OS X v10.5. They did a little research and discovered that, prior to the introduction of Time Machine, only 4 percent of Mac users were backing up their data on a regular basis. This was an unacceptable number, so Apple decided that the only way to convince users to do so on a regular basis was to create a new backup process that would be as easy as possible to set up and also surprisingly fun to use. The Apple solution was Time Machine.

In this lesson you will learn how Time Machine allows users to easily browse the backup history of their entire file system. Details regarding the configuration of Time Machine settings are also covered. Finally, you will explore multiple methods for recovering data from Time Machine backups.

GOALS

- Understand the technology behind Time Machine
- Configure Time Machine to back up important data
- Restore data or entire systems from a Time Machine backup

Reference 18.1
Time Machine Architecture

Aside from being built into the operating system, Time Machine has two features that make it fundamentally different from any other solution currently out there. First, configuring Time Machine is so easy it's nearly automatic. The system practically begs you to set up Time Machine if you haven't done so already, and with as little as one click it's configured.

The second, more significant feature is that Time Machine is so tightly integrated with the operating system that users don't even have to exit the application they are currently using to recover data. Applications, both built-in and third-party, can tie directly into the Time Machine backup system. From applications supporting Time Machine, a user can activate the visually striking Time Machine interface and travel back through time to see the application's data as it was in the past. If an application doesn't yet support Time Machine, you can use the Finder while in the Time Machine interface to browse the entire file system through time.

Time Machine Disks

Time Machine can back up to any locally connected Mac OS Extended volume that is not the startup volume. You are allowed to select a backup disk that resides as another partition on the system disk, but this is an incredibly bad idea—if the system disk dies, so does your backup. As such, many chose an external USB, FireWire, or Thunderbolt disk as their Time Machine backup disk.

External disks though have the potential to be lost or stolen. Thus, OS X Lion introduced support for an encrypted local backup disk. This option automatically reformats the backup disk as Mac OS Extended (Journaled, Encrypted). Using this option requires setting a password, which is used to access the encrypted Time Machine backup volume. When configured, the password is saved to the local system keychain for automatic retrieval. However, if the encrypted Time Machine backup volume is connected to another system, the user has to manually enter the password to access the backup items.

If you don't have a local volume suited for backup, you can also select a shared network volume as your backup disk. Time Machine supports network shares by creating a disk image on the share to store the backups. Time Machine currently only supports backing up to Apple Filing Protocol (AFP) network shares hosted from OS X Server or Time Capsule wireless base stations.

> **MORE INFO ▶** You can find out more about configuring OS X Server as a Time Machine backup disk from *Apple Pro Training Series: OS X Server Essentials.*

> **MORE INFO ▶** You can find out more about the Apple Time Capsule wireless base station at www.apple.com/timecapsule.

New in OS X Mountain Lion is support for selecting more than one Time Machine backup disk. This is especially useful for those who are away from their primary Time Machine backup disk for extended periods. For example, you can choose to back up to a Time Capsule wireless base station at home, and also use a portable external disk when traveling.

Time Machine Schedule

Logistically, Time Machine uses a sophisticated background process, named `backupd`, to automatically create new backups of the entire file system every hour. This only works, though, if the backup disk is readily available. As more users go for portable Macs, it's becoming increasingly possible that a user may be away from his backup disk for quite a while.

Introduced with OS X Lion, Time Machine supports local snapshots. As the name implies, Time Machine takes local snapshots if the backup disk is unavailable. Even if the user is away from the backup disk, he at least has access to restore from the local snapshots. This feature is only enabled on Mac portables with Time Machine left in the "on" state. Once the Mac can locate the backup disk again, the local snapshots are converted to traditional backups and saved to the disk. Time Machine attempts to keep a history of local snapshots available as well, in case you need to restore when the backup disk is offline. To save space though, this local snapshot history is not as deep as the full backup.

While the Time Machine local snapshots are a convenient new feature, they certainly aren't true backups, as they are located on the same disk they are backing up. If the system disk fails, the local snapshots are lost as well. This is why, after not backing up to the backup disk for ten days, the system warns the user on a regular basis to reconnect that disk. Train your users to ensure their Macs are connected to their Time Machine disks on a regular basis. Again, as long as the Mac can connect to the disk, Time Machine automatically handles the backup maintenance.

Another issue that may prevent Time Machine backups is system sleep. Quite simply, if the computer is asleep it may not run the backup job. To rectify this situation, OS X Mountain Lion includes the ability to back up to Time Machine while the system is in Power Nap mode. For Mac systems that support Power Nap, even while the system is "sleeping" it still attempts to perform Time Machine backups or local snapshots every hour. Obviously, the availability of the backup disk likewise affects the ability of a sleeping system to back up even with Power Nap enabled.

> **MORE INFO ▸** Power Nap details are covered in Lesson 29, "Startup, Shutdown, and Sleep Modes."

Time Machine Backup Format

Time Machine uses several tricks to keep backups as small as possible so that you can maintain a deep history. The initial Time Machine backup copies almost the entire contents of your file system to the specified backup volume.

In order to provide fast backups and convenient restores, Time Machine does not use a compressed archive format common to many other backup systems. Instead, Time Machine simply copies the items as is to the backup disk. As you'll see later, this allows for easy access to those items.

The space saving comes into play with each subsequent backup. Between backups, a background process, similar to the one used by the Spotlight search service, automatically tracks any changes to the original file system. When the next scheduled backup occurs, only the items that have changed are copied to the backup volume. Time Machine then combines this new content with hard link file system pointers (which occupy nearly zero disk space) to the previous backup content, and creates a simulated view of the entire file system at that point in time.

Time Machine also saves space by ignoring files that do not need to be backed up, as they can be re-created after a restoration. Generally speaking, Time Machine ignores temporary files, Spotlight indexes, items in the Trash, and anything that can be considered a cache. Of particular note, Time Machine doesn't back up system log files, which you could need for later troubleshooting. Software developers can also tell Time Machine to ignore specific application data that does not need to be backed up.

> **MORE INFO ▸** Specifically, Time Machine always ignores files as defined by a configuration file that lives at /System/Library/CoreServices/backupd.bundle/Contents/Resources/StdExclusions.plist. You may find it beneficial to modify this file to suit your own backup needs.

Eventually, so as not to waste space on your backup volume with historical data that has outlived its usefulness, Time Machine starts "aging out" backups. Time Machine only keeps hourly backups for a day, daily backups for a week, and weekly backups until your backup volume is full. After your backup volume is full, Time Machine starts deleting the oldest items first. However, Time Machine always keeps at least one copy of every item that is still on your current file system.

NOTE ▶ Do not confuse Time Machine with snapshot technology common on other operating systems. While snapshots do create multiple instances of a file system through time, they do not provide you with a backup, as they don't actually copy data to another storage device. In other words, if a disk containing file system snapshots dies, those snapshots are just as lost as the current data on the dead disk.

Time Machine Caveats

Although Apple has put a lot of work into Time Machine, it is not without flaws. The Time Machine backup architecture does not lend itself well to large files that change often. For example, many database files appear as large, single files to the file system. While the database application may be able to change just a few bytes of the large file as a user edits the database, Time Machine doesn't recognize this, and it has to create another copy of the entire database file during the next backup. This obviously fills your backup volume much quicker than if the database had been stored as many smaller files.

This leads to the next Time Machine issue: running out of backup space. Once Time Machine fills up the backup volume, it begins deleting older items to make room for newer ones. Therefore, the depth of your backup history varies based not only on the size of your backup volume, but also on how often you change your files and how Time Machine recognizes those changes. Because you cannot change how Time Machine chooses to delete older items, you may discover that items you thought would still be on the backup volume have already been deleted.

TIP ▶ By default, Time Machine lets you know if it needs to delete older items to make space for new backups.

One final issue is that Time Machine can only back up Legacy FileVault accounts when the user is logged out of the system. The solution to this problem is to simply stop using Legacy FileVault in favor of OS X FileVault 2, as covered in Lesson 11, "FileVault 2.".

Reference 18.2
Configuring Time Machine

Despite the rather complex process going on behind the scenes to make Time Machine possible, configuration couldn't be easier. In fact, Time Machine is enabled by default and simply waiting for you to pick a backup disk. If you haven't configured a Time Machine backup disk, the system automatically scans the network for a Time Machine network share or waits for you to attach an external disk. If the system locates either, you are prompted to select it as your backup disk. If you select your backup disk with this method, after you click the "Use as Backup Disk" button, Time Machine is fully configured. It's just that easy.

Depending on the amount of data that has to be backed up, it can take from minutes to hours for the initial backup to complete. Time Machine opens a small progress dialog that also allows you to cancel the backup by clicking the small "X" button to the right of the progress bar. The Time Machine preferences have a similar progress bar.

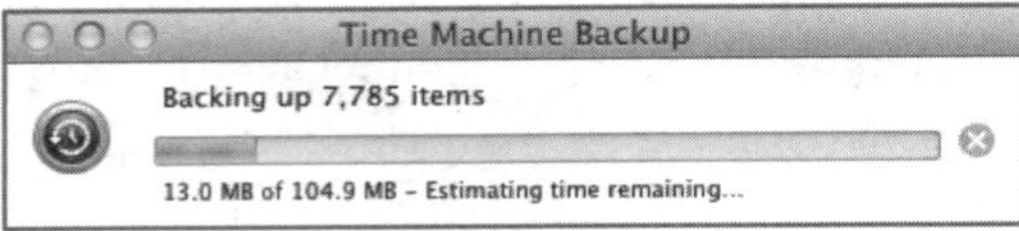

Subsequent backups occur automatically in the background. You can verify the last backup and force an immediate backup from the Time Machine menu near the clock in the menu bar. From this menu you can also open the Time Machine preferences, which show you the time and date of the oldest, last, and next backup.

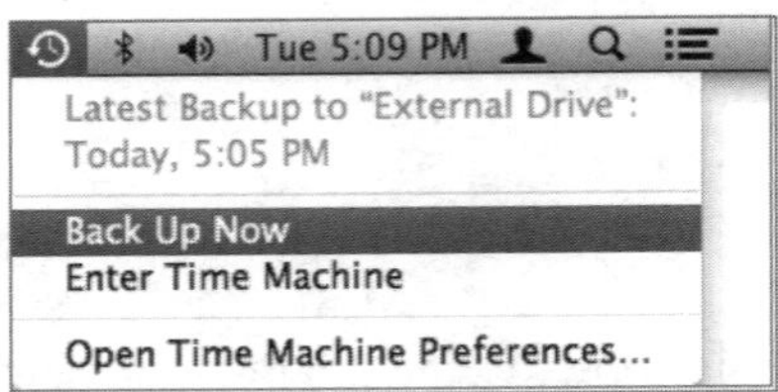

Time Machine Preferences

If you need to select a network backup disk or you want to manually configure backup settings to better suit your needs, you can do so from the Time Machine preferences. You can open the Time Machine preferences from the System Preferences application, the Time Machine menu, or by using secondary (or Control) click on the Time Machine icon if it's in the Dock.

TIP If you only want Time Machine to back up when you say so, simply turn it "off" in the Time Machine preferences and use the Time Machine menu to initiate manual backups. You can also postpone backups by disconnecting from the backup volume, though this works only for locally attached backup volumes.

Configure Backup Disks

Again, OS X Mountain Lion includes the ability to select multiple Time Machine backup disks. Depending on the number of backup disks currently configured, the Time Machine preferences will look a bit different.

To add the first backup disk, click the Select Backup Disk button. If you want to modify the configuration of a single backup disk, click the Select Disk button. Finally, if you want to modify the configuration of multiple backup disks, select the text that reads, "Add or

Remove Backup Disks." Any of these methods reveals the Time Machine backup disk management dialog, which allows you to both add and remove backup disks.

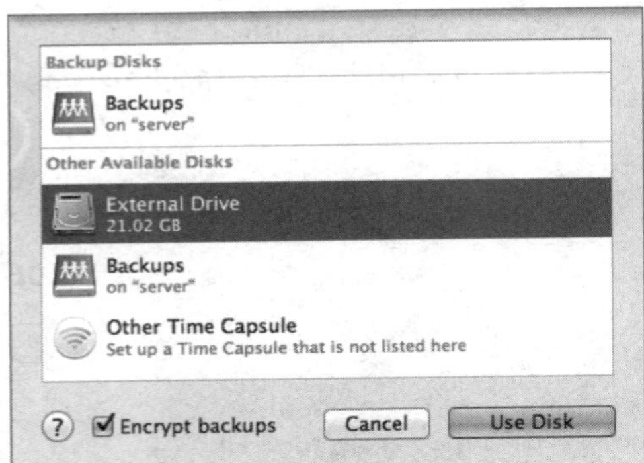

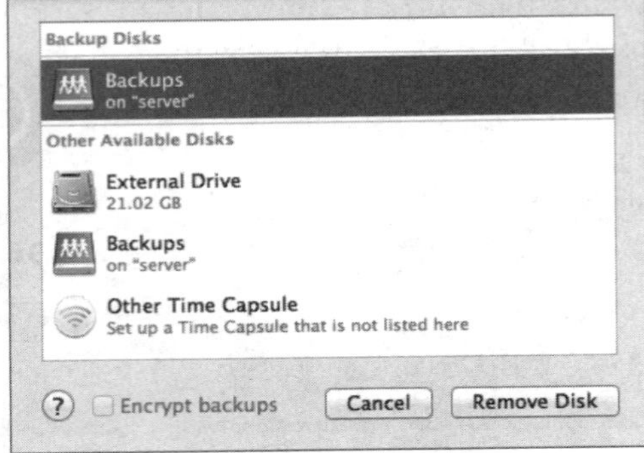

If you selected a locally connected external disk and the encryption option, you need to specify a password to protect the encryption along with a password hint. This password is saved to the local Mac computer's System keychain so backups can occur unattended. If you forget the password used to encrypt the Time Machine backup disk, its contents are lost forever. Not even Apple can recover the data.

NOTE ► Selecting the option to encrypt the Time Machine backup disk erases the disk's contents.

If you selected a network share or Time Capsule as the disk, you need to specify an authentication that allows you to access the share. This authentication information is saved to the local Mac computer's System keychain so backups can occur unattended.

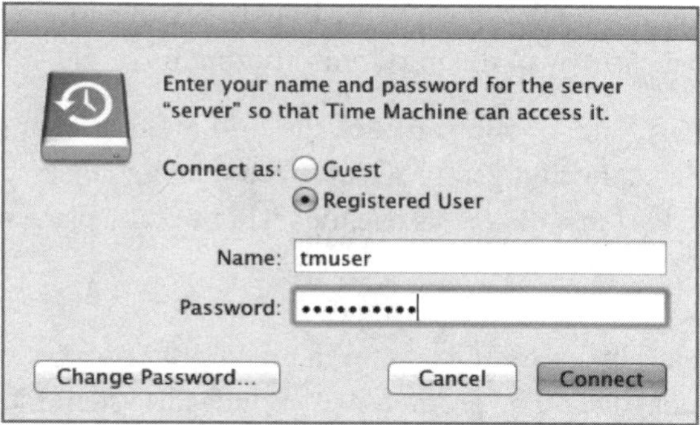

If you configure a new backup disk, Time Machine waits two minutes, allowing you to make further configuration changes, before it starts the first backup to the new disk. Again, you can always return to the Time Machine backup disk management dialog to add or remove backup disks.

NOTE ► If your portable Mac supports local backup snapshots, this is configured automatically.

Time Machine Options

Clicking the Options button at the bottom of the Time Machine preferences reveals a dialog allowing you to adjust backup settings.

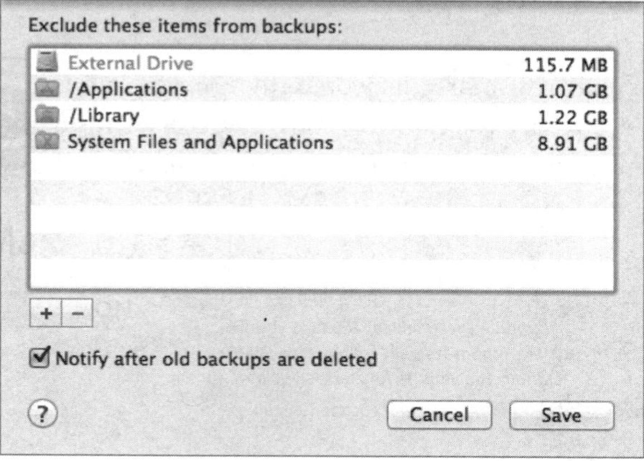

The most important configuration choice you can make with Time Machine is to exclude items from the backup. Excluding items obviously reduces the amount of space required to maintain your backups. It's not uncommon for users to leave only the /Users folder as the single item to back up; after all, that's where all the important user items reside.

You can drag and drop items into the list field, or you can click the Add (+) button at the bottom of the list to reveal a file browser, allowing you to select specific folders or volumes to exclude. Make sure to click Save to close this dialog, as backups will not take place until you have set the options here.

NOTE ▶ If you're going to save space by excluding system items, simply add the /System folder to the exclude list and you will be prompted to exclude all system files or just the /System folder. It's best to exclude all system files.

NOTE ▶ If you do not perform a full backup of your system volume, you will not be able to perform a full restoration of it. Instead, you will have to install OS X first, and then restore the remainder using Migration Assistant, as covered later in this lesson.

Reference 18.3
Restoring from Time Machine

Using Time Machine to restore data is what many consider its best feature because of the dynamic interface Apple has created to "look through time." This interface is available by opening the Time Machine application or using the Time Machine menu. Few applications currently support the Time Machine interface, so in most cases you are presented with a historical view in the Finder.

For quick access to Time Machine, you can also drag its icon to the Dock. From the Time Machine icon in the Dock, you can secondary (or Control) click to reveal a shortcut menu allowing you to adjust Time Machine preferences, start a backup immediately, or browse another Time Machine backup.

Restore via Time Machine

The Finder windows let you browse as usual, with one significant addition. You can use the navigation arrows on the bottom right, or the navigation timeline on the right side, to view Finder contents as they change through time.

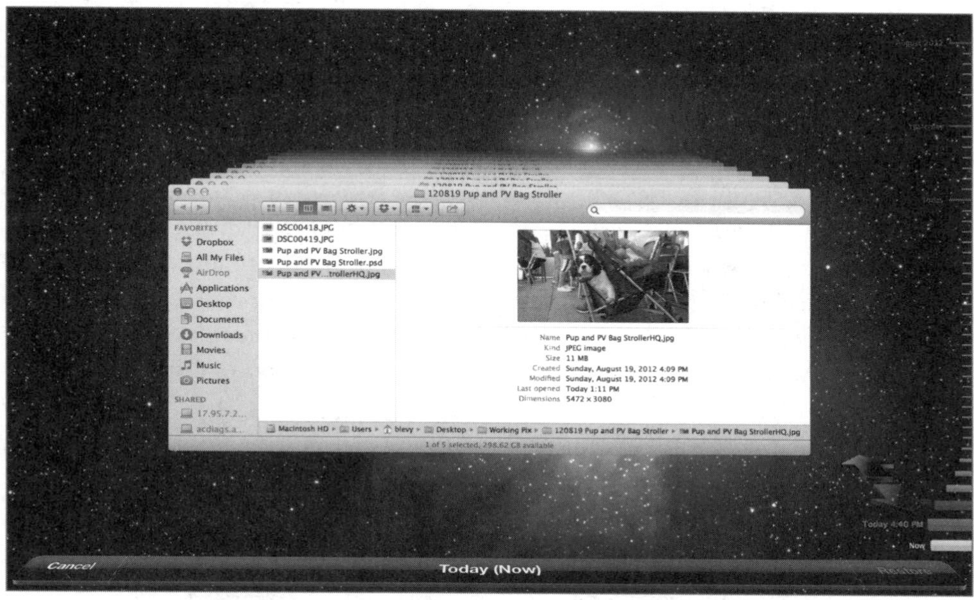

NOTE ▸ If you use an encrypted disk or network share for your backup disk, and you are trying to restore to a different system, you have to enter a password to access the backup data.

If the local snapshots feature is enabled, the local non-backed-up snapshots show as gray tick marks in the navigation timeline. Normal snapshots, which are backed up to the Time Machine disk, show as pink tick marks in this timeline. If any of the pink tick marks appear dimmed, it's because the Time Machine backup disk is currently unavailable.

TIP You can examine the amount of disk space used for local snapshots by opening the About This Mac dialog (from the Apple menu). Click More Info, and then select the Storage tab. Any space on the system volume used for local snapshots will appear as "Backups."

To aid in your search through time, the Spotlight search field remains active, and you can quickly preview any item using the Quick Look feature in the Finder (by pressing the

Spacebar). Once you have found the item you were looking for, simply click the Restore button and the Finder returns to "the present" with your recovered file intact where it once was.

NOTE ► Legacy FileVault users cannot access their home folder backup via the standard Time Machine interface. They can, however, use the following three methods to restore their home folder from a Time Machine backup.

Restore via Migration Assistant

You can restore a complete user home folder or other nonsystem data from a Time Machine backup using the Migration Assistant. When the Migration Assistant opens, either during new system setup or when opened from /Applications/Utilities, simply choose to restore from a Time Machine backup. Once you have selected the backup disk, the remainder of the Migration Assistant process is similar to the standard migration process covered in Lesson 3, "Setup and Configuration," for applications and settings, or Lesson 7, "User Home Folders," for user-specific items.

NOTE ► Legacy FileVault user accounts can only be fully restored by using the Migration Assistant during the initial OS X system setup.

Restore an Entire System

You can restore an entire system volume when started up from OS X Recovery. This technique assumes you did not exclude any items from your system volume; thus, you have backed up the entire system volume.

When started up from OS X Recovery, as covered in Lesson 4, select Restore From Time Machine Backup in the OS X Utilities window to open the Time Machine System Restore Assistant. The assistant first scans for local and network Time Machine backup volumes. Once you have selected the Time Machine volume, you can restore the entire system from any backup instance on that volume to your new system disk.

Manually Restore via Finder

If you are experiencing problems using one of the other Time Machine restoration interfaces, you can always browse the backup from the Finder. The Time Machine backup technology uses file system features that are part of standard Mac OS Extended volumes, so no special software is needed to browse through backup contents.

NOTE ► Do not directly modify the contents of a Time Machine backup, as doing so could damage the backup hierarchy. The default file system permissions will not give you write access to these items.

NOTE ► Legacy FileVault home folders remain inside an encrypted disk image in the Time Machine backup. Thus you need the user's password to access the secure home folder contents.

NOTE ► If your Time Machine configuration supports local snapshots, those snapshots are cached locally to a hidden /Volumes/MobileBackups folder. While you can navigate here and look around, the items in this location aren't permanent, as they will eventually be copied to the backup disk and then erased on the local disk to save space.

If you're accessing a locally attached disk for Time Machine, the backups are located on the root of your backup volume in a folder named Backups.backupdb. Inside the backup database folder are folders with the name of each computer backed up to that volume. Inside each computer folder are folders named with a date and time indicating each backup. Finally, inside each dated folder are folders representing each backed-up volume.

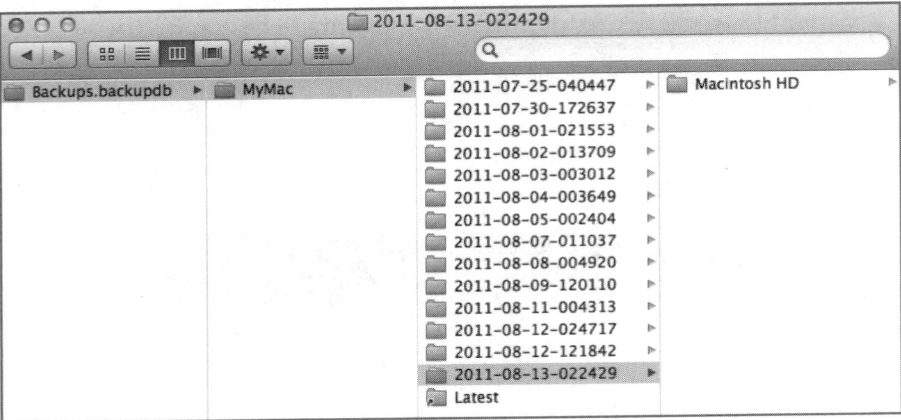

If you're accessing Time Machine over a network, you need to manually connect to the Time Machine share first. (Connecting to shares is covered in Lesson 25, "Network Services.") Once connected, you need to locate the Time Machine backup disk images. They are at the root of the Time Machine share, most commonly named Backups. Each Mac computer's backup is saved as a separate sparse disk image file named with the computer's sharing name.

Double-click to mount the Time Machine backup disk image volume, which will be named "Backup of" followed by the computer's name. Inside this volume is the same Backups.backupdb folder and contents you would find on a directly connected Time Machine backup.

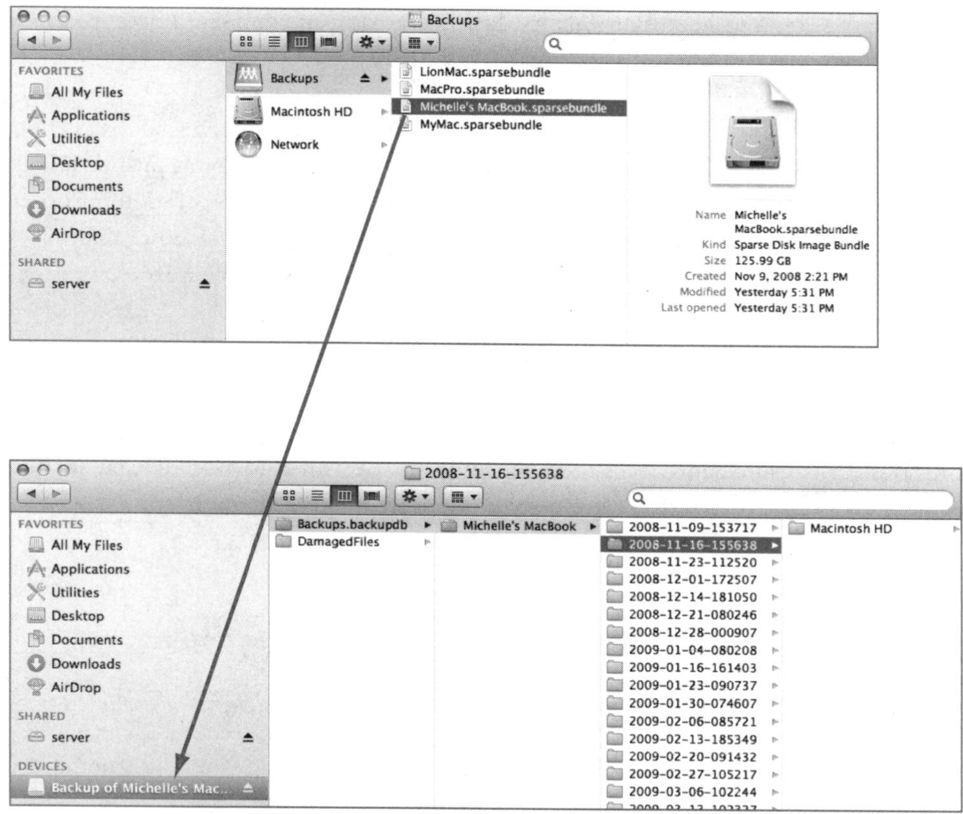

Exercise 18.1
Enable and Configure Time Machine

Prerequisites

- You must have created the Local Admin (Exercise 3.1 or 3.2) and Chris Johnson (Exercise 6.1) accounts.
- You must have partitioned your internal disk to create a Backup partition (Exercise 10.1), or have an external disk in Mac OS Extended format, or have a Time Capsule appliance to use for backups.

In this exercise, you will configure Time Machine to back up your user home folders to either its Backup partition, or to an external disk drive.

> **NOTE ▶** Backing up to a second partition on your computer's internal disk is not a recommended backup strategy, because it provides no protection against disk failure or loss of the computer. It is presented in this exercise for demonstration purposes only. If you are performing these exercises on a computer you use other than for exercises, configure it to back up to an external disk or Time Capsule instead.

Configure Exclusions for Time Machine

By default, Time Machine backs up the entire startup volume (excluding some types of files), but for this exercise you will configure it to back up only user files. In most situations, this is sufficient, since the system and applications can always be reinstalled; but if you want to be able to do a full system restore, do not exclude anything from the backup.

1. If necessary, log in as Chris Johnson.

2. Open System Preferences, and select the Time Machine preference pane.

3. If necessary, click the lock icon and authenticate as Local Admin.

4. Select the "Show Time Machine status in the menu bar" checkbox if it is not already selected.

5. Click the Options button to reveal a dialog allowing you to exclude folders from backup.

6. Click the Add (+) button at the bottom of the dialog.

7. Navigate to your startup volume (generally Macintosh HD), and select the Applications, Library, and System folders.

   Note that you can Command-click folders to add them to the selection.

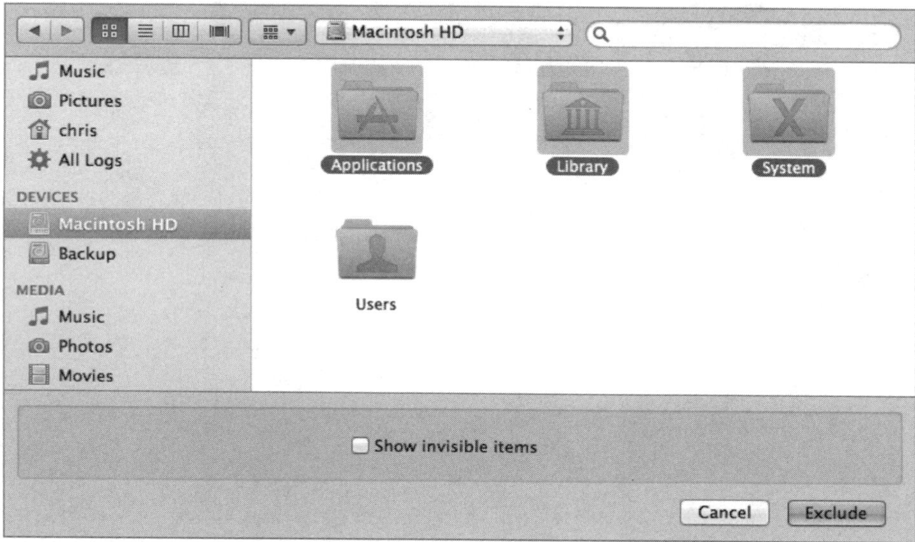

8 Click Exclude.

9 When you see the dialog "You've chosen to exclude the System folder," click Exclude All System Files.

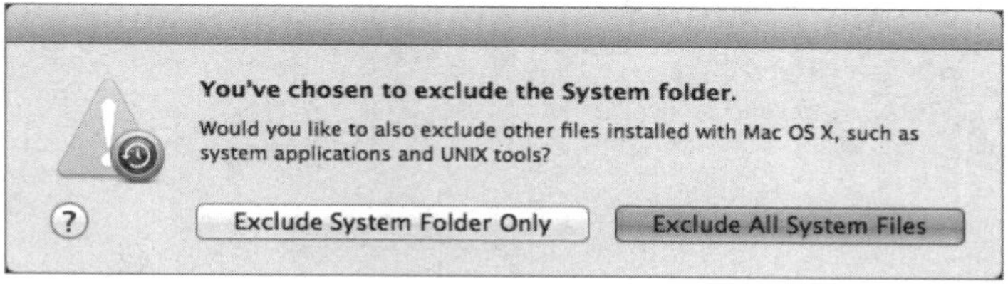

10 Click the Add (+) button again to add another exclusion.

11 This time, exclude the /Users/Shared/StudentMaterials/Software Updates folder from the backup.

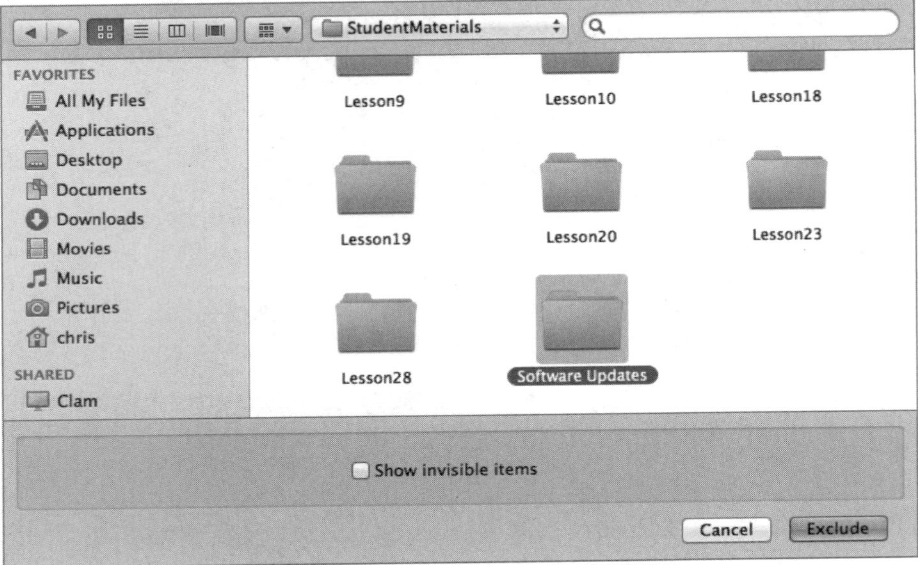

12 Click Exclude.

Your exclusion list now looks like this (although the sizes may be different):

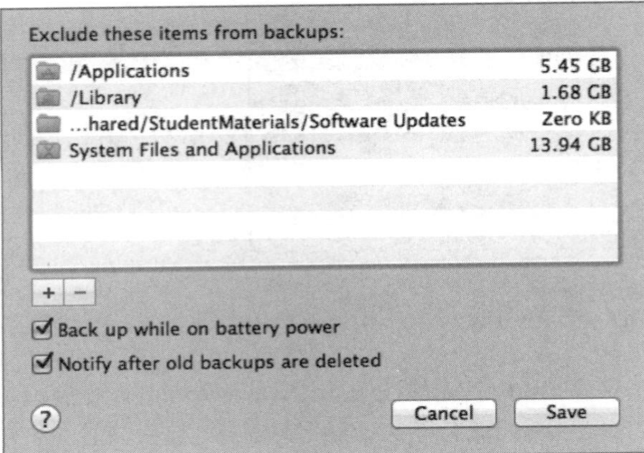

Note that the option to back up while on battery power only appears on laptop computers.

13 Click Save.

Select a Backup Volume

1 If you want to back up this computer to an external disk, connect the disk to the computer now.

2 If a dialog appears asking if you want to use the disk to back up with Time Machine, click Decide Later so that you can configure the backup manually.

3 Turn on Time Machine by sliding the switch to On.

A dialog appears with a choice of backup targets.

4 Select the Volume or Time Capsule you want to back up to. If you do not have an external disk or Time Capsule, use the Backup volume for demonstration purposes.

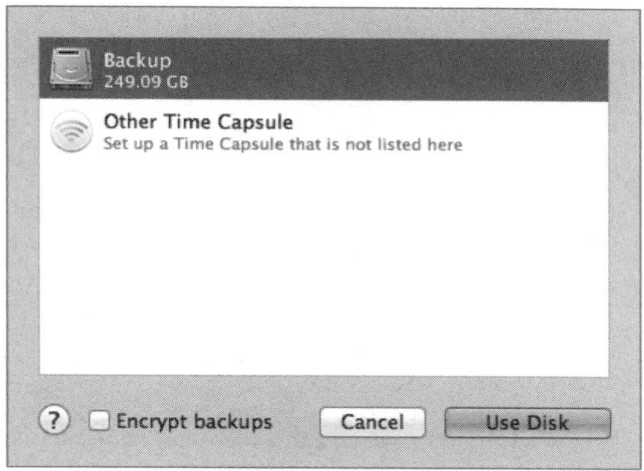

Storing the backup on the same disk as your original data will not protect you in the event of a hard disk failure. It will, however, be sufficient for the purposes of these exercises.

Note the checkbox that allows you to encrypt the backups. This encrypts the backup volume the same way as encrypting it in the Finder, as you did in Exercise 10.5.

If you are performing these exercises in a class, do not encrypt the volume, since backups would not start until the disk finished encrypting. If you are performing them on your own, you can encrypt the backup volume if you want to; however, you have to wait for the encryption to finish before you can start Exercise 18.2.

5 Click Use Disk.

6 If a dialog appears asking if you are sure you want to back up to the same disk, click Use Selected Volume.

Time Machine will start backing up in two minutes. When the backup starts, a progress indicator may appear, showing you the backup status.

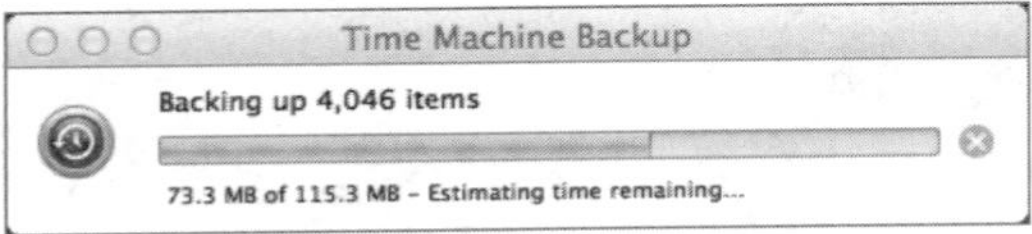

You do not have to wait for it before proceeding.

7 Quit System Preferences.

Import vCards into Contacts

In order to demonstrate Time Machine, you will import some contacts that you can delete and then recover.

1 Open /Users/Shared/StudentMaterials/Lesson18.

2 Open the vCards.vcf file.

The Contacts app opens, and a dialog appears to confirm that you want to add the contacts to your Contacts.

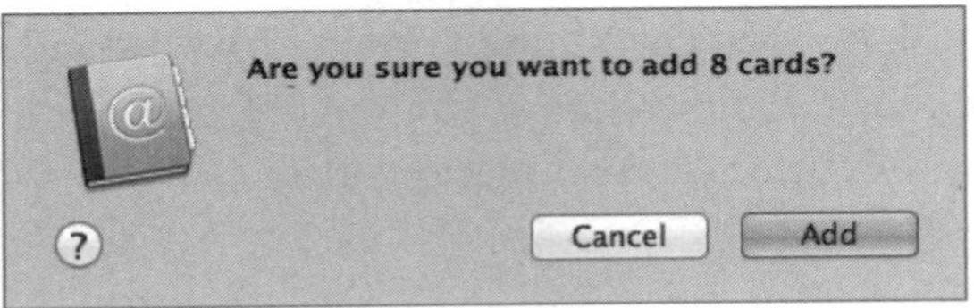

If the dialog indicates that some cards are duplicates, this may be because a previous student left them in the iCloud account you are using.

3 Click Add or Import.

This imports eight vCards into Contacts. Since you have set up iCloud, they are also pushed to the iCloud servers.

4 Quit Contacts.

You should now perform Exercise 18.2 to test the backup.

Exercise 18.2
Restore Using Time Machine

Prerequisites

- You must have performed Exercise 18.1.

In this exercise, you will learn how to use the Time Machine interface to recover lost files from the backup. You will use Time Machine to recover an accidentally deleted entry in your Contacts and a deleted file from the Downloads folder.

Make a New Snapshot

Before testing the backup, make sure it has finished backing up and is up to date.

1 If necessary, log in as Chris Johnson.

2 Click the Time Machine menu. If its menu indicates that it is still backing up, wait for it to finish.

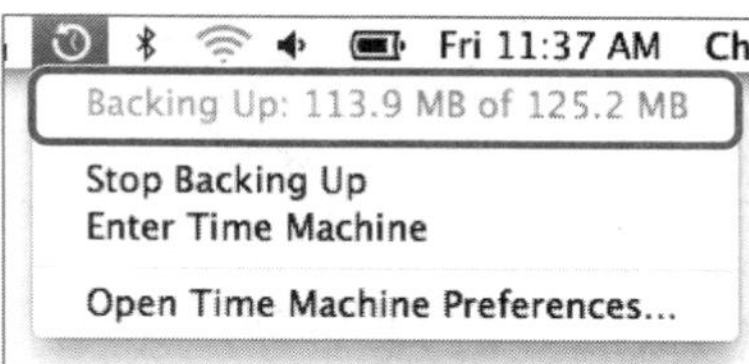

3 From the Time Machine menu, choose Back Up Now.

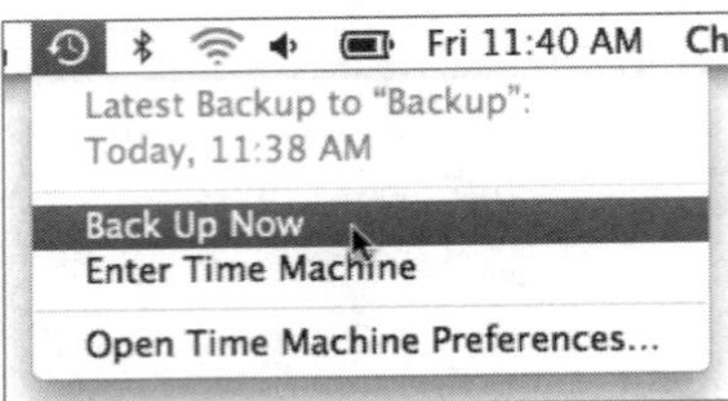

This creates a new backup snapshot. Since very little has changed since the initial backup, it should finish very quickly.

4 Wait for the new backup to finish before proceeding.

Delete a Contact

Here you will delete one of the new contacts, and the vCard file it was imported from.

1 Open the Contacts app.

You are going to delete some data so that you can test restoring it.

2 Select Carl Dunn.

3 Press Delete.

4 When asked if you are sure, click Delete.

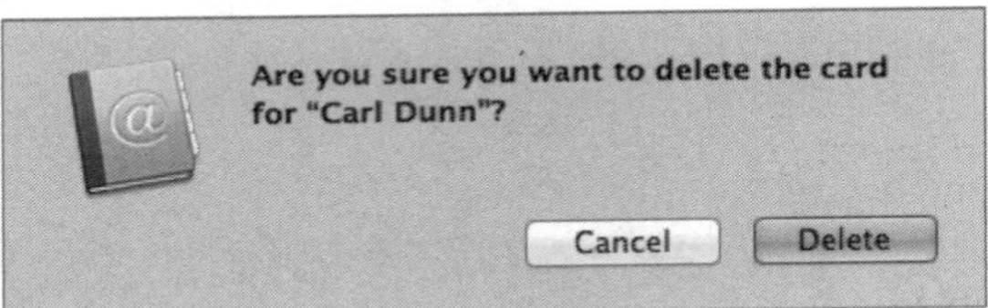

5 Quit Contacts.

6 In the Finder, open /Users/Shared/StudentMaterials/Lesson18.

7 Move the vCards.vcf file to the Trash.

8 When you are prompted, authenticate as Local Admin.

9 Choose Finder > Empty Trash. In the confirmation dialog, click Empty Trash.

You have now removed all copies of Carl's contact information from your startup volume.

Restore a Contact Using Time Machine

Some apps integrate the Time Machine restore capability to allow you to restore their contents without needing to know how it is stored in the file system. You will test this capability with the Contacts app.

1 Now imagine you are trying to call Carl Dunn. Open Contacts and search for his phone number.

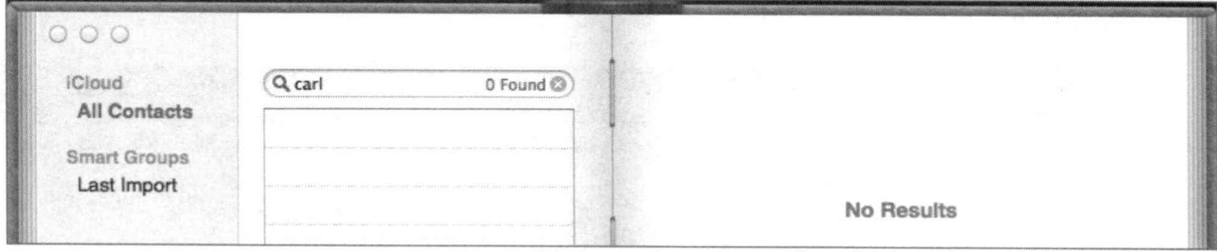

2 With Contacts the active application, choose Enter Time Machine from the Time Machine menu.

Time Machine opens and shows snapshots of your Contacts fading into the past.

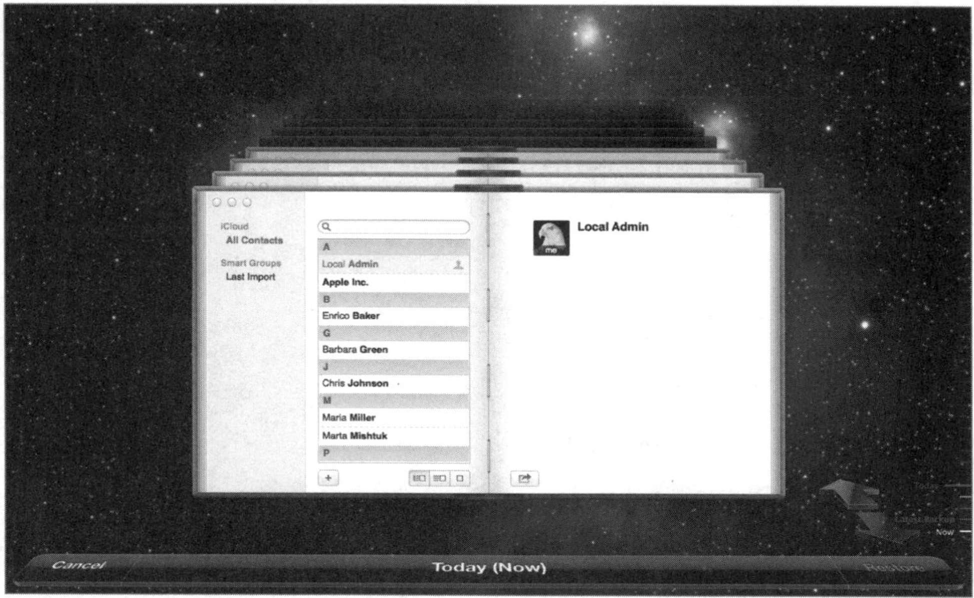

3 Navigate to an earlier time by clicking the up arrow. This arrow points back in time.

You can also navigate through time using the timeline along the right side of the screen.

Carl Dunn's entry will appear in Contacts.

4 Type carl in the search field.

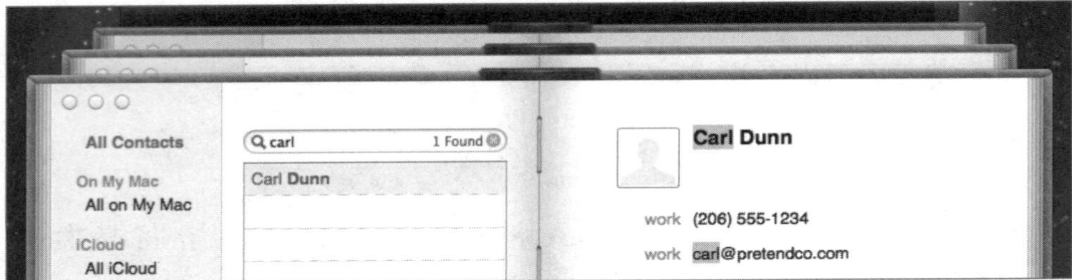

Time Machine finds Carl's entry in the old version of your Contacts.

5 Select Carl's card and click Restore.

Time Machine mode ends and you are returned to Contacts. Contacts asks if you are sure you want to add 1 card to your Contacts.

If you are not prompted to add the contact, you may not have selected the card before clicking Restore. Return to step 2 and try again.

6 Click Add.

Carl's entry is added back into your live Contacts.

7 Quit Contacts.

Restore a File Using Time Machine

1 Switch to the Finder and if necessary, navigate to /Users/Shared/StudentMaterials/Lesson18.

The Lesson18 folder is empty.

2 From the Time Machine menu, choose Enter Time Machine.

3 Navigate back in time until the vCards.vcf file appears.

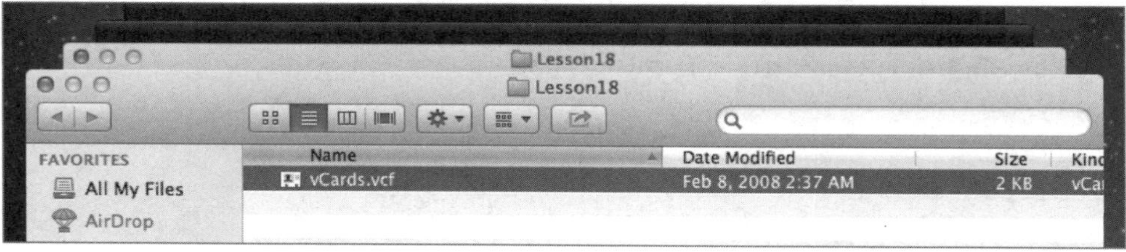

4 Select vCards.vcf and click Restore.

5 If you are prompted to, authenticate as Local Admin.

You are returned to the Finder, and vCards.vcf is restored into the Lesson18 folder.

Restore Directly from Time Machine

When backing up to a local volume, Time Machine stores its backups in the file system. This nice feature means that you can restore files by directly inspecting the backup and copying files out of it.

If you are backing up to a Time Capsule, directly accessing backups is more complex; in this case, you should skip this section of the exercise.

1 In the Finder, open the volume you have chosen to back up to.

2 Open the Backups.backupdb folder. In this folder is a folder for your client. Open it.

This folder contains a series of folders, the names of which are date/time stamps. There is also an alias named Latest that always points to the latest backup.

3. Browse through these folders: Latest/Macintosh HD/Users/Shared/StudentMaterials/Lesson18.
4. Drag a copy of vCards.vcf to your desktop.
5. If prompted, authenticate as Local Admin.

Applications and Processes

Lesson **19**

Application Installation

People use computers because they want to run applications, not operating systems. Most users don't care about the technologies underneath as long as the applications they want run smoothly. This is why, despite the growing popularity of Macs, non-Mac users are apprehensive about switching. It cannot be ignored that there are many applications that run only on Windows-based computers.

GOALS

- Install applications from the Mac App Store
- Understand application support and security issues
- Use traditional installation methods

Yet many Mac-only applications tempt non-Mac users because they represent the best solutions available. For several years now, Apple has held a strong lead on media creation applications with the iLife and Pro production suites. Third-party developers have stepped up their game in the last few years as well, as OS X provides a robust development platform with many unique features. For hundreds of examples, look no further than the Mac App Store.

In this lesson you will install applications using both the Mac App Store and traditional installation methods. You will also explore the various application environments and application security measures used in OS X.

Reference 19.1
The Mac App Store

With traditional installation methods, acquiring the software is often more difficult than actually installing it. Taking a page from the iOS playbook, Apple has solved this issue with the Mac App Store included in OS X. It gives users a single easy-to-use interface for locating, downloading, and installing software via the Internet.

Chances are you are already familiar with the Mac App Store, as it's the primary distribution method for installation and updates of all Apple software. However, if you purchased a Mac with OS X preinstalled, you may not have used the Mac App Store yet. Even if you have used it, you may not be familiar with all its features. This section provides an introduction to the Mac App Store from a support perspective.

Mac App Store Requirements

Introduced in OS X v10.6.6, the Mac App Store is the premier location for Mac-compatible software, and it's increasingly the only location for new Apple software. The Mac App Store combines all the steps of acquiring new software into a single interface. These steps, covered in greater detail later in this section, include browsing and searching for new software, downloading and installing software, managing an account for purchasing software, updating installed software, and managing purchased software.

Aside from having OS X v10.6.6 or later, there are a few requirements for installing software via the Mac App Store:

- An Internet connection—Obviously you must have an Internet connection to access content from the Mac App Store. A fast broadband connection is recommended, but slower connections are adequate as long as you have the time to wait for the download.
- An Apple ID—Identification with Apple is required to install anything from the Mac App Store, free or otherwise. If you intend to purchase items, you must also associate a valid credit card with your Apple ID. However, free items can be purchased without a credit card, but this type of non-credit-card Apple ID can only be set up via the iTunes Store or iOS App Store. All Apple ID account management can be handled via the Mac App Store as covered in the "Store Account Management" section later in this lesson.
- Authorization as an administrative user—You do not have to be logged in to the Mac with an administrator account to open the Mac App Store. However, to install applications via the Mac App Store, you must authenticate as an administrative user. This is because the Mac App Store installs new applications in the /Applications folder, the contents of which are only modifiable by the system or administrative users.

MORE INFO ▶ The Mac App Store has its own support site with even more details than are covered in this guide. You can find the site at www.apple.com/support/mac/app-store/.

Browse, Search, and Install

Even if you don't have an Apple ID, you can easily browse and search the Mac App Store. To get started, open the Mac App Store in the Dock, or choose App Store from the Apple menu. When the Mac App Store opens, you are greeted with the Featured view.

Browse the Mac App Store

The main area of the Featured view allows you to browse new, popular, and staff favorite items. To the right of the Featured view you'll find Quick Links, which link to specific categories and Mac App Store management features. Across the top of the Mac App Store window is a toolbar. Note the arrow buttons in the top-left corner that allow you to navigate back and forward much like a web browser's history. If you're still browsing for new applications, you can click Top Charts to see the most downloaded items or click Categories to browse for a specific type of application.

TIP The buttons in the Mac App Store toolbar correspond to keyboard shortcuts Command-1 through Command-5. For example, use the Command-2 keyboard shortcut to quickly navigate to the Top Charts page.

Search the Mac App Store

The most direct route is the Spotlight search in the top right of the window. Simply start typing part of the name of an application, and the search immediately returns a list of matching items.

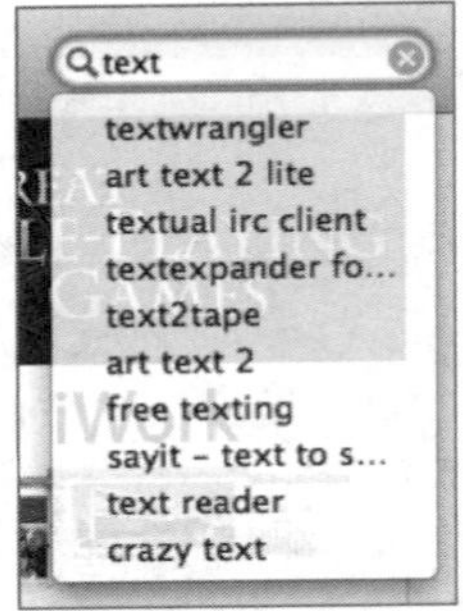

Selecting an item from the list returns a search results page, giving you a more detailed view of the matching items. Click an application's icon or name to view the details page.

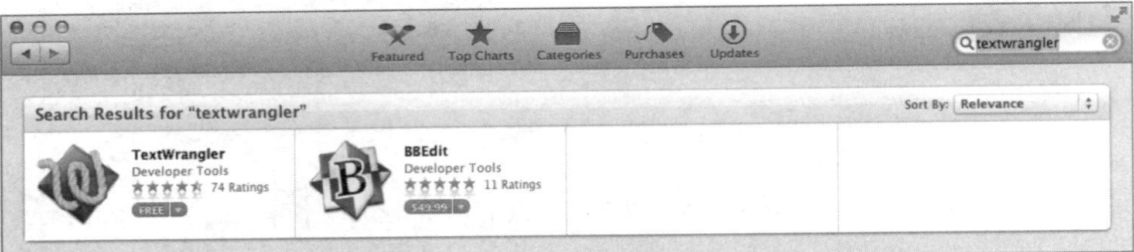

Once you're at an application's details page, you can read more about the application, view application screenshots, and at the bottom browse or write your own customer ratings and reviews. To the far right you'll also see developer and application information, including version, download size, and system requirements.

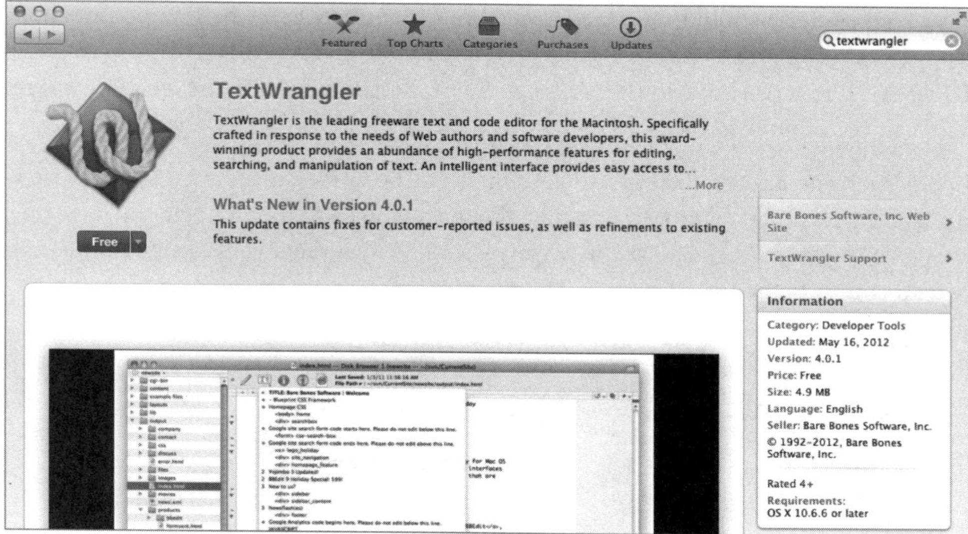

Install from the Mac App Store

Directly under the application's icon, you'll see the application's price. Some applications on the Mac App Store are free, and you can download those items without entering payment information. Paid items obviously require that you enter valid credit card or PayPal information. To download and install an item, click the price button. The button changes to Install App (for a free application) or Buy App (for a paid application). Click either to start the installation process.

TIP Clicking the small arrow to the right of the install button reveals a pop-up menu allowing you to copy or share a link to the selected application.

If you have yet to sign in to the Mac App Store with an Apple ID, or you did not enter an Apple ID during system setup, you are prompted to do so now. If you don't have an Apple ID yet, you can create one in the Mac App Store. Details regarding the creation and management of accounts in the Mac App Store are covered in the next section.

If, however, you already have an Apple ID that has been previously used to purchase items from an Apple store, enter it to continue the installation process. Also, if you have opened the Mac App Store as a standard user, you are asked to authenticate as an administrative user to complete the installation.

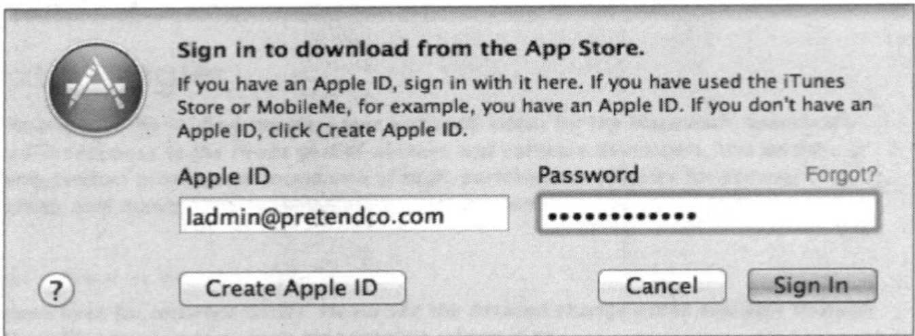

Once your Apple ID is validated, the selected application downloads and installs directly to what appears to be the Launchpad. In reality the application is being installed to the /Applications folder. Thus, if you prefer to use the Finder, you can also open the application from this folder. Note that the progress bar in the following screenshot, as shown in both Launchpad and Finder, indicates the application is still downloading.

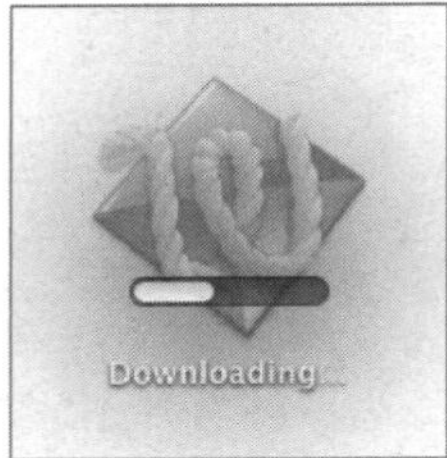

Any item your Apple ID has purchased is always available to update or reinstall from the Mac App Store. You can find out more about this in the "Updating and Managing Purchases" section later in this lesson.

Store Account Management

Again, an Apple ID is required to purchase anything from the Mac App Store. If you have purchased items from Apple previously using the Apple Web Store, iTunes Store, or the iOS App Store, you can use the same Apple ID you used for those previous purchases. If you have not purchased anything from Apple via an online store, you can add purchasing information to an existing Apple ID or create a new Apple ID.

The only requirement for creating a new Apple ID is a unique email address, which is used for contact and verification. If your primary email address is from a non-Apple source, you can use that email to define an Apple ID. Alternatively, you can use a free iCloud account, which also provides a free email address, acts an Apple ID, and can be used to make Apple store purchases.

You can begin any account management process by clicking the Sign In link or by choosing Store > Sign In.

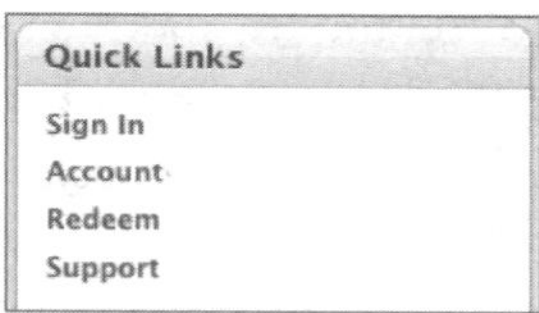

The Mac App Store authentication dialog appears. If you already have an Apple ID, enter it now. If you don't have an Apple ID, or you want to create a new one just for purchases, click Create Apple ID.

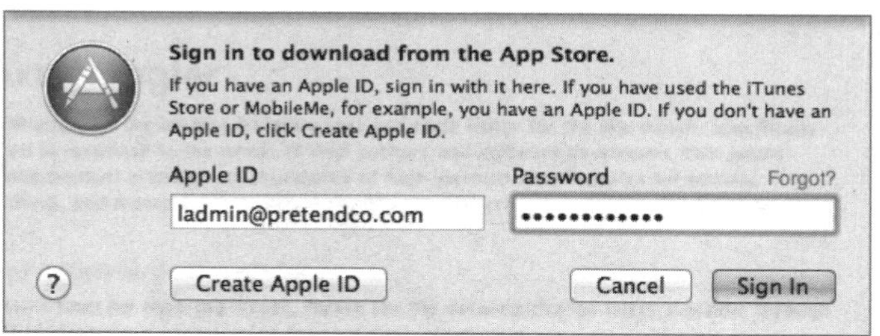

NOTE ▶ Apple IDs created previously with .Mac, MobileMe, or iCloud can be used for the Mac App Store.

Depending on the state of your Apple ID, one of the following situations occurs: your Apple ID is ready to install items, your Apple ID information needs to be verified or updated, or you're creating a new Apple ID.

Your Apple ID Is Ready to Install

If your Apple ID has been used to purchase items from Apple previously, it may be ready to go for the Mac App Store. If this is the case, you don't see any other screens. When you are signed in, the first Quick Links item is Welcome, followed by your first name. You can also verify the signed-in Apple ID by clicking the Store menu. Note that you can sign out from the Store menu as well.

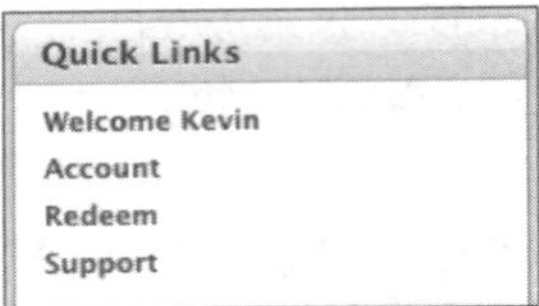

Your Apple ID Needs Updating

If your Apple ID information needs to be verified or updated, you're prompted to review your account. You first need to agree to the App Store terms and conditions, and then you need to verify your Apple ID security details. Sometimes this is all the verification that's needed. There may, however, come a time where you must enter or update your account with a valid credit card and billing address for purchasing items.

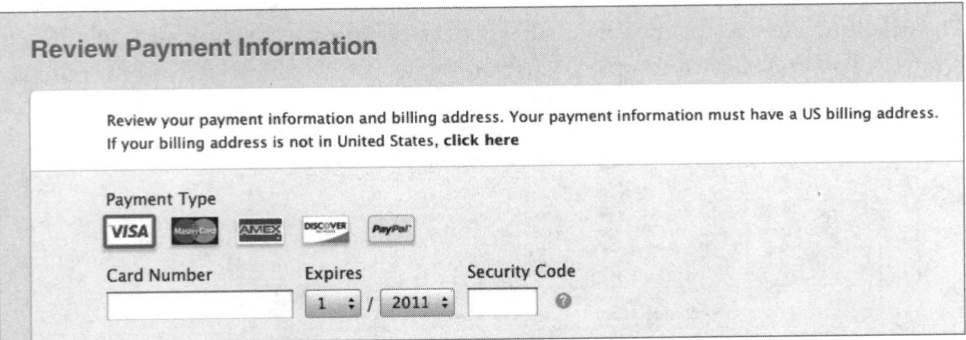

When using an existing Apple ID, you must always enter credit card information even if you plan to install only free items. If you need to create an Apple ID that can only install free items, you must create a brand new Apple ID. Once you have completed updating your account, you have to sign in to the Mac App Store again to purchase or install any items.

You're Creating a New Apple ID

If you don't have an Apple ID, or you want to create a new one just for making purchases, you can do so almost entirely from the Mac App Store. After agreeing to the terms and conditions, you are prompted to enter details for a new Apple ID. Any time you create a new Apple ID, you must first provide account details that include a verifiable email address, three security questions, and your birthday.

NOTE ▶ An individual must be over the age of 13 to create an Apple ID.

NOTE ▶ If you want to create a new iCloud account that will also be used for Apple store purchases, you must first create the account in the iCloud preferences. Once the account has been created, you can return to the Mac App Store to update your account's purchasing information.

NOTE ▶ If you want to create an Apple ID that can only install free items, you must do so from the iTunes Store, or the iOS App Store. You can find out more about this process from Knowledge Base document HT2534, "Creating an iTunes Store, App Store, iBookstore, and Mac App Store account without a credit card."

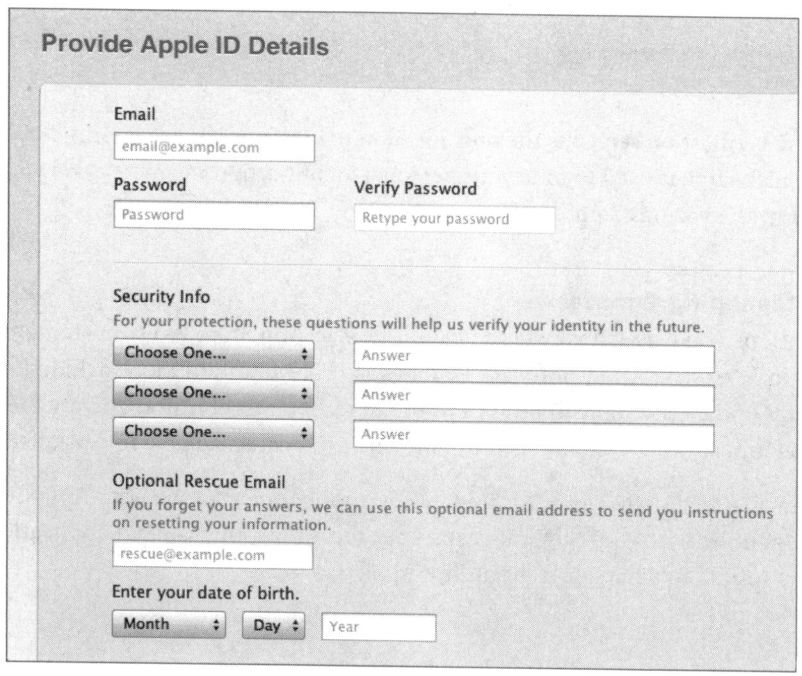

After entering your details, you're prompted to provide a payment method. Finally, when creating a new Apple ID, you have to verify the email address specified. The App Store system sends an email verification; click the link inside the email to open a web page allowing you to authenticate and verify the account. Once you have verified it, you have to sign in to the Mac App Store again to purchase or install any items.

Verify and Manage Apple ID

Any time you want to make changes to your Apple ID, you can do so from within the Mac App Store by clicking the Account link in the Quick Links section or by choosing Store > View My Account. From the Account Information page, you can change your Apple ID, payment information, and country or region setting.

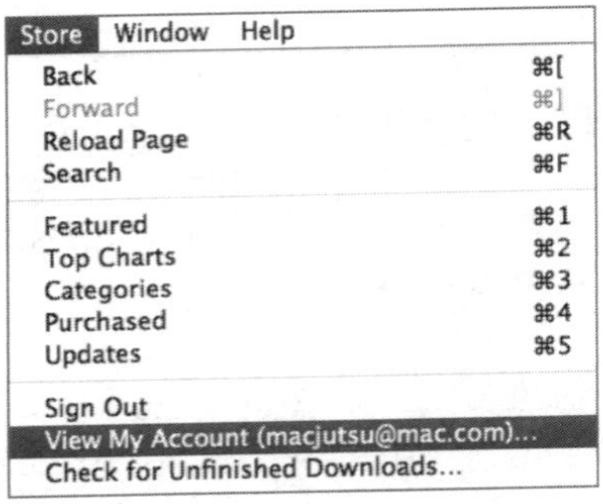

Store Window Help
Back ⌘[
Forward ⌘]
Reload Page ⌘R
Search ⌘F
Featured ⌘1
Top Charts ⌘2
Categories ⌘3
Purchased ⌘4
Updates ⌘5
Sign Out
View My Account (macjutsu@mac.com)...
Check for Unfinished Downloads...

Also, the Apple ID verification screen is the only location to create or change your nickname. Your Apple store nickname is used to hide your personal identification in any reviews you may have posted in the various Apple stores.

Updating and Managing Purchases

Updating applications you originally installed from the Mac App Store is also extremely easy. As covered in Lesson 5, "OS X Software Updates," OS X Mountain Lion includes an automatic software update mechanism built in to the Mac App Store. Automatic updates are enabled by default, and the system reminds you when they are available for installation.

However, you can also manually check for updates by simply opening the Mac App Store. Every time you open the Mac App Store, it scans your local Mac for installed applications and compares the results to what's current on the Apple servers.

TIP If the proper updates don't seem to be appearing for your system, you can force the Mac App Store to reevaluate your installed software by holding the Option key while opening the Mac App Store. Continue to hold the Option key while you click the Updates button as well.

If updates are available, you may notice in the toolbar that the Updates button has a small number by it. This represents applications that have updates available. Click the Updates button to reveal the list of available updates. You can choose to install individual updates by clicking specific Update buttons, or you can click the Update All button to install all updates.

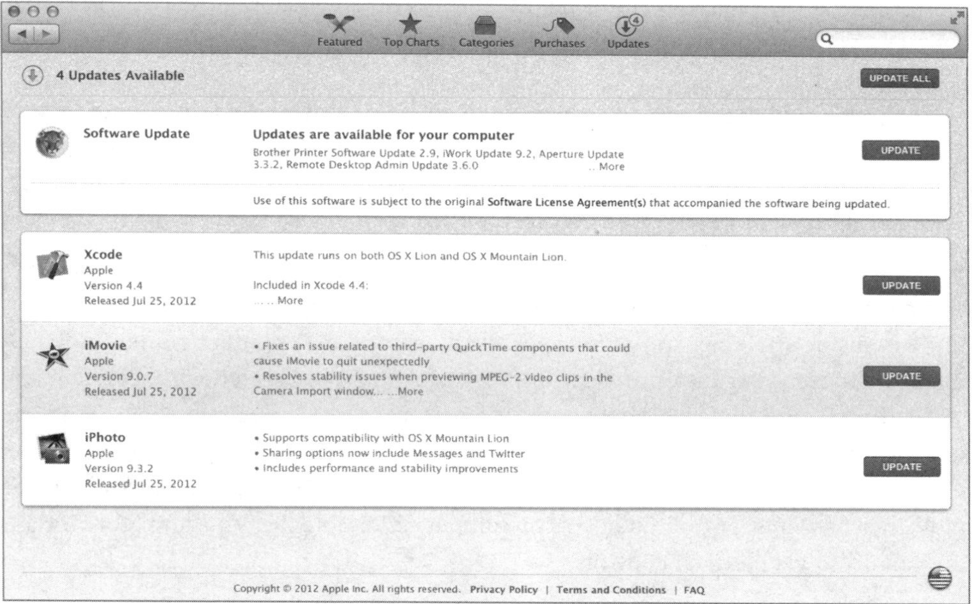

A significant feature of the Mac App Store is that applications are "owned" by your Apple ID. According to Apple, "Apps from the Mac App Store may be used on any Macs that you own or control for your personal use." This means that if you personally use multiple Macs, you can install items from the Mac App Store on all of them. This is possible because Apple keeps track of the items purchased or installed by your Apple ID.

To install an application you already own on a new Mac, open the Mac App Store, sign in with your Apple ID, and then click the Purchases icon in the toolbar. The Purchases page shows all the items owned by the signed-in Apple ID, both installed and not installed on the Mac. Obviously, clicking the Install button will download and install the latest version of the application to the local Mac.

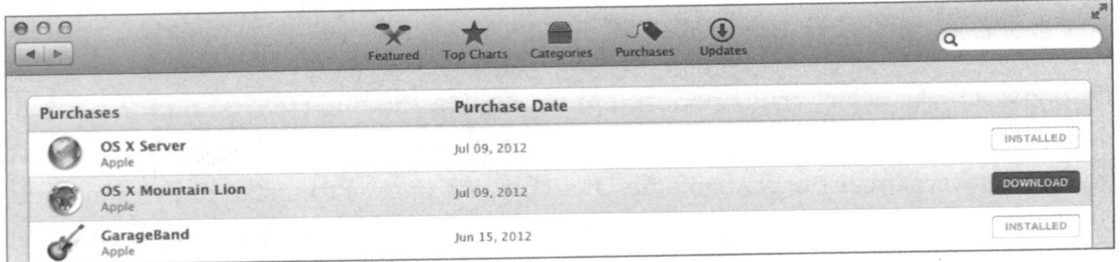

TIP ▶ If the Mac App Store is in the process of downloading a particularly large item, you can check the item's progress from the Purchases page.

TIP ▶ If purchases are made using an iCloud account, and you use more than one Mac, you may want to enable the automatic downloading of purchased applications. This can be set from the Software Update preferences for every Mac that has been configured with your iCloud account.

Limit Access to the Mac App Store

Some items on the Mac App Store, specifically games, may contain content not suitable for children. Because software on the Mac App Store is rated with a system similar to that for motion pictures, you can limit a user's access to specific ratings. Further, if your organization prevents users from installing their own applications, or users are not allowed administrative access, then you may want to disable access to the Mac App Store altogether. If you want to limit access or completely disable the Mac App Store for a user, you can do so via parental controls.

NOTE ▶ Do not attempt to delete the Mac App Store, as you will not be able to perform system updates without this application.

In the Parental Controls preferences, you have several methods to limit applications from the Mac App Store. The easiest method is to simply choose an age requirement from the Allow App Store Apps pop-up menu. Selecting a minimum age here limits both the purchasing of new applications and the opening of any applications already installed from the Mac App Store.

Alternatively you can click the disclosure triangle next to App Store and then individually deselect the applications you want to disallow. Scrolling down through the allowed applications list also reveals an option to disallow the Mac App Store itself. This obviously prevents the installation or updating of any application available from the Mac App Store.

MORE INFO ▸ Parental controls are further covered in Lesson 6, "User Accounts."

Reference 19.2
Application Environments

Obviously, applications from the Mac App Store are made specifically to work for OS X. Once you venture beyond the Mac App Store, though you'll find there are thousands of other applications that also work on OS X. Before the Mac App Store, software was delivered through a variety of mechanisms, and was created with a variety of different technologies.

This is because OS X supports several different application environments. Application developers create their products based on support for these environments. Several are specific to OS X, while others add support for popular UNIX-based tools. Most important, though, average users do not need to concern themselves about which environment their application is using—the system will provide the appropriate resources automatically. The four primary application environments in OS X are native OS X applications, UNIX commands, Java applications, and UNIX applications that use the X Window System.

MORE INFO ▶ To learn more about OS X system architecture and application environments, see the Apple development resources at http://developer.apple.com/technologies/mac.

Native OS X Applications

Most native OS X applications are created using a development environment known as Cocoa. Unsurprisingly, Cocoa is the application environment most specific to OS X, as Cocoa-based applications run only on iOS and OS X. Cocoa is primarily based on the Objective-C object-oriented programming language.

MORE INFO ▶ To learn more about the Cocoa application environment, refer to the Apple development resources at http://developer.apple.com/technologies/mac/cocoa.html.

OS X Mountain Lion continues to support older OS X applications created using a development environment known as Carbon. The Carbon application environment is a streamlined and significantly updated version of the previous Mac OS 9 environment. Developers could update their legacy Mac applications, often with little work, to run natively in OS X. Carbon is based on the industry standard C and C++ programming languages.

MORE INFO ▶ To learn more about Carbon, see the Apple development resources at http://developer.apple.com/carbon.

On the surface, it's hard for a user to identify any differences between Carbon and Cocoa applications. As OS X advanced, Apple further blurred the lines between Cocoa and Carbon by allowing applications to use a mix of both environments.

However, Apple drew the line in OS X v10.6 by adding full 64-bit support for Cocoa graphical applications but not for Carbon graphical applications. Apple has made it clear that going forward, new development for OS X should be exclusively in Cocoa. Often, developers must use the Cocoa environment if they want to take advantage of the latest OS X features. As an example, only Cocoa-based applications can integrate with Auto Save and iCloud services.

For this reason, nearly all Apple software and most third-party software available from the Mac App Store is developed for the Cocoa application environment. Further, while OS X Mountain Lion still supports Carbon applications, the technology has officially been deprecated, indicating future releases of OS X may not support Carbon-based applications.

Legacy Mac Applications

Previous versions of OS X supported applications created for Mac OS 9 and PowerPC processors. The Classic compatibility environment, which enables users to run software created for Mac OS 9, is not supported as of OS X v10.5 or later. The Rosetta compatibility environment, which enables users to run software created for PowerPC processors, is not supported as of OS X Lion or later.

UNIX Applications

Since the introduction of OS X v10.5, the system has been both POSIX- and UNIX 03–compliant. Thus, OS X is compatible with most UNIX software. The Mac OS X system foundation, named Darwin, is based on the open source Free Berkeley Software Distribution (FreeBSD) UNIX command-line interface. The command line is most often accessed via the /Applications/Utilities/Terminal application.

> **MORE INFO ▸** To learn more about Darwin, see the Apple open source development resources at http://developer.apple.com/opensource/.

Java Applications

Java is an application environment originally developed by Sun Microsystems but is now owned and primarily maintained by Oracle Corporation. The goal of developing software in Java is to create nonplatform-specific applications. This means a developer can create software code once and it can run on many environments. At the time of this writing, there are two versions of the Java runtime available for OS X; Apple supplies the older Java SE 6, while Oracle supplies the latest Java SE 7.

> **NOTE ▸** JavaScript, another technology, is used almost exclusively by web browsers and is fundamentally quite different than the Java application runtime. The included web browser in OS X, Safari, provides robust support for JavaScript.

Java SE 6 from Apple

While there is Java application runtime support for OS X, it is not included with the default OS X system installation. The first time you run a Java applet or application in OS X, the Software Update mechanism engages to automatically download Java SE 6 (Standard Edition) for OS X from the Apple servers. Interestingly, OS X includes one application that needs the Java runtime, the Java Preferences application. Thus, opening

/Applications/Utilities/Java Preferences for the first time prompts the user to install the Java runtime.

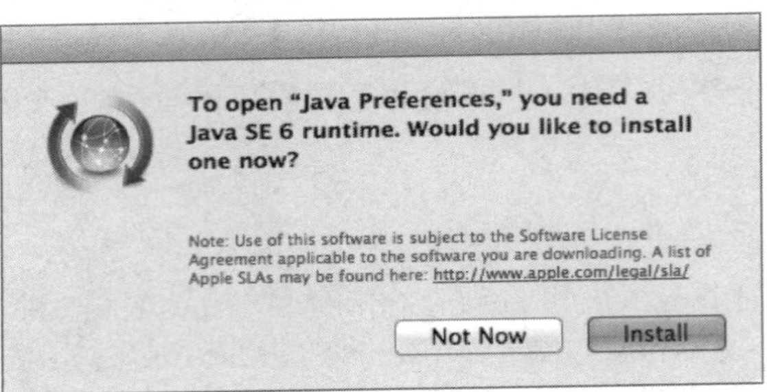

As with any Apple Software Update, administrative user access is required to install the Java runtime. Thus, if you know that your users require access to Java applications, you may want to manually download and install the Java runtime as part of your standard OS X configuration. At the time of this writing, the Java runtime for OS X was available for download in Knowledge Base document DL1572, "Java for OS X 2012-005."

MORE INFO ▶ It's highly likely that future versions of the Java runtime will be maintained directly by Oracle Corporation. You can find out more at www.oracle.com/technetwork/java/.

With Java from Apple installed, the system supports both 32-bit and 64-bit Java SE 6 version 1.6.x. You can verify the specific Java version supplied by Apple when you open the /Utilities/Java Preferences application. Going forward Apple will only be providing updates for this older Java technology. Similar to other Apple-supplied software, updates to Java SE 6 from Apple can be automatically installed via the OS X software update mechanism.

Java SE 7 from Oracle

Historically, Java for other computing platforms was delivered by Java's primary developers, originally Sun and now Oracle. Starting with Java SE 7, Oracle is now the official developer for OS X versions of the Java runtime. Thus, to acquire the latest versions of Java for OS X, you must download and install the Java runtime from http:/java.com/.

This website provides the Java runtime in the form of a standard Apple installer package. Note that the installation of this package requires administrator authentication. Again, if you know that your users require access to Java applications, you may want to manually download and install the Java SE 7 runtime as part of your standard OS X configuration.

Also note that you can have both the Apple-supplied Java SE 6 and the Oracle-supplied Java SE 6 installed at the same time.

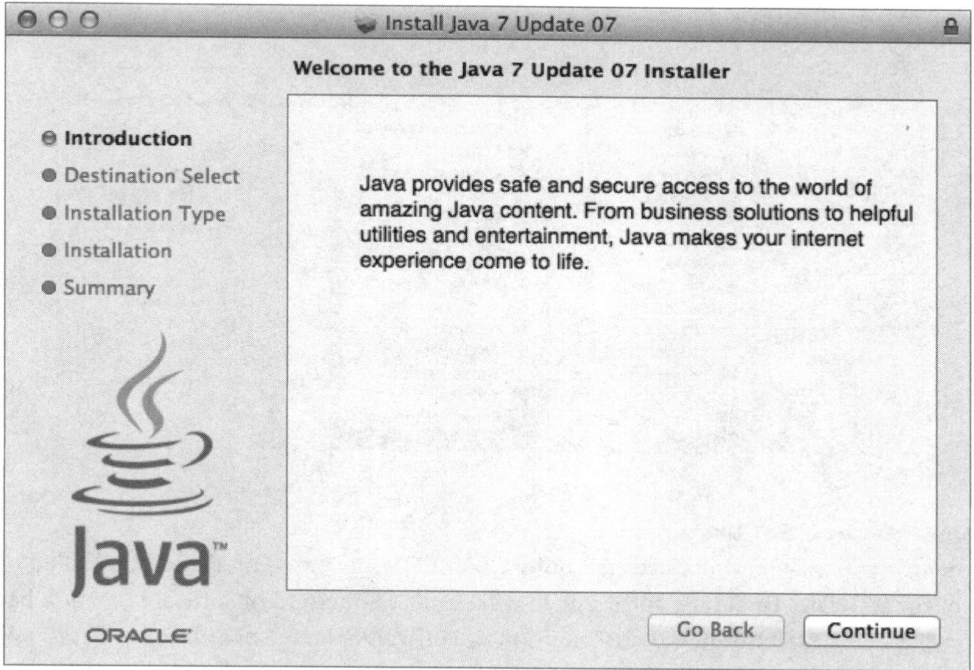

With Java from Oracle installed, the system supports 64-bit Java SE 7 version 1.7.x. You can verify the specific Java version supplied by Oracle and adjust other Java settings by opening the Java preference, which appears in the Other section of System Preferences. Oracle's implementation of the Java runtime features its own proprietary updater mechanism, which can also be managed from the Java preference.

X Window System Applications

The X Window System is an extension of the UNIX environment that provides a common graphical applications platform for UNIX workstations. Previous versions of OS X included the Apple version of a popular implementation of the X Window System known as X11. You could access X Window System applications by opening /Applications/Utilities/X11.

However, opening this application in OS X Mountain Lion redirects you to Knowledge Base document HT5293, "About X11 and OS X Mountain Lion." From that document you are redirected to an open source implementation known as XQuartz, available at http://xquartz.macosforge.org. Going forward this is the Apple-supported implementation of the X Windowing System on OS X. Upon installation the /Applications/Utilities/X11 application is replaced with /Applications/Utilities/XQuartz.

Open Source Software

By now you may have noticed that quite a bit of OS X is based on something called open source software. Generally speaking, open source is a method of software creation based on the free distribution and contribution of software source code. In other words, it's software whose code is available at no cost to anyone for general use or further modification. Interested individuals are expected and usually encouraged to provide improvements to open source software by adding to the software's code. It's expected that over time this community involvement will yield software products of exceptional quality, often free of cost.

Apple is deeply involved with many open source projects; this includes not just borrowing from open source but also contributing to existing projects and creating entirely new open source projects as well. In fact, the core of OS X, Darwin, is an entirely open source operating system that includes more than 200 individual open source projects. Keep in mind, though, that Apple maintains proprietary closed software solutions as part of OS X as well. Apple charges for these proprietary parts of OS X, but this is what allows Apple to employ hundreds of talented developers to create exceptional software.

> **MORE INFO ▸** To learn more about how Apple is involved in open source development, visit http://developer.apple.com/opensource/.

The astounding growth of open source software in the last decade has not only produced some great software but also led to the rise of an entirely new operating system, Linux. With the growing popularity of Linux, high-quality open source applications have taken off as well. Because of the open source and UNIX heritage of OS X, you can also take advantage of many of these open source applications on your Mac. Some open source applications run in the command line, others through XQuartz, and some have even been converted to full-fledged Mac applications. Take some time to explore these free open source solutions for your Mac, as they may be suitable replacements for commercially purchased software.

MORE INFO ► The MacPorts project hosts over 15,000 open source software titles for OS X at www.macports.org.

Reference 19.3
Application Security

One of the primary benefits of acquiring applications from the Mac App Store is knowing that Apple has processes for ensuring the applications are free of malicious software, also known as malware. No system is perfect, but even if a bad application slips by the Apple procedures, they can quickly pull the application from their store.

Despite the popularity of the Mac App Store, there are many thousands of Mac applications that are only available outside of this store. The engineers at Apple recognize the need for software developers to distribute their wares outside of the Mac App Store. At the same time, though, there is the need to ensure that OS X users are protected from bad software. To this end, OS X includes several application security technologies that help protect users when they install third-party applications.

Process Security

OS X inherits relatively robust process security due to its UNIX foundation. At both the command line and graphical interface, applications and processes are not allowed to access resources unless they are authorized. Access restrictions in the form of file system permissions are responsible for much of the security here. Simply, a running process is owned by a user, and is therefore granted file system access similar to that of the user.

However, system privileges are allowed when needed. The most obvious example of this is the Installer application, which requires administrative authorization to install software that affects more than one user. The moral of this story is to beware applications that require administrator authorization, as you are granting that application system level access.

Application Sandboxing

Even with the OS X default process security mechanism in place, an application could still access all the files owned by a user. This gives an application the potential to read all your files and potentially gain unauthorized access to personal information.

A significant security feature in OS X is support for full application and process sandboxing. As the name implies, applications and processes in OS X can "play" inside a protected environment that has little or no access to other parts of the system. With application sandboxing, applications are granted access only to the items they need through a sophisticated arrangement of rules.

Apple developer requirements govern the majority of sandbox rules, but some of these rules are user-initiated. For example, if a user opens a specific document, the user is implying her intent to allow that application to access that file; thus the application is granted access to that file outside of the sandbox. Other examples of user-initiated access can be found in the Privacy pane of the Security & Privacy preferences, as detailed in Lesson 8, "System Security."

It's important to note that application sandboxing is an optional feature. Despite this, Apple has already sandboxed any application or process built into OS X that could benefit from this feature. Further, as of June of 2012, all applications available from the Mac App Store must use application sandboxing.

Code Signing

OS X v10.5 introduced support for secure signed application and process code. Signed applications and processes include a digital signature, which is used by the system to verify the authenticity and integrity of the software code and resources. Code is verified not only on disk but also as it is running. Therefore, even if some part of the application's or process's code is inappropriately changed while it's active, the system can automatically quit it.

In addition to identifying changes to applications, code signing provides guaranteed application identification for other parts of the system, including the keychain, the personal application firewall, Parental Controls preferences, application sandboxing, and Managed Client settings.

Finally, in OS X Mountain Lion, code signing is used as the basis of identification for trusting newly installed items. Though code signing is optional, applications with this are automatically trusted by the system. All Apple software and applications from the Mac App Store are always code signed, and thus trusted by OS X upon installation.

If a software developer chooses not to use the Mac App Store, they can still take advantage of this system. A developer can code sign their installers and applications using an Apple-granted Developer ID. In this way, code signed applications installed from any origin can be trusted by OS X.

File Quarantine

OS X v10.5 also introduced a file quarantine service that displays a warning when you attempt to open an item downloaded from an external source like the Internet. Quarantined items include many file types, including documents, scripts, and disk images. This lesson focuses primarily on quarantine as it relates to downloaded applications.

File quarantine goes into effect only when an item is marked for quarantine by the application that downloaded it. This is true for all applications built into OS X, but it may not be true for third-party applications that can download files. Also, files copied to the Mac using any other method are not marked for quarantine. For example, using the Finder to copy an application from a USB disk does not engage the quarantine system.

When a file is marked, the system requires you to verify your intent to open the item or cancel if you have any suspicions about the safety of an item. Any administrative user can permanently clear the quarantine by clicking Open. When a standard user clicks Open, the item opens but the quarantine remains. Thus, subsequent users who try to open the item still get the quarantine warning.

Apple further enhanced this feature in OS X v10.6 by starting to maintain a list of known malicious software. If you attempt to open any software on this list, the system presents a warning dialog suggesting that you move the item to the Trash. The list of malicious software is automatically updated via the OS X software update mechanism and is located on your Mac in the file /System/Library/CoreServices/CoreTypes.bundle/Contents/Resources/XProtect.plist.

MORE INFO ▶ To find out more about file quarantine, see Knowledge Base document HT3662, "About file quarantine in OS X."

Gatekeeper

OS X Mountain Lion introduces a significant new security model for application installation via Gatekeeper. Gatekeeper is a new system that leverages both code signing and file quarantine to further protect your Mac from malicious applications. It does this by giving you the choice to only allow trusted application sources.

NOTE ▶ Because Gatekeeper relies on the file quarantine system, it restricts only applications that were downloaded by applications that properly set file quarantine.

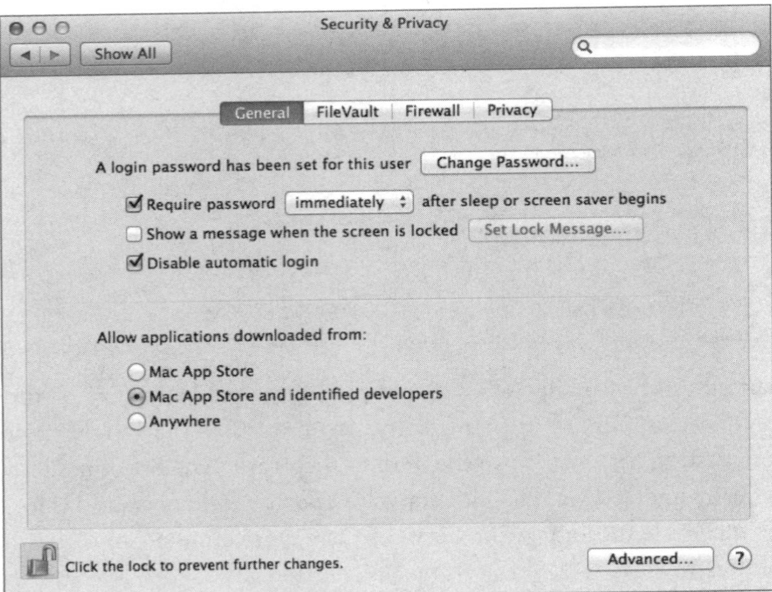

From the General pane of the Security & Privacy settings, you can adjust the settings for Gatekeeper. Gatekeeper allows for three modes of application restriction:

- Mac App Store—This is the most limited option as it only allows applications from the Mac App Store to open. Even when a version of the application is available from the Mac App Store, if you download the application from somewhere else, it will still be blocked.

- Mac App Store and identified developers—This is the default option for OS X Mountain Lion. As covered previously, developers can use an Apple-verified code signing certificate to identify their application. If a developer has done this, the application is allowed to open but the system still presents the file quarantine dialog for downloaded items. If an application isn't properly signed, it will be blocked.

- Anywhere—This option is similar to the behavior of previous versions of OS X. All applications are allowed regardless of source, but again the system presents the file quarantine dialog for downloaded items.

Gatekeeper also identifies modified or damaged applications regardless of your security settings. In this case you are seeing code signing at work, as the system has identified changes to an application from its original state. Thus, the application is either damaged due to file corruption, or someone other than the original developer has modified it. In either case you will not be allowed to open the application as it may cause harm.

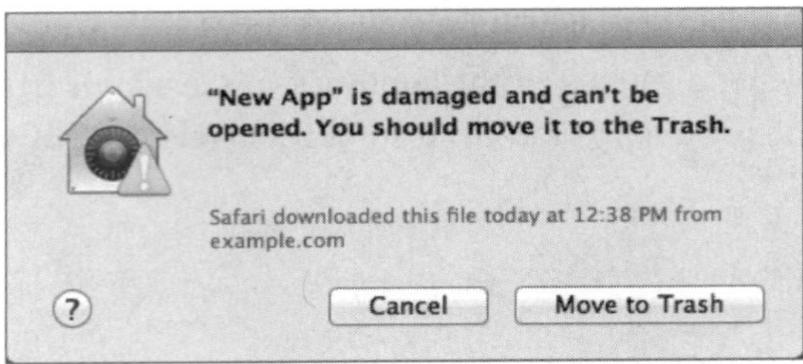

MORE INFO ▶ To find out more about Gatekeeper, see Knowledge Base document HT5290, "Mountain Lion: About Gatekeeper."

Temporarily Bypassing Gatekeeper

Even with Gatekeeper in place, an administrative user can override the system's settings and allow untrusted applications. In the Finder an administrative user can secondary (or Control) click on the application file and then choose Open from the shortcut menu. The Gatekeeper warning appears to verify the administrator's intent.

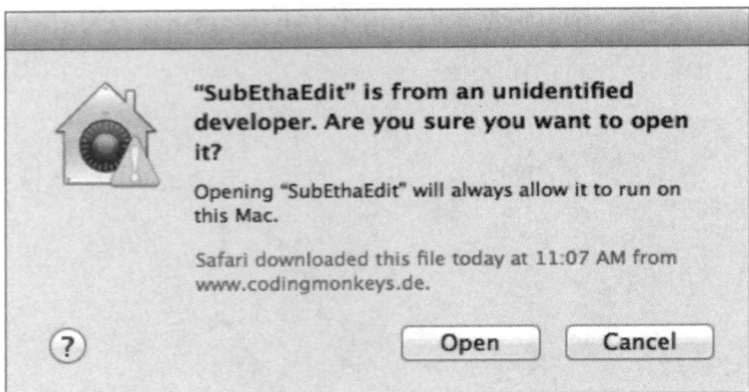

Clicking Open opens the application and clears the file quarantine. However, this may not be enough for all unsigned applications, because some applications may automatically open other background or child applications. Examples include applications that also provide background software to facilitate hardware functionality.

These secondary applications also trigger Gatekeeper. Unfortunately you may not be able to override the appropriate files from the Finder. In these cases you may have to temporarily allow "Anywhere" in the General tab of the Security & Privacy preferences. Once you have launched the application and verified its full functionality, the quarantine is cleared and you can return the Gatekeeper settings to something more secure.

Reference 19.4
Traditional Installation Methods

Traditional installation methods fall into one of two categories: drag-and-drop installations or installation packages. Application developers can choose any method they want to deploy their wares. Often the distinction between the two traditional methods is the complexity of the software being deployed.

If a software developer creates a product that only requires a folder of a few items or even one single item, it's often deployed as a drag-and-drop installation. However, if a software developer creates a product that requires a more complex set of items that must be installed in multiple specific locations throughout the system, it's often deployed as an installation package.

> **NOTE ►** As covered previously in this lesson, applications downloaded from any source outside of the Mac App Store are subject to file quarantine and Gatekeeper rules.

Drag-and-Drop Installations

Apple pioneered the era of drag-and-drop in computing, so it should come as no surprise that many traditional software installations in OS X are of the simple drag-and-drop variety. In general, OS X doesn't care where an application or process resides. So long as the application itself doesn't have a specific location requirement, applications can run from any location on the Mac. That said, as covered in previous lessons, some locations are more appropriate and secure than others.

Specifically, OS X includes the /Applications folder as the default location for applications available to all users. Only administrative users can make changes to the /Applications folder. If users want to install their own drag-and-drop applications, they can create their own ~/Applications folder. However, a user can place an application anywhere she pleases inside her own home folder. Again, many drag-and-drop applications work from any location on the system.

Drag-and-Drop Application Security

Also, it's important to recognize that because of the default security and permissions model in OS X, any application a standard user is allowed to install and open cannot interfere with other users on the system. Poorly written or malicious software could potentially harm items in the user's home folder, but as long as the user is not allowed to authenticate as an administrator, it is extremely difficult for the software to cause damage to the system or other users.

Keep in mind, the same is true for a user's intentional actions as well. A user could, by his own hand, cause similar damage. In short, allowing nonadministrative users the ability to install software is no more dangerous than allowing them to use the computer in the first place.

Installing Drag-and-Drop Items

Drag-and-drop software deployed via optical disc, or any other physical disk, is often ready to copy to wherever the user wants to install it. On the other hand, software downloaded from the Internet is almost always deployed in some kind of archive format. As covered in Lesson 17, "File Archives," zip files and disk images are the most common archive formats for OS X.

In OS X the Safari browser automatically unarchives zip files, by default, to the ~/Downloads folder. The user could technically leave the application in the ~/Downloads folder and continue to open it from there, but she should be trained to move the new application to a more appropriate location in her home folder. An example of this type of installation is SubEthaEdit by the Coding Monkeys, available at www.codingmonkeys.de/subethaedit/.

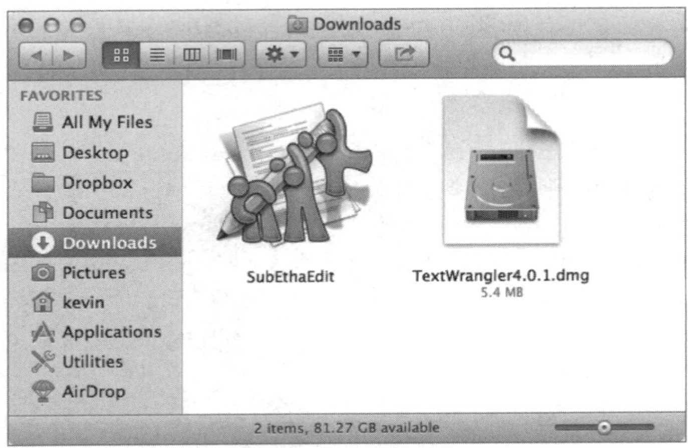

In OS X the Safari browser does not, however, automatically mount a downloaded disk image. A user must double-click a disk image to make its contents available to the Finder. Once the disk image volume is mounted, again the user could technically leave the application inside the disk image and open it from there, but he should be trained to move the new application to another location. This is especially true of disk images because if the user logs out or restarts the computer, the disk image unmounts.

For many novice users, this would result in their "losing" the application. Fortunately, many developers use a helpful Finder window background graphic that should encourage the user to copy the software to a more appropriate location. An example of this type of installation is TextWrangler by Barebones Software, available at www.barebones.com/products/TextWrangler/.

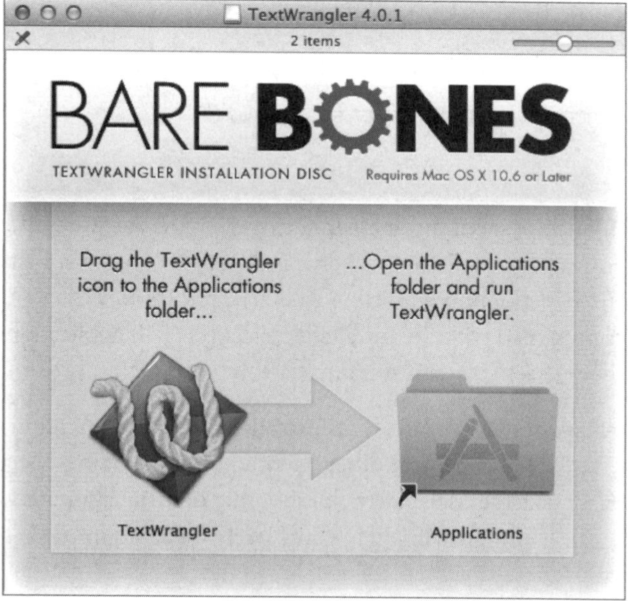

Similar to a drag-and-drop install is the double-click install. Instead of the user dragging the item into place, she double-clicks the item, and the system prompts her with an offer to copy the item into place. In most cases when a double-click install is required, moving the item into a specific location is necessary for the item to work properly.

The user can still drag and drop the item into the appropriate location, often in a Library folder, if desired. Items the system will install for you when double-clicked include fonts, preference panes, screen savers, and widgets. An example of this type of installation is Perian by the Perian Project, available at http://perian.org.

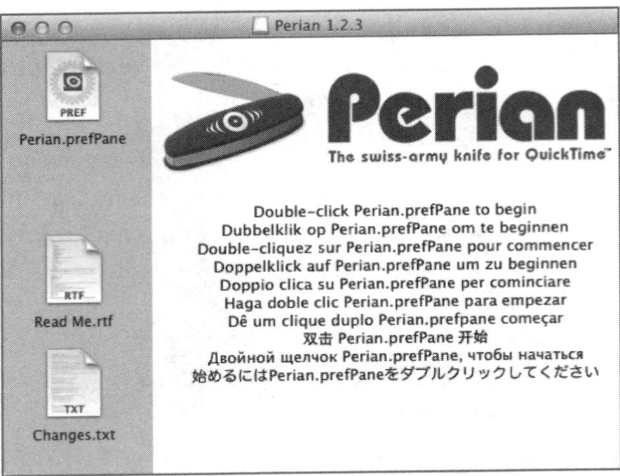

Installation Packages

Installation packages are the default deployment mechanism for most Apple software updates and third-party software that requires the installation of items in multiple locations. Installation packages are deployed via user interaction with the Installer application. When a user opens an installation package, he is presented with the Installer application. This application has the user walk through a few simple screens to configure and initiate the installation process.

Most significantly, installation packages often require administrative user authentication, as they are frequently used to install items that can affect other users and the operating system. Lesson 5, "OS X Software Updates," details the use and troubleshooting of installation packages for Apple software updates. The same techniques apply to third-party installation packages deployed via the Installer application.

That said, on occasion you will find third-party installers that do not use the Apple Installer application. These installations are easily identified because the installation assets are themselves an application using the .app filename extension. The Apple native installation assets come only in the form of installation packages using the .pkg or .mpkg filename extensions. If you have problems with a third-party installer, you must contact the developer for any issues regarding installation, as it has elected to use a proprietary installation mechanism.

Updating Installed Software

Similar to installation, there are a variety of methods for keeping installed software up-to-date:

- Apple software and Mac App Store software—Any software acquired via the Mac App Store, including both Apple software and third-party software, is also updated via the Mac App Store software update mechanism, as covered previously in this lesson and in Lesson 5, "OS X Software Updates."
- Automatically updating third-party software—Automatic update mechanisms for third-party software vary widely. Prior to the Mac App Store, no unified method for providing third-party software updates existed. Thus, software developers often implemented their own automatic update methods. Unfortunately, this means there is no standard method to determine if an application has automatic update capability. You can start by looking in common locations, including the application menu (the menu that appears with the application's name), the application's preferences window, or the application's Help menu. If the third-party item installed a preference pane, it's highly likely any automatic update mechanism will be found within. Finally, it's important to note that nearly all automatic update mechanisms require administrative user authentication.
- Manually update third-party software—In some cases the only update mechanism for third-party software is to simply install a newer version. Keep in mind, only administrative users can replace or update software in the /Applications folder. Further, many package installations require administrative user authentication.

Reference 19.5
Removing Installed Software

In many cases removing installed software is much easier than installing it in the first place. One thing that often surprises veteran Windows support specialists who are new to the Mac is that there's no default Apple software removal mechanism. This is because the vast majority of Mac software can simply be thrown in the Trash. That being said, it's never recommended to remove any part of the OS X system software.

Software removal methods include:

- Mac App Store software—While it's true that applications installed via the Mac App Store can be dragged to the Trash, you can also remove these applications from Launchpad. To engage Launchpad, double-click its icon in the /Applications folder, or from a Multi-Touch trackpad use the "pinch with thumb and three fingers" gesture. In Launchpad, hold down the Option key and a small "x" button appears next to Mac App Store installed applications. Click one of the buttons and the system will remove that application.
- Drag and drop to the Trash—Yes, it's true that most applications are "removed enough" if you simply move the primary application icon into the Trash. If the software item is a type of resource, like a preference pane or font, just locate the item in one of the Library folders and drag it to the Trash. This method may leave some residual support files, but by removing the primary application or resource file you have rendered the software inoperable. This method works for applications installed using a traditional method and via the Mac App Store. Just don't forget to empty the Trash before continuing with your work, and a user logout wouldn't hurt either.
- Application uninstaller—Only in very rare occasions will third-party software require an uninstaller. The only times you will find an uninstaller are in situations where the software's developer has deemed the removal process complicated enough to warrant an uninstaller. If this is the case, the software developer must provide the uninstaller, often along with the original software installer.

Exercise 19.1
Use the Mac App Store

Prerequisites

- You must have created the Local Admin (Exercise 3.1 or 3.2) and Chris Johnson (Exercise 6.1) accounts.

In this exercise, you will use the Mac App Store to purchase, download, and install a free application on your computer.

Select an App to Purchase

1 If necessary, log in as Chris Johnson (password: **chris**, or whatever you chose when you created the account).

2 Open System Preferences, and select the Software Update preference pane.

The settings in this preference pane allow you to automate updating and downloading App Store purchases. The options to check for and install updates (which are selected by default) make the App Store automatically update both system software and installed apps. The option to automatically download apps is useful if you have several computers linked to the same Apple ID; if you enable this option, purchasing an app on one linked computer automatically downloads and installs the app on all linked computers.

3 If "Automatically download apps purchased on other Macs" is selected, click the lock, authenticate as Local Admin, and turn it off.

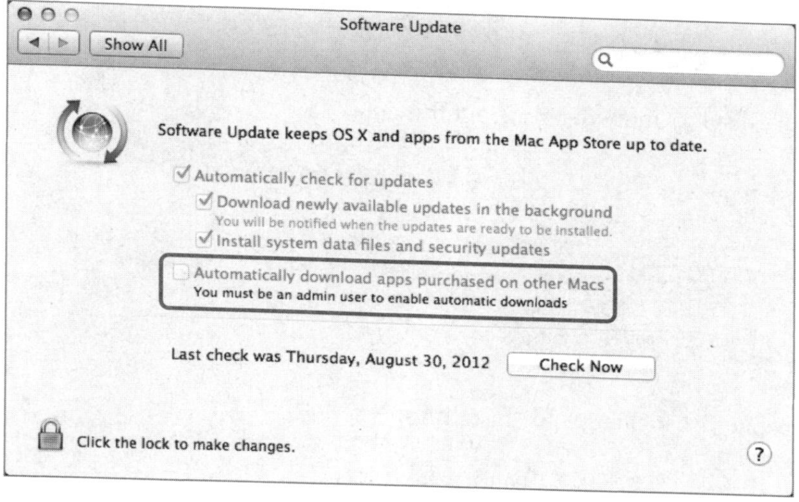

4 Close System Preferences.

5 From the Apple menu, choose App Store.

6 Type **helvetica weather** into the search field and press Return.

NOTE ▶ If you are performing these exercises in a class, the instructor may recommend a different app for this exercise; in this case, substitute his recommendation for Helvetica Weather throughout this exercise.

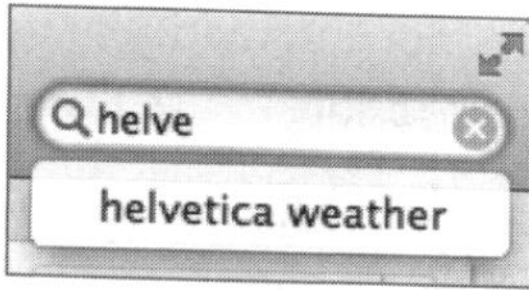

The App Store may find more than one relevant app. Find a free app named Helvetica Weather (or the app your instructor recommended).

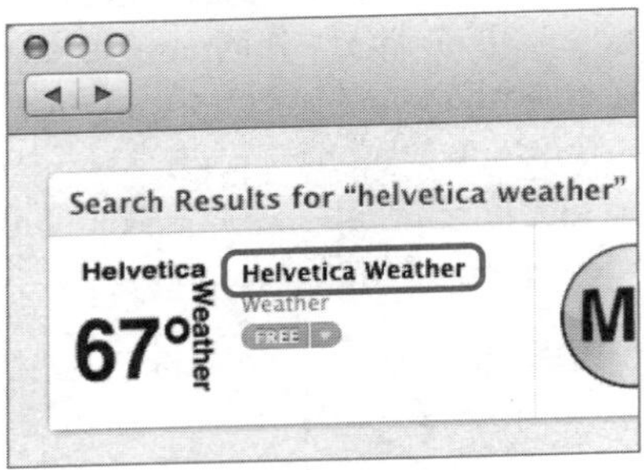

7 Click the free app's name.

The App Store displays more details about this app.

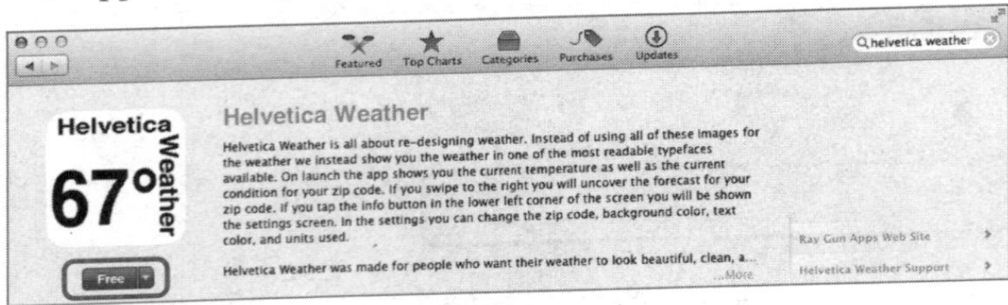

8 Click the Free button. It changes to "Install App".

9 Click the Install App button.

Since you are logged in as a standard user, you are required to provide an administrator's name and password to install this app.

10 Authenticate as Local Admin (remember that you can use the short account name **ladmin** to save typing), and click Install Software.

A dialog appears asking you to sign in to download the app. Note that an Apple ID is required even though this is a free application. Also, it does not automatically use your iCloud Apple ID for App Store purchases (although it is possible to use the same Apple ID for both).

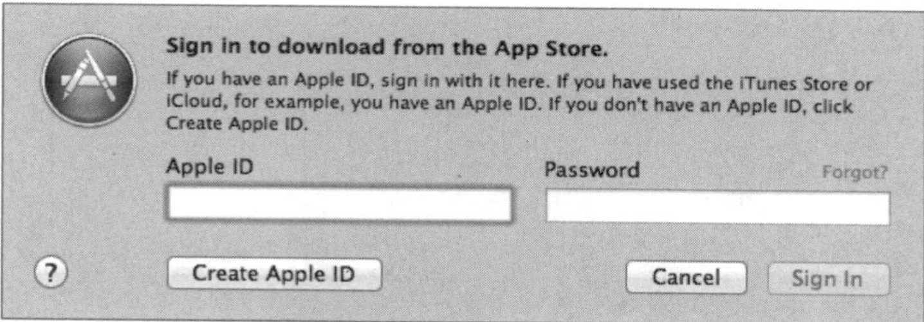

You have several choices for which account to use:

- If you have an existing Apple ID set up for use with the App Store or iTunes, you can use that.
- If you are performing this exercises as part of a class, the instructor can provide an Apple ID for this exercise.
- You can use the iCloud account you created earlier with the App Store.
- If you have access to an existing email account, you can create a new Apple ID linked to it and use that for the App Store.

Depending on which choice you prefer, perform the steps in the corresponding section:

Option 1: Use an Existing Apple ID (Either Yours or Provided by an Instructor)

Follow these steps if you have an Apple ID set up for use with iTunes and the App Store, or if you are performing the exercise in class and the instructor has provided an Apple ID for you to use.

NOTE ► If you choose to use your own Apple ID for this exercise, you need to authorize it on the computer you are using. Unlike iTunes music authorization, this does not count against a limit for your account. As of this writing, the Mac App Store Product Usage Rules state that:

> (i) You may download and use an application from the Mac App Store ("Mac App Store Product") for personal, non-commercial use on any Apple-branded products running Mac OS X ("Mac Computer") that you own or control.

See http://www.apple.com/legal/itunes/us/terms.html for the current terms and conditions. You may also need to verify your payment information, and will be notified by email that your account has been used.

If you are in a class and have any reservations about using your own Apple ID on a classroom computer, feel free to use the instructor-provided Apple ID instead.

1 Enter the Apple ID and password, and click Sign In.

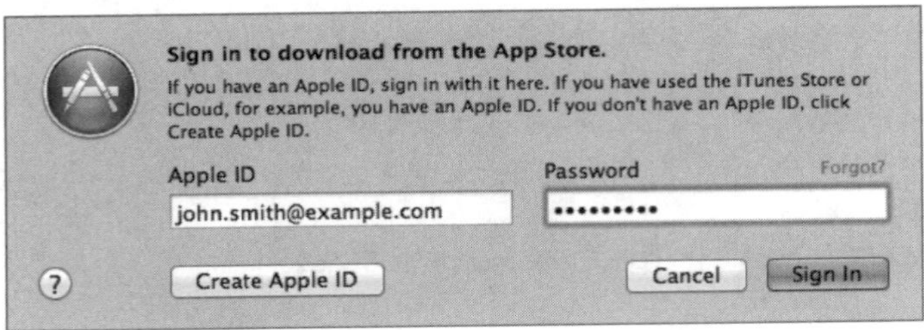

2 If you receive a message that this Apple ID has not been used with the iTunes Store, click Cancel and either restart from step 8 of the previous section (clicking the Free button) using an instructor-provided Apple ID instead of your own, or use one of the other options for an Apple ID.

3 If you are asked to verify payment information for your Apple ID account, enter it as requested. If the requested information is not available, click Cancel, and then choose Store > Sign Out and either restart from step 8 of the previous section (clicking the Free button) using an instructor-provided Apple ID instead of your own, or use one of the other options for an Apple ID.

4 If you receive a warning that the terms and conditions have changed, click OK and read the new terms. If you are using your own Apple ID and do not want to agree to them, click Cancel, and then choose Store > Sign Out and either restart from step 8 of the previous section (clicking the Free button) using an instructor-provided Apple ID instead of your own, or use one of the other options for an Apple ID.

5 Once the app starts downloading (shown under the Launchpad icon in the Dock), skip ahead to the "Test the App" section.

Option 2: Use the iCloud Account You Created Earlier

Follow these steps if you want to use the same Apple ID for both iCloud and the App Store.

1 Enter the iCloud Apple ID (including the domain name) and password, and click Sign In.

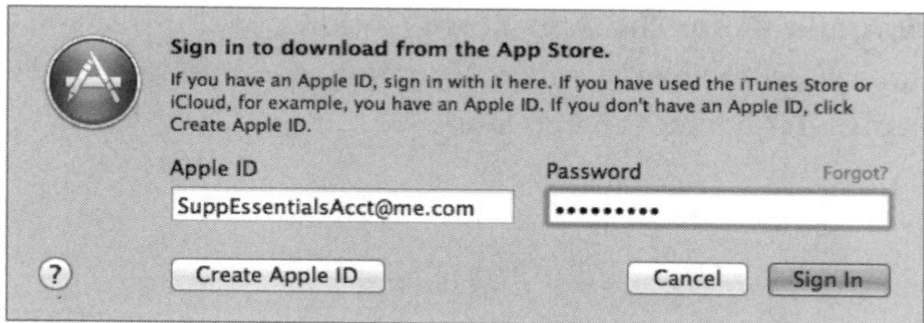

You are notified that this Apple ID has not been used with the iTunes store.

2. Click Review.

3. In the "Welcome to the App Store" screen, click Continue.

4. In the "Terms and Conditions" screen, review the terms.

   If the terms are not acceptable to you, you cannot use the App Store. Quit the App Store, and proceed to the next exercise.

5. If the terms are acceptable, select "I have read and agree to these terms and conditions," and then click Agree.

6. In the Review Your Address screen, select None as the payment type, and enter your billing address. Click Continue.

7. In the Congratulations screen, click Start Shopping.

   Since you have now signed into a new account, the App Store may reset back to its starting screen. You need to find the app (generally Helvetica Weather) and reselect it for purchase. See the earlier section "Select an App to Purchase" for details.

8. Once the app starts downloading (shown under the Launchpad icon in the Dock), skip ahead to the "Test the App" section.

Option 3: Create a New Apple ID for the App Store

Follow these steps if you have access to an existing email account, and want to create an Apple ID linked to that email and use it for the App Store.

1. Click the Create Apple ID button.

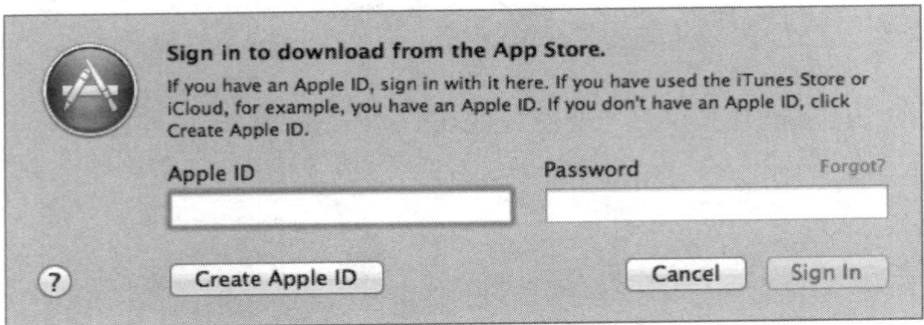

2. In the "Welcome to the App Store" screen, click Continue.

3. In the "Terms and Conditions" screen, review the terms.

   If the terms are not acceptable to you, you cannot use the App Store. Quit the App Store, and proceed to the next exercise.

   If the terms are acceptable, select "I have read and agree to these terms and conditions," and then click Agree.

4. In the Provide Apple ID Details screen, enter your existing email address, choose a (new) password and security questions, enter your date of birth, and adjust the email options to your preferences.

5. In the "Provide a Payment Method" screen, select None as the payment type, and enter your name and billing address. Click Create Apple ID.

   Apple sends a test message to verify the email address you provided.

6. Check your email. When you receive the verification message from Apple, click the Verify Now link in the message.

   This link takes you to a web form where you can verify the address.

7. In the web form that opens, enter your Apple ID (the email address you provided) and the password you chose, and then click Verify Address.

8. When the email address has been verified, quit the browser.

9 In the App Store, click OK.

10 In the Congratulations screen, click Start Shopping.

Since you have now signed into a new account, the App Store may reset back to its starting screen. You need to find the app (generally Helvetica Weather) and reselect it for purchase. See the earlier section "Select an App to Purchase" for details.

11 Once the app starts downloading (shown under the Launchpad icon in the Dock), proceed with the "Test the App" section.

Test the App

1 In the Dock, click the Launchpad icon.

If Helvetica Weather has not finished downloading, Launchpad displays its progress. When it finishes, you will see the app's regular icon.

2 Click the Helvetica Weather icon.

Helvetica Weather launches.

3 Quit Helvetica Weather.

Examine the App Store

1 In the App Store toolbar, click the Purchases icon.

The App Store lists all the applications purchased with this Apple ID. If you are using your own Apple ID, you see your previous purchases; if you are using an instructor-supplied Apple ID, you may see apps that previous students purchased.

Note that if you had enabled the "Automatically download apps purchased on other Macs" option in the Software Update preferences, any additional apps would be automatically downloaded and installed. Since this option is disabled, you see Install buttons that allow you to download and install them manually.

NOTE ► The Mac App Store terms and conditions limit the situations in which an app may be installed on several computers. See www.apple.com/legal/itunes/us/terms.html for the current terms and conditions.

If any other apps are listed, do not install them at this time.

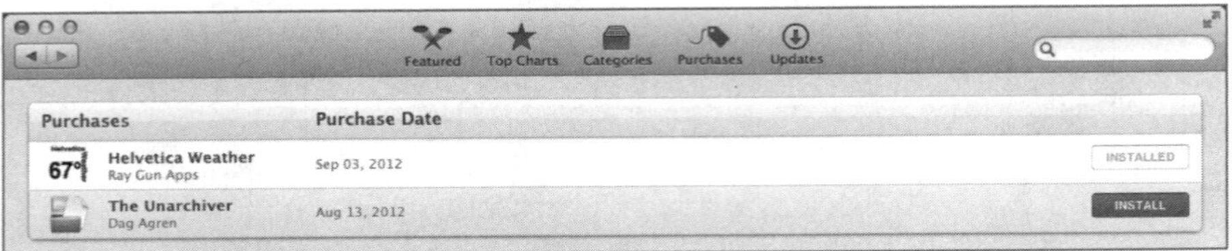

2 In the App Store toolbar, click the Updates button. If you are prompted to, authenticate as Local Admin.

This displays updates available for both system software and App Store purchases installed on this computer.

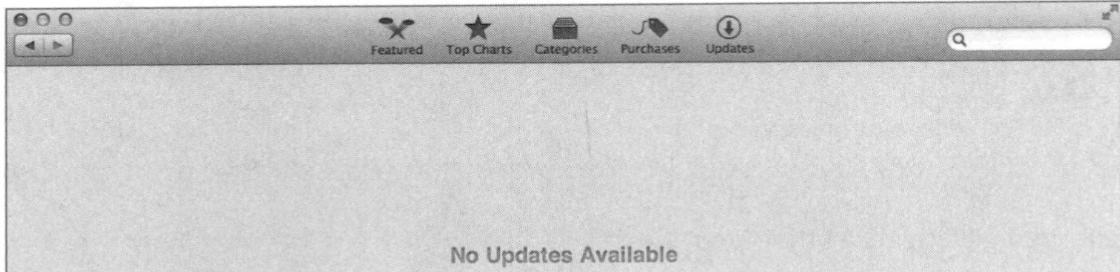

3 Quit the App Store.

Exercise 19.2
Use an Installer Package

► Prerequisites

- ► You must have created the Local Admin (Exercise 3.1 or 3.2) and Chris Johnson (Exercise 6.1) accounts.

Traditionally, one common way of distributing software is in the form of an installer package. While this installation process involves more steps than the App Store method, it also offers some additional capabilities, such as allowing the developer to install files outside of /Applications, allowing the user to choose which optional components to install, and so on. Packages can also be distributed on physical media (CDs and DVDs), as well as by download. For these reasons, package-based installation is likely to continue to be used for complex applications and other software. In this exercise, you will use it to install a simple application.

Install an App with an Installer Package

1 If necessary, log in as Chris Johnson.

2 Open the /Users/Shared/StudentMaterials/Lesson19 folder.

3 Open Hello World.dmg.

The image mounts, with the Hello World package inside it.

4 Open Hello World.pkg.

The Installer opens and prepares to install the Hello World application.

5 Click the lock icon at the upper right of the Installer window.

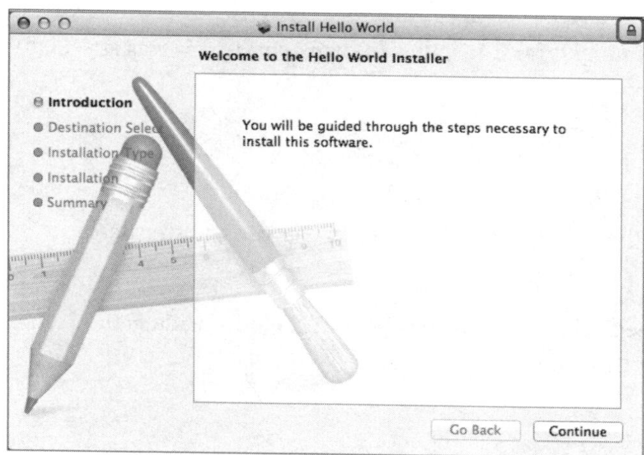

The lock icon indicates that this is a signed package; clicking it displays information about the certificate it was signed with. In this case, it was signed with Gordon Davisson's Developer ID Installer certificate, which was signed by the Developer ID Certification Authority, which in turn was signed by the Apple Root CA. Essentially, this means that the Apple Root CA vouches for the authenticity of the Developer ID Certification Authority, which vouches for the authenticity of Gordon Davisson's certificate, which vouches for the authenticity of the installer package.

This is the standard format of an Apple-issued Developer ID certificate.

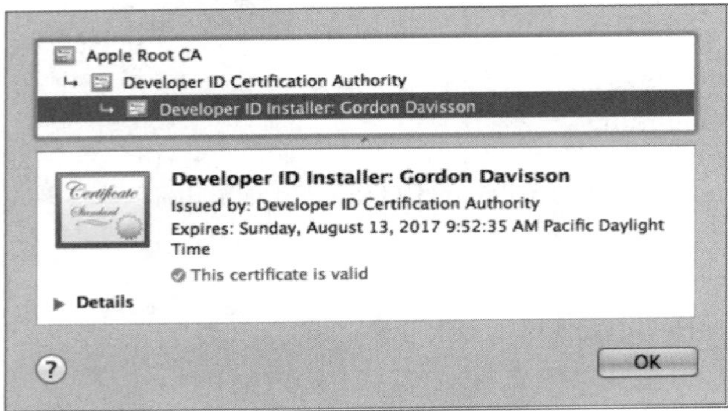

6 Click OK to dismiss the certificate dialog.

Some packages include additional steps, such as readme info, license agreements, choices of components to install, and so forth. This is a very simple package, so it proceeds straight to the install pane.

7 At the Standard Install pane, click Install.

8 Authenticate as Local Admin when prompted.

The installation completes quickly, and Installer informs you that it was successful.

9 Click Close, and Installer exits.

10 Eject the disk image.

11 In the Finder, navigate to the Applications folder (you can use the shortcut Command-Shift-A).

Note that a subfolder named "Hello World" has been installed. Inside is the Hello World application, and an Uninstall script.

12 Open Launchpad.

Even though it was installed in a subfolder, the new app is displayed along with your other applications.

13 Open Hello World.

Because this application was installed with a package (and the package was properly signed), Gatekeeper does not activate and no warning is displayed. You will see what happens with an untrusted application in the next exercise.

14 Quit Hello World.

Note that unlike the Mac App Store, there is no standard update process for package-installed applications. Some apps manage their own updates, while others require you to manually download and install updates.

Exercise 19.3
Use a Drag-and-Drop Install

> **Prerequisites**
>
> - You must have created the Local Admin (Exercise 3.1 or 3.2) and Chris Johnson (Exercise 6.1) accounts.

In this exercise, you will examine the process of installing a downloaded application via the drag-and-drop method. The way you will get this application depends on whether you have a server available to support these exercises (either one provided by the classroom, or one you set up yourself). If you have a "Mainserver" available, follow option 1; otherwise, follow option 2.

Option 1: Download an Application from Mainserver

Follow these steps if you have an OS X server configured to support these exercises.

1 If necessary, log in as Chris Johnson.

2 Open Safari.

3 Enter **mainserver.local/Downloads**.

4 When the page loads, click the link to download Dead End. When the download is complete, quit Safari.

5 Open Dead-End.dmg from your Downloads folder. Note that there is a shortcut to Downloads in your Dock.

Option 2: Use an Application from StudentMaterials

Follow these steps if you do not have an OS X server configured to support these exercises.

1 If necessary, log in as Chris Johnson.

2 Open the /Users/Shared/StudentMaterials/Lesson19 folder.

3 Open Dead-End.dmg.

Note that this disk image contains an application that was previously downloaded from a website and is still in quarantine, so OS X treats it as coming from an untrusted source.

Copy the Application to /Applications

Some applications distributed for drag-and-drop installations come with instructions or hints about how to install them, while others simply assume the user will know what to do. The Dead End app comes as a disk image with instructions in the background image.

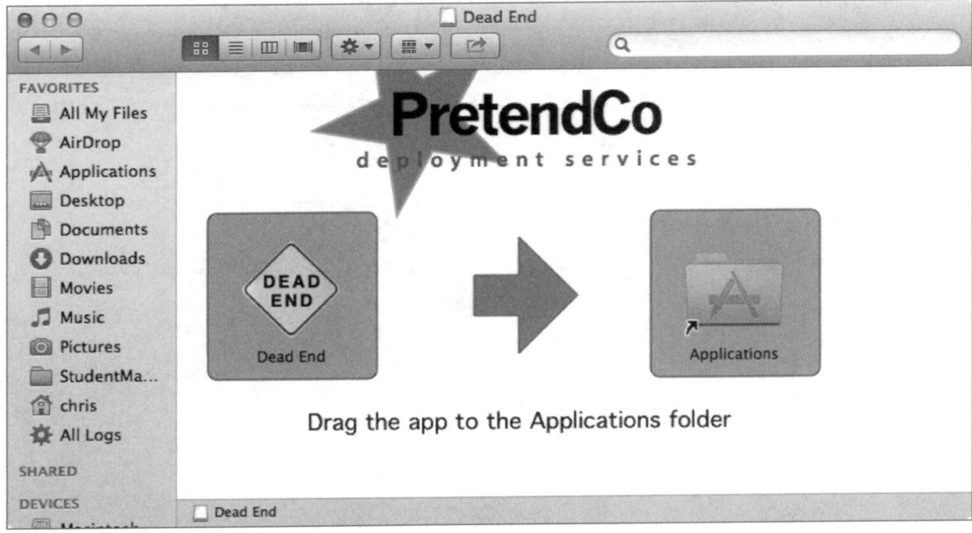

1 Drag the Dead End icon onto the Applications icon (which is actually a symbolic link to /Applications).

A dialog appears telling you that the Applications folder can't be modified. This is because you are logged in as a standard user, and the file permissions on /Applications allow only administrators to write to it.

2 Click the Authenticate button, authenticate as Local Admin, and click OK.

The Finder now copies Dead End into /Applications.

OS X is very tolerant, and it allows you to run applications no matter where they're stored. Because of this, users sometimes do not realize they should put applications into /Applications. Instead, they run the copy in the disk image they downloaded, or make any of a variety of similar mistakes. This is generally OK but may cause confusion or slightly odd Mac behavior.

Do not launch the Dead End app yet.

3 Eject the disk image.

Test the Gatekeeper Security Settings

1 Open System Preferences, and select the Security & Privacy pane.

2 Click the General tab.

3 If necessary, authenticate and set the "Allow applications downloaded from" option to "Mac App Store and identified developers."

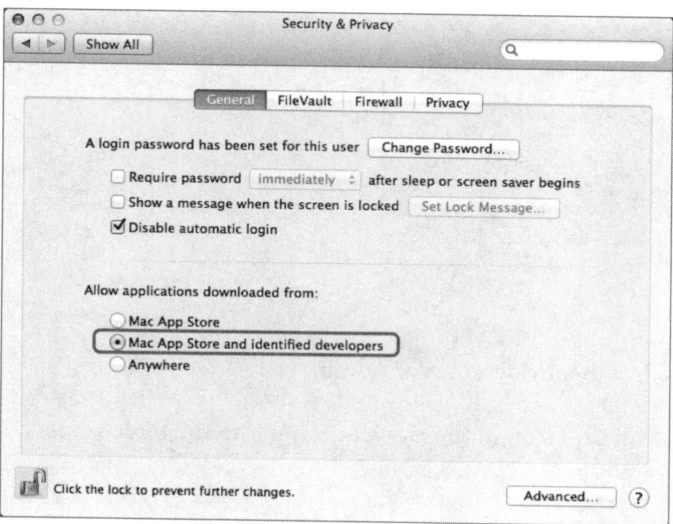

4 Quit System Preferences.

5 In the Finder, navigate to the Applications folder (you can use the shortcut Command-Shift-A).

6 Double-click Dead End.

The file was tagged with some additional metadata to indicate that it is in quarantine because it was downloaded from the Internet. The first time you open it, Gatekeeper checks it against your allowed applications policy. Since the application is not signed with a Developer ID, Gatekeeper does not allow it to open.

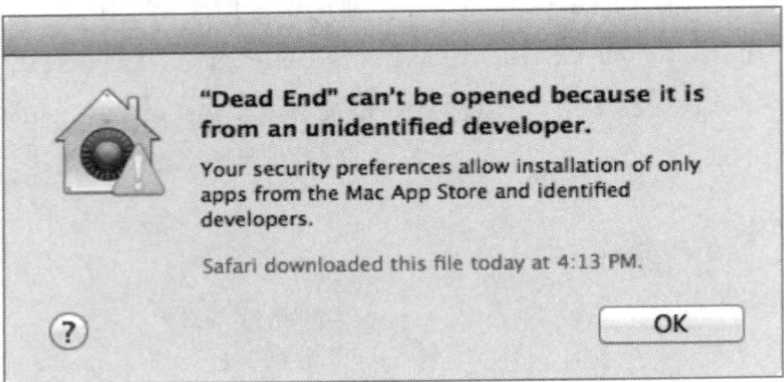

7 Click OK.

8 Control-click Dead End, and choose Open from the shortcut menu.

This time, Gatekeeper warns you about the app, but gives you the option to bypass its normal policy and open the application.

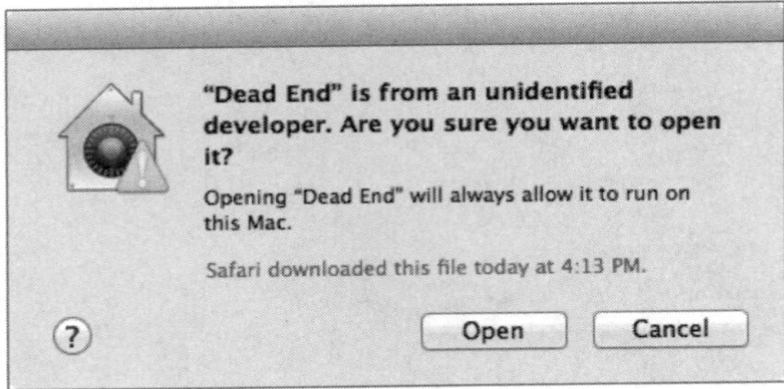

9 Click Open.

10 When you are prompted, authenticate as Local Admin.

11 If necessary, click the Dead End icon in the Dock to bring it to the foreground.

Do not click "Download the Internet" at this time. If you do, see Exercise 21.1 for information on forcing applications to quit. While this app is not particularly malicious, it doesn't do anything useful either.

12 Quit Dead End.

13 Double-click Dead End to reopen it.

This time it opens without the warning. Since you opened it once, its quarantine metadata has been removed and it is no longer subject to the Gatekeeper policy.

14 Quit Dead End again.

Note that unlike the Mac App Store, there is no standard update process for drag-and-drop-installed applications. Some apps manage their own updates, while others require you to manually download and install updates.

Exercise 19.4
Remove Applications

Prerequisites

- You must have performed Exercises 19.1 and 19.2.

Since OS X applications are usually just packages (or even single files), all that's necessary to remove them is to drag them to the Trash. A few more complex programs consist of more than just an application, and these will generally include their own uninstaller.

View Installed Applications

1 Open System Information by holding the Option key and choosing Apple menu > System Information.

System Information opens directly to the full system report.

2 From the Software section of the sidebar, select Installations.

This part of the report shows software that has been installed on the computer by both the App Store and by package, so it shows both Helvetica Weather (or whatever app you installed in Exercise 19.1) and Hello World. It does not show software installed by other methods, so even if you installed Dead End (by the drag-and-drop method) it is not shown here.

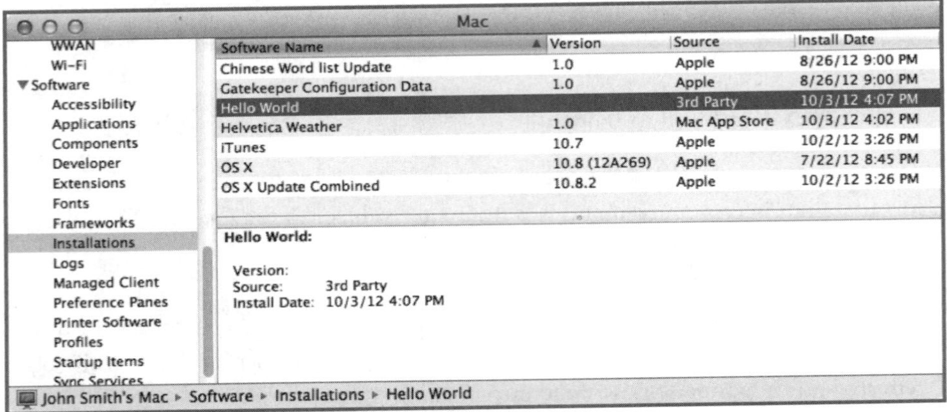

3 Quit System Information.

Remove an Application in Launchpad

1 Open Launchpad.

2 Click Helvetica Weather and hold down the mouse until an X appears at its top left, and the other icons begin to wobble.

In this mode, Launchpad lets you drag app icons around to rearrange them, and also use the X button to delete apps purchased from the App Store. Since Helvetica Weather is the only one you purchased from the App Store, it is the only one that has an X by its icon.

3 Click Helvetica Weather's X button.

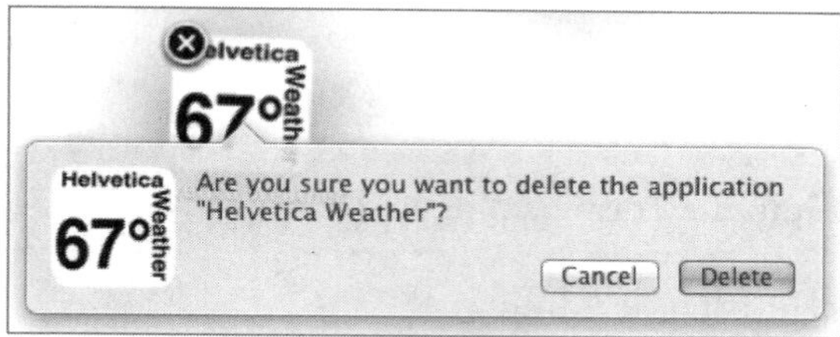

4 In the confirmation dialog that appears, click Delete.

5 If you are prompted, authenticate as Local Admin.

Helvetica Weather is now uninstalled from your computer. Note that your preference file(s) and user data still exist, so if you ever decide to reinstall the program all of your settings are kept.

Reinstall an Application in the App Store

1 Open the App Store.

2 In the toolbar, click the Purchases icon.

Since you purchased Helvetica Weather, it is listed here and available to reinstall. Depending on the history of the Apple ID you are using, other apps may be listed as well.

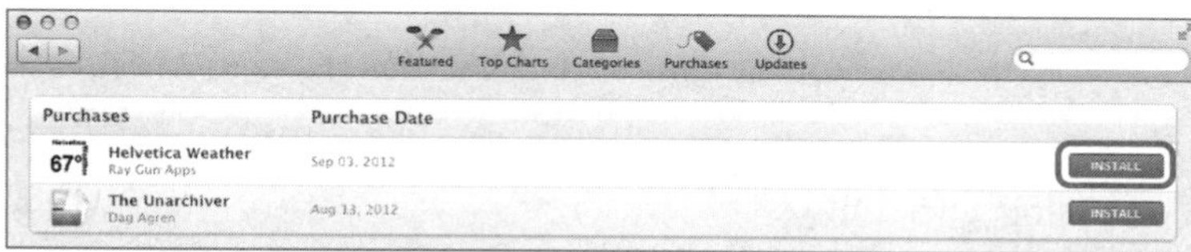

3 Click the Install button for Helvetica Weather.

4 When you are prompted, authenticate as Local Admin.

5 When you are prompted, enter your Apple ID's password to authenticate to the App Store.

The app is downloaded and reinstalled.

6 Wait for the download to finish, and then quit the App Store.

Remove an Application in the Finder

1. In the Finder, navigate to the Applications folder.
2. Select Helvetica Weather, and drag it to the Trash icon in your Dock.
3. When you are prompted, authenticate as Local Admin.
4. Choose Finder > Empty Trash.

   Helvetica Weather is now uninstalled from your computer.

Remove an Application with an Uninstaller

Since most applications can be uninstalled with the Finder, they don't provide any special uninstaller. Applications that do will vary as to how they provide the uninstaller, and exactly how it works. This exercise presents a simple example.

1. In the Finder, navigate to the Applications folder.
2. Open the Hello World folder.
3. Open the Uninstall script in the Hello World folder.

   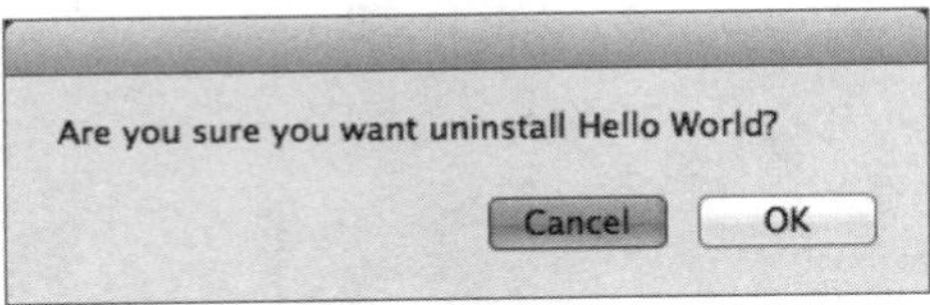

4. At the confirmation dialog, click OK.
5. When you are prompted, authenticate as Local Admin.
6. Reopen the Applications folder.

   The entire Hello World folder has been removed from your computer.

Lesson **20**

Document Management

For most users, document management is one of their primary day-to-day computing tasks. For many years the act of opening and saving documents on a Mac system has remained the same. Yet, with the introduction and ultimate success of iOS, Apple has been seriously rethinking how Mac users interact with documents. OS X Lion introduced significant changes to how documents are saved with Auto Save and Versions. Now OS X Mountain Lion changes where users can save their documents with full iCloud integration.

This lesson first introduces the OS X Launch Services, which is the system that determines an action when the user double-clicks a document. You will also learn to use Quick Look for previewing most common document types. Then a significant portion of this lesson is dedicated to document management via Auto Save, Versions, and documents in iCloud. Finally, you will see how OS X attempts to automatically resume documents and applications on the users' behalf.

GOALS

- Manage Launch Services settings
- Use Quick Look to preview documents
- Work with applications that support Auto Save and Versions
- Save and open documents in iCloud

Reference 20.1
Launch Services

Aside from a file's name, the most fundamentally important piece of information about a file is its type. Identifying a file's type allows OS X to almost always choose the correct application to open when you double-click a file. Launch Services is the technology responsible for helping OS X make the connection between a file's type and the appropriate application. When you double-click a file from the Finder, it asks Launch Services to open the file with the appropriate application. Launch Services identifies the file based on its type and then references an application registration database to determine which application should open the file.

File Type Identification

Apple pioneered file type identification when it first introduced the Mac OS. Apple designed the file identification system to use four-character file type and creator signature file attributes, which were normally hidden from the user. This was a brilliant design that separated the file's type and default application binding from the file's name.

Unfortunately, the popularity of other operating systems forced the awkward practice of adding a file type identifier to the end of a file's name. This complicated the practice of naming files by requiring the user to identify and maintain the appropriate filename extension such as .mp3 for compressed audio files, .jpg for compressed picture files, or .doc for Microsoft Word files.

Using filename extensions has become standard practice, so modern operating systems have been designed to work around this poor design choice by simply hiding the filename extension from the user. For the sake of compatibility, Apple adopted this later method of file type identification as the default for all versions of OS X.

> **NOTE ►** OS X still supports the legacy file type attribute but no longer supports the creator code attribute. Thus some files may not default to opening in the application that created them. However, you can change the default behavior, as covered later in this section.

Since the Finder hides many filename extensions by default, you can toggle file type extension visibility from the Finder preferences by choosing Finder > Preferences. Then click the Advanced button and select or deselect the checkbox next to "Show all filename extensions."

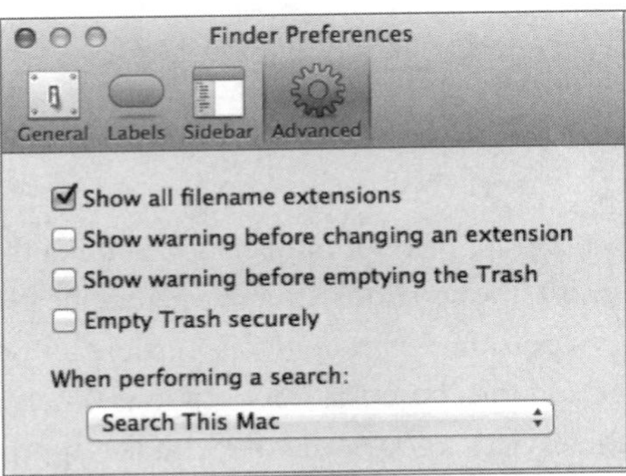

NOTE ▶ Choosing to show all file extensions in the Finder overrides the individual file attribute for hiding the extension as configured from the Get Info and Inspector windows in the Finder.

Application Registration

When a user attempts to open a file of a certain type, Launch Services reads from a database of applications and the types of files each can open to determine a match. Successful file and application match information is cached, so future attempts to open an application are as quick as possible. However, after every startup or login, a background process automatically scans for new applications and updates this database. Further, both the Finder and Installer keep track of new applications as they arrive on your system and add their supported file types to the database.

The application registration system is pretty good at finding matches, so odds are if the system gives you an error message, then you probably don't have the correct application for the file. In OS X, Launch Services maps many common file types to the built-in Preview and TextEdit applications if the primary application is missing. For example, Numbers or Excel documents open in Preview and Pages, and Word documents open in TextEdit.

TIP The OS X Quick Look feature can also preview many common file types even without the applications installed. This includes both iWork and Microsoft Office documents. Quick Look details are covered later in this lesson.

If Preview, or any other application, cannot properly open a specific file type, you can change the Launch Services settings to force those files to open in a more appropriate application, as outlined in the following section. Other times, though, Launch Services may not have any idea which application to use for the file type. If you attempt to open a file type that is not stored in the Launch Services database, the computer prompts you to find an application that supports the file. Alternatively, you can use a new feature in OS X that searches the Mac App Store for a compatible application.

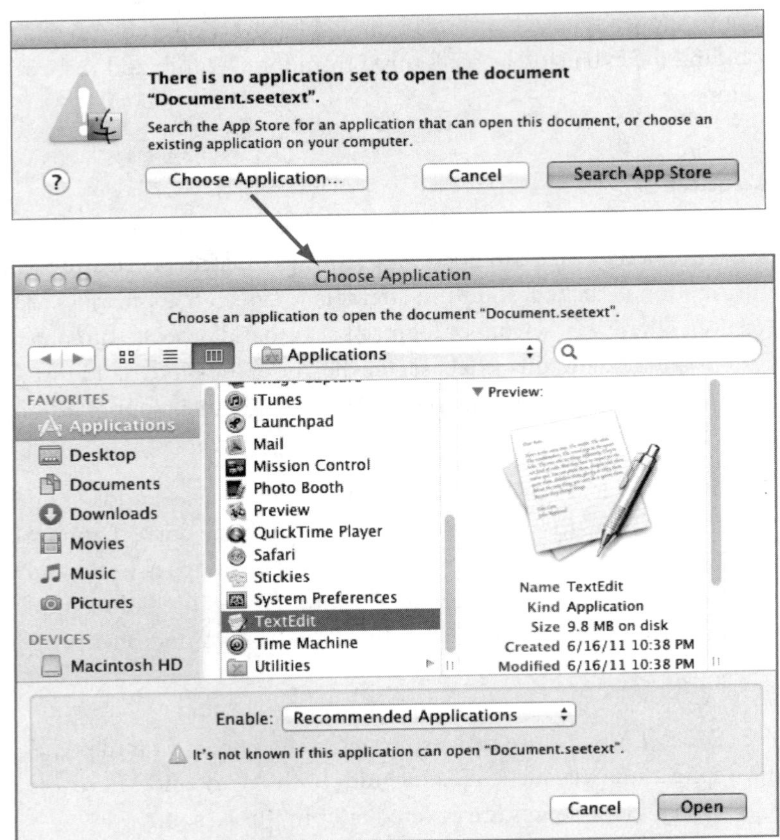

Launch Services Settings

From the Get Info or Inspector windows in the Finder, you can override the Launch Services default application settings for any specific file type.

> **MORE INFO ▶** Using the Info window to inspect files and folders is detailed in Lesson 12, "Permissions and Sharing."

Once you have selected the files you want to change Launch Services settings for and have opened an Info window, click the "Open with" disclosure triangle to reveal the default application selected by Launch Services. To change just the selected files' default application, simply select another application from the pop-up menu. This information is saved to the files' metadata and only defines Launch Services settings for the selected items.

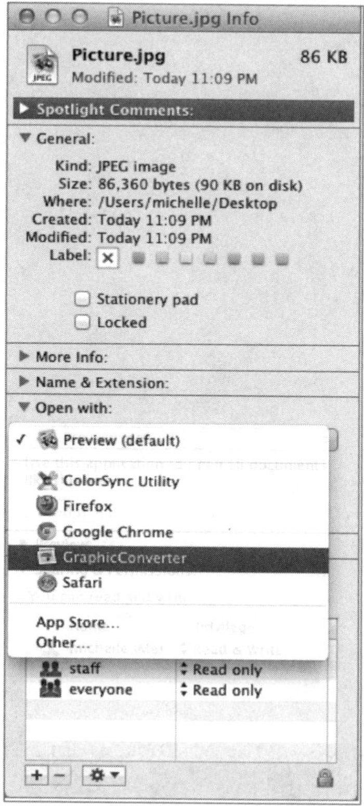

To change the default application for all files of this type, select the application you want to define as the default, and then click the Change All button. This setting is saved per user, so one user's application preferences do not override another user's preferences. A user's custom Launch Service settings are saved to the com.apple.LaunchServices.plist preference file in each user's ~/Library/Preferences folder.

TIP You can also modify Launch Services settings in the Finder by secondary (or Control) clicking on the selected files and then choosing Open With from the shortcut menu. Additionally, holding down the Option key changes the menu command to Always Open With.

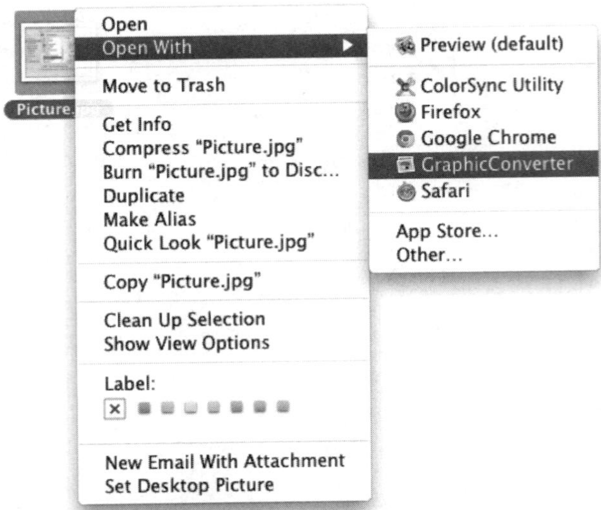

Reference 20.2
Quick Look

Quick Look allows you to preview nearly any file type without having to open any additional applications, or even having those applications installed on your Mac. This makes Quick Look the most convenient method to view the contents of any file.

Quick Look previews can be accessed, or dismissed, by pressing the Spacebar from any Finder view, the Time Machine restore interface, most open and save browser dialogs, the Mail application, or any other application that supports Quick Look. Later versions of OS X keep the Quick Look preview window open in the Finder until closed. Selecting another item in the Finder changes the Quick Look preview to the newly selected item. The Quick Look close button is in the top-left corner, just like in a traditional window. You can also quickly dismiss the Quick Look preview by pressing the Spacebar again.

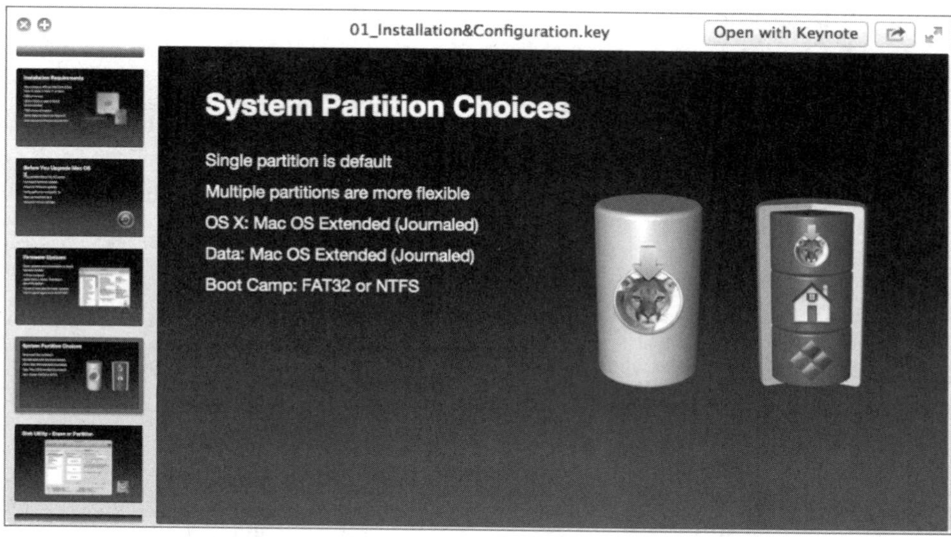

Quick Look technology is also used to provide the Finder with previews for files in icon view, previews in column view, and the preview section of the Get Info and Inspector windows. Finally, Quick Look also provides previews for the Cover Flow view. This view allows you to browse folder content in a similar way to browsing on other Apple mobile devices or in iTunes. Cover Flow view can be accessed from any Finder window by selecting its icon in the toolbar, which you can find directly to the left of the action (gear icon) menu also in the toolbar.

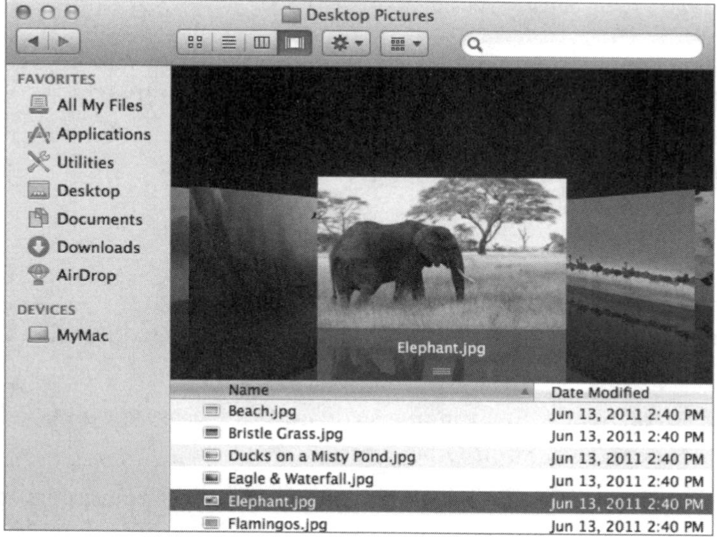

The Quick Look Window

With the Quick Look preview window open, you can resize the window by clicking and dragging any edge of the window, or you can go full-screen by clicking the twin arrow button at the top right of the preview window. Note the "Open with Application" button next to the full-screen button for opening the selected file in its native application. New in OS X Mountain Lion is the Share button (box with rightward arrow) that allows you to quickly share the document.

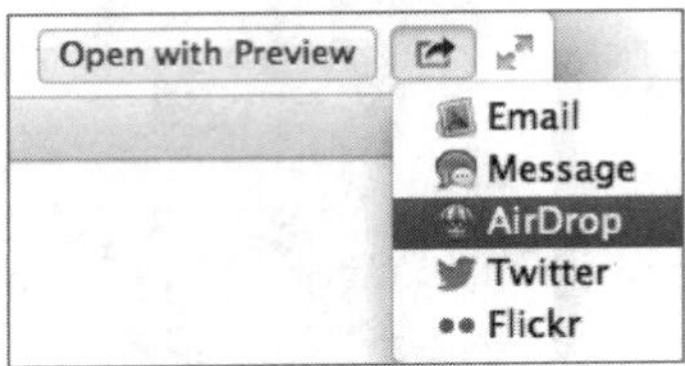

Use the arrow keys to navigate and preview the items adjacent to the original previewed item in the Finder. If the previewed file has multiple pages, you'll be able to scroll through the document. In some cases—Keynote presentations, for example—Quick Look shows a thumbnail preview of each slide, allowing you to scroll through the thumbnails as well. Finally, if you select multiple items to preview, the Quick Look window allows some basic slideshow features via buttons at the top left of the window.

Quick Look Plug-ins

Quick Look is able to preview an ever-growing variety of file types using a plug-in technology. Each Quick Look plug-in is designed to preview specific types of files. Many Quick Look plug-ins are included by default, but Apple and third-party developers can create additional plug-ins to expand the Quick Look preview capabilities.

Included Quick Look plug-ins enable you to:

- Preview any audio or video file that can be decoded by QuickTime
- Preview a variety of graphics files, including many digital camera files, PDF files, EPS files, and any standard graphics file
- Preview a variety of productivity files, including standard text files, script files, and files created by the iWork and Microsoft Office suites
- Preview a variety of Internet-centric files, including mailboxes, iChat transcripts, and web archives

Quick Look plug-ins, like any other system resource, are stored inside the various Library folders. The built-in Apple Quick Look plug-ins are always found in the /System/Library/QuickLook folder and sometimes appear in the /Library/QuickLook folder. Third-party plug-ins should always be installed in either /Library/QuickLook or the ~/Library/QuickLook folder, depending on who needs access to them.

Reference 20.3
Auto Save and Versions

For over 30 years most applications have relied on users to remember to save their work. It's true that for many years some applications have featured optional Auto Save features. In fact, many Apple applications have always provided an environment where users don't have to remember to save. Examples include Aperture, iPhoto, and iTunes.

With OS X Lion, Apple introduced a sophisticated automatic document management model that can be used by any application. Not only does the system automatically save for the user, it also automatically maintains a history of versions for the user's documents as well.

In this section you will learn how the new Auto Save and Versions features work together. These two features also work hand in hand with another OS X feature, document locking and resume, to maintain a current state of the user's work environment even if he logs out or restarts the computer.

Auto Save and Versions Architecture

A primary goal of later versions of OS X is to incorporate many of the iOS features and workflows. One of the main tenets of iOS application design is that the user never has to remember to save her work. However, Mac users are accustomed to having more control over their documents. Further, Mac computers in general have more storage and computing resources than iOS devices. Thus, with OS X Lion Apple took the Auto Save concept and extended it with support for document versions.

For applications that support Auto Save, once the user saves the first time, he is never again bothered by dialogs asking if the application should save changes. In addition, if the user wants to use the document in another application or share it with another user, he doesn't have to remember to save the latest version of the document. From the user's point of view, the document seen in the Finder is always the same as the document seen in the application—the location where the document was first saved will always be the latest version.

In addition, applications that support Auto Save also support document Versions. This provides an environment where the system automatically maintains a history of changes for any document. The user can easily return a document to a previous state with just a few clicks. Or she can navigate to an earlier version of a document and quickly copy specific elements to the latest version of the document.

The user can access a document's version history using an interface very similar to the Time Machine Restore interface. However, from a technical perspective, the document version histories are saved in a hidden folder, /.DocumentRevisions-V100, at the root of the disk containing the original document. Again, the most recent version of a document is always automatically saved to its original location and can be copied or shared with other applications or users immediately after a change is made. Finally, in order to avoid unintentional changes, older documents are automatically locked, but as you'll see later, the user can easily manage this behavior as well.

Applications that support OS X Auto Save and Versions are easily identified by the content of the File menu in the application. Applications that support Auto Save can be most easily identified by a File > Duplicate menu option, instead of the traditional Save As menu option. Auto Save–compatible applications in OS X Mountain Lion also add File > Rename and File > Move To menu options. Updated applications still feature File > Save for saving a document the first time, but upon subsequent usage the behavior of this menu option changes to saving a version of the document. Most Apple-designed applications already support Auto Save and Versions, including TextEdit, Preview, Pages, Numbers, and Keynote.

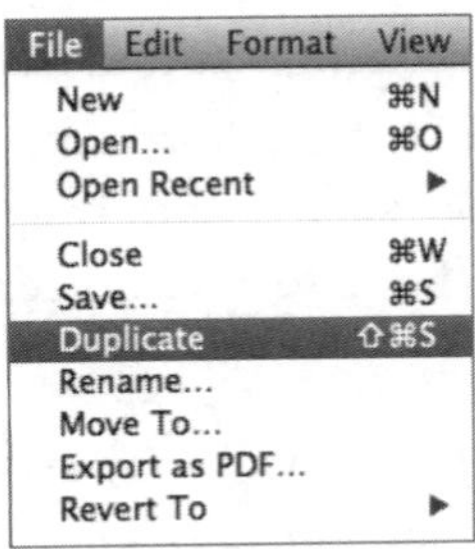

Auto Save

Saving the first time in an application that supports Auto Save is much like using a traditional application. Users may not be prepared for what comes next, though. The irony is that many users may find it difficult to move to this new method even though it requires less work. Simply, most users have grown accustomed to the traditional save methods and will have to "unlearn" them. Thus, training may be required for users to get the most out of OS X Auto Save and Versions.

TIP TextEdit is a great application for testing Auto Save and Versions techniques.

When you open an application that supports Auto Save for the first time, one of two things happens. If you are not signed in to iCloud, or the application does not support saving to iCloud, the application automatically opens a new document. If you are signed in to iCloud and the application supports saving documents to iCloud, you are prompted with an open dialog. Saving documents to iCloud is covered in the next section of this lesson.

When you start a new document in an application that supports Auto Save, it's actually already saved even though you've not yet set a location for it. In other words, changes you make to the new document are automatically saved, even if you have yet to "save" the document. This is because the document is actually saved to the versions history database on the system volume. By default, if you choose to close the document window or application, the system prompts you to save the document. Obviously you can also manually choose File > Save. The resulting save dialog is similar to previous versions of OS X, allowing you to choose a name and location for the document.

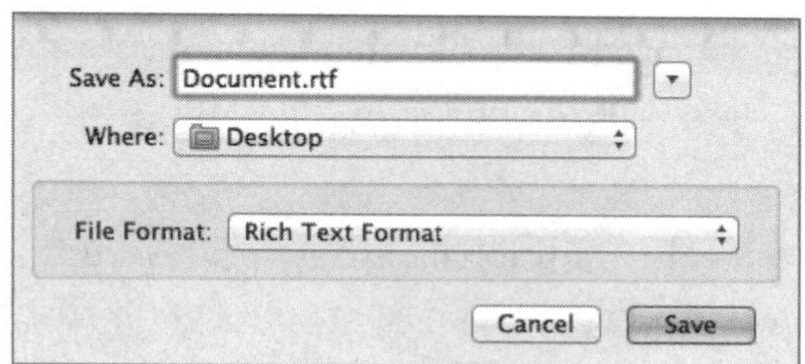

TIP When you open an existing document, you'll never have to save even the first time because the document already has a storage location.

After you have picked a location for the document, you'll never have to save it again. There are many instances that will trigger an Auto Save event, including making a significant change to the document, closing the document window, closing the application, selecting the Finder, or attempting to access the document from another application.

As you make changes to the document, you may notice the word "Edited" in the document title bar. This is also a visual cue to let the user know the system is automatically saving changes. You can test this by making some changes to the document, and then immediately using Quick Look to preview the document by selecting it in the Finder and pressing the Spacebar. The Quick Look preview is identical to the open document in the application.

Duplicate and Save As

If you need to save another copy of a document, you do so by using the Duplicate option. With the document open, choose File > Duplicate or select the document's filename in the title bar to reveal a pop-up menu allowing you to choose Duplicate.

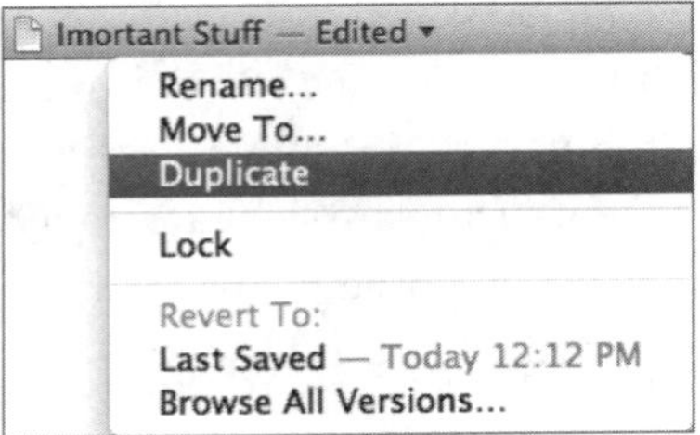

TIP The Move To command in the document menu moves the original document to a new location without creating a new copy.

TIP Holding the Command key and clicking the document's filename in the menu bar reveals its path in the file system.

A new window appears with a copy of the document. Note that the filename in the title bar is highlighted, indicating you can change the name of the duplicated document. The document itself is saved in the same folder as the original document. Again, because Auto Save is at work, you never have to manually "save" this document again, as the system always saves the changes for you.

If you or your users are more comfortable with the traditional Save As process, this is available as well. While holding the Option key the File > Duplicate menu option changes to File > Save As. As of OS X 10.8.2, performing Save As here gives you the option to also save the changes to the original document. This option is disabled by default, giving the Save As procedure behavior similar to that as found in an application that does not support Auto Save.

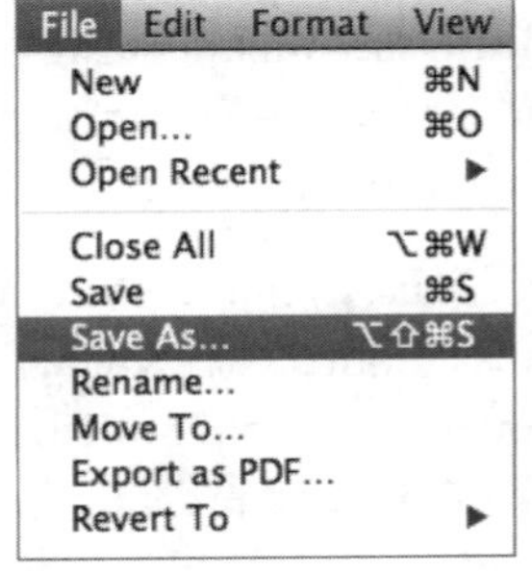

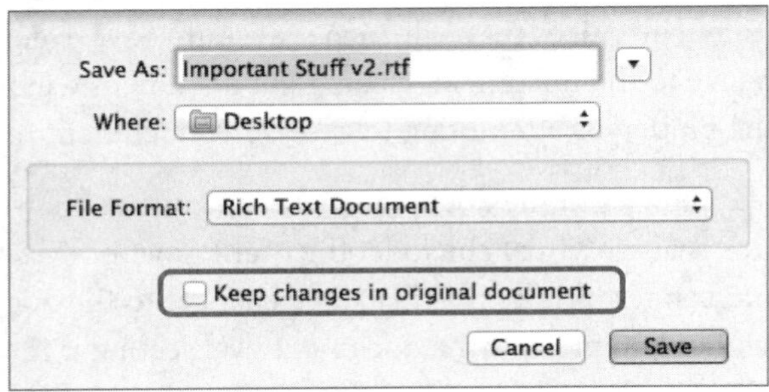

TIP The Save keyboard shortcut remains the same as previous versions of OS X: Command-S. On the other hand, there is no Duplicate keyboard shortcut; instead the Save As command gets a new keyboard shortcut: Option-Shift-Command-S.

Selecting the Save As command is effectively the same process as Duplicate, only it also presents the save dialog, allowing you to choose a different filename and location, and then "closes" the original document. Note that this "close" is quite subtle as the new document replaces the original document in the active window without any obvious animation.

Document Versions

With Versions in OS X, applications always maintain a history of your changes. Any time an application automatically saves, a new document version is also saved. If the user, perhaps out of habit, attempts to manually save by choosing File > Save or by pressing Command-S, he is essentially telling the system to save another version of the document in the version history.

If you're editing a document and have yet to trigger a manual or automatic save, you can easily revert to the previously saved state by choosing File > Revert To > Last Saved. Alternatively, you can select the document's filename in the title bar to reveal a pop-up menu allowing you to choose Revert To: Last Saved.

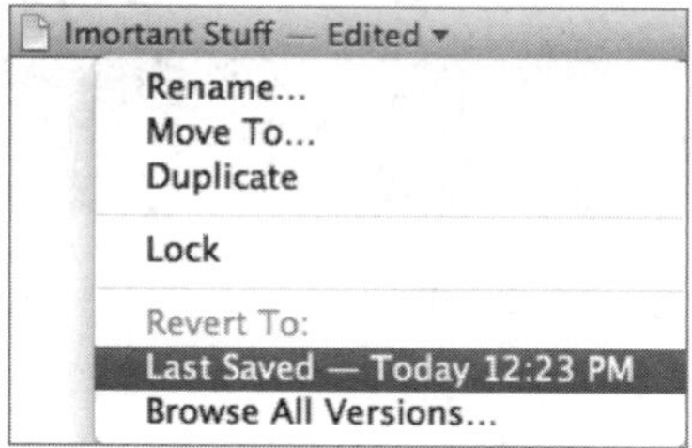

If a deeper history of versions is available, OS X allows you to browse the entire version history of a document. To open the versions history browser, choose File > Revert To > Browse All Versions, or again select the document's filename in the title bar and from the pop-up menu choose Browse All Versions.

NOTE ► A document's versions history is maintained only on the volume where the original document is saved. If you share a document by creating or sending a copy of the document, other users will not have access to the document's version history.

NOTE ▶ Version history is not maintained on files being edited from a shared network volume. If you want to maintain version history, you must copy the shared file to a local disk.

If you've ever used Time Machine, the versions browser interface will look pretty familiar. To the left you'll see the current version of the document, and to the right you can see previous versions. Navigate by either clicking a previous version's title bar or using the timeline to the right.

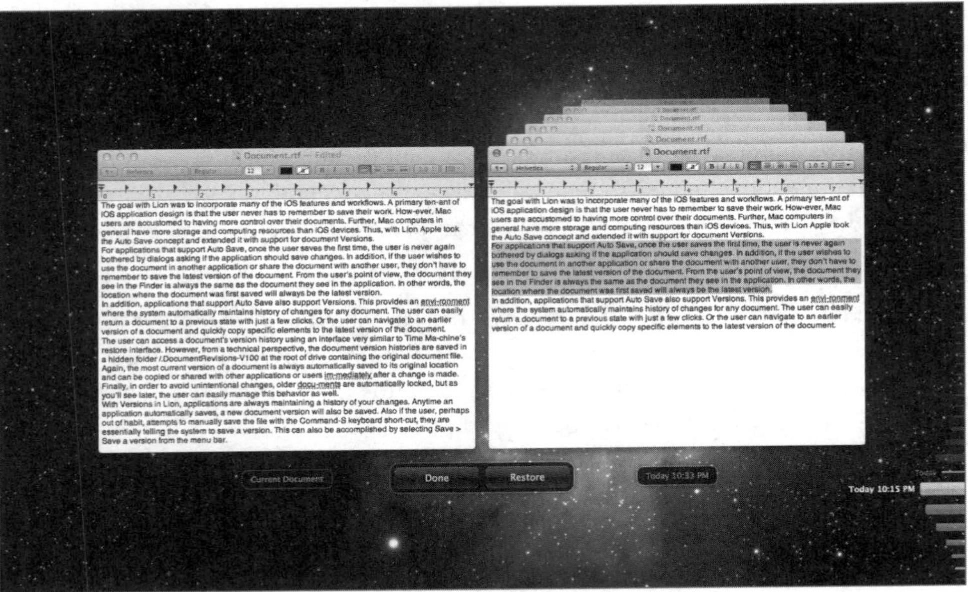

If you would like to restore a previous version in its entirety, click Restore. However, if you just want a specific section of a previous version copied to the latest version, simply make a selection inside the previous document, and then copy and paste to the current document. When you are done making targeted edits, click Done to return to the standard application interface.

TIP In the versions browser, you can copy and paste using the Command-C and Command-V keyboard shortcuts, or by using the secondary (or Control) click to reveal a shortcut menu.

TIP To delete a previous document version, in the versions browser select the document name in the title bar to reveal a pop-up menu allowing you to choose Delete This Version.

TIP ▶ If you have Time Machine enabled, as covered in Lesson 18, an application's version history can go much deeper by showing you versions in the Time Machine backup.

Reference 20.4
Document Locking

OS X includes a special file and folder attribute that trumps all write privileges and even administrative user access. Users can choose to lock a file or folder that they own from any application that supports Auto Save or the Finder Info window.

Locking an item renders it completely unchangeable to all users except the item's owner. Even administrative users are prevented from making changes to another user's locked file in the graphical interface. In other words, a standard user could potentially lock an item that the administrative user would have no ability to change in the graphical interface.

Manage Locking via Finder

The Finder Get Info or Inspector windows can be used to view and change a file's lock state. Once an item is locked, no other users can modify, move, delete, or rename it in the Finder.

MORE INFO ▶ Using the Info window to inspect files and folders is detailed in Lesson 12, "Permissions and Sharing."

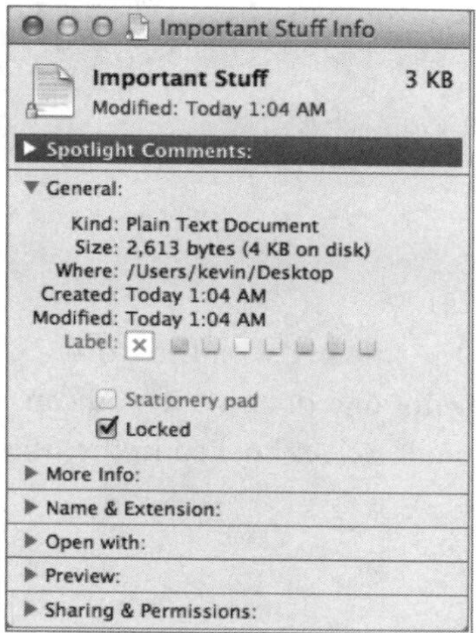

Once the file is locked, the Finder prevents the owner from moving, renaming, or changing ownership and permissions for the locked item. In fact, if you as the owner try to move a locked item, the Finder defaults to making a copy. The owner can return the file to the normal state by disabling the locked attribute from the Get Info or Inspector windows.

> **NOTE ►** Duplicating a locked document in the Finder simply results in another locked copy of the document. In OS X, only applications that support Auto Save can create an unlocked duplicate of a locked file.

Manage Locking via Applications

Applications that support Auto Save also provide easy access to document locking. Document locking may seem like an inconvenience, but in a system where changes are automatically saved, document locking provides a useful service. Specifically, locking a document prevents users, or more appropriately their applications, from accidentally auto saving changes. Users can choose to manually lock or unlock documents within applications that support Auto Save.

> **NOTE ►** OS X Lion automatically locked documents if they had not been edited after a certain amount of time. This feature confused a lot of users, as such it is no longer available in OS X Mountain Lion.

As long as you are the owner of a document, which is often the case if you created the document or are editing a copy of the document, you can manually lock it to prevent further changes. To manually lock a document in an application that supports Auto Save, select the document's filename in the title bar to reveal a pop-up menu allowing you to choose Lock.

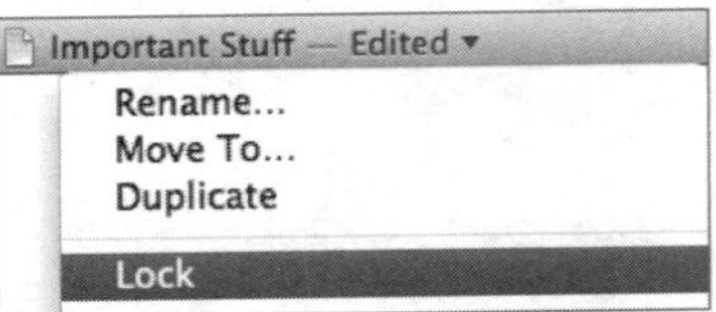

You'll note that locked documents are clearly marked in the title bar with the word "Locked" and a small lock icon. As long as you are the owner of a document, you can manually unlock it to enable changes. To unlock a document, select Locked in the title bar to reveal a pop-up menu allowing you to choose Unlock.

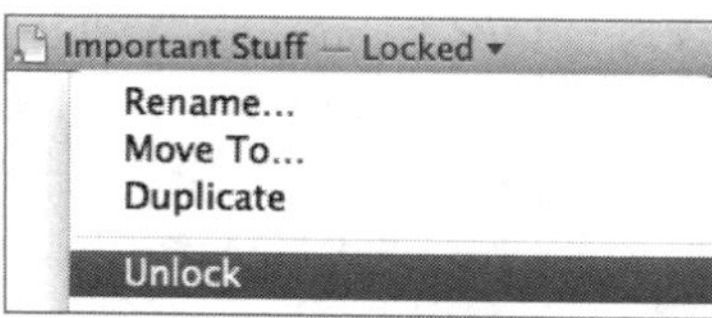

Alternatively, you can simply start modifying a locked document that you own. A dialog appears, allowing you to verify your intent to unlock and edit the document.

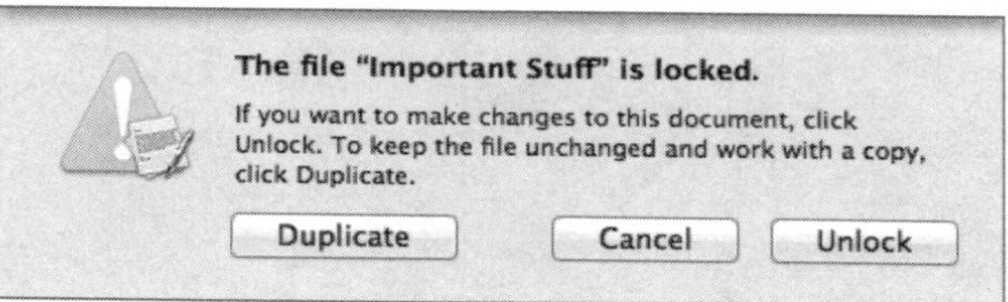

If you aren't the owner of a locked document, you aren't allowed to unlock it; thus you aren't allowed to edit it. Also, as covered in Lesson 12, "Permissions and Sharing," if you don't have write file permissions, you are not allowed to edit a document. In both cases the title bar shows the document as "Locked."

However, you can treat a locked document as a template by duplicating the document and then editing the duplicate copy. Attempting to edit a locked, or otherwise unwriteable, document reveals a prompt that allows the user to duplicate the document.

As covered previously, you can also manually duplicate a locked document by choosing File > Duplicate from the menu bar or by choosing the document's filename in the title bar and from the pop-up menu choosing Browse All Versions. Again, once the application has duplicated a copy, you can then save the copy as you would a new document.

Reference 20.5
Documents in iCloud

The introduction of Auto Save and Versions in OS X Lion was ultimately a precursor for what was to come in OS X Mountain Lion: documents in iCloud. By allowing OS X applications to automatically open and save documents to iCloud, Apple has added the last fundamental bit of feature parity between iOS and OS X. Quite simply, saving your documents in iCloud is the easiest way to manage documents between multiple Apple devices.

To use documents in iCloud, you must first make sure that you are signed in to iCloud and have Documents & Data enabled. Enabling this, or even signing up for iCloud in the first place, can be accomplished via the iCloud or Mail, Contacts & Calendars preferences.

Saving Documents to iCloud

Again, taking a page from the iOS playbook, instead of using a file manager application like the Finder, a user interacts with her documents in iCloud via a compatible application. For example, to manage text documents in iCloud, a user would first open the TextEdit application. With Documents & Data enabled on your Mac for your iCloud account, when you open an iCloud-compatible application, it reveals a new iCloud document browser interface.

> **NOTE ▶** Only applications available from the Mac App Store are capable of saving documents to iCloud. At the time of this writing, iCloud-compatible applications include TextEdit, Preview, Pages, Numbers, and Keynote.

As the iCloud document browser clearly states, you can drag existing TextEdit-compatible documents to this browser. This simple process automatically pushes those documents to iCloud. Another method for moving your existing local documents to iCloud involves first opening a local document. Then when the local document is open in an application window, you can easily move it to iCloud by clicking the document's filename in the title bar and from the pop-up menu choosing Move To iCloud.

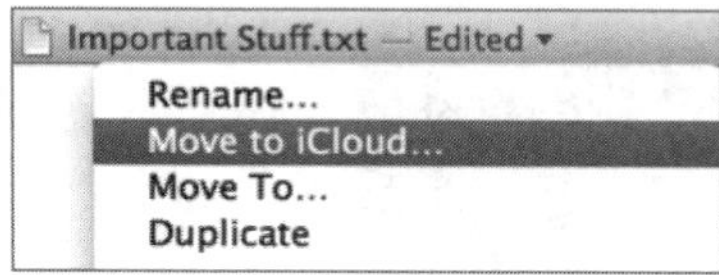

In the application's iCloud browser, you can click New Document to create a new document that automatically saves to iCloud. Alternatively, if you start a new document in an iCloud-compatible application, the save dialog has iCloud selected as the default save destination.

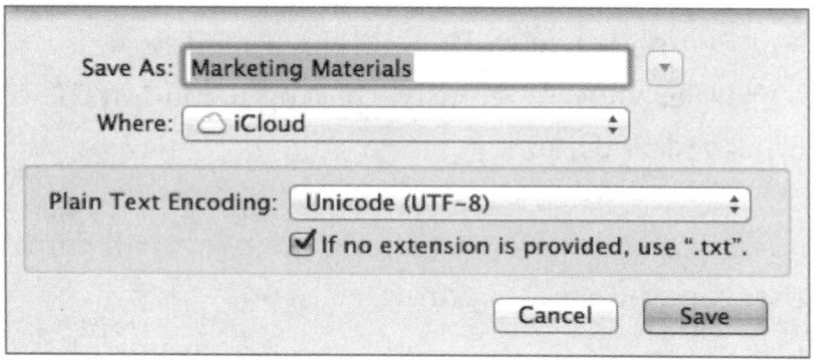

Managing Documents in iCloud

Courtesy of Auto Save and Versions, once a document is saved to iCloud, the user never has to return to the Finder for handling document management tasks. The acts of saving, renaming, duplicating, reverting to previous versions, and locking can all be handled by the application. Any changes the user makes while using an iCloud-compatible application are automatically pushed to the Apple iCloud servers and then in turn pushed to all other OS X or iOS devices configured for iCloud.

> **TIP** You can also manage iCloud documents via any modern web browser by logging into www.icloud.com

Further, other document management tasks previously handled by the Finder can be accomplished from the in-application iCloud document browser. The iCloud document browser appears automatically any time an application is opened without an active document window. You can also manually open the iCloud document browser by choosing File > Open.

> **TIP** Clicking "On My Mac" in the title bar of the iCloud document browser returns to the standard local file browser view. Obviously, clicking iCloud in the title bar returns to viewing documents saved to iCloud.

> **TIP** You can switch between icon and list view by clicking the two small combined buttons at the bottom of the iCloud document browser.

As you can see from the previous screenshot, a user can even create and manage folders from the iCloud document browser. Again, taking inspiration from iOS, dragging a document on top of another in the iCloud document browser creates a new folder. You can also drag items in and out of folders, and rename folders by double-clicking the folder's name when the folder is open.

Several other document management options are available by using secondary (or Control) click on a document. This includes rather important document management tasks like moving something to the Trash and sharing files via other services. Sharing files from the iCloud document browser is of particular importance because these items cannot be easily accessed outside the iCloud browser window. For example, from the Mail application you cannot create a message with an attached document from iCloud. Instead you would use secondary (or Control) click on a document in the iCloud browser, and then from the shortcut menu choose Share > Email.

TIP You can also share selected documents from the iCloud browser by clicking the small share button (a box with a rightward arrow) at the bottom of the window.

Finally, a couple very useful system tricks are always available from the iCloud document browser. Of note, you can quickly preview any document by pressing the Spacebar to open a Quick View window. Also, for users with lots of files, don't forget the Spotlight search field in the top-right corner of the window. Note, however, the Spotlight search is limited to only those documents saved to iCloud in the current application.

iCloud Document Architecture

Saving documents to iCloud represents a fundamentally different way of thinking about how a user approaches document management. The most challenging issue for many will likely be that each application's iCloud document browser shows only files managed by that particular application. For example, if you create and save a text document to iCloud from TextEdit, it isn't available in the iCloud document browser for the Pages application, even though both applications are capable of handling text documents.

This is because each iCloud-compatible application maintains its own collection of documents and folders. A user can drag a document out of one application's iCloud document browser to the Finder, and then back into another application, but this is rather inconvenient. Also, a user can accidentally drag a document that's not compatible with the application into its iCloud document collection. For example, you can drag a PDF document into the TextEdit iCloud document browser, even though TextEdit can't properly open or edit a PDF.

If you want to manage an application's iCloud documents in a more familiar fashion, they can be reached via the Finder. Documents saved in iCloud are maintained locally in each user's ~/Library/Mobile Documents/ folder. In here you will find folders named for each application or service that saves to iCloud.

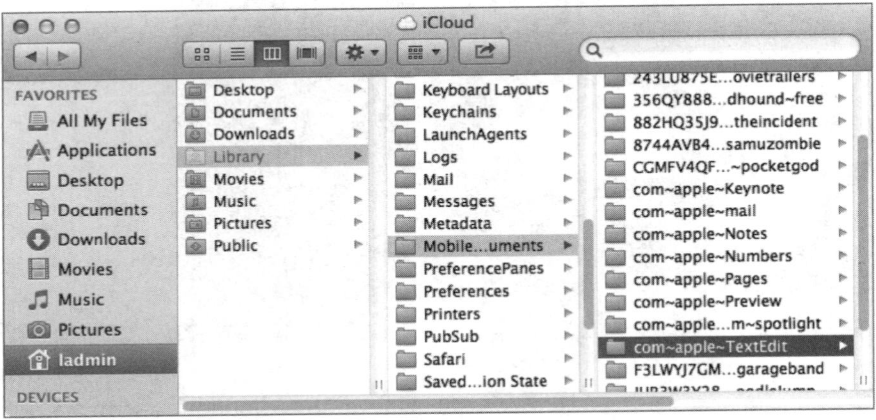

In the Mobile Documents folder, avoid modifying the content of folders with unclear names. On the other hand, applications that support iCloud documents are clearly named, and the content is easily editable using standard Finder methods. Even folder management via the Finder is properly respected by the iCloud document browser. Further, any changes automatically save to iCloud the moment you make them.

Speaking of iCloud documents, the actual transfer process is highly sophisticated and efficient. In the worst case, a user should only notice a few moments delay before the changes are reflected to all iCloud-configured devices. This is because if multiple devices on the same network share an iCloud account, they transfer the data locally to improve performance. Also, if you make changes to iCloud documents while offline, the system caches the changes and then silently pushes them the very next moment an Internet connection to the Apple servers becomes available.

Reference 20.6
Automatic Resume

An ancillary OS X feature to Auto Save is automatic application resume. This feature allows supported applications to maintain their current state even if the user logs out or the application is quit. When an application quits, not only are any open documents automatically saved, the state of the application is saved as well.

Upon application restart, everything returns to how it was when the user quit the application. This includes automatically saving and restoring documents and windows open in the application, the view and scrolling position of each window, and even the last user selection in the application.

> **NOTE ▶** Applications that support resume can also be automatically quit by the system when it's determined that the system resources, specifically memory, are running low. The system quits only applications that are sitting idle for the user.

Resume After Log Out

Automatic resume of applications and windows after logout is, by default, enabled in OS X. You can however, permanently prevent this behavior by deselecting the option when prompted to verify logout. Unlike in previous versions of OS X, this option stays disabled once a user deselects it in the logout dialog.

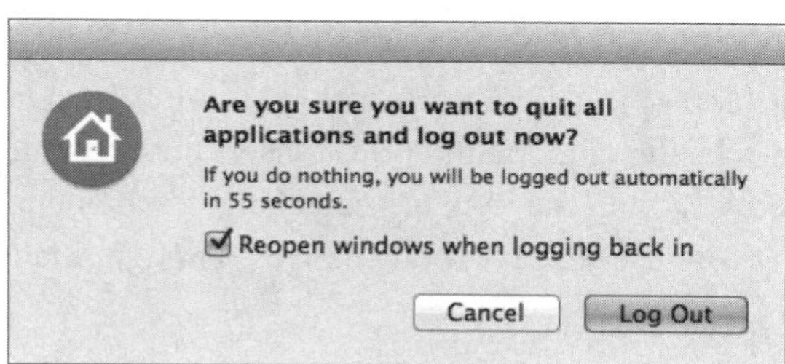

TIP If the resume after logout feature is disabled, you can temporarily force it by holding the Option key when you log out.

Resume After Quit

A different type of automatic resume is to do so after a user quits an application. This feature however is not enabled by default on OS X Mountain Lion. This returns OS X to the pre-Lion behavior that if a user quits an application, all the open documents are closed as well.

If you prefer the OS X Lion behavior of always resuming open documents and windows, you can do so from the General preferences. Deselect the "Close windows when quitting an application" checkbox to effectively enable automatic resume of an application's state if the user quits it.

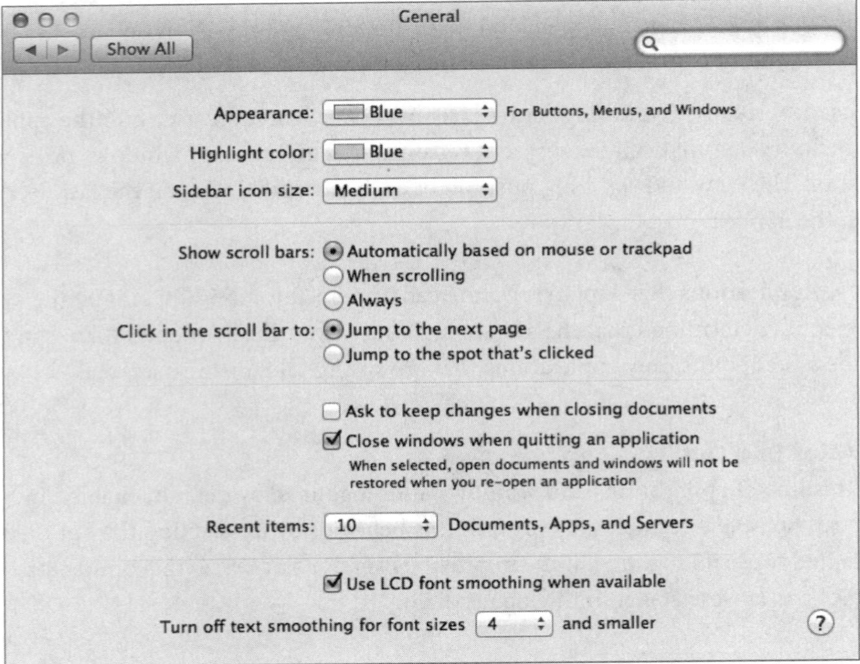

Another new feature in OS X Mountain Lion optionally returns the pre-Lion behavior of asking the user to save changes upon the closing of a document. For users comfortable with how the legacy save system behaved, enabling the "Ask to keep changes when closing documents" checkbox will always prompt the user to save final changes. Though, many would argue this feature defeats one of the primary advantages of Auto Save: less bother for the user. Enabling this option may also cause an inconvenient delay or cancellation of the logout process as it waits for applications to quit.

MORE INFO ► Details regarding the user logout process can be found in Lesson 29, "Startup, Shutdown, and Sleep Modes."

Exercise 20.1
Use Alternate Applications

► Prerequisites

- ► You must have created the Chris Johnson account (Exercise 6.1).

In this exercise, you will learn different ways to choose applications to open files, either when you want to make a one-time choice of a different application, or permanently change the default application for a particular file type. You will also use the OS X Quick Look feature, which lets you see the contents of common file types without opening an application at all.

View a File with Quick Look

1. If necessary, log in as Chris Johnson.
2. In the Finder, open the StudentMaterials/Lesson20 folder.
3. Copy the file Pet Sitter Notes to your desktop.

   The file has no visible extension, so it may not be obvious what type of file it is.
4. Select (single-click) the Pet Sitter Notes document on your desktop.
5. Choose File > Quick Look "Pet Sitter Notes" (or press Command-Y).

   Quick Look displays a preview of the document. Note that it has a button near the top right that allows you to open the document in TextEdit (currently the default application for this type of document).

TIP You can also use Quick Look to view a document by selecting it in the Finder and pressing Spacebar. However, if you have the filename selected rather than the file itself, pressing Spacebar will begin to edit the filename. If you do this by mistake, you can delete the filename and press Return; since the filename cannot be blank, the Finder displays an error and puts the original filename back.

TIP Yet another way to use Quick Look is to Control-click the document and choose Quick Look "filename" from the shortcut menu.

6 Press Command-Y to close the Quick Look preview.

Choose an Application to Open a File Once

1 Double-click Pet Sitter Notes on your desktop.

The file opens in TextEdit. Note that TextEdit does not display the document's headings or background image.

2 On your desktop Control-click the file.

3 In the shortcut menu, mouse over the Open With choice.

A submenu opens showing the applications available that can open this type of document.

4 In the Open With submenu, choose Preview.

The file opens in Preview.

Note that editing the same file in two different applications at the same time can lead to unpredictable results. In this case you are only viewing the file, so it is not a problem.

5 Compare how the file is displayed in TextEdit versus Preview.

Preview gives a richer view of the file, showing a background image and headings that TextEdit does not show. On the other hand, TextEdit lets you edit its content, while Preview does not. Depending on what you wanted to do with the document, you might prefer either one.

6 Close the document in both applications.

7 Double-click the document again.

It opens in TextEdit, because the Open With choice you made earlier was not a permanent setting.

8 Close the document.

Permanently Change the Default Application for a File Type

1 In the Finder, select the Pet Sitter Notes document.

2 Choose File > Get Info (Command-I).

3 If necessary, expand the General and Name & Extension sections of the Info window.

This is a Word 97 document, and it has a file extension of .doc, which is hidden.

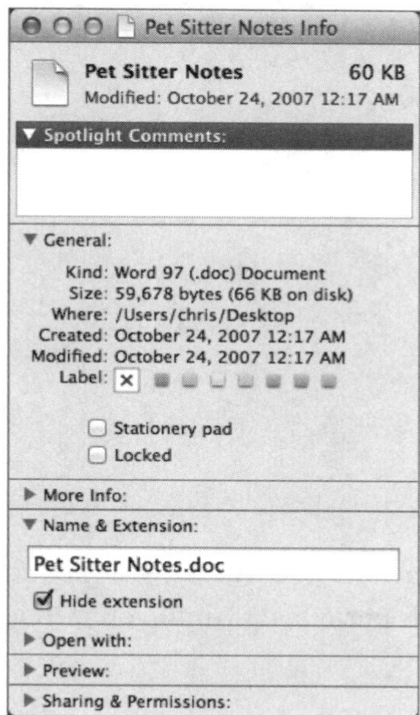

4 Deselect "Hide extension." The extension will now be visible in the view of your desktop in the Finder.

5 Expand the "Open with" section of the Info window, and then choose Preview from its pop-up menu.

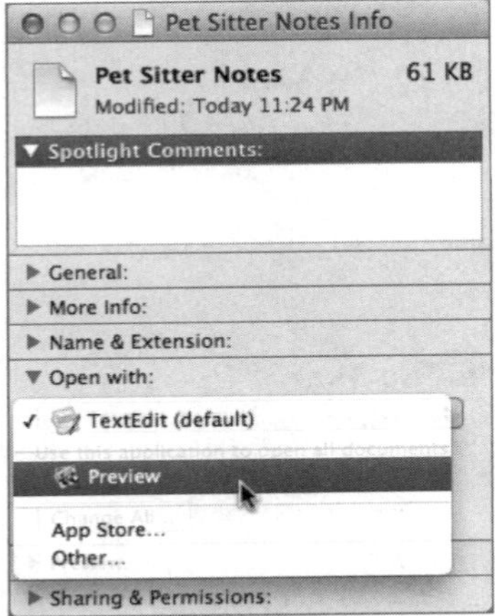

Note that this menu shows the same possible applications as the Open With submenu in the Finder. Choosing an application here makes a permanent setting, but only for this specific file.

6 Click Change All.

7 In the confirmation dialog, click Continue.

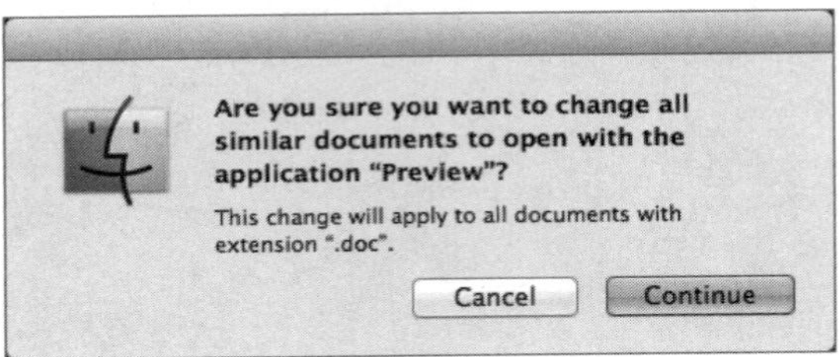

You have now changed the default application for opening documents with the extension ".doc" in Chris Johnson's account. This setting is permanent (until you change it to something else).

8 Close the Info window.

9 Double-click the document on your desktop.

   It now opens in Preview.

10 Quit Preview.

11 Move Pet Sitter Notes.doc from your desktop to the Trash.

Configure the Finder to Show All Extensions

1 In the Finder, reopen the StudentMaterials/Lesson20 folder and examine the original Pet Sitter Notes document there.

   Note that its filename extension is not shown. When you used Get Info to show the extension of the copy on your desktop, it affected only that specific file.

2 Control-click the original Pet Sitter Notes, and examine the Open With submenu.

   The default application is now Preview, because you used Change All in the Info window to apply the setting to all Word 97 documents.

3 Click in the desktop to close the shortcut menu.

4 Choose Finder > Preferences (Command-comma).

5 Click Advanced.

6 Select "Show all filename extensions."

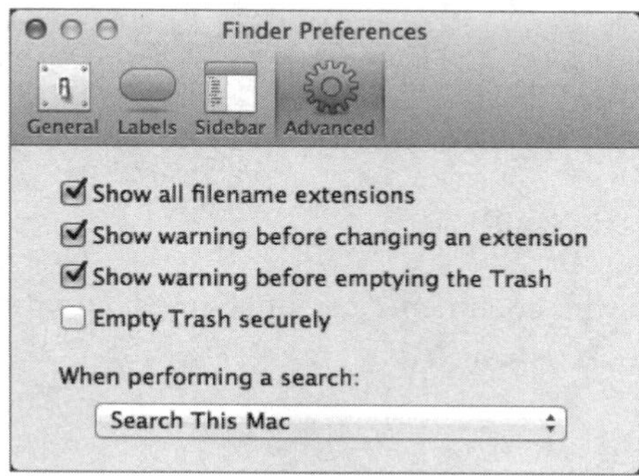

   The ".doc" extension on the original Pet Sitter Notes will now be visible.

7 Select the original Pet Sitter Notes document, and choose File > Get Info (Command-I).

8 If necessary, expand the Name & Extension section of the Info window.

Note that the "Hide extension" checkbox is selected. This setting is overridden by your Finder preference.

9 Close the Info window.

Exercise 20.2
Use Auto Save and Versions

Prerequisites

- You must have created the Chris Johnson account (Exercise 6.1).

Many support issues derive from users losing work either because they forgot to save changes to a document, or because they did save after making unfortunate changes. In applications that support it, OS X provides the capability to periodically save changes automatically, and to keep multiple previous versions of a document. This means users don't have to worry about whether they should—or shouldn't—save the documents they're working on.

In this exercise, you will edit a file in TextEdit, save several versions, and roll back to an earlier version.

Experiment with Auto Save

1 If necessary, log in as Chris Johnson.

2 Open System Preferences, and select the General pane.

3 Ensure that "Ask to keep changes when closing documents" is not selected, and that "Close windows when quitting an application" is selected.

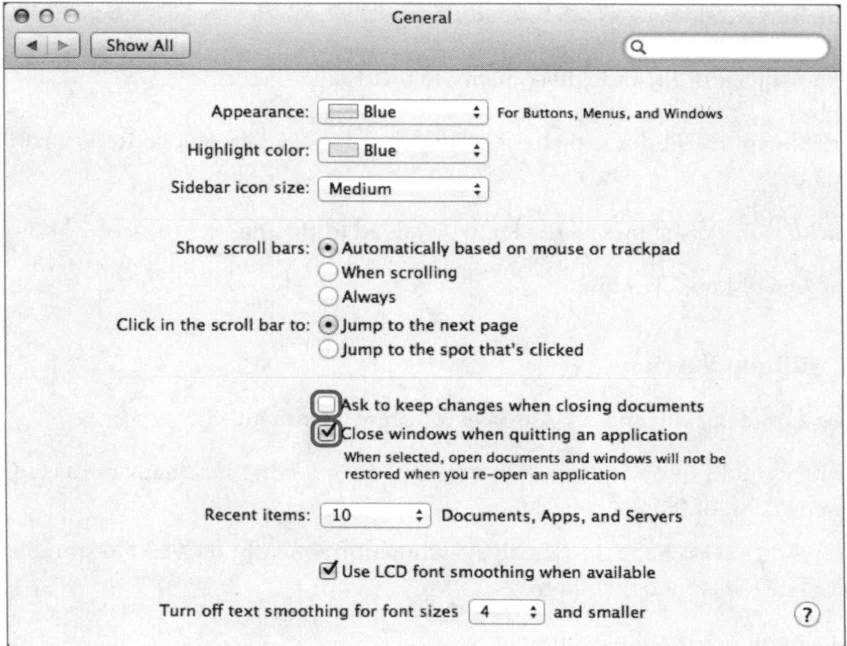

4 Quit System Preferences.

5 If necessary, navigate to /Users/Shared/StudentMaterials/Lesson20.

6 Copy Pretendco Report.rtfd to your desktop, and open the copy.

7 Add some text to the file.

Notice that the window's title bar now indicates its status as Edited.

8 Switch to the Finder, and Get Info on the Pretendco Report file.

Notice that it has been modified within the last minute or so (your edits were saved automatically).

9 Close the Info window.

10 Switch back to TextEdit, and add some more text to the file.

11 Select the file in the Finder and choose File > Quick Look “Pretendco Report.rtfd” (Command-Y).

 The Quick Look view shows all the text you added to the file.

12 Close the Quick Look window.

Work with Multiple Versions

1 Switch back to TextEdit, and choose Save (or press Command-S).

 Note that this looks like a “normal” save command, but what it actually does is save a restorable version of the file.

 While TextEdit saves changes to the live document frequently, it saves a restorable version only when explicitly told to.

2 Delete the graphic from the document.

3 Quit TextEdit.

 Notice that you are not prompted to save changes; they were saved automatically.

4 Reopen the Pretendco Report.rtfd file.

5 Choose File > Revert To > Previous Save.

 The graphic is restored.

6 Add more text to the document, and choose File > Save (Command-S) again.

7 Add still more text, and examine the File > Revert To submenu.

 It now lists options to restore to the Last Saved version, the Last Opened version, or to Browse All Versions.

8 Choose File > Revert To > Browse All Versions.

 TextEdit displays a full-screen version browser, showing the current document state on the left and saved versions on the right. This view is similar to the Time Machine Restore interface, and actually shows versions from the Time Machine backups as well as restorable versions created by the application.

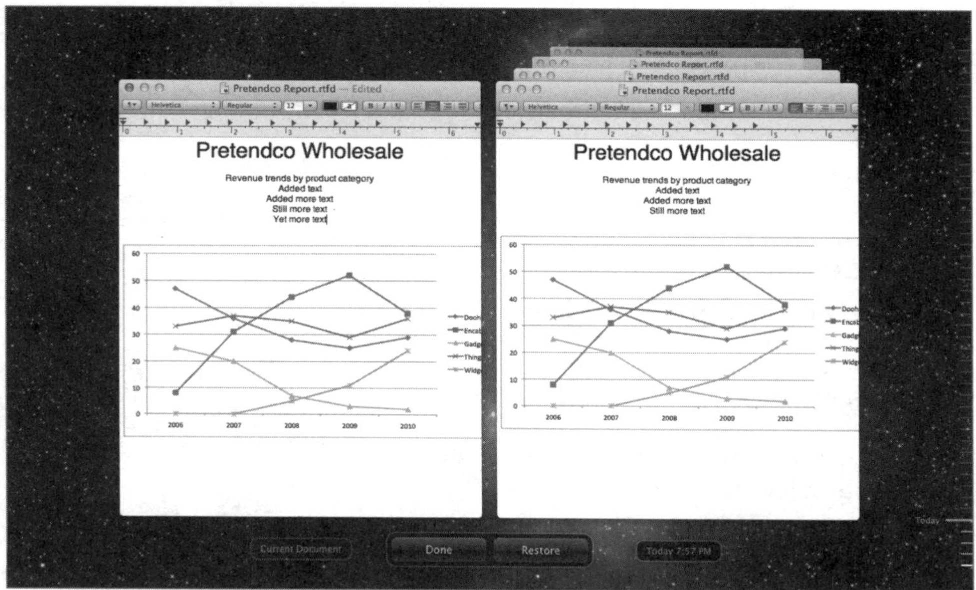

9 Experiment with the two windows. Note that you can switch between saved versions either by clicking their title bars in the stack, or by using the timeline on the right side of the screen. You can also use editing controls, including copying and pasting content between versions.

10 Scroll back to the oldest version and click Restore.

The document reverts to its original state.

11 Hover your pointer over the title bar of the window, and note that a small triangle appears to the right of the document name.

12 Click the triangle, and choose Browse All Versions from the pop-up menu.

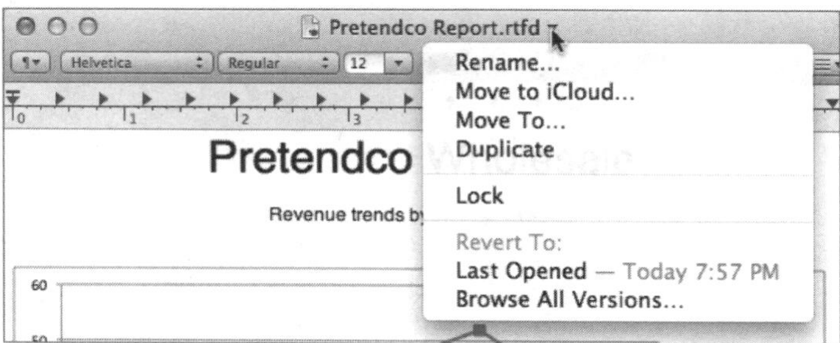

TextEdit again switches to the full-screen version browser. Note that "newer" versions are still available, even though you reverted to the original state.

13 Click Done to exit the history browser.

14 Quit TextEdit.

Exercise 20.3
Manage Document Locking

Prerequisites

- You must have created the Local Admin (Exercise 3.1 or 3.2) and Chris Johnson (Exercise 6.1) accounts.

In this exercise you will explore options for locking documents to prevent accidental changes.

Lock and Unlock a Document

1 If necessary, log in as Chris Johnson.

2 If you have not performed Exercise 20.2, copy /Users/Shared/StudentMaterials/Lesson20/Pretendco Report.rtfd to your desktop.

3 Get Info on the Pretendco Report.rtdf document.

4 In the General section of the Info window, select the Locked checkbox.

Notice that the document's icon now has a small padlock in its corner.

5 Close the Info window.

6 Open the document.

Notice that the window's title bar now indicates its status as Locked.

7 Attempt to add some text to the document.

A dialog appears telling you the file is locked, and giving options for how to deal with the locked file.

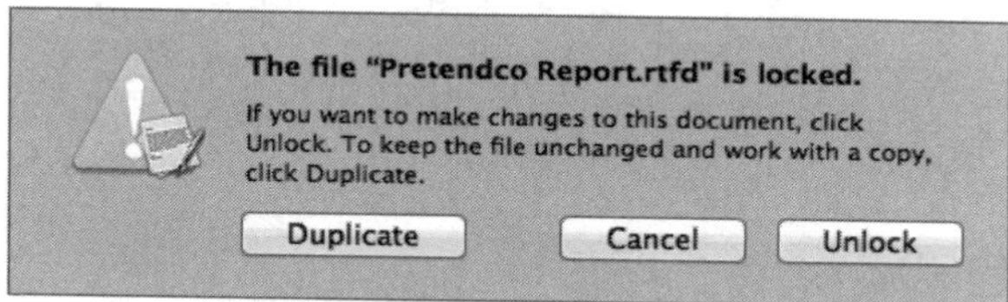

8 Click Unlock.

The padlock vanishes from the document's icon on your desktop.

9 Add some text to the document.

10 In the window's title bar, click the document's name and choose Lock from the pop-up menu.

The padlock reappears on the document's icon on your desktop.

Since you are the owner of the document, you can lock and unlock it freely, in either the Finder or an editor that supports Auto Save.

11 Quit TextEdit.

Exercise 20.4
Store Documents in iCloud

Prerequisites

- You must have created the Chris Johnson (Exercise 6.1) and Mayta Mishtuk (Exercise 7.1) accounts.

OS X Mountain Lion allows applications to save documents to the Internet by way of iCloud, and then access them from any computer tied to the same iCloud account.

Save a Document to iCloud

1 If necessary, log in as Chris Johnson.

2 If you have not performed Exercise 20.2, copy /Users/Shared/StudentMaterials/Lesson20/Pretendco Report.rtfd to your desktop.

3 Open the Pretendco Report.rtfd document.

4 If necessary, click in the window's title bar and choose Unlock" from the pop-up menu.

5 Click in the window's title bar again, and choose "Move to iCloud" from the pop-up menu.

A confirmation dialog appears.

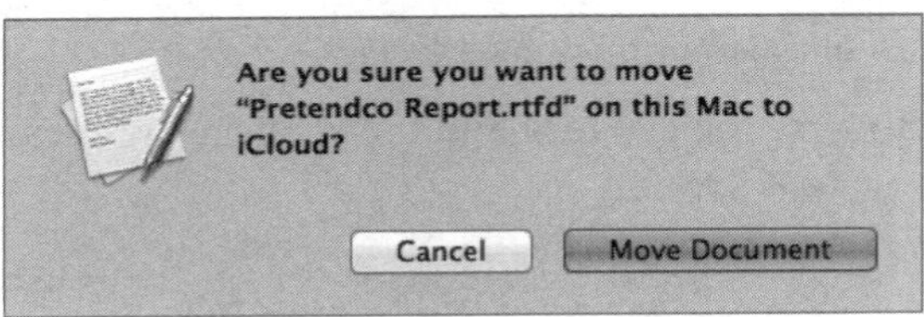

6 Click Move Document.

7 If a dialog appears indicating that an item named "Pretendco Report.rtfd" already exists in this location, a previous student may have left this item in the iCloud account. Click Replace to replace the old copy with yours.

   The document's icon vanishes from your desktop.

8 Quit TextEdit.

9 Open the Contacts application.

   If you performed Exercise 18.1, the contacts you imported in that lesson are listed.

10 If the contacts from Exercise 18.1 (Enrico Baker, Carl Dunn, Barbara Green, and so on) are not listed, open the file /Users/Shared/StudentMaterials/Lesson18/vCards.vcf, to import them into Contacts.

11 Wait a few moments as your contacts list is pushed to the iCloud servers.

12 Quit Contacts and log out as Chris Johnson.

Open a Document from iCloud

Now that your document and contacts are stored in iCloud, they are available from any computer account tied to the same iCloud account. For simplicity, you will demonstrate this using the Mayta Mishtuk account on your computer, but iCloud could push the documents and contacts to an account on a different computer just as well.

1 Log in to the Mayta Mishtuk account (password: **mayta**, or whatever you chose when you created the account).

2 Open System Preferences, and select the iCloud preference pane.

   You are prompted for an iCloud account to use.

3 Enter the iCloud Apple ID and password you used with the Chris Johnson account, and click Sign In.

4 Make sure "Use iCloud for contacts …" is selected, but that Use Find My Mac is not. Click Next.

5 Make sure that Documents & Data is selected.

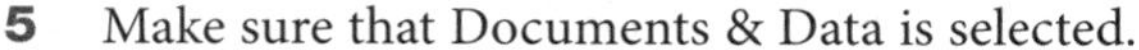

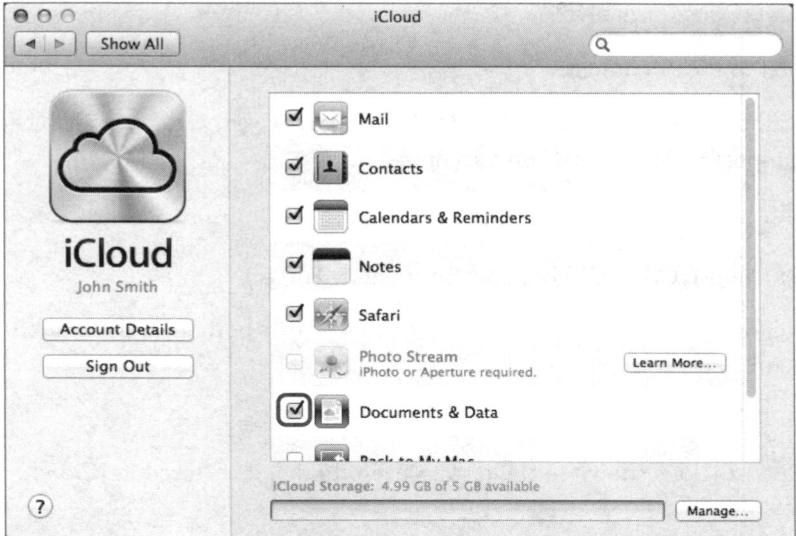

6 Close System Preferences.

7 Open TextEdit.

The TextEdit open dialog has buttons near the top left to show documents in iCloud or On My Mac.

8 If necessary, click iCloud.

The Pretendco Report.rtfd file you saved to iCloud is shown (there may be short delay before the document appears).

9 Double-click Pretendco Report.rtfd.

The document opens normally.

10 Add some text to the document.

Your edits are automatically pushed back to the iCloud servers, and are available to any other computers using this iCloud account.

11 Quit TextEdit.

12 In the Finder, choose Go > All My Files (Command-Shift-F).

Pretendco Report.rtfd is listed; the All My Files view shows both local documents and those in iCloud.

13 In the search field, enter **wholesale**.

Pretendco Report.rtfd is shown in the results, even though it is stored in iCloud.

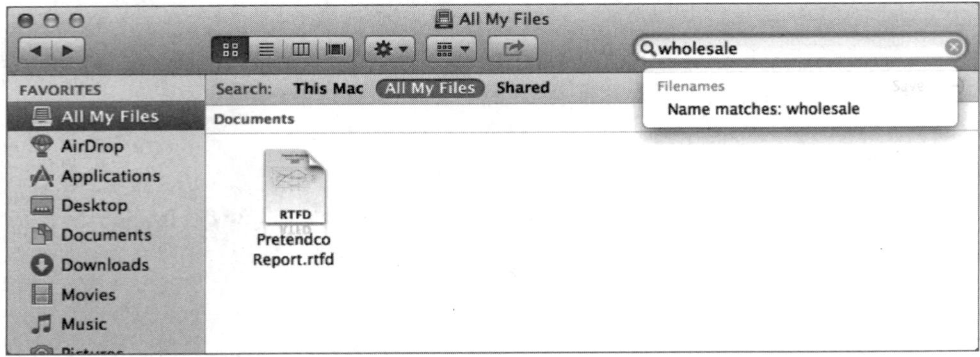

Use Contacts from iCloud

1 Open the Contacts application.

After a few moments, the contacts from the Chris Johnson account appear.

2 Quit Contacts and log out as Mayta Mishtuk.

Exercise 20.5
Manage Automatic Resume

Prerequisites

- You must have created the Chris Johnson account (Exercise 6.1).
- You must have performed Exercise 20.4.

By default, OS X Mountain Lion remembers what apps were open when you log out, but the apps themselves do not reopen the documents they had open before. In this exercise, you will experiment with changing these defaults.

Examine the Default Behavior

1. Log in as Chris Johnson.
2. Open System Preferences and select the General preference pane.
3. If necessary, select the checkbox for "Close windows when quitting an application."

   This is the default setting in OS X Mountain Lion.
4. Leave System Preferences open, and open TextEdit.
5. In the TextEdit open dialog, open the Pretendco Report.rtfd you saved in iCloud in the last exercise.

   Note that the edit you made in a different account in the last exercise is included in the document.
6. Create a new TextEdit document by choosing File > New (Command-N).
7. Type some text into the new document.
8. From the Apple menu, choose Log Out Chris Johnson (Command-Shift-Q).

9 In the confirmation dialog, make sure that "Reopen windows when logging back in" is selected, and click Log Out.

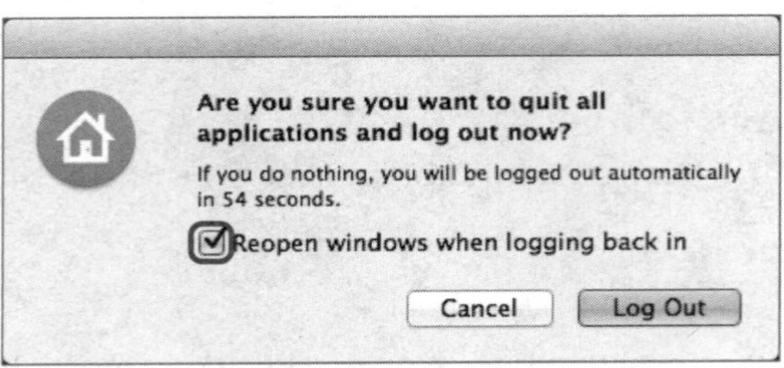

10 At the login screen, log back in as Chris Johnson.

System Preferences and TextEdit both automatically reopen, and TextEdit opens both of the documents it had open before.

11 Quit TextEdit.

Since the option to close windows when quitting is selected, you are prompted for whether you want to keep the new (unsaved) document.

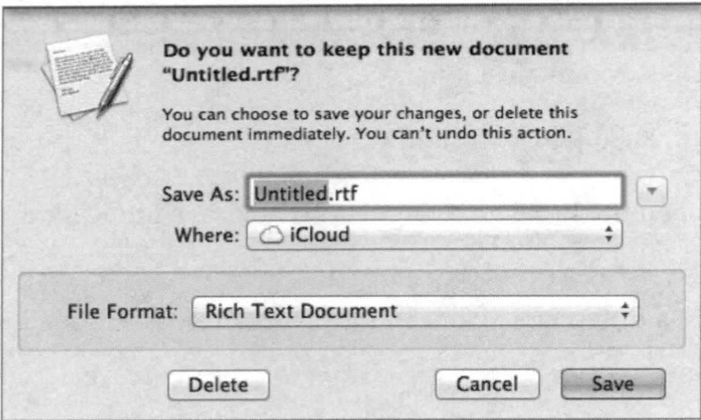

12 Click Delete.

13 Reopen TextEdit.

This time it does not automatically open any documents but instead shows the dialog to let you select a document to open.

14 Reopen Pretendco Report.rtfd.

Experiment with Other Options

1. In System Preferences, reselect the General preference pane.
2. Deselect "Close windows when quitting an application."
3. Bring TextEdit to the foreground (you can do this by clicking in its window, or its icon in the Dock).
4. Quit TextEdit.
5. Reopen TextEdit.

   This time it automatically reopens Pretendco Report.rtfd.
6. Switch to System Preferences, and select "Close windows when quitting an application."
7. Quit System Preferences.
8. From the Apple menu, choose Log Out Chris Johnson (Command-Shift-Q).
9. This time, delesect "Reopen windows when logging back in" and click Log Out.

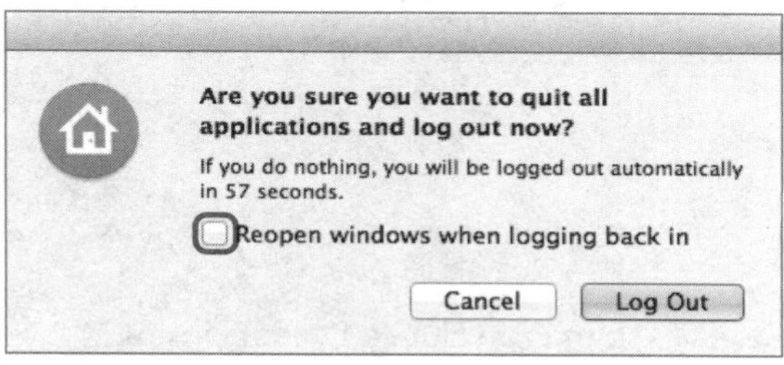

10. At the login screen, log back in as Chris Johnson.

    This time, neither System Preferences nor TextEdit reopen.
11. From the Apple menu, choose Log Out Chris Johnson.

    Note that the "Reopen windows…" option is deselected. This setting is remembered, although you can always change it when logging out.
12. Click Cancel to remain logged in.

Disable Auto Save

1 Open System Preferences, and select the General preference pane.

2 Select "Ask to keep changes when closing documents."

3 Open TextEdit, and reopen Pretendco Report.rtfd.

4 Add some more text to the Pretendco Report document.

   As before, the title bar shows its status as Edited, but now there is also a dot in the close button, which indicates unsaved changes in the document.

5 Click the close button for the document (Command-W).

   You are asked whether you want to save changes to the document.

   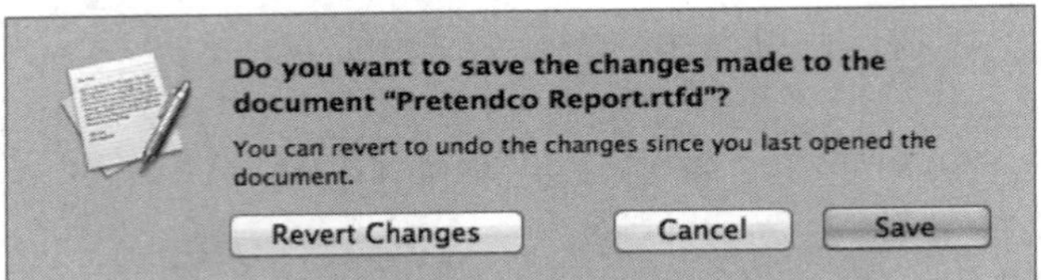

6 Click Save.

7 Quit TextEdit.

8 In the General preference pane, deselect "Ask to keep changes when closing documents."

   This restores the normal Auto Save behavior.

9 Close System Preferences.

Lesson **21**

Application Management and Troubleshooting

GOALS

- Understand and support the various application types
- Monitor and control processes and applications
- Explore various application troubleshooting techniques
- Manage and troubleshoot widgets and the Dashboard

For many OS X support professionals, their most common day-to-day task is troubleshooting application issues. The successful resolution of an application issue is most often due to previous experience with the specific application. Specific application issues, however, are beyond the scope of this guide.

On the other hand, support professionals dealing with new applications or new issues must rely on their ability to effectively gather relevant information and their knowledge of general system technologies. This lesson primarily addresses these later two application troubleshooting aspects. So you have a better understanding of the pieces in play, this lesson first defines key elements of the OS X process architecture. You will then learn to gather information about applications and processes. The remainder of this lesson covers a variety of general troubleshooting techniques that can be used for any type of application.

Reference 21.1
Applications and Processes

A process is any instance of executable code that is currently activated and addressed in system memory. In other words, a process is anything that is currently "running" or "open." OS X handles processes very efficiently, so although an idle process will likely consume zero processor resources, it's still considered an active process because it has dedicated address space in system memory. The four general process types are applications, commands, daemons, and agents.

OS X Process Types

Applications are a specific category of process that is generally identified as something the user opened in the graphical interface. *Commands* are also normally opened by the user but are only available at the command-line interface. The key similarity between most applications and commands is that they are running in the user's space. In other words, most applications and commands are started, stopped, and limited to accessing resources available only to the user.

Processes that run on behalf of the system fall into another category, *daemons*, also referred to as background processes because they rarely have any user interface. Daemons usually launch during system startup and remain active the entire time the Mac is up and running; as such, most daemons run with root or systemwide access to all resources. These background daemons are responsible for most of the automatic system features like detecting network changes and maintaining the Spotlight search metadata index.

Agents are technically also daemons, or background processes. The primary difference is that agents run only when a user is logged in to the system. Agents are always started automatically for the user by the system. While applications and commands can also be opened automatically, they are not controlled by the system the way agents are. Most important, all three of these process types are considered part of the user's space because they are executed with the same access privileges the user has.

OS X Process Features

OS X is a desirable platform for running applications and other processes because it combines a rock-solid UNIX foundation with an advanced graphical user interface. Users will most likely recognize the graphical interface elements right away, but it's the underlying foundation that keeps things running so smoothly. Specifically, a few fundamental features of OS X are responsible for providing a high level of performance and reliability.

OS X Process Performance Features

- Preemptive multitasking—This gives OS X the ability to balance computing resources without letting any single process take over. It allows the system to run dozens of processes without significantly slowing down user applications.
- Symmetric multiprocessing—Whenever possible the system uses all available computing resources to provide the best performance. This is a key feature since every currently shipping Mac includes at least two processor cores. OS X v10.6 introduced two new unique multiprocessing features, Grand Central Dispatch and OpenCL, which provide for even greater performance than previous versions of OS X. Grand Central Dispatch makes it much easier for application developers to take full advantage of not just multiprocessor systems but also multicore processors. OpenCL takes this even

further by allowing applications to use your Mac computer's powerful graphics processor to accelerate general computing tasks.

- Simultaneous 32-bit and 64-bit support—OS X supports both 32-bit and 64-bit modes simultaneously. A process running in 64-bit mode has the ability to individually access more than 4 GB of system memory, can perform higher-precision computational functions much faster, and can take advantage of Intel's updated x86-64 architecture for improved performance and security. All OS X Mountain Lion–compatible Macs feature 64-bit-capable processors and can take advantage of 64-bit system features. With the previous version, OS X v10.6, Apple updated nearly all included software to take advantage of 64-bit resources, including the core of OS X, the system kernel.

OS X Memory Management Features

- Protected memory—Similar to how the file system prevents users from meddling with items they shouldn't, processes are also kept separate and secure in system memory. The system manages all memory allocation so processes are not allowed to interfere with each other's system memory space. In other words, an ill-behaved or crashed application does not normally affect any other process on the system.
- Dynamic memory allocation—The operating system automatically manages system memory for processes at their request. Though real system memory is clearly limited by hardware, the system dynamically allocates both real and virtual memory when needed. Thus, the only memory limitations in OS X are the size of installed RAM and the amount of free space you have available on your system volume.
- Secure memory allocation—OS X Mountain Lion includes two new memory management features that further protect the system from malicious processes. The first feature is known as "execute disable" memory, which creates a strong barrier between memory used for data and memory used for executable instructions within an individual process. This helps prevent malicious process code from improperly accessing user data. Another feature is known as Address Space Layout Randomization, which changes the location in memory where a process stores key items, thus, making it much more difficult for an attack that attempts to inject malicious actions into a normally benign process.

64-Bit vs. 32-Bit Mode

In OS X Mountain Lion, nearly all the operating system and included applications run in 64-bit mode. In fact, only two of the main built-in applications are still limited to 32-bit mode: DVD Player and Grapher.

While moving most of the applications to support 64-bit mode generally improves performance, this advancement is not without drawbacks. Namely, applications that run in

64-bit mode can't take advantage of any 32-bit code. This means any application that uses plug-in technology may suffer from compatibility issues with third-party plug-ins that have not been updated to support 64-bit mode.

Examples of plug-in software affected by this issue include:

- Printer drivers that add additional interfaces for the printer dialog
- Screen savers
- Audio device drivers known as audio units
- Spotlight metadata import plug-ins
- Quick Look preview plug-ins
- Dashboard widgets that require plug-in code, though most widgets don't use extra code, so they should work without issues
- Safari plug-ins

In short, applications running in 64-bit mode will not load 32-bit plug-ins. If you need to use a third-party 32-bit plug-in with a 64-bit-capable application, you have to force the application to run in 32-bit mode on most Macs. This can be accomplished from the Finder Get Info or Inspector windows by simply selecting the "Open in 32-bit mode" checkbox. Obviously, forcing 32-bit mode may make the application run slower, but this is required to use nonupdated plug-ins.

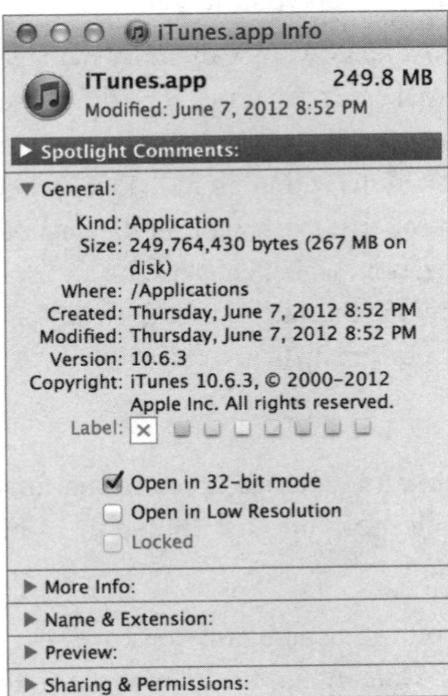

TIP ▶ The "Open in Low Resolution" checkbox appears only on new Macs featuring Retina displays. This option disables the use of high-resolution application assets, which also may not be compatible with older application plug-ins.

One system application automatically switches modes for you: System Preferences. When a user tries to open a third-party 32-bit System Preferences plug-in, often called a System Preferences pane, it prompts her to restart System Preferences. If the user clicks OK (the default), System Preferences restarts in 32-bit mode and loads the selected pane.

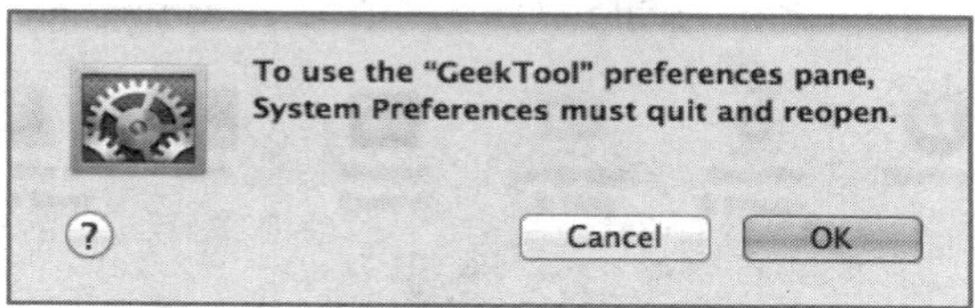

NOTE ▶ The process that handles Dashboard automatically runs both 64-bit and 32-bit widgets. Dashboard is detailed in the "Managing Dashboard" section later in this lesson.

NOTE ▶ With the exception of Dashboard and System Preferences, third-party plug-ins that tie into a system resource or background process must support 64-bit mode in order to work with OS X.

Reference 21.2
Monitoring Applications and Processes

OS X provides several methods for identifying and managing applications and processes. You can use the Finder or System Information to identify application and command information, including what processor architectures the item supports. On the other hand, the Activity Monitor application is used for viewing and managing all currently running processes on your Mac.

Application Identification via Finder

You can quickly locate basic application information from the Finder. To do so in the Finder, select the application you want to identify, and then open the Get Info or Inspector window.

MORE INFO ▶ Using the Finder Get Info window to inspect files and folders is detailed in Lesson 12, "Permissions and Sharing."

Once you have opened a Get Info or Inspector window, click the General disclosure triangle to reveal general application information. This reveals that the selected application is one of three types:

- Application—Designed for OS X on Intel-based Macs, runs in 64-bit mode and possibly 32-bit mode for plug-in compatibility.
- Application (32-bit)—Designed for OS X on Intel-based Macs, runs only in 32-bit mode.
- Application with a prohibitory icon—Designed only for OS X on PowerPC-based Macs, or the classic Mac OS. These applications will not open in OS X, as indicated by the prohibitory sign on top of the application icon.

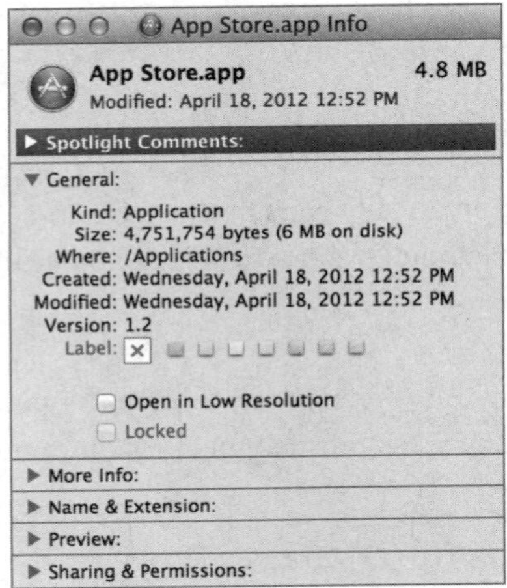

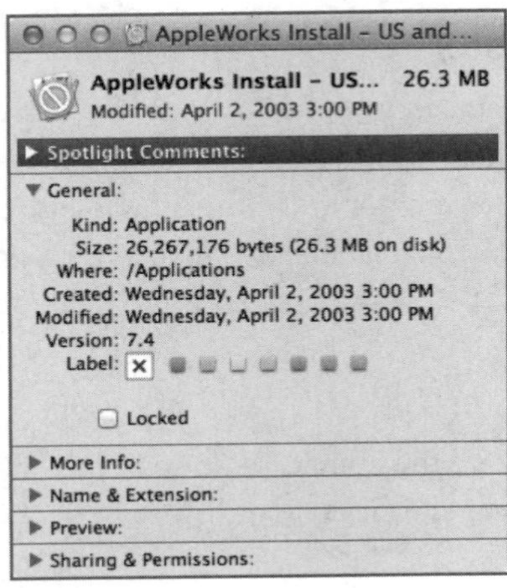

NOTE ▶ Classic applications, though identifiable from the Get Info window, are not compatible with OS X.

Applications via System Information

If you want to quickly gather information about all the applications on your Mac, try the /Applications/Utilities/System Information application. Upon opening, System Information scans the contents of all available Application folders. This includes /Applications, /Applications/Utilities, ~/Applications, /System/Library/CoreServices, and any other Applications folders at the root of any mounted volumes.

From the Contents list, select Applications to see which applications System Information found. Selecting an application from the list reveals its name, version number, modification date, application type, and whether it was purchased from the Mac App Store. Note that applications installed as part of OS X do not show as being purchased from the Mac App Store.

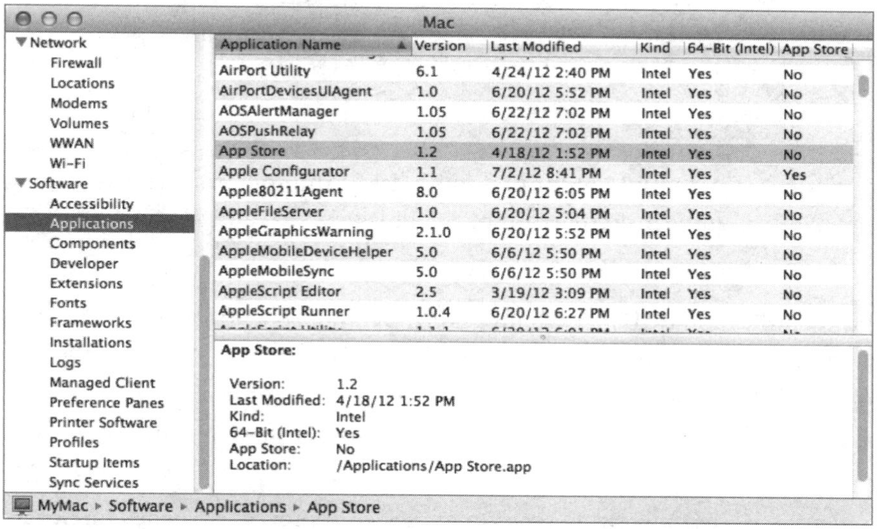

Monitoring Processes via Activity Monitor

The primary application in OS X for monitoring processes as they are running is /Applications/Utilities/Activity Monitor. This extremely useful tool shows you the vital signs of any currently running process and the system as a whole. If an application has stopped responding or has become noticeably slow, check Activity Monitor. Also check here if the overall system is running noticeably slower. Activity Monitor helps you identify an application or background process that is using a significant percentage of system memory or processor resources.

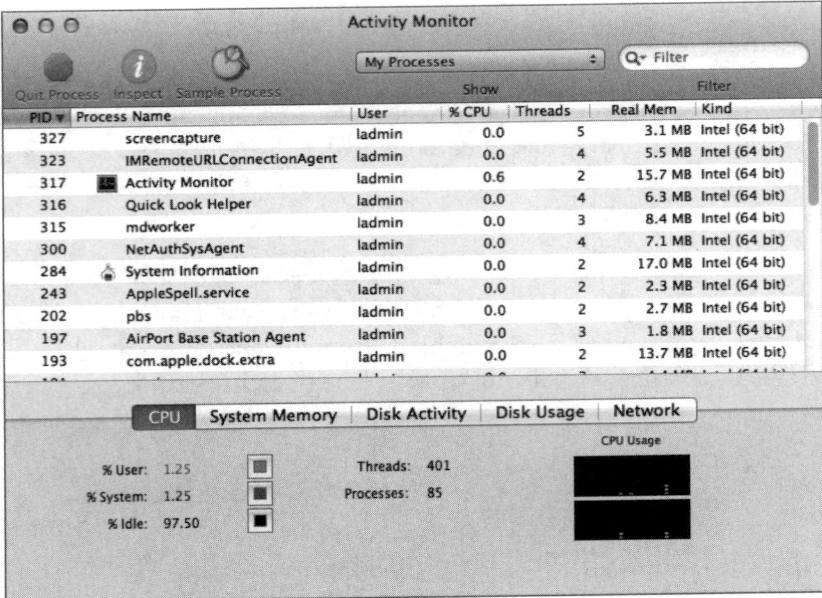

The main window of Activity Monitor presents a list of running processes and applications. The default columns in Activity Monitor allow you to examine various process statistics:

- Process Identification (PID)—Each process has a unique identifier that is chosen based on the order in which it was opened since system startup. Note that the PIDs are "recycled" after number 65,535 has been reached.
- Process Name—This is the name of the running process chosen by the developer who created it.
- User—Per the UNIX application security model, each process is opened on behalf of a particular user. Thus, each application has file system access based on the assigned user account.
- % CPU—This number is the percentage of total CPU usage the process is consuming. Note that the maximum percentage possible is 100 percent times the number of

processor cores. For example, a Mac featuring an Intel Core i7 presents a total of eight processor cores to the system.

- Threads—Each process is further broken down into the number of thread operations. Multithreading helps increase a process's responsiveness by enabling it to perform multiple simultaneous tasks. Multithreading also increases performance as each thread of a single process can run on a separate processor core.
- Real Mem—This represents the amount of physical memory that the process is currently occupying.
- Kind—This shows what processor architecture the application is currently using: Intel (64 bit) or Intel.

By default, Activity Monitor only shows processes running for the currently logged-in user. To increase your view of all active processes, choose All Processes from the Show pop-up menu. To narrow down your view, use the Spotlight search filter in the upper-right corner of the Activity Monitor window.

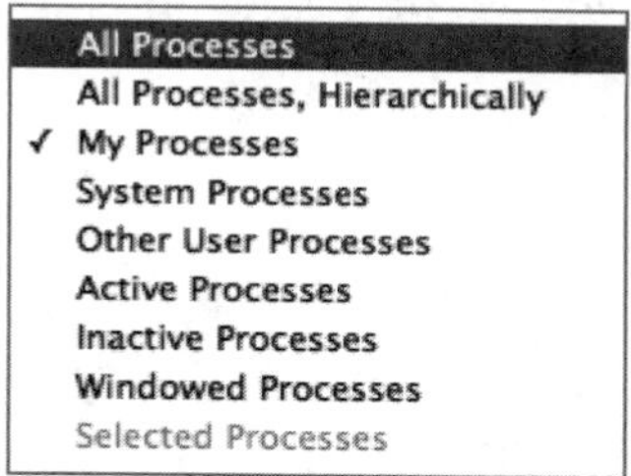

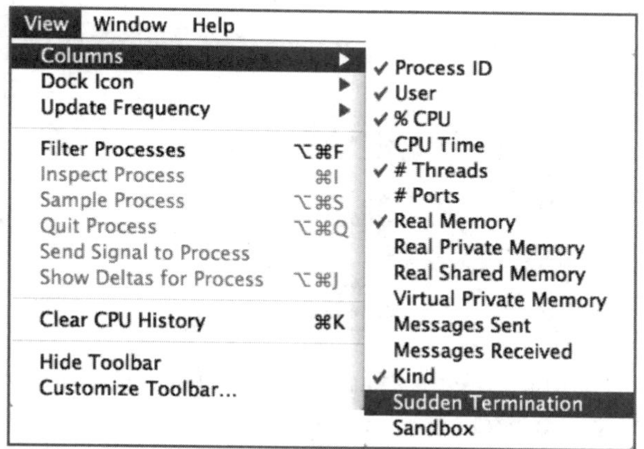

You can also adjust the number of statistics shown in the columns and the update frequency from the View menu. To sort the process list by a column, simply click any column title. Click the column title again to toggle between ascending and descending sorts. By viewing all processes and then re-sorting the list by either % CPU or Real Mem, you can determine whether any process is using excessive resources.

To further inspect an individual process, double-click its name in the Activity Monitor list. This reveals a window showing detailed process information.

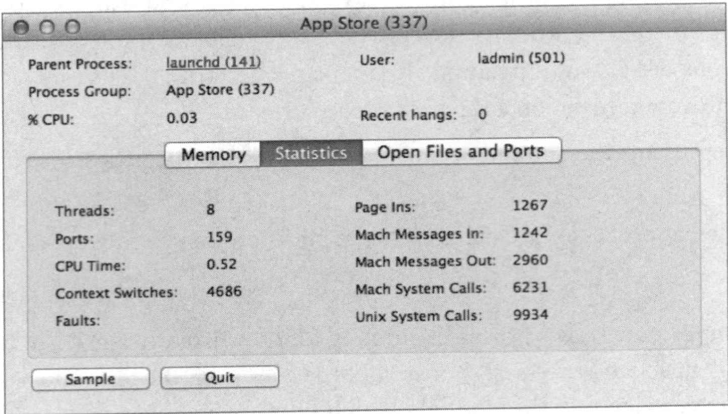

Finally, to inspect overall system information, click through the tabs at the bottom of the Activity Monitor window. These monitoring features are invaluable for troubleshooting, as they show you real-time system statistics.

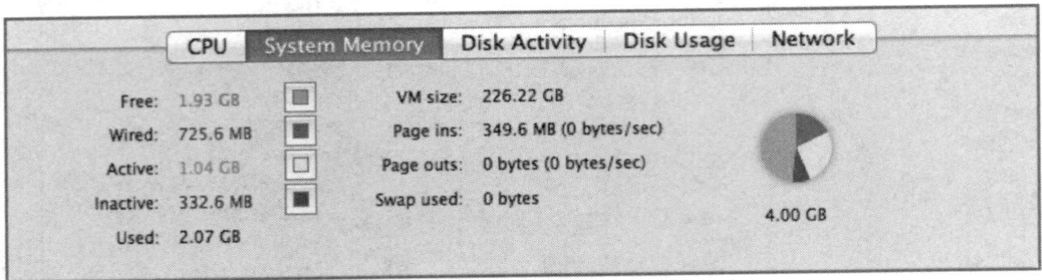

Of particular note are the "Page ins" and "Page outs" statistics under the System Memory tab. These numbers are a historical account, since last system startup, of how much active process data has been read in and out of memory. A high number of page ins is acceptable, but a high number of page outs is an indication of a system that does not have enough real memory to meet the user's application demands. In other words, the system only "pages out" when it does not have enough real memory, thus slowing system performance.

TIP Take time to explore all the features available from the Activity Monitor menu options. For an even more detailed process inspector, check out the Instruments application installed as part of the optional Xcode Developer Tools package that can be found on the Mac App Store.

Reference 21.3
Application Troubleshooting

Application issues are as diverse as the applications themselves. Just as each application is designed to provide unique features, problems often manifest in unique ways as well. Fortunately, there are a variety of general troubleshooting steps you can take when diagnosing and resolving an application issue.

> **NOTE ▶** Some software is just incompatible with OS X. Apple maintains a list of software known to be incompatible in the Knowledge Base document HT3258, "About incompatible software (Mac OS X v10.6, OS X Lion, OS X Mountain Lion)."

General Application Troubleshooting

The actions in the following list are in order from the least invasive and time-consuming to the most invasive and time-consuming. Actions are also generally presented by the likelihood of their success in resolving the issue, from most to least likely. General application troubleshooting methods include:

- Restart the application—Often, restarting an application resolves the issue, or at least resolves application responsiveness. In some cases, the application may become unresponsive and you may have to forcibly quit it to restart it, as detailed later in this lesson.
- Try another known working document—This is an excellent method to determine if a document has become corrupted and is the cause of the problem. If you discover that the problem's source is a corrupted document file, usually the best solution is to restore the document from an earlier backup. As covered in Lesson 18, "Time Machine," OS X includes a sophisticated and easy-to-use backup system.
- Try another application—Many common document types can be opened by multiple Mac applications. Try opening the troublesome document in another application. If this works, save a new "clean" version of the document from the alternate application.
- Try another user account—Use this method to determine if a user-specific resource file is the cause of the problem. If the application problem doesn't appear when using another account, search for corrupted application caches, preferences, and resource files in the suspect user's Library folder. Creating a temporary account to test and then delete is quite easy, as covered in Lesson 6, "User Accounts."

- Check diagnostic reports and log files—This is the last information-gathering step to take before you start replacing items. Few applications keep detailed log files; however, every time an application crashes, the OS X diagnostic reporting feature saves a diagnostic report of the crash information. Using the Console application to view diagnostic reports is detailed later in this lesson.
- Delete cache files—To increase performance, many applications create cache folders in the /Library/Caches, ~/Library/Caches, and ~/Library/Saved Application State folders. A specific application's cache folder almost always matches the application's name. While not the most likely application resource to cause problems, cache folders can be easily deleted without affecting the user's information. Once you delete an application's cache folder, the application creates a new one the next time you open it. One cache type that can't be removed easily from the Finder is the various font caches. However, the system font caches are cleared during a Safe Boot, as covered in Lesson 30, "System Troubleshooting."

  TIP The ~/Library folder is hidden by default in OS X. The easiest method to reveal this folder in the Finder is to hold the Option key and choose Go > Library.

- Replace preference files—Corrupted preference files are one of the most likely of all application resources to cause problems, as they change often and are required for the application to function properly. Application preference troubleshooting is detailed later in this lesson.
- Replace application resources—Although corrupted application resources can certainly cause problems, they are the least likely source of problems, since application resources are rarely changed. Application resource troubleshooting is also detailed later in this lesson.

Forcibly Quit Applications

It's pretty easy to tell when an application becomes unresponsive—it stops reacting to your mouse clicks, and the cursor often changes to a wait cursor (spinning pinwheel) for more than a minute. Hence, the terms "spinning-wheel" or "beach-balling" have become slang for a frozen Mac application.

Because the forward-most application controls the menu bar, it may seem as if the application has locked you out of the Mac entirely. But moving the cursor from the frozen application window to another application window or the desktop usually returns the cursor to normal—and you can then click another application or the desktop to regain control of your Mac.

OS X provides no less than three methods for forcibly quitting applications from the graphical interface:

- From the Force Quit Applications dialog—Choose Apple menu > Force Quit or press Command-Option-Escape to open the Force Quit Applications dialog. A frozen application appears in red text with "(not responding)" next to it. To forcibly quit, select any application and click Force Quit. Note that you can only restart the Finder from this dialog.
- From the Dock—Control-click, right-click, or click and hold the application's icon in the Dock to display the application shortcut menu. If the Dock has recognized that the application is frozen, simply choose Force Quit from this menu. Otherwise, hold down the Option key to change the Quit menu command to Force Quit.
- From Activity Monitor—Open /Applications/Utilities/Activity Monitor and select the application you want to quit from the process list. Next, click the Quit Process button in the Activity Monitor toolbar, and then click Force Quit. Activity Monitor is the only built-in graphical application that also allows administrative users to quit or forcibly quit any other user processes or background system process.

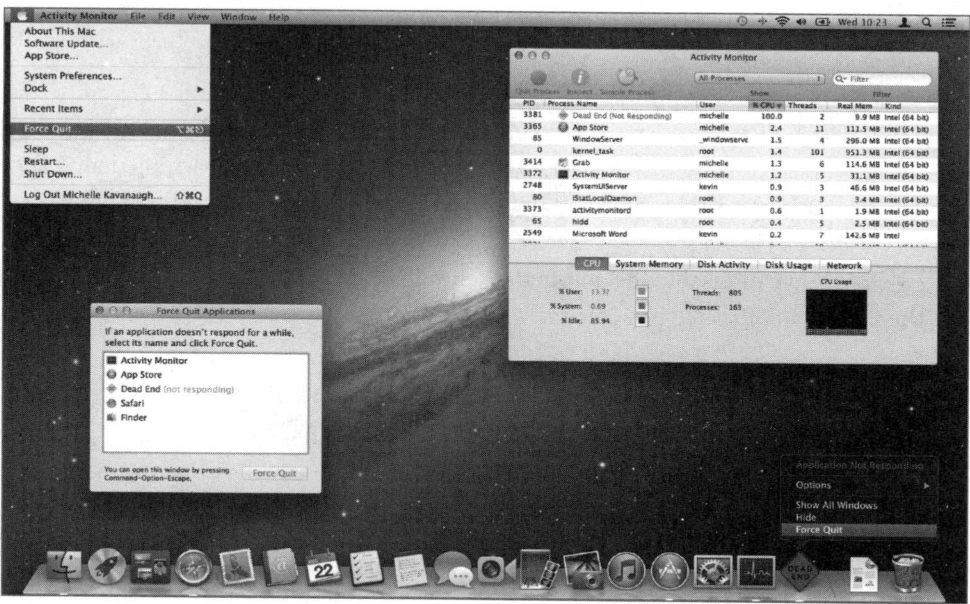

Diagnostic Reports

To help diagnose persistent issues, the OS X diagnostic reporting feature springs into action any time an application quits unexpectedly, commonly known as a *crash*, or stops functioning and you have to forcibly quit it, commonly known as a *hang*. This process displays a warning dialog to the user, letting her know a problem has occurred.

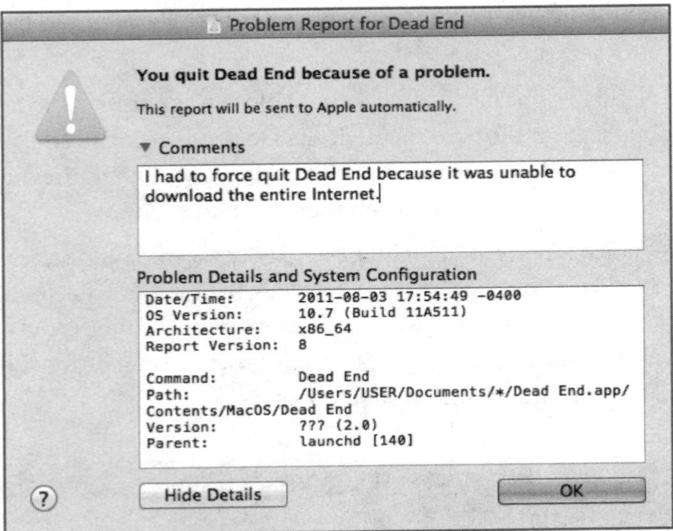

More important, this process records log files that detail the circumstances surrounding the application's crash or hang. If you click the Report button when the warning dialog appears, you can see the diagnostic report and optionally add comments to send to Apple.

> **TIP** You can disable the automatic sending of diagnostic reports to Apple from the Security & Privacy preferences.

Viewing Diagnostics via Console

Even if you don't send the report to Apple, you can revisit diagnostic reports again, as they are always saved to the system volume. If the application crashed, a diagnostic report log with the name of the application followed by ".crash" is saved in the user's ~/Library/Logs/DiagnosticReports folder. However, if the application hung, a diagnostic report log with the name of the application followed by .hang or .spin is saved in the local /Library/Logs/DiagnosticReports folder.

The easiest way to view these reports is to open the /Applications/Utilities/Console application, and then click the Show Log List button in the toolbar. The diagnostic reports are chronologically listed in the Diagnostic and Usage Information section.

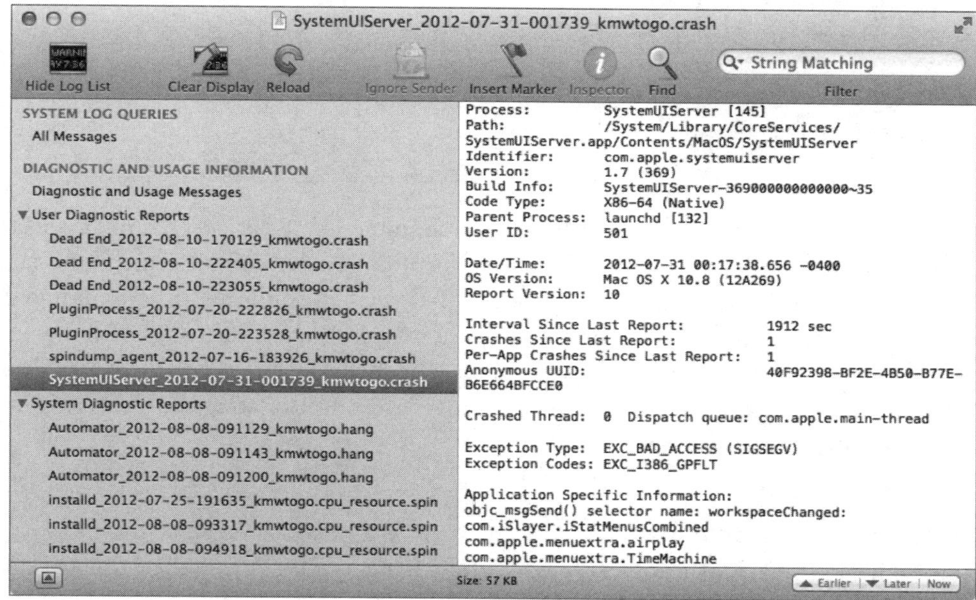

These diagnostic report logs include highly technical information that many may not understand, but they also include key pieces of information that may help the average troubleshooter diagnose the issue. For example, diagnostic reports often indicate which files were being used by the application at the time. One of the reported files could be the source of the problem due to corruption.

Another method in the Console application for reviewing hangs and crashes is to choose File > New System Log Query, which allows you to construct a custom search to precisely target key items across the most common logs.

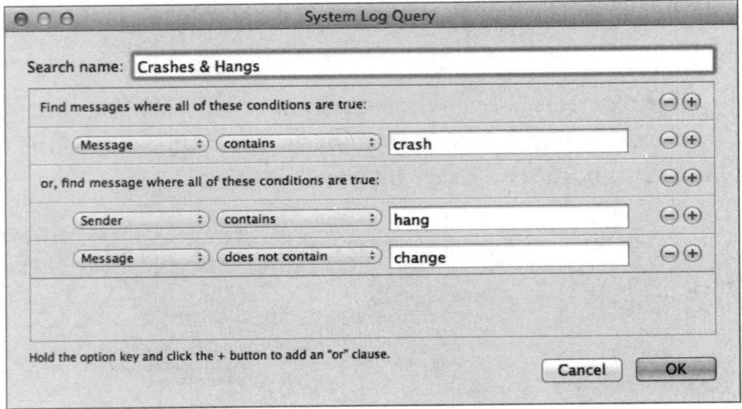

Much like constructing a custom Spotlight search in the Finder, as covered in Lesson 16, "Metadata and Spotlight," you can click the plus button to add multiple search criteria. Each new search criteria is an "and" by default, but you can define an "or" by holding the Option key when you click the plus button. For example, the prior screenshot shows a search that looks for any log entry that contains "crash" or "hang" but not "change." Note the word "hang" is contained in the word "change," thus necessitating the final criteria to avoid log entries with just the word "change."

Preference Troubleshooting

Applications primarily access two types of often-changing files during their use: the documents that the application is responsible for viewing or editing, and the preference files that contain all the application's settings. From an administration perspective, preference files are often more important, as they may contain important settings that are required for an application to work properly. For instance, an application's serial number or registration information is often stored in a preference file.

Preference files can be found in any Library folder, but most application preferences end up in the user's Library, specifically in the ~/Library/Preferences folder. This is because the local Library should only be used for system preferences. More important, it enables each user to have his own application settings that do not interfere with other users' application settings. By this logic, it's clear that if you're troubleshooting a system process, then you should look for its preferences in the /Library folder.

TIP The ~/Library folder is hidden by default in OS X. The easiest method to reveal this folder in the Finder is to hold the Option key and choose Go > Library.

Most application and system preference files are saved as property list files. The naming scheme for a property list file is usually in the form of a reverse domain name, followed by the program name, ending with the file type .plist. For example, the Finder preference file is named com.apple.finder.plist. This naming scheme may seem strange at first, but it helps avoid confusion by identifying the software's maker along with the application.

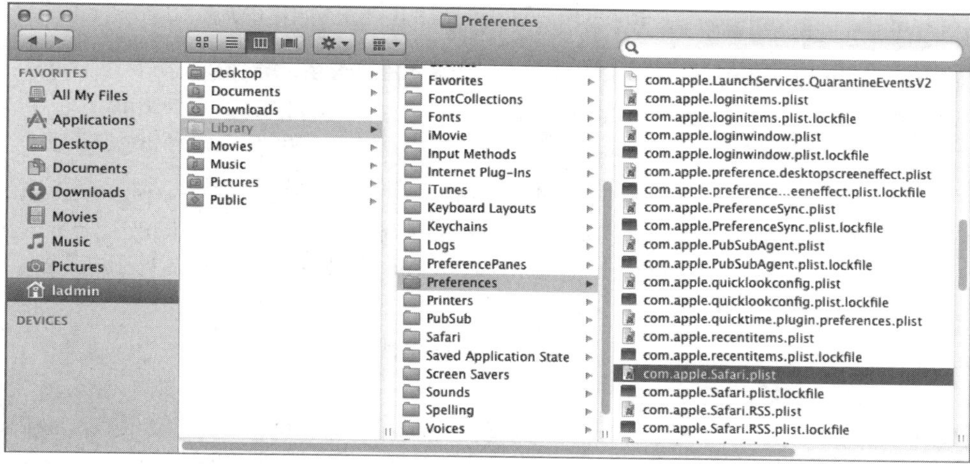

NOTE ▶ Any lock files associated with a preference file can be largely ignored as they don't contain any data and are simply the result of a legacy OS X Lion behavior.

Application preference files are historically one of the most common application resources to cause problems. Because these files can contain both internal application configuration information and user-configured preferences, even if you haven't changed any preferences, odds are the application is constantly storing new information in this file. It is the only file required by most applications that is regularly being rewritten, so it's a potential target for corruption.

Apple has worked hard to make its own applications and the user preference system wary of corrupt preference files. Many applications, including third-party applications, that use the Apple preference model simply recognize the corrupt preference file, ignore it, and create a new one. On the other hand, many third-party applications use their own proprietary preference models that are not as resilient. If this is the case, corrupted preferences typically result in an application that crashes frequently or during startup.

Resolving Corrupted Preferences

The most convenient method of isolating a corrupted preference in this case is to rename the suspect preference file. If any part of the preference filename is different than expected, the application ignores it and creates a new preference file. In the Finder, add an identifier to the end of the suspect preference filename—something like .bad. Alternatively you could simply put a tilde (~) at the beginning of the preference file, which will cause the Finder to put it at the beginning of the file listing when sorted alphabetically.

Restarting the application or process creates a new preference file based on the code's defaults. If this resolves the issue and doesn't remove any irreplaceable settings, go ahead and trash the old preference file; if not, move on to resource troubleshooting.

If you eventually resolve the problem elsewhere, you can then restore the previous settings by deleting the newer preference file and then removing the filename identifier you added to the original preference file. The benefit is that you don't lose any of the settings or custom configuration from the previous preference file.

Viewing and Editing Preferences

One of the primary advantages of using the property list file format is that it can generally be understood by humans. During your troubleshooting, you may find it advantageous to verify settings by directly viewing the contents of the configuration property list file. Many applications and processes keep additional settings items in these files that may not have a graphical interface for configuration.

> **NOTE ▶** Some third-party applications do not store their preference files as property lists. Thus, they will likely sport a different naming convention, and you will probably not be able to view or edit the file's contents.

The content of a property list file is formatted either as plain-text Extensible Markup Language (XML) or binary. The XML format is relatively human-readable with normal text interspersed alongside special text tags that define the data structure for the information. Thus, you can view and attempt to decipher the XML code of plain-text-formatted property list files using any text-reading application.

Binary-encoded files are, on the other hand, only readable using special tools designed to convert the binary code into human-readable format. Fortunately, OS X includes a Quick Look plug-in that allows you to easily view the contents of either type of property list file by simply pressing the Spacebar while you have the file selected in the Finder.

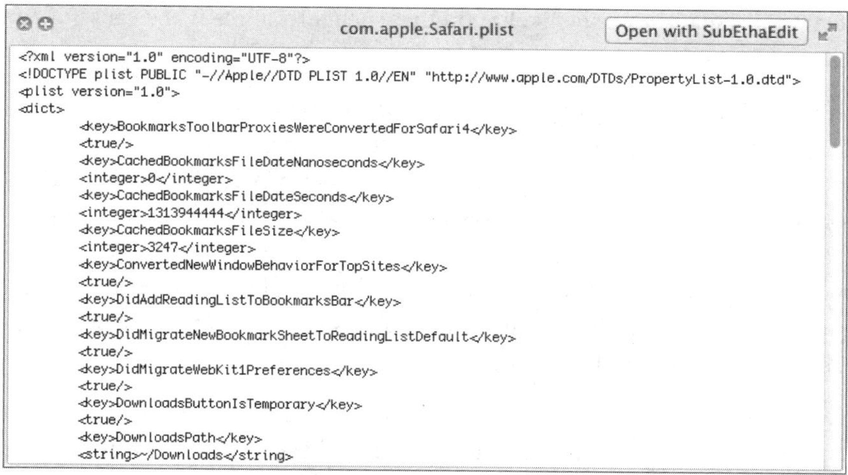

If you need to edit a property list file, the most complete graphical application for doing so is Xcode. The Xcode application can decode binary property list files, and it enables you to view and edit any property list in an easy-to-read hierarchical format. Again, Xcode is an optional install with OS X and can be found on the Mac App Store.

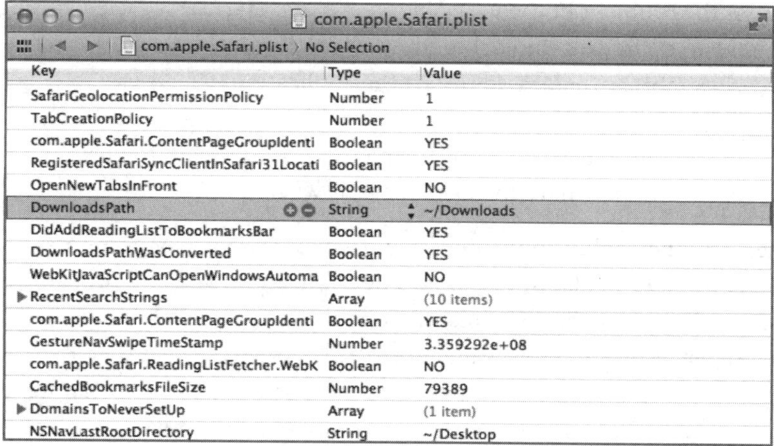

Application Resource Troubleshooting

Although rare, corrupted application software and associated nonpreference resources can be a source of application problems. These types of files rarely, if ever, change after the initial application installation, so the likelihood that such a resource is the cause of a problem is low.

However, keep in mind that many applications use *other* resources from the local and user Library folders, such as fonts, plug-ins, and keychains, as well as items in the Application Support folder. The hard part is locating the suspect resource; once you have, the fix is to simply remove or replace the corrupted resource and restart the application.

> **NOTE ►** Applications running in 64-bit mode will not load plug-in resources that only support 32-bit mode. This compatibility issue is covered in the "64-bit vs. 32-bit Mode" section previously in this lesson.

Remember that corrupted resources in the user's home folder Library affect only that user, whereas corrupted resources in the local Library affect all users. Use this fact to narrow your search when looking for a corrupted resource. Further, application and diagnostic report logs, covered earlier in this section, may tell you which resources the application was attempting to access when it crashed. Obviously, those resources should be your primary suspects.

If the application exhibits problems with only one user, attempt to locate the specific resource at the root of the problem in the user's Library folder. Start with the usual suspects; if you find a resource that you think could be causing the problem, move that resource out of the user's Library folder and restart the application.

> **NOTE ►** Some applications have a habit of storing their resources in the user's Documents folder, so you may have to check there as well.

If you've determined that the application issue is persistent across all user accounts, start by reinstalling or upgrading to the latest version of the application. You will probably find that a newer version of the application is available—one that likely includes bug fixes. At the very least, by reinstalling you replace any potentially corrupted files that are part of the standard application. If you continue to experience problems after reinstalling the application, search through the local Library resources to find and remove or replace the corrupted resource.

> **NOTE ►** If you are discovering a large number of corrupted files, this probably indicates a much more serious file system or storage hardware issue. Troubleshooting these items is covered in Lesson 13, "File System Troubleshooting."

Reference 21.4
Assistive Technologies

Apple has worked hard to ensure that OS X remains approachable for all users, including those who have trouble using the standard Mac interface via keyboard, mouse, and video display. Apple has built an extensive accessibility architecture into OS X called Universal Access. Universal Access enables assistive interaction features for Apple and many third-party applications.

Even if you don't need to use the assistive technologies in OS X, you may find many of the accessibility features extremely useful. This includes one of the most innovative OS X Mountain Lion features, a systemwide Dictation feature that requires no voice training.

> **MORE INFO ▶** This guide provides a cursory overview of the accessibility options in OS X. You can find out more by visiting the Apple Accessibility resource website (www.apple.com/accessibility).

Universal Access

The majority of the OS X accessibility features are available from the Accessibility preferences. (Choose Apple menu > System Preferences, and then click the Accessibility icon.) General preferences include showing the Universal Access menu item and enabling access for assistive devices like electronic Braille interfaces.

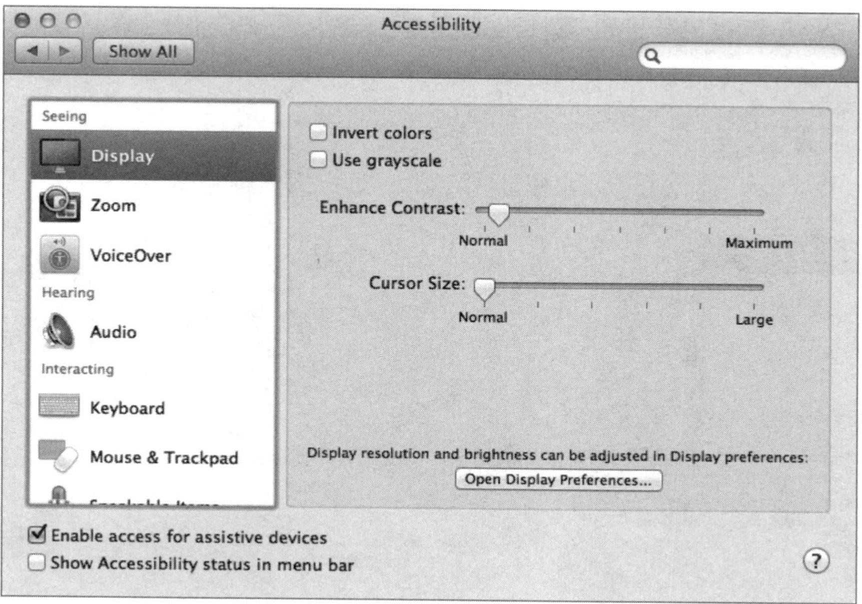

The remaining Universal Access preferences are presented in three categories representing different assistance features:

- Seeing—The accessibility features in this section are designed to assist those who have difficulty viewing the screen or who are unable to view the screen at all. Options include enabling dynamic screen zooming and adjusting display settings to enhance clarity. The VoiceOver spoken-word interface, covered next in this section, is also enabled here.
- Hearing—The accessibility features in this section are designed to assist those who have difficulty hearing or who cannot hear sound. The primary option here is to enable screen flashing as an alternative to the alert sound.
- Interacting—The accessibility features in this section are designed to assist those who have difficulty using a keyboard, mouse, or trackpad. Keyboard options include enabling sticky keys to assist with using keyboard combinations and slow keys to help with initial or repeated keystrokes. Mouse and trackpad options include increasing the cursor size so it's easier to see and enabling mouse keys that allow you to use the keyboard arrow keys in place of a mouse or trackpad. Finally, the Speakable Items options allow you to adjust control of your computer using spoken commands, as covered later in this section.

VoiceOver

VoiceOver is an interface mode that enables you to navigate the OS X user interface using only keyboard control and spoken English descriptions of what's happening onscreen. You enable VoiceOver from the VoiceOver pane of the Accessibility preferences.

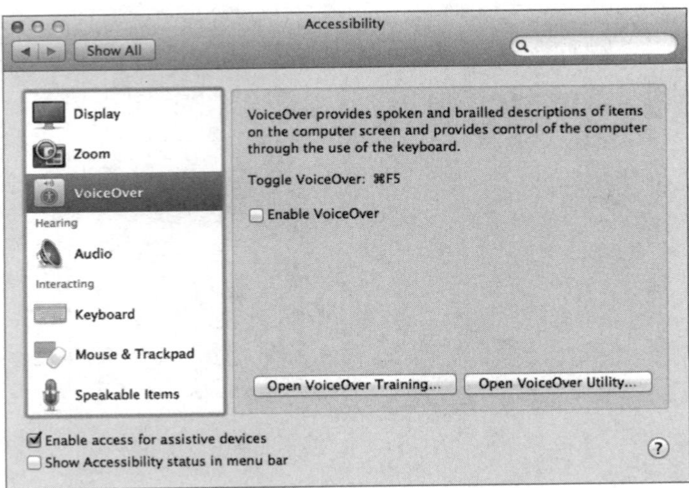

The first time you enable VoiceOver, it automatically launches an interactive tour of the VoiceOver interface. This tour can also be reopened at any time by clicking the Open VoiceOver Training button. This spoken tour teaches how to use the various VoiceOver keyboard shortcuts that are used in lieu of a mouse or trackpad.

VoiceOver is a highly customizable interface, allowing the user to adjust almost every interaction parameter by opening the /Applications/Utilities/VoiceOver Utility application. Alternatively, you can open this application from the VoiceOver pane of the Accessibility preferences.

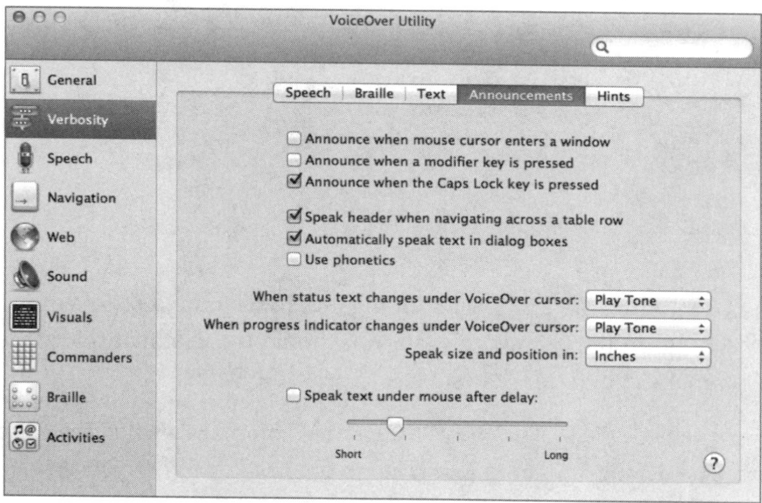

MORE INFO ► To learn more, visit the Apple VoiceOver resource website at www.apple.com/accessibility/voiceover.

Speakable Items

For many years OS X has offered a simple command dictation system that allows the user to speak common commands. This system can be enabled and managed via the Speakable Items pane of the Accessibility preferences.

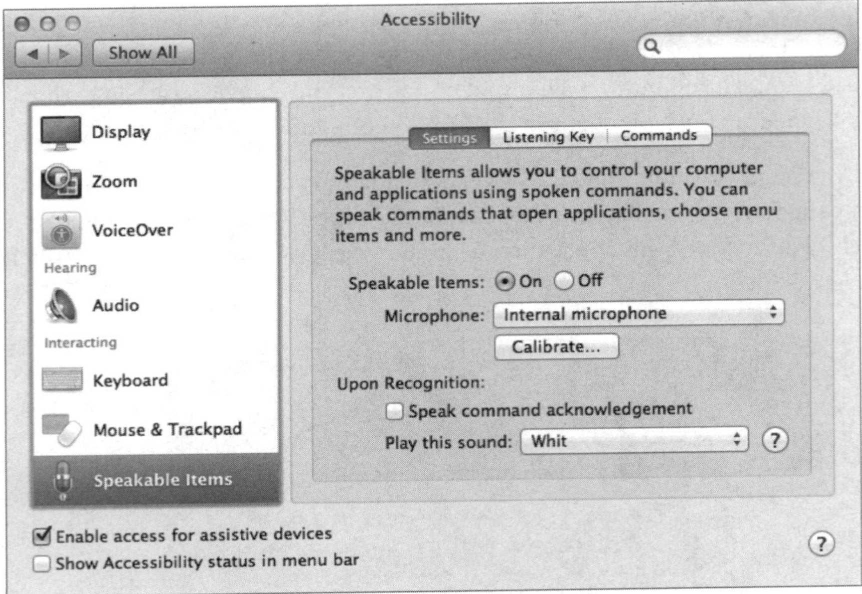

OS X Speakable Items do not require any voice training, but has a limited set of commands as defined by settings in the Commands tab. You should thoroughly explore the options under the Commands tab to make best use of Speakable Items.

With Speakable Items enabled, the system only "listens" for commands when the Listening Key is held down. The default Listening Key is set to the Esc key. When Speakable Items are enabled, a small round indicator appears, letting you know when the system is listening.

When a command is recognized, the command text appears above the Speakable Items indicator. Many spoken commands respond using both a spoken response and a visual response below the Speakable Items indicator.

TIP The voice used to provide the spoken response in Speakable Items can be adjusted from the Dictation & Speech preferences.

Dictation

The Speakable Items system does not take dictation; as such OS X Mountain Lion has borrowed another technology from iOS: systemwide Dictation. The OS X Dictation feature actually sends the spoken audio to the Apple servers across the Internet. This may seem like an excessively complex solution, but it's the only way to create a dictation system that contains a huge library of words and doesn't require any user training or excessive local storage. The OS X Dictation feature is enabled and managed via the Dictation & Speech preferences.

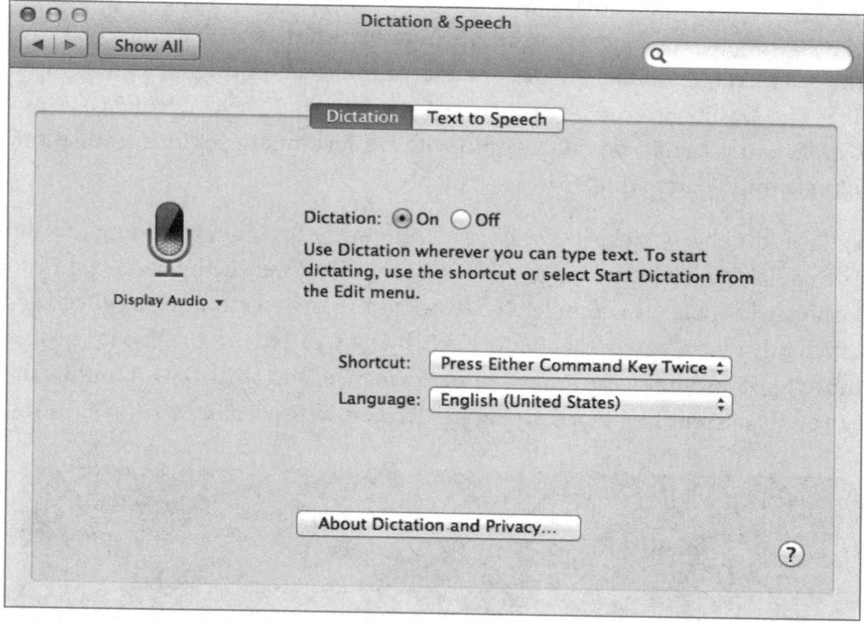

Much like Speakable Items, the Dictation system engages only when the user-defined keyboard shortcut is pressed. When you want to dictate text to the computer, simply make sure the text entry (blinking) cursor is active in the location where you want the resulting text to go, and then use the Dictation shortcut. The computer starts recording your voice as indicated by the Dictation pop-up indicator.

When you have completed a few moments of dictation, click Done, or quickly press the shortcut key, and the Dictation system begins transcribing the text. Depending on the length of your dictation and the speed of your Internet connection, the response could be nearly instantaneous, or a few seconds.

Reference 21.5
Managing Dashboard

OS X v10.4 introduced Dashboard as a new interface concept that provides instant access to narrowly focused, but usually very attractive, mini-applications called widgets. When activated, the full screen Dashboard slides out and your chosen mini-applications instantly springs to life. The Dashboard can be dismissed just as quickly. The convenience of using these mini-applications caught on quickly, and within a few months of its introduction hundreds of new third-party widgets were available.

Apple has been adding new tricks to Dashboard with every revision, including the ability for any user to quickly make new widgets in Safari from any website by choosing File > Open in Dashboard. Apple also completely reworked the widget runtime architecture to run more efficiently and securely than before. With OS X v10.6, the Dashboard process made the move to 64-bit mode for improved performance, and with OS X Lion, Dashboard was given its current home occupying the farthest left space in Mission Control.

Dashboard can be activated by opening the Dashboard application, pressing F12 on older Macs, pressing F4 on later Macs, or using the multi-finger swiping gesture to the right on a Multi-Touch input device. If you don't like the default shortcuts, you can adjust the Dashboard key from the Mission Control preferences, or adjust the Dashboard device gestures from the Mouse or Trackpad preferences. Further, you can activate a Hot Corner for Dashboard from the Mission Control preferences.

Adding More Widgets

To easily locate, test, and install a new widget, start by opening Dashboard using one of the methods outlined previously. Once in Dashboard, click the Open (+) button to reveal the new full-screen widget browser.

The widget browser is modeled after the Launchpad application in that it presents an icon view of all the installed items as it covers the existing background. To add an installed widget to your Dashboard area, simply click the widget's icon. Conversely, you can remove widgets from the Dashboard by clicking the Remove (–) button, and then clicking the "X" button next to the widget you want to remove.

Finally, from the widget browser, click the More Widgets button, and it automatically opens the default web browser and takes you to the Apple online widget repository. At this point you can browse and download any additional widgets that strike your fancy. Alternatively, you can acquire widgets using any method you like, including from other websites or via file sharing.

> **TIP** You can also create your own custom widgets from webpages in Safari by choosing File > Open in Dashboard.

If you downloaded the widget with Safari, it automatically prompts for installation. However, if you acquired the widget through other means, you have to double-click the widget file in the Finder to start the widget installer. When the Widget Installer dialog appears, click Install to open the widget in Dashboard for installation. The widget first appears in the widget browser, so the user must click the widget again to add it to her Dashboard.

NOTE ▸ Widget files are subject to quarantine and Gatekeeper just like any other OS X application. Thus, third-party unsigned widgets are not allowed unless overridden using the techniques covered in Lesson 19, "Application Installation."

The widget is installed in the currently logged-in user's home folder in the ~/Library/Widgets folder, and is always available to that user in Dashboard from the widget browser. Built-in Apple widgets are located in /Library/Widgets, while third-party widgets are typically installed in ~/Library/Widgets in the user's home folder. Most users will use the automatic widget install mechanisms in OS X to add new widgets to their Dashboard, thus keeping the /Library/Widgets folder clean.

Manually Manage Widgets

You can also manually install widgets by simply dragging them into one of the Library Widgets folders. This is necessary if you want to install a widget for all users of the system.

Similar to other system resources, widgets installed in the user's home folder are only available to that user, and widgets installed in the local Library folder are available to all local users. If you manually install a widget, thus bypassing the automatic widget installer, users still have to manually add that widget to Dashboard from the widget browser.

To remove a widget, locate it in either the local or user ~/Library/Widgets folder and drag it to the Trash. If the widget is still active in Dashboard after you have removed it from the Widgets folder, log the user out and then back in again to restart the Dashboard process.

The Dashboard Process

The widget runtime architecture was reworked for Mac OS X v10.5 to provide a more efficient and secure Dashboard environment. When a user logs in, the launchd process starts the Dock process. The first time a user attempts to access Dashboard, the Dock process starts the Dashboard process. The Dashboard process is responsible for running the Dashboard environment, including all widgets.

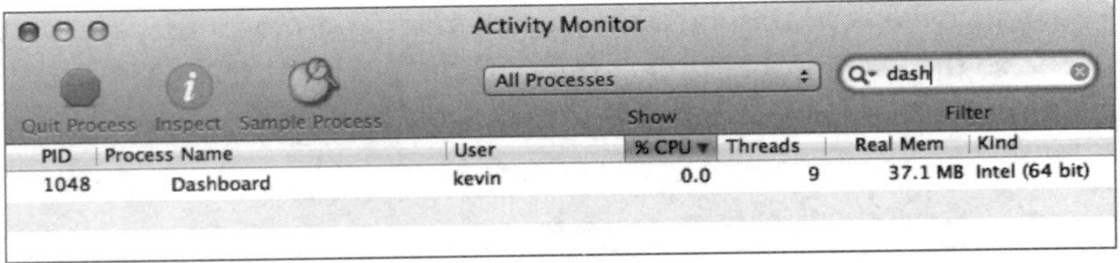

The Dashboard process maintains two general Dashboard preference files in the ~/Library/Preferences folder: com.apple.dashboard.client.plist and com.apple.dashboard.plist. Each open widget also maintains its own preference file in the user Preferences folder named widget-com.*widgetmaker*.widget.*widgetname*.plist, where *widgetmaker* is the name of the software developer who created the widget, and *widgetname* is the name of the widget.

The Dashboard process has the same access privileges as the user. So generally, widgets are as secure as any other normal application. Nevertheless, it is possible for someone to create and distribute widgets that have a negative effect. Widgets are basically miniature specialized web browsers, so just about any data transfer or software that can run from a web browser can also be run by a widget. Dashboard is only as safe as the widgets a user chooses to run. If you are at all suspicious of a third-party widget, simply avoid using it.

> **TIP** Although an administrator can't prevent a user from downloading third-party widgets, she can limit a user's ability to use third-party widgets with the Parental Controls preferences, as covered in Lesson 6, "User Accounts."

Troubleshooting Widgets

If a widget appears to stop working or becomes unresponsive, your first step should be to attempt to reset it. From Dashboard, click once on the widget, and then press Command-R to reset the widget. Widgets use a swirling animation to indicate that they have reset.

If the widget is still having problems, or you're having trouble using all the widgets, restart the Dashboard process associated with the user account. You can forcibly quit the Dashboard process by using /Applications/Utilities/Activity Monitor. More information about forcibly quitting processes is available in the "Forcibly Quit Applications" section earlier in this lesson. After you quit the Dashboard process, reactivate Dashboard and the Dashboard process, and all open widgets reopen. Another method is to restart all user processes by logging the user out and then back in again.

If restarting the widget and the Dashboard process doesn't work, you may have a corrupted widget or widget preference file. Widgets are similar to other applications in that they are susceptible to errors from corrupted files. Start by removing the specific widget preference file, and then restart the Dashboard process. If you're having trouble with a third-party widget, download a new copy and replace the widget itself. Finally, you can reset the entire Dashboard system by removing all Dashboard and widget preference files and then logging the user out and back in again.

Exercise 21.1
Force Applications to Quit

Prerequisites

- You must have created the Chris Johnson account (Exercise 6.1).
- You must have installed the Dead End application (Exercise 19.3).

In this exercise, you will learn how to determine when an application has become unresponsive. You will learn different ways to force unresponsive applications to quit: from the Dock, using the keyboard shortcut, and using Activity Monitor. Even background processes without a user interface can have issues and stop running, so you'll learn how to manage these processes as well. You will also see how to open an application in 32-bit mode.

Force an Application to Quit via the Dock

1. If necessary, log in as Chris Johnson.

2. Open the Dead End application you installed earlier.

   Dead End is an application whose sole purpose is to become unresponsive, giving you an opportunity to practice different ways to force an application to quit.

   Dead End opens a window with a button labeled "Download the Internet."

3. Click "Download the Internet."

   Dead End becomes unresponsive. After a few seconds you may see the wait cursor (looks like a colored pinwheel). Note that the wait cursor appears only when you mouse over the Dead End window or (if Dead End is in the foreground) the menu bar.

4 Control-click (or secondary-click) the Dead End icon in the Dock, and then choose Force Quit from the shortcut menu. Alternatively, you could click and hold the Dead End icon in the Dock, and then choose Force Quit from the pop-up menu.

If Force Quit does not appear in the menu, repeat step 3 or hold down the Option key. When you hold down the Option key, Quit changes to Force Quit and you then choose it to force Dead End to quit.

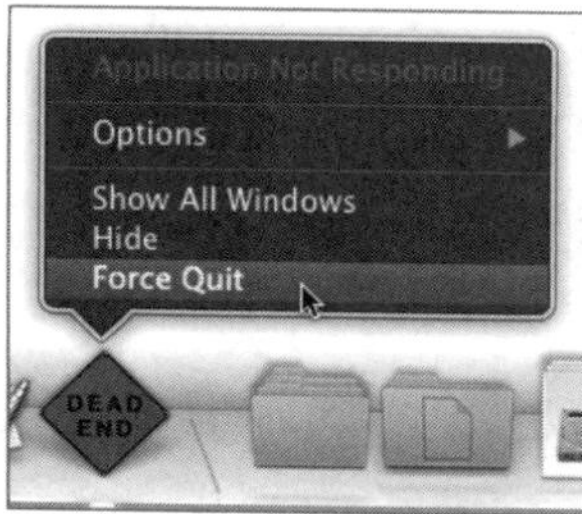

Use the Force Quit Window

1 Open the Dead End application again, so you can try another method of forcibly quitting.

One way to open applications you've used recently is by going to the Apple menu and choosing Recent Items. By default, the system remembers the last ten applications you've opened.

2 Click "Download the Internet."

3 Press Command-Option-Esc (or choose Force Quit from the Apple menu) to open the Force Quit Applications window.

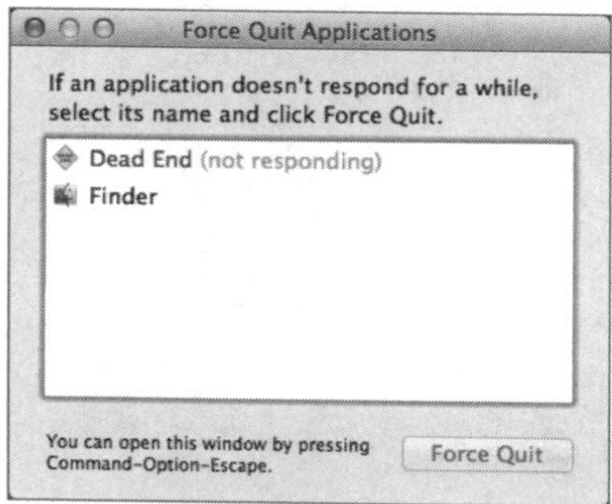

Note that it will take around 15 seconds before Dead End is shown as "not responding."

4 Select Dead End, and click Force Quit.

5 In the confirmation dialog, click Force Quit.

6 If you are given the opportunity to send a report to Apple, click Ignore.

7 Close the Force Quit Applications window.

Use Activity Monitor

There may be times when you need another method to force an application to quit. Activity Monitor not only forces applications to quit, but also allows you to review all processes running on the computer, gather information, and quit them when necessary.

1 Open Dead End.

2 Click "Download the Internet".

3 Open Activity Monitor (from the Utilities folder).

Even though the wait cursor appears in Dead End, you can still click the desktop to make the Finder active, or in the Dock to use Launchpad. A single unresponsive application should not affect the rest of the system.

Activity Monitor displays a list of all running processes. When you open this window, it shows processes that you will recognize as applications. It also shows other processes running in the background that do not have a graphical user interface.

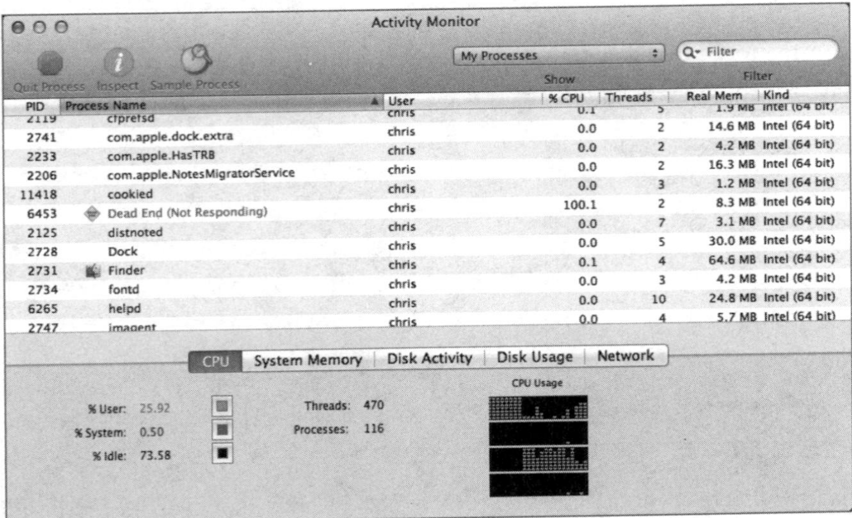

4 In the Activity Monitor window, click "% CPU" in the table header twice to get a top-down (most to least) list of processes in terms of their CPU usage. The triangle that appears next to % CPU should point downward.

5 Look for the Dead End process by name. It should be at the top.

The name of an unresponsive application appears in red with a note declaring the application is "Not Responding." As you look at the Dead End process, notice how the CPU usage is close to 100%. You can see how an application can hijack your CPU, even though the application is not responding and appears to be doing nothing.

Note that the % CPU statistic can be misleading, since it refers to the percentage of a CPU core being used. Recent Macs have multiple cores, so "100%" CPU utilization is not fully using the computer's CPU power. For instance, on a 12-core Mac Pro, full utilization would be listed as 1200%.

6 Select Dead End in the process list, and then click the Quit Process button on the toolbar.

7 When asked to confirm, click Force Quit.

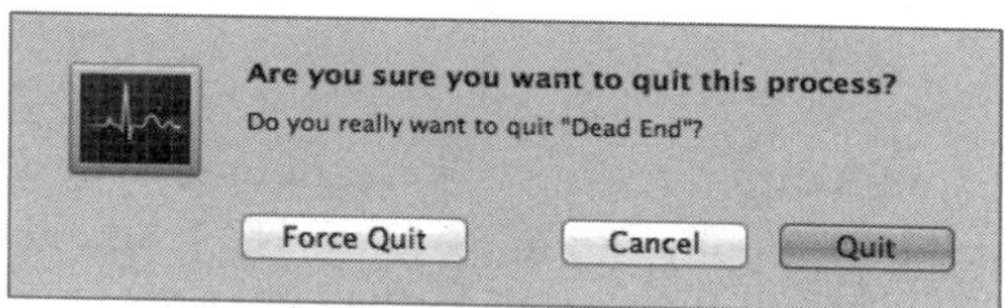

Note that Quit is the default option in the dialog that appears. However, since Dead End is not responding to its own Quit command, you need to choose Force Quit in order to stop this process from running.

Dead End disappears from the process list in the Activity Monitor window and from the Dock.

Unlike the Dock and Force Quit Applications window, Activity Monitor is capable of forcing background processes to quit. Background processes are generally programs that are launched automatically to provide some part of the system's functionality. Normally, you will not have to manage them explicitly, but in a few cases forcing them to quit is useful.

8 Select SystemUIServer in the process list. It may help to click Process Name in the table header. Remember its PID (process ID) number.

SystemUIServer is the program that manages the menu items on the right side of the menu bar. Each menu item runs as a plug-in inside of the SystemUIServer, and if one of them locks up it might be necessary to force SystemUIServer to quit.

9 With SystemUIServer selected, click the Quit Process button, and then watch the right side of the menu bar as you click Force Quit.

The right side of the menu bar goes blank, and then the menu items reappear. Examine your process list, and notice that SystemUIServer is running, but with a different process ID than it had before.

What has happened is that the user launchd process (another background process) has detected that SystemUIServer exited, and has automatically relaunched it. launchd is responsible for starting and monitoring many of the system's background processes, and will restart them if necessary.

Not all processes can be safely forced to quit this way. For example, forcing launchd itself to quit would leave your login session in a degraded state. We discuss launchd more in the final lesson.

10 Leave Activity Monitor open for the next section.

Open an App in 32-Bit Mode

Most applications that come with OS X Mountain Lion can only run in 64-bit mode. Some can run in either 32- or 64-bit mode but normally run in 64-bit mode. If you need to, you can run them in 32-bit mode (for example, in case they need to load a 32-bit-only plug-in).

1 If necessary, expand the Activity Monitor window until you can see the Kind column on the right.

Normally, all the processes have the kind "Intel (64 bit)."

2 Open Dead End.

3 In Activity Monitor, find the Dead End process, and note that its Kind is also listed as "Intel (64 bit)."

4 Quit Dead End.

5 In the Finder, Get Info on the Dead End application.

6 In the General section of the Info window, select "Open in 32-bit mode."

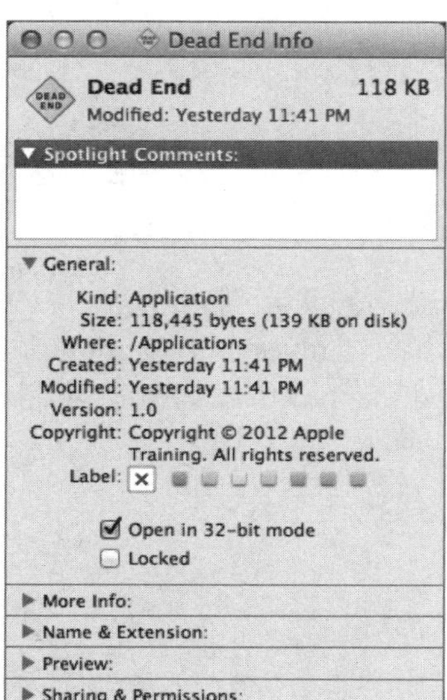

7 Close the Info window, and reopen the Dead End app.

8 In Activity Monitor, find the new Dead End process.

Its Kind is listed as Intel, indicating that it is running in 32-bit mode.

9 Quit Dead End.

View System Processes and Usage

1 In Activity Monitor, choose All Processes from the pop-up menu in the toolbar.

You see many more processes appear in the process list. In addition to the background processes within your user session (sometimes called agents), OS X has many background processes (sometimes called daemons) running outside of your login session.

2 At the bottom of the Activity Monitor window, switch through the CPU, System Memory, Disk Activity, Disk Usage, and Network tabs, and examine the information they display.

3 Quit Activity Monitor.

Exercise 21.2
Troubleshoot Preferences

Prerequisites

- You must have created the Chris Johnson account (Exercise 6.1).

Most application preferences are created and stored for individual users in their personal Library folder. This compartmental approach can help when troubleshooting application issues. You'll learn how to set and restore a preference and see the effect of moving a preference file out of the ~/Library/Preferences folder.

Create and Locate the Preview Preferences

1. If necessary, log in as Chris Johnson.

2. Open Preview from the Applications folder.

3. Open the Preview preferences by choosing Preview > Preferences (Command-comma).

   Note that the default setting for "When opening files" is "Open groups of files in the same window."

4. Select "Open all files in one window."

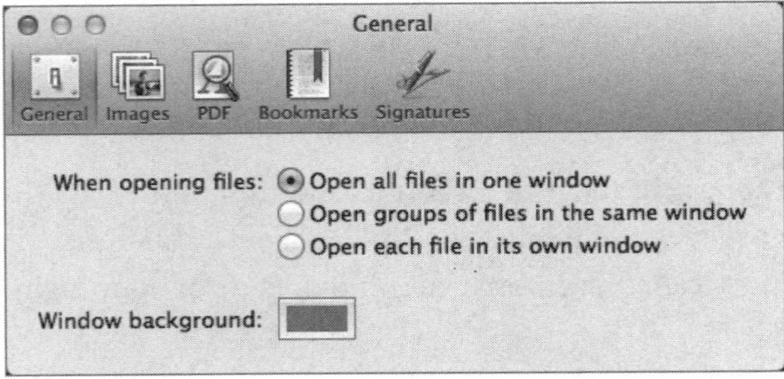

5. Close the Preferences window and quit Preview.

6. In the Finder, open ~/Library.

Remember that since the user Library folder is invisible, the easiest way to navigate to this folder is to hold down the Option key, and choose Go > Library.

7 Open the Preferences subfolder, and look for files with names starting with "com. apple.Preview".

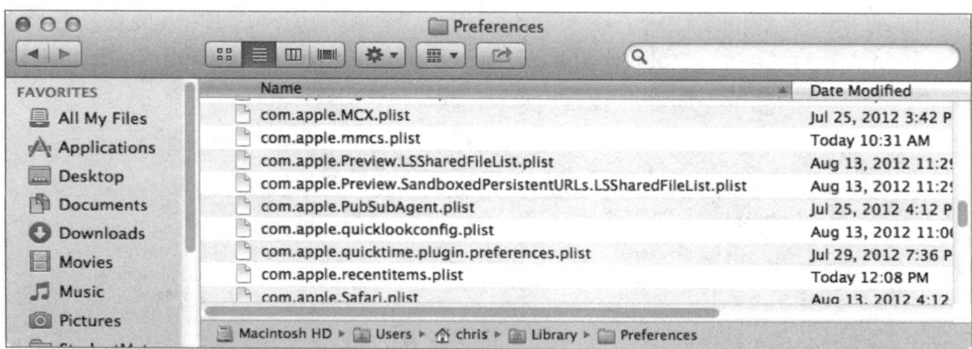

Normally, an application's preference file starts with the developer's domain name in reverse order, followed by the application's name or ID, with the extension ".plist". In this case, there is no file by the expected name "com.apple.Preview.plist," although there are a few with similar names. These files are not Preview's own preferences, but files used by Launch Services and the sandbox to keep track of files Preview has used.

This is because of the way Preview is sandboxed. It does not have direct access to your user Library, so it stores its preferences inside a special sandbox container.

8 Back out of the Preferences folder, and open the Containers folder (under ~/Library).

This folder is part of the OS X application sandbox system. Sandboxed applications like Preview are provided with a private folder inside ~/Library/Containers to store their settings, caches, and so on.

9 Locate the com.apple.Preview folder inside ~/Library/Containers, and examine its contents.

It contains a Data subfolder, with a structure that mirrors your home folder. Most of its contents are aliases, pointing to their "real" counterparts.

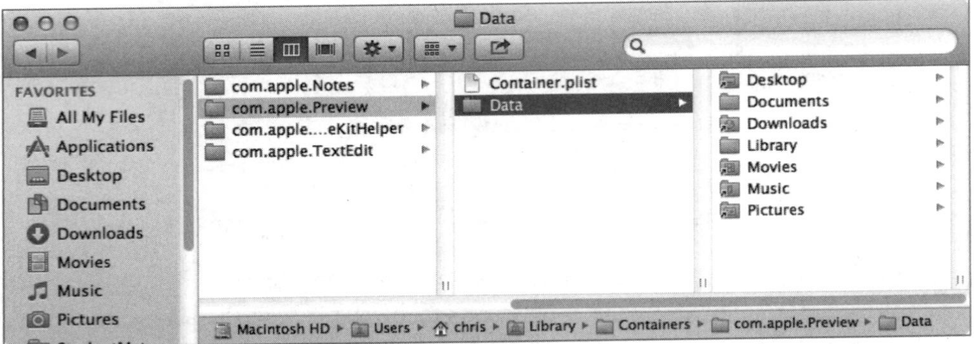

10 Navigate down to com.apple.Preview/Data/Library/Preferences.

There is a file here named com.apple.Preview.plist.

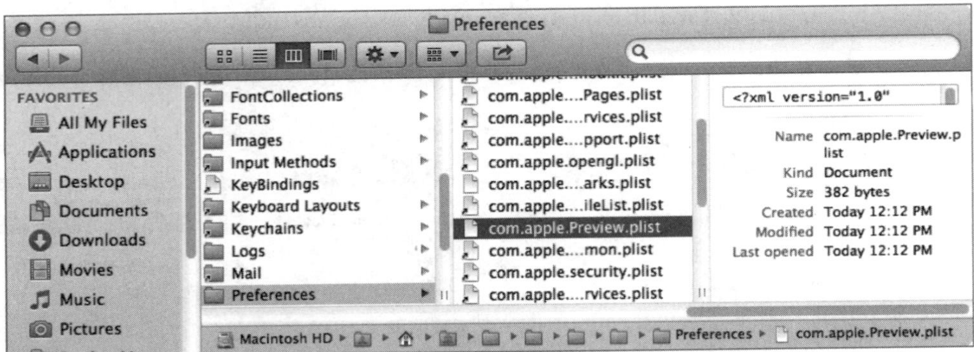

11 Use Quick Look to view the preference file's contents (select it and press Command-Y).

The preference setting you made is listed here, although in somewhat cryptic form.

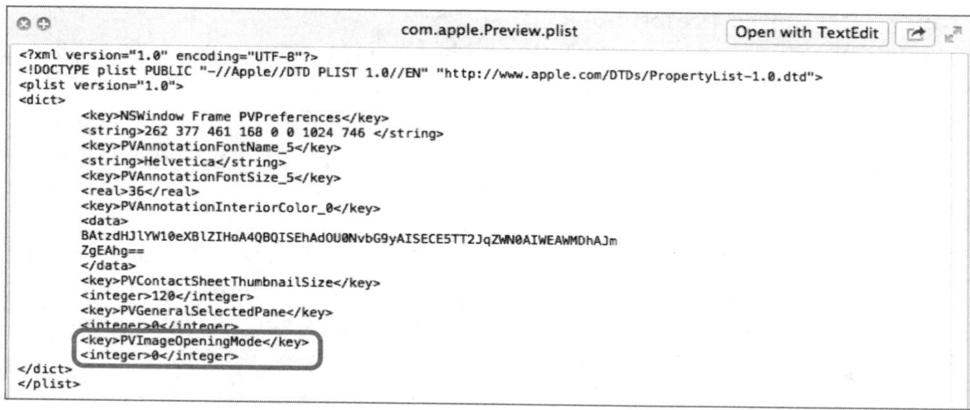

12 Close the Quick Look window

Disable and Restore Preferences

1 Drag the com.apple.Preview.plist file to your desktop. Leave the Preferences folder open for later.

   Since the file is no longer in the expected place, Preview is not able to find it or use the settings in it.

2 Open Preview again, and open its preferences.

   The setting for "When opening files" has reset back to its default of "Open groups of files in the same window."

3 Quit Preview.

4 Move the com.apple.Preview.plist file from your desktop back into the Preferences folder.

5 If you are notified that a newer item named com.apple.Preview.plist already exists, click Replace.

6 Open Preview again, and open its preferences.

   This time your custom preference setting ("Open all files in one window") has been restored.

7 Quit Preview.

Manage Corrupted Preferences

OS X has some built-in features for dealing with corrupted preference files. You will explore what happens when a preference file becomes corrupt.

1. Control-click the com.apple.Preview.plist file, and choose Open With > TextEdit from the shortcut menu.

   Some .plist files are stored in an XML/text format, which TextEdit can edit like any other text document. This .plist file, however, is stored in a binary format TextEdit cannot fully display or edit. As a result, you see only part of the file's contents.

   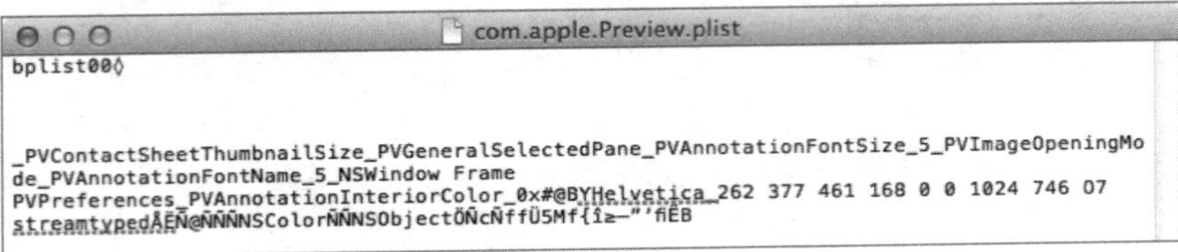

2. Add some new text anywhere in the document.

3. Quit TextEdit. Note that the changes are saved automatically.

4. Quick Look the file (select it and press Command-Y).

   By editing the file as if it were plain text, you have damaged its binary structure. As a result, Quick Look cannot display its contents and shows a generic view.

   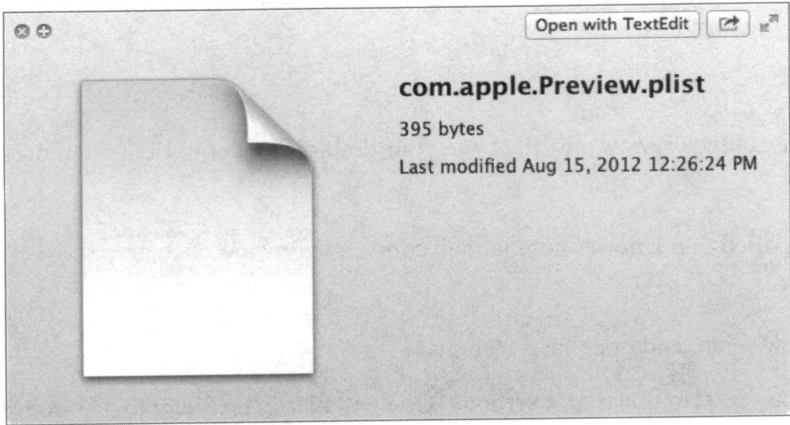

5. Close the Quick Look window.

6 Reopen Preview, and open its preferences.

Since the preferences file was damaged, the system has reset it, and the setting for "When opening files" has reset back to its default of "Open groups of files in the same window."

7 Quit Preview.

8 Use Quick Look to view com.apple.Preview.plist again.

Preview has rewritten its preference file, removing the corruption you introduced.

Exercise 21.3
Examine Application Diagnostics

Prerequisites

- You must have created the Local Admin (Exercise 3.1 or 3.2) and Chris Johnson (Exercise 6.1) accounts.
- You must have performed Exercise 21.1.

The Console utility is the primary tool in OS X for viewing system logs. In this exercise, you will use it to view application diagnostic logs and to search the system log for application events.

View a Diagnostic Report

1 If necessary, log out as Chris Johnson.

2 Log in as Local Admin.

Some of the log files you will examine in this exercise are only readable by administrators.

3 Open the Console utility.

Console is the primary tool in OS X for viewing log files. Its Log List sidebar lets you view specific log files, or the catchall All Messages.

4 In the Log List, examine the entries under User Diagnostic Reports and System Diagnostic Reports. If necessary, click the disclosure triangles next to each one to show the individual reports.

A separate log file is created each time a program crashes or is force-quit while hung, so you should have a number of entries from force-quitting Dead End in Exercise 21.1. Note that these are listed under System Diagnostic Reports, even though it was Chris Johnson that force-quit them.

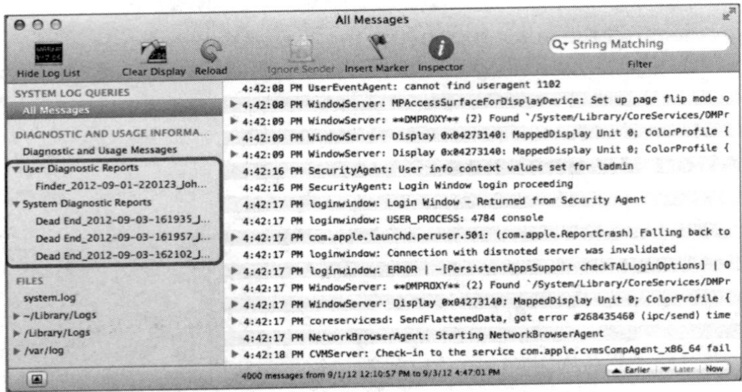

5 Select one of the diagnostic reports. It includes detailed information about what the program was doing when it crashed or hung.

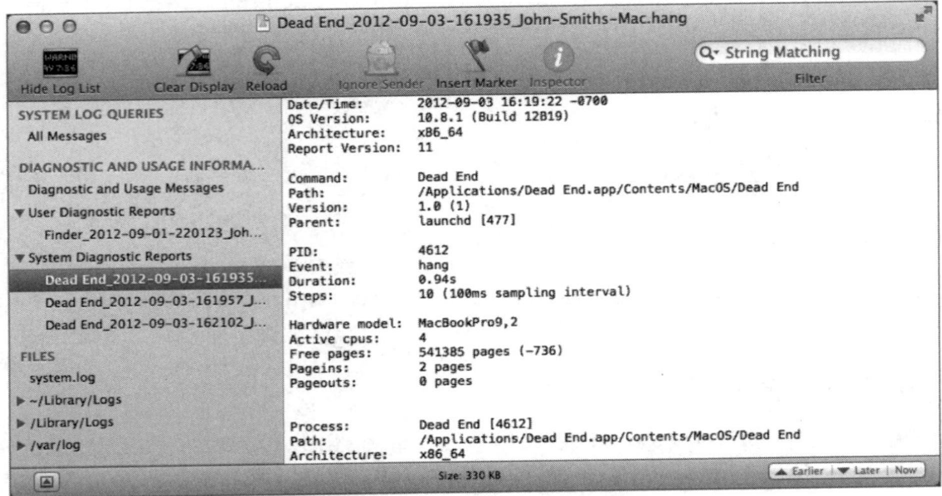

Create a Custom Search Query

You can also use Console to search for particular types of events in the computer's logs.

1 Choose File > New System Log Query (Command-Option-N).

2 Change the Search Name to **Crashes**.

3 Click the Message and "contains" pop-up menus, and look at the options for filtering messages.

4 Leave the pop-up menus set to Message and "contains," and enter **crash** in the field to the right.

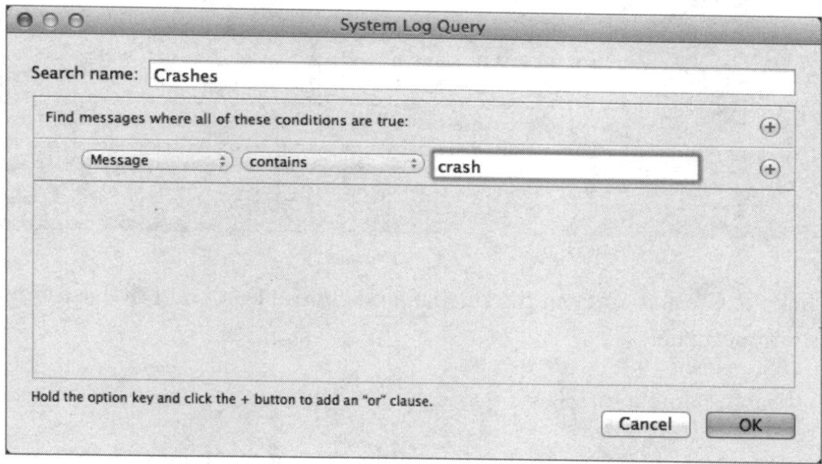

5 Click OK.

A new window opens showing entries in the system log that contain "crash." Depending on your computer's history, there might not be any messages to show.

Your custom query is also added to the Log List sidebar, in the System Log Queries section.

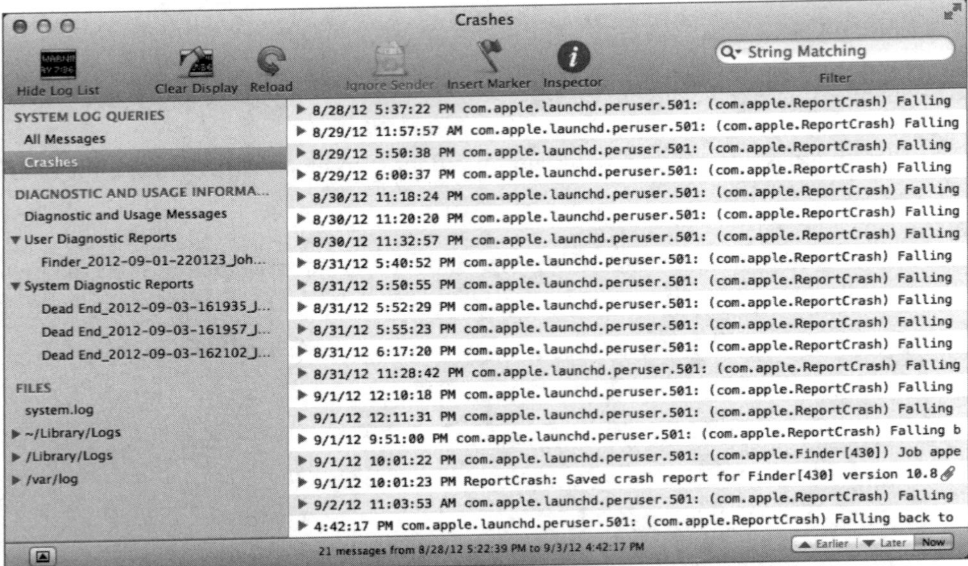

6 Control-click the Crashes entry in the sidebar, and choose Edit Log Database Query from the shortcut menu.

7 Change the search name to **Crashes & Hangs**.

8 Option-click the Add (+) button to the right of the "Message contains crash" line.

Holding Option makes it create an "or" clause, that is, makes it display entries that match one search criterion *or* the other.

9 Change the new search clause to "Message contains **hang**".

This search now includes all messages containing the text "hang." Unfortunately, this also matches other words, such as "change," "changed," and so on.

10 Without holding down the Option key, click the Add (+) button to the right of the "Message contains hang" line.

11 Set the new search clause to “Message does not contain `change`”.

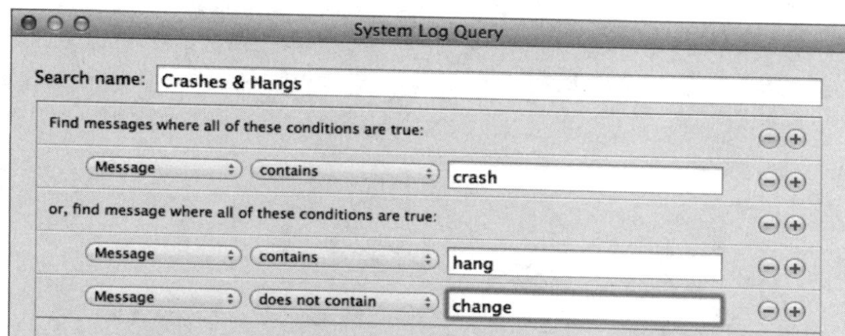

12 Click OK.

The new search criteria are applied, and messages mentioning either “crash” or “hang” are displayed.

This custom search query is stored in Local Admin’s preferences, and will be available in the Console sidebar anytime you want to check for recent crash and hang events.

13 Quit Console.

14 Log out as Local Admin.

Network Configuration

Lesson **22**

Network Essentials

The capability to share information between computers across a network has always been important. During the early years of personal computer development, vendors designed their own proprietary local network systems. Apple was no exception with its implementation of AppleTalk and LocalTalk network standards for file sharing and network printing. Yet although these vendor-specific technologies were suitable for private networks, they didn't allow for direct communication between dissimilar networks. Special hardware or software had to be put in place to translate from one vendor's network to another.

GOALS

- Understand fundamental TCP/IP network concepts
- Configure and monitor basic network settings
- Connect to a Wi-Fi network

Around the same time, researchers were working at the behest of various U.S. organizations to create a wide area network (WAN) standard for military and governmental use. From this research was born the Internet protocol suite known as TCP/IP. The marriage of the Transmission Control Protocol (TCP) and the Internet Protocol (IP) became the universal language that allows computers to communicate on the Internet. This standard became so pervasive that nearly every network today, from small local networks all the way up to the largest long-distance network on Earth, the Internet, is based on the TCP/IP suite.

It should come as no surprise, then, that OS X includes a robust TCP/IP implementation. In fact, the first computer systems to popularize the use of TCP/IP were UNIX systems. Thus, much of the TCP/IP software built into every version of OS X is based on open source UNIX software that was established long before OS X ever existed as a product from Apple.

In this lesson, you will configure basic settings for both Ethernet and Wi-Fi networks. Before that, though, you must have a fundamental understanding of core network concepts, to which the first part of this lesson is devoted.

Reference 22.1 Network Concepts

Properly configuring and troubleshooting networking on any operating system requires a basic understanding of fundamental network concepts. Due to the widespread adoption of standardized network technology, the following network overview applies to nearly any operating system, OS X included. Basic network terminology is covered first, followed by an overview of the processes involved in actual data delivery across a network.

Network Terminology

It's best to explore networking from a layered perspective. In fact, there is an established seven-layer model used to describe network technologies: the Open Systems Interconnection Reference Model (known as the OSI model). Exploring networking using the OSI model goes well beyond the scope of this guide. Consequently, networking concepts will be presented in a more simplistic abstraction of three basic elements:

- Network interface—The network interface is the medium through which network data flows. Network interfaces can be physical or virtual. The most common physical network interfaces for computers are Ethernet and 802.11 wireless Ethernet, which is known most commonly as Wi-Fi. Virtual network interfaces are also available that can be used to increase the functionality of the physical interface: for example, a virtual private network (VPN) that uses the existing physical network interface to provide a secure connection without the need for a dedicated physical interface.
- Network protocol—A protocol defines a set of standard rules used for data representation, signaling, authentication, or error detection across network interfaces. Primarily, protocols are designed to ensure that all data is communicated properly and completely. Specific protocols have a narrow focus, so often multiple protocols are combined or layered to provide a complete network solution. For example, the combined TCP/IP protocol suite provides only for the addressing and end-to-end transport of data across the Internet; dozens of other protocols are required for something as simple as checking your email or browsing a website.
- Network service—In the context of the Network preferences, the term "network service" describes a configuration assigned to a network interface. For example, in Network preferences, you will see listed the Wi-Fi service, which represents the connection settings for the Wi-Fi network interface. A fundamental feature of OS X is

the ability to support multiple network services, or connections, per each individual network interface be it physical or virtual.

A different definition of "network service" is sometimes used in Lessons 25 and 26, wherein a network service is information provided on the network by a server for use by clients. Common examples in these lessons include file sharing services, messaging services, and collaboration services. Often a specific set of protocols is used to define how the particular service works.

MORE INFO ▸ For more details on the OSI model for describing computer networks, refer to the Wikipedia entry http://en.wikipedia.org/wiki/OSI_model.

Simplifying computer network technology to only three distinct elements does not provide a detailed abstraction, but it still shows clearly how each is related. When a network interface, service, or protocol is created, it is often put through a review process before it's deemed a network standard. Standards committees are formed with members from multiple network organizations and vendors to ensure that new network standards remain interoperable with existing network standards. Most networking technologies in use today have been ratified by some standards body, so you may often come across an interface, protocol, or service labeled as a "standard."

Media Access Control (MAC) Address

The Media Access Control (MAC) address is used to uniquely identify a physical network interface on a local network. Each physical network interface has at least one MAC address associated with it.

Because the most common network interface is Ethernet, people often refer to MAC addresses as "Ethernet addresses." Still, nearly every other network interface type also uses some type of MAC address for unique identification. This includes, but isn't limited to, Wi-Fi, Bluetooth, and FireWire.

A MAC address is usually a 48-bit number represented by six groups of two-digit hexadecimal numbers each separated by colons. For example, a typical MAC address would look something like this: 00:1C:B3:D7:2F:99. The first three number groups are the Organizationally Unique Identifier (OUI), and the last three number groups identify the network device itself. In other words, you can use the first three number groups of a MAC address to identify who made the network device.

MORE INFO ▸ The Institute of Electrical and Electronics Engineers (IEEE) maintains a searchable database of publicly listed OUIs at its website http://standards.ieee.org/regauth/oui/index.shtml.

Internet Protocol (IP) Address

Communicating with computers on both local and remote networks requires an Internet Protocol (IP) address. IP addresses, unlike MAC addresses, are not permanently tied to a network interface. Instead, they are assigned to the network interface based on the local network it's connected to. This means if you have a portable computer, every new network you connect to will probably require a new IP address. If necessary, you can assign multiple IP addresses to each network interface, but this approach is often only used for computers that are providing network services.

There are currently two standards for IP addresses: IPv4 and IPv6. IPv4 was the first widely used IP addressing scheme and is the most common today. An IPv4 address is a 32-bit number represented by four groups of three-digit numbers, also known as octets, separated by periods. Each octet has a value between 0 and 255. For example, a typical IPv4 address would look something like this: 10.1.45.186.

With IPv4, a little over 4 billon unique addresses exist. This may seem like a lot, but considering how many new network-ready devices come out and the number of people who want to own multiple network-ready gadgets, this number isn't really big enough. For the time being, the available IPv4 addresses are extended by using network routers that can share a single routable, or "real world," IPv4 address to a range of reusable private network addresses. This is how most home networks are configured, but it is only a temporary solution for what's to come next.

The successor to IPv4 is IPv6, but because IPv4 is so entrenched in the backbone of the Internet, the transition to IPv6 has been slow. The main advantage to IPv6 is a much larger address space—so large, in fact, that every person on Earth could have roughly 1.2 × 1019 copies of the entire IPv4 address range. This may appear to be a ridiculous number of IP addresses, but the design goal of IPv6 was to eliminate the need for private addressing and allow for easier address reassignment and changing to a new network.

An IPv6 address is a 128-bit number that is presented in eight groups of four-digit hexadecimal numbers separated by colons. Hexadecimal numbers use a base-16 digit system, so after the number 9 you use the letters A through F. For example, a typical IPv6 address would look something like this: 2C01:0EF9:0000:0000:0000:0000:142D:57AB. Large strings of zeros in an IPv6 address can be abbreviated using a double colon, resulting in an address more like this: 2C01:0EF9::142D:57AB.

Subnet Mask

The computer uses the subnet mask to determine the IPv4 address range of the local network. Networks based on the IPv6 protocol do not require subnet masks. A subnet mask is similar to an IPv4 address in that it's a 32-bit number arranged in four groups of octets. The computer applies the subnet mask to its own IP address to determine the local network's address range. The nonzero bits in a subnet mask (typically 255) correspond to the portion of the IP address that determines which network the address is on. The zero bits correspond to the portion of the IP address that differs between hosts on the same network.

For example, assuming your computer has an IP address of 10.1.5.3 and a commonly used subnet mask of 255.255.255.0, the local network is defined as hosts that have IP addresses ranging from 10.1.5.1 to 10.1.5.254.

> **MORE INFO ▶** Another way of writing the subnet mask is known as CIDR notation. This is written as the IP address, a slash, and then the number of 1 bits in the subnet mask. The previous subnet example would be 10.1.5.3/24. You can find out more about CIDR notation from Wikipedia: http://en.wikipedia.org/wiki/Classless_Inter-Domain_Routing.

Whenever the computer attempts to communicate with another network device, it applies the subnet mask to the destination IP address of the other device to determine if it's on the local network as well. If so, the computer attempts to directly access the other network device. If not, the other device is clearly on another network, and the computer sends all communications bound for that other device to the router address.

Router Address

Routers are network devices that manage connections between separate networks; as their name implies, they route network traffic between the networks they bridge. Routing tables are maintained by routers to determine where network traffic goes. Even if a router is presented with traffic destined for a network that the router is unaware of, it still routes the traffic to another router that it thinks is closer to the final destination. Thus, routers literally are the brains of the Internet.

In order to be able to reach computers beyond the local network, your computer needs to be configured with the IP address of the router that connects the local network with another network or, more commonly in residential situations, an Internet service provider. Typically the router's address is at the beginning of the local address range, and it's always in the same subnet. Using the previous example, assuming your computer has an IP address of 10.1.5.3 and a commonly used subnet mask of 255.255.255.0, the local network IP address range would be 10.1.5.0 to 10.1.5.255 and the router address would most likely be 10.1.5.1.

Transmission Control Protocol (TCP)

TCP is the primary protocol used to facilitate end-to-end data connectivity between two IP devices. TCP is the preferred transport mechanism for many Internet services because it guarantees reliable and in-order delivery of data. In other words, IP provides network addressing and data routing, and TCP ensures that the data arrives at its destination complete. The combination of these two protocols encompasses the TCP/IP suite, commonly known as the Internet protocol suite.

The TCP/IP protocol suite chops continuous data streams into many individual packets of information before they are sent across the network. This is because IP networks use packet-switching technology to route and transmit data. Almost all digital networking technologies are packet-based because this provides efficient transport for network connections that aren't always reliable. Remember, the TCP/IP protocol was originally designed with the military in mind, so packet-based network technology is ideal because it's designed to work around communications link failure. This is why sophisticated routing hardware was originally developed for TCP/IP networks, so data could be literally rerouted and re-sent should a network link go down.

A lesser-used protocol known as User Datagram Protocol (UDP) is also attached to the TCP/IP suite. UDP is a simpler protocol that does not guarantee the reliability or ordering of data sent across networks. This may seem like a poor choice for networking, but in some cases UDP is preferred because it provides better performance than TCP. Examples of network services that use UDP include Domain Name System (DNS), media streaming, voice over IP (VoIP), and online gaming. These services have been designed to tolerate lost or out-of-order data so they can benefit from UDP's increased performance.

MORE INFO ▶ For more information regarding the Internet protocol suite, refer to this Wikipedia entry: http://en.wikipedia.org/wiki/internet_protocol_suite.

Reference 22.2
Networks in Action

Manually assigning an IP address, a subnet mask, and a router address is technically all that is needed to configure a computer to use TCP/IP-based networking on both local area networks (LANs) and wide area networks (WANs). Yet two other network services are almost always involved in basic network functionality: Dynamic Host Configuration Protocol (DHCP) and DNS. These two services, combined with TCP/IP, characterize core network functionality that provides the foundation for nearly any network service.

Local Area Network (LAN) Traffic

Most LANs use some form of wired or wireless connection. Once the network interface has been established, TCP/IP networking must be configured, either manually or via DHCP. Once both these steps are complete, network communication can begin.

Is it on this subnet?

	Origin				Destination			
IP address	10	1	5	9	10	1	7	5
Subnet	255	255	0	0	255	255	0	0
	10	1	0	0	10	1	0	0

If so, communicate via Ethernet to MAC address

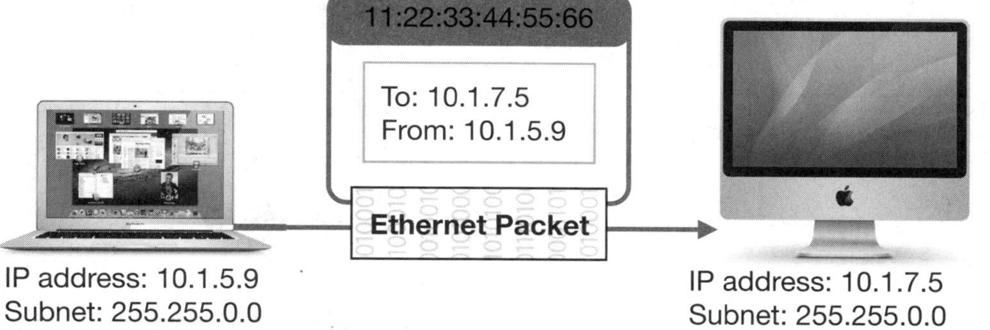

TCP/IP packets are encased inside Ethernet frames to travel across the local network. The TCP/IP packet includes the originating IP and destination IP addresses along with the data to be sent. The network device applies the subnet mask setting to determine if the destination IP address is on the local network. If so, it consults its Address Resolution Protocol (ARP) table to see if it knows the MAC address corresponding to the destination IP address.

Each network host maintains and continuously updates an ARP table of known MAC addresses that correspond to IP addresses on the local network. If the MAC address is not listed yet, it broadcasts an ARP request to the local network asking the destination device to reply with its MAC address, and adds the reply to its ARP table for next time. Once the MAC address is determined, an outgoing Ethernet frame, encasing the TCP/IP packet, is sent using the destination MAC address.

The other network device likely returns some information as well using the same technique of transferring TCP/IP packets inside of MAC-addressed Ethernet frames. This goes on and on for thousands of packets every second to complete a data stream. For standard Ethernet the maximum frame size is only 1,500 bytes (that's roughly 1.5 kilobytes or 0.0015 megabytes), so you can imagine how many Ethernet frames are necessary to transmit even a small file.

Wide Area Network (WAN) Traffic

Sending data over a WAN differs only in that data is sent through one or more network routers to reach its intended destination. WANs exist in all shapes and sizes, from a small WAN perhaps used to connect separate LANs in a large building all the way up to the biggest and most popular WAN, the Internet.

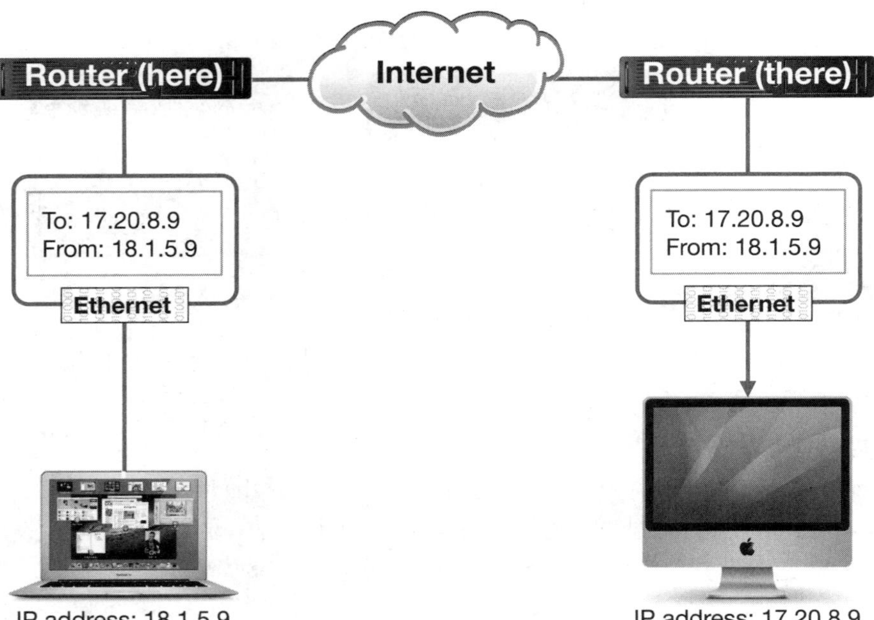

Initially, transferring data across a WAN is similar to transferring data on a LAN. After all, the first stop for the data destined for the WAN is at the network router on the local network. The network device prepares the packets as before by encasing the TCP/IP packets inside Ethernet frames. Once again, the subnet mask is applied to the destination IP address to determine if the address is on the local network. In this case, the network device determines that the destination is not on the local network, so it sends the data to the router. Because the router is on the local network, the transmission between the local network client and the router is identical to standard LAN traffic.

Once the router receives the Ethernet-encased TCP/IP packets, it examines the destination IP address and uses a routing table to determine the next closest destination for this packet. This almost always involves sending the packet to another router closer to the destination. In fact, only the last router in the path sends the data to the destination network device.

Network routers also often perform some sort of hardware interface conversion, as WAN network links are rarely standard copper Ethernet connections. The router strips the Ethernet container away from the original TCP/IP packet and then rewraps it in another container that is appropriate for the WAN connection. Obviously, the final router has to prepare the TCP/IP packet for the last leg of the journey on the destination device's local network by rewrapping it in an Ethernet frame addressed to the destination's MAC address.

In most cases, network data is transferred back and forth several times to establish a complete connection. Remember, these packet sizes are very small. The default packet size for Internet traffic is also 1,500 bytes with a maximum packet size of 65,535 bytes for most TCP/IP connections.

Network routers are highly optimized devices that can easily handle thousands of data packets every second, so for small amounts of data many WAN connections "feel" as fast as LAN connections. Conversely, a lot of latency is introduced from all the different routers and network connections involved in transferring data across a WAN, so often sending large amounts of data across a WAN is much slower than across a LAN. Thus, many a user's favorite time-wasting computer practice was born: waiting for an Internet download or upload.

Domain Name System (DNS)

Most people are bad at remembering strings of seemingly arbitrary numbers used to define addresses, so additional technology is often implemented to help users find addresses. Even the simplest cell phones feature a contact list so users don't have to remember phone numbers. For TCP/IP networks, DNS makes network addressing much more approachable to normal humans.

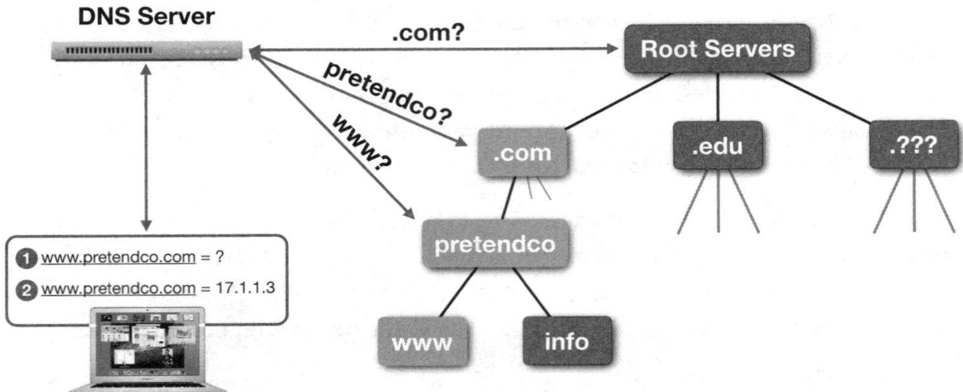

In essence, DNS is a worldwide network of domain servers with the task of maintaining human-friendly host names used to easily locate specific network IP addresses. If you've spent any time at all on the Internet, you're already familiar with the DNS naming convention: For example, the Apple website is located at www.apple.com. Any network device can have a host name, but only those network devices providing a service that needs to be easily located need to have host name entries on a DNS server. Devices providing shared services, such as printers and server computers, are the most common devices to have DNS entries.

The hierarchical DNS naming convention relates directly to the hierarchical structure of the DNS domain architecture. As you know, DNS names are broken into labels separated by periods. Each label represents a different level, or domain, of the DNS hierarchy.

The top of the DNS hierarchy is the "root" or "." domain. The names that are part of the root domain are the familiar abbreviations at the end of nearly every Internet resource. Common examples are .com, .edu, .gov, and others, including various country codes. These top-level domains (TLDs) are hosted by a consortium of commercial and governmental organizations.

Below the TLDs, individual organizations or users host or rent their own DNS domains. For example, Apple hosts several DNS servers that are known by the TLD servers in order to maintain the apple.com domain. Apple can host an unlimited number of host names inside the apple.com domain. Apple can create unlimited domain names by preceding apple.com with any text. Examples include www.apple.com, training.apple.com, and developer.apple.com.

When a local network device needs to resolve a DNS name into the corresponding IP address, it sends the name query to the IP address of a DNS server. The IP address for a DNS server is usually configured along with the other TCP/IP address information for the network device. The DNS server searches its local and cached name records first. If the requested name isn't found locally, the server queries other domain servers in the DNS hierarchy.

This process may take a while, so DNS servers temporarily cache any names they have recently resolved to provide a quicker response for future requests. Querying a DNS server to resolve an IP address given a known host name is called a forward lookup, whereas querying a DNS server to resolve a host name from a known IP address is called a reverse lookup. When initially configured, network clients query the DNS server with a reverse lookup of its own IP address to determine if the network client has its own DNS name.

MORE INFO ▶ For more information regarding DNS, refer to this Wikipedia entry: http://en.wikipedia.org/wiki/Domain_Name_System.

MORE INFO ▶ Bonjour is a name discovery service that uses a name space similar to DNS. Bonjour is covered in Lesson 26, "Host Sharing and Personal Firewall."

Dynamic Host Configuration Protocol (DHCP)

Although not required to provide network functionality, DHCP is used by nearly all network clients to automatically acquire preliminary TCP/IP configuration. In some situations, an administrative user may still choose to manually enter TCP/IP networking configuration information. This is often the case with network devices that are providing network services. However, manually configuring multitudes of network clients is tedious work that is prone to human error. Thus, even on rigorously managed networks, DHCP is still widely used to configure network clients.

NOTE ▶ DHCP is specifically designed to assign IPv4 addressing, as IPv6 addressing is handled automatically via other mechanisms.

NOTE ▸ A precursor to DHCP is Bootstrap Protocol (BOOTP). DHCP is backward compatible with BOOTP but provides greater functionality and reliability.

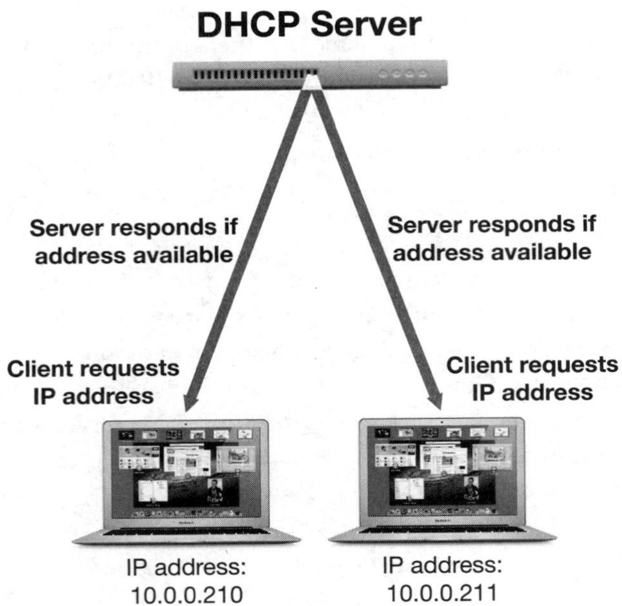

A DHCP server is required to provide the service. On many networks, the network routers provide the DHCP service, but in some cases a dedicated server or network appliance can be used for this purpose. When a network device becomes active on the network, it first negotiates a link with the hardware interface, and then sends out a broadcast to the local network requesting DHCP information. Because the new network client doesn't yet have an IP address, it uses the network interface's MAC address for identification.

If a DHCP server that is listening has available addresses, it sends back a reply to the client with TCP/IP configuration information. At a minimum, this information includes IP address, subnet mask, router, and a DHCP lease time that defines how long the client can retain the address before it's given away. Ancillary DHCP information can include DNS information and NetBoot information.

MORE INFO ▸ For more information regarding DHCP, refer to this Wikipedia entry: http://en.wikipedia.org/wiki/Dhcp.

Reference 22.3
Basic Network Configuration

Initial networking configuration is handled by Setup Assistant, which runs the first time you start up a new Mac or a fresh OS X system installation. Setup Assistant makes it easy for even a novice user to configure network settings. Yet even if you choose to not set up networking during the initial system setup process, the Mac automatically enables any active network interface, including connecting to unrestricted wireless networks, and attempts to configure TCP/IP via DHCP. Consequently, for many users OS X does not require any initial network configuration at all.

MORE INFO ▸ Advanced network configuration techniques are covered in Lesson 23, "Advanced Network Configuration."

Network Preferences

If network changes are required after initial setup, you can still use Network Setup Assistant to help guide you through the network configuration process. You can access Network Setup Assistant by clicking the "Assist me" button at the bottom of the Network preferences.

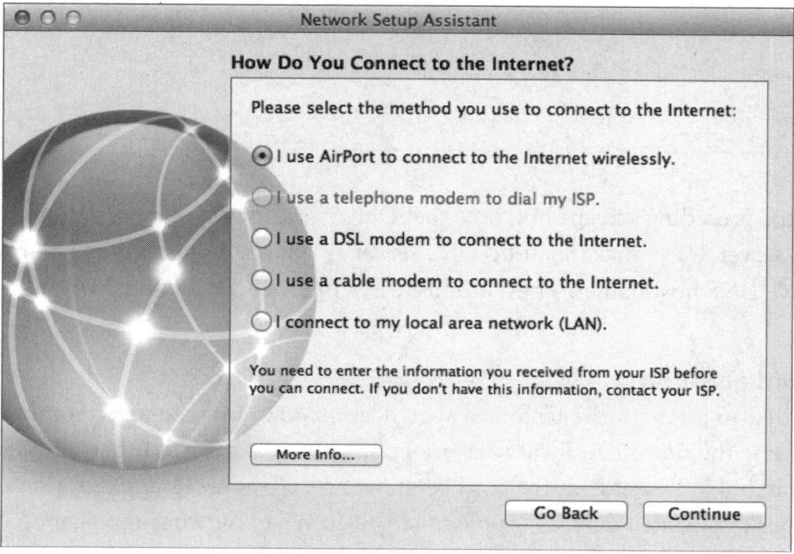

Although this assistant is helpful for novice users, get familiar with all network configuration options so you're prepared for any potential network situation or troubleshooting issue. All Network preferences and configuration windows are consolidated into a unified interface. Thus, all network settings can be found in the Network preferences. Note that the Network preferences are locked, indicating that only administrative users have access to most of these settings. However, because DHCP is enabled by default for Ethernet and Wi-Fi interfaces, for most situations network configuration is automatic.

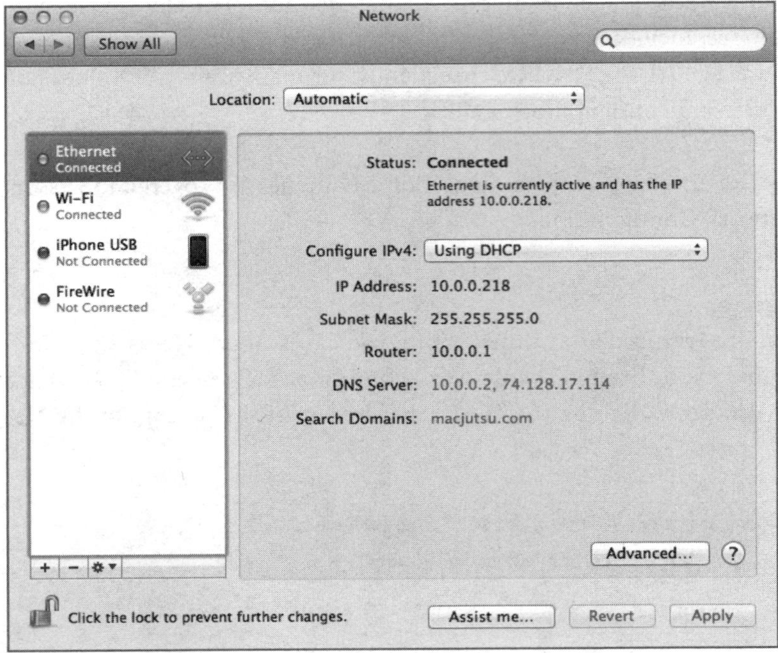

NOTE ► In the preceding screen shot, note that DHCP is also providing configuration for the DNS server. Recognize that if no DNS server IP address is configured, your Mac cannot resolve DNS host names. Thus, in most cases Internet connections will fail.

Basic Wi-Fi Configuration

Wireless Ethernet, also know by the technical specification 802.11 or the more common "Wi-Fi," has become the dominant local network connectivity standard. Ethernet is certainly still popular, but Wi-Fi has cut the cord by allowing easy network access for an ever increasing number of portable devices. Apple made basic Wi-Fi network management a breeze with automatic Wi-Fi network discovery and the Wi-Fi status menu. These Wi-Fi setup mechanisms give nonadministrative users access to the most commonly needed Wi-Fi network settings.

By default, if you start up or wake your Mac, and it cannot establish a valid network connection, the system automatically scans for new local Wi-Fi networks. If the Mac discovers an open wireless network that doesn't require authentication, it automatically connects to that network. However, if wireless networks requiring authentication are found or multiple new networks are found, the system then prompts the user to join a Wi-Fi network.

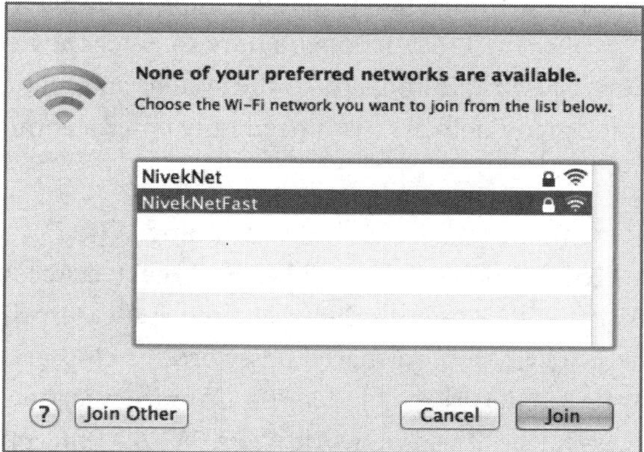

If the Mac doesn't automatically prompt you for Wi-Fi configuration, you can manually select a wireless network from the Wi-Fi status menu near the top-right corner of the display. When you select this menu, the Wi-Fi background process automatically scans for any advertised networks that are within range for you to choose from.

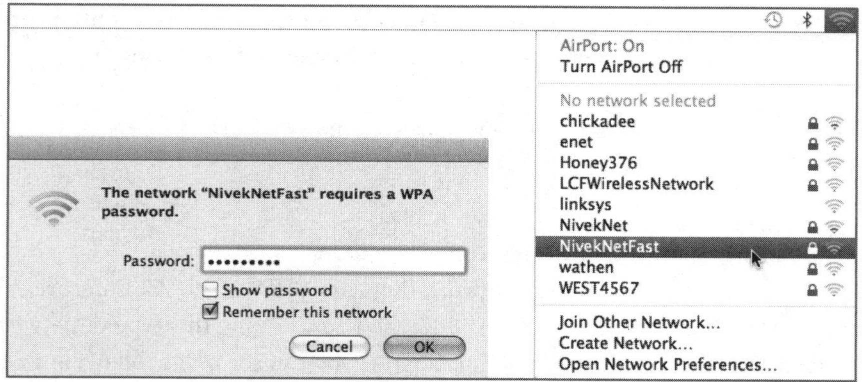

A Service Set Identifier, or SSID identifies a Wi-Fi network's name and associated configuration information. An administrator of the devices providing Wi-Fi services sets the network's name and configuration settings. OS X uses the information in the SSID configuration to automatically establish Wi-Fi network communications.

Aside from Wi-Fi network names, the most important indicator this menu shows is the relative strength of any Wi-Fi network, as indicated by the number of black bars to gray bars. The more black bars displayed, the higher the relative strength of the Wi-Fi signal.

Wi-Fi Authentication

If you select an open wireless network, the Mac immediately connects, but if you select a secure wireless network, as indicated by the small lock icon, you have to enter the network password. When you select a secure network, in most cases the system automatically negotiates the authentication type, and for many networks you need only enter a common shared Wi-Fi password.

OS X supports the most common Wi-Fi authentication standards including Wired Equivalent Privacy (WEP), Wi-Fi Protected Access (WPA), and Wi-Fi Protected Access II (WPA2). This includes support for WPA/WPA2 in both their personal and enterprise forms. Essentially WPA/WPA2 Personal uses a common shared password for all users of the Wi-Fi network, whereas WPA/WPA2 Enterprise includes 802.1X authentication, which allows for per-user password access to the Wi-Fi network. WPA/WPA2 Enterprise authentication is covered in the next section of this lesson.

By default, if you join a WEP or WPA/WPA2 Personal Wi-Fi network as an administrative user, the system automatically saves the passwords to the system keychain. This allows the Mac to automatically connect to the Wi-Fi network immediately after startup or waking up. Thus, all users can access the wireless network without needing to reenter the password. On the other hand, if you join a Wi-Fi network as a standard user the password is only saved to the user's keychain, and thus only automatically connects when that user is logged in.

> **MORE INFO ▸** Details regarding the Keychain system are covered in Lesson 8, "System Security."

Automatic WPA Enterprise Configuration

If you join and authenticate to a wireless network that uses WPA or WPA2 Enterprise, it's implied that the authentication is handled via 802.1X. Thus, joining this type of network automatically creates an 802.1X service configuration. As you can see in the following screenshot, when 802.1X is used you must enter both a username and password to authenticate the connection. You may also be prompted with a certificate verification dialog that requires administrative authentication to bypass. Again, the system saves this information to the system keychain by default.

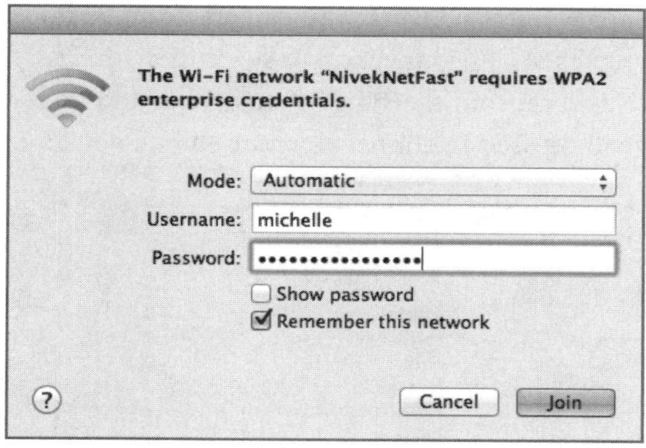

Wi-Fi Status Menu Options

In some cases, to increase security, wireless networks may not advertise their availability. You can connect to these hidden wireless networks (also called closed networks) as long as you know their network name (or Service Set Identifier, aka SSID) by choosing Join Other Network from the Wi-Fi status menu. In the dialog you can enter all the appropriate information to join the hidden wireless network.

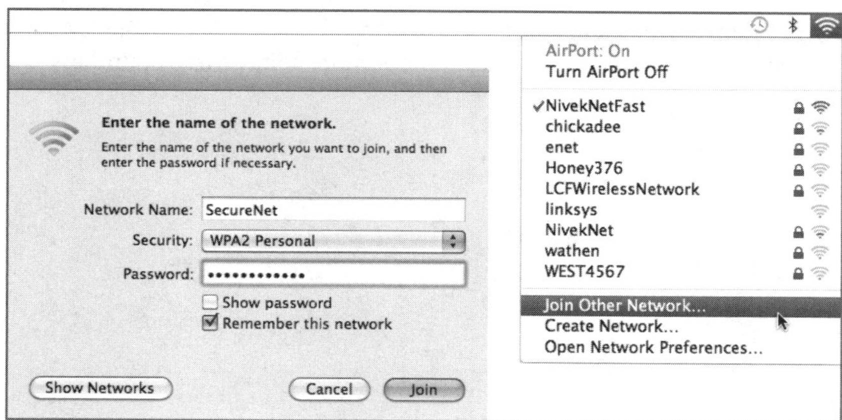

If you are unable to connect to a standard wireless network, you can create an ad hoc wireless network using your Mac computer's Wi-Fi connection to share files wirelessly with other computers. Choose Create Network from the Wi-Fi status menu and then enter the wireless network information that will be used to connect to your ad hoc network.

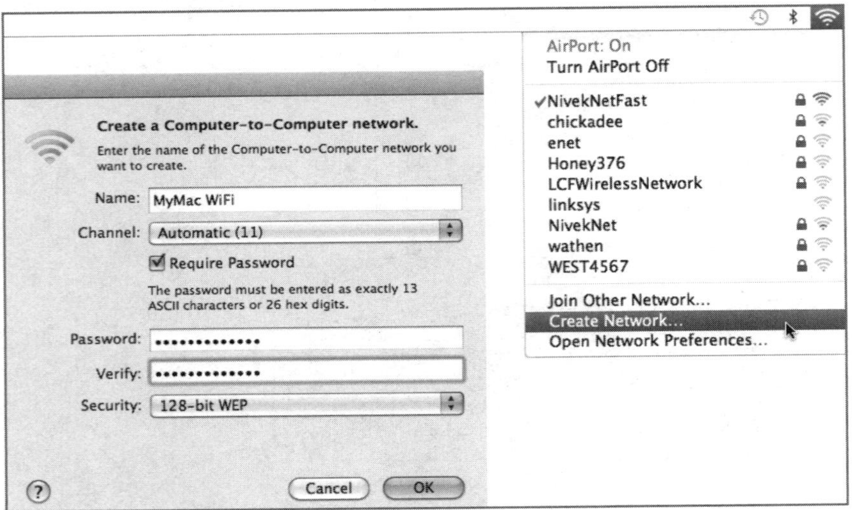

NOTE ▶ Leaving an ad hoc network enabled on your Mac is a security risk. To disable the ad hoc network, turn off the Wi-Fi hardware or choose another wireless network from the Wi-Fi status menu.

NOTE ▶ Do not confuse the creation of an ad hoc Wi-Fi network with the new OS X AirDrop Wi-Fi sharing feature. Creating a Wi-Fi network has permanence, and it can be used by other non–OS X systems, while AirDrop allows for only temporary connections between OS X systems. You can find out more about AirDrop in Lesson 26, "Host Sharing and Personal Firewall."

Exercise 22.1
Connect to a Wi-Fi Network

Prerequisites

- You must have created the Local Admin (Exercise 3.1 or 3.2) and Chris Johnson (Exercise 6.1) accounts.
- Your computer must have a Wi-Fi interface, and you must have access to an available Wi-Fi network that you are not already connected to.

OS X makes joining a wireless network simple. In this exercise, you will examine the process of finding and joining a wireless network.

Verify Your Network Settings

1. If necessary, log in as Chris Johnson.
2. Open System Preferences, and select the Network preference pane.
3. If necessary, click the padlock, and authenticate as Local Admin.
4. Select the Wi-Fi service from the sidebar. If you do not have Wi-Fi service, you cannot perform this exercise.
5. If necessary, click the Turn Wi-Fi On button.
6. If necessary, select "Show Wi-Fi status in menu bar."
7. Click Advanced.
8. Examine the options available under the Wi-Fi tab.

   The Preferred Networks list allows you to control which networks this computer joins automatically, and has an option to add networks to this list as your computer joins them. You can also control whether admin authorization is required for certain operations.

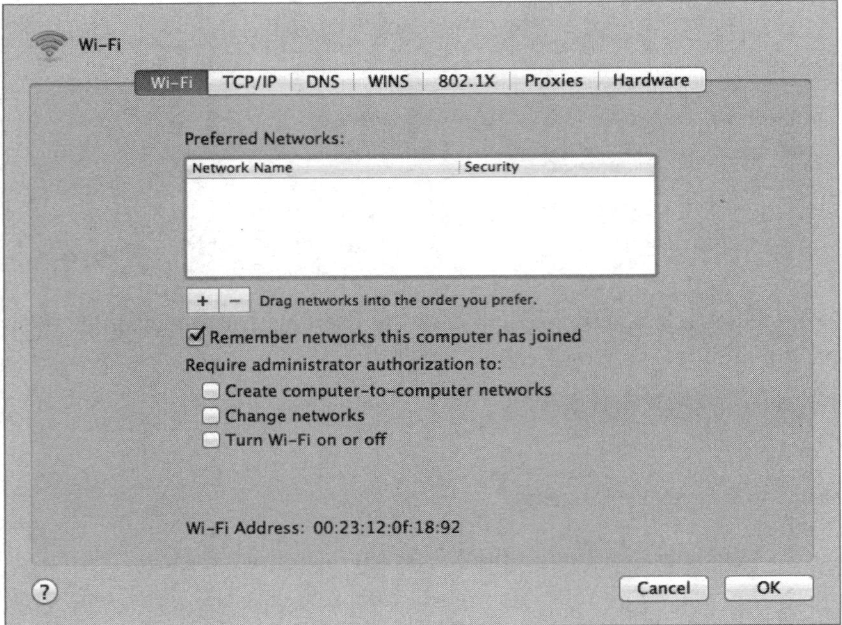

9 Click OK.

10 If you made any changes, click Apply.

11 Click the Wi-Fi status menu.

A list of visible networks in your area is shown. Note that it may take a few seconds for your computer to discover all the local networks.

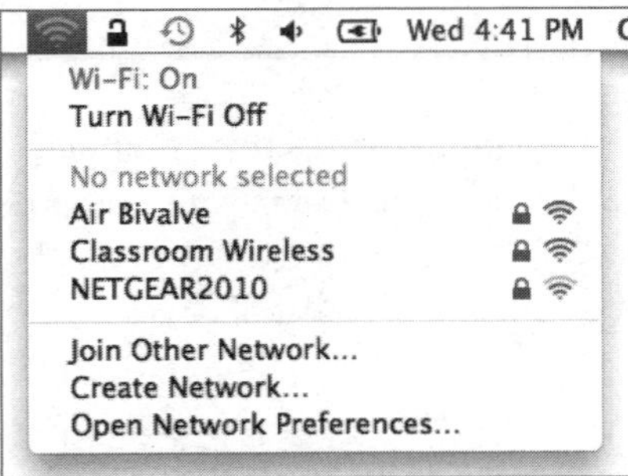

Also, note that this list is also available in Network preferences, in the Network Name pop-up menu.

If you are performing these exercises in a class, the instructor provides you with the name of the network to join (and if necessary, security information for it).

If the network you want to join is shown in the list, follow the section "Join a Visible Network." If it is not shown, the network may be configured as invisible (or "SSID broadcast disabled"), in which case you need to follow the section "Join an Invisible Network."

Option 1: Join a Visible Network

1 Choose the network you want to join from the Wi-Fi status menu.

If the wireless network is encrypted, you are prompted for the network password. Selecting the "Remember this network" option allows your computer to automatically reconnect to this network whenever it is available.

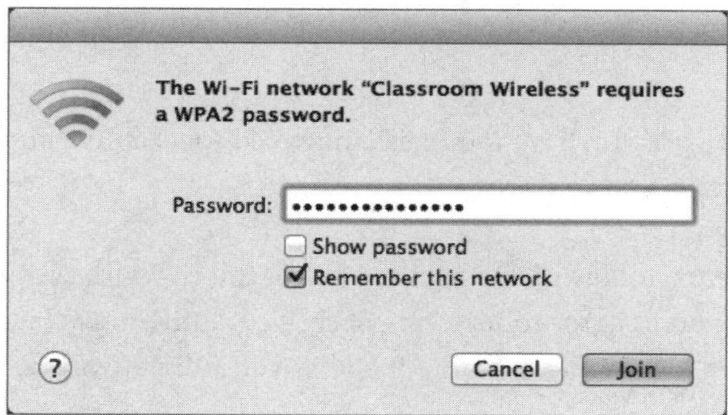

2 If you are prompted to, enter the network password and click Join.

Skip ahead to the "Verify Your Connection" section.

Option 2: Join an Invisible Network

1 Choose Join Other Network from the Wi-Fi status menu.

2 Enter the network's name (SSID).

3 If the network is encrypted, you need to know its encryption type as well as the password. Choose the encryption type from the Security pop-up menu, and then enter the

network password. Selecting the "Remember this network" option allows your computer to automatically reconnect to this network whenever it is available.

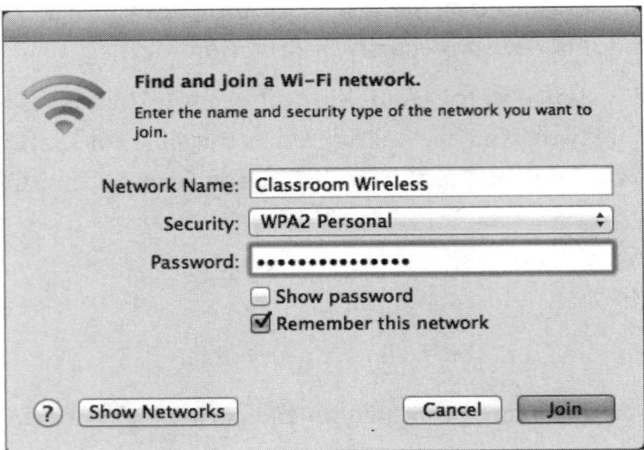

4 Enter the security information, and click Join.

Verify Your Connection

If OS X detects that the wireless network you have joined is connected to a captive portal, it opens a window showing the portal's sign-in page.

1 If a captive portal window appears, follow its instructions to get full network access.
A captive portal might require you to agree to its terms of service, authenticate, watch an advertisement, or meet other requirements before it allows you full network access.

2 In the Network preferences, check the status indicator next to the Wi-Fi service.

The status indicator will be green if the computer is connected to a network and has address information configured. If the indicator is not green, you did not successfully join the network and may have to troubleshoot the connection.

3 Click the Wi-Fi status menu.

It shows a number of arcs to indicate the signal strength of the wireless network. If all the arcs are light gray, you are not joined to a wireless network or are receiving only a very weak signal.

4 Option-click the Wi-Fi status menu.

The menu opens and displays additional information about your connection, including the current wireless speed ("Transmit rate") and signal strength (RSSI; note that –50 is a very strong signal, while –100 is a very weak one).

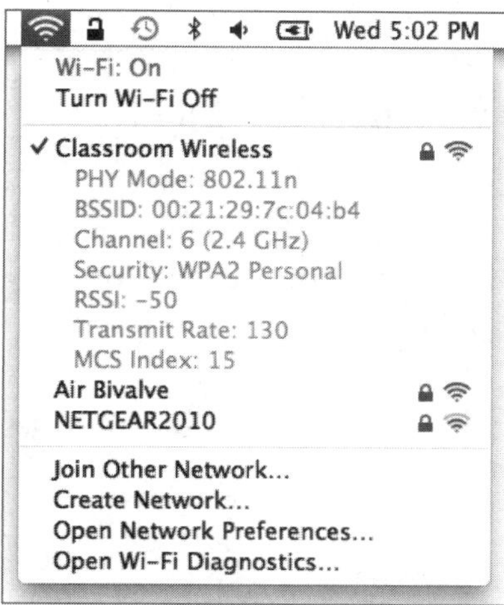

Exercise 22.2
Monitor Network Connectivity

Prerequisites

- You must have created the Chris Johnson account (Exercise 6.1).

In this exercise you will break your primary network connection and observe how that change is reflected in the Network pane of System Preferences. The Network pane dynamically updates as network connectivity changes, so it is a valuable tool for troubleshooting connectivity issues.

Monitor Connectivity via Network Preferences

The Network Status view of Network preferences shows the status of all active configured network interfaces. User-initiated connections like PPP and VPN are also listed. Users can view the Network Status pane to verify their active connections in order of priority.

1. If necessary, log in as Chris Johnson.

2. If necessary, open System Preferences and select the Network preference pane.

   Notice the status of your network connections on the left side of the window. The green status indicators show which network service(s) are active, and their order shows their priority. Whichever service is at the top of the list is your current "primary" service, and it is used for all Internet connectivity. Make a note of which service is currently the primary service.

   If you do not have any services with green status indicators, you do not have a network connection and cannot perform this exercise.

3. Select the current primary service.

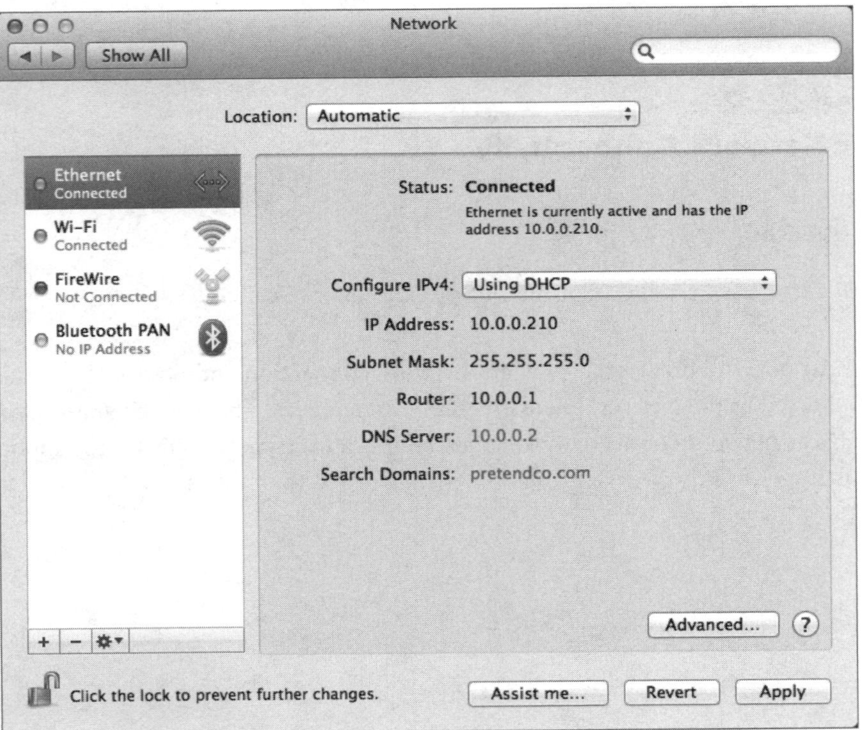

4 Watch the status indicators and service order as you disable the connection for your primary network service. How to do this depends on what type of service it is:

- If it is an Ethernet service, unplug the Ethernet connector from your computer.
- If it is a Wi-Fi service, click the Turn Wi-Fi Off button.
- If it is a dial-in or mobile broadband service, click the Disconnect button.

When the service is disabled, its status indicator turns red or yellow, and it drops down in the service order. If you had another active service, it becomes the new primary service.

The detailed view on the right also changes to indicate why the service is disabled.

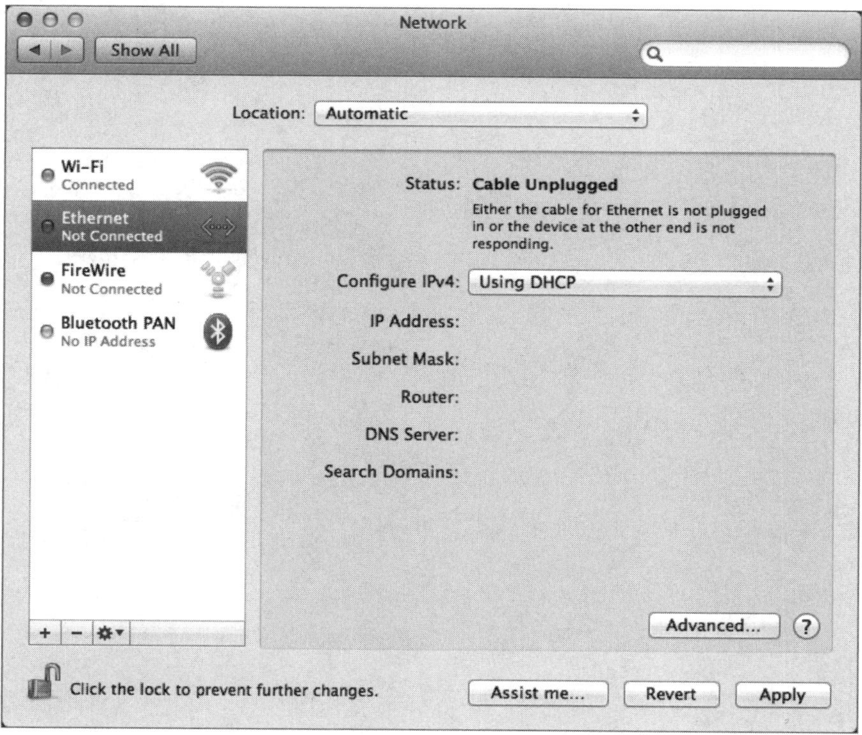

5 Again, watch the status indicators and service order as you reenable the connection. How to do this depends on what type of service it is:

- If it is an Ethernet service, plug the Ethernet connector back into your computer.

- If it is a Wi-Fi service, click the Turn Wi-Fi On button, and if necessary choose the network from the Network Name pop-up menu.
- If it is a dial-in or mobile broadband service, click the Connect button.

It may take a few seconds for the network connection to come up and the service to reconfigure itself. When the service becomes fully active, its status indicator turns green and it rises back to the top of the service list.

Lesson **23**

Advanced Network Configuration

A strong understanding of network fundamentals is required to properly configure advanced network settings without error. As such, this lesson builds on the network essentials topics covered in the previous lesson. The focus of this lesson is squarely upon the unique and powerful OS X user interface for managing network configuration, the Network preferences. First, this lesson presents an overview of the OS X network configuration architecture and supported network interfaces and protocols. You will then dive deeper into the more advanced network configuration options.

GOALS

- Understand the OS X network configuration architecture
- Manage multiple network locations and service interfaces
- Configure advanced network settings

Reference 23.1 Network Locations

Similar to how applications are designed to save information to any number of individual documents, OS X allows you to save network settings to any number of individual network configurations known as network locations. A network location contains all network interface, service, and protocol settings, allowing you to configure as many unique network locations as you need for different situations. For example, you could create one network location for home and a different one for work. Each location would contain all the appropriate settings for that location's network state.

A network location can contain any number of active network service interfaces. This allows you to define a single location with multiple network connections. The system automatically prioritizes multiple service interfaces based on a service order that you set. Details about using multiple network service interfaces are covered in the "Multiple Simultaneous Interfaces" section later in this lesson.

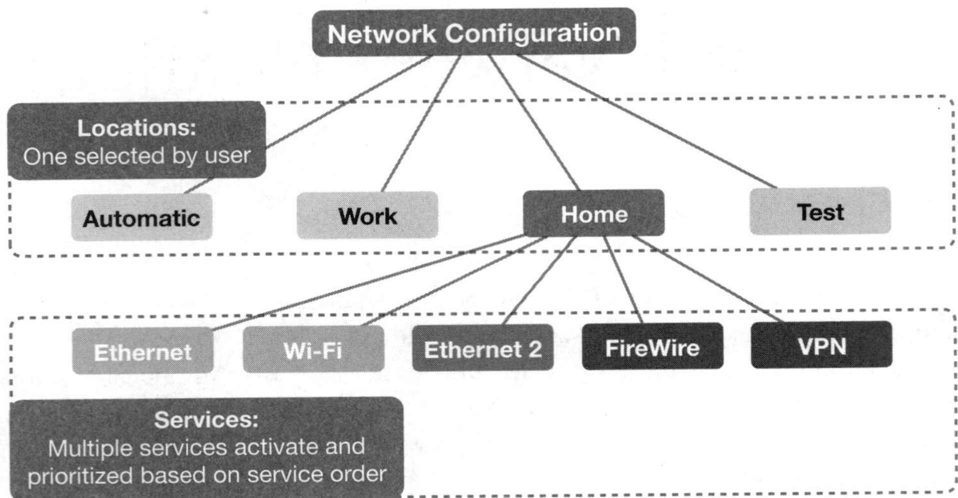

It is not necessary to add new network locations to change network settings, but it is more convenient as you can easily switch back to the previous network location should you make a mistake. Thus, creating additional network locations is an essential network troubleshooting technique. Also, because OS X always requires one active network location, if you ever want to temporarily turn off networking, you have to create a new location with all the network service interfaces disabled.

Configuring Network Locations

The default network location on OS X is called Automatic. Despite this, this first location is no more automatic than any other network location you create. The initial location is simply called Automatic to indicate that it attempts to automatically initialize any network service interface to establish a TCP/IP connection via DHCP, but all network locations regardless of their name attempt this as well.

To configure network locations, open the Network preferences by choosing Apple menu > System Preferences, and then clicking the Network icon. You may have to click the lock icon in the bottom-left corner and authenticate as an administrative user to unlock the Network preferences. Choose Edit Locations from the Location pop-up menu to reveal the interface for editing network locations.

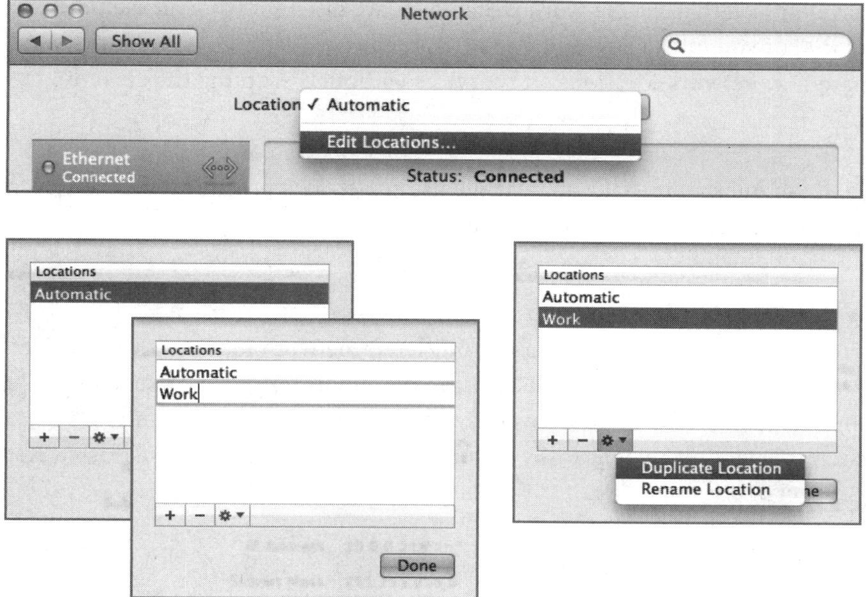

To add a new location with default settings, click the Add (+) button, and then enter a new name for the location. Or, you can duplicate an existing location by selecting its name from the locations list and clicking the Action (gear icon) button, and then choosing Duplicate Location from the pop-up menu. Finally, double-clicking a location name allows you to rename it.

When you are finished making location changes, click Done to return to the Network preferences. The Network preferences automatically load the newly created location but won't apply the location settings to the system. If you want to work with another location, simply choose it from the Location pop-up menu, and the Network preferences load it but won't apply it to the system.

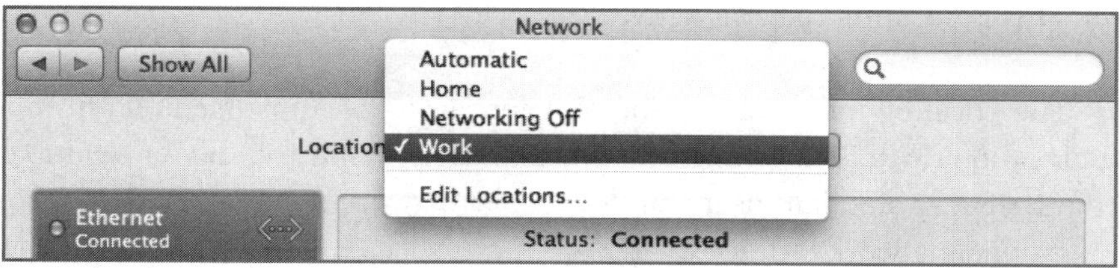

You may have noticed that the Network preferences are different from all the other system preferences in that you must click Apply to activate the new settings. This allows you to easily prepare new network locations and services without disrupting the current network configuration.

> **TIP** If you make a mistake at any time using Network preferences, click Revert to return to the current active network configuration.

Changing Network Locations

Though you can certainly choose and apply a different network location from the Network preferences, only administrative users have this ability, as normal users do not have access to the Network preferences. Conversely, all users who can log in to the OS X graphical user interface can quickly and easily change the network location by choosing Apple menu > Location > *location name.*

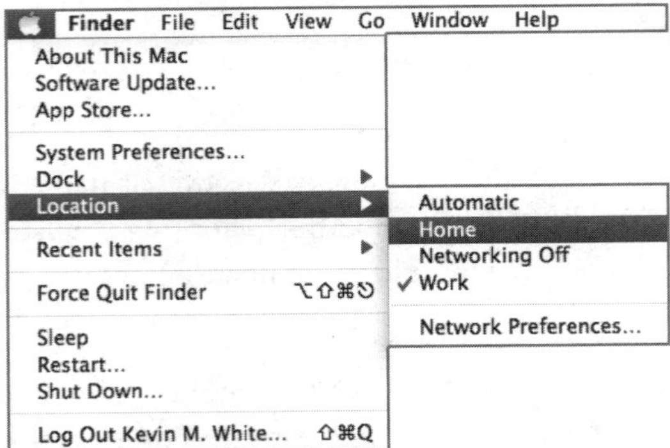

This applies the selected network location. Keep in mind that changing locations may interrupt network connections. Once a network location is selected, it remains active until another location is selected. Even as other users log in to the Mac, or the Mac is restarted, the selected network location remains active.

> **NOTE ▸** The Location menu option does not appear in the Apple menu if only one network location exists. Thus, from an administrative perspective, if you want to configure the system so standard users cannot change network preferences, do not configure additional network locations.

Reference 23.2
Network Interfaces and Protocols

Mac hardware has a long history of providing built-in network connectivity. Apple started including Ethernet on Macs as early as 1991 and was the first manufacturer to have wireless as a built-in option when it introduced the iBook in 1999. Mac models have varied over the years as network technologies have grown increasingly faster and more affordable.

Network Hardware Interfaces

You can identify the hardware network service interfaces available to your Mac from the /Applications/Utilities/System Information or /Applications/Utilities/Network Utility applications. Many of these interfaces automatically appear as a network service in the Network preferences.

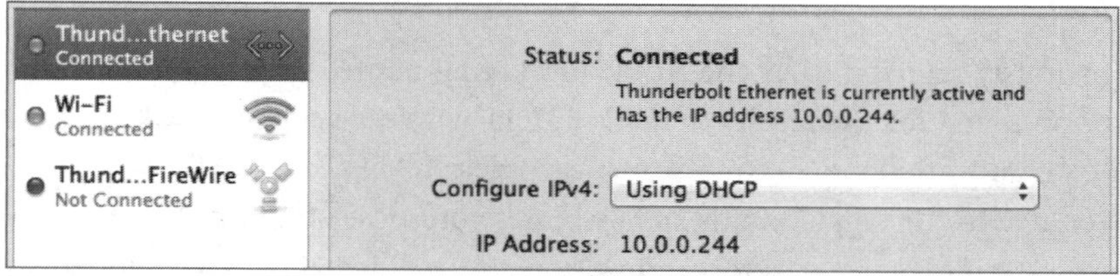

NOTE ▶ The newest hardware interface on Mac systems is Thunderbolt. While not a network interface, Thunderbolt adapters allow for connectivity to other hardware interfaces that do support networking. For example, Apple offers a Thunderbolt to Ethernet adapter and a Thunderbolt to FireWire adapter.

OS X includes built-in support for the following hardware network interfaces:

- Bluetooth—This relatively low-speed wireless interface has become popular as a short-range connectivity standard. Every recent Mac that includes Wi-Fi support also includes Bluetooth. OS X supports Bluetooth as a network bridge to some cellular phones and hotspots, like iPhones, that can provide Internet connectivity via a cellular network.
- Ethernet—Ethernet is the family of IEEE 802.3 standards that define most modern wired LANs. Every Mac desktop since 1997 has included standard built-in Ethernet connectivity, with some models even featuring multiple Ethernet interfaces. Until

recently most Mac portables also included standard built-in Ethernet connectivity. However, with the prevalence of Wi-Fi networks, and the popularity of smaller portable devices, recent Mac portables are dropping standard Ethernet connectivity. For these systems Apple offers an optional USB to Ethernet (100baseT) adapter or Thunderbolt to Gigabit Ethernet adapter.

- FireWire—FireWire is the Apple marketing name for the IEEE 1394 connection standard. Though not a common network standard, OS X includes software that allows you to create small ad hoc networks using daisy-chained FireWire cables. FireWire is standard on many Mac models.
- USB—While not technically a network connectivity standard, OS X supports a variety of USB adapters that provide Internet access via cellular networks. Also, many modern phones feature a "tethering" service that provides Internet access via a USB connection to the phone. The iPhone is an example of a device that offers tethering connectivity.
- Wi-Fi—Previously referred to by the Apple marketing name AirPort, Wi-Fi is the more common name for the family of IEEE 802.11 wireless standards, which have become the default implementation for most wireless LANs. The AirPort name is still used in reference to the Apple family of Wi-Fi network base stations, AirPort Express and AirPort Extreme. Every desktop and portable Mac since 2006 has included standard built-in Wi-Fi connectivity. Wi-Fi remains an option for the Mac Pro as well.

Cellular Internet Connections

Internet access via cellular networks is nothing new, but in the last few years this type of connectivity has seen a huge growth in popularity. With most major carriers offering ever-faster near-broadband speeds and expanded geographical coverage, many are relying on cellular networks as their primary Internet access. As such, a variety of devices and methods are available for providing cellular Internet access for your Mac computer.

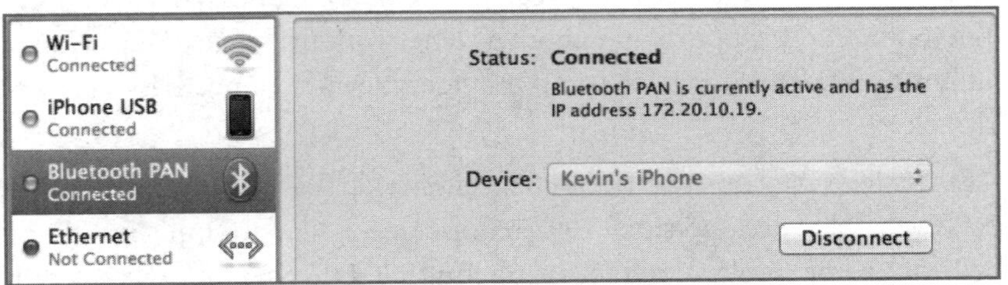

NOTE ▶ The capabilities and configuration of cellular devices vary greatly. Check with your cellular device vendor regarding how to enable Internet access for your specific device.

OS X supports use of cellular Internet connections via:

- Bluetooth personal area network (PAN)—Modern cellular devices allow for Internet connectivity by acting as a small router providing a PAN available via Bluetooth wireless. For example, an iPhone can provide Internet access via Bluetooth PAN. As with any Bluetooth device, you must first pair your Mac with the mobile device as covered in Lesson 27, "Peripherals and Drivers." Once paired, configuration should be automatic, as the Mac should configure TCP/IP using DHCP hosted from the cellular device. You have to initiate the connection by clicking the Connect button in Network preferences or by choosing the device and "Connect to Network" in the Bluetooth status menu.
- USB cellular network adapters—Again, USB is not technically a network connectivity standard, but OS X supports a variety of USB adapters and tethered phones that provide cellular Internet access. The iPhone is an example of such a device, and in typical Apple fashion all configuration on the Mac is automatic. If tethering is available on your cell phone data plan, simply plug an iPhone in via the USB adapter cable, and then on the iPhone turn on the Personal Hotspot feature. Conversely, third-party cellular Internet devices vary, and many require the installation and configuration of third-party drivers.
- Wi-Fi personal area network—In a move to simplify the connection and configuration of cellular Internet devices, many can act as a small Wi-Fi router. Thus, any device that supports Wi-Fi can connect to the cellular device without any special software. On the Mac, simply select the Wi-Fi network the cellular device is hosting and provide authentication if necessary. Inspecting the Wi-Fi connection in Network preferences reveals that the cellular Internet device appears identical to a traditional Wi-Fi router. Again, an iPhone can provide cellular Internet access via Wi-Fi.

Virtual Network Services

A virtual network service is a logical network within a hardware network interface. Think of a virtual network service as providing another unique network interface by carving out a section of an established network connection.

Some virtual network services are used to increase security by encrypting data before it travels across an IP network, and others are used to segregate or aggregate network traffic across LAN connections. OS X includes the necessary client software that allows you to connect to many common virtual network services and establish a virtual network service interface.

If necessary, you can define multiple separate virtual network service interfaces for each network location. Virtual network service interfaces are not always tied to a specific physical network interface, as the system attempts to seek out the most appropriate route when there are multiple active connections. Likewise, any virtual network service interface that is not destined for a LAN connection is always routed to the primary active network service interface.

NOTE ▸ Third-party virtualization tools, like Parallels Desktop and VMware Fusion, also use virtual network interfaces to provide networking for multiple simultaneous operating systems.

OS X includes built-in support for the following virtual network services:

- Point-to-Point Protocol over Ethernet (PPPoE)—Used by some service providers for directly connecting your Mac to a modem providing a high-speed Digital Subscriber Line (DSL) Internet connection.
- Virtual private network (VPN)—By far the most commonly used virtual network service, VPNs are primarily used to create secure virtual connections to private LANs over the Internet.
- Virtual local area network (VLAN)—The OS X VLAN implementation allows you to define separate independent LAN services on a single physical network interface.
- Link aggregate—Allows you to define a single virtual LAN service using multiple physical network interfaces.
- 6 to 4—Creates a VPN of sorts to transfer IPv6 packets across an IPv4 network. There is no enhanced security when using a 6 to 4 connection, but your Mac will appear to be directly connected to a remote IPv6 LAN. The differences between IPv4 and IPv6 were covered earlier in this lesson.

Network Protocols

Each network service interface provides connectivity for a number of standard networking protocols. The Network preferences show primary protocol settings whenever you select a service from the services list, but many protocol configuration options are only available by clicking the Advanced button.

NOTE ▶ AppleTalk is not supported on OS X v10.6 or later.

OS X includes built-in support for the following network protocols:

- TCP/IP configured via DHCP—As explained previously in this lesson, TCP/IP is the primary network protocol for LANs and WANs, and DHCP is a popular network service that automatically configures TCP/IP clients.
- TCP/IP configured manually—If you do not have DHCP service on your local network or if you want to ensure that the TCP/IP settings never change, you can manually configure TCP/IP settings.
- DNS—As covered previously, DNS provides host names for IP network devices. DNS settings are often configured alongside TCP/IP settings either by DHCP or manual configuration. OS X supports multiple DNS servers and search domains.
- Wireless Ethernet (Wi-Fi) protocol options—The wireless nature of Wi-Fi often requires additional configuration to facilitate network selection and authentication.
- Authenticated Ethernet via 802.1X—The 802.1X protocol is used to secure Ethernet networks (both wired and Wi-Fi) by allowing only properly authenticated network clients to join the LAN.
- Network Basic Input/Output System (NetBIOS) and Windows Internet Naming Service (WINS)—NetBIOS and WINS are protocols most often used by older Windows-based computers to provide network identification and service discovery.
- IP proxies—Proxy servers act as intermediaries between a network client and a requested service and are used to enhance performance or provide an additional layer of security and content filtering.
- Ethernet hardware options—OS X supports both automatic and manual Ethernet hardware configuration, as covered later in this lesson.
- External (analog) modem with PPP—For many years this was the only method for accomplishing any sort of digital computer-based communication. OS X still supports this, though the rarity of analog modems in the age of broadband Internet has put an end to coverage of analog modem configuration in this guide.
- Point-to-Point Protocol (PPP)—PPP is an older protocol originally intended for use with analog modems. Again, OS X still supports PPP for analog modems, but it also supports PPP for Bluetooth DUN, and PPPoE connectivity. Also the rarity of these protocols in the age of broadband Internet has put an end to coverage of PPP configuration in this guide.

Reference 23.3
Network Services

Typically, having multiple active network service interfaces means you will also have multiple active IP addresses. To handle multiple IP addresses, OS X also features IP network multihoming. In fact, OS X supports multiple IP addresses for each physical network interface. Thus, the network service list can contain multiple instances of the same physical network interface. Again, a "network service" in this context is a single configuration of a physical network interface.

Multiple Simultaneous Interfaces

OS X supports a multilink networking architecture, which means that OS X supports multiple simultaneous network service interfaces. For example, you can have both an active wired Ethernet connection and an active Wi-Fi, or wireless Ethernet, connection at the same time. In other words, you can configure as many separate network service interfaces with as many unique IP addresses as you need. This may seem like overkill for most Mac clients, but remember OS X and OS X Server share the same underlying network architecture.

For some servers, multilink multihoming networking is a requirement, but Mac clients can also benefit from this technology. You may have a work environment where you have one insecure network for general Internet traffic and another network for secure internal transactions. With OS X, you can be on both of these networks at the same time. However, the first fully configured active service in the list is the primary network service interface.

In most cases the primary network service interface is used for all WAN connectivity, Internet connectivity, and DNS host name resolution. The exception to this is if the primary network interface is lacking a router configuration. In this case, the system treats the next fully configured active service as the primary network service interface.

When multiple IP addresses are available, the system can communicate via any of those network service interfaces but will attempt to pick the most appropriate route for every network connection. As described in the previous lesson, a network client uses the subnet mask to determine if an outgoing transmission is on the LAN. OS X takes this a step further by examining all active LANs when determining a destination for outgoing transmission. Because a LAN connection is always faster than a WAN connection, OS X always routes outgoing transmissions to the most appropriate LAN.

Any network connections that are not destined for a LAN that your Mac is connected to are sent to the router address of the primary active network service interface, which should be the topmost service listed in Network preferences. Again, in most cases this means the primary active network service interface is responsible for all WAN connections, Internet connections, and DNS host name resolution. Any active network service interface with a valid TCP/IP setting is considered, but the primary active network service interface is automatically selected based on the network service order. You can manually configure the network service order, as outlined later in this lesson.

Using the previous example where you have a Mac active on both wired Ethernet and Wi-Fi, the default network service order prioritizes wired Ethernet over Wi-Fi because wired is almost always faster. Thus, in this example, even though you have two active valid network service interfaces, the primary active network service interface is the wired Ethernet connection.

NOTE ▶ OS X features automatic source routing. This means incoming connections to your Mac over a specific network service interface are always responded to on the same interface, regardless of the service order.

Network Services List

Every time you open the Network preferences, the system identifies all available network service interfaces. Even if a physical network interface is not connected or properly configured, it creates a configuration for that interface, which shows up in the network services list. In the Network preferences, each network interface is tied to one or more network services.

A quick glance at the network services list clearly shows the status of all network interfaces and their configured services. Network services with a red indicator are not connected, a yellow indicator shows services that are connected but not properly configured, and a green indicator shows connected and configured network services.

The active service at the top of this list is the primary network service interface as defined by the network service order. This list updates dynamically as new services become active or as active services become disconnected, so it's always the first place to check when attempting to troubleshoot a network issue.

Manage Network Services

To manage network interfaces and their configured services, open and if necessary, unlock the Network preferences. First, make sure the network location you want to edit from the Location pop-up menu is selected, or configure a new network location, as detailed previously in this lesson. To configure a particular network service, simply select it from the network services list.

Remember, each network service has its own settings separate from the other services. The configuration area to the right of the list changes to reflect primary options available to the selected service. Clicking Advanced reveals all the advanced network protocol options available to the selected network service. Advanced network configuration is covered later in this lesson.

NOTE ▶ The following screenshot shows a system connected to the Apple Thunderbolt to Ethernet adapter and Thunderbolt to FireWire adapter. Unfortunately, the Network preference truncates the interface names in an awkward manner.

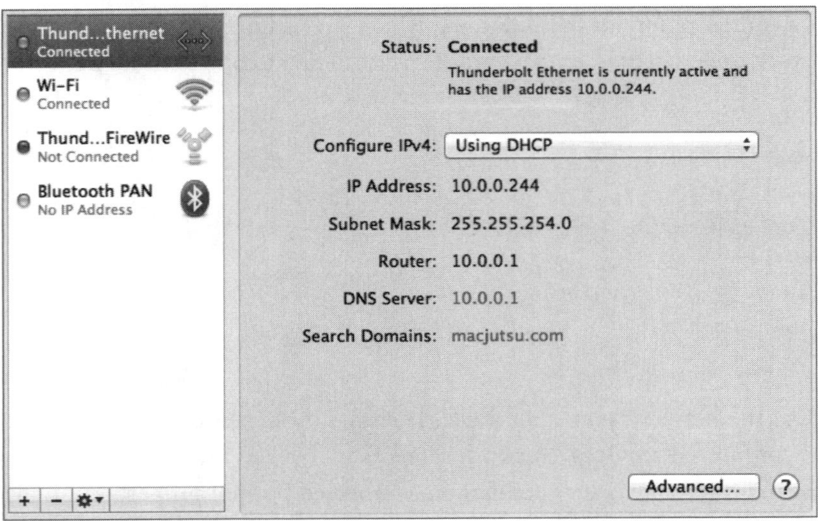

To create another configurable instance of a network interface, click the Add (+) button at the bottom of the network services list. This reveals a dialog that allows you to choose a new interface instance from the pop-up menu and then assign it a unique service name to identify it in the services list. Creating additional instances of a network service allows you to assign multiple IP addresses to a single network interface.

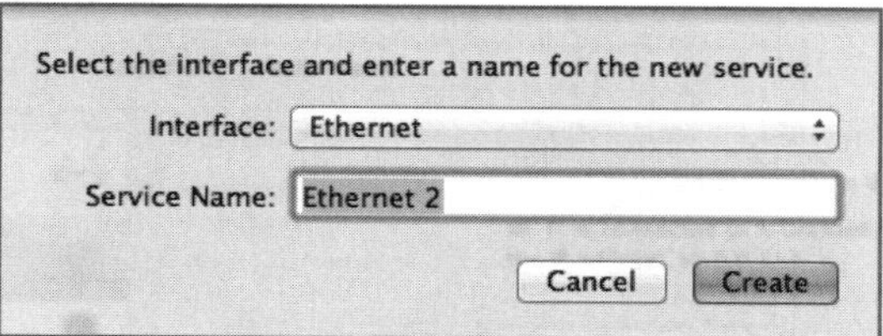

To make a service inactive, select it from the services list, click the Action (gear icon) button, and then choose Make Service Inactive from the pop-up menu. An inactive service never activates, even if connected and properly configured. You can also delete an existing network service by selecting its name from the services list and then clicking the Delete (–) button at the bottom of the list. Deactivating or deleting a network service from this list is the only way to disable a hardware network interface in OS X.

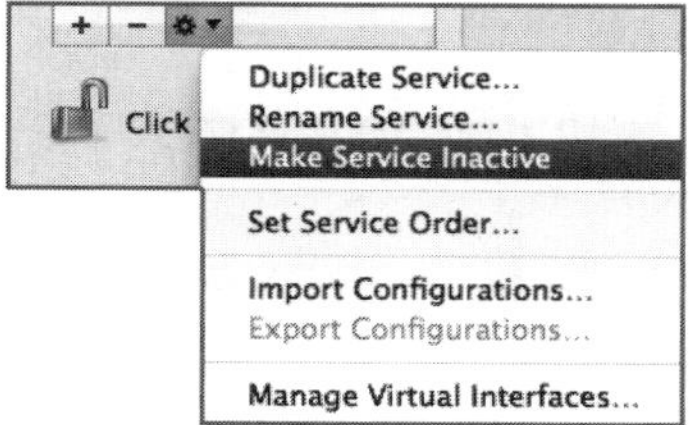

NOTE ▶ You are not allowed to delete network service interfaces configured as part of a configuration profile. To delete these network services, you must delete their associated configuration profile from the Profiles system preference.

Clicking the Action (gear) button at the bottom of the network services list reveals a pop-up menu with several management options. For example, you can duplicate an existing network service by selecting its name from the services list, and then choosing Duplicate Service from the pop-up menu. Using this menu, you can also rename an existing network service. Finally, you can modify the active network service interface order by choosing Set Service Order from the pop-up menu.

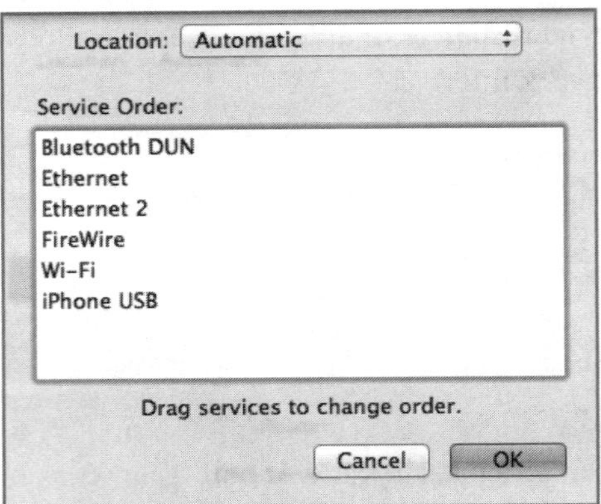

The service order dialog allows you to click and drag network services into your preferred order for selection as the primary network interface. Click OK when you have finished reordering, and the system automatically reevaluates the active network service interfaces based on the new order. Also, don't forget that you must also click Apply in Network preferences to activate and save all the changes to the currently selected network location.

TIP If you make a mistake at any time using the Network preferences, click Revert to return to the currently active network configuration.

Reference 23.4
VPN Configuration

A VPN is an encrypted tunnel from your client to the network routing device providing the VPN service. Once it is established, your Mac will appear to have a direct connection to the LAN that the VPN device is sharing. So even if you're on a wireless Internet connection thousands of miles away from your LAN, a VPN connection provides a virtual network interface as if your computer were directly attached to that LAN. OS X supports three common VPN protocols: the Layer 2 Tunneling Protocol over Internet Protocol Security (L2TP over IPSec), Point-to-Point Tunneling Protocol (PPTP), and Cisco's version of IPSec.

NOTE ► Some VPN services require a third-party VPN client. Third-party VPN clients usually include a custom interface for managing the connection. Although you may see the virtual network interface provided by the third-party VPN client appear in the Network preferences, it's usually not configurable from there.

VPN Configuration Profile

By far the easiest method for managing VPN configuration is to do so via a configuration profile. As detailed in Lesson 3, "Setup and Configuration," a configuration profile is a document that contains instructions for specific settings. The administrator of a VPN system can provide a VPN profile that a user need only double-click to configure all the relevant settings.

Installed configuration profiles can be verified from the Profiles preference. Once a configuration profile is installed, all the appropriate VPN settings should be configured for you. To establish the VPN tunnel, a user need only initiate the VPN connection, as covered in the "Establish VPN Connection" section later in this lesson.

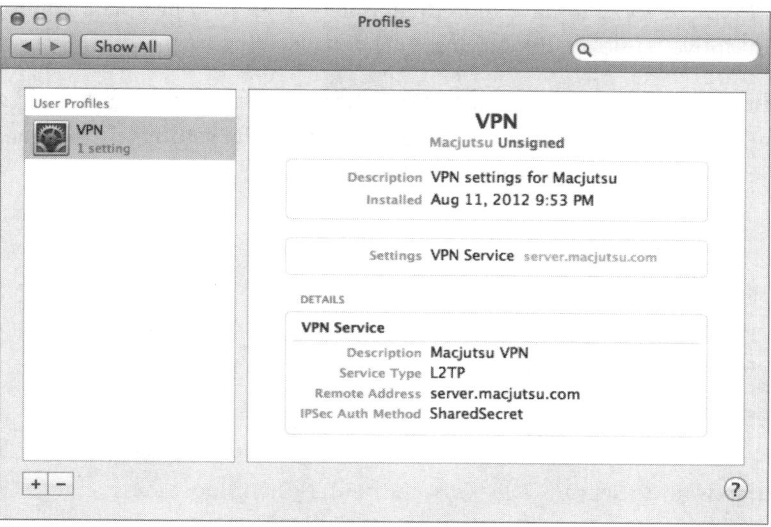

Manual VPN Configuration

Even with a VPN configuration profile, you may find it necessary to verify or further manage VPN connections from the Network preferences. Or if the administrator of the

VPN service is unable to provide a configuration profile, you need to manually configure VPN services. To add a VPN interface, click the Add (+) button at the bottom of the network services list in the Network preferences. This reveals a dialog that allows you to add a new network service interface.

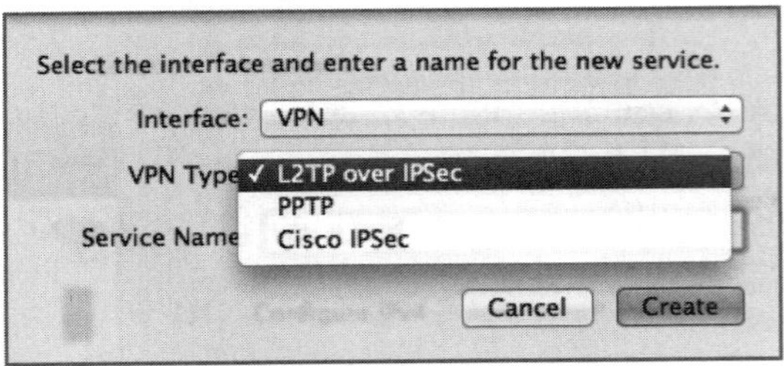

From the new network service interface dialog you must choose the appropriate VPN protocol from the VPN Type pop-up menu. Again, OS X supports the L2TP over IPSec, PPTP, and Cisco IPSec VPN protocols. All three have similar configuration options, but for the purposes of this lesson L2TP is used because it has a few more authentication and advanced options. If you're going to have more than one type of VPN protocol, you may want to enter a descriptive name for the service.

Once you create the new VPN interface, select it from the network services list, and basic VPN configuration settings appear to the right. To configure VPN settings, first enter the VPN server address and if you use user-based authentication, an account name.

TIP If you do want to set multiple VPN configurations, choose Add Configuration from the Configuration pop-up menu. In the dialog you can name and create a new VPN configuration. You can also delete and rename your configuration from this pop-up menu.

You must also define authentication methods by clicking the Authentication Settings button, and then specifying user and computer authentication settings. The VPN administrator can provide you with the appropriate authentication settings. Supplying a password here adds it to the system keychain. If the field is left blank, the user is prompted for the password when connecting.

To configure advanced VPN settings, click the Advanced button in the Network preferences. In the advanced settings dialog, click the Options tab to view general VPN options. The most important optional setting is to send all traffic over the VPN connection. By default, active VPN connections do not move to the top of the network service list. Thus, the system only routes traffic to the VPN service if the destination IP address is part of the LAN that the VPN service is providing or the VPN server supplies special routing information.

NOTE ► The built-in Cisco IPSec client does not feature any advanced options or VPN on demand settings.

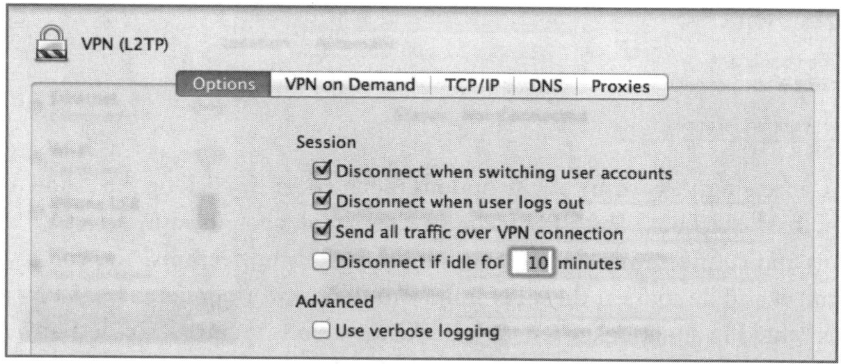

If you are using certificate-based VPN authentication, you can enable automatic VPN connections by clicking the "VPN on Demand" tab. The options on this tab allow you to assign domains that, when accessed, automatically activate specific VPN configurations.

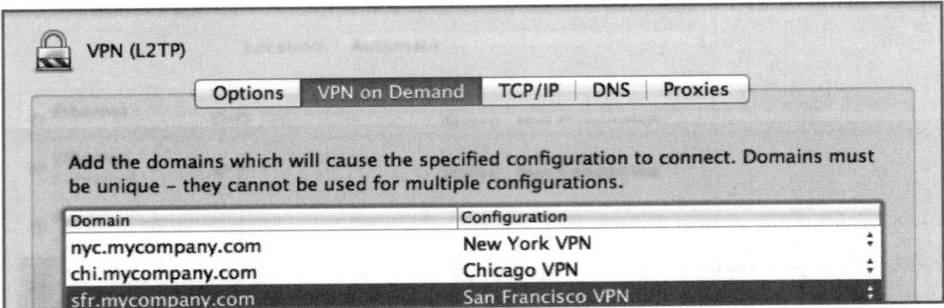

Click the Add (+) button at the bottom of the list to add a domain and an associated VPN configuration. Double-click a domain name to change it, and click once on the VPN configuration name to choose an alternate configuration from the pop-up menu. When you have finished, click OK to save the "VPN on Demand" settings. Also, don't forget to click Apply in Network preferences to save and activate the changes.

Establish VPN Connection

VPN connections are not typically always-on connections. As you saw in the instructions, OS X supports automatic VPN connections with the "VPN on Demand" feature, but many users may still manually enable VPN connections when necessary.

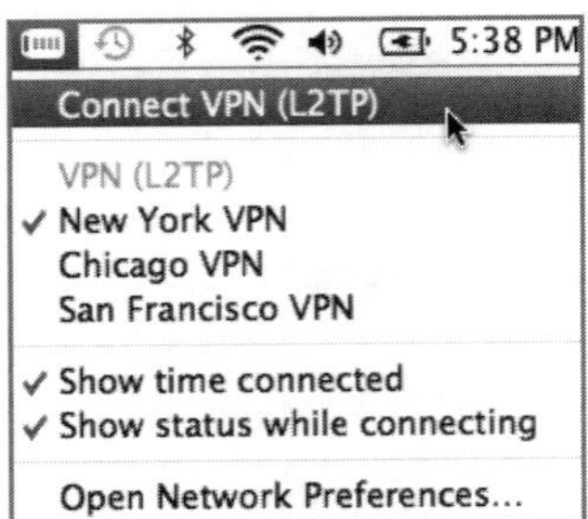

You can make accessing VPN connectivity options much easier by clicking the "Show VPN status in menu bar" checkbox. The VPN menu bar item allows you to easily select VPN configurations and connect, disconnect, and monitor VPN connections. You can also manually connect and disconnect the VPN link from the Network preferences. VPNs are usually implemented in situations where user authentication is required, so for many, initiating a VPN connection prompts an authentication dialog.

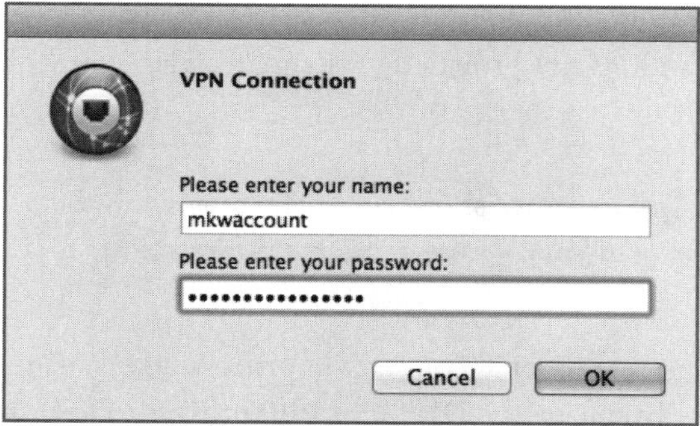

Once the connection is authenticated and established, the VPN process automatically configures TCP/IP and DNS settings using the PPP protocol. VPN interfaces are, by default, set at the bottom of the network service order, so they do not automatically become the primary network interface when activated. This behavior is overridden when the optional "Send all traffic over VPN connection" checkbox is enabled, as covered in the previous instructions. You can also manually reorder the network service order, as explained previously in this lesson.

TIP When troubleshooting VPN connections, it's useful to view the connection log info in /var/log/system.log. You can view the system log from the /Application/Utilities/Console application.

Reference 23.5
Advanced Network Configuration

The advanced network configuration techniques covered in this section are largely optional for many configurations. However, for those who are tasked with supporting OS X systems, it's important to have a full understanding of all the configuration choices available in the Network preferences.

Manual TCP/IP Configuration

Many network situations do not require any manual intervention to configure TCP/IP and DNS, as the DHCP or PPP services automatically acquire these settings. The default configuration for all Ethernet and Wi-Fi services is to automatically engage the DHCP process as soon as the interface becomes active. To verify TCP/IP and DNS settings for hardware or virtual Ethernet services when using the DHCP service, simply select the service from the Network preferences.

NOTE ► IPv6 addressing information is automatically detected as well, if available. However, automatic IPv6 configuration is not provided by standard DHCP or PPP services.

NOTE ► Automatically configured DNS settings show as gray text, which indicates that you can override these settings by manually entering DNS information, as covered later in this section.

Network service interfaces that may require a manual connection process, like Wi-Fi, VPN, and PPPoE interfaces, automatically engage the DHCP or PPP process to acquire TCP/IP and DNS settings. To verify TCP/IP and DNS settings when using these interfaces, select the service from the services list, and then click Advanced in Network preferences. In the advanced settings dialog, you can click the TCP/IP or DNS tabs to view their respective settings. You can also verify network settings of any other interface this way.

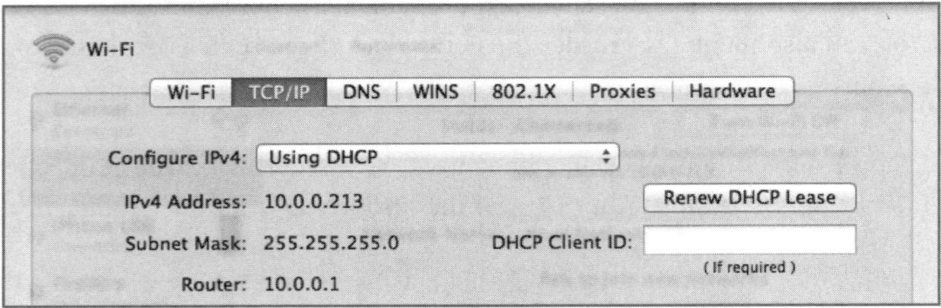

Despite the convenience of automatic TCP/IP and DNS configuration, there may be times where manual configuration is required. For example, the network server providing the DHCP service requires a manual configuration. In fact, most network devices that provide services, like servers or printers, use manually entered network configuration information so they don't run the risk of changing to a different TCP/IP address should DHCP reset.

NOTE ► In some DHCP configurations, a DHCP client ID must be set. You can access this setting by clicking Advanced and then selecting the TCP/IP tab.

If you want to keep using DHCP but manually assign just the IP address, choose "Using DHCP with manual address" from the Configure IPv4 pop-up menu. You only have to manually enter an IPv4 address for the Mac, as the rest of the TCP/IP settings remain as populated by DHCP.

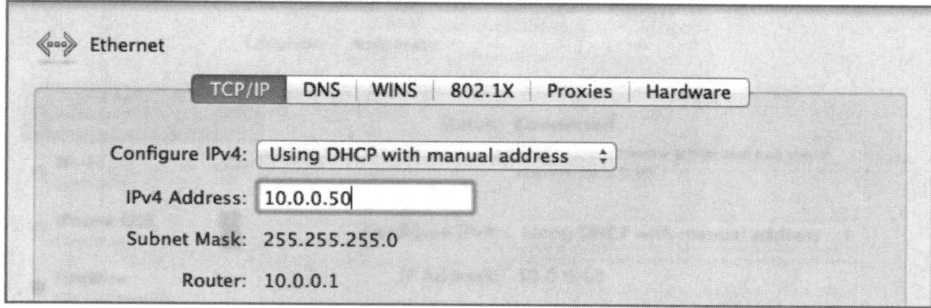

However, if you want to manually enter all TCP/IP settings, choose Manually from the Configure IPv4 pop-up menu. At a minimum you have to manually enter the IP address, the subnet mask (for this you can also use CIDR notation), and the router address. The user interface caches the TCP/IP settings from the DHCP service, so you may only have to enter a new IPv4 address.

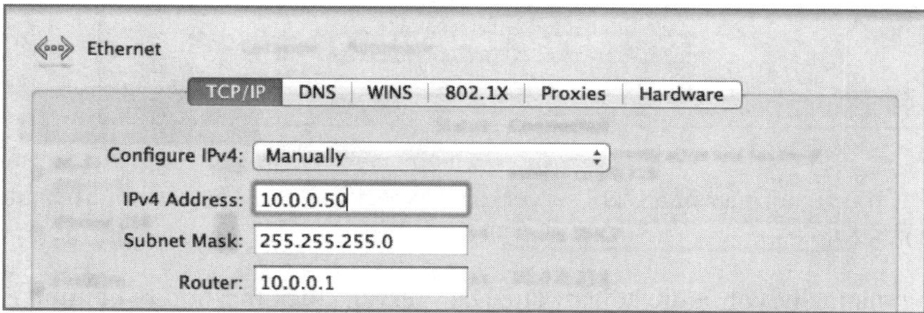

If you have to manually set up IPv6 settings as well, choose Manually from the Configure IPv6 pop-up menu. At a minimum you have to manually enter the IPv6 address, router address, and prefix length. The user interface caches any automatic IPv6 settings, so you may only have to enter a new IPv6 address.

Any time you choose to manually configure IPv4, you should also verify DNS server settings. To configure DNS, click the DNS tab to view the DNS settings. Again, the user interface caches the DNS settings from the DHCP service, so you may not have to enter any DNS settings at all.

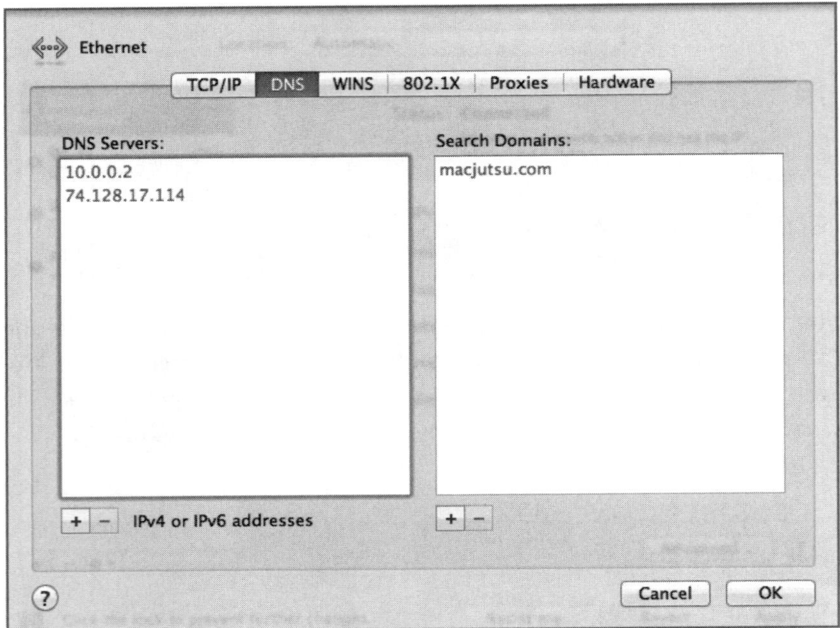

NOTE ▶ If the IP address of a DNS server is not specified, the Mac will not be able to resolve DNS host names.

If configuring manually, configure at least one DNS server. Click the Add (+) button at the bottom of the DNS server list to add a new server, and then enter the server's IP address. Entering a search domain is optional. Click the Add (+) button at the bottom of the Search Domains list, and then enter the domain name.

If you configure multiple DNS servers or search domains, the system attempts to access those resources in the order in which they appear in the list. To edit an address, double-click its entry in the list, or you can delete an entry by selecting it and clicking the Delete (–) button at the bottom of the list.

When you have entered all the appropriate IP and DNS settings, click OK to dismiss the advanced network options dialog, and then click Apply in Network preferences to save and activate the changes.

Whenever you manually configure TCP/IP or DNS settings, always test network connectivity to verify that you properly entered all information. Using standard applications to access network and Internet resources is one basic test, but you could also test more thoroughly using the included network diagnostic utilities, as covered in Lesson 24, "Network Troubleshooting."

Advanced Wi-Fi Configuration

Some administrators may find the need to restrict some of the wireless features. You may want to require that the Mac connect only to specific secure wireless networks, or that the Mac always connect to one particular network. In these situations, you can use the advanced Wi-Fi configuration options in the Network preferences.

To manage advanced Wi-Fi options and connections, open and unlock the Network preferences, and then select the Wi-Fi service from the services list. At this point you can configure basic Wi-Fi settings in a manner similar to how you would do it from the Wi-Fi status menu, including the ability to join or create another wireless network, from the Network Name pop-up menu.

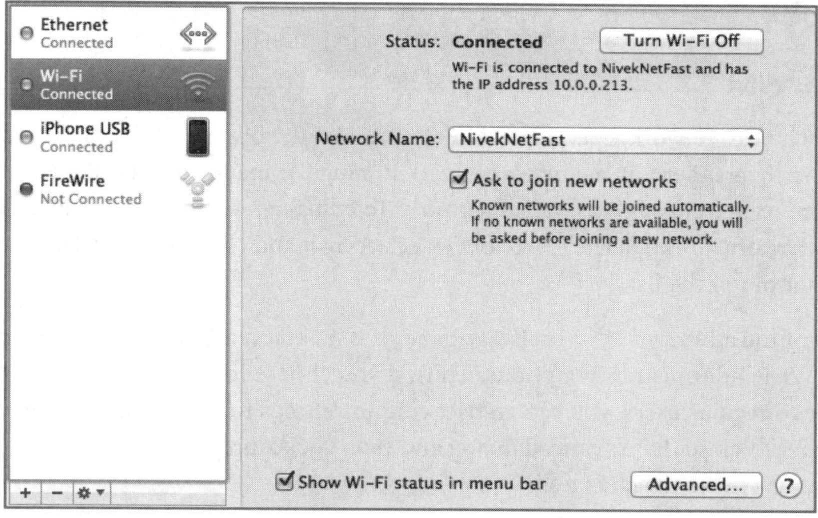

At this point you can also prevent nonadministrative users from accessing Wi-Fi settings:

- Deselect the "Ask to join new networks" checkbox to prevent the user from being prompted when the Mac can't find a preconfigured wireless network but there are other networks in the area.
- Deselect the "Show Wi-Fi status in menu bar" checkbox to disable the Wi-Fi status menu; however, this doesn't prevent a user from choosing a wireless network if the Mac presents a wireless discovery dialog.

Clicking the Advanced button reveals the advanced settings dialog. If the Wi-Fi tab at the top is not selected, click it to view the advanced Wi-Fi settings.

From the top half of the advanced Wi-Fi settings pane, you can manage a list of preferred wireless networks. By default, wireless networks that were added previously appear here as well. If you disable user access to Wi-Fi settings as just described, the system connects only to the preferred wireless networks in this list.

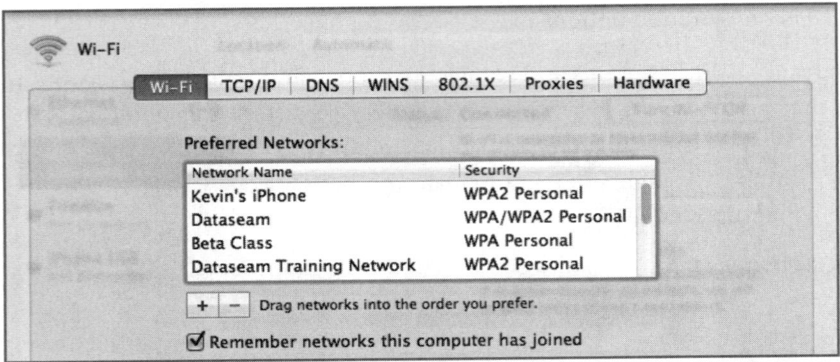

To add a new wireless network, click the Add (+) button at the bottom of the preferred network list, and then either join a wireless network in range or manually enter the information for a hidden or not-currently-in-range network. To edit a network, simply double-click its entry in the list, or you can delete a network by selecting it and clicking the Delete (–) button at the bottom of the list.

At the bottom of the advanced Wi-Fi settings pane, you have several settings that allow for more specific Wi-Fi administration options. Thus, if you choose to leave the Wi-Fi status menu available to regular users, you can restrict certain settings to only administrative users. Remember to close the Advanced dialog and then click Apply in Network preferences to save and activate the changes.

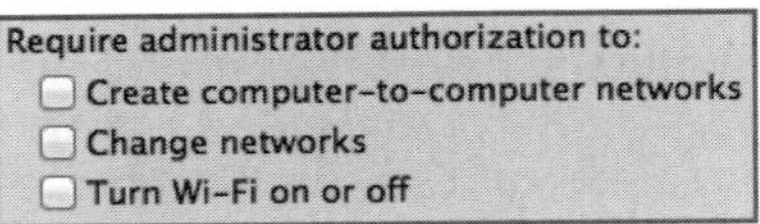

802.1X Configuration

The 802.1X protocol is used to secure both wired and wireless (Wi-Fi) Ethernet networks by only allowing properly authenticated network clients to join the LAN. Networks using 802.1X do not allow any traffic until the network client properly authenticates to the network.

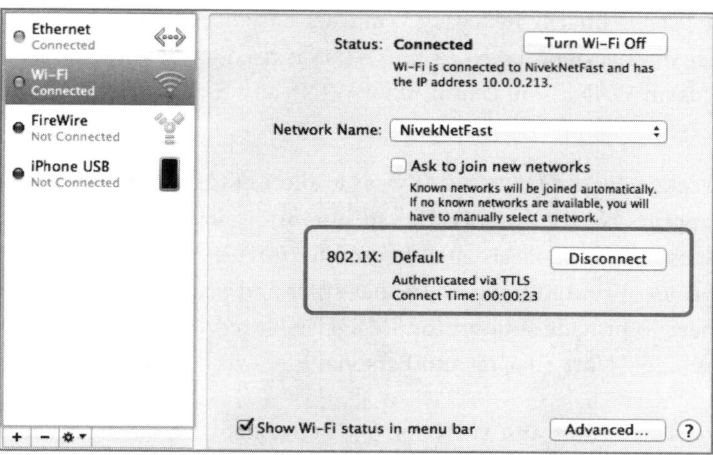

To facilitate 802.1X authentication, OS X provides two methods for automatic configuration:

- User-selected Wi-Fi network with WPA or WPA2 Enterprise authentication—As covered in the previous lesson, if a Wi-Fi network is selected that uses WPA or WPA2 Enterprise authentication, the system automatically configures 802.1X. You can verify the 802.1X configuration by selecting Wi-Fi in the Network preferences, though you cannot modify the connection details in any way.
- Administrator-provided 802.1X configuration profile—The 802.1X architecture often relies on shared secrets or certificates to validate client connections; thus a network administrator must securely deploy these items to client computers. In OS X, the only mechanism for non-Wi-Fi or managed 802.1X configuration is via a configuration profile. This profile can be deployed by simply double-clicking a local copy of a configuration profile, or by having the Mac managed by a Mobile Device Management (MDM) solution. From the local Mac, however, you can verify the 802.1X configuration by selecting the 802.1X tab among the advanced configuration panes of the Network preferences.

  MORE INFO ▶ OS X Server can provide MDM services through Profile Manager, as covered in *Apple Pro Training Series: OS X Server Essentials: Using and Supporting OS X Server on Mountain Lion.*

NetBIOS and WINS

Network Basic Input/Output System (NetBIOS) and Windows Internet Naming Service (WINS) run on top of TCP/IP to provide network identification and service discovery.

NetBIOS and WINS are used primarily by legacy Windows-based systems to provide identification and service discovery on LANs, while WINS is used to identify and locate NetBIOS network devices on WANs. You can think of WINS as a form of DNS for NetBIOS network clients.

Modern Windows networks now use Dynamic DNS as a solution for network client discovery, but OS X still supports NetBIOS and WINS to support legacy network configurations. Further, these discovery protocols are mainly used to provide naming for the Server Message Block (SMB) protocol commonly used to share files and printers. In other words, the NetBIOS name is there to provide support for SMB sharing services hosted from your Mac, as covered in Lesson 26, "Host Sharing and Personal Firewall."

> **NOTE ►** OS X supports NetBIOS and WINS on any active network interface except for VPN connections.

OS X automatically configures your computer's NetBIOS name based on your Mac computer's sharing name, and for many networks this should be sufficient. If your Mac is on a larger legacy Windows network and you want to share resources from your Mac with other network clients, you may want to manually select the NetBIOS workgroup. NetBIOS workgroups are used to make navigation easier on large networks by grouping devices into smaller collections. You may have to manually configure the WINS service to provide faster NetBIOS resolution.

> **NOTE ►** It's not required to configure NetBIOS and WINS in order to connect to Windows resources. For certain legacy Windows clients, however, it may help when attempting to connect to those resources.

To manually configure NetBIOS and WINS settings, open and unlock the Network preferences, select the network service you want to configure from the network services list, and then click Advanced. In the advanced settings dialog, click the WINS tab to view the NetBIOS and WINS settings.

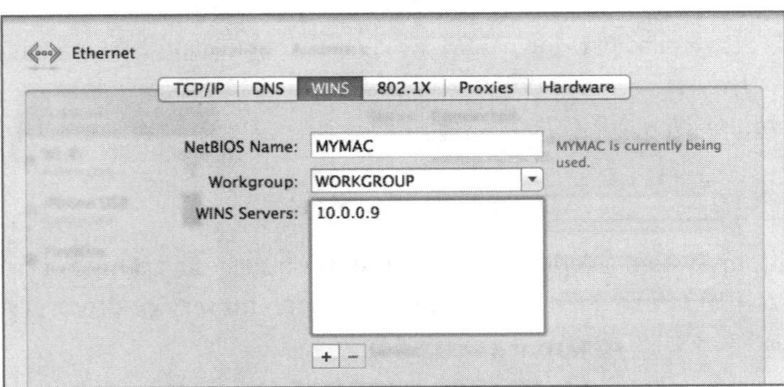

To manually configure NetBIOS, start by entering a unique name, and then choose a workgroup from the pop-up menu. It may take a while for the NetBIOS workgroup list to refresh, thus preventing you from selecting it via the pop-up menu. If you already know the name of the workgroup you want the Mac to be in, you can manually enter the workgroup name.

> **NOTE ▶** NetBIOS names and workgroup names are in all capital letters and cannot contain any special characters or spaces.

To enable WINS, enter at least one WINS server IP address. Click the Add (+) button at the bottom of the WINS server list to add a new server, and then enter the server's IP address. If you configure multiple WINS servers, the system attempts to access those resources in the order in which they appear in the list. To edit a server address, double-click its entry in the list, or you can delete a server by selecting it and clicking the Delete (–) button at the bottom of the list.

When you have entered all the appropriate NetBIOS and WINS settings, remember to close the Advanced dialog and then click Apply in Network preferences to save and activate the changes.

IP Proxies

Proxy servers act as intermediaries between a network client and a requested service. Proxy servers are often used to enhance the performance of slow WAN or Internet connections by caching recently requested data so future connections appear faster to local network clients. Primarily, though, proxy servers are implemented so network administrators can limit network connections to unauthorized servers or resources. Administrators can manage lists of approved resources, having the proxy servers allow access only to those resources.

OS X supports proxy services for File Transfer Protocol (FTP), web protocols (HTTP and HTTPS), streaming (RTSP), SOCKS, and Gopher. For proxy configuration, OS X supports manual configurations, automatic proxy configuration using local or network-hosted proxy auto-config (PAC) files, and full auto proxy discovery via the Web Proxy Autodiscovery Protocol (WPAD).

> **NOTE ▶** It's highly likely that you will have to acquire specific proxy configuration instructions from a network administrator.

To enable and configure proxy settings, open and unlock the Network preferences, select the network service you want to configure from the network services list, and then click Advanced. Click the Proxies tab at the top to view the proxy settings.

At this point you will perform one of three routines based on your network's proxy implementation:

- If your proxy service supports the Web Proxy Autodiscovery Protocol (WPAD), simply enable the Auto Proxy Discovery checkbox.

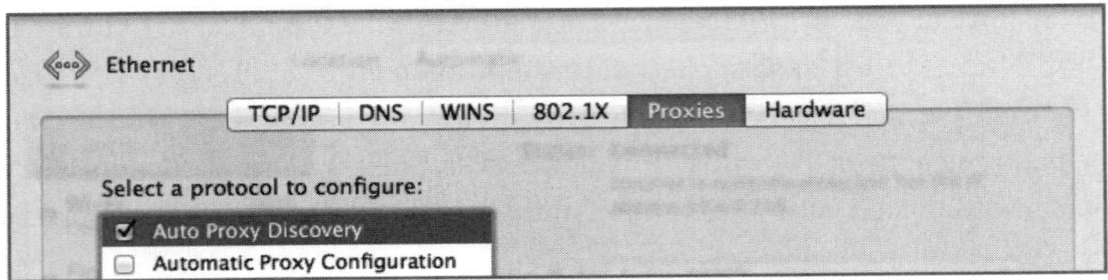

- If you have access to a proxy auto-config (PAC) file, enable the Automatic Proxy Configuration checkbox at the bottom of the proxy protocols list. You must then specify a PAX proxy configuration file. To specify a local file, click the Choose File button and then select the file using the file browser dialog. To specify a network-hosted file, enter the full network path to the file in the URL field.

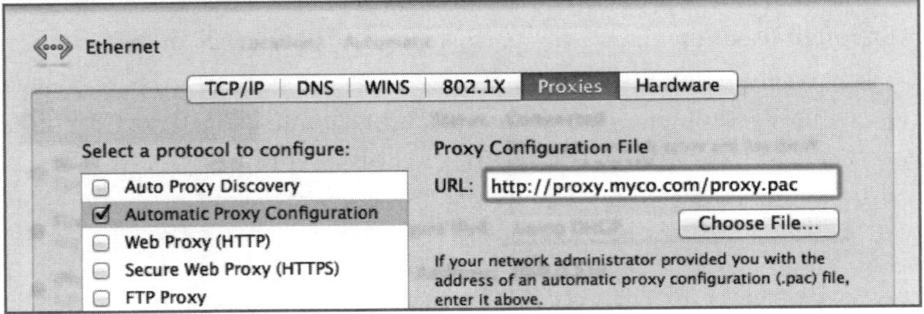

- To manually configure proxy settings, select the checkboxes next to each protocol you want to send through the proxy servers. Select each protocol individually to enter the proxy connection information provided by the network administrator. At the bottom you can also elect to bypass the proxy for specific additional hosts and domains.

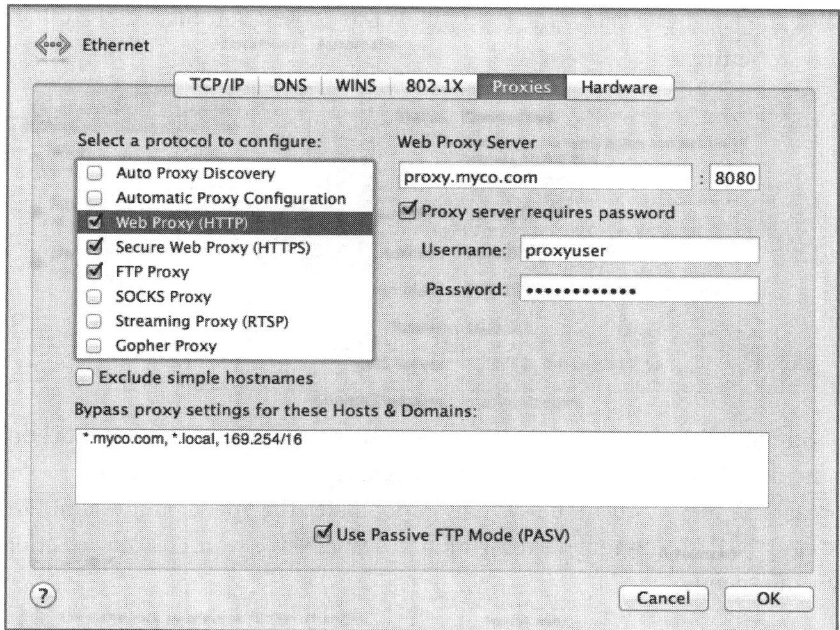

When you have entered all the appropriate proxy information, remember to close the Advanced dialog and then click Apply in Network preferences to save and activate the changes.

Manual Ethernet Configuration

Ethernet connections are designed to establish connection settings automatically. Yet OS X allows you to manually configure Ethernet options from the Network preferences should the automatic selections prove problematic.

The most common case for this is when you have an environment with fast gigabit Ethernet switches and old or substandard wired infrastructure. In this case it's common for the Mac to attempt to automatically establish a gigabit connection but ultimately fail because the wired infrastructure doesn't support the high speeds. The most common symptom is that even with the Ethernet switch showing that the Mac has an active connection, Network preferences on the Mac show Ethernet as disconnected.

To manually configure Ethernet settings, open and unlock the Network preferences, select the Ethernet service you want to configure from the network services list, and then click

Advanced. Click the Hardware tab at the top to view the current automatically configured Ethernet hardware settings.

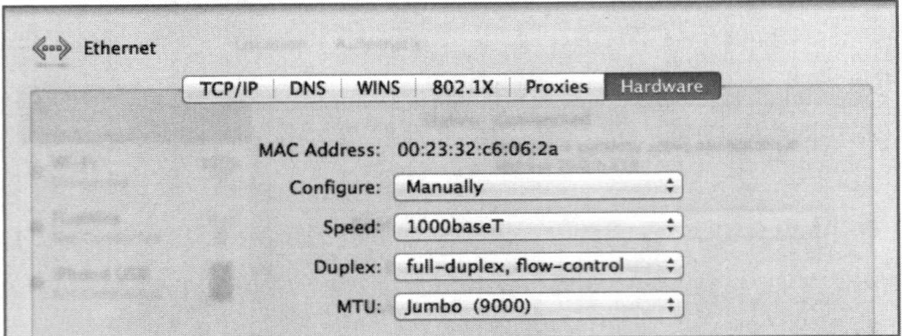

To manually configure Ethernet options, choose Manually from the Configure pop-up menu. The system caches the current automatically configured Ethernet settings so you do not have to change all the settings. The system prepopulates the Speed, Duplex, and MTU options based on your Mac computer's network hardware. Make your custom selections from these pop-up menus.

When you have selected all the appropriate Ethernet hardware settings, remember to close the Advanced dialog and then click Apply in Network preferences to save and activate the changes.

Exercise 23.1
Configure Network Locations

Prerequisites

- You must have created the Local Admin (Exercise 3.1 or 3.2) and Chris Johnson (Exercise 6.1) accounts.
- This exercise requires a very specific network configuration; it can only be performed in a classroom with the proper network setup, or if you have configured your network according to the Optional Network Setup Instructions (available in the Bonus Content for this guide after you register at www.peachpit.com/apts.osxmountainlion).

Some network configurations do not have a DHCP (Dynamic Host Configuration Protocol) server, or there may be times when the DHCP server fails. In these instances, to establish and maintain network access, a OS X computer configured to obtain an IP address via DHCP self-assigns an IP address.

Turn Off DHCP Service

If you are performing these exercises in a class, the instructor will turn the classroom DHCP service off.

If you are performing these exercises on your own, follow the instructions in the "Turn Off DHCP for Exercise 32.1" section of Optional Network Setup Instructions.

Examine Your DHCP-Supplied Configuration

1 If necessary, open System Preferences and select the Network preference pane.

2 If necessary, click the padlock and authenticate as Local Admin.

3 Select the primary network service.

Even though DHCP service has been disabled, the service still indicates that it is configured using DHCP, and has valid network settings. This is because the DHCP service gave it the configuration information before it shut down, and the information is still valid.

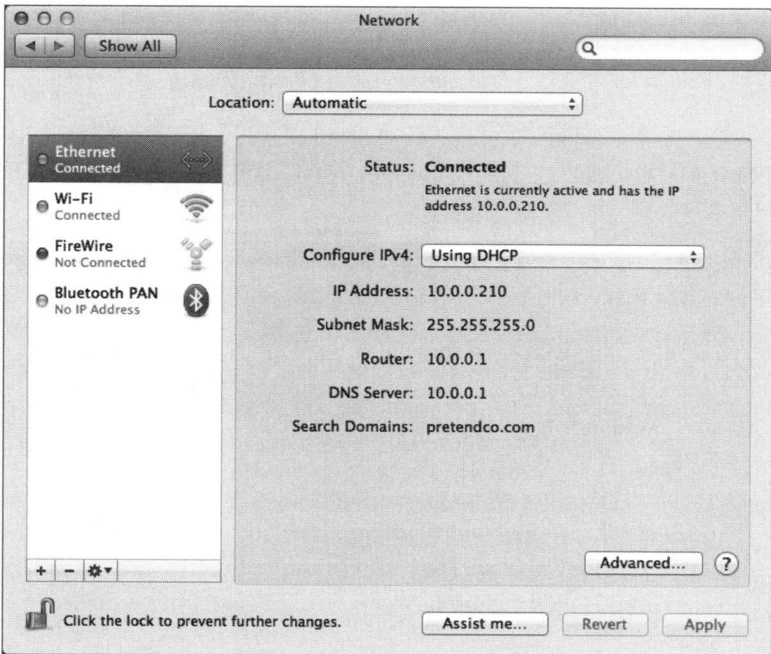

Note that your display probably appears different than this screenshot, especially if you have different network services connected.

Create a DHCP-Based Network Location

1 From the Location pop-up menu, choose Edit Locations.

2 Click the Add (+) button under the Locations list to create a new location.

3 Enter **Dynamic** as the name of the new location.

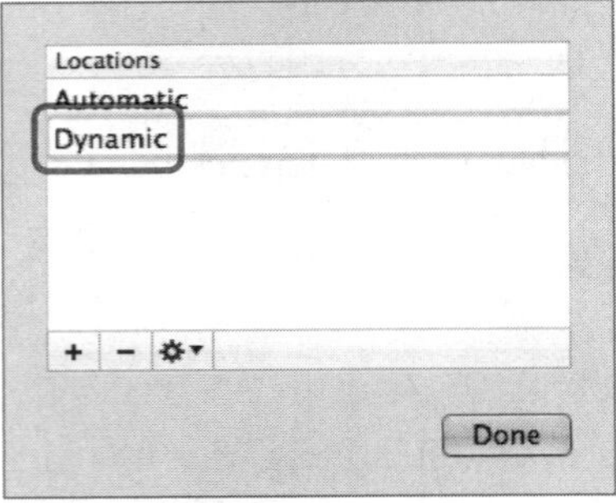

4 Click Done.

5 If necessary, choose the new Dynamic location from the Location pop-up menu.

6 Click Apply.

Network preferences is one of a few places in OS X where you must click Apply before your settings take effect.

7 If necessary, select the network service that is set up for these exercises (that is, the one that DHCP was just turned off for). If it is a wireless network, rejoin it.

The network service enters an Unknown state with no IP address as it tries to acquire new DHCP configuration information. After a few seconds, it gives up and selects a "self-assigned" IP address beginning with 169.254.

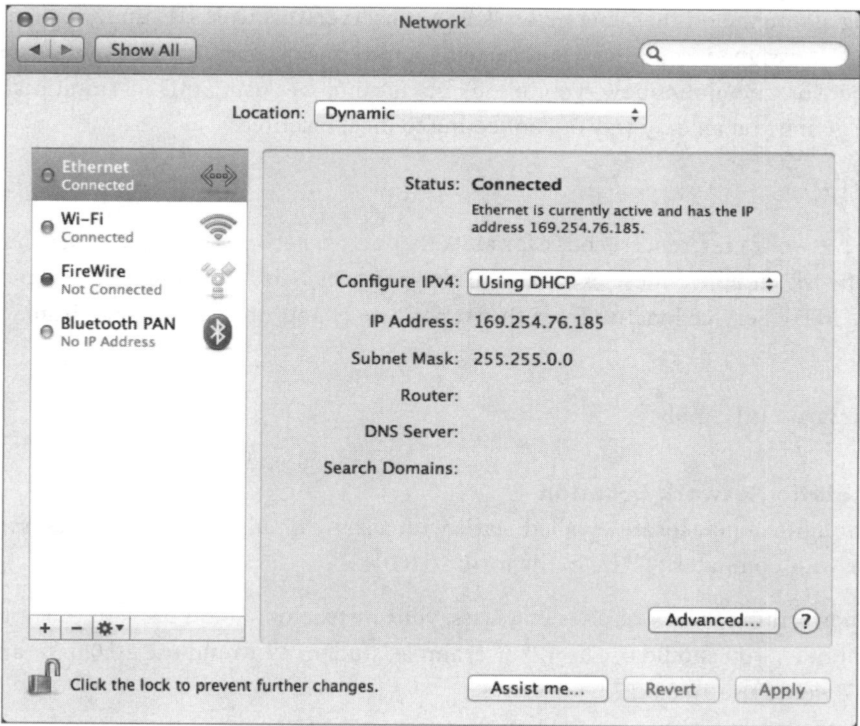

If this is an Ethernet interface, the status indicator is green despite it being in self-assigned mode. If this is a Wi-Fi interface, the indicator is yellow instead.

Note that with this "self-assigned" configuration, there is no router or DNS server for that service. Therefore, this network service cannot be used to reach the Internet.

8 Open Safari, and try to browse the web.

If you have another active network service with a valid Internet connection, you can still reach the Internet. OS X Mountain Lion uses the router and DNS from lower-priority network services if the primary service does not have a router configured.

If you do not have another active network service, you cannot reach the Internet. Internet connectivity is available on the network you are connected to, but you cannot use it without proper IP settings.

9 If you have a server set up to support these exercises (either in a classroom or because you set one up according to the Mainserver Setup Instructions), try to browse to mainserver.local.

As long as you are on the same network as Mainserver, this works. Even though you have a self-assigned IP address, you can still communicate with other computers on your network. Bonjour allows you to look up .local names using mDNS (multicast DNS), giving you an easy way of connecting to local resources.

10 Quit Safari.

11 In the Network preferences, check for any other active network services (other than the network set up for these exercises). If there are any, select them one by one and choose Make Service Inactive from the Action (gear) pop-up menu to inactivate them.

12 If necessary, click Apply.

Create a Static Network Location

You will configure a new location called Static with a static IP address. The IP address you will use for your computer will be in the form 10.0.0.*n*2.

If you are performing these exercises in a class, your instructor should provide you with a student number you should use as *n*. For example, student #3 would use 10.0.0.32, and student #17 would use 10.0.0.172.

If you are performing these exercises on your own, use the address 10.0.0.12.

1 From the Location pop-up menu, choose Edit Locations.

2 From the Action (gear icon) pop-up menu, choose Duplicate Location.

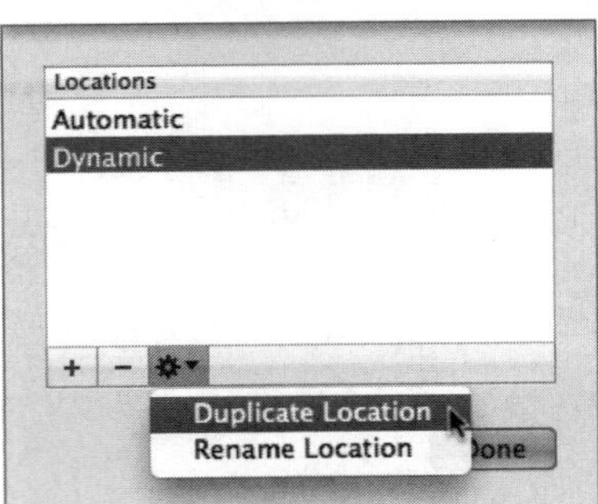

3 Rename the Untitled location **Static**.

4 Click Done.

5 Use the Location pop-up menu to switch to the new Static location, if it is not already selected.

6 Click Apply.

7 Select the network service that is set up for these exercises from the service list on the left. It will most likely be either Ethernet or Wi-Fi.

8 Click Advanced.

9 If necessary, click the TCP/IP tab.

10 From the Configure IPv4 pop-up menu, choose Manually.

11 In the IPv4 Address field, enter **10.0.0.*n*2/24** (where *n* is either your student number if you are in class, or **1** if you are on your own).

So if you are on your own, you enter **10.0.0.12/24**; if you are student #17 in a class, you enter **10.0.0.172/24**.

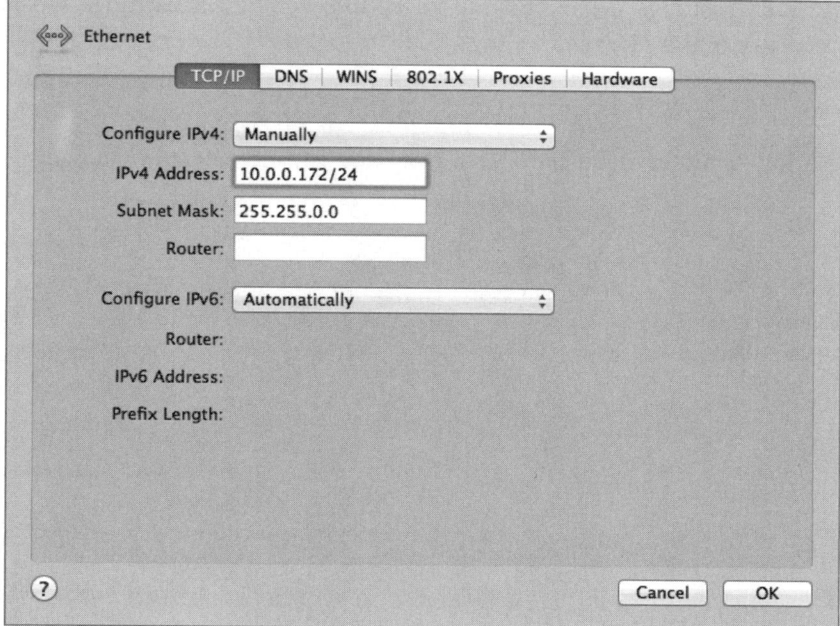

12 Press Tab.

This fills in the subnet mask (255.255.255.0) and router (10.0.0.1) when you tab out of the field.

You are using a shortcut to fill in the subnet mask and router information. 10.0.0.*n*2/24 is CIDR (pronounced *cider* and short for Classless Interdomain Routing) notation. It specifies an IP address and subnet mask by indicating the number of on bits (1s) in the subnet mask. In CIDR notation, a /24 subnet equates to a 255.255.255.0 subnet mask (binary 11111111 11111111 11111111 00000000). Once it has an address and the subnet mask, it can figure other things out.

It also assumes that the default gateway (router) is the first usable address on the subnet. While common practice, this is not a given. Some network administrators place the default router at the last usable address on the subnet. The gateway can be at any address on the subnet, so you may need to edit the router information to reflect the configuration of your network. Addressing doesn't tell the computer anything about the DNS environment, so you still have to enter that information manually.

13 Click DNS.

Note that for an Ethernet service, TCP/IP IPv4 settings are available without going into the advanced settings; however, we also need to get at the DNS settings, which are only available in the advanced settings.

14 Click the Add (+) button under the DNS Servers list, and enter **10.0.0.1**.

15 Click the Add (+) button under the Search Domains list, and enter **pretendco.com**.

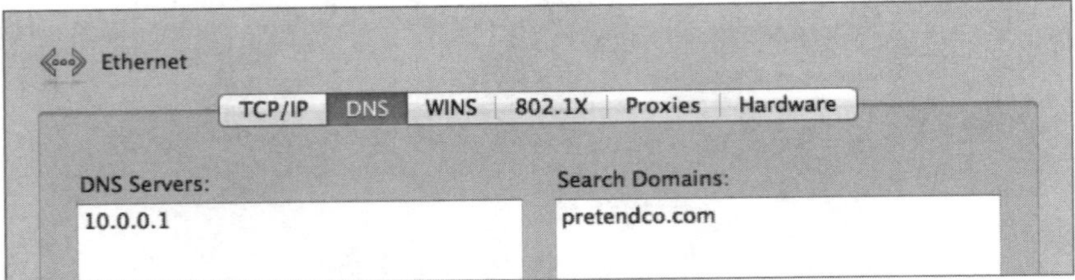

16 Click OK to dismiss the advanced settings dialog.

17 Click Apply.

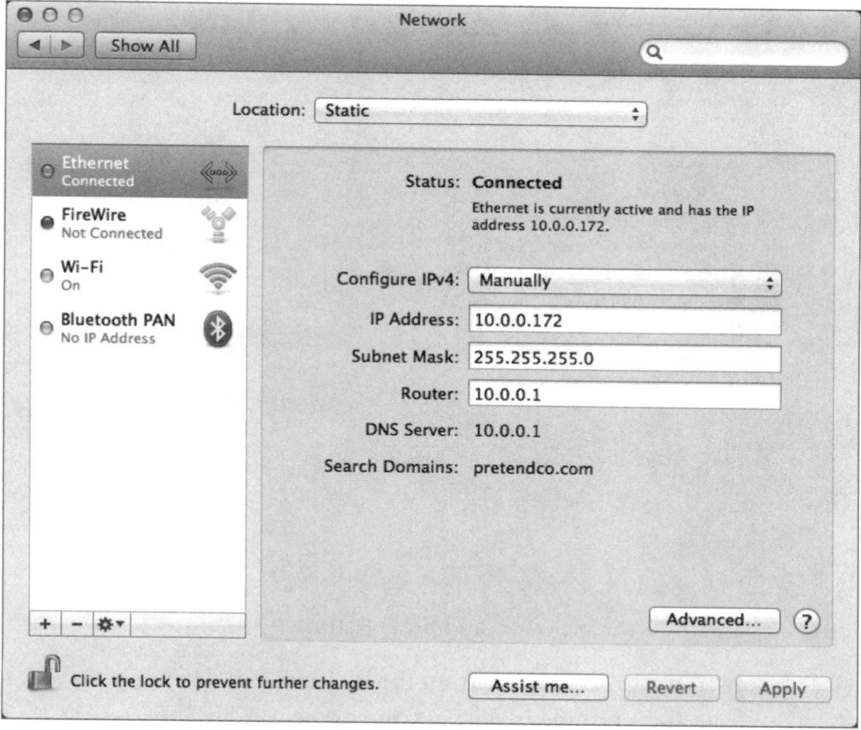

18 Quit System Preferences.

Test Web Access

At this point you have correctly configured your computer to work on the network. Now you will use Safari to verify that you can access the Apple.com website.

1 Open Safari.

2 Choose Safari > Reset Safari.

Browser caches can make testing websites rather challenging because it is often unclear whether what you see in the browser has been freshly downloaded from the server or retrieved from the cache. The reset function clears more than just the caches, but that is not a problem here.

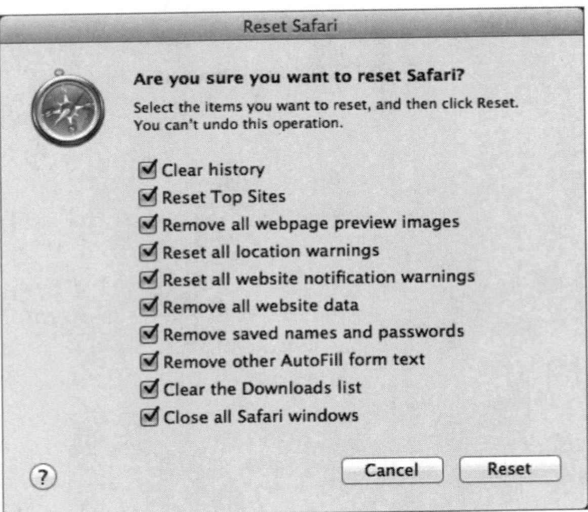

3 Click Reset.

4 In the address bar, type www.apple.com and press Return.

If Safari is already trying to load a page from the Internet, you don't need to wait for it to finish or time out. If everything is working, the Apple website appears.

5 Quit Safari.

Exercise 23.2
Configure Network Service Order

Prerequisites

- You must have created the Local Admin (Exercise 3.1 or 3.2) and Chris Johnson (Exercise 6.1) accounts.
- You must have performed Exercise 23.1.

The network service order determines which service is used to reach the Internet. Because of this, it is important to understand how network service order is determined, and what its effects are.

Create a Multi-Homed Location

1 If necessary, open the Network pane in System Preferences and authenticate as Local Admin.

2 Note the currently selected Location.

3 From the Location pop-up menu, choose Edit Locations.

4 Select the Static location, and then choose Duplicate Location from the Action (gear) menu below the location list.

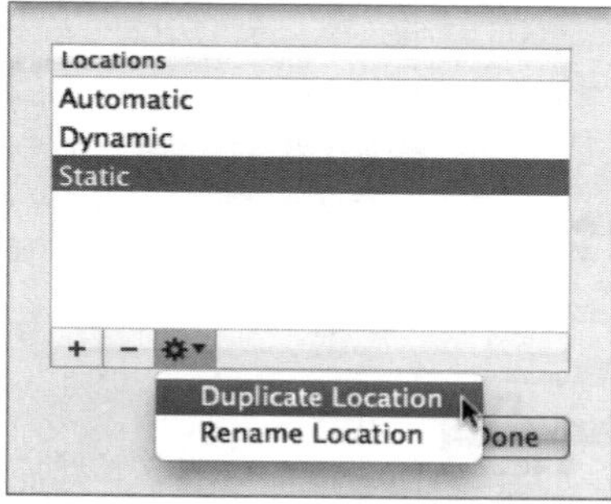

5 Name the new location **Multi-homed**.

6 Click Done.

7 Switch to the Multi-homed location, if necessary.

8 Click Apply.

9 Select the primary network service (the one at the top of the list on the left).

10 From the Action (gear) pop-up menu, choose Rename Service.

11 Enter **With DNS** in the New Name field and click Rename.

12 Click Apply.

13 From the Action (gear) pop-up menu, choose Duplicate Service.

14 Enter **Without DNS** in the Name field.

15 Click Duplicate.

You now have two network services using the same interface. Essentially, this means that you have two sets of network configurations (IP address, subnet mask, and so on) running through the same connector (or wireless network).

16 Select the Without DNS service and click Advanced.

17 Click TCP/IP.

18 Increase the last number of the IPv4 address by 1 (for example, if it was 10.0.0.172, change it to 10.0.0.173).

19 Click DNS.

20 Select the entry in the DNS Servers list, and click the Delete (–) button below the list to remove it.

The DNS Servers list is now empty.

21 Click OK to dismiss the advanced settings.

22 Click Apply.

At this point, both the With DNS and Without DNS services have a green status indicator, and the With DNS service is at the top of the list.

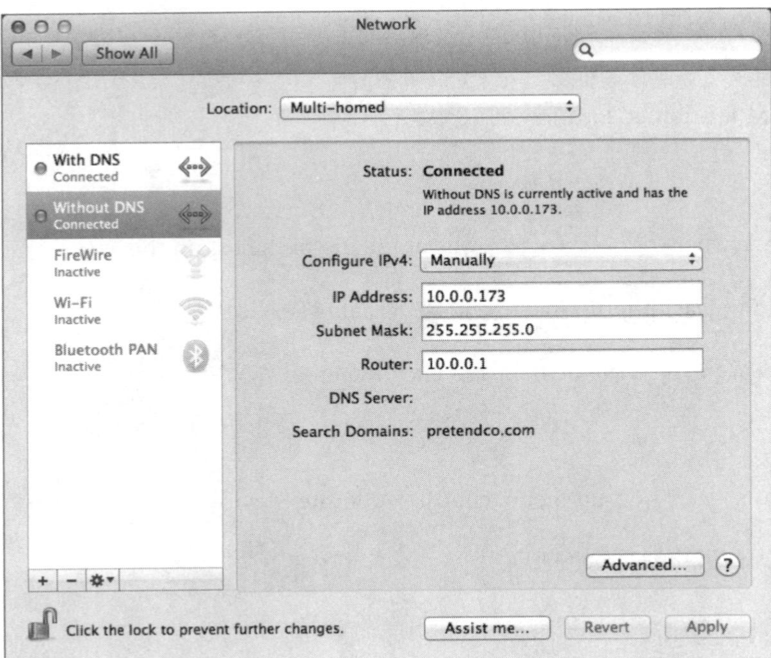

23 Open Safari, and attempt to browse the web.

You can now browse the web normally. If it does not work, go back and recheck the setup you have done.

Change the Service Order

1 Switch back to the Network preferences.

2 From the Action (gear) pop-up menu, choose Set Service Order.

This list controls the normal order of the services. The system always reprioritizes the services based on their status (active services always bubble up to the top), but among the active services this controls which is the primary.

3 Drag the Without DNS service to the top of the list, and then click OK.

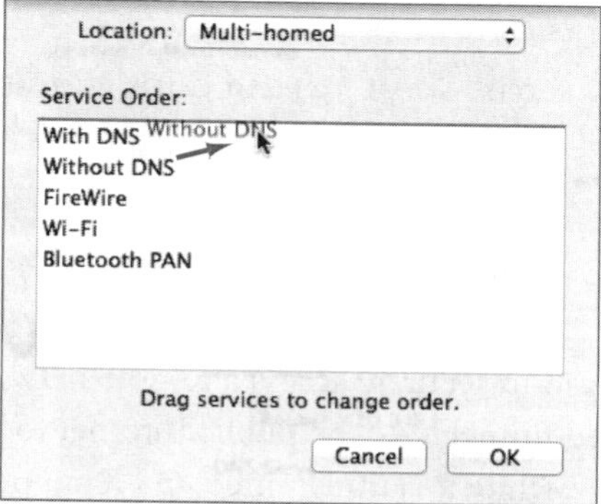

The Without DNS service now moves to the top of the service list, but it is not actually used as the primary service until you apply the change.

4 Click Apply.

5 Switch back to Safari.

6 Press Command-R to reload the current page.

You are presented with a page that tells you that Safari couldn't load the site because "Your computer is not connected to the Internet." Specifically what it means is that it cannot find a name server to resolve the name.

The Without DNS service now has priority over the With DNS service (it is higher on the list). Because Without DNS is not configured with any name servers, it cannot look up any websites by name and so fails with this message.

7 From the Apple menu, choose Location > Static.

   This submenu allows you to switch locations without having to open the Network preferences.

8 Reload the page in Safari (note that it may reload automatically after a short delay). This time it works because the Static location has DNS settings associated with its highest-priority (and only) service.

9 Quit Safari.

Exercise 23.3
Configure VPN Settings

Prerequisites

- You must have created the Local Admin (Exercise 3.1 or 3.2) and Chris Johnson (Exercise 6.1) accounts.
- You must be performing these exercises in a class, or have set up your own server configured as in the Mainserver Setup Instructions.

Virtual private networks (VPNs) are commonly used to securely access a remote network. With a VPN connection you establish an encrypted tunnel over the public Internet to the remote network. The encryption protects your data while it is transmitted. OS X supports three types of VPN: Point to Point Tunneling Protocol (PPTP), Layer 2 Tunneling Protocol over IPSec (L2TP), and Cisco IPSec. You can configure a VPN service manually in OS X, but the preferred way to set one up is with a configuration profile.

In this exercise, you will use a configuration profile to set up a VPN connection from your computer to the Mainserver server's private network.

Configure a VPN Service

1 If necessary, log in as Chris Johnson.

2 Open the file StudentMaterials/Lesson23/VPN.mobileconfig.

   The profile opens in the Profiles pane of System Preferences.

3 Click Show Profile.

The profile contains the settings to connect to mainserver.local over the L2TP protocol.

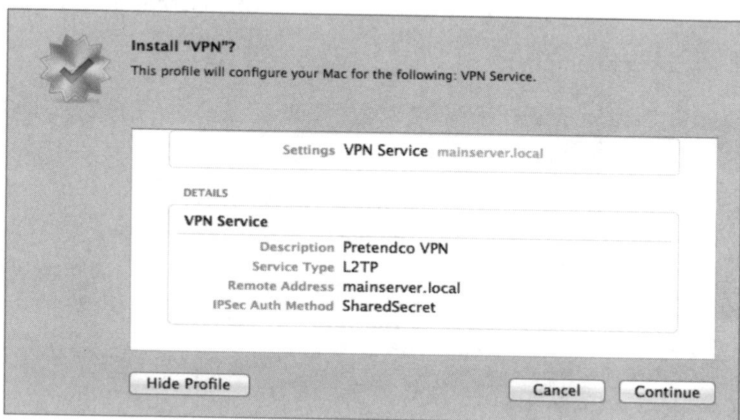

4 Click Continue, and then click Continue again to install the profile.

The profile does not specify a username to authenticate to the VPN server, so you need to enter one.

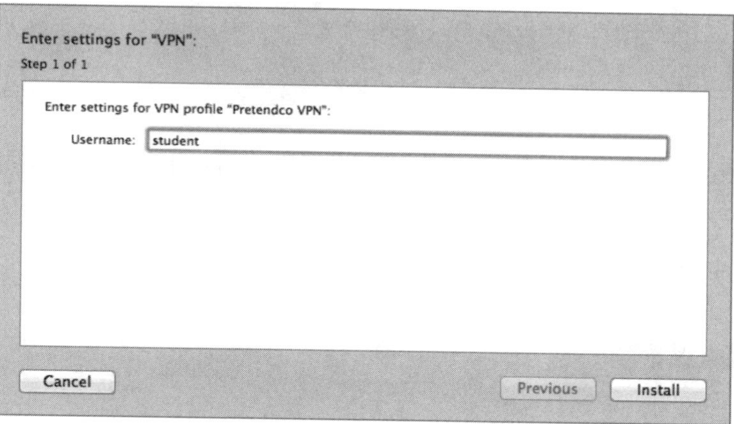

5 Enter the username **student**, and click Install.

6 When you are prompted, authenticate as Local Admin.

The Profile preferences now list the VPN profile as installed on this computer.

7 Click Show All, and then select the Network preference pane.

8 Select the VPN service that has been added to your current location.

All the settings in the profile have been applied, along with the username you entered.

9 Select "Show VPN status in menu bar."

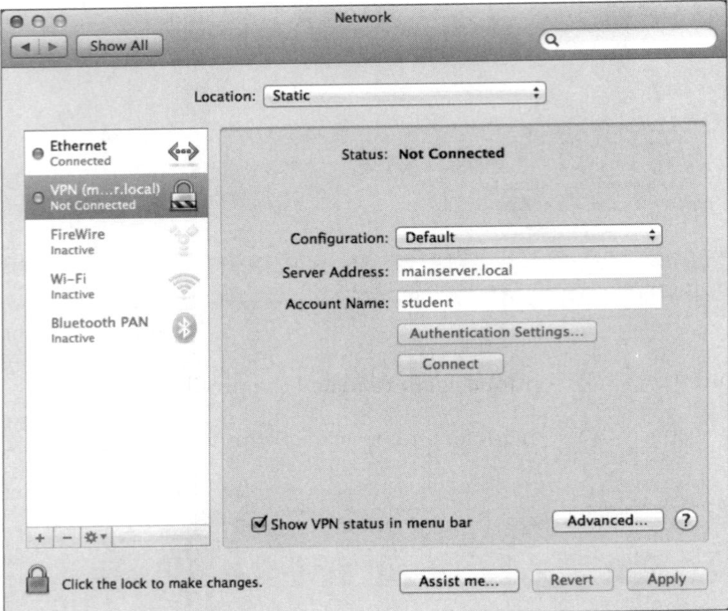

The Connect button in the Network preferences may be dimmed, but you can still use the menu item to connect.

10 From the VPN menu item, choose Connect VPN.

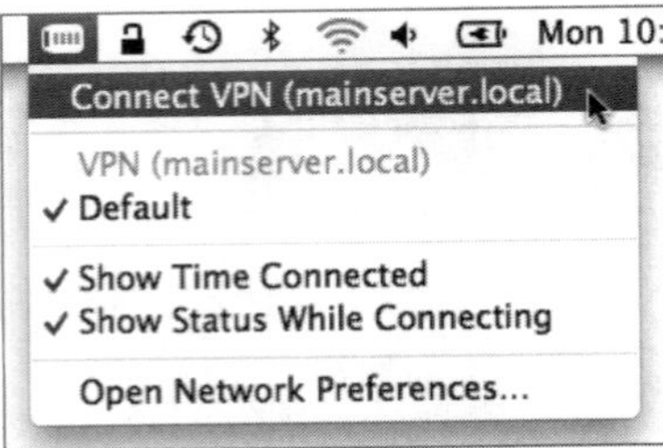

11 When you are prompted to authenticate to the VPN server, enter the password **student** (the username is already filled in).

It may take a few seconds to connect. When it does, the VPN service's status changes.

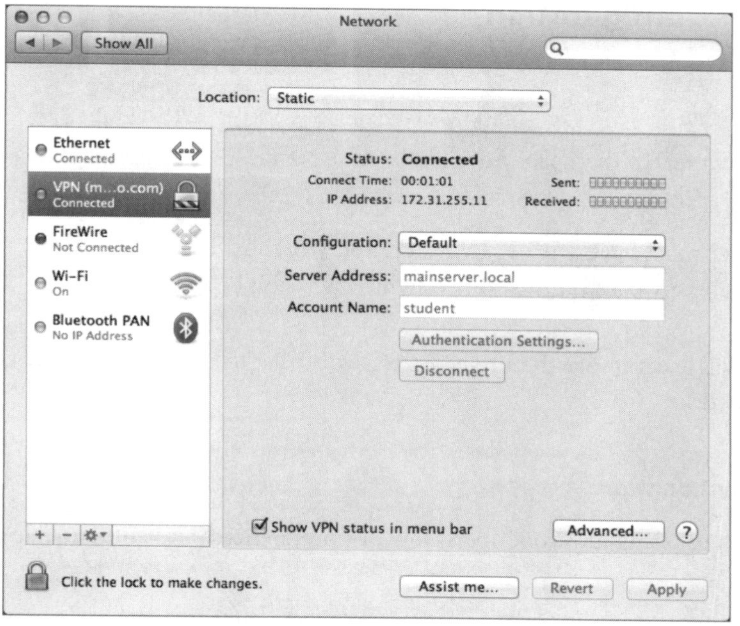

Check Your VPN Connectivity

Now that you are connected to the classroom network via VPN, you will access a network resource that was previously unreachable.

1 Open Safari.

2 Use the address bar to access **internal.pretendco.com**.

   You have just opened an internal website. You will now verify that it was only accessible from a VPN connection.

3 From the VPN menu bar, choose Disconnect VPN (mainserver.local).

4 In Safari, press Command-R to reload the internal website.

   The website does not load, and if you wait long enough you'll see an error page telling you that "Safari can't open the page."

5 Quit Safari.

Exercise 23.4
Advanced Wi-Fi Configuration

Prerequisites

- You must have created the Local Admin (Exercise 3.1 or 3.2) and Chris Johnson (Exercise 6.1) accounts.
- Your computer must have a Wi-Fi interface, and you must have access to at least two Wi-Fi networks (at least one of which is visible).

In this exercise, you will learn to use the Preferred Networks list to control how your computer joins Wi-Fi networks.

Create a Wi-Fi-Only Location

1. If necessary, log in as Chris Johnson, open Network preferences, and authenticate as Local Admin.
2. Note the currently selected Location, so that you can return to it at the end of the exercise.
3. From the Location pop-up menu, choose Edit Locations.
4. Click the Add (+) button under the Locations list to create a new location.
5. Enter **Wi-Fi Only** as the name of the new location.

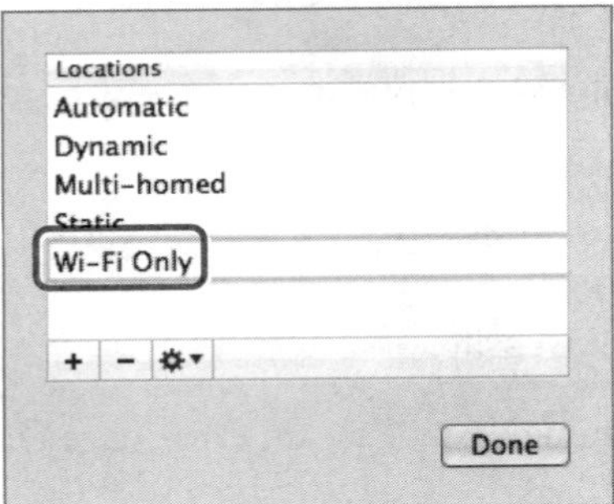

6. Click Done.

7 If necessary, choose the new Wi-Fi location from the Location pop-up menu.

8 Click Apply.

9 In the network service list, make the services other than Wi-Fi inactive. Do this one-by-one by selecting a service, and then from the Action (gear) pop-up menu choosing Make Service Inactive.

When you are done, all services except Wi-Fi are listed as Inactive.

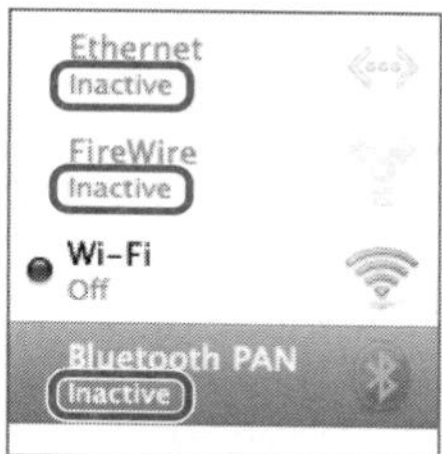

10 Click Apply.

11 Select the Wi-Fi service.

12 If necessary, click Turn On Wi-Fi.

13 If necessary, deselect "Ask to join new networks."

This prevents your computer from suggesting networks to you when it can't find any of your preferred networks.

14 If necessary, select "Show Wi-Fi status in menu bar."

15 If your computer has not already joined a wireless network, join one by following the instructions in Exercise 22.1.

Clear the Preferred Network List

1 Click Advanced.

2 Examine the Preferred Networks list.

This is the list of wireless networks that your computer will join automatically anytime it is in range of them. If there is more than one in range, it joins the one that is highest on the list.

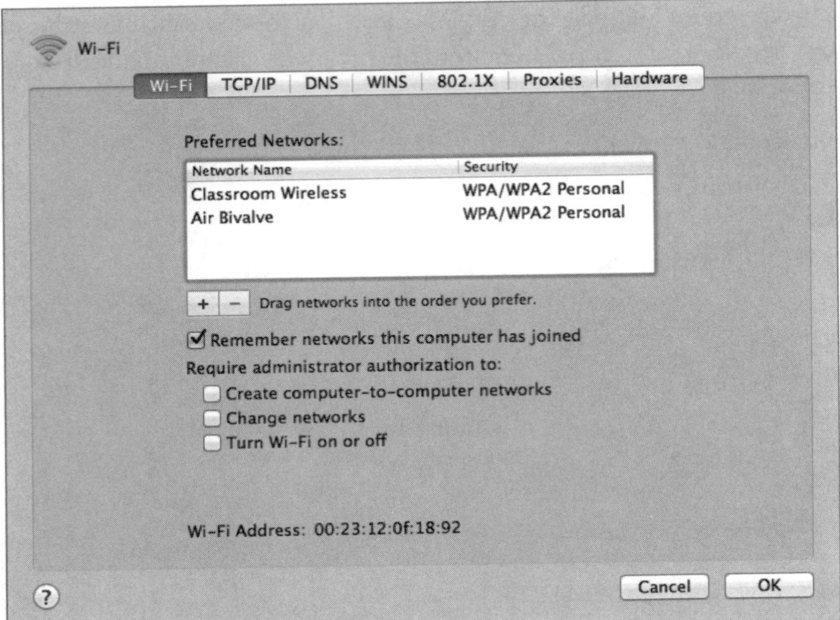

3 Clear the list by selecting each entry, and then clicking the Delete (–) button at the bottom of the list to remove it.

4 When the list is empty, click OK and then click Apply. If prompted, authenticate as Local Admin.

Note that your computer is still joined to the same wireless network. The Preferred Networks list controls which networks your computer joins automatically, but once it is joined to a network it stays joined until it loses the connection or you tell it to disconnect.

5 Click Turn Wi-Fi Off.

6 Wait 10 seconds, and then click Turn Wi-Fi On.

The wireless interface turns on, but does not connect to any network.

Add a Network to the Preferred List by Joining It

1. From the Network Name pop-up menu, choose one of the wireless networks you have access to.

2. If necessary, enter the network password to join it.

   Note that you may not be prompted for a password if you have joined the network before, and its password is recorded in your keychain. Removing a network from the preferred list does not remove its password from the keychain.

3. Click Advanced.

   The network you joined has been added to the preferred list. This is because the "Remember networks this computer has joined" option is selected.

Add a Network to the Preferred List Manually

1. Click the Add (+) button under the Preferred Networks list.

2. Enter the network name and security information for another network you have access to.

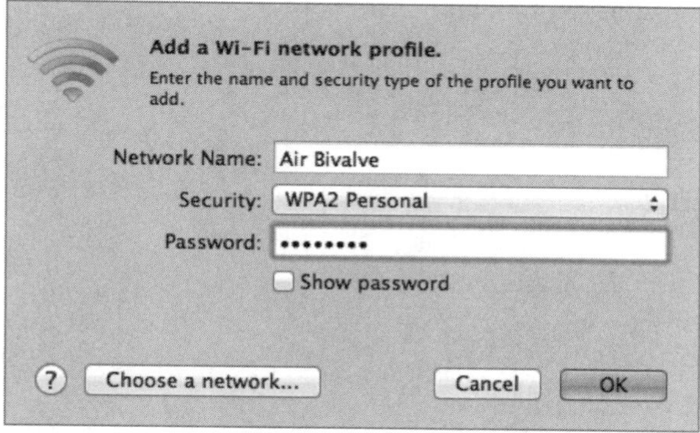

   Note that you have to enter the network's security mode and password even if they are recorded in your keychain.

3. Click OK to add the entry.

   Note that the new entry is added to the bottom of the list.

4. Click OK to dismiss the advanced settings, and then click Apply. If prompted, authenticate as Local Admin.

Test the Network Preference Order

1 Click Turn Wi-Fi Off. Wait 10 seconds, and then click Turn Wi-Fi On.

After a short delay, your computer rejoins the first network you joined it to.

2 Click Advanced.

3 Drag the current wireless network to the bottom of the list.

The network you added manually is now at the top of the list.

4 Click OK, and then click Apply.

5 Click Turn Wi-Fi Off. Wait 10 seconds, and then click Turn Wi-Fi On.

This time, your computer joins the network you added manually, because it is first in the preferred network list.

If your computer joins the other network instead, there may be a problem with the manual entry such as a typo in the name or password, or an incorrect security mode. In this case, you could remove it from the list and try adding it back in.

6 Switch back to the network location you were in at the beginning of the exercise (generally the Static location, if you have one), and click Apply.

Lesson **24**

Network Troubleshooting

This lesson builds on the network topics covered previously in Lessons 22 and 23. A solid understanding of general network technologies and the OS X network configuration architecture is necessary to effectively troubleshoot network issues from a Mac system. This lesson first covers general network troubleshooting and common network issues. Again, digging deeper, you will then learn how to use the built-in OS X network troubleshooting tools, including the Network Diagnostics and Network Utility applications.

GOALS

- Identify and resolve network configuration issues
- Verify network configuration via the Network preferences
- Understand how to use the Network Utility to aid in troubleshooting

Reference 24.1
General Network Troubleshooting

The most important thing to remember about troubleshooting network issues is that it is often not the computer's fault. There are many other points of failure to consider when dealing with LAN and Internet connection issues. So the second most important thing to remember about troubleshooting network issues is to isolate the cause of the problem before attempting generic resolutions.

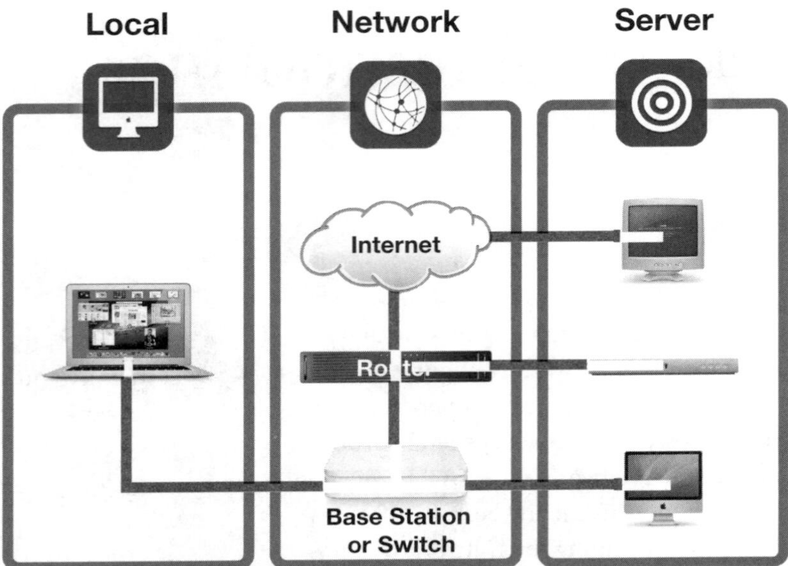

To help isolate network issues, you can categorize them into three general areas:

- Local issues—These are usually related to either improperly configured network settings or disconnected network connections.
- Network issues—These are by far the hardest to pinpoint, as there could be literally hundreds of points of failure involved. It always helps to be familiar with the physical topology of your network. Start by checking the devices that provide network access closest to your Mac. Something as simple as a bad Ethernet port on a network switch can cause problems. As you move on to investigating devices farther away from your Mac, you will find that it's often easiest to start your investigation using the network diagnostic utilities included with OS X.
- Service issues—These issues are related to the actual network device or service you are trying to access. For example, the devices providing DHCP or DNS services could be temporarily down or improperly configured. It's often easy to determine if the problem is with the service alone by testing other network services. If the other network services work, you're probably not dealing with network or local issues. Again, OS X provides some useful diagnostic tools for testing service availability. Troubleshooting network services is also covered in Lesson 25, "Network Services."

You will be using three main tools for diagnosing network issues in OS X: the Network preferences, Network Diagnostics, and Network Utility.

MORE INFO ▶ Many of the issues beyond the general scope of this guide are covered by the Apple networking support website at www.apple.com/support/networking/.

Network Preference Status

One of the first diagnostic tools you should always check is the Network preferences. Network preferences features a dynamically updating list that shows you the current status of any network interface. If a network connection is not working, you will find out about it here first.

Network status indicators include:

- Green status—The connection is active and configured with TCP/IP settings. This, however, does not guarantee that the service is using the proper TCP/IP settings.
- Yellow status—The connection is active but the TCP/IP settings are not properly configured. If you are still experiencing problems with this service, double-check the network settings. If the settings appear sound, move on to the other diagnostic utilities.
- Red status—This status usually indicates either improperly configured network settings or disconnected network interfaces. If this is an always-on interface, check for proper physical connectivity. If this is a virtual or PPP connection, double-check the settings and attempt to reconnect.

Common Network Issues

A good starting point for resolving network issues is to quickly verify some of the most common causes. You can think of this list as items you should check every time you're having an issue. To put it another way, verify common issues before hunting down exotic issues. This includes verifying Ethernet connectivity, Wi-Fi connectivity, DHCP services, and DNS services.

Ethernet Connectivity Issues

For well over a century those supporting any electronic device have been able to heed these words, "Check the cable first!" If you're using an Ethernet connection, always verify the physical connection to the system and if possible verify the entire Ethernet run back to the switch. If that's not possible, try swapping your local Ethernet cable or use a different Ethernet port.

You should also verify the Ethernet status from Network preferences, as detailed in the next section. Also, keep an eye out for substandard Ethernet cabling or problematic switching hardware. A symptom of these issues would be a large amount of packet errors, which you can verify with Network Utility, as covered later in this lesson.

You may also find that while the Ethernet switch registers a link, Network preferences still shows the link as down. This issue may be resolved by manually setting a slower speed in the advanced hardware settings of the Network preferences, as covered previously in Lesson 23, "Advanced Network Configuration."

Wi-Fi Connectivity Issues

A modern version of "Check the cable first!" would certainly be "Check the Wi-Fi first!" After all, when using Wi-Fi networking, the wireless signal represents the "physical" network connection. Start by verifying you are connected to the correct SSID from the Wi-Fi status menu or Network preferences.

The Wi-Fi status menu can also serve as a diagnostic tool when you hold the Option key when choosing this menu item. This shows connection statistics for the currently selected Wi-Fi network. Of particular note is the Transmit Rate, which shows (in megabits per second) the current data rate for the selected Wi-Fi network.

MORE INFO ▸ The Wi-Fi status menu is capable of other diagnostic tricks, including helping you quickly identify network issues and opening the advanced Wi-Fi Diagnostics application. You can find out more in Knowledge Base document HT3821, "Mac OS X 10.6 Snow Leopard: The AirPort status menu (AirPort Menu Extra) FAQ."

DHCP Service Issues

Most client network connections are configured automatically via DHCP. If the DHCP server has run out of available network addresses, or there is no DHCP service available, as is the case with small ad hoc networks, the client automatically generates a self-assigned address. Sometimes this automatic assignment of addressing is referred to as "link-local addressing," but the Network preferences shows it as Self-Assigned.

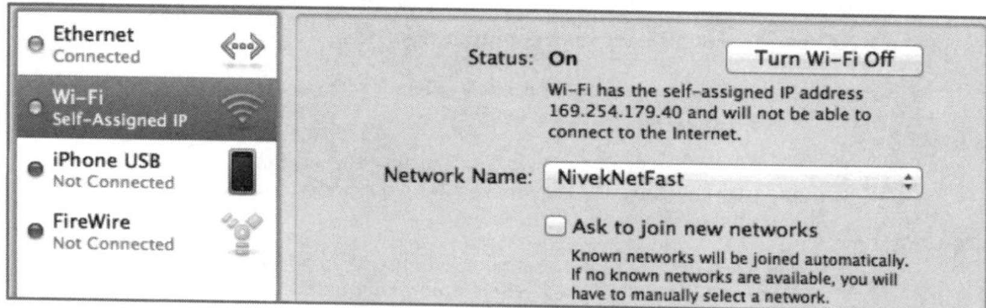

Self-assigned addresses are always in the IP address range of 169.254.xxx.xxx with a subnet mask of 255.255.0.0. The network client automatically generates a random self-assigned address and then checks the local network to make sure no other network device is using that address. Once a unique self-assigned address is established, the network client can only establish connections with other network devices on the local network.

As such, a client configured with a self-assigned address may be able to communicate with other devices on the LAN, but it doesn't have access to WAN or Internet resources.

DNS Service Issues

Aside from TCP/IP settings, DNS is a requirement for most network services. As always, you should start by verifying the DNS server configuration in Network preferences. Remember, in most cases the topmost network service interface is the primary, and as such is used for all DNS resolution. The exception is if the primary network service is lacking a router configuration, in which case DNS resolution falls to the next fully configured network service interface.

Though rare, the OS X DNS resolution services can sometimes cache out-of-date DNS information and return inaccurate results. If you suspect your DNS issues are due to old information, you can either restart the system or flush the DNS service caches. You can find out more about this process from Knowledge Base document HT5343, "OS X: How to reset the DNS cache."

Network Diagnostics

OS X includes Network Diagnostics assistant to help you troubleshoot common network issues. Some networking applications automatically open this assistant when they encounter a network issue. You can also open it manually by clicking the Assist Me button at the bottom of the Network preferences, and then clicking the Diagnostics button.

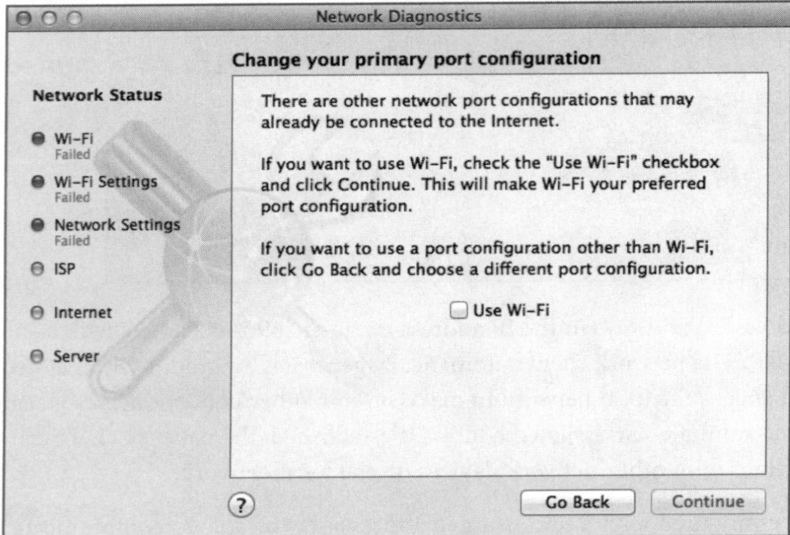

Network Diagnostics assistant asks you a few simple questions about your network setup, and then, based on your answers, it runs a battery of tests to determine where the problem might be occurring. Test results are displayed using colored indicators on the left side of the window. If there are problems, the assistant makes suggestions for resolution.

Reference 24.2
Network Utility

The Network preferences and Network Diagnostics assistant are good places to start troubleshooting network issues, but the most powerful application in OS X for diagnosing network issues is /Applications/Utilities/Network Utility. Network Utility provides a selection of popular network identification and diagnostic tools. In fact, most of the tools in Network Utility are based on UNIX command-line network utilities that have been used by network administrators for years.

Network Utility is broken up into the following sections:

- Info—Allows you to inspect details regarding hardware network interfaces.
- Netstat—Shows routing information and network statistics.
- Ping—This fundamental network troubleshooting tool lets you test network connectivity and latency.
- Lookup—Lets you test DNS resolution.
- Traceroute—Helps you analyze how your network connections are routed to their destination.
- Whois—Lets you query whois database servers and find the owner of a DNS domain name or IP address of registered hosts.
- Finger—Enables you to gather information based on a user account name from a network service.
- Port Scan—A handy tool for determining if a network device has services available.

Network Utility can also be opened when your Mac is started from OS X Recovery as covered in Lesson 4. Any time the Mac is started from OS X Recovery, you can open Network Utility by choosing it from the Utilities menu. However, when running from an OS X Recovery system, you do not have access to the Network preferences. This means that the Mac will automatically activate built-in wired Ethernet connections and attempt to acquire configuration via DHCP. Alternatively, the Wi-Fi status menu is available, allowing you to temporarily connect to wireless networks.

Network Utility: Interface Information

When you open Network Utility, you will first see the Info section. This section lets you view the detailed status of any hardware network interface. Even if you've opened Network Utility to use another section, always take a few moments to verify that the network interface is properly activated.

Start by selecting the specific interface you're having issues with from the pop-up menu. You'll notice the selections here do not necessarily match the service names given in the Network preferences. Instead, this menu shows the interfaces using their interface type and UNIX-given names. When working properly, the en0 interface is the first internal Ethernet port, and in most cases the en1 interface is the Wi-Fi interface. If you have a Mac with two internal Ethernet ports, the second internal port is en1 and the Wi-Fi interface is bumped to en2. The FireWire interface is labeled as "fw0".

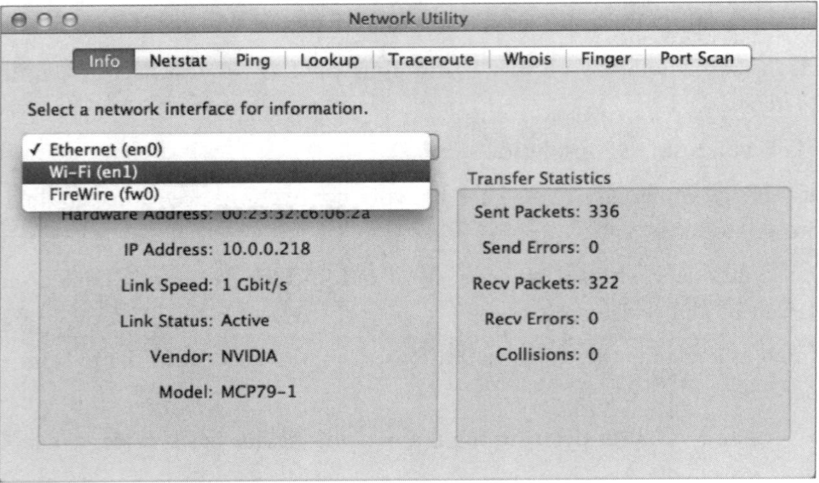

Once you have selected an interface, you can view general interface information to the left and transfer statistics to the right. The primary pieces of information you're looking for here are Link Status, Link Speed, and IP Address(es). Only active hardware network interfaces show as such, and the link speed indicates if the interface is establishing a proper connection. Obviously, a proper IP address is required to establish a TCP/IP connection. You can also identify the selected interface's MAC address, which is used to identify this particular interface on the LAN.

As a final validation of the selected network interface, you can view recent transfer statistics. If you open other network applications to stir up some network traffic, you can verify that packets are being sent and received from this interface. If you are seeing activity here but still experiencing problems, the issue is most likely due to a network or service problem and not the actual network interface. Or, if this interface is experiencing transfer errors, a local network hardware connectivity issue may be the root of your problem.

To resolve hardware network interface issues, always start by checking the physical connection. With wired networks, try different network ports or cabling to rule out physical connection issues. With wireless networks, double-check the Wi-Fi settings and the configuration of any wireless base stations. On rare occasions, you may find that the Mac computer's network hardware is somehow no longer working properly, in which case you should take your Mac to an Apple Authorized Service Provider.

Network Utility: Ping

If you have determined that your network settings are properly configured and the hardware network interface appears to be working correctly, but you are still experiencing network issues, your next step is to test network connectivity using the ping tool. The ping tool is the most fundamental network test to determine if your Mac can successfully send and receive data to another network device. Your Mac sends a ping data packet to the destination IP address, and the other device returns the ping packet to indicate connectivity.

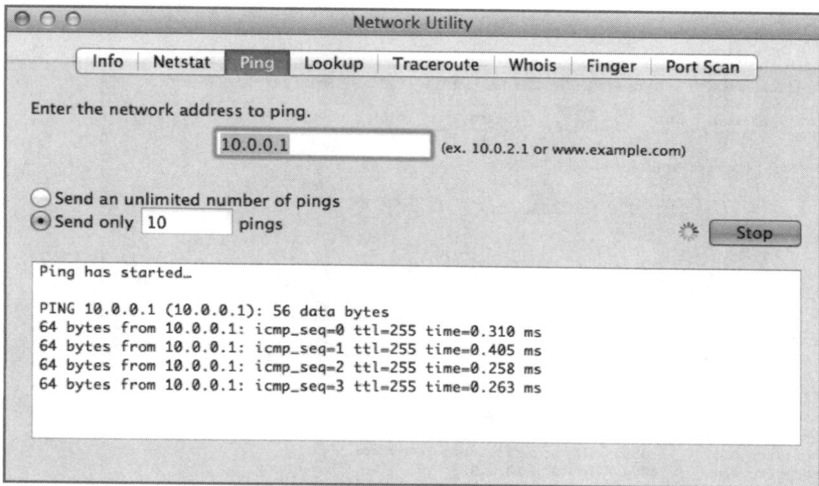

To use ping, open Network Utility, and then click the Ping tab. Start by entering an IP address to a device on the LAN that should always be accessible, like the network router. Remember, using a domain name assumes that your Mac is properly communicating with a DNS server, which might not be the case if you're troubleshooting connectivity issues.

Click the Ping button to initiate the ping process. If the ping is successful, it returns the amount of time it took for the ping to travel to the network device and back. This is typically within milliseconds; experiencing ping times any longer than a full second is unusual.

> **NOTE ►** Some network administrators view excessive pinging as a threat, so many configure their firewalls to block pings or network devices to not respond to any network pings.

Once you have established successful pings to local devices, you can branch out to WAN or Internet addresses. Using the ping tool, you may find that everything works except for the one service you were looking for that prompted you to start troubleshooting the network.

Network Utility: Lookup

If you are able to successfully ping other network devices by their IP address, but attempting to connect to another device by its host name doesn't work, you are experiencing issues related to DNS. The network lookup process allows you to test name resolution against your DNS server.

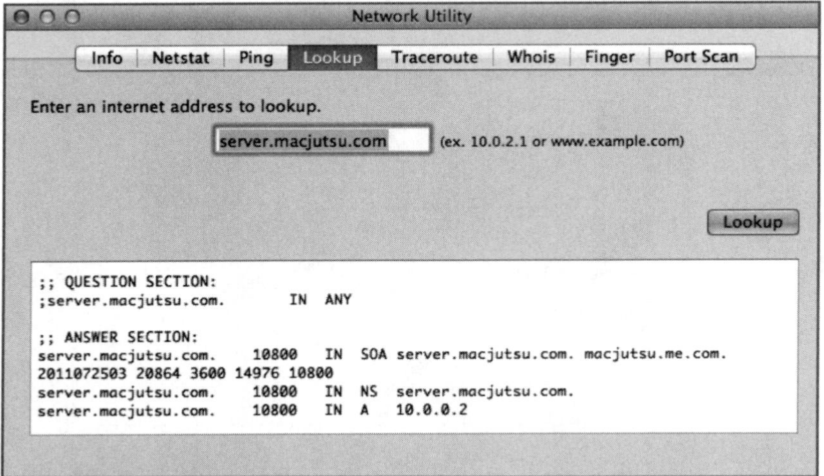

To verify DNS lookup, open Network Utility, and then click the Lookup tab. Start by entering the host name of a device or service in your local domain. If you can resolve local host names but not Internet host names, this indicates that your local DNS server is resolving local names but it's not properly connecting to the worldwide DNS network. If you don't have a local domain, you can use any Internet host name.

Click the Lookup button to initiate the network lookup process. A successful forward lookup returns the IP address of the host name you entered. A successful reverse lookup returns the host name of the IP address you entered. If you are unable to successfully return any lookups, your Mac is not connecting to the DNS server. You can verify this by pinging the DNS server IP address to test for basic connectivity.

Network Utility: Traceroute

If you are able to connect to some network resources but not others, use the network traceroute utility to determine where the connection is breaking down. Remember that WAN and Internet connections require the data to travel through many network routers to find their destination. The traceroute tool examines every network hop between routers using the ping tool to determine where connections fail or slow down.

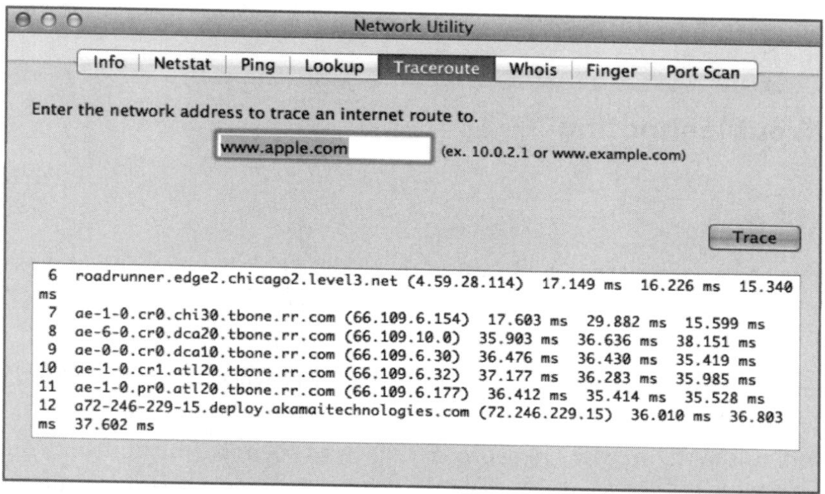

To verify a network TCP/IP route, open Network Utility, and then click the Traceroute tab. Start by entering an IP address to a device on the LAN that should always be accessible, like the network router. Remember, using a domain name assumes that your Mac is properly communicating with a DNS server, which might not be the case if you're troubleshooting connectivity issues.

Click the Trace button to initiate the traceroute process. If traceroute is successful, it returns with the list of routers required to complete the connection and the amount of time it took for the ping to travel to each network router. Note that it sends three probes at each distance, so three times will be listed for each hop. Again, the delay is typically measured within milliseconds; experiencing delay times of any longer than a full second is unusual.

NOTE ► If traceroute doesn't get a reply from any router along the way, it shows an asterisk instead of listing the router address.

NOTE ▶ Some network administrators view excessive pinging as a threat, so many configure their firewalls to block pings or set up network devices to not respond to any network pings.

Once you have established successful routes to local devices, you can branch out to WAN or Internet addresses. Using the traceroute tool, you may find that a specific network router is the cause of the problem.

Exercise 24.1
Network Troubleshooting

▶ Prerequisites

- ▶ You must have created the Local Admin (Exercise 3.1 or 3.2) and Chris Johnson (Exercise 6.1) accounts.

Network connectivity issues can be complex, but familiarity with the arsenal of tools included in OS X will help you develop a solid plan of attack for their resolution. In this exercise you will misconfigure your network settings, and then use the built-in troubleshooting tools in OS X to see how they show the symptoms of the problem and allow you to isolate the problem.

Break Your Network Settings

First, you will run an application that modifies your network settings.

1. If necessary, log in as Chris Johnson.
2. If necessary, open the Network pane in System Preferences and authenticate as Local Admin.
3. Note the currently selected Location so that you can return to it at the end of the exercise.
4. From the Location pop-up menu, choose Edit Locations.
5. Select the current location, and then choose Duplicate Location from the Action (gear) menu below the location list.

6 Name the new location **Broken DNS**.

7 Click Done.

8 Switch to the Broken DNS location, if necessary.

9 Click Apply.

10 Select the primary network service (the one at the top of the list on the left), and click Advanced.

11 Click DNS.

12 If any entries are in the DNS Servers list, make a note of them so you can add them back later, then use the Delete (–) button to remove them.

13 Click the Add (+) button under the DNS Servers list, and add the server address **127.0.0.55**.

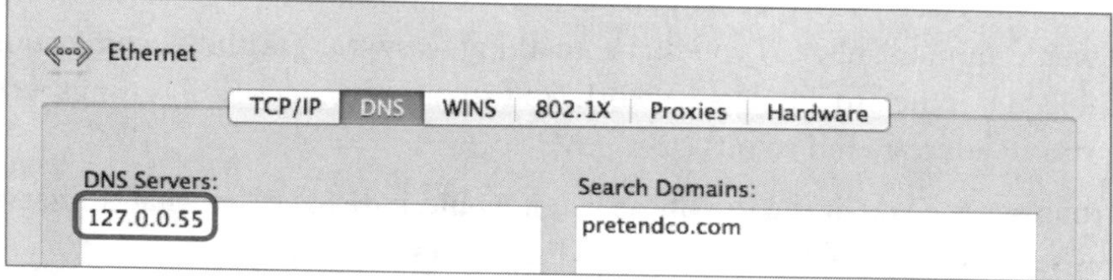

No DNS server is available at this address. The 127.0.0 prefix is reserved for computers to talk to themselves (known as "local loopback" addresses), but OS X actually only uses 127.0.0.1 for this. As a result, this is effectively an invalid address.

14 Click OK, and then click Apply.

Observe the Problem

1 Open Safari.

Safari attempts to load a webpage, but is not able to reach anything. If you leave it long enough it will eventually give up and display an error, but you do not need to wait for this.

2 Enter **www.apple.com** in the address bar and press Return.

Again, Safari is not able to load the page.

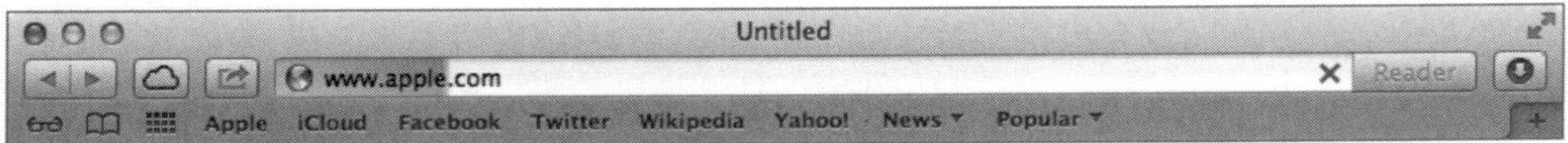

3 Quit Safari.

Check Network Status in the Network Preferences

When you are experiencing a network problem, one of the first things to check is the network service status in the Network preference pane. This allows you to spot simple problems without having to go into more detailed diagnostics.

1 If necessary, open System Preferences and select the Network preference pane.

2 Examine the status indicators next to the network services, and the order they appear in the list.

 If the network service you expected to be active was not showing a green status indicator, it would immediately tell you that something was wrong with the connection (loose cable, not joined to wireless network, and so on) or that critical settings were missing (no IP address, and so on).

 If the wrong service was at the top of the list, it would indicate either that the service order was set incorrectly, or that unexpected services were active.

 In this case, the expected service is green and at the top of the list, so more detailed troubleshooting is necessary.

Use Ping to Test Connectivity

This section walks you through the steps required to determine whether a computer is reachable using ping.

1 Open Network Utility from the Utilities folder.

2 Click the Ping tab.

3 In the "Enter the network address to ping" field, type the domain name of the server you are trying to reach: www.apple.com.

4 Enter 5 in the "Send only" field and make sure it is selected.

5 Click the Ping button.

After a minute or so, you receive a message telling you that it could not resolve www.apple.com. This message indicates that it was not able to use DNS to look up ("resolve") the name www.apple.com and match it to an IP address to send the ping to. In this case, we know that the name www.apple.com is valid because we have used it before, so this indicates that something is wrong with DNS.

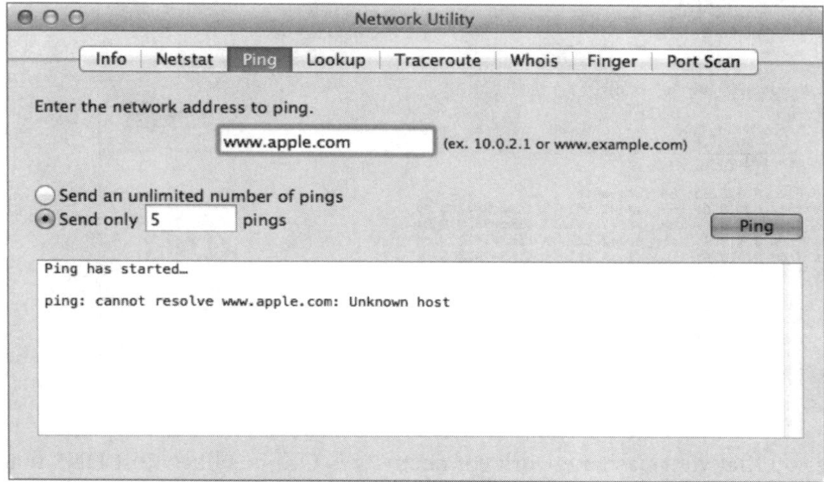

While this gives us some information about the problem, it does not really tell us where the problem lies. It can be very hard to tell the difference between a DNS problem and a complete network failure. If DNS resolution is the only thing failing, it can mimic a complete failure because almost all network access starts with (and depends on) a DNS lookup. On the other hand, if the network is completely disconnected, most attempts to use the network fail at the DNS step, so the only visible symptoms will be DNS errors.

NOTE ▶ At this point you could use the Network Utility Lookup feature to test DNS lookups more directly, but it would not tell you anything you don't already know from the ping error.

One good way to distinguish between a DNS-only problem and a complete network failure is to try to reach a server by its numeric IP address. This bypasses the usual DNS lookup, and hence will work even if DNS is broken.

6 In the "Enter the network address to ping" field, enter the numeric IP address **8.8.8.8**. This is an easy-to-remember address of a public server maintained by Google.

7 Click Ping.

This time, ping reaches the remote computer successfully, and shows statistics for its five test pings.

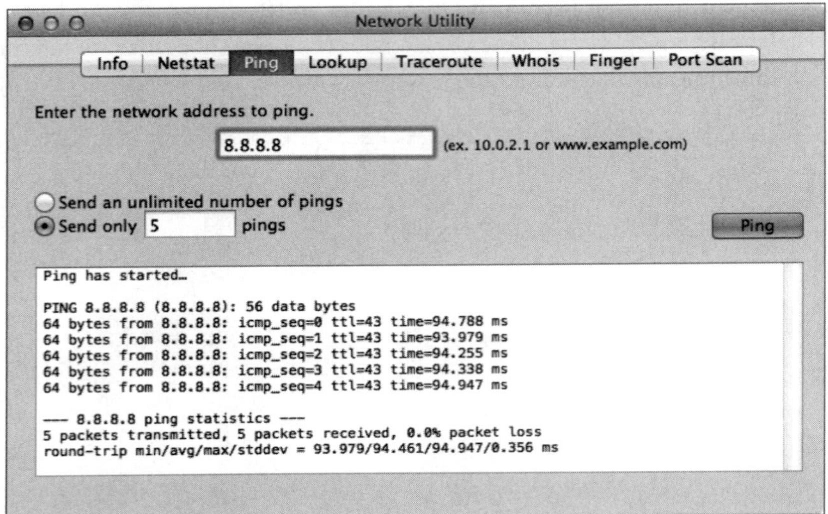

This tells you that your basic network connectivity is OK; it is likely just DNS that is not working.

NOTE ▶ If ping is unable to reach the server at 8.8.8.8, it may indicate that your computer is behind a tightly locked-down firewall. Ping probes are sometimes used in network attacks, and as a result some firewalls are configured to block them. Firewalls increase network security, but they can also complicate troubleshooting considerably.

TIP If ping was not able to reach the remote server, you could use the traceroute tool to test connectivity in more detail. Traceroute attempts to find out what network routers your packets go through on their way to the remote computer. If your packets are not making it all the way to the remote computer, traceroute can often tell you how far they are getting, which tells you more about where the problem is.

Use Network Diagnostics

Network Diagnostics is a program Apple includes in OS X to help users diagnose and fix basic network problems. Now that we've determined that there's something seriously wrong and have some idea where the problem is (DNS), let's see what Network Diagnostics can do to help.

1 If necessary, open System Preferences and select the Network preference pane.

2 Click Assist Me.

It asks if you want assistance setting up a new network configuration or solving a problem.

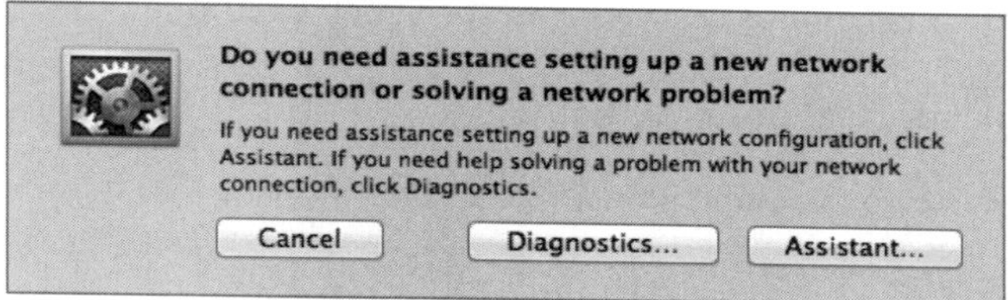

3 Click Diagnostics.

Network Diagnostics opens and automatically runs some basic tests. Several status indicators show the results.

In the following example, the Ethernet, Network Settings, and ISP tests passed (that is, there is a live Ethernet connection, and it has network settings associated with it, and can reach as far as your Internet provider), but the Internet and Server tests failed. Your results may differ depending on what type of connection you have.

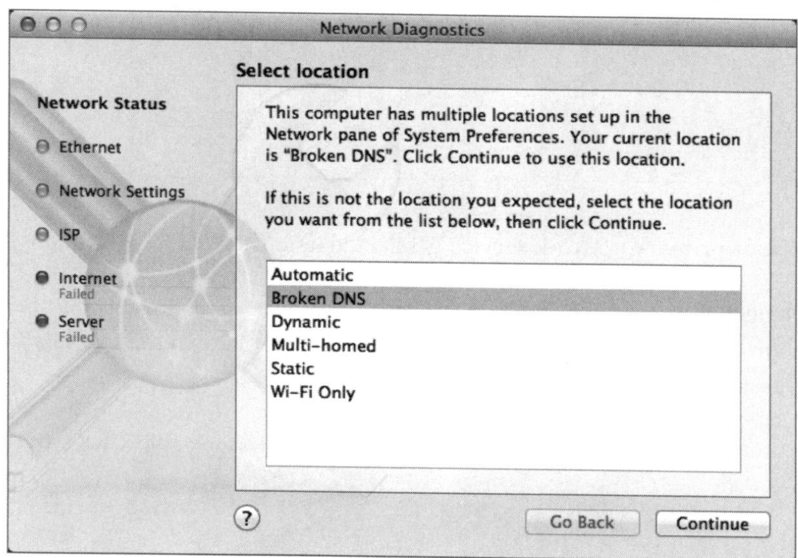

NOTE ▸ The exact results that Network Diagnostics gets depend on what type of network service and configuration you are using. While the following steps include most of the possibilities, you may run into a test result or prompt that is not covered. If this happens, use your best judgment on how to proceed.

Network Diagnostics can troubleshoot this problem further, but you need to tell it what to test and how it's supposed to work. First, you need to tell it which network location to test.

4 Ensure that the Broken DNS location is selected, and then click Continue.

5 If you are prompted, authenticate as Local Admin.

It asks which network service you use to connect to the Internet.

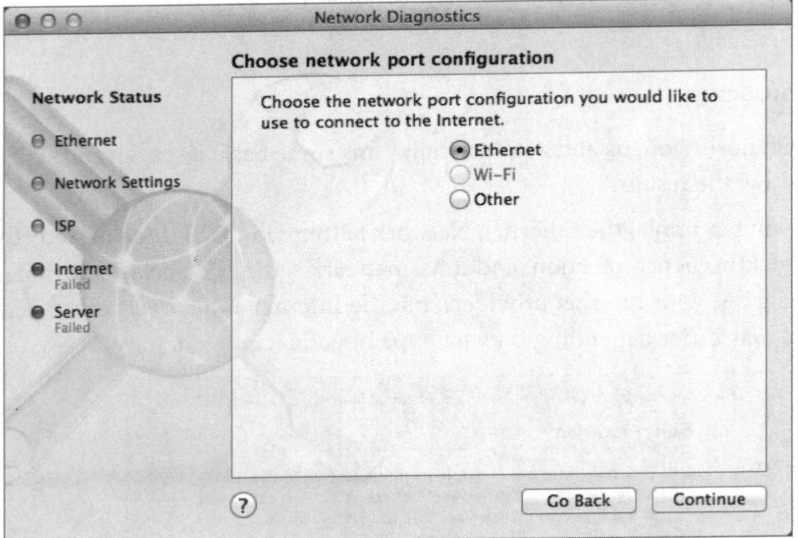

6 Ensure that your primary network service is selected, and then click Continue.

7 If you are using a Wi-Fi service, it asks which wireless network you want to join. Select the appropriate network and click Continue. Authenticate to the wireless network if necessary.

8 If it asks if you are sure you want to use manual settings, select Yes and click Continue.

9 If your primary network service is configured manually, it asks you to verify the current settings. In this situation you need to know how computers on this network should be configured in order to work properly.

The current settings include the invalid DNS server 127.0.0.55, which you configured at the beginning of the exercise.

▶ Change the DNS Servers list back to what it should be. If you are using the Static location you created in Exercise 23.1, it should be **10.0.0.1**. If you do not remember what the old DNS server list was, enter **8.8.8.8** as a temporary fix (you will switch back to the old location with the proper settings later).

▶ When you have corrected the manual settings, click Continue.

10 If your primary service is configured using DHCP, it reports that the DNS server is unavailable, and gives you the option to use DNS servers provided by DHCP.

Select "Use DNS servers provided by DHCP," and click Continue.

If the bad DNS server setting was coming from the DHCP service, this would not help; in this case, however, the problem was the incorrect setting you entered manually, so this solves the problem.

11 If it requires you to authenticate to make the change, authenticate as Local Admin.

12 If it asks if you use a DSL or cable modem, select No and click Continue.

If you select Yes here, it simply suggests restarting the device. This is generally a good troubleshooting step, but irrelevant to the current problem so you can skip it.

At this point, Network Diagnostics reports that your Internet connection appears to be working correctly.

Since the problem in this case was a misconfiguration on your computer, changing your computer's settings was sufficient to fix the problem. If your computer was properly configured but the DNS server was offline or unreachable, you would have seen essentially the same symptoms. Often, telling the difference between a network or server problem and misconfiguration on the client requires knowing the correct settings for a particular network.

13 Click Quit to close Network Diagnostics.

Use Lookup to Test DNS

At this point, you have fixed the problem with the DNS settings on your computer. You will use the Network Utility Lookup pane to verify that it is working properly.

1 In Network Utility, click the Lookup tab.

2 In the "Enter an Internet address to look up" field, enter the address **www.apple.com**.

3 Click Lookup.

The lookup tool queries your configured DNS server for the IP address corresponding to the domain name www.apple.com.

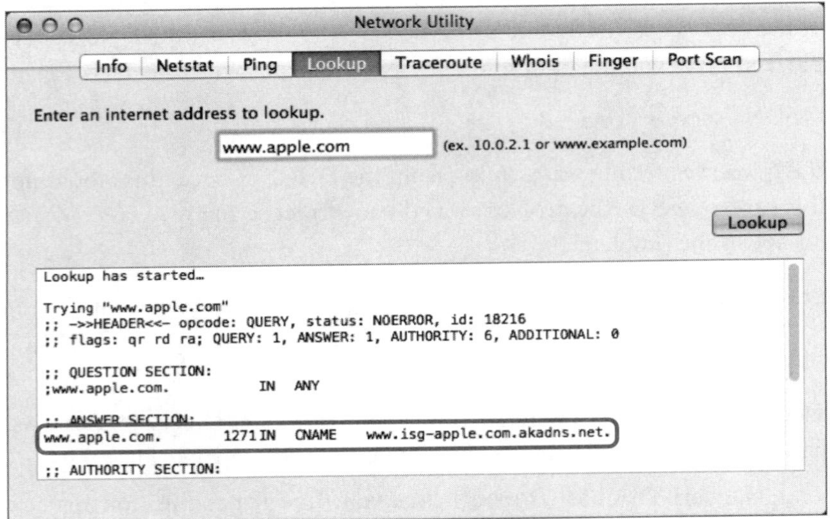

The answer it gets is a bit cryptic. If you examine the "Answer Section," it says (in DNS notation) that www.apple.com has the CNAME (canonical name) www.isg-apple.com.akadns.net. This means that www.apple.com is really just an alias, and that to find its address you should look up www.isg-apple.com.akadns.net. If you looked that up (and probably followed several more layers of aliases), you would eventually get an answer listing "A" (for address) instead of CNAME, and giving the actual IP address where you can reach the www.apple.com server.

This would be useful if you were trying to track down a glitch in the Apple DNS setup, but in this case all you really need to know is that the DNS server gave you an answer, and thus that DNS is working for your computer.

Use Safari to Test Web Access

Different applications rely on different network components to work properly. In the last step, you corrected your network settings. In this step, you will use Safari to test browsing with your current network settings.

1 Open Safari.

This time, Safari is able to successfully load its start page. If you want, you may test browsing other sites to make sure it is fully functional.

Monitor Network Traffic

The Network Utility Info pane can be used to view low-level network interface settings, and also to monitor network throughput on a per-interface basis.

1 Switch to the Network Utility, and click the Info tab.

2 Select your computer's primary network interface from the pop-up menu.

The left side of the pane shows information about the active network connection, and the right side shows statistics about the network packets sent and received through this interface.

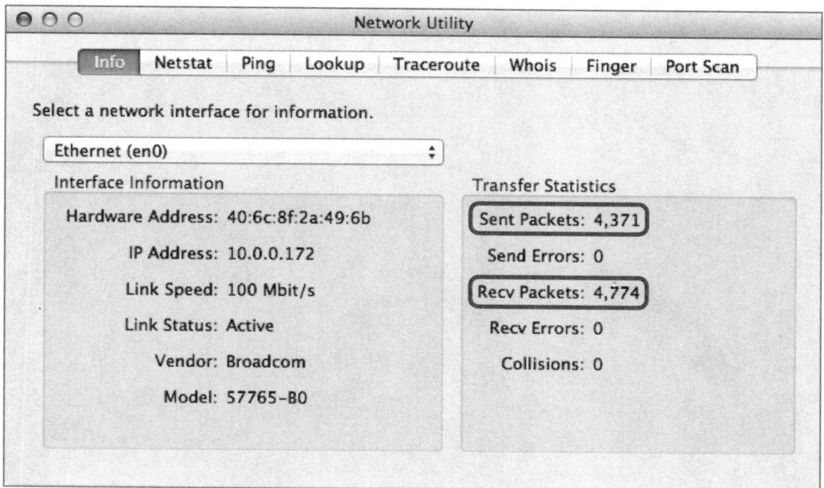

3 Arrange the Safari and Network Utility windows so that Safari is in front, but you can see the Transfer Statistics section of the Network Utility window.

4 In Safari, press Command-R to reload the current page.

   The Sent and Received Packets increase as Safari reloads the current page.

5 In Network Utility, select another network interface from the pop-up menu.

6 Switch to Safari, and reload again.

   The packet counts for this interface might increase slightly due to miscellaneous network chatter, but should not respond specifically to refreshing in Safari.

   You can use this feature of Network Utility to see which network interface your connections are actually running through.

Set Your Network Back to Normal

1 Use the Apple menu's Location submenu to switch from the Broken DNS location to the one you were using at the beginning of this exercise.

2 Reload again in Safari to make sure this location is working as well.

3 Quit Safari, Network Utility, and System Preferences.

Network Services

Lesson **25**

Network Services

Modern operating systems provide a wide range of network and Internet service options, but all of them share the basic network architecture of client software, which accesses network services, and server software, which provides network services. OS X includes support for many popular network protocols, allowing you to connect and access a wide variety of shared network services.

This lesson first discusses the architecture of network services, in a general sense. Then, you will be introduced to the key network service applications built into OS X. You will then learn how OS X can access popular file sharing services. Finally, this lesson covers techniques for troubleshooting network services when problems arise.

GOALS

- Understand how OS X accesses shared network services
- Configure built-in OS X network applications
- Browse and access network file services using the Finder
- Troubleshoot network shared service issues

Reference 25.1
Network Services Architecture

From an architectural standpoint, shared network services are defined by client software (designed to access the service) and server software (designed to provide the service). The network service communication between the client and server software is facilitated by commonly known network protocols or standards.

By adhering to such standards, software developers can create unique yet compatible network client and server software. This allows you to choose the software tool that best fits your needs. For instance, you can use the built-in OS X Mail client created by Apple to access mail services provided by Apple, Google, Yahoo, or Microsoft.

Network Services Software

Some client software takes the form of dedicated applications, as is the case with many Internet services like email and web browsing. Other client software is integrated into the operating system—file and print services, for example. In either case, when you establish a network service connection, settings for that service are saved on the local computer to preference files. These client preferences often include resource locations and authentication information.

On the other side of this relationship is the server software, which is responsible for providing access to the shared resource. Properly setting up server software is usually a much more complicated affair. Server administrators may spend weeks designing, configuring, and administering the software that provides network services. Server-side settings include configuration options, protocol settings, and account information.

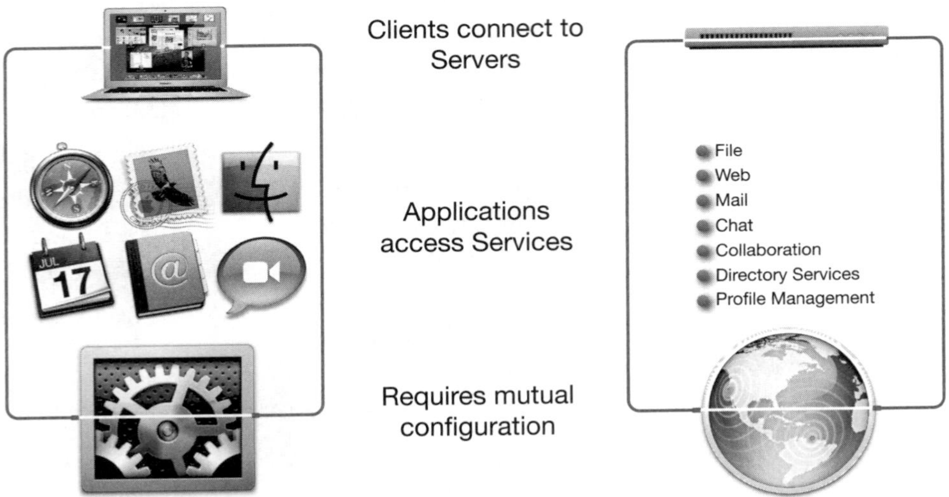

Network Services Communication

Network clients and servers, sometimes of different makes, communicate using commonly known network protocols or network standards. A protocol becomes a standard once it is widely adopted and ratified by a standards committee. Part of what defines a specific network protocol is which TCP or UDP ports are used for communications.

A primary feature of both the TCP and UDP transport mechanisms is the ability to handle multiple simultaneous connections and service protocols. This is accomplished by assigning each communication service to a specific port number or port range. Both TCP and UDP connection ports are defined between 0 and 65,535.

For instance, the standard TCP port for web traffic is port 80. When troubleshooting a network service, you must know the port numbers or ranges for that service. Apple maintains a list of commonly used network services and their associated TCP or UDP ports at Knowledge Base document TS1629, "'Well Known' TCP and UDP ports used by Apple software products."

NOTE ► This guide assumes the default port numbers and port ranges for each network service. Network administrators may choose to use a different port number than the default for testing, to "hide" a service or to bypass router restrictions.

Network Service Identification

At a minimum, accessing a network service requires you to know the service's network location and often requires some way to prove your identity to the service provider. For some network services, you must manually identify the service's location with an Internet Protocol (IP) address or Domain Name Service (DNS) host name. Others feature dynamic service discovery, which allows you to easily locate a network service by simply browsing a list of available services. Details regarding dynamic network service discovery are covered in Lesson 26, "Host Sharing and Personal Firewall."

Once you have selected a network service, you may need to prove your identity to that service provider. This process is called authentication. Successful authentication to a network service is usually the last step in establishing a connection to that service. Once a connection is established, security technologies are normally in place to ensure that you're allowed to access only certain resources. This process is called authorization. Both of these fundamental network service concepts, authentication and authorization, will be covered throughout this lesson and Lesson 26, "Host Sharing and Personal Firewall."

Reference 25.2
Network Service Applications

Because of the widespread adoption of TCP/IP for nearly all LAN, WAN, and Internet communications, there really isn't any difference between how you access a "standard network service" and an "Internet service." With few exceptions, nearly all network services work the same way across a LAN as they do across the Internet. The primary difference between the two is the scope of service. Services like email and instant messaging can certainly work on a local level, but these services are also designed to communicate across separate networks and between servers. OS X includes a range of client applications designed to access different network services.

TIP Although this guide focuses on the network client software built into OS X, many excellent third-party network clients are available for the Mac. In fact, when troubleshooting a network access problem, using an alternative network client is an excellent way to determine if the issue is specific to your primary client software.

Mail, Contacts & Calendars

A feature clearly influenced by iOS, the Mail, Contacts & Calendars preferences provide a single unified interface for configuring network service accounts to be used in a variety of OS X applications and services. In other words, entering a single network service account in the Mail, Contacts & Calendars preferences configures all appropriate network service applications built into OS X.

Through the Mail, Contacts & Calendars preferences, OS X can be configured to use network service accounts for Apple iCloud, Microsoft Exchange, Gmail, Twitter, Facebook, Yahoo, AOL, Vimeo, Flickr, and other common network service protocols including those hosted from a system running OS X Server.

Each different service type includes varying levels of support for built-in OS X applications and services. For example, signing in with a Twitter account configures the system so you can tweet from the Notification Center or any supported application. Whereas signing in to a service that provides multiple features, like Google or Yahoo, in turn configures multiple applications including Mail, Contacts, Calendars, Reminders, Messages, and Notes. The Apple iCloud includes support for even more features, including Photo Stream, saving your Documents & Data, Back to My Mac, and Find My Mac.

Configuring Network Service Accounts

The best method for configuring network service accounts in OS X is by using the Mail, Contacts & Calendars preferences. Simply click an included service provider to get the signup process started. This reveals a service sign-in dialog.

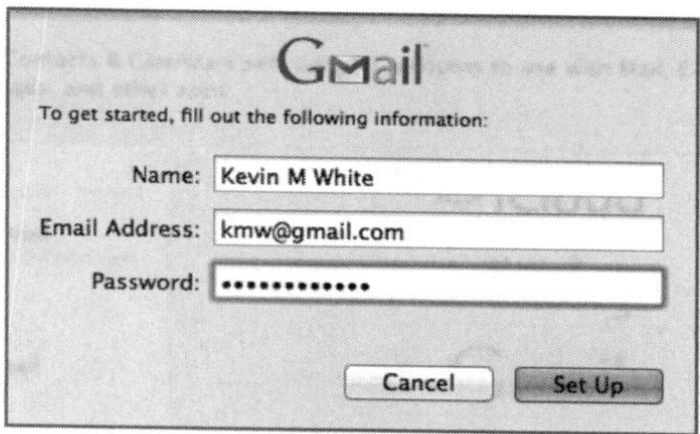

TIP If you don't see the Mail, Contacts & Calendars list of services, simply click the small plus button at the bottom right corner of the preference pane.

If you are signing in to a service with multiple features, after you successfully authenticate, you will be allowed to enable any available options for the service. You can also return to the Mail, Contacts & Calendars preferences at any point to enable or disable a service feature. Additionally, from there you can verify or reenter account information by clicking the Details button.

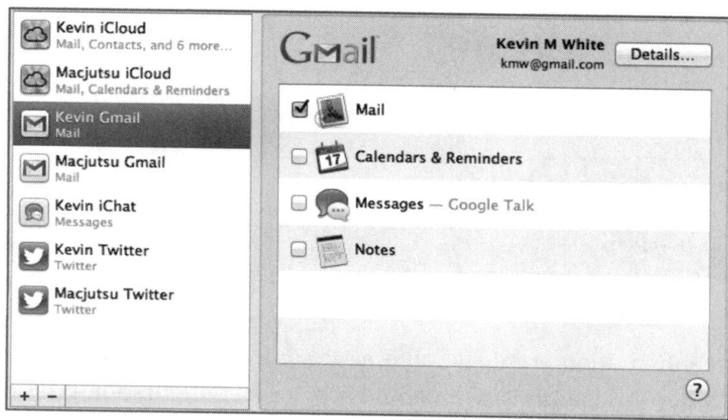

If you need to configure an Internet service that's not listed in the Mail, Contacts & Calendars preferences, or you need to configure a local service provided by your organization, you should click Add Other Account at the bottom of the services list. This reveals a dialog allowing you to manually configure services for Mail, Messages, Calendar, and Contacts. In many cases, if you add a service via this method you will likely have to define additional configuration information. This information should be provided to you by an administrator of the service in question.

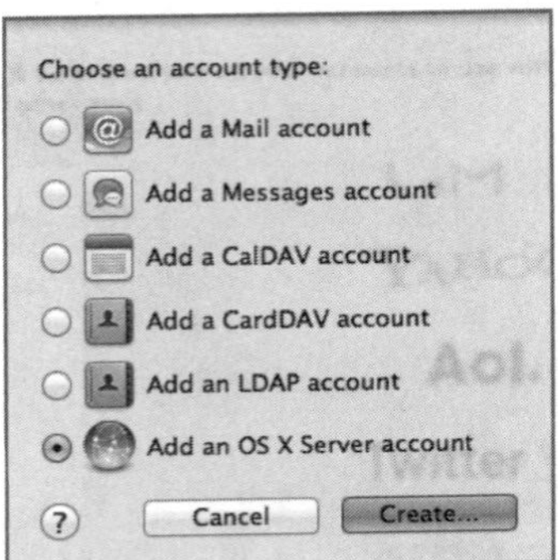

If you choose "Add an OS X Server account," the following dialog searches the local network for an OS X Server v10.7 or newer system that provides compatible services. You can select your server from the list or enter the hostname of a server that's not on your local network. Because OS X can automatically detect OS X Server services, you'll only need to enter network account authentication to complete the setup.

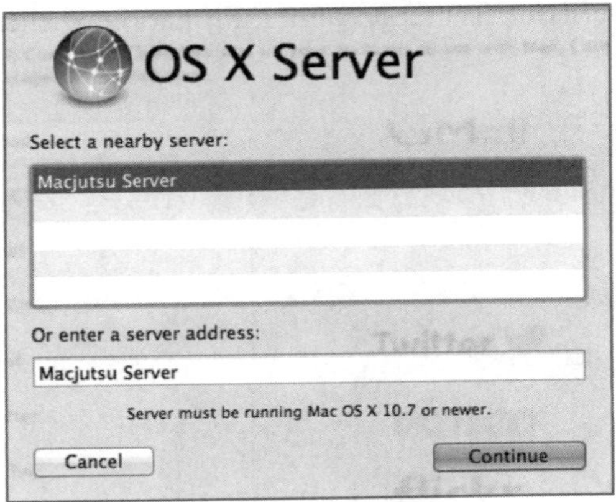

OS X can also accept a configuration profile for automatic configuration of network service accounts settings. A network administrator would provide a configuration profile containing all the necessary settings to properly configure the OS X network applications for a specific network service account. These settings can be deployed by simply double-clicking a local copy of a configuration profile or by having the Mac computer managed by a Mobile Device Management (MDM) solution.

MORE INFO ▶ OS X Server can provide MDM services through Profile Manager, as covered in *Apple Pro Training Series: OS X Server Essentials*.

Safari Web Browser

OS X Mountain Lion includes the updated Safari 6 web browser. Safari is an efficient and robust browser that supports most websites. Apple continues to add new features to Safari with every new version of OS X. For example, Safari in OS X Mountain Lion features a unified search bar that can accept both web URLs and web search queries. Also, Safari now automatically saves all your open tabs to iCloud so they can easily be accessed from any other device also signed in to your iCloud account.

By far the most popular and ubiquitous network service, the Hypertext Transfer Protocol (HTTP), handles web communication using TCP port 80. Secure web communication, known by the acronym HTTPS, encrypts HTTP over a Secure Sockets Layer (SSL) connection and by default uses TCP port 443. Generally, little additional network configuration is required to use web services, as you only need to provide the web browser with the Uniform Resource Locator (URL) or web address of the resource to which you desire to connect. The only exception is if you have to configure web proxies, as described in Lesson 23, "Advanced Network Configuration."

MORE INFO ▶ You can find out more about Safari from the Apple website, www.apple.com/safari.

Mail and Notes

OS X Mountain Lion includes an updated email client, Mail version 6, for handling email communications. Mail supports all standard email protocols and their encrypted counterparts, along with a variety of authentication standards. Mail also includes support for Microsoft Exchange Server 2007 or newer via Exchange Web Services.

NOTE ▶ Mail in OS X requires Microsoft Exchange Server 2007 Service Pack 1 Update Rollup 4 or newer, with Exchange Web Services enabled.

With this many service options, properly configuring mail service settings can be quite daunting. Ideally Mail is configured automatically via the Mail, Contacts & Calendars preferences or via a configuration profile. However, Mail also includes its own Account Setup Assistant to walk you through the process of configuring mail account settings. The assistant even attempts to automatically determine the appropriate mail protocol security and authentication mail protocol settings. This includes support for the Autodiscovery feature of Microsoft Exchange Server. Further, when you set up Mail to use Exchange, the system automatically configures Notes, Contacts, and Calendar to use Exchange as well.

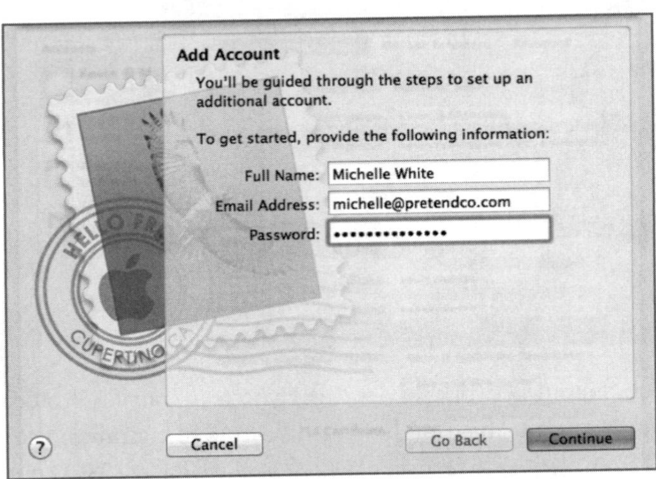

Closely related to the Mail application is the new OS X Mountain Lion Notes application, which allows you to maintain a library of personal notes. The Notes application allows for saving notes on the local system, but it can also save notes to a network mail service to make them available on multiple devices.

The Notes application can only access a network service when configured via the Mail, Contacts & Calendars preferences, and only when the network service provides access to mail services. This is because the Notes application utilizes IMAP mail services as the mechanism for saving the notes. The Notes application creates a special Notes mailbox in your mail service. The Notes application automatically manages this mailbox, thus the OS X Mountain Lion Mail application ignores this mailbox. However, you may notice this mailbox when using older versions of the Mail application or third-party mail clients.

> **TIP** In the Mail, Contacts & Calendars preference you can enable Notes independently from Mail. This includes the ability to enable Notes without enabling Mail. However, Notes still requires use of the IMAP mail service from the network service provider.

> **TIP** Notes can also be shared through other network services by clicking the Share button (rightward arrow inside a box icon) at the bottom of the Notes window.

In summary, the OS X Mountain Lion Mail and Notes supports the following email services:

- Standard mailbox access protocols—The standard protocol used between mail clients and mail servers for receiving mail is either Post Office Protocol (POP) on TCP port 110 or Internet Message Access Protocol (IMAP) on TCP port 143. However, the Notes application can only utilize servers that host IMAP mailboxes. Both protocols can also be encrypted with an SSL connection. By default, encrypted POP uses TCP port 995 and encrypted IMAP uses TCP port 993. Finally, the Apple iCloud service defaults to secure IMAP.
- Standard mail sending protocols—The standard protocol used for sending mail from clients to servers and from server to server is Simple Mail Transfer Protocol (SMTP) on TCP port 25. Again, SMTP can be encrypted with an SSL connection on ports 25, 465, or 587. The ports used for secure SMTP vary based on mail server function and administrator preference. Finally, the Apple iCloud service defaults to secure SMTP.
- Microsoft Exchange Server 2007 or newer—Although popular, this does not use mail standards for client communication. Instead, the Mail application relies on the Exchange Web Services (EWS) protocol for client communication. EWS, as its name implies, uses the standard ports for web traffic: TCP port 80 for standard transport and TCP port 443 for secure transport. Further, though the Exchange server itself uses SMTP for sending mail to other servers, the Mail client again uses the EWS protocol to send the outgoing mail message to the Exchange server.

Calendar and Reminders

OS X Mountain Lion includes an updated scheduling application, Calendar version 6, previously known as iCal. While the Calendar application can certainly work on its own for managing your calendar information on your local Mac, it also integrates with a variety of network calendar services. Again, ideally the Calendar application is configured automatically via the Mail, Contacts & Calendars preferences or via a configuration profile. However, the Calendar application also features an easy-to-use Setup Assistant for configuring specific calendar network service accounts.

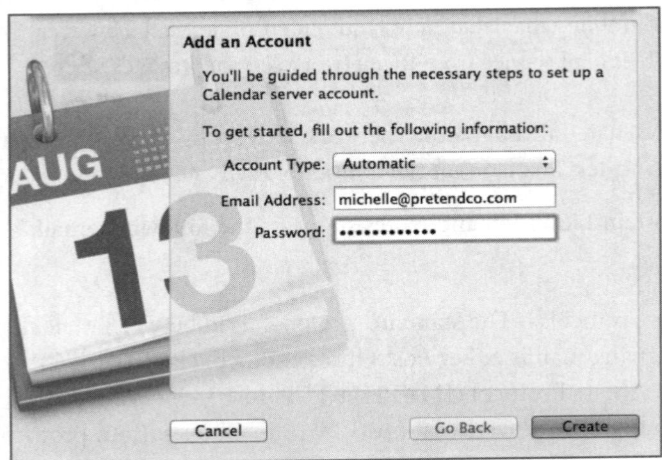

Closely related to the Calendar application is the new OS X Mountain Lion Reminders application, which allows you to maintain a personal to-do list. The Reminders application allows for saving to-do items on the local system, but it can also save reminders to a network calendar service so they are available on multiple devices.

NOTE ▸ You cannot configure Reminders independently of Calendar services.

The Reminders application can only access a network service when configured via the Mail, Contacts & Calendars preferences, and only when the network service provides access to calendar services. This is because the Reminders application utilizes network calendar services as the mechanism for saving the notes. The Reminders application creates to-do calendar events and automatically manages these events. Thus, the OS X Mountain Lion Calendar application ignores to-do events. However, many third-party calendar applications support to-do events within their interface; this includes previous versions of the OS X iCal.

In summary, the OS X Mountain Lion Calendar and Reminders applications support the following network calendar services:

- Internet-based calendar services—Calendars and Reminders can use a variety of Internet-based calendar services, including iCloud, Yahoo, and Google calendar services. All three of these services use the encrypted HTTPS protocol over TCP port 443.
- CalDAV collaborative calendaring—The Calendar application supports a network calendar standard known as CalDAV. As the name implies, this standard uses WebDAV as a transport mechanism on TCP port 8008 or 8443 for encrypted, but CalDAV adds the administrative processes required to facilitate calendar and scheduling collaboration. The OS X Server Calendar service is based on CalDAV. Furthermore, CalDAV is being developed as an open standard so any vendor can create software that provides or connects to CalDAV services.
- Exchange 2007 or newer collaborative calendaring—The Calendar application includes support for this popular calendar service. Again, the OS X Exchange integration relies on EWS, which uses TCP port 80 for standard transport and TCP port 443 for secure transport.
- Calendar web publishing and subscription—The Calendar application allows you to share your calendar information by publishing iCalendar files to WebDAV-enabled web servers. Web-based Distributed Authoring and Versioning (WebDAV) is an extension to the HTTP protocol, so it runs over TCP port 80 or TCP port 443 if encrypted. You can also subscribe to iCalendar files, identified by the filename extension ".ics," hosted on WebDAV servers. Configuration is fairly easy, as accessing a shared calendar is identical to accessing a webpage. Simply provide the Calendar application with the URL of the iCalendar file. Although calendar publishing allows you to easily share calendars one way over the web, it doesn't provide a true collaborative calendaring environment.

  MORE INFO ▶ Apple hosts dozens of compatible calendars at www.apple.com/downloads/macosx/calendars.

- Calendar email invitation—The Calendar application, again using iCalendar files, is integrated with Mail to automatically send and receive calendar invitations as email attachments. In this case the transport mechanism is whatever your primary mail account is configured to use. While this method isn't a calendaring standard, most popular mail and calendar clients can use this method.

Contacts

OS X Mountain Lion includes an updated contact management application, Contacts version 7, previously known as Address Book. Similar to other OS X network applications, while the Contacts application can certainly work on its own for managing nonshared contact information on your Mac, it also integrates with a variety of network contact services.

Again, ideally the Contacts application is configured automatically via the Mail, Contacts & Calendars preferences or via a configuration profile. However, the Contacts application also features an easy-to-use Setup Assistant for configuring specific address or directory network service accounts.

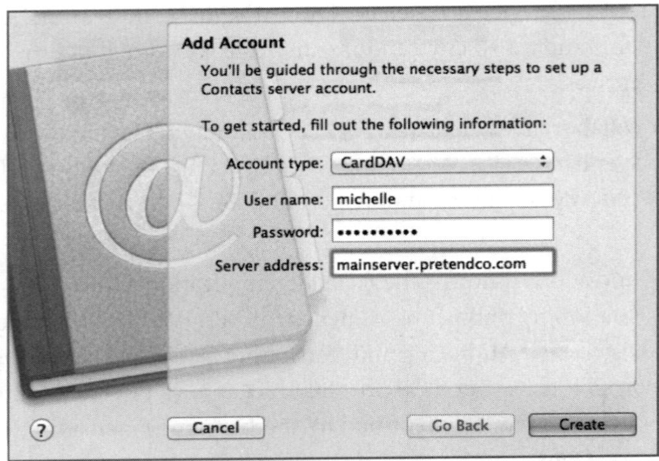

TIP Contacts can also share through other network services by clicking the Share button (rightward arrow inside a box icon) at the bottom of the Contacts window.

TIP You can update contact information from other services in the Mail, Contacts & Calendars preferences by selecting the service and clicking the Update Contacts button. For example, using this feature you can automatically update Twitter handles saved to the Contacts application.

In summary, the OS X Mountain Lion Contacts application supports the following network contact services:

- Internet-based contact services—Contacts can use a variety of Internet-based contact services, including iCloud, Yahoo, and Google contact services. All three of these services use the encrypted HTTPS protocol over TCP port 443.

- CardDAV contact sharing—Contacts supports a network calendar standard known as CardDAV. Again, as the name implies, this standard uses WebDAV as a transport mechanism on TCP port 8800 or 8843 for encrypted, but CardDAV adds the administrative processes required to facilitate contact sharing. The OS X Server Contacts service is based on CardDAV. Furthermore, CardDAV is being developed as an open standard so any vendor can create software that provides or connects to CardDAV services.

  NOTE ▶ The Apple selection of TCP ports 8800 and 8843 for CardDAV is not based on any assigned standard. Some implementations of CardDAV may use the standard ports for HTTP(S) and TCP ports 80 and 443 for encrypted.

- Exchange 2007 or newer contact sharing—The Contacts application includes support for this popular contact sharing service. Again, the OS X Exchange integration relies on Exchange Web Services (EWS), which uses TCP port 80 for standard transport and TCP port 443 for secure transport.
- Directory service contacts—The Contacts application can search contact databases via the standard for network directory services, the Lightweight Directory Access Protocol (LDAP). The Contacts application can be configured for LDAP services either directly from its account Setup Assistant or via integration with the OS X systemwide directory service, as configured in the User & Groups preferences.

Messages

Instant messaging has grown well beyond text chatting with Messages version 7, formerly known as iChat, included with OS X Mountain Lion. The Messages application supports ten-way audio conferencing, four-way video conferencing, peer-to-peer file sharing, remote screen sharing, and high-resolution Messages Theater for sharing video from supported applications. This latest version of the Messages application also introduces support for iCloud iMessage push-based messaging service, which allows you to communicate with iOS devices as well.

Again, ideally Messages is configured automatically via the Mail, Contacts & Calendars preferences or via a configuration profile. In fact, you can only enable iCloud iMessage services from the Mail, Contacts & Calendars preferences or the iCloud preferences. However, Messages also features an easy-to-use Setup Assistant for configuring most chat network service accounts.

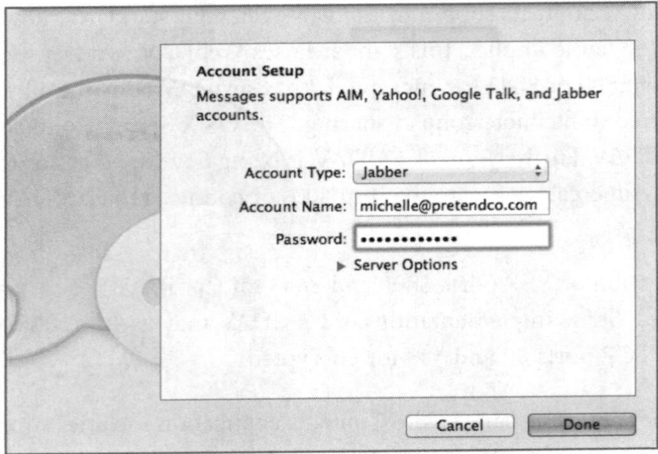

NOTE ▶ The Messages application's advanced features, such as video conferencing, screen sharing, and Messages Theater, are not supported by many third-party chat clients. When you select a chat participant, the Messages application automatically determines the client software's messaging capabilities and allows you to use only supported features.

In summary, the OS X Mountain Lion Messages application supports the following categories of chat services:

- Internet messaging services—The Messages application supports AOL Instant Messenger (AIM), Google Talk, and Yahoo chat accounts. Assuming you have already registered for an account through one of these service providers, configuring Messages simply involves entering your account name and password.
- iCloud iMessage—Based on the Apple push technology, the iMessage service is unique among chat services. The Apple push technology is highly efficient for devices that rely on battery power and may occasionally lose network connectivity. This makes the iMessage service ideal for messaging with iOS devices. Again, you can only configure iMessage via the Mail, Contacts & Calendars preferences or the iCloud preferences.

NOTE ▶ The iCloud iMessage service does not support advanced features such as video conferencing, screen sharing, and Messages Theater. These services are only available when using traditional chat services like AIM or Jabber.

- Privately hosted messaging services—The Messages application supports open source Jabber servers, including the OS X Server Messages service. Jabber servers are based on the Extensible Messaging and Presence Protocol (XMPP), which uses TCP port 5222 or 5223 for encrypted.
- Ad hoc messaging—The Messages application can use the Bonjour network discovery protocol to automatically find other Messages or iChat users. No configuration is necessary to access Bonjour messaging. Bonjour details are covered in Lesson 26, "Host Sharing and Personal Firewall."

The Messages application supports a wide variety of messaging features and instant messaging protocols—which means it uses far too many TCP and UDP ports to list here. However, an older Knowledge Base document HT1507, "Using iChat with a firewall or NAT router," lists some the possible ports Messages may attempt to use.

Reference 25.3
File Sharing Protocols

Many protocols exist for transferring files across networks and the Internet, but the most efficient are those designed specifically to share file systems. Network file servers can make entire file systems available to your client computer across the network.

Client software built into the OS X Finder can mount a network file service much as it would mount a locally connected storage volume. Once a network file service is mounted to the Mac, you can read, write, and manipulate files and folders as if you were accessing a local file system.

Additionally, access privileges to network file services are defined by the same ownership and permissions architecture used by local file systems. Details regarding file systems, ownership, and permissions are covered in Lesson 12, "Permissions and Sharing."

OS X provides built-in support for these network file service protocols:

- Apple Filing Protocol (AFP) version 3 on TCP port 548 or encrypted over SSH on TCP port 22—This is the Apple native network file service. The current version of AFP supports all the features of the Apple native file system, Mac OS Extended.

- Server Message Block (SMB) on TCP ports 139 and 445—This network file service is mainly used by Windows systems, but many other platforms have adopted support for this protocol. SMB also supports many of the advanced file system features used by OS X. Further, new in OS X is support for Distributed File Service (DFS) referrals. DFS allows Windows administrators to distribute SMB services across multiple servers.
- Network File System (NFS) version 4, which may use a variety of TCP or UDP ports—Used primarily by UNIX systems, it supports many advanced file system features used by OS X.
- Web-based Distributed Authoring and Versioning (WebDAV) on TCP port 80 (HTTP) or encrypted on TCP port 443 (HTTPS)—This protocol is an extension to the common HTTP service and provides basic read/write file services.
- File Transfer Protocol (FTP) on TCP ports 20 and 21 or encrypted on TCP port 989 and 990 (FTPS)—This protocol is in many ways the lowest common denominator of file systems. FTP is supported by nearly every computing platform, but it provides only the most basic file system functionality. Further, the Finder supports only read capability for FTP or FTPS shares.

  NOTE ▸ Don't confuse FTPS with another similar protocol, SFTP. The distinction is that FTPS uses SSL encryption on TCP port 990 and SFTP uses SSH encryption on TCP port 22. The Finder does not support FTPS. However, both are supported in the Terminal.

Reference 25.4
Connecting to File Shares

The Finder provides two methods for connecting to a network file system: automatically discovering shared resources by browsing them in the Finder Network folder or manually connecting by entering the address of the server providing the file service.

Browsing to File Shares

You can browse for dynamically discovered file services from two locations in the Finder. The first location is the Shared list located in the Finder sidebar. If enabled in the Finder preferences, the Shared list is ideal for quickly discovering computers providing file services on a small network. The Shared list shows only the first eight discovered computers providing services. If additional servers are discovered, the last item in the Shared list, All Items, is a link to the Finder Network folder.

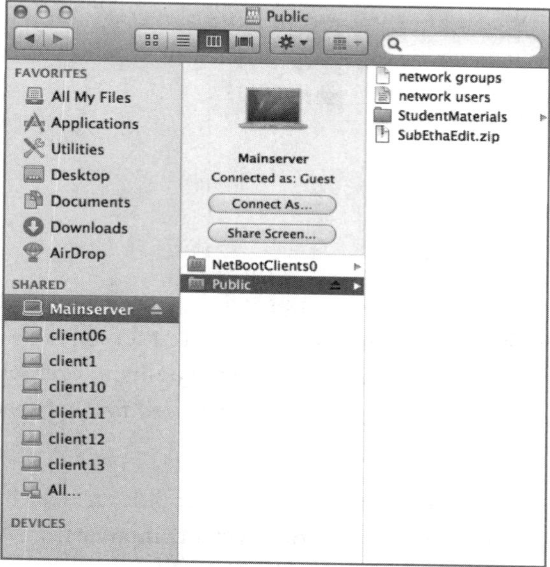

TIP The sidebar also appears in any application's Open dialog with exactly the same items as are available from the Finder.

TIP The Finder Shared list shows servers that you are currently connected to even if they didn't originally appear in the Shared list.

TIP The Finder also lets you browse to screen sharing (VNC) hosts via Bonjour, as covered in Lesson 26, "Host Sharing and Personal Firewall."

The Finder Network folder is a special place in OS X. The Network folder is not a standard folder at all; it's an amalgamation of all dynamically discovered network file services and all currently mounted file systems, including manually mounted file systems. Obviously, the Network folder is constantly changing based on information gathered from the two dynamic network service discovery protocols supported by OS X—Bonjour and SMB/NetBIOS/WINS—so you can only browse AFP or SMB file services from the Network folder.

On smaller networks there may only be one level of network services. Conversely, if you have a larger network that features multiple service discovery domains, they appear as subfolders inside the Network folder. Each subfolder is named by the domain it represents. Items inside the domain subfolders represent shared resources configured for that specific network area.

To browse and connect to an AFP or SMB file service from the Finder Sidebar, select the computer you wish to connect to from the Shared list, or select a computer from the Finder Network folder. In the Finder, the quickest routes to the Network folder are to either choose Go > Network from the menu bar or press Shift-Command-K. Selecting a computer from either the Shared list or the Network folder yields similar results.

Automatic File Service Authentication

The moment you select a computer providing services, the Mac attempts to automatically authenticate using one of three methods:

- If you are using Kerberos single sign-on authentication, the Mac attempts to authenticate to the selected computer using your Kerberos credentials.
- If you are using non-Kerberos authentication but you connected to the selected computer previously and chose to save the authentication information to your keychain, the Mac attempts to use the saved authentication information.
- The Mac attempts to authenticate as a guest user. Keep in mind that guest access is an option on file servers that many administrators disable.

If the Mac succeeds in authenticating to the selected computer, the Finder shows you the account name it connected with and also lists the shared volumes available to this account.

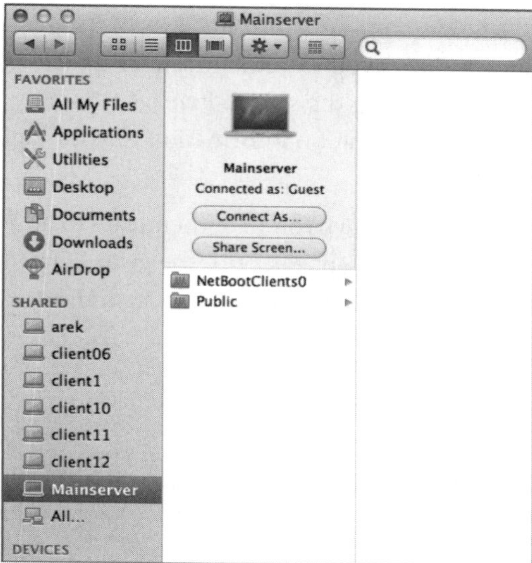

Manual File Service Authentication

If the Mac was unable to automatically connect to the selected computer, or you need to authenticate with a different account, click the Connect As button to open an authentication dialog.

You can authenticate to a sharing service using one of three methods:

- Selecting the Guest radio button, if available, indicates that you wish to connect anonymously to the file service.
- Selecting the Registered User radio button allows you to authenticate using a local or network account known by the computer providing the shared items. Optionally, you can select the checkbox that will save this authentication information to your login keychain.
- Selecting the "Using an Apple ID" radio button allows you to authenticate to an AFP share using an Apple ID. In order for this option to appear, both the local Mac and the computer hosting the share must be running OS X or a newer system. Further, the local account on your Mac must be tied to an Apple ID as covered in Lesson 6, "User Accounts."

Mounting a Share Item When Browsing

Click the Connect button, and the Mac authenticates and shows you a new list of shared volumes available to the account. Each available share appears as a folder. Click once on a shared item to connect and mount its file system.

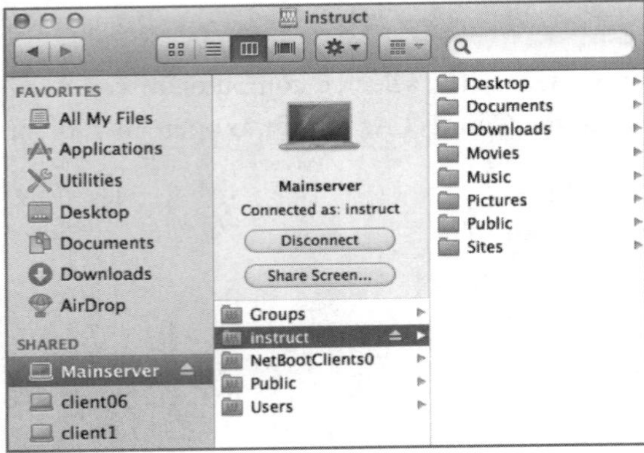

Once the Mac has mounted the network file share, it can appear in several locations from the Finder or any application's open dialog, including the Computer location, the desktop, and the sidebar's Shared list, depending on configuration. By default, connected network volumes do not show up on the desktop. You can change this behavior from the General tab of the Finder Preferences dialog.

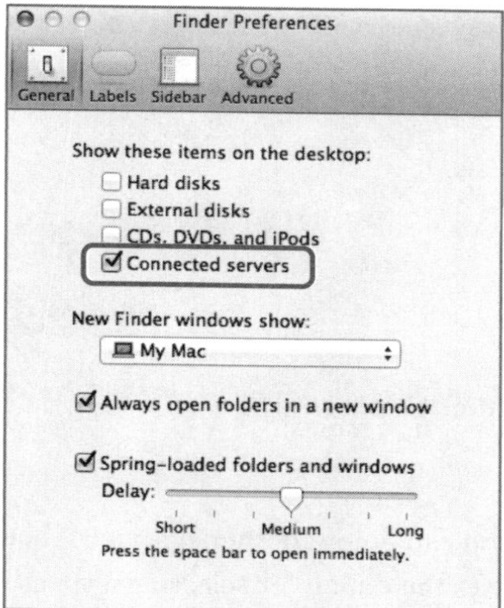

TIP Again, the sidebar also appears in any application's Open dialog with exactly the same items that are available from the Finder.

Manually Connecting File Services

To manually connect to a file service, you must specify a network identifier (URL) for the file server providing the service. You may also have to enter authentication information and choose or enter the name of a specific shared resource path. When connecting to an AFP or SMB service, you can authenticate first and then choose a shared item, or optionally provide a path. Conversely, when connecting to an NFS, WebDAV (HTTP), or FTP service, you may have to specify the shared items or full path as part of the server address and then authenticate if required.

Manually Connect to AFP or SMB

To manually connect to an AFP or SMB file service from the Finder, choose Go > Connect to Server, or press Command-K to open the Finder "Connect to Server" dialog. In the Server Address field, enter `afp://` or `smb://` followed by the server's IP address, DNS host name, computer name, or Bonjour name.

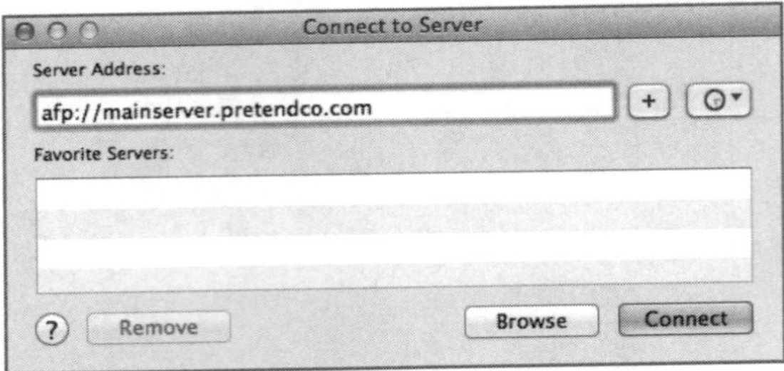

TIP If you don't specify a protocol prefix, the "Connect to Server" dialog defaults to the AFP protocol.

TIP Optionally, after the server address, you can enter another slash and then the name of a specific shared item. This bypasses the dialog for selecting a specific file share.

TIP When connecting to DFS via SMB, make sure to follow the guidelines as outlined in Knowledge Base document HT4794, "OS X Lion: Guidelines for connecting to a DFS namespace via SMB."

If automatic file service authentication is available, as covered earlier in the "Automatic File Service Authentication" section of this lesson, you will not have to enter authentication information. If not, a dialog appears requiring you to enter authentication information. This authentication dialog is identical to the one covered earlier in the "Manual File Service Authentication" section of this lesson.

Once you have authenticated to the file service, you are presented with the list of shared volumes that your account is allowed to access. Select the shared item you wish to mount. Optionally you can hold down the Command key to select multiple shared items from the list.

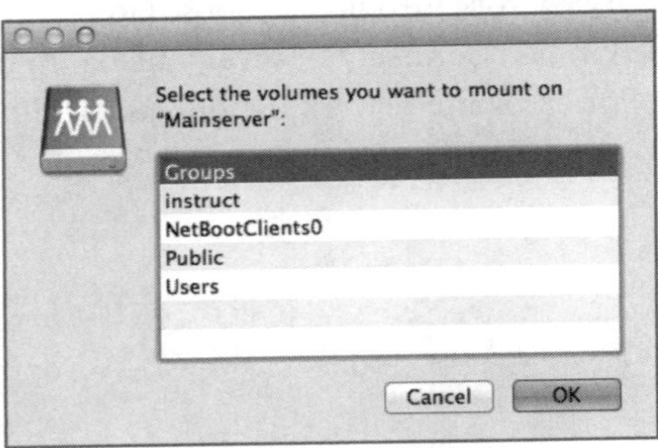

Manually Connect to NFS, WebDAV, or FTP

To manually connect to an NFS, WebDAV, or FTP file service from the Finder, choose Go > Connect to Server, or press Command-K to open the Finder "Connect to Server" dialog.

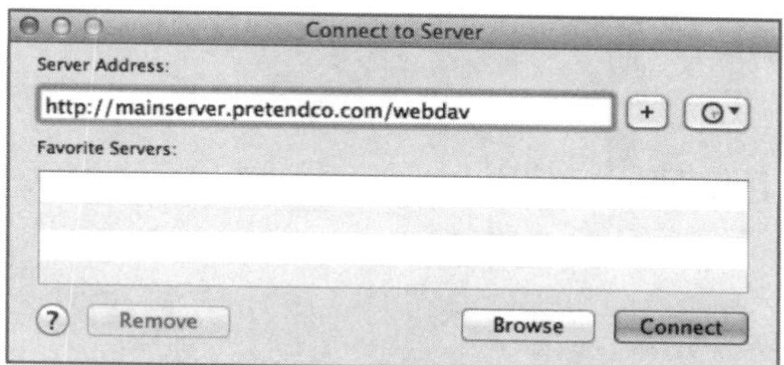

TIP Clicking Browse in the "Connect to Server" dialog brings you to the Finder Network folder, allowing you to browse for a server, as covered in the previous section of this lesson.

In the Server Address field, enter one of the following:

- nfs:// followed by the server address, another slash, and then the absolute file path of the shared items.
- http:// for WebDAV (or https:// for WebDAV encrypted via SSL), followed by the server address. Each WebDAV site has only one mountable share, but you can optionally enter another slash and then specify a folder inside the WebDAV share.
- ftp:// (or ftps:// for FTP encrypted via SSL), followed by the server address. FTP servers also have only one mountable root share, but you can optionally enter another slash and then specify a folder inside the FTP share.

Depending on the protocol settings, you may be presented with an authentication dialog. Specifically, NFS connections never display an authentication dialog. The NFS protocol uses the local user that you're already logged in as for authorization purposes or Kerberos single sign-on authentication.

If you are presented with an authentication dialog, enter the appropriate authentication information here. Optionally, you can select the checkbox that will save this authentication information to your login keychain. When connecting to NFS, WebDAV, or FTP file services, the share mounts immediately after authentication.

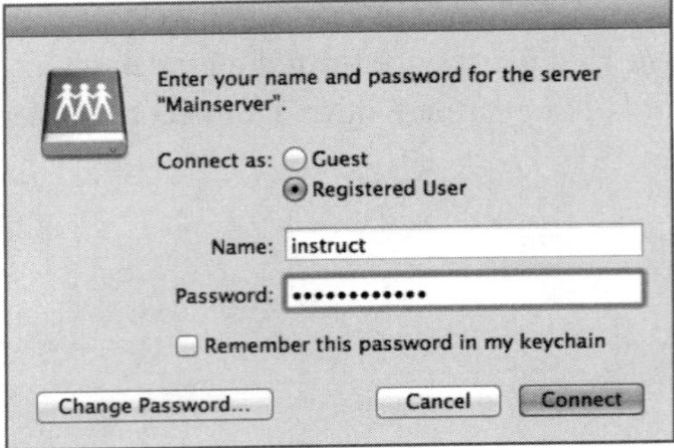

Manually Mounted Shares

Again, once the Mac has mounted the network file share, it can appear in several locations from the Finder, including the Computer location, the desktop, and the sidebar's Shared list, depending on configuration. However, mounted network volumes *always* appear at the Computer location in the Finder, accessible by choosing Go > Computer or by pressing Shift-Command-C. Again, you can also set Finder preferences to show mounted network volumes on the desktop and in the sidebar's Shared list, as covered in the previous section.

TIP Remember, the sidebar also appears in any application's Open dialog with exactly the same items as are available from the Finder.

Manually entering server information every time you connect to a server is a hassle. Two features in the "Connect to Server" dialog make this process efficient for your users. The dialog maintains a history of your past server connections. You can access this history by clicking the small clock icon to the right of the Server Address field. Also, you can create a list of favorite servers by clicking the plus button to the right of the Server Address field.

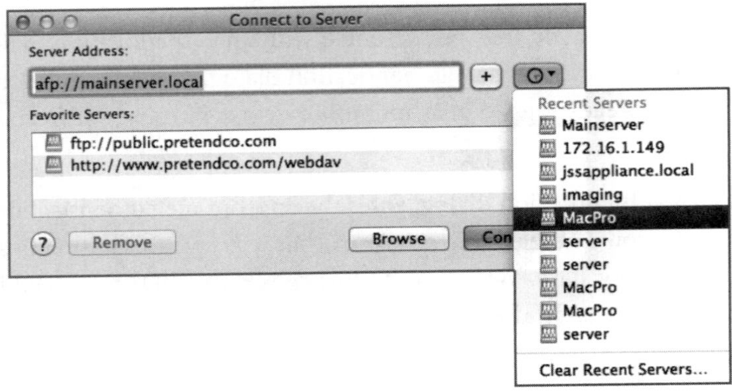

Disconnecting Mounted Shares

It is important to recognize that the Mac treats mounted network volumes similarly to locally attached volumes, so you must remember to always properly unmount and eject network volumes when you're done with them. Mounted network volumes are unmounted and ejected from the Finder using the same techniques you would use on a locally connected volume. Unmounting and ejecting volumes is covered in Lesson 10, "File Systems and Storage." One difference in working with mounted volumes is that the Eject button appears multiple times in the Finder wherever the server name or the shared items appear.

In practice, though, it's difficult for users to remember they have network shares mounted, as there is no locally attached hardware device to remind them. Further, laptop users often roam out of wireless network range without even thinking about what network shares they may have mounted.

If a network change or problem disconnects the Mac from a mounted network share, the Mac spends several minutes attempting to reconnect to the server hosting the shared items. If after several minutes the Mac cannot reconnect to the server, the user sees an error dialog allowing him to fully disconnect from the server.

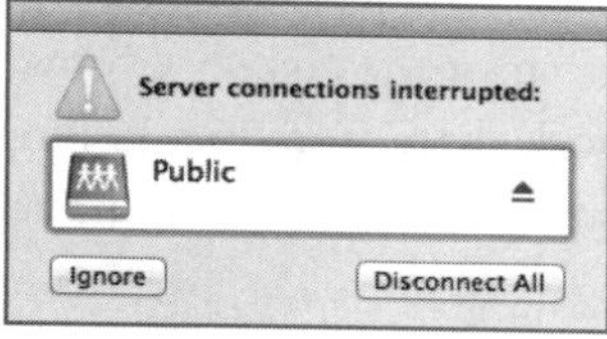

Automatically Connecting File Shares

On a positive note, because the Finder treats mounted network shares as similar to other file system items, you can save time and make life easier for you and your users by creating automatic connections to network shared items. One method is to have a network share mount automatically when a user logs in by adding the network share to the user's login items. Managing login items is covered in Lesson 6, "User Accounts."

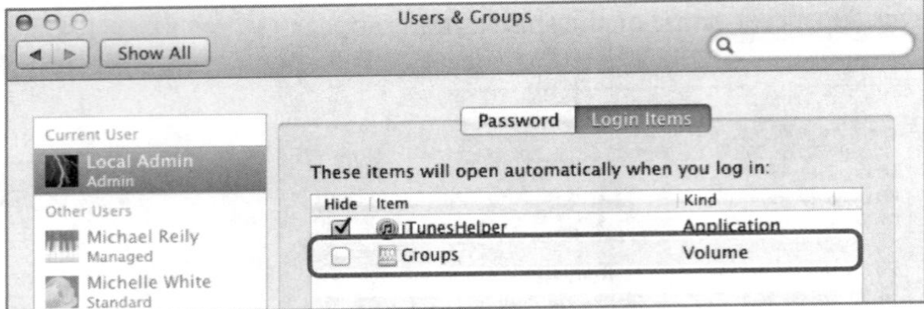

Alternately, you can create easy-to-use shortcuts to often-used network shares. One method involves creating Dock shortcuts by dragging network shares or their enclosed items to the right side of the Dock. You can also create aliases on the user's desktop that link to often-used network shares or even specific items inside a network share. Creating aliases is covered in Lesson 14, "Hidden Items and Shortcuts." Either method you use automatically connects to the network share when the item is selected.

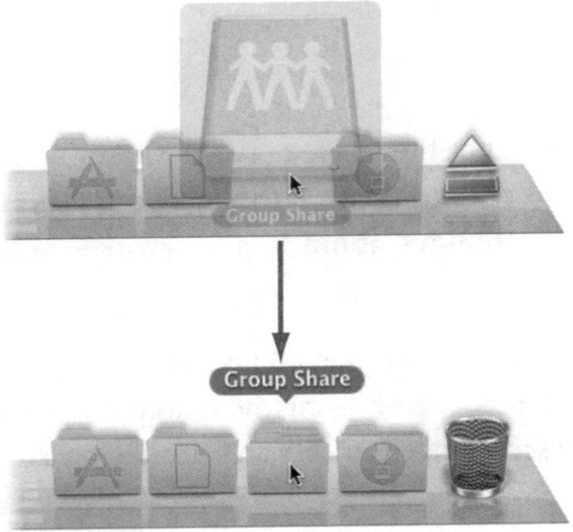

TIP You cannot drag and drop from the Finder sidebar or the Network browser to the login items on the Dock. Instead, select the network share from the desktop or the Computer location in the Finder. You can access the Computer location in the Finder by choosing Go > Computer.

TIP Remember that by using Kerberos single sign-on authentication or by saving authentication information to the keychain, you can bypass authentication dialogs as well.

Reference 25.5
Network Service Troubleshooting

To effectively troubleshoot a network issue, you must isolate the issue into one of three categories: local, network, or service. Most issues involving failure to access network services probably fall under the service category. This means that you should probably focus most of your efforts toward troubleshooting the specific service you're having issues with.

However, before digging too deep into troubleshooting the specific network service, quickly check for general network issues. First, check to see if other network services are working. Opening a web browser and navigating to a few different local and Internet websites is always a good general network connectivity test.

To be thorough, also test other network services, or test from other computers on the same network. If you're experiencing problems connecting to a file server but you can connect to web servers, chances are your TCP/IP configuration is fine, and you should concentrate on the specifics of the file server. If you're only experiencing problems with one particular service, you probably don't have local or network issues and you should focus your efforts on troubleshooting just that service.

Conversely, if other network clients or services aren't working either, your issue is likely related to local or network issues. Double-check local network settings to ensure proper configuration from both the Network preferences and Network Utility. If you find that other computers aren't working, you might have a widespread network issue that goes beyond troubleshooting the client computers. For more information on general network troubleshooting, see Lesson 24, "Network Troubleshooting."

Network Utility: Port Scan

Once you decide to focus on troubleshooting a problematic network service, one of your most important diagnostic tools is the network port scan utility. Part of the Network Utility application, port scan scans for any open network service ports on the specified network address.

As covered earlier in this lesson, network service protocols are tied to specific TCP and UDP network ports. Network devices providing a service must leave the appropriate network ports open in order to accept incoming connections from other network clients. A port scan reveals whether the required ports are indeed open. If the ports aren't open, that device is either not providing the expected service or is configured to provide the service in a nonstandard method. Either way, this indicates that the issue lies with the device providing the service, not your Mac.

NOTE ► Network administrators view repeated network pings and broad port scans as a threat. Thus, some network devices are configured to not respond even when working properly. In general, you should avoid excessive network pinging and scanning an unnecessarily broad range of ports when testing others' servers.

To verify network service availability, start by opening Network Utility and clicking the Ping tab at the top. Before performing a port scan, check for basic network connectivity by attempting to ping the device that is supposed to be providing the service. Enter the device's network address or host name and click the Ping button. If the ping is successful, it returns with the amount of time it took for the ping to travel to the network device and then return. Assuming you have network connectivity to the other device, continue to the port scan.

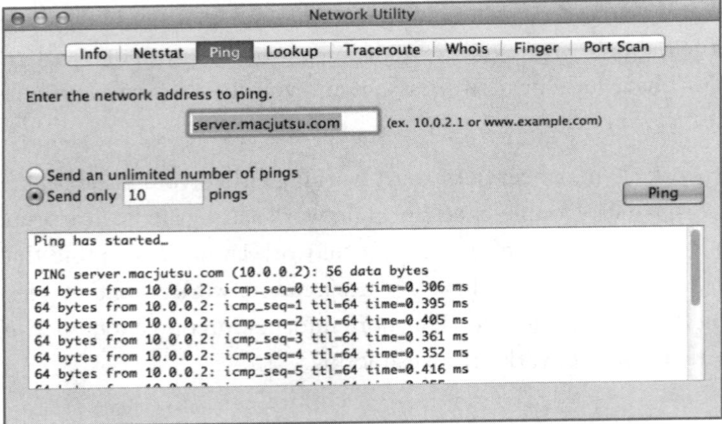

To scan for a network service, click the Port Scan tab. Again, enter the network address or host name of the device that is supposed to be providing the service. If you're only troubleshooting a specific service, limit the port scan to just that service's default ports by selecting the appropriate checkbox and entering a beginning and ending port range. Click the Scan button to initiate the port scan process.

NOTE ▶ There are 65,535 available TCP and UDP network ports, so a full port scan is unnecessary and overly time intensive. Even if you don't know the specific port, most common ports are between 0 and 1024.

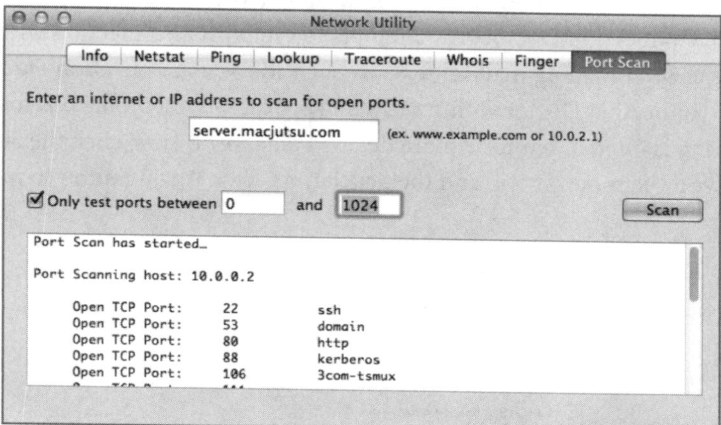

Depending on the scan range you choose, it may take several minutes to complete the scan. Any open ports discovered will be listed along with the associated network protocol if known.

NOTE ▶ There are some inaccuracies with the protocol reporting of the port scan feature. For example, port 106 (listed as 3com-tsmux) is actually the OS X Server password service, and port 625 (listed as dec_dlm) is actually the directory service proxy. This is because these ports are registered by the IANA (iana.org) for the reported protocols. However, Apple is using these numbers for its own purposes.

Troubleshooting Network Applications

Aside from general network service troubleshooting, there are a few application-specific troubleshooting techniques you can try. First, double-check any application-specific configuration and preference settings. It takes only a few moments, and you may find that users have inadvertently caused the problem by changing a setting they shouldn't have.

Be aware of these specifics when troubleshooting network applications:

- Safari—Safari is a good web browser, but it's not perfect. You may find that some websites do not render properly or work correctly with Safari. If you are unable to access certain websites with Safari, try a third-party web browser. Several are available for the Mac, including Google Chrome, Firefox, OmniWeb, and Opera.

- Mail—Improper mail account configuration settings are the most common cause of Mail application issues. Fortunately, the Mail application includes a built-in account diagnostic tool called the Mail Connection Doctor that attempts to establish a connection with all configured incoming and outgoing mail servers. To open the Mail Connection Doctor, choose Window > Connection Doctor within the Mail application. If a problem is found, a suggested resolution is offered, but for a more detailed diagnostic view, click the Show Detail button to reveal the progress log, and then click the Check Again button to rerun the tests.

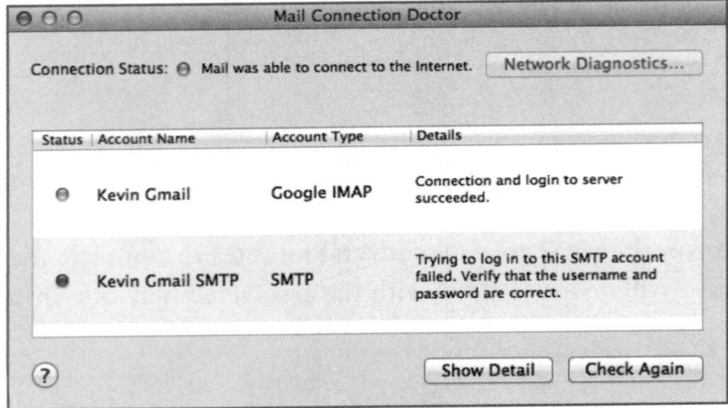

TIP Apple also provides an online mail Setup Assistant database that may help you identify mail client configuration issues: www.apple.com/support/macosx/mailassistant/.

- Messages—The Messages application also suffers from occasional improper account configuration, but it's a less frequent occurrence than with the Mail application. More often, Messages experiences connectivity issues when attempting advanced messaging features like voice and video conferencing. As such, Messages also features a Connection Doctor that lets you view conference statistics, chat capabilities, and the Messages error log. Within the Message application, choose Video > Connection Doctor. If you have experienced recent errors, the Connection Doctor opens to the error log, but you can view other information from the Show pop-up menu.

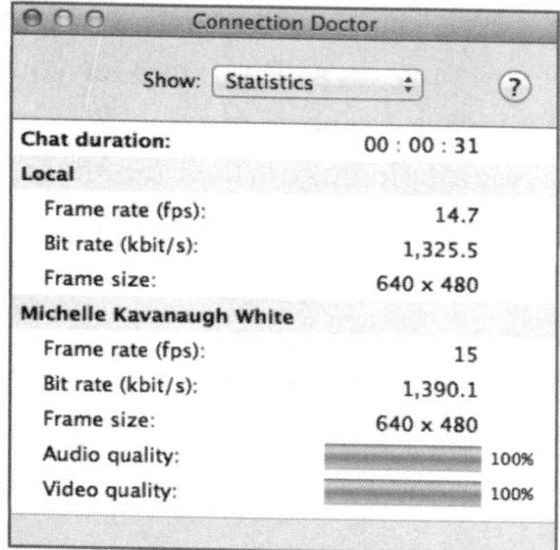

File Sharing Service Troubleshooting

There are a few known OS X file service issues of which you should be aware. They aren't software bugs in the sense that something is broken and requires a fix. These issues represent compatibility and design choices that are intentional but may still cause you problems.

AppleDouble Issues

As covered in Lesson 16, "Metadata and Spotlight," OS X uses separate metadata stores. The NFS and WebDAV file sharing protocols do not support metadata of this type. Thus, when files are written to a mounted NFS or WebDAV volume, OS X automatically splits these files into two separate files.

With this practice, commonly known as AppleDouble, the data retains the original name, but the metadata will be saved with a period and underscore before the original name. The Finder recognizes these split files and shows only a single file to the user. However, users on other operating systems see two separate files and may have trouble accessing the appropriate file.

Microsoft's Services for Macintosh Issues

You may encounter another issue when trying to access an AFP network volume from a Windows file server. Windows servers prior to 2008 include Services for Macintosh (SFM), which provides only the legacy AFP 2 file service. OS X is still compatible with AFP 2 but is optimized for AFP 3.1.

There are many known performance issues with AFP 2, so you should avoid it at all costs. Ideally, you should use a system running OS X Server to provide AFP services for your network. However, if you must keep the Windows file server, you can add AFP 3.1 support by installing the Group Logic ExtremeZ-IP (www.grouplogic.com). Also remember that OS X clients include a robust SMB client that natively connects to your Windows server with a high degree of reliability and performance.

MORE INFO ▶ OS X only supports legacy AFP if you follow the steps in Knowledge Base document HT4700, "Connecting to legacy AFP services."

Exercise 25.1
Configure a Network Service Account

▶ Prerequisites

- ▶ You must have created the Chris Johnson account (Exercise 6.1).
- ▶ You must be performing these exercises in a class, or have set up your own server configured as in the Mainserver Setup Instructions.

The client applications built into OS X can use a wide variety of network services, and the Mail, Contacts & Calendars preference pane makes setting up suites of services easy. You have already set up iCloud-based services on your computer. In this exercise, you will also configure your computer to use services provided by an OS X Mountain Lion server.

View Your Existing Network Accounts

1. If necessary, log in as Chris Johnson.
2. Open the Contacts application.
3. Open the Contacts preferences by choosing Contacts > Preferences (Command-comma).
4. Click the Accounts button to see the accounts your Contacts application is configured to use.

You see two accounts listed, the iCloud account you configured when you created the Chris Johnson account, and a local On My Mac account for contacts that are not shared via iCloud.

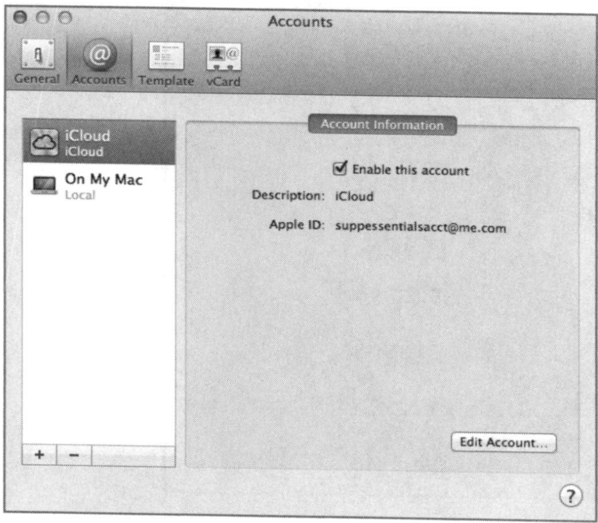

This pane of the Contacts preferences can be used to view and add network accounts for Contacts, but often you have accounts that are used for groups of related services.

5 Close the Preferences window and quit Contacts.

6 Open System Preferences, and select the Mail, Contacts & Calendars preference pane.

7 Select your iCloud account from the accounts list.

Your iCloud account information appears, along with options for controlling which apps and capabilities are enabled for iCloud. Note that these settings are also available in the iCloud preference pane.

8 If necessary, deselect the Mail service for your iCloud account.

Not having iCloud mail mixed with the new account will simplify testing later in the exercise.

Set Up a New Network Account

1 Click the Add (+) button under the account list.

A list of account types that this preference pane supports appears.

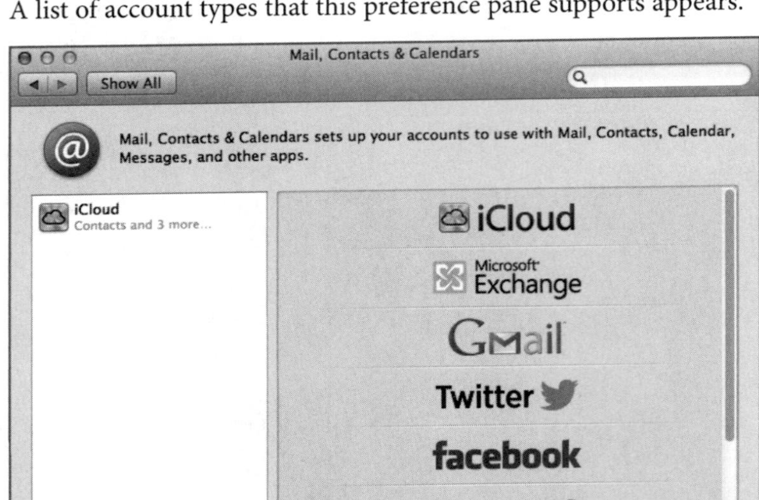

2 Scroll to the bottom of the list, and click Add Other Account.

This option lists additional account types you can set up.

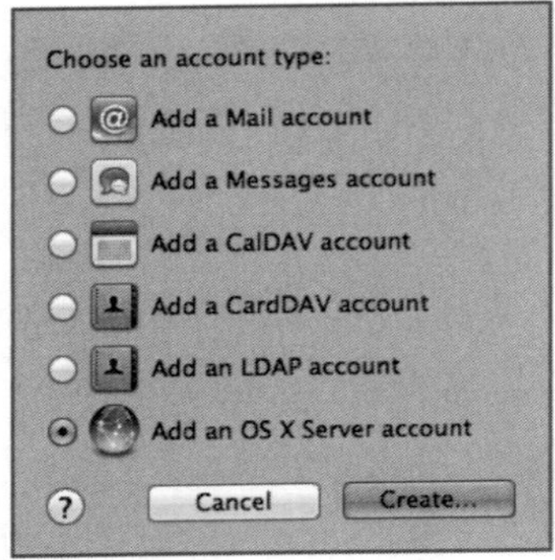

3 Select “Add an OS X Server account” and click Create.

Mainserver is available in the nearby server list.

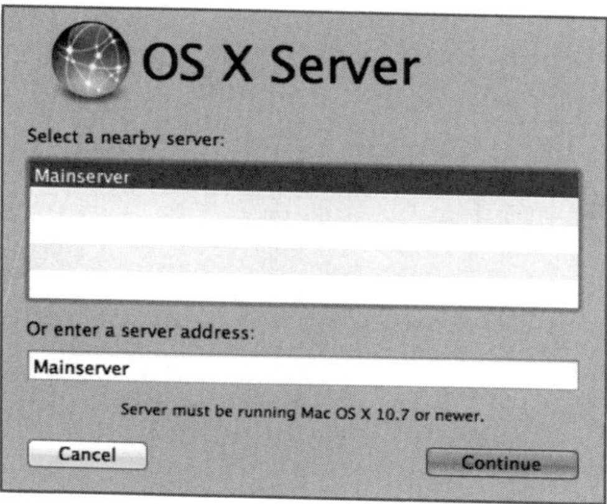

4 Select Mainserver and click Continue.

You are prompted for the server account you want to use. If you are performing these exercises in a class, your account name will include your student number or seat number. If you are performing these exercises on your own, use "1" as your student number.

5 Enter the following for your account information:

Name: **Student *n*** (where *n* is your student number)

Account: **student*n*** (where *n* is your student number)

Password: **student**

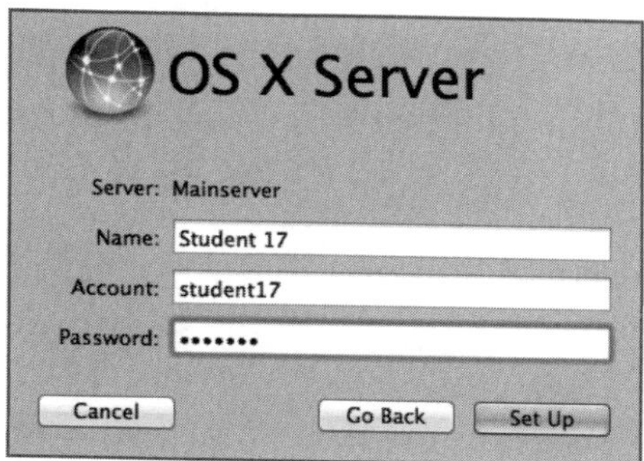

6 Click Set Up. If you receive an error message, check the settings and try again.

7 In the Use With dialog, deselect Notes and click Add Account.

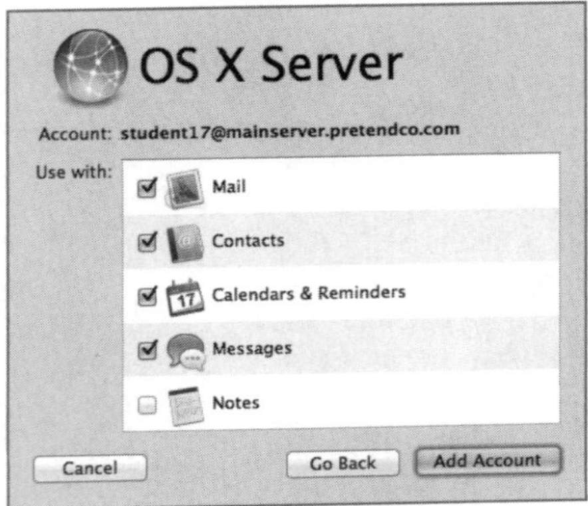

8 If you receive a message that a secure connection couldn't be established, click Continue.

It may take a few moments to set up all of the accounts.

9 When the account setup finishes, quit System Preferences.

Test Your New Account

1 Open the Contacts application.

2 If you are prompted to allow Contacts to use your "login" keychain, enter Chris's keychain password (**chris**, or whatever you chose when you created the account) and click OK.

You see an OS X Server account listed in the left side of the window.

3 Open the Contacts preferences by choosing Contacts > Preferences (Command-comma).

Your OS X Server account is now listed here as well as the iCloud account.

4 Close the Preferences window and quit Contacts.

5 Open the Mail application.

Mail checks for new messages in your OS X Server account. You should have a welcome message from the server team.

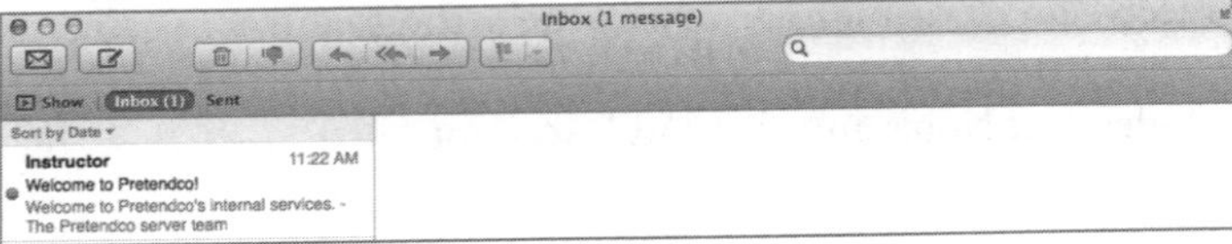

6 Quit Mail.

If you also had iCloud messages, you may have missed the step to turn iCloud mail off; return to the iCloud preference pane and disable its Mail service.

Scan the Server

To prepare for Exercise 25.3, "Troubleshoot Network Services," you will record a baseline of what services Mainserver provides when everything is working normally.

1 Open the Network Utility.

2 Click the Port Scan tab.

The Port Scan pane scans a server or other IP address to see what network ports are accepting connections. This is explored in more detail in Exercise 25.3.

3 Enter the server address **mainserver.local** in the IP address field.

4 Select the "Only test ports between" option, and set the range to **1** through **1024**.

5 Click Scan.

6 Wait for it to finish scanning, then expand the Network Utility window until the entire results are visible.

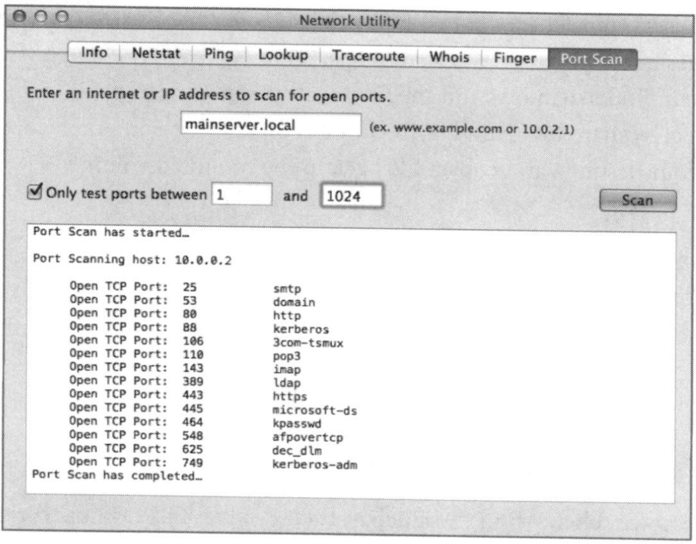

Your results may not exactly match those above. To record your results, you will take a screenshot of the Network Utility window. The options for taking screenshots in OS X are explained in more detail in Exercise 7.1.

7 Press Command-Shift-4 and then press Spacebar.

The cursor changes into a camera icon, and the region of the screen it is over is highlighted in blue.

8 Move the pointer over the Network Utility window, then click to record its contents.

The image is saved to your desktop with the name "Screen Shot" followed by the date and time it was taken.

9 Quit the Network Utility.

Exercise 25.2
Use File Sharing Services

Prerequisites

- You must have created the Chris Johnson account (Exercise 6.1).
- You must be performing these exercises in a class or have set up your own server configured as in the Mainserver Setup Instructions.

Many protocols can be used to transfer files across networks and over the Internet, but some of the most efficient are designed specifically to share file systems, such as AFP and SMB. In this exercise, you will use a Finder window and the Connect to Server command from the Finder Go menu to connect to shared AFP and SMB volumes on another computer, copy a file from that volume to your desktop, and copy a file back to the mounted volume.

Browse to an AFP Share

These steps will lead you through the process of using the sidebar to mount an AFP volume on the desktop.

1 If necessary, log in as Chris Johnson.

2 In a Finder window, select Mainserver in the Shared section of the sidebar.

If Mainserver is not shown, click All in the sidebar, then double-click Mainserver in the network view.

Your computer contacts Mainserver and logs in automatically as a guest.

3 Click the Connect As button.

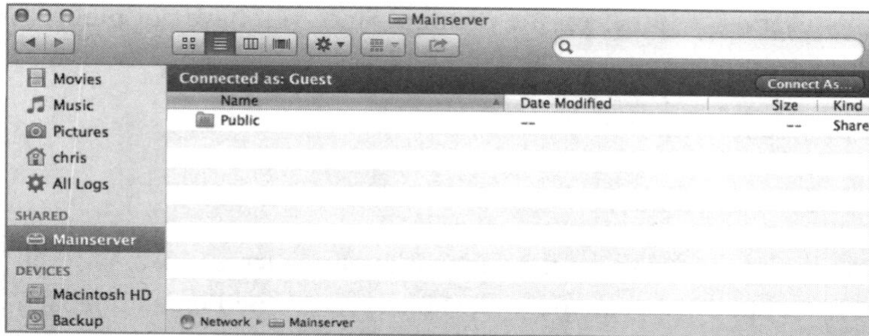

4 When prompted to authenticate, select Registered User and enter the Name **student** and the password **student**, then select "Remember this password in my keychain" and click Connect.

You are now connected to Mainserver with the "student" account.

The Finder window shows all the shared folders to which you have access.

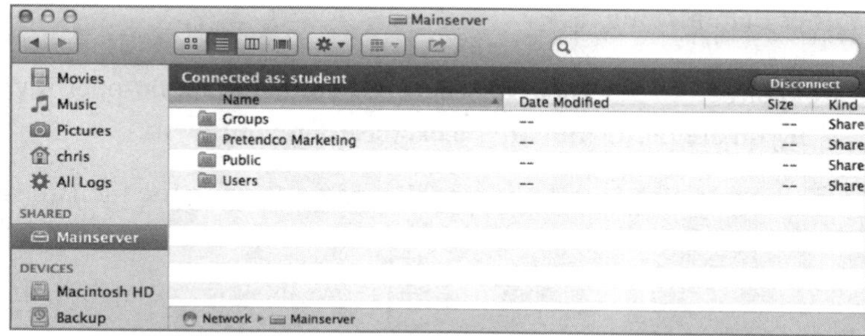

Now you will take a look at what you can see in the Public folder on the server.

5 Open the Finder preferences using Finder > Preferences (or Command-comma), click General, and select "Connected servers," if it is not already selected.

This shows mounted server volumes on the desktop. Since you have not mounted any shared folders yet, nothing new appears on the desktop at this point.

6 Close the Finder preferences window.

7 Open the shared folder named Public.

The folder displays in the Finder and a new network volume icon appears on the desktop. Also, an Eject button appears next to Mainserver in the Finder sidebar.

In the Public folder you see a file (copy.rtf) and two folders (DropBox and SMB_DropBox) along with the StudentMaterials folder. Note the icon badge on the two folders indicating that they are write-only.

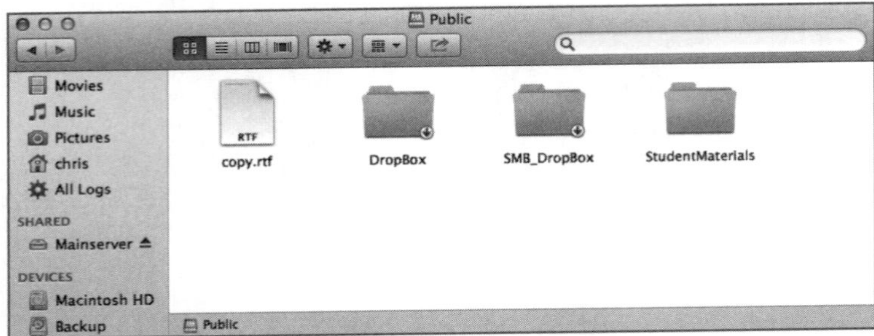

Copy Files to a Network Share

You will use the Finder to copy files to a shared folder mounted over Apple Filing Protocol (AFP).

1 Drag copy.rtf to your desktop. Since you are dragging from one volume to another, it copies the file rather than moving it.

2 Rename your copy of copy.rtf to **Student *n*.rtf** (where *n* is your student number if you are in a class, or "1" if you are performing these exercises on your own).

You can rename a file by selecting it and pressing Return or clicking the filename and waiting a moment.

3 Drag the renamed file from your desktop onto the DropBox folder on the mounted Public volume.

The DropBox folder is a write-only folder, so you won't be able to see the results of this action.

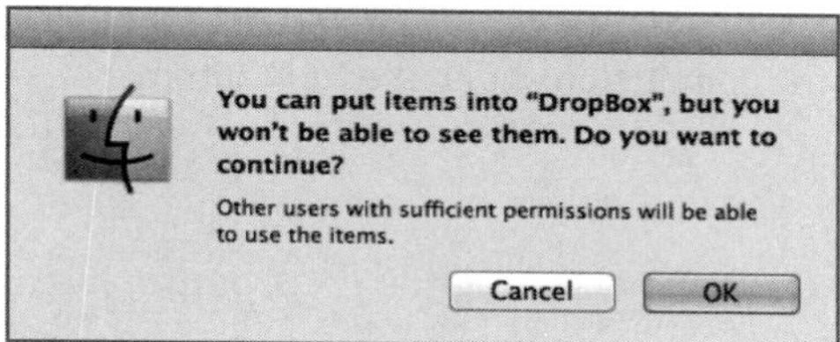

4 Click OK.

Automatically Mount a Network Share

OS X provides several ways to memorize a share point to allow easy access to it. In this section, you will configure your user preferences to automatically mount a share point whenever you log in.

1 Open System Preferences and select the Users & Groups preference pane.

2 With Chris Johnson selected in the user list, click the Login Items tab.

Note that you do not need to authenticate as an administrator to access your login items; they are a personal preference, so standard users can manage their own login items.

3 Drag the Public icon from your Desktop to the login items list.

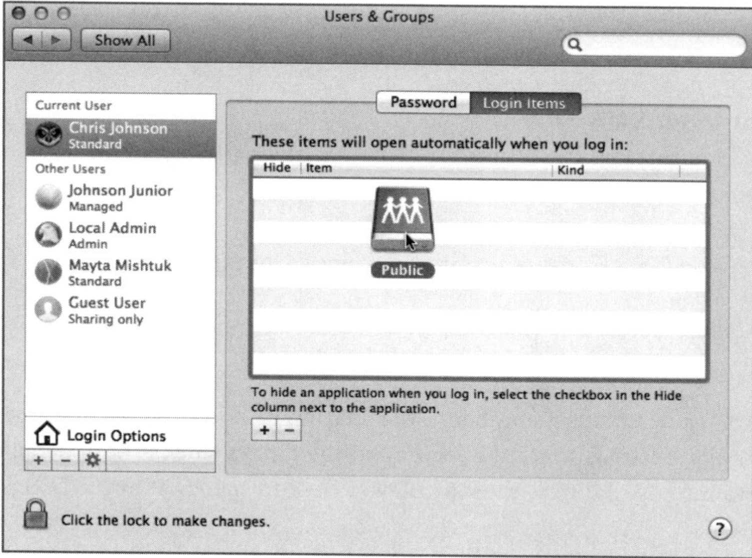

Anything in your login items list will be automatically opened every time you log in. It can include applications, documents, folders, and so on. By adding a shared folder, you have configured it to mount every time you log in. Since you also memorized the server account name and password when you connected, the connection should be fully automatic.

4 Quit System Preferences.

5 Disconnect from Mainserver (unmount Public) by clicking the Eject button next to Mainserver in the Finder sidebar.

6 Log out and back in as Chris Johnson.

The Public folder is automatically remounted and opened in the Finder. Note that if you are connecting via Wi-Fi, it may take a minute or so to reconnect.

7 Disconnect from Mainserver again.

8 Reopen the Users & Groups preferences.

9 Click Login Items.

10 Remove Public from the login items list by selecting it, and then clicking the Delete (-) button under the list.

11 Quit System Preferences.

Manually Connect to an SMB Share

These steps will lead you through the process of using "Connect to Server" (in the Finder) to mount an SMB volume on the desktop.

1 In the Finder, choose Go > Connect to Server (or press Command-K).

2 In the Server Address field, enter **smb://mainserver.local** to connect using the SMB protocol.

Connect to Server understands a number of file-sharing protocols which you can specify with familiar URLs. Connect to Server and the Finder sidebar both default to AFP, so if you want to use a different protocol, you need to specify it in the URL, as you have done here.

3 Before you click Connect, click the Add (+) button to the right of the Server Address field.

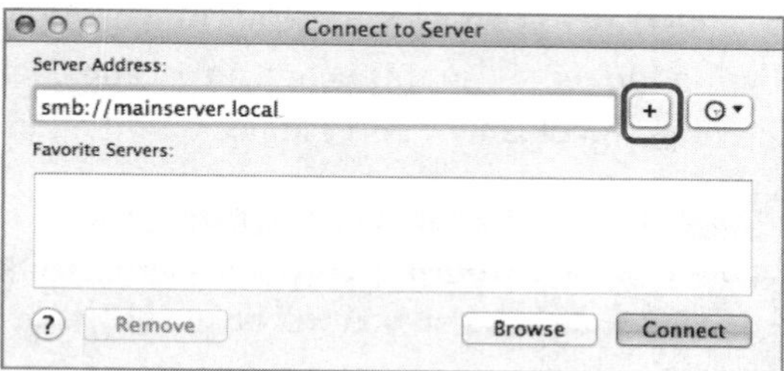

This adds the server URL to your Favorite Servers list. This is another way to allow easy access to a shared folder.

4 Click Connect.

5 Use the same credentials you used when connecting over AFP, and select "Remember this password in my keychain." Click Connect.

Note that while you have already memorized the AFP password for the server, this is a different file service and its password must be memorized separately.

Since you entered a connection URL that did not specify a shared folder to mount, you will be asked which folder(s) you want to mount.

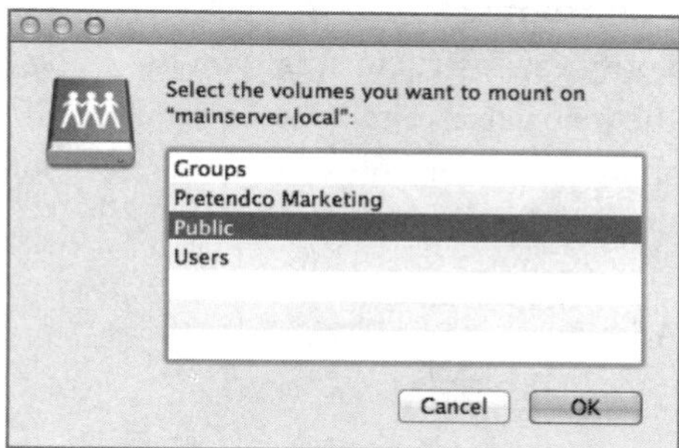

6 Select the Public folder and click OK.

The volume mounts and you see the same files you saw when connecting using AFP. You have connected to the same folder on the server, so this is not surprising. Note that since you connected over a different protocol, a new entry appears in the Finder sidebar for mainserver.pretendco.com.

7 Drag the Student *n*.rtf file from your desktop to the SMB_DropBox folder. SMB_DropBox is also write-only, so you see the same dialog telling you that you will be unable to see the results.

8 Click OK.

9 Disconnect from the server, either by dragging the Public icon to the Trash or by clicking the Eject button in the Finder sidebar.

Exercise 25.3
Troubleshoot Network Services

Prerequisites

- You must have created the Chris Johnson account (Exercise 6.1).
- You must be performing these exercises in a class or have set up your own server configured as in the Mainserver Setup Instructions.
- You must have performed Exercise 25.1.

In this exercise, the mail service will fail, and you will use several network service troubleshooting tools to investigate the problem.

Turn Off the Mail Service or Wait for the Instructor to Do So

If you are performing these exercises in class, notify the instructor that you are ready for the mail service to be turned off, and wait for the instructor to tell you to proceed. If you are performing these exercises on your own, follow these steps on your server computer to turn off the mail service:

1 On your server computer, log in as Local Admin.

2 Open the Server application.

3 Select Mail from the sidebar.

4 Switch the service off.

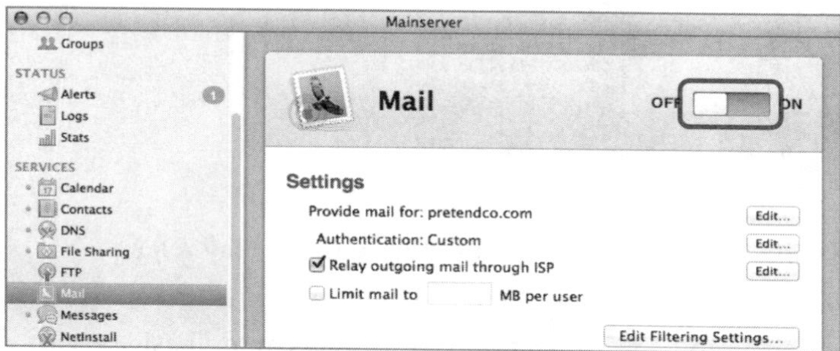

5 Quit the Server application and return to your regular exercise computer.

Troubleshoot with the Mail.app Connection Doctor

1 If necessary, log in as Chris Johnson.

2 Open the Mail application.

3 Choose File > New Message (Command-N).

4 Address the message to **david@pretendco.com** and add a Subject.

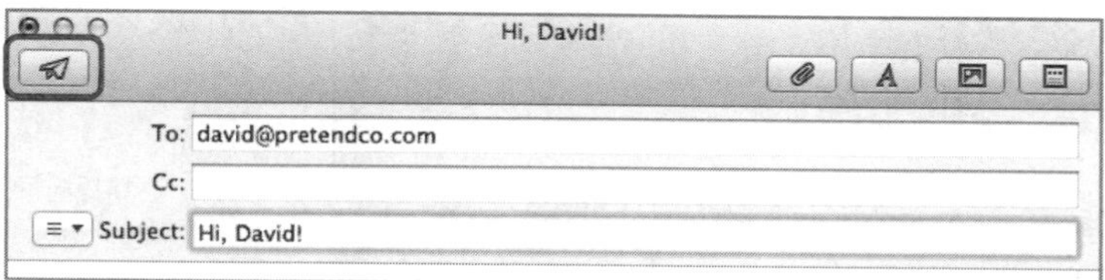

5 Click the Send button (the paper airplane icon near the top left).

You are notified that the message cannot be sent, because the server refused to allow a connection.

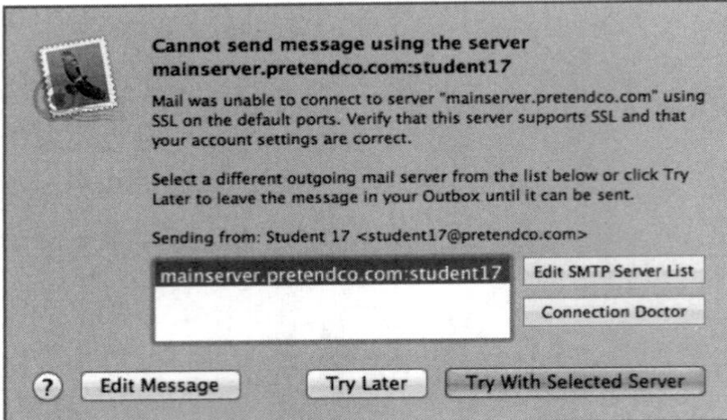

Note that depending on your network setup, the error you see may refer to "mainserver.local" instead of "mainserver.pretendco.com."

The Mail application has a built-in Connection Doctor that can do basic service diagnostics.

6 Click Connection Doctor in the error dialog.

The Connection Doctor opens, and runs a series of tests to see which parts of your mail service are working. In this case, it detects that your Internet connection is working (the green Connection Status indicator at the top), but neither the mail sending service (SMTP) nor the receiving service (IMAP) are working because it cannot connect to either service. It may take it a while to evaluate your iCloud service, but since you are not using that you don't have to wait for it to finish.

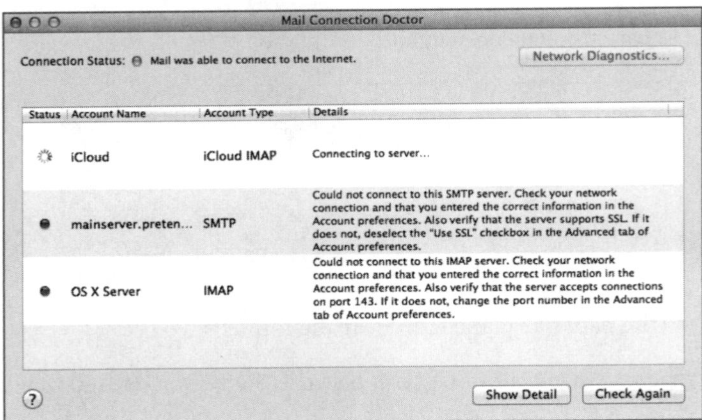

If this were a minor glitch, the Mail Connection Doctor might be able to point you to a solution. Since the server appears to be completely unreachable, you will now turn to the Network Utility for further troubleshooting.

7 Close the Mail Connection Doctor window.

8 In the outgoing message error dialog, click Try Later.

9 Quit Mail.

Troubleshoot with the Network Utility

1 Open the Network Utility.

Since Mail is unable to reach the server at all, you should first test to make sure the network connection(s) between your computer and the server are working.

2 Click the Ping tab.

3 In the "Enter the network address to ping" field, enter mainserver.local.

4 Click Ping.

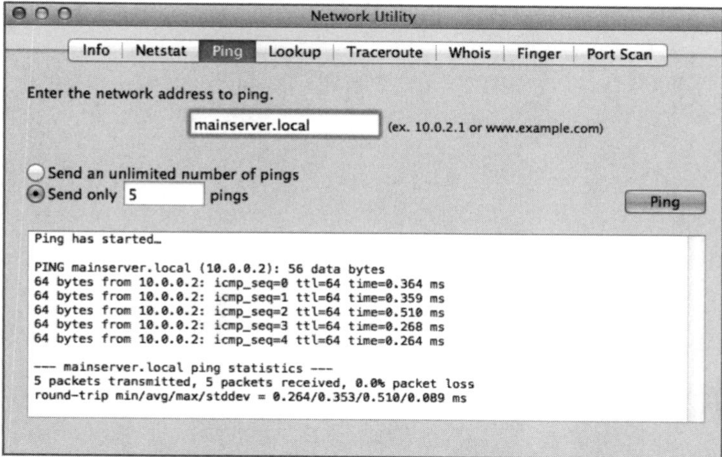

The ping probes are able to reach the server. This tells your that the network connection between your computer and the server is working, so you need to move on to the services you are trying to use.

5 Click the Port Scan tab.

The Port Scan can scan a server to see what TCP port numbers it has services running on; usually, you can tell what services are available based on the port numbers.

NOTE ▶ Many malicious network attacks start with or employ port scans, so this type of troubleshooting might be interpreted as an attack. Before you scan ports on a target computer, request permission from its owner or a network or server administrator, if possible. As a general rule, only port-scan computers you have responsibility for. Many environments employ automatic countermeasures. Simply scanning a server may get your computer or IP address blacklisted, preventing you from knowing if you have resolved the problem you are troubleshooting.

6 Enter the server address **mainserver.local** in the IP address field.

7 Select the "Only test ports between" option, and set the range to **1** through **1024**.

8 Click Scan.

9 Watch the scan as it identifies the open ports.

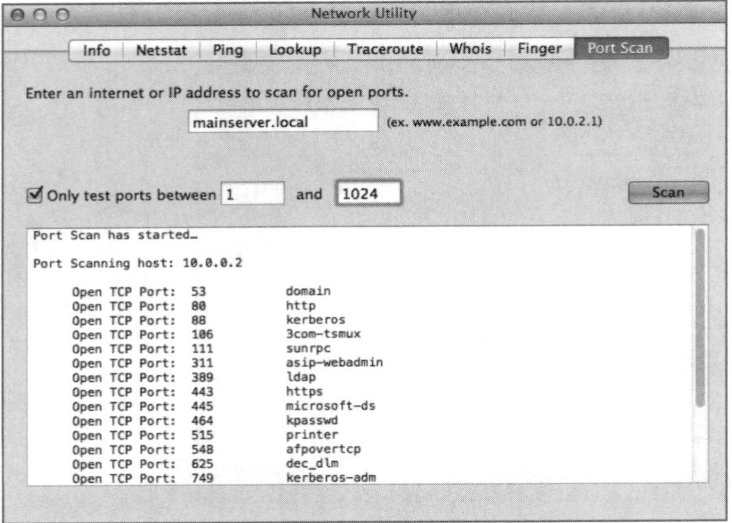

Port scan lists the open ports it finds, along with the names of the services usually associated with them. For example, port 80 is the standard (or "well-known") port for the web service (the HTTP protocol), and port 548 is the standard port for the Apple Filing Protocol ("afpovertcp"). These well-known ports are commonly used in the industry and facilitate interoperability across different vendors' implementations of the same protocols. To test whether a computer has an HTTP (web) server, you would run a port scan on it and test whether or not TCP port 80 is open. HTTPS (SSL secured web service)

normally uses TCP port 443, so if HTTPS requests are not working, port 443 might be blocked or inactive.

For a listing of many ports used by Apple products, see Apple Knowledge Base document #TS1629, "Well known TCP and UDP ports used by Apple software products."

10 Open the Screen Shot you took in Exercise 25.1 showing which ports were open when the services were working, and compare it with the current scan.

In this case, you are trying to troubleshoot the mail service, which normally involves TCP ports 25 (SMTP), 110 (POP3), and 143 (IMAP), and sometimes 587 (message submission) and 933 (IMAPS). Note that mail servers that use proprietary protocols such as Exchange provide access to those protocols over other port numbers.

Ports 25, 110, and 143 are all listed in the earlier scan, but not in the current scan. This indicates that either the server does not offer mail service (which is true here, since the service is switched off) or that a firewall is blocking access to the service.

This is as far as you can resolve this problem from the client side; further troubleshooting would mean looking in detail at the server and/or network firewall(s), which is beyond the scope of this exercise.

11 Quit the Network Utility.

Lesson **26**

Host Sharing and Personal Firewall

One of Apple's worst kept secrets is that OS X already includes many of the core technologies that make OS X Server possible. Although OS X Server supports additional advanced network services and administration tools, the two systems share the same software for providing several network services.

In this lesson, you will focus on using OS X as both a network client and a shared resource for a variety of network and Internet services. After an introduction to the general concepts of providing shared services, you will delve into remotely controlling OS X systems via screen sharing. Then you will see how to use AirDrop—the easiest way to share files between Mac systems. You will also learn how to secure access to shared resources from an OS X system using the built-in firewall. Finally, this lesson covers some general troubleshooting methods to resolve issues that may arise when you attempt to share services from your Mac.

GOALS

- Examine the host sharing services built into OS X
- Use screen sharing tools to access other network hosts
- Use AirDrop to quickly and easily share files
- Secure shared services by configuring the firewall
- Troubleshoot shared service issues

Reference 26.1
Host Sharing Services

OS X includes an assortment of shared network services, which you'll now see how to manage. These shared services vary in implementation and purpose, but they all allow users to remotely access resources on the Mac providing the service. They are also all easily enabled and managed from the Sharing preferences.

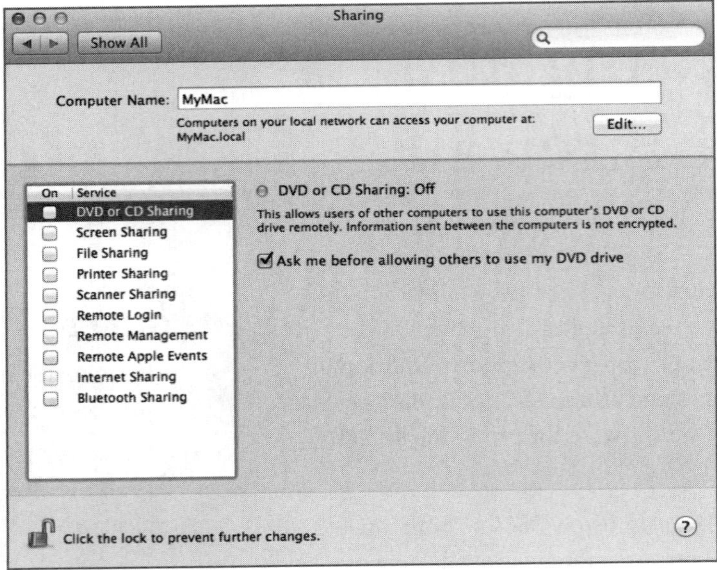

NOTE ► Users cannot access services on a Mac in sleep mode. You can disable your Mac computer's automatic sleep activation or enable automatic waking for network access from the Energy Saver preferences. OS X supports automatic wake on both wired and wireless networks if your network hardware supports it. You can find out more from Knowledge Base document HT3774, "About Wake on Demand."

It's important to recognize the security risk involved in providing a service that allows other users to control processes on your Mac. Obviously, if you're providing a service that allows remote control and execution of software, it's certainly possible for an attacker to cause trouble. Thus, it's paramount that when you enable these types of services, you choose strong security settings. Using strong passwords is a good start, but you can also configure limited access to these services from the Sharing preferences.

Shared Services

The OS X sharing services include:

- DVD or CD Sharing (Remote Disc)— Allows you to share your Mac computer's optical disc via the network. It's primarily designed to let you install software for Mac systems that lack a built-in optical disc. Do not confuse Remote Disc with standard file sharing services covered later in this lesson. This service differs in several key respects; it shares only what is in the optical disc, you cannot configure user-specific access, and it can only be accessed via Bonjour. By enabling this service, the launchd control process starts the ODSAgent background process, which listens for Remote Disc requests on a very high randomly selected TCP port. This service can be accessed only by other Macs from the Finder sidebar or the Migration Assistant application.

MORE INFO ▶ For more information about Remote Disc, see Apple Knowledge Base document HT5287, "DVD or CD sharing: Using Remote Disc."

- **MORE INFO** ▶ Details regarding the launchd control process are covered in Lesson 29, "Startup, Shutdown, and Sleep Modes."
- Screen Sharing—Allows remote control of your Mac. Using this service is covered later in this lesson.
- File Sharing—Allows remote access to your Mac computer's file system via the Apple Filling Protocol (AFP) or Server Message Blocks (SMB) network file sharing services. When you enable the File Sharing service, the launchd control process listens for AFP service requests on TCP port 548 and automatically starts the AppleFileServer process as necessary to handle any requests. Further, you can enable SMB in the optional File Sharing settings. When SMB is enabled, the launchd control process listens for SMB service requests on TCP ports 139 and 445 and automatically starts the smbd process as necessary to handle any requests. By default on OS X Mountain Lion, only standard and administrative users have access to File Sharing services, but you can modify access for other users as outlined in Lesson 12, "Permissions and Sharing."

  MORE INFO ▶ Connecting OS X systems to file sharing services is covered in Lesson 25, "Network Services."

- Printer Sharing—Allows network access to printers that are directly attached to your Mac. Using this service is covered in Lesson 28, "Print and Scan."
- Scanner Sharing—Allows network access to document scanners that are configured for your Mac. This service only works with other Macs on a local network (Bonjour) via the Image Capture application. This service is also enabled only on a per-user basis, and available only when the user is logged in. By enabling this service, the launchd control process listens for scanner sharing requests on a very high randomly selected TCP port and starts the Image Capture Extension background process as needed to handle any requests. The only additional configuration is that you can, from the Sharing preferences, enable specific scanners if you have more than one attached.
- Remote Login—Allows remote control of your Mac computer's command line via Secure Shell (SSH). Further, SSH remote login allows you to securely transfer files using Secure File Transfer Protocol (SFTP) or the secure copy command scp. With Remote Login enabled, the launchd control process listens for remote login service

requests on TCP 22 and starts the sshd background process as needed to handle any requests. By default, all standard and administrative user accounts are allowed to access the service. Command-line usage is beyond the scope of this guide, thus using SSH is beyond the scope of this guide.

- Remote Management—Augments the screen sharing service to allow remote administration of your Mac via the Apple Remote Desktop (ARD) application. Using this service is covered later in this lesson.
- Remote Apple Events—Allows applications and AppleScripts on another Mac to communicate with applications and services on your Mac. This service is most often used to facilitate automated AppleScript workflows between applications running on separate Macs. By enabling this service, the launchd control process listens for remote Apple Events requests on TCP and UDP port 3130 and starts the AEServer background process as needed to handle any requests. By default, all non-guest user accounts are allowed to access the service, but this can be limited to specific users from the Sharing preferences.
- Internet Sharing—Allows your Mac to "reshare" a single network or Internet connection with any other network interface. For example, if your Mac had Internet access via a cellular network USB adapter, you could enable Internet Sharing for the Mac computer's Wi-Fi and turn it into a wireless access point for the other computers. When you enable the Internet Sharing service, the launchd process starts several background processes. The natd process performs the Network Address Translation (NAT) service that allows multiple network clients to share a single network or Internet connection. The bootpd process provides the DHCP automatic network configuration service for the network devices connected via your Mac. When a network device connects to your Mac computer's shared network connection, it automatically obtains an IP address, usually in the 10.0.2.X range. Finally, the named process provides DNS resolution for network devices connected to the Internet via your Mac.
- Bluetooth Sharing—Allows access to your Mac via Bluetooth short-range wireless. Using this service is covered in Lesson 27, "Peripherals and Drivers."

NOTE ▸ OS X Mountain Lion no longer supports Xgrid sharing or services.

NOTE ▸ OS X Mountain Lion no longer includes a graphical interface for enabling web sharing services. To find out more about alternatives to Web Sharing, see Knowledge Base document, HT5230, "OS X Mountain Lion: Options for web sharing."

Dynamic Service Discovery

Requiring users to manually enter network addresses to access a network service isn't very user-friendly. What if you join a new network without knowing the exact names of all its available resources? Or what if the shared resource you need is hosted from another client computer that doesn't have a DNS host name or the same IP address every time? To address these issues, OS X supports dynamic network service discovery protocols.

Dynamic network service discovery protocols allow you to browse local area and wide area network resources without knowing specific service addresses. In a nutshell, network devices providing services advertise the availability of their services on the network. As available network resources change, or as you move your client to different networks, the service discovery protocols dynamically update the list of available services.

OS X makes ample use of dynamic network service discovery throughout. For example, dynamic network service discovery allows you to browse for available network file shares with the Finder, or locate new network printers from the Print & Scan preferences. Other network applications built into OS X use service discovery to locate a variety of shared resources, including Messages, Image Capture, iPhoto, iTunes, Safari, and the OS X Server application. Third-party network applications also take advantage of dynamic network service discovery.

It is important to remember the discovery protocol is only used to help you and the system locate available services. Once the discovery protocol provides your computer with a list of available services, its job is done. When you connect to a discovered service, the Mac establishes a connection to the service using the service's protocol. For example, the Bonjour service discovery protocol can provide the Mac with a list of available screen sharing systems, but when you select a Mac server from this list, the Mac establishes a screen sharing connection to the server using the VNC protocol.

NOTE ▶ OS X v10.6 and later no longer support the AppleTalk network browsing protocol.

Bonjour

Bonjour is the Apple implementation of Zero Configuration Networking, or Zeroconf, a collection of standards drafts that provide automatic local network configuration, naming, and service discovery. Bonjour uses a broadcast discovery protocol known as multicast DNS (mDNS) on UDP port 5353.

MORE INFO ▶ You can find out more about Zeroconf at www.zeroconf.org.

Bonjour is the primary set of dynamic network service discovery protocols used by OS X native services and applications. Bonjour is preferred because it is based on TCP/IP standards, and so integrates well with other TCP/IP-based network services. OS X v10.5 added support for Wide-Area Bonjour, allowing you to browse WAN resources as well as LAN resources.

While local Bonjour requires no configuration, Wide-Area Bonjour requires that your Mac be configured to use a DNS server and search domain that supports the protocol. Configuring DNS is covered in Lesson 22, "Network Essentials," and Lesson 23, "Advanced Network Configuration."

> **MORE INFO ▸** OS X also supports network identification via the iCloud "Back to My Mac" feature. However, "Back to My Mac" systems can only be located by the iCloud user that set it up. In other words, it doesn't help other users locate your system. You can find out more about "Back to My Mac" from www.apple.com/support/icloud/back-to-my-mac/.

Server Message Block (SMB)

Originally designed by Microsoft, SMB has become the most common network service for sharing files and printers. SMB includes a network discovery service that runs on UDP ports 137 and 138. Most modern operating systems that provide support for SMB sharing also support dynamic discovery via SMB.

The Apple implementation of SMB also supports browsing through the legacy Network Basic Input/Output System (NetBIOS) and Windows Internet Naming Service (WINS) protocols. Details regarding configuration of NetBIOS and WINS are also covered in Lesson 23, "Advanced Network Configuration."

> **NOTE ▸** On OS X v10.5 and later, you can no longer disable Bonjour or SMB network discovery protocols from the graphical interface.

Host Network Identification

If you want to provide network services from your Mac or otherwise identify your Mac from another computer, you must configure it so that other network hosts can easily reach it. Even if you aren't providing sharing services from your Mac clients, if you plan to use any network administration tools, then you must have some way of identifying your Mac clients from across the network.

At a minimum your Mac can be reached by its IP address, but IP addresses are hard to remember and can change if your Mac is acquiring its IP address via DHCP. Thus, it is much more convenient for you and other network clients to locate your Mac using a network name and discovery service.

OS X network identification methods include:

- IP address(es)—The primary network identifier for your Mac, an IP address, can always be used to establish a network connection.
- DNS host name—All Macs have a host name configured via one of two methods. Traditionally, these names are hosted on a DNS server configured by administration at the DNS server. The Mac attempts to resolve its host name by performing a DNS reverse lookup on its primary IP address. However, many network clients don't have properly configured DNS host names because of the administrative overhead required to create and update client DNS entries. As such, if the Mac can't resolve a host name from the DNS server, it instead uses the Bonjour name.
- Computer name—This name is used by other Apple systems to identify your Mac. The computer name is part of the Apple Bonjour implementation and is set in the Sharing preferences. The computer name is also used by AirDrop peer-to-peer file sharing.
- Bonjour name—As covered previously, Bonjour is the OS X primary dynamic network discovery protocol; in addition, Bonjour provides a convenient naming system for use on a local network. The Bonjour name is usually similar to the computer name but differs in that it conforms to DNS naming standards and ends with .local. This allows the Bonjour name to be supported by more network devices than the standard computer name, which is generally recognized only by Apple systems. This name is also set in the Sharing preferences.
- NetBIOS/WINS name—This name is used for the legacy Windows dynamic network discovery protocols as part of the SMB service. This name is set by either the Sharing or Network preferences.

Identifier	Example	Set by	Used by
IP address	10.1.17.2	Network preferences	Any network host
DNS host name	client17.pretendco.com	Defined by DNS server	Any network host
Computer name	Client 17	Sharing preferences	Mac systems (Bonjour or AirDrop)
Bonjour name	Client-17.local	Sharing preferences	Any Bonjour host
NetBIOS name	CLIENT17	Network preferences	Any SMB host

Configuring Network Identification

You may be unable to control your Mac computer's IP address or DNS host name; the network administrator usually controls these. But as long as the Mac has properly configured TCP/IP settings as outlined in Lesson 22, "Network Essentials," your configuration is complete for these two identifiers. If your Mac has multiple IP addresses or DNS host names properly configured, it also accepts connections from those.

For dynamic network discovery protocols, though, your Mac uses network identification that can be set locally by an administrator. By default, your Mac automatically chooses a name based either on its DNS name or on the name of the user created with the Setup Assistant. However, at any time an administrative user can change the Mac computer's network identifier from the Sharing preferences. Simply enter a name in the Computer Name field, and the system sets the name for each available discovery protocol.

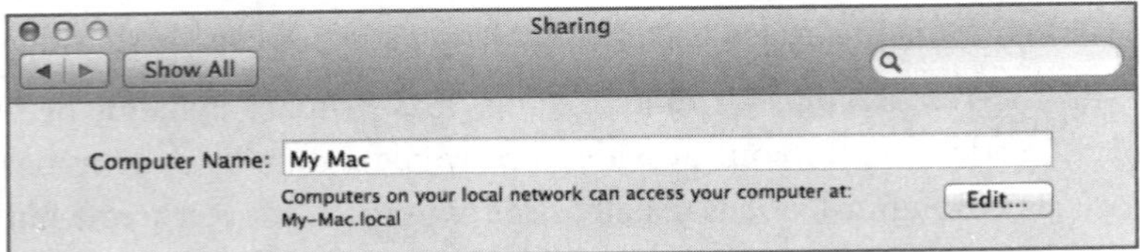

For example, if you enter the computer name "My Mac," the Bonjour name is set to "My-Mac .local" and the NetBIOS/WINS name is set to "MY_MAC." If the name you choose is already taken by another local device, the Mac automatically appends a number on the end of the name. NetBIOS/WINS may require additional configuration if your network uses multiple domains or workgroups, as covered in Lesson 23, "Advanced Network Configuration."

The local Bonjour service needs no additional configuration, but if you want to set a custom Bonjour name, click the Edit button below the Computer Name field to reveal the Local Hostname field. From this interface you can also register your Mac computer's identification for Wide-Area Bonjour. To do so, select the "Use dynamic global hostname" checkbox to reveal the Wide-Area Bonjour settings.

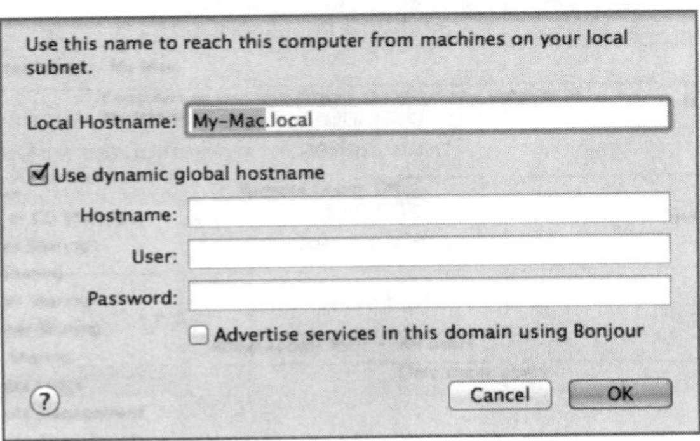

Reference 26.2
Screen Sharing

Providing remote phone support can be arduous. Inexperienced users don't know how to properly communicate the issues they are experiencing and may not be able to describe what they are seeing on the screen. Further, attempting to describe the steps involved in performing troubleshooting or administrative tasks to an inexperienced user over the phone is at best time consuming for both parties.

When it comes to troubleshooting or administration, nothing beats actually seeing the computer's screen and controlling its mouse and keyboard. OS X includes built-in software that allows you to view and control the graphical interface via three methods: system screen sharing, Messages screen sharing, and Apple Remote Desktop (ARD) remote management.

Screen Sharing Architecture

Both system screen sharing and Messages screen sharing are included with the standard system software, and their use is covered in the following sections of this lesson. However, the standard installation of OS X includes only the client-side software for ARD, as the administrative side of ARD used to control other Macs is a separate purchase.

Yet, screen sharing is a subset of ARD, so when you enable ARD remote management, you are also enabling screen sharing. This may seem a bit confusing if you look at the Sharing preferences interface, which disables the screen sharing checkbox when remote management is enabled. Rest assured, though, enabling remote management also enables screen sharing. Thus, you can save yourself a step by initially configuring remote management, which allows for both ARD and screen sharing access. Configuring ARD remote management is also covered later in this lesson, as it can still be used to provide system screen sharing.

All Apple screen sharing is based on a modified version of the Virtual Network Computing (VNC) protocol. The primary modification is the use of optional encryption for both viewing and controlling traffic. Another change is the ability to copy files and clipboard content between Macs using screen sharing.

Further, OS X allows you to access a virtual desktop on another Mac via screen sharing. In other words, on OS X systems screen sharing allows you to have your own virtual login on another Mac, completely separate from the login currently being used by the local user. This feature is similar to fast user switching, covered in Lesson 6, "User Accounts," except the second user is entirely remote via screen sharing and potentially using the computer at the same time as the local user.

NOTE ► OS X screen sharing is backward compatible with OS X v10.5 or later screen sharing. Further, OS X can control previous OS X systems that have ARD remote management or other VNC software enabled.

NOTE ► Using screen sharing to copy files and clipboard content is only supported when using ARD or when using OS X Lion or later. Using screen sharing to a virtual desktop is only supported when using OS X Lion or later.

NOTE ► VNC is a cross-platform standard for remote control; so, if configured properly, the OS X screen sharing technology integrates well with other third-party VNC-based systems. Thus, your Mac can control (or be controlled by) any other VNC-based software regardless of operating system or platform.

Enable System Screen Sharing

Obviously, in order to access a Mac remotely via screen sharing, the remote Mac must first have screen sharing enabled. To enable screen sharing, open the Sharing preferences and click the lock icon in the bottom-left corner and authenticate as an administrative user to unlock the Sharing preferences.

NOTE ► The screen sharing service is part of the ARD remote management service. Thus, if Remote Management is enabled, the Screen Sharing checkbox is inaccessible.

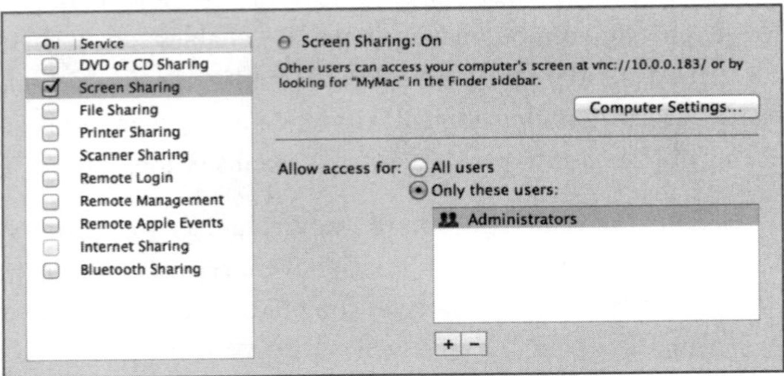

Select the Screen Sharing checkbox in the Service list to enable screen sharing. The launchd control process starts the AppleVNCServer background process, which listens for screen sharing service requests on TCP and UDP port 5900. By default, only administrative user accounts are allowed to access the service.

Optionally, you can adjust screen sharing access by selecting the "All users" radio button, or using the Add (+) and Delete (-) buttons at the bottom of the users list. When adding accounts, a dialog appears allowing you to select the specific users or groups for whom you wish to grant screen sharing access. You can select existing users or groups, or create a new Sharing user account by clicking the New Person button or selecting a contact from your Contacts.

Also optional, you can allow a wider range of operating systems to access your Mac computer's screen sharing service by clicking the Computer Settings button. This reveals a dialog allowing you to enable guest and standard VNC screen sharing access.

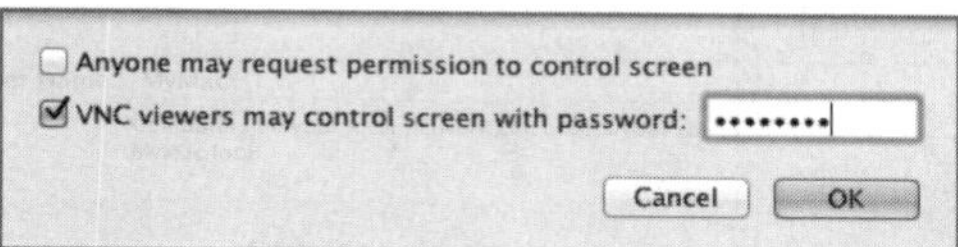

When attempting to access your Mac computer's screen sharing, the currently logged-in user must authorize the session. By default, only local authorized users and groups are allowed to use screen sharing. Select the "Anyone may request permission to control screen" checkbox to allow anyone (from another Mac) to ask permission to share the screen.

Standard third-party VNC viewers cannot authenticate using the secure methods employed by the OS X screen sharing service. Thus, if you enable the "VNC viewers may control screen with password" checkbox, you must also set a specific password for VNC access. Remember that all standard VNC traffic is unencrypted. Further, standard VNC viewers cannot use screen sharing's clipboard copy, file copy, or virtual desktop features.

Control via Screen Sharing

The process to connect to and control another computer for screen sharing is similar to how you connect to a shared file system. From the Finder you can connect to another computer with screen sharing, ARD 3 remote management, or VNC enabled. You can initiate the connection using one of two methods. The first method only works for screen sharing or ARD hosts on the local network. In the Finder, browse to and select the computer from the Finder sidebar Shared list or the Finder Network folder, and then click the Share Screen button.

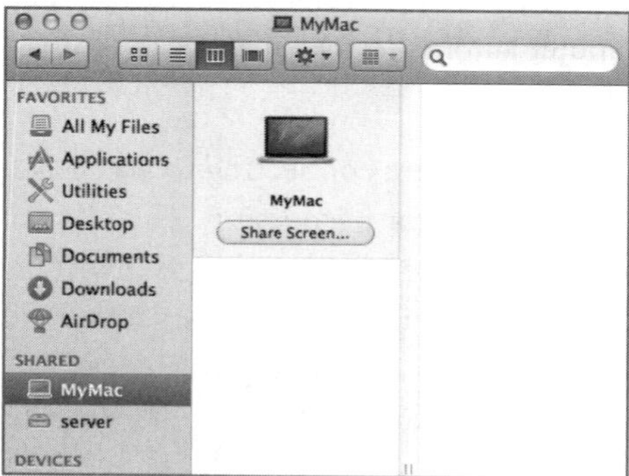

The second method allows you to connect to and control any host providing screen sharing, ARD, or standard VNC services. In the Finder choose Go > Connect to Server. In the Connect to Server dialog, enter vnc:// followed by the computer's IP address, DNS host name, or Bonjour name, and then click Connect.

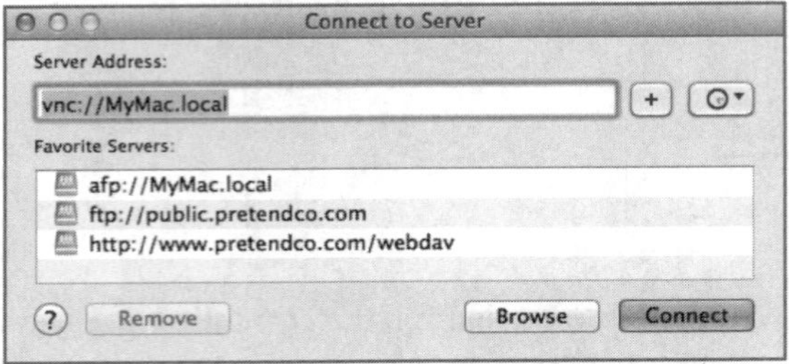

Regardless of the connection method, the system automatically opens the /System/Library/CoreServices/Screen Sharing application and initiates a connection to the specified host. You are presented with a dialog that requires you to make an authentication choice.

NOTE ► If you are using Kerberos single sign-on or have previously saved your authentication information to a keychain, the computer automatically authenticates for you and doesn't present the authentication dialog.

The first authentication choice, which appears only if you are connecting to an OS X system with this option enabled, is to ask the current user for permission. The second authentication choice, the default for any system, is to authenticate with a user account. The last choice, whether to authenticate with an Apple ID, also only appears if you are connecting to an OS X system with this option enabled. As a final option, you can select the checkbox that saves this information to your login keychain. Once you have made your authentication selection, click Connect to continue.

Depending on the remote computer's system, one of three situations occurs when the screen sharing establishes the connection:

- If the remote computer is not a Mac running OS X, you instantly connect to the current screen of the remote computer.
- If the remote computer is a Mac running OS X and no one is logged in, or if you authenticated as the currently logged-in user, you instantly connect to the current screen of the remote Mac.
- If the remote computer is a Mac running OS X and you authenticated using a different user than the one currently using the Mac, you are presented with a dialog allowing you to choose between the currently logged-in user and a virtual desktop for your user account. If you select the first choice, the remote user is prompted with a dialog to either allow or deny you access. The remote user's choice dictates whether you can connect. If, however, you select the second choice, you are instantly connected to a new virtual screen that logs in to your account. The other user does not know that you are remotely using the computer.

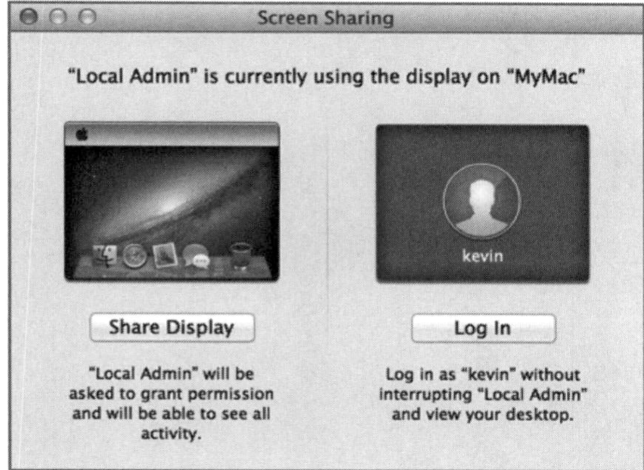

Once connected to the remote computer, a new window opens, titled with the controlled computer's name, showing a live view of the controlled computer's screen(s). Any time this window is active, all keyboard entries and mouse movements are sent to the controlled computer. For example, pressing Command-Q quits the active application on the computer being controlled. Thus, in order to quit the Screen Sharing application, you have to click the close (X) button at the top-left corner of the window.

Note the buttons in the toolbar reveal additional screen sharing features, including the option of taking a screen shot of the remote Mac and sharing clipboard content between your Mac and the remote Mac. Optionally, if the remote computer is running OS X, you can drag and drop files from your Finder to the Mac computer's remote desktop. Doing so opens a File Transfers dialog allowing you to verify the transfer progress or cancel the file transfer.

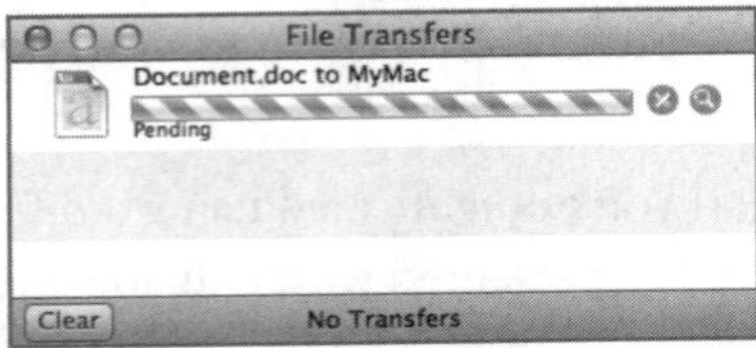

While using the Screen Sharing application, be sure to check out the preference options by choosing Screen Sharing > Preferences. Use these preferences to adjust screen size, encryption, and quality settings. If you are experiencing slow performance, adjust these settings for faster performance. Keep in mind that some network connections, such as crowded wireless or dial-up connections, are so slow that these preferences don't matter much and you simply have to wait for the screen to redraw.

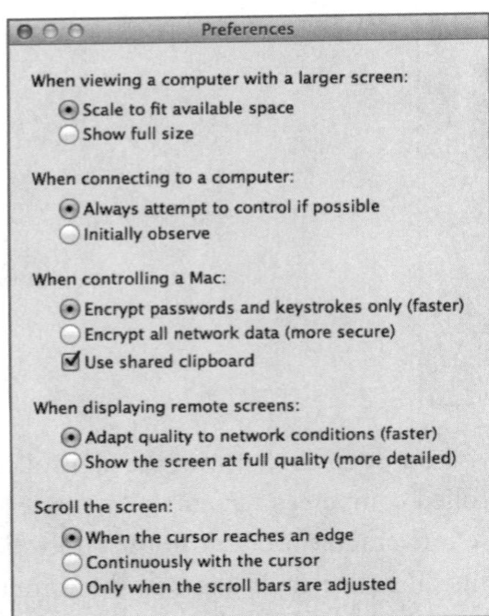

Messages Screen Sharing

The included Messages application can be used to initiate screen sharing, and as an added bonus simultaneously provides voice chat services between the administrator Mac and the controlled Mac. Messages screen sharing also makes it much easier to locate other Macs to control, as the Messages application automatically resolves the location of remote computers based on your active chats or available buddies. Further, Messages also supports reverse screen sharing—the administrator Mac can push its screen to display on another Mac for demonstration purposes.

NOTE ► The Messages application does not require either Mac to have screen sharing enabled in the Sharing preferences. This is because the Messages application includes a quick and easy authorization process to initiate each screen sharing session.

NOTE ► Messages screen sharing is only compatible with other Macs running OS X v10.5 or later. When you select chat participants, the Messages application automatically determines if their computer is using a compatible version of iChat or Messages.

To initiate a Messages screen sharing session, select an available chat user from a buddy list and then click the Screen Sharing button at the bottom of the buddy list. This opens a pop-up menu where you can choose "Share My Screen with <chatuser>" or "Ask to Share <chatuser>'s Screen," where <chatuser> is the name of the user whose computer you are asking to control.

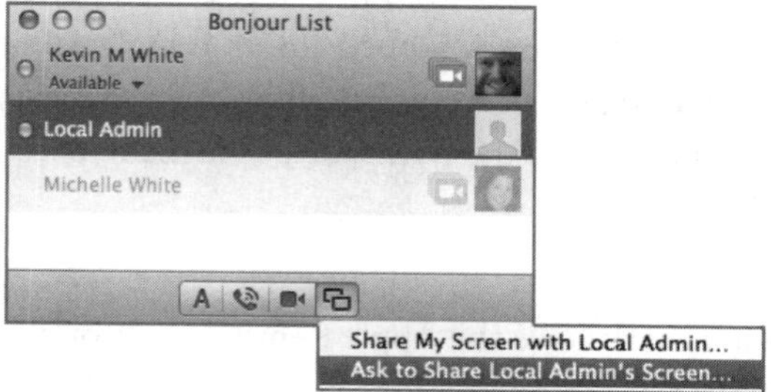

The user on the other computer sees an authorization dialog where he can choose to accept or decline your request to share screens. If the other user clicks the Accept button, the screen sharing session begins.

NOTE ► Even as an administrative user, you cannot force other users to share screens using Messages; they have the sole power to allow or deny your request.

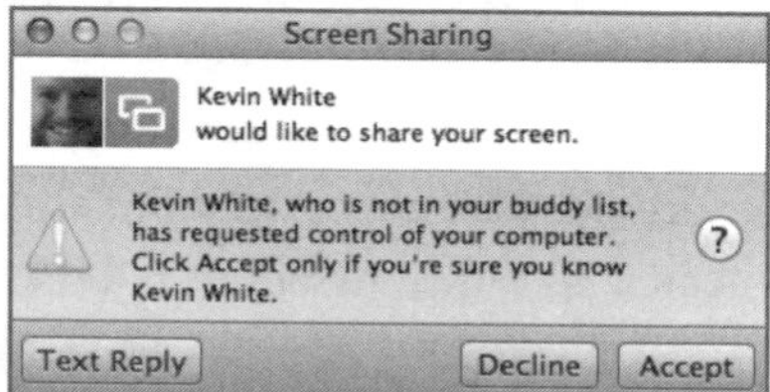

The following screen capture is from the screen sharing "controller's" point of view. The full screen shows the remote Mac and the small My Computer window is the local Mac. The other user does not see the small My Computer window. Clicking the My Computer window allows you to switch back and forth between your local Mac and the remote Mac.

Further, if both computers support voice chat, the Messages application automatically starts a voice chat session between the two computers. You may need to configure Audio/Video settings in the Messages preferences for this feature to work properly. Both users have simultaneous control of the Mac being shared, including the ability to end the screen sharing session at any time from the Screen Sharing menu item on the right side of the menu bar.

Enable ARD Remote Management

Remote Management is client-side software that allows the Apple Remote Desktop (ARD) administration tool to access your Mac. ARD, at version 3.6 for OS X Mountain Lion support, is the ultimate remote management tool for OS X computers. In addition to screen sharing, ARD allows administrators to remotely gather system information and usage statistics, change settings, add or remove files and software, install software packages, send UNIX commands, and perform nearly any other management task you can think of.

The real power of ARD is that you can execute all these tasks simultaneously on dozens of Macs with just a few clicks. Again, if you plan to use ARD in the future, but you want to enable screen sharing for now, you can enable remote management in one step and take advantage of both remote control features.

MORE INFO ▶ The ARD administration software provides advanced functionality that goes well beyond simple screen sharing. You can find out more about ARD at www.apple.com/remotedesktop.

To enable ARD remote management, open the Sharing preferences and authenticate as an administrative user to unlock the preferences. Select the Remote Management checkbox to enable both screen sharing and the ARD client-side services. The launchd control process then starts the ARDAgent background process, which listens for incoming administration requests on UDP port 3283, and also starts AppleVNCServer, which listens for screen sharing requests on TCP port 5900.

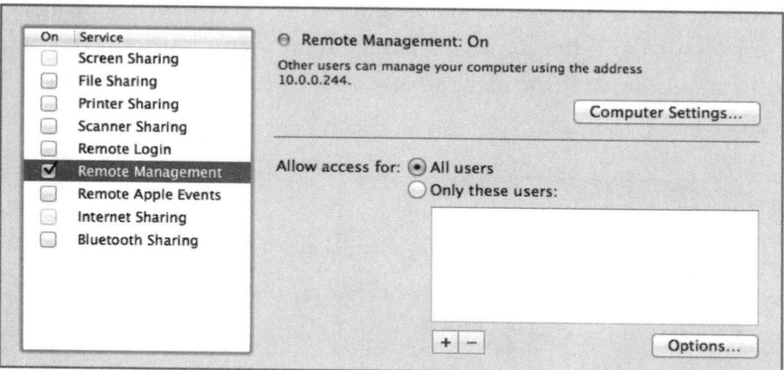

NOTE ▶ The screen sharing service is part of the ARD remote management service. Thus, if Remote Management is selected, the Screen Sharing checkbox is inaccessible.

If this is the first time you have enabled remote management, you'll see a dialog that allows you to select the ARD options you wish to allow for all non-guest local users. You can individually select options, or you can hold down the Option key and then select any checkbox to enable all options.

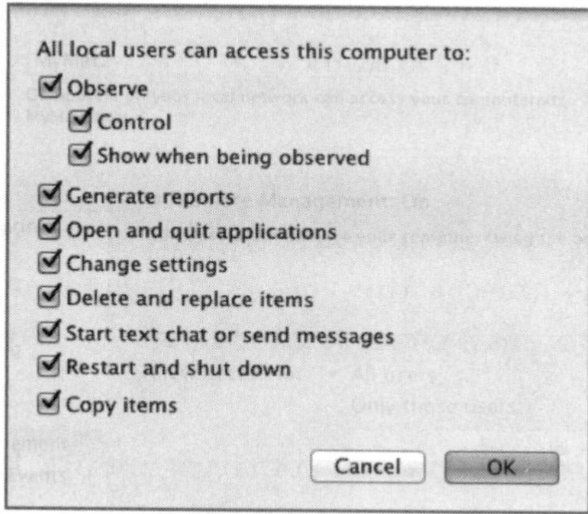

Optionally, to further limit ARD access, select "Only these users" and click the Add (+) button. Then select a standard or administrative local user for whom you wish to grant ARD access. When you're done, another dialog appears, from which you select the ARD options this particular user can access. You can further edit a user's ARD options at any time by double-clicking that user's name in the user access list.

Additional optional ARD computer options are available by clicking the Computer Settings button. This opens a dialog that allows you to enable guest and VNC screen sharing access (covered earlier in this lesson) and the Remote Management menu bar item that allows users to request help from administrators, and add any additional information to help identify this particular Mac.

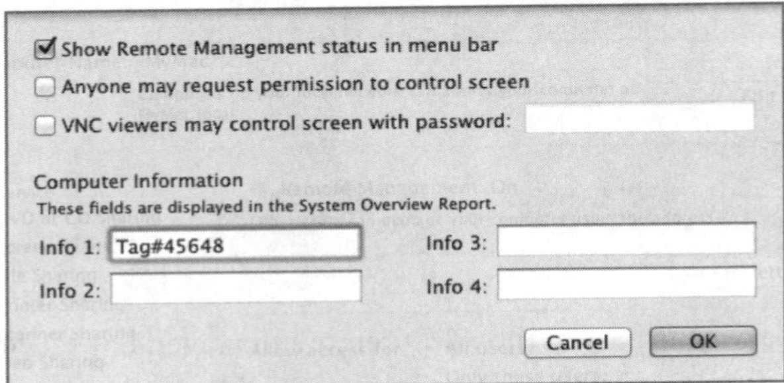

Reference 26.3 AirDrop

In addition to traditional file sharing services, OS X features a peer-to-peer Wi-Fi file sharing service called AirDrop. Although AirDrop is only available on newer Mac models, it's the easiest method to share files between Macs in close proximity.

AirDrop Architecture

While AirDrop does use Wi-Fi networking, it uses radio frequencies outside the Mac computer's normal network connection; thus it does not travel across your established network. In fact, you don't need a network at all to use AirDrop, as it creates a closed network between local Macs.

The most significant feature of AirDrop is that it requires no setup or configuration. Users who want to share items need only navigate to the AirDrop window in the Finder, and the system presents an interface allowing those users to easily share files. AirDrop handles all the details of peer-to-peer file sharing, including discovery, easy authentication, and secure file transfer, using TLS encryption.

AirDrop does have a few significant caveats. First, it only works between computers within the Mac computers' local Wi-Fi range. This range varies based on many factors, but it's generally limited to within 150 feet in an open space or less than 50 feet in a space with heavy interference. Also, AirDrop was specifically designed to provide direct file sharing for selected items, as opposed to traditional file sharing, which allows the user to browse another computer's file system. Finally, AirDrop is not supported on older Macs or Macs lacking Wi-Fi support. You can verify if a Mac supports AirDrop in the Finder by clicking the Go menu. If an AirDrop menu option appears, the Mac supports AirDrop.

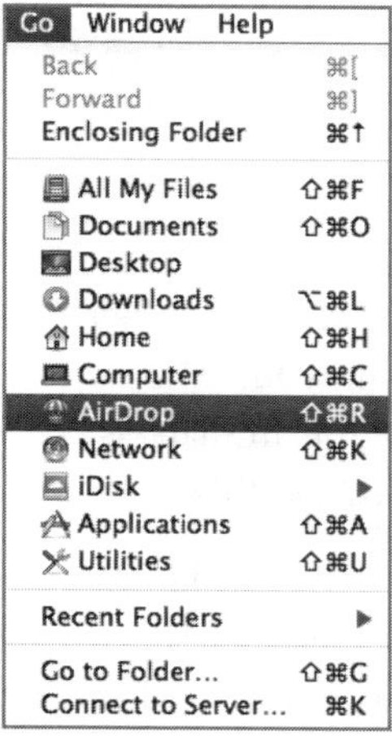

MORE INFO ▶ A list of Macs that support AirDrop can be found in Knowledge Base document HT4783, "OS X Lion: Can I use AirDrop with my computer?"

Using AirDrop

To quickly share files between Macs that support AirDrop, start by choosing the AirDrop icon in the Finder sidebar, choosing Go > AirDrop, or pressing Shift-Command-R. Any of these methods opens the AirDrop Finder window.

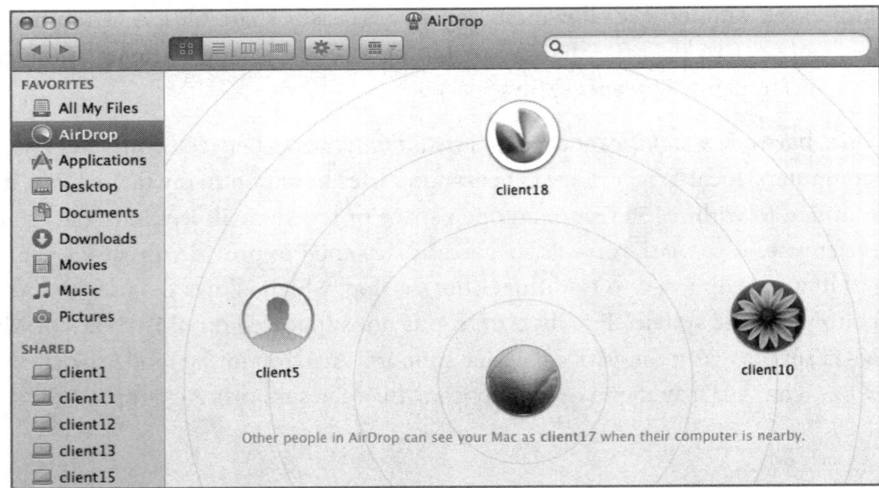

NOTE ► If the Mac computer's Wi-Fi interface is turned off, click the Turn Wi-Fi On button to enable AirDrop.

Any time you select the AirDrop window, the system automatically scans for other AirDrop Macs within local Wi-Fi range. For another Mac to show up within your AirDrop range, it must also have the AirDrop window selected in the Finder. Note the animated sweeping AirDrop icon in the Finder sidebar, indicating that AirDrop is active for this Mac.

The icons that appear in AirDrop are based on the Mac computer's currently logged-in user account. The names that appear in AirDrop default to the Mac computer's computer name set in the Sharing preferences, as covered earlier in this lesson. If the currently logged-in user has an Apple ID associated with her account, and you have that Apple ID in your Contacts, the name that appears in AirDrop is the user's human name from the associated Contacts entry.

Once AirDrop has found the other Mac you wish to transfer an item to, drag a file or folder from another Finder window to the icon representing the other Mac. A pop-up appears to verify that you want to transfer the item. Click Send to initiate the AirDrop connection.

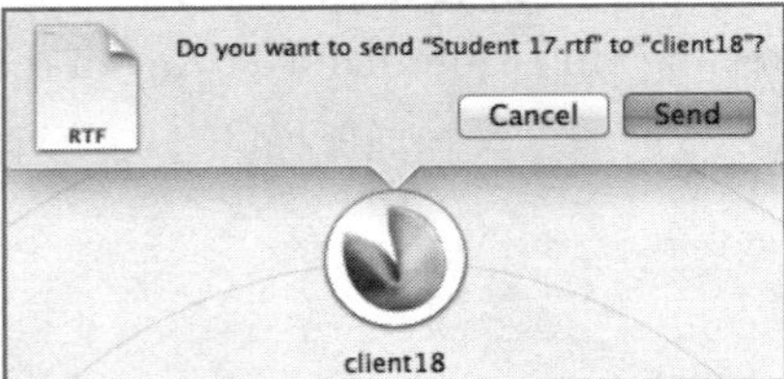

Once you click Send, the pop-up shows that AirDrop has sent a request to the other Mac.

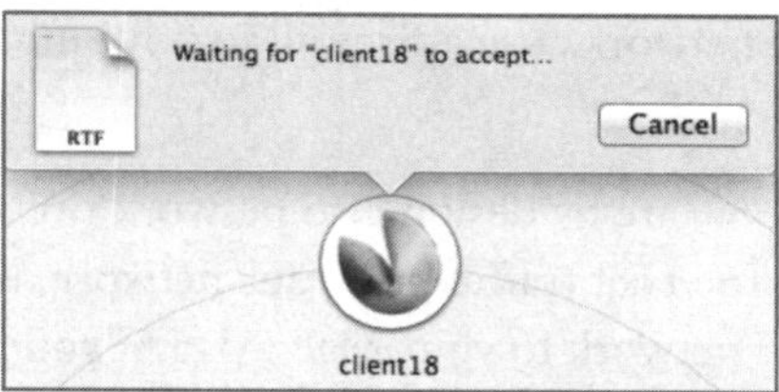

From the other Mac, a pop-up appears, allowing the user to accept the incoming item. If Save is clicked, the item is transferred to the user's Downloads folder. Clicking "Save and Open" saves to the same location, and then automatically opens the item. Clicking Decline cancels the transfer and notifies the other user in the AirDrop window.

Reference 26.4
Personal Firewall

From a network services standpoint, your Mac is already very secure because, by default, there are only a few essential services running that respond to external requests. Even once you start providing individual shared services, your Mac is designed to respond only to those services that are enabled.

Further, services that could cause trouble if compromised, like file or screen sharing, can be configured to have limited access authorization, as covered previously in this lesson. Still, users can open third-party applications or background services that could leave a Mac vulnerable to a network attack.

TIP To maintain a high level of network security, you should leave sharing services disabled unless absolutely necessary. If you do enable sharing services, be sure to limit authorization access as best you can.

Personal Application Firewall

The most common method to secure network services is to configure a firewall, which blocks unauthorized network service access. Most networks use a firewall to limit inbound traffic from an Internet connection.

In fact, most home routers, like AirPort base stations, are by design also network firewalls. While network-level firewalls block unauthorized Internet traffic into your network, they don't block traffic that originated from inside your network to your Mac. Also, if your Mac is mobile and is often joining new networks, odds are that every new network you join will have different firewall rules.

Thus, to prevent unauthorized network services from allowing incoming connections to your specific Mac, you can enable the built-in personal application firewall. A personal firewall blocks unauthorized connections to your Mac no matter where they originated. The OS X firewall also features a single-click configuration that provides a high level of network service security, which works for most users.

A standard firewall uses rules based on service port numbers. As you've learned previously in this lesson, each service defaults to a standard port or set of ports. However, some network services, like the Messages application, use a wide range of dynamic ports. If we were to manually configure a traditional firewall, we would have to make dozens of rules for every potential port that the user may need.

To resolve this issue, the OS X firewall uses an adaptive technology that allows connections based on applications and service needs, without you having to know the specific ports they use. For example, you can authorize the Messages application to accept any incoming connection without configuring all of the individual TCP and UDP ports used by the Messages application.

> **TIP** A more traditional port-based firewall, `ipfw`, is still in place in OS X and can be configured from the Terminal or the `ipfw` configuration files if that's your preferred method.

The personal application firewall also leverages another built-in feature, code signing, to ensure that allowed applications and services aren't changed without your knowledge. Further, code signing allows Apple and third-party developers to provide a guarantee that their software hasn't been tampered with. This level of verifiable trust allows you to configure the firewall in default mode with a single click, automatically allowing signed applications and services to receive incoming connections.

Finally, because the personal application firewall is fully dynamic, it opens only the necessary ports when the application or service is running. Again, using the Messages application as an example, the personal application firewall allows only incoming connections to the required ports if the Messages application is running. If the application quits because the user logs out, the firewall closes the associated ports. Having the required ports open only when an application or service needs them provides an extra layer of security not found with traditional firewalls.

Configure the Personal Firewall

To enable and configure the OS X personal application firewall, open the Security & Privacy preferences then click the lock icon in the bottom-left corner and authenticate as an administrative user to unlock the Security & Privacy preferences. Select the Firewall tab, and then click the Turn On Firewall button to enable the default firewall rules. Once enabled, this button changes to a Turn Off Firewall button, allowing you to disable the firewall.

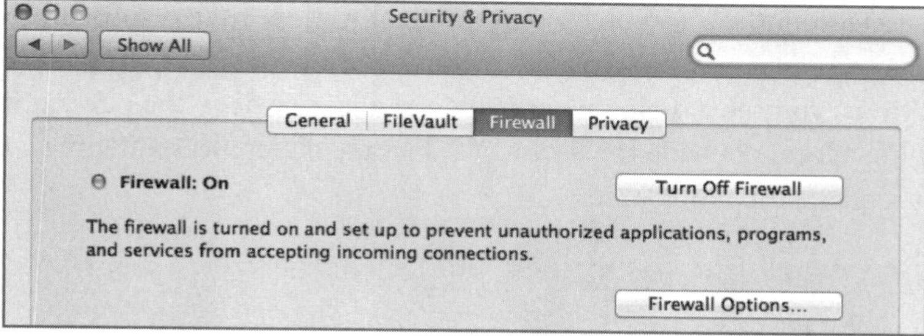

The default firewall configuration is to allow incoming traffic for established connections (connections that were initiated from your Mac and are expecting a return) and for any signed software or enabled service. This level of security is adequate for most users.

> **TIP** Firewall logging is always enabled and can be viewed from the Console application. The firewall log is located at /private/var/log/appfirewall.log.

Advanced Firewall Configuration

If you want to customize the firewall, you can reveal any additional firewall configuration by clicking the Firewall Options button. From the firewall options window, a list of services currently allowed appears. Without any additional configuration, sharing services enabled from the Sharing preferences automatically appear in the list of allowed services. Conversely, disabling a shared service from the Sharing preference removes the service from the list of allowed services.

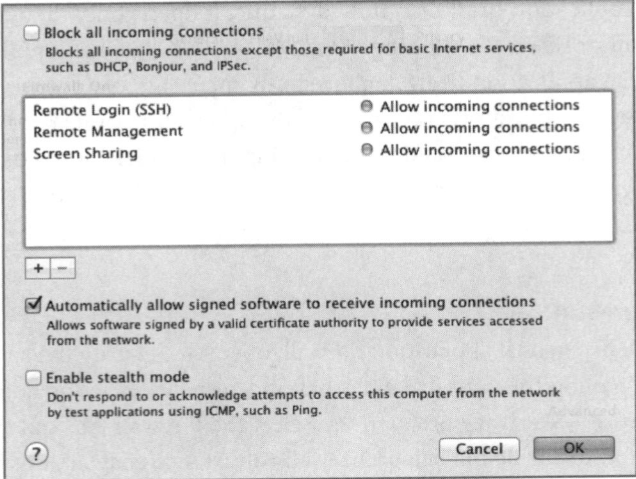

Optionally, for a bit more control, you can manually set which applications and services the firewall allows by deselecting the checkbox to automatically allow signed software. With this firewall choice, as you open new network applications for the first time or update existing network applications, you see a dialog where you can allow or deny the new network application. This dialog appears outside the Security & Privacy preferences any time a new network application requests incoming access.

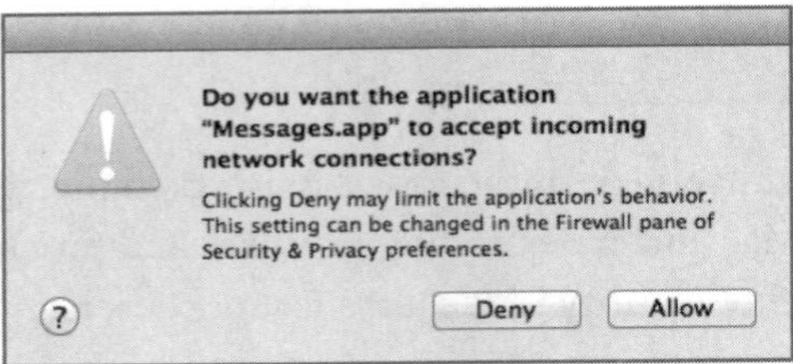

If you are manually setting network application and service firewall access, you can always return to the Advanced firewall dialog to review the list of items, and either delete items from the list or specifically disallow certain items.

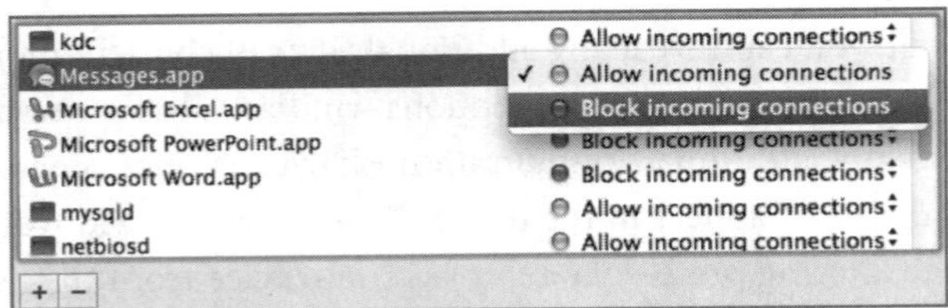

For a bit more security, you can select the "Enable stealth mode" checkbox to prevent response or acknowledgement of a failed attempt to the requesting host. With this enabled, your Mac does not respond to any unauthorized network connections, including network diagnostic protocols like ping, traceroute, and port scan.

In other words, your computer simply ignores the request instead of returning a response of failure to the requesting host. However, your Mac still responds to other allowed services. This includes, by default, Bonjour, which dutifully announces your Mac computer's presence, thus preventing your Mac from being truly hidden on the network.

When the utmost security is needed, you can select the "Block all incoming connections" checkbox. Notice that selecting this option automatically selects stealth mode as well.

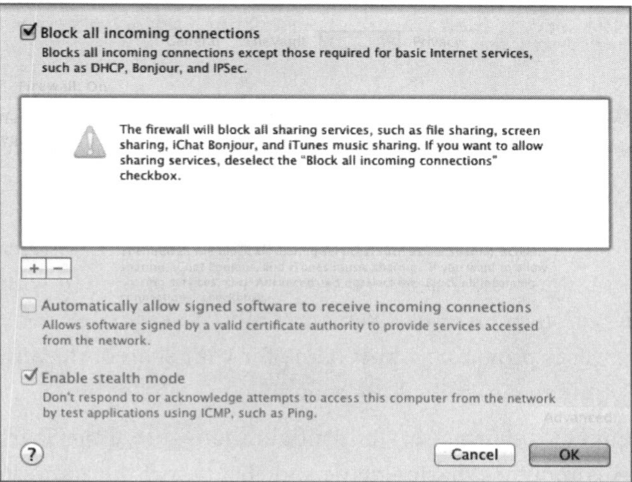

When blocking all incoming connections, your Mac does not respond to any incoming network connections except for those required for basic network services or established connections, such as those needed to browse the web or check email. Obviously, this prevents any shared service or application hosted on your Mac from working remotely.

Reference 26.5
Shared Service Troubleshooting

If you're providing a shared service from your Mac, and others are having trouble reaching it, you must first consider how established the service is to determine where to focus your efforts. So, if your Mac has been reliably providing a shared service for a while, but now a single client computer has trouble accessing the service, troubleshoot the client computer before troubleshooting your shared Mac.

Otherwise, if multiple clients cannot access your shared Mac, you may indeed have an issue with the sharing service. After ruling out other potential local client and network issues, you can safely assume that the problem lies with the Mac providing shared services. If so, shared network service issues fall into two general categories: service communication or service access.

Service communication issues are manifested by an inability to establish a connection to the shared service. Keep in mind that if you are presented with an authentication dialog, the client and server are establishing a proper connection, and you should troubleshoot the issue as a service access issue. However, if you are unable to authenticate, or you can authenticate but you're not authorized to access the service, then you are experiencing a service access issue.

Network Service Communication Issues

If you are unable to establish a connection to the shared service, this may signal a network service communication issue:

- Double-check the shared Mac network configuration—From the Network preferences, make sure the Mac computer's network interfaces are active and configured with the appropriate TCP/IP settings. You can also use Network Utility to verify the network configuration. If a DNS server is providing a host name for your shared Mac, use the Lookup tool in Network Utility to verify the host name.
- Double-check the Mac computer's sharing service configuration—From the Sharing preferences, verify the Mac computer's sharing name and ensure that the appropriate services are enabled and configured.
- Double-check the Mac computer's firewall configuration—From the Security & Privacy preferences, first temporarily stop the firewall to see if disabling it makes a difference. If you are able to establish a connection, adjust the list of allowed services and applications before you restart the firewall.
- Check for basic network connectivity to the shared Mac—First, turn off the firewall's stealth mode, and then, from another Mac, use the Network Utility ping tool to check for basic connectivity to the shared Mac. If you can't ping the shared Mac, you're probably having a network-level issue that goes beyond service troubleshooting.
- Check for network service port connectivity to the shared Mac—First, turn off the firewall's stealth mode, and then, from another Mac, use the Network Utility port scan tool to verify whether the expected network service ports are accessible. If the shared Mac

is configured properly, the appropriate network service ports should register as open. If network routers exist between the network clients and the shared Mac, consider the possibility that a network administrator has decided to block access to those ports.

Network Service Access Issues

Failure to authenticate or be granted authorization to a shared service is considered a network service access issue. The following list provides methods for troubleshooting these access issues:

- Verify the local user account settings—When using local user accounts, make sure the correct authentication information is being used. You may find that the user is not using the right information, and you may have to reset the account password. (Troubleshooting user account issues was covered in Lesson 6, "User Accounts.") Also, keep in mind that some services do not allow the use of guest and sharing-only user accounts. Further, the standard VNC service uses password information that is not directly linked to a user account.
- Double-check directory service settings—If you use a network directory service in your environment, verify that the Mac is properly communicating with the directory service by checking its status in the Directory Utility application. Even if you're only trying to use local accounts, any directory service issues can cause authentication problems. Also, keep in mind that some services, like ARD remote management, do not by default allow you to authenticate with accounts hosted from network directories.
- Double-check shared service access settings—Several authenticated sharing services allow you to configure access lists. Use the Sharing preferences to verify that the appropriate user accounts are allowed to access the shared service.

Exercise 26.1
Use Host Sharing Services

Prerequisites

- You must have created the Local Admin (Exercise 3.1 or 3.2) and Chris Johnson (Exercise 6.1) accounts.
- You need another computer running OS X Mountain Lion on the same network as your primary computer. If you are performing these exercises in a class, you will work with a partner.

In this exercise, you will use the OS X screen sharing capability to control another computer remotely. You will use both the option to share the current user's session, and the option to use a virtual display to log in as a different user.

Enable Screen Sharing

1 If necessary, log in as Chris Johnson.

2 Open System Preferences and select the Sharing preference pane.

3 Click the lock and authenticate as Local Admin.

4 Select the checkbox next to Remote Management, if it is not already selected.

   Note that although you will be using screen sharing, you are configuring it via the Remote Management service. Remote Management includes screen sharing as an optional capability. If you look at the checkbox for the Screen Sharing service, you'll see that it is dimmed; this does not mean that the service is disabled, but that it is being controlled by Remote Management.

5 Ensure that "All users" is selected for "Allow access for."

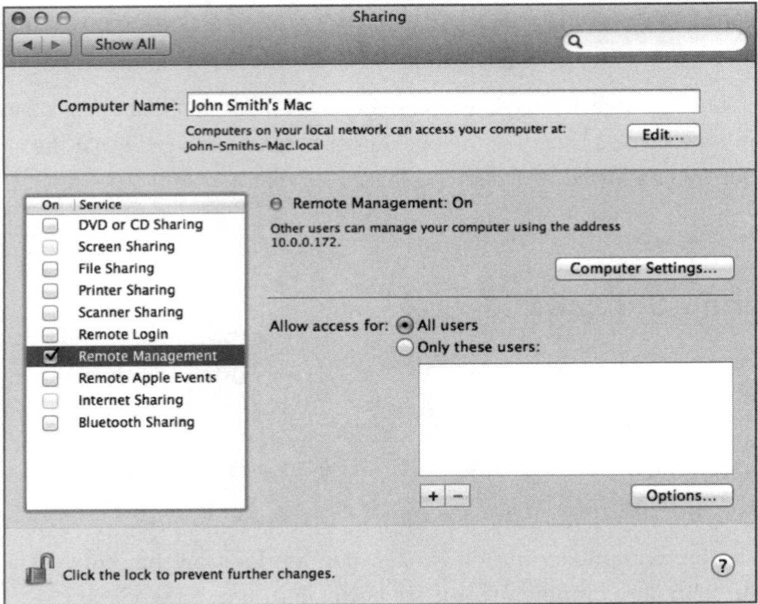

6 Click Options.

7 Ensure that all options are selected. An easy way to do this is to Option-click a checkbox until all of the checkboxes are selected.

8 Click OK, then quit System Preferences.

Remotely Control Another Computer's Screen

In this section you will use screen sharing to control another computer. Which computer you will control depends on whether you are performing these exercises in a class or on your own:

- If you are in a class, you will work with a partner and take turns controlling each other's computers.
- If you are performing these exercises on your own, you will perform this section from another computer and use it to control your primary exercise computer.

1 If you are working with a partner, wait for her to finish enabling and configuring Remote Management, then decide who will go first. If your partner goes first, wait for her to finish this section before starting.

2 If you are on your own, log into the other computer.

3 In the Finder, choose Go > Network (or press Command-Shift-K).

The computer you are going to control appears in the display of shared computers on the local network. Note that this shows computers offering file sharing, screen sharing, or both.

The Finder sidebar also displays local computers offering sharing services, but it only shows a limited number. The network view shows all of them.

4 Double-click the computer you will control in the Network window.

Since the other computer does not offer file-sharing service, your computer only has the option to share its screen.

5 Click Share Screen.

6 Authenticate as Chris Johnson (note that you can use the account's short name, **chris**), and click Connect.

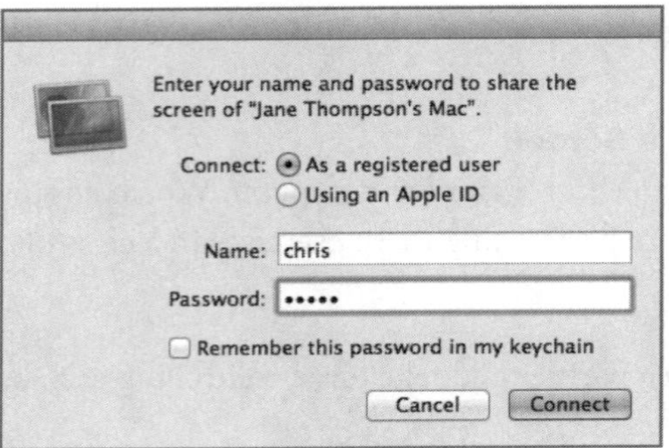

Screen sharing begins and you see a window with a live, interactive picture of the other computer's desktop.

7 Open System Preferences on the other computer and select the "Desktop & Screen Saver" preference pane.

8 Select a different picture for the other computer's desktop.

9 Press Command-Q.

This quits the System Preferences application on the other computer. You cannot use standard shortcuts to control the Screen Sharing application itself.

10 Click the Full Screen button at the right end title bar of the Screen Sharing window.

Like many OS X apps, Screen Sharing supports a full-screen mode. In full-screen mode, your display is a virtual mirror of the other computer's.

11 Move your mouse to the very top of the screen.

The Screen Sharing menu and toolbar appear at the top of the screen. This allows you to exit full-screen mode, or access the Screen Sharing controls.

12 Choose Screen Sharing > Quit Screen Sharing.

13 If asked if you are sure you want to quit, click Quit.

14 If you are working with a partner, switch roles and have your partner repeat these steps.

Connect to a Virtual Display

By connecting to another computer as a different user, you can work with a virtual display instead of sharing the local user's display. As in the last section, you will either work with a partner (although this time you can both work at once, rather than taking turns) or connect to your primary exercise computer from another computer.

1 If necessary, wait for your partner to finish the previous section.

2 If necessary, reopen the Network view (press Command-Shift-K), and select the computer you will control.

3 Click Share Screen.

4 This time authenticate as Local Admin (you can use the short name **ladmin**), and click Connect.

Since you authenticated as a different user than is logged into the other computer, you are now presented with the choice of sharing the current user's display or logging in as a different user with a virtual display.

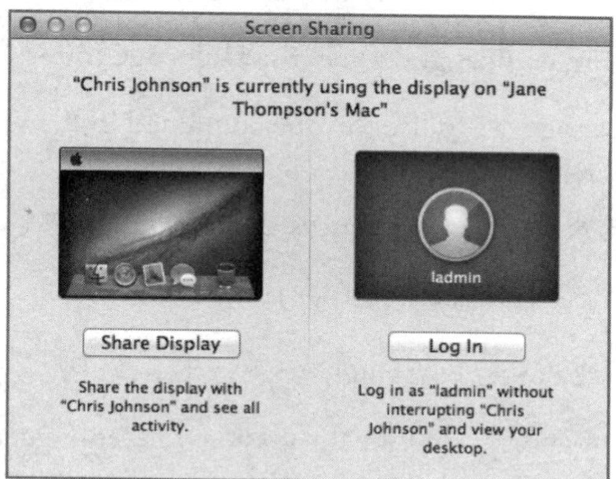

5 Click Log In.

A screen-sharing window opens and displays a login screen for your partner's computer.

6 Log in to your partner's computer as Local Admin.

This virtual screen capability makes it easy to remotely manage users' computers without disturbing them. Note that if you are in a class, your partner is connecting to your computer at the same time, but you do not see any indication of this.

7 On the other computer, open System Preferences and select the Users & Groups pane.

If you use the Apple menu or the Dock, be sure to use the one contained in the window, not the one at the edge of your screen.

Do not make any changes in the Users & Groups preferences at this time.

8 Quit System Preferences on your partner's computer.

9 Click the fast user switching menu on the other computer.

You see that both Chris Johnson (either your partner or the session you left logged in there) and Local Admin (actually, you) are logged in to the other computer. Your virtual display is treated as a fast user switching session.

10 From the remote menu bar, choose Apple menu > Log Out Local Admin, then click the Log Out button.

If you disconnect screen sharing without logging out first, you leave behind an orphaned fast user switching session.

11 From the menu bar at the top of the screen, choose Screen Sharing > Quit Screen Sharing.

12 If you are working with a partner, wait for him to finish before starting the next exercise.

13 If you are working on your own, move back to your primary exercise computer for the first part of the next exercise.

Exercise 26.2
Configure the Personal Firewall

Prerequisites

- You must have created the Local Admin (Exercise 3.1 or 3.2) and Chris Johnson (Exercise 6.1) accounts.
- You need another computer running OS X Mountain Lion on the same network as your primary computer. If you are performing these exercises in a class, you will work with a partner.

A firewall blocks network traffic based on port numbers and protocols. The OS X firewall allows only ports based on application and service requests. The OS X built-in firewall is simple to configure from the user interface. In this exercise you will turn on the firewall and start a network-aware application. Then, you will view the firewall log. You will also configure the advanced Stealth option and see that it disables responses to network pings.

Enable the Firewall

1. If necessary, log in as Chris Johnson.
2. Open the Security & Privacy pane in System Preferences.
3. Click the Firewall tab.
4. Click the lock and authenticate as Local Admin.
5. Click Turn On Firewall.
6. Click Firewall Options.

   Notice that Remote Management and Screen Sharing are already on the list as "Allow incoming connections." The system assumes that if you enable a service in the Sharing pane, you must want users to be able to connect to it, so it automatically allows those services through the firewall.

   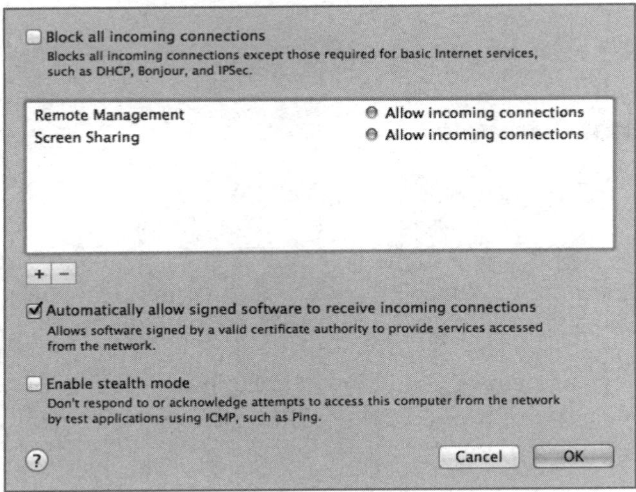

7. Deselect "Automatically allow signed software to receive incoming connections."

8 Click OK.

9 Quit System Preferences.

NOTE ▶ With the firewall in this mode, you may receive alerts about various system components attempting to accept incoming connections. "ubd" (the ubiquity daemon, part of iCloud) is a common example. It is generally safe to allow these through the firewall.

Test Firewall Settings

1 Open iTunes, which can be found in the Applications folder.

2 If it presents you with the iTunes Software License Agreement, click Agree.

3 If it tells you a new version of iTunes is available, click "Don't Download."

4 If an iTunes Tutorials window opens, close it.

5 Choose iTunes > Preferences (Command-comma).

6 Click the Sharing icon.

7 Select the checkbox for "Share my library on my local network."

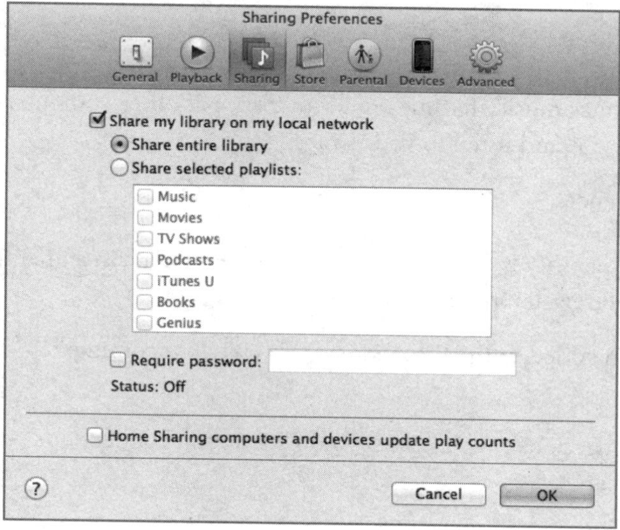

8 Click OK.

9 In the copyright reminder dialog, click OK (you may need to drag an iTunes dialog out of the way to get to it).

10 If a dialog appears asking if you want the application "iTunes.app" to accept incoming connections, click Deny. Note that clicking Allow would prompt for an admin password to allow the exception to the firewall rules.

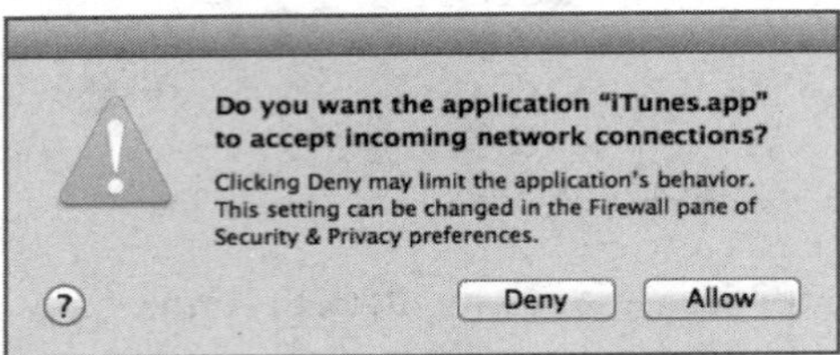

iTunes displays a dialog indicating that the firewall settings prevent you from using some iTunes features.

If you click Ignore here, iTunes music sharing would turn on, but other computers would not be able connect to it and listen to your songs.

11 Click Open Firewall Preferences.

12 In the Firewall pane of the Security & Privacy pane of System Preferences, authenticate if necessary and then click Firewall Options.

Notice that iTunes has been added to the list, and is set to "Block incoming connections."

13 Click "Block incoming connections", and choose "Allow incoming connections" from the pop-up menu that appears.

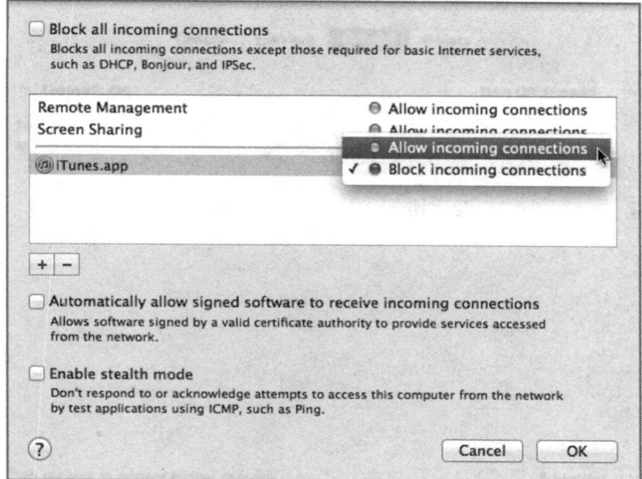

Since you have authenticated as an administrator, you can change the firewall policy for any specific application.

14. Click OK to dismiss the Firewall Options dialog.

15. Quit iTunes, but leave System Preferences open.

View the Firewall Log

1. Open Console from the Utilities folder.

2. If the source list sidebar is not shown, click the Show Log List button in the toolbar to enable it.

3. In the files section of the source list on the left, select /var/log. This is one of the standard log locations on the system.

4. Click the disclosure triangle next to /var/log and select appfirewall.log. This is the log file that the firewall service logs to, and that records which applications have attempted to listen for network connections.

5. Quit the Console utility.

Test Stealth Mode

As in the last section, you will either work with a partner or connect to your primary exercise computer from another computer.

1 In System Preferences, switch to the Sharing preference pane.

   Note your computer's Bonjour name, listed beneath its computer name.

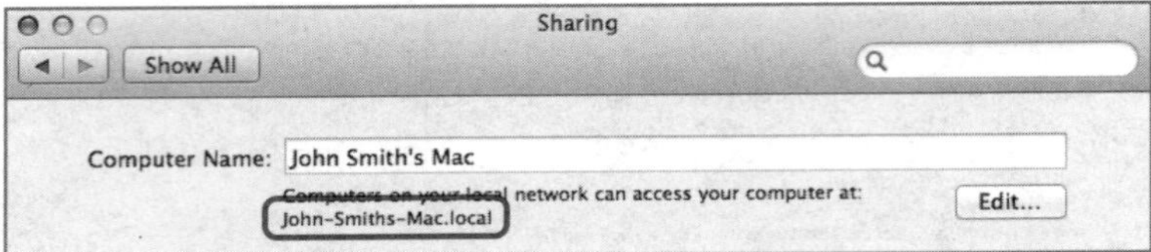

2 If you are working on your own, switch to your other computer.

3 Open Network Utility from /Applications/Utilities.

4 Click the Ping tab.

5 If you are working with a partner, ask him for his computer's Bonjour name and enter it as the network address to ping. If you are working on your own, enter the Bonjour name of your primary exercise computer.

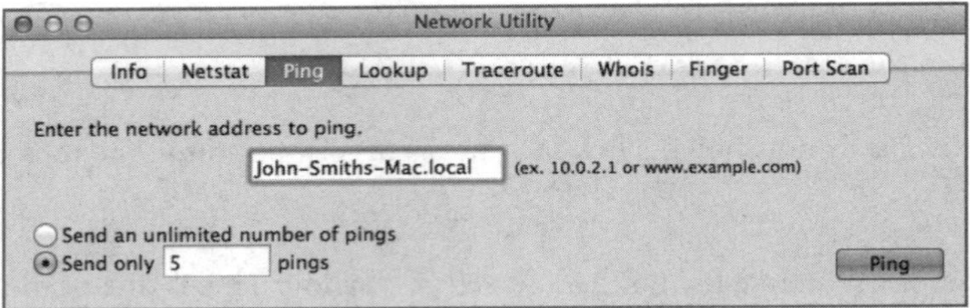

6 If necessary, set it to send only 5 pings and click Ping.

   You should see successful pings.

7 If you are working with a partner, wait for him to finish pinging your computer. If you are working on your own, switch back to your primary exercise computer.

8 Switch to System Preferences, switch to the Security & Privacy pane, and open the Firewall Options.

9 Select “Enable Stealth mode” and click OK.

10 If you are working with a partner, wait for him to finish enabling stealth mode. If you are working on your own, switch back to your other computer.

11 Switch to Network Utility and click Ping to rerun the connectivity test.

After about 30 seconds, “Request timeout” messages appear in Network Utility.

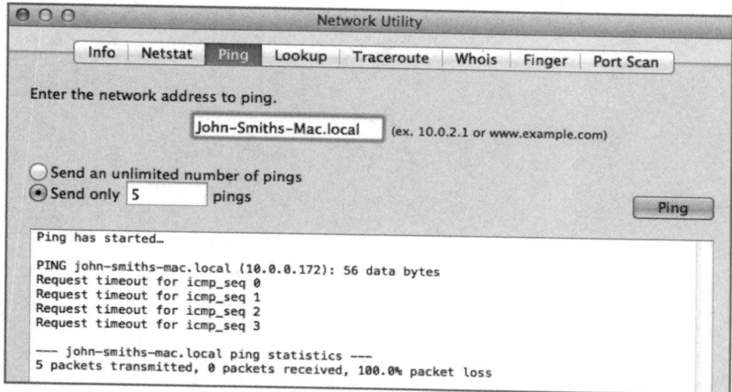

NOTE ► While Stealth mode is an excellent security feature, it interferes with network troubleshooting. If a computer does not respond to a ping, in addition to checking cables, you should check firewall settings.

12 On your computer, turn off the firewall.

13 Quit all running programs.

Peripherals and Printing

Lesson **27**

Peripherals and Drivers

Apple pioneered the concept of automatic peripheral support with the original Mac. This feature, commonly known as plug-and-play, is now supported with varying success in all modern operating systems. Peripheral hardware has also improved, as now the most common connectivity standards support hot-pluggable or even wireless connections. OS X supports all popular modern peripheral standards, demonstrating Apple's continued commitment to making peripheral use as easy as possible.

At the start of this lesson, you'll learn how OS X supports different peripheral technologies. Then you'll learn how to manage and troubleshoot peripherals connected to OS X systems.

GOALS

- Understand and manage OS X peripheral connectivity
- Pair Bluetooth devices to your Mac
- Troubleshoot peripheral and driver issues

Reference 27.1
Peripheral Technologies

For the purposes of this lesson, a peripheral is any non-networked device to which your computer system can be directly connected. A peripheral is also controlled by the computer, whereas network devices are shared.

Given the wide range of devices included in this definition, this lesson shows you how to categorize devices based on their connectivity type and device class. Understanding the available connection methods and device types is necessary to manage and troubleshoot peripherals, which is the goal of this lesson.

NOTE ▸ This lesson only covers connection technologies included with Mac systems that support OS X Mountain Lion.

Peripheral Connectivity

Most peripherals communicate with the Mac system via a connection mechanism commonly known as a bus. Bus connections are the most common peripheral connection type because they allow multiple peripherals to connect to your Mac simultaneously. In fact, the only connection types that are not buses are those used strictly for audio and video connectivity. Even then, your Mac is connected via a peripheral bus to intermediary hardware responsible for encoding or decoding the audio and video signals.

We can categorize peripheral connectivity into four types:

- Peripheral buses—General-purpose buses primarily used to connect an external device to your Mac.
- Expansion buses—Designed to expand your Mac computer's hardware capabilities, often by adding extra connectivity options.
- Storage buses—Used only for accessing storage devices.
- Audio and video connectivity—Standard interfaces used to send audio or video signals from one device to another.

Each connection is specialized for a particular type of communication, so a combination of technologies is often required to use a peripheral. For example, your Mac computer's graphics hardware is obviously designed to output a standard video signal, but it communicates with the processor via an expansion bus. You'll see many examples of combined connection types as you explore various peripheral devices.

Given this, it's a good thing OS X includes the System Information application to help you identify connected peripherals, including their connection types. Access System Information by holding the Option key and choosing Apple menu > System Information. Once System Information is open, select a hardware interface from the Contents list to view its information. Using System Information for further troubleshooting peripherals is covered later in this lesson.

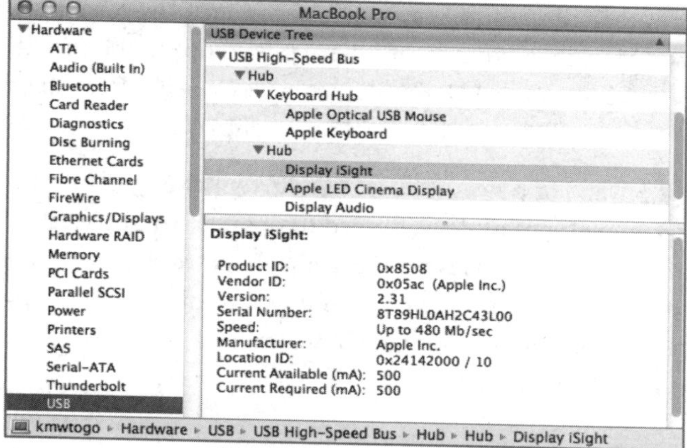

Peripheral Buses

Peripheral buses are the connection type most commonly associated with computer peripherals. Because they are designed to provide a general-purpose communications link between the computer and the peripheral, a variety of devices can use them. There have been dozens of peripheral connectivity standards developed over the years, but in the last decade three have dominated the market: Universal Serial Bus (USB), FireWire, and Bluetooth.

Universal Serial Bus (USB) 1.1/2.0/3.0

Standard on every Mac that supports OS X, USB is by far the most popular peripheral connection. In fact, every single type of peripheral can be found in USB versions. You're probably already aware of the external USB ports on your Mac, but you may not know that Intel-based Macs also use USB for internal connectivity. For example, the MacBook keyboard, trackpad, infrared receiver, iSight camera, and Bluetooth controller are all connected via internal USB connections.

USB was originally designed by Intel and is a hot-pluggable interface that allows the user to connect and disconnect devices while they are on, or "hot." USB is also a highly expandable connection platform that allows for daisy-chained connections. So, you can connect one USB device to your Mac, then connect another USB device to the first, and so on. The USB specification allows for up to 127 simultaneous devices per host controller. Most Macs have at least two externally accessible USB host controllers.

A USB port may supply up to 2.5 watts of power (500 mA of current at 5 volts) to the connected devices, which is all that some types of devices need to operate. Unpowered hubs, including those built into many USB keyboards, split the available power between their ports, usually supplying only 0.5 watts (100 mA) to each, enough for only very low-power devices. When the system detects that there is not enough power for a connected device, it displays a low-power warning and disables the device.

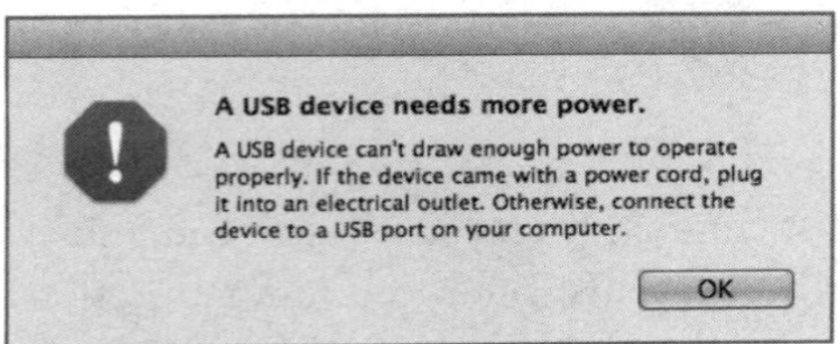

If you see this dialog, you can verify the power issue by opening /Applications/Utilities/System Information and selecting USB from the report list. Selecting any USB device displays the electric current available to, and desired by, the device.

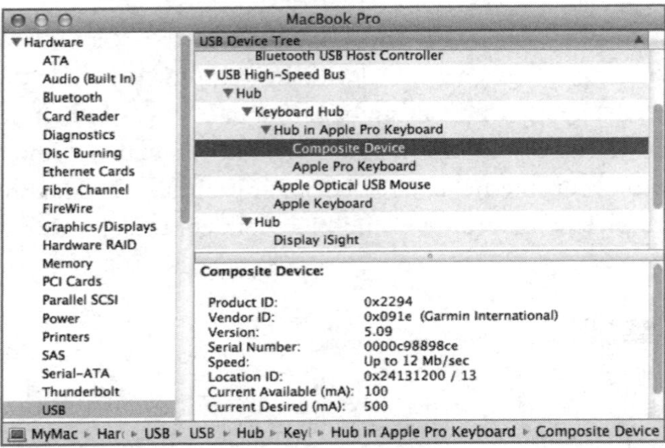

You can try resolving USB power issues by connecting the peripheral directly to the Mac or through a powered hub, which uses an external power connection to supply full power to the attached device. Peripherals that require even more power to operate, such as printers or large disk drives, generally also include a separate power source.

There are currently three USB versions supported by Apple hardware: USB 1.1, USB 2.0, and USB 3.0. Despite significant upgrades in performance, all USB ports on Mac systems are backward compatible with USB 1.1 cabling and devices. The various USB versions offer the following performance characteristics:

- USB 1.1 supports low-speed connections at 1.5 megabits per second (Mbit/s) and full-speed connections at up to 12 Mbit/s. All Mac systems that support OS X Mountain Lion also support USB 1.1.
- USB 2.0 supports high-speed connections up to a theoretical maximum of 480 Mbit/s. In practice, though, high-speed USB 2.0 connections fall short of the theoretical maximum due to the compression algorithms in use. All Mac systems that support OS X Mountain Lion also support USB 2.0.
- USB 3.0 supports super-speed connections up to a theoretical maximum of 5 Gbit/s (~5000 Mbit/s). Peripherals and devices that support USB 3.0 are often identified by the use of bright-blue plastic for the interior of the physical connection, although no Apple device uses this for identification. Mac systems introduced in mid 2012 or newer support USB 3.0.

MORE INFO ▶ You can find out more about USB at the official USB Implementers Forum website: www.usb.org.

FireWire 400/800

Also standard on most Macs that support OS X, FireWire is a high-speed, general-purpose peripheral connection originally developed by Apple. FireWire has been ratified as an Institute of Electrical and Electronics Engineers (IEEE) standard known as IEEE-1394 and has been adopted as a standard interface for many digital video devices.

Like USB, FireWire supports hot-pluggable and daisy-chained connections. Using hubs, each FireWire host controller can support up to 63 devices simultaneously. FireWire host controllers also allow your Mac to be used in target disk mode without the need for a functional operating system, as covered in Lesson 13, "File System Troubleshooting."

All Macs with FireWire ports support FireWire 400 with a maximum transfer rate of up to 400 Mbit/s, and most newer Macs support FireWire 800 with a maximum transfer rate of up to 800 Mbit/s. These two FireWire standards use different port connections, but Macs with FireWire 800 ports can connect to FireWire 400 devices with the appropriate adapter. Newer Mac systems that feature Thunderbolt ports also support FireWire via the Apple Thunderbolt to FireWire Adapter.

Finally, FireWire ports on Mac systems generally supply about 7 watts per port, compared with the 2.5 watts of a USB. This increased power capacity makes FireWire ideal for use with external portable hard drives, as no additional power source is required to run the disk.

Alas, the FireWire standard's days are numbered, as the additional cost and complexity of FireWire host controllers makes the technology overkill for many simple peripherals, such as mice, keyboards, and flash drives, which are well served by USB. At the high-end, the tremendous speed and flexibility of the newer Thunderbolt standard puts FireWire to shame.

MORE INFO ▶ You can find out more about FireWire at the official 1394 Trade Association website: www.1394ta.org.

Thunderbolt

Originally designed by Intel, then later in collaboration with Apple, Thunderbolt represents the latest in peripheral connectivity. This new standard folds PCI Express and DisplayPort data into a single connection and cable. One Thunderbolt host computer connection supports a hub or daisy chain of up to six devices, with up to two of these devices being high-resolution displays. Further, Macs with Thunderbolt can be used in target disk mode without the need for a functional operating system, as covered in Lesson 13, "File System Troubleshooting."

Thunderbolt provides for unmatched peripheral flexibility given its mix of PCI Express and DisplayPort connectivity. As detailed later in this lesson, PCI Express is actually an expansion bus, and DisplayPort provides digital video and audio connectivity. Each Thunderbolt port on a Mac system supports up to seven devices in a daisy chain configuration. With the appropriate adapters, a single Thunderbolt connection can provide access to any other networking, storage, peripheral, video, or audio connection.

For example, the Apple Thunderbolt display not only provides a high-definition digital display, but also a built-in camera, a microphone, audio speakers, a three-port USB hub, a FireWire port, a Gigabit Ethernet port, and an additional Thunderbolt port for another display—all this through a single Thunderbolt cable from the Mac to the display.

All this connectivity through one cable means that Thunderbolt provides significant data rates. In fact, Thunderbolt is the fastest external peripheral bus to date, providing two bidirectional 10 Gbit/s (10 gigabits per second, or 10,000 Mbit/s) channels. This means a total of 20 Gbit/s outbound and 20 Gbit/s inbound. Future versions of Thunderbolt are planned to provide up to 100 Gbit/s channels. While this technology isn't available yet, the plan bodes well for Thunderbolt's prospects for future expansion.

Copper Thunderbolt cabling also supplies up to 10W of power to connected devices, again providing more power than any previous external peripheral bus. Unfortunately, copper Thunderbolt cabling is limited to a maximum 3 meter length. However, optical Thunderbolt cabling is soon to be available in lengths of up to 100 meters, albeit sans power for peripheral devices.

Apple's contribution to the Thunderbolt standard brought the inclusion of the DisplayPort standard and use of the Mini DisplayPort connection. Thunderbolt connections are physically identical to Mini DisplayPort connections, but they provide both PCI Express and DisplayPort data via this single connection. As a result, Thunderbolt devices and cables provide full support for DisplayPort data.

However, older Mini DisplayPort devices and cables don't support the additional PCI Express data. Thus, items that only support Mini DisplayPort should be the last connection in a Thunderbolt daisy chain. You can identify items compatible with Thunderbolt by an icon that looks like a thunderbolt, while items compatible with only Mini DisplayPort feature an icon that looks like a flat-panel display.

MORE INFO ▸ You can find out more about Thunderbolt at Intel's official website: www.intel.com/technology/io/thunderbolt/index.htm.

Bluetooth

Bluetooth is a short-range wireless peripheral connection standard originally developed by Ericsson for cell phone headsets. Most Bluetooth devices have a range of only 1 to 10 meters, ideal for peripherals but inadequate for wireless networking. Further, Bluetooth is not designed for connections nearly as fast as wireless Ethernet. However, the primary advantage of Bluetooth is that it works with low-power devices.

As Bluetooth increased in popularity, computer manufacturers adopted it for wireless peripherals as well. In addition to providing a wireless connection between your Mac and cell phone, Bluetooth allows your Mac to use wireless headsets, mice, keyboards, and printers. Most Macs that support OS X include Bluetooth wireless, and for those that don't, you can easily add it with a USB-to-Bluetooth adapter. Configuring Bluetooth is covered later in this lesson.

All OS X Mountain Lion-compatible Mac systems, except for the Xserve, include built-in support for Bluetooth. Depending on the age of the Mac, one of two Bluetooth variations is included:

- All OS X Mountain Lion-compatible Macs (without Xserve) support Bluetooth 1.2 with a maximum transfer rate of 721 kilobits per second (kbit/s) and Bluetooth 2.1 + Extended Data Rate (EDR) with a maximum transfer speed of up to 3 Mbit/s.
- Newer Mac systems starting in 2011 support all previous versions of Bluetooth in addition to Bluetooth 3.0 + High Speed (HS) with a maximum transfer speed of up to 24 Mbit/s and Bluetooth 4.0 with low energy support. Bluetooth low energy (BLE) mode isn't very fast, at a maximum of 200 kbit/s, but it uses much less energy, is quicker to pair with devices, and sports a larger maximum range.

MORE INFO ▶ You can find out more about Bluetooth at the official Bluetooth Technology Information website: www.bluetooth.com.

Expansion Buses

With expansion buses, you can add hardware functionality to your Mac, usually in the form of a small computer board, often referred to as a *card*. Expansion buses are only found built into the main computer board inside your Mac. Though designed to allow for the addition of any type of technology, they are most often used to add support for another type of bus or connection. For example, most graphics cards are connected to your Mac via an expansion bus. Other common expansion cards add network ports, peripheral bus ports, storage bus connections, or audio and video input/output connections.

Even if you never add an expansion card to your Mac, several internal components are actually connected via an expansion bus. Many Mac computers feature a space-saving design that accommodates most users' needs without additional expansion connections. Yet, for those who require hardware expansion, certain OS X–compatible computers have additional expansion bus connections: Mac Pros, older model 15-inch MacBook Pros, and 17-inch MacBook Pros. The specific type of expansion ports varies by Mac model. As always, you can use the System Information application to identify your Mac computer's expansion bus capabilities.

As of this writing, the three main expansion buses supported by OS X–compatible hardware are:

- PCI Express 1.x (PCIe)—This more recent version of the PCI standard supports a maximum connection bandwidth of up to 32 Gbit/s, depending on configuration. All Intel-based Macs use PCIe internally, and Mac Pro features PCIe expansion ports.
- PCI Express 2.x (PCIe)—This latest version of the PCI standard supports a maximum connection bandwidth of up to 64 Gbit/s, depending on configuration, and is backward compatible with PCIe 1.0 cards. The latest Mac Pros feature PCIe 2.0 expansion ports.
- ExpressCard 34—Based on PCIe and USB technology, this expansion format is primarily designed for portable computers and features a maximum connection bandwidth of up to 2.5 Gbit/s. The slot supports both PCIe and USB signaling, so it uses whichever is most appropriate for the inserted card. Some MacBook Pro models feature a single ExpressCard 34 slot.

NOTE ▶ Some Mac models feature an SD card slot. While convenient for those needing regular access to SD cards, this is not an expansion-bus technology, as it only allows for connections to SD cards.

Storage Buses

Storage buses are designed to connect your computer to disk or optical storage drives. The age and model of your Mac determines which storage bus technologies are used. But if your Mac features free expansion bus connections, you can generally add any storage bus connections you require via an expansion card.

Some storage buses are designed for internal use, and others can be used externally as well. It's important to know that external storage disk and optical drives connected via USB, FireWire, or Thunderbolt are still using a dedicated storage bus inside the external disk case. So, every disk or optical disk is designed to use a specific storage bus, but those signals can also be retransmitted via a USB, FireWire, or Thunderbolt connection.

Therefore, you can purchase empty external disk enclosures that include hardware that bridges the storage bus connection to USB, FireWire, or Thunderbolt, and then install your own internal disk in the case. This is extremely useful for recovering data from a Mac with a functional internal disk but otherwise inoperable hardware.

Storage buses supported in various Mac hardware include:

- Advanced Technology Attachment (ATA)—Sometimes called Parallel ATA, this storage bus was the most common standard for internal storage for many years and supports a maximum connection bandwidth of up to 133 megabytes per second (MB/s). ATA host controllers are inexpensive because they support only two drives per controller. Some older Macs still use ATA-based internal optical drives to reduce product costs.
- Serial ATA (SATA)—This improvement on ATA is now the most common storage bus for internal storage. Older Macs support SATA 3 Gbit/s, which has a maximum connection bandwidth of ~300 MB/s. Newer Macs support SATA 6 Gbit/s, which sports a maximum connection bandwidth of ~600 MB/s. External SATA connectivity can be added to your Mac via an expansion bus.
- Small Computer System Interface (SCSI)—Sometimes also called Parallel SCSI, this was the original disk interface designed for personal computers. Over the years SCSI has evolved to become the most common storage bus for use in high-end or server computers, and though it supports internal storage, it's more often used for external

storage. The latest SCSI supports a maximum connection bandwidth of up to 320 MB/s and up to 16 drives per controller. SCSI connectivity can be added to the Mac Pro via an expansion card.

- Serial Attached SCSI (SAS)—This improvement on SCSI is becoming a popular storage bus for use in high-end or server computers. SAS also allows internal and external connections and currently supports a maximum connection bandwidth of up to 3 Gbit/s or 384 MB/s and up to 16,384 devices through the use of expanders. The Intel-based Xserve supports internal SAS drives, but again, you can add SAS connectivity to your Mac via an expansion card.
- Fibre Channel—This networking technology is most often used for high-end SCSI connectivity. Fibre Channel can offer speeds up to several gigabytes per second (GB/s) depending on the specification and adds features important for large-scale storage solutions such as long-distance cabling and packet-based communication switching. Fibre Channel host controllers are more complicated than other storage controllers, so they are relatively expensive and only available via an expansion card or Thunderbolt adapter. The Apple Xsan network storage technology is built around Fibre Channel hardware.

Audio and Video Connectivity

Most dedicated audio and video connections are point-to-point and don't support multiple devices. An audio or video signal is typically output from one device and directly connected to another single device designed to receive the signal.

All Macs, with the exception of some Xserve computers, have a variety of audio and video output connections. Many Macs also include audio input connections that allow you to record audio to digital files. Conversely, no Mac includes built-in support for direct video input. Nevertheless, a wide variety of video input options allow you to capture video files to your Mac via USB, FireWire, Thunderbolt, or expansion card.

Audio connections supported by various Macs include:

- Analog stereo audio—The standard stereo signal used by most consumer-grade audio equipment, which takes the form of either the 3.5 mm minijack or twin RCA connectors. Nearly every device made by Apple features built-in analog stereo output via minijack, and many Macs also feature analog stereo input.
- TOSLINK digital audio—This optical connection has become the most common digital audio connection for consumer-grade audio equipment. While both analog and digital audio connections support varying audio resolutions, digital audio connections

do not suffer from electromagnetic interference; thus they typically provide a much clearer audio signal. Many Intel-based Macs feature digital audio input and output. The Mac Pro uses standard TOSLINK ports, while all other Macs use special audio ports that support both analog stereo minijack and mini-TOSLINK connections.

Video connections supported by various Macs include:

- Composite video—This RCA connection is the most common connection for analog, standard-definition, consumer-grade video. Many older Intel-based Macs can output a composite video signal using an Apple video adapter. However, composite video has an effective resolution of only 640 × 480 pixels, so it's not ideal for computer use.
- S-Video—This mini-DIN connection is also a common connection for analog, standard-definition, consumer-grade video, but it provides a slightly better picture than composite video. Many older Intel-based Macs can output an S-Video signal using an Apple video adapter. S-Video is also hindered by an effective resolution of 640 × 480 pixels.
- Video Graphics Array (VGA)—This is the most common connection used for analog computer video displays. Most Macs can output a VGA signal up to a resolution of 1600 × 1200 pixels, with some going as high as 2048 × 1536 pixels. Although older Macs feature built-in VGA ports, Intel-based Macs all require some form of VGA adapter.
- Digital Video Interface (DVI)—This is the most common connection used for digital computer video displays and high-definition televisions. DVI supports resolutions of up to 1920 × 1200 pixels. For a while Apple used smaller connections for DVI on some Macs to save space. These connections, known as mini-DVI and micro-DVI, are electronically identical to DVI; they simply use smaller connections. Many older Macs feature built-in DVI ports, but more recent Macs require an Apple DVI adapter.
- Dual-Link DVI (DVI-DL)—This is an extension to the DVI standard that supports resolutions of up to 2560 by 1600 pixels. Older high-end Macs directly support DVI-DL connections, while some newer Macs support this through an Apple DVI-DL adapter.
- Mini DisplayPort—The most recent display standard used by Apple, this is based on a smaller connector version of the DisplayPort standard. DisplayPort is quickly becoming the standard connection for computer-based digital displays because of its support of new technologies and less complicated, ultimately less expensive, display hardware. Apple has stated that going forward, all Macs will be compatible with Mini DisplayPort for external displays. Both Apple and third parties have created adapters for Mini DisplayPort to allow the use of most other video standards.

NOTE ▶ The Mini DisplayPort connector is also used for Thunderbolt; however, Thunderbolt provides more than just video connectivity. Details regarding compatibility between these two technologies is covered previously in this lesson.

- High-Definition Multimedia Interface (HDMI)—This is fast becoming the standard connection for consumer-grade digital audio and high-definition video equipment. HDMI combines a DVI-based digital video signal with multichannel digital audio signals in a single, inexpensive copper connection. A few newer Mac models feature built-in HDMI ports, but you can convert any DVI or Mini DisplayPort connection to HDMI by using an inexpensive cable adapter. However, all DVI connections and certain older Macs with Mini DisplayPort do not support HDMI audio. For a full list of Macs with Mini DisplayPort that support HDMI audio, please refer to Apple Knowledge Base document HT4241, "About Mini DisplayPort to HDMI adapters."

MORE INFO ▶ To identify the various Apple video adapters available, see Apple Knowledge Base document HT3235, "Monitor and Display Adapter Table."

Reference 27.2
Bluetooth Peripherals

Because Bluetooth is a wireless technology, some configuration is required to connect your Mac to a Bluetooth peripheral. The process of connecting Bluetooth devices is known as *pairing*. Once two devices are paired, they act as if they were directly connected to each other. The OS X Bluetooth interface makes the process of configuring peripherals easy.

NOTE ▶ Desktop Macs can be purchased with only Bluetooth wireless input devices. If this is the case, the Mac and its associated peripherals are factory-paired and require no further pairing.

The quickest way to manage Bluetooth peripherals is to click the Bluetooth status menu. First, make sure your Mac computer's Bluetooth is turned on. It's also advisable to disable Discoverable mode, as leaving it enabled is a potential security risk.

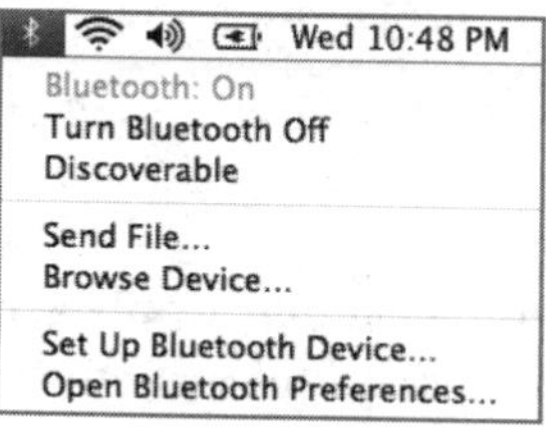

NOTE ▸ Discoverable mode advertises your Mac as a Bluetooth resource to any device within range, which could invite unwanted attention to your Mac. The only time you should enable Discoverable mode is when you are having difficulty pairing from your Mac to a Bluetooth peripheral; then you can try it the other way around and attempt to pair from peripheral to your Mac.

Pairing a Bluetooth Peripheral

Before you begin the pairing process, you will need to enable Discoverable mode on the Bluetooth peripheral you're going to pair with your Mac. Each device is different, so you may need to consult the device's user guide to enable Discoverable mode. In this example you will be pairing to an iPhone, which is only discoverable when enabled from the iPhone General settings.

From the Bluetooth menu extra, select Set Up Bluetooth Device to open the Bluetooth Setup Assistant, which walks you through the setup process. Once open, the Bluetooth Setup Assistant scans for any Bluetooth peripherals in range that are in Discoverable mode. It may take several moments for the device's name to appear; once it does, select it and click Continue.

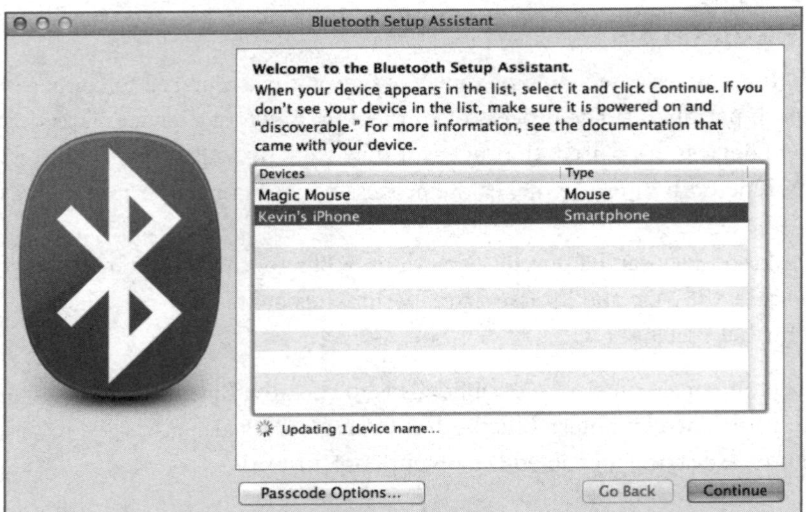

For Bluetooth peripherals, a passkey must be used to authorize pairing. Depending on the device, you will perform one of the following:

- The pairing automatically completes in the background with an automatically generated passkey. This is often the case for a device that has no method to verify the passkey, such as a Bluetooth mouse.

- On your Mac, enter a predefined passkey, as given in the device's user guide, and click Continue to authorize the pairing.
- Allow the Bluetooth Setup Assistant to create a random passkey that you then enter or verify on the Bluetooth device to authorize the pairing. In this example of pairing to an iPhone, the passkey is generated for you automatically.

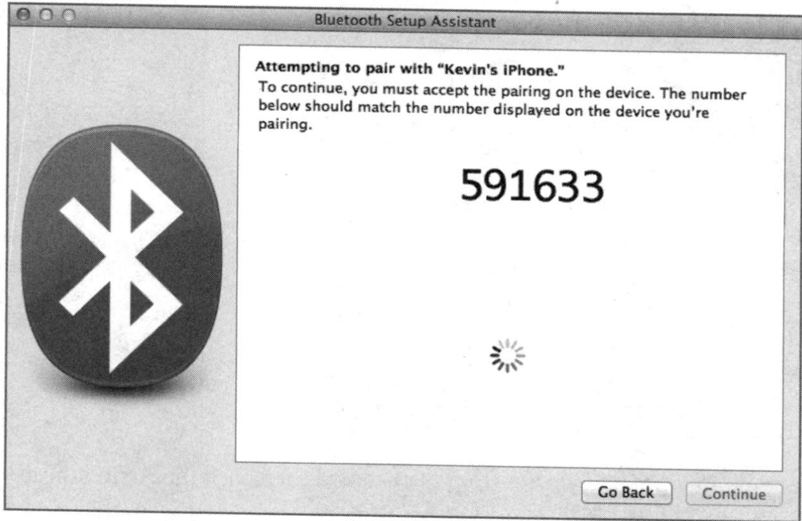

The Bluetooth Setup Assistant automatically detects the capabilities of your Bluetooth peripheral and may present you with additional configuration screens. Continue through these screens until you complete the setup process. When the pairing is complete, you can choose Quit the Bluetooth Setup Assistant or Set Up Another Device.

Verify that your Mac is paired to the device by again clicking the Bluetooth status menu. Notice that it indicates a connected device by using bold letters. You can adjust settings such as the peripheral's name from the Bluetooth preferences.

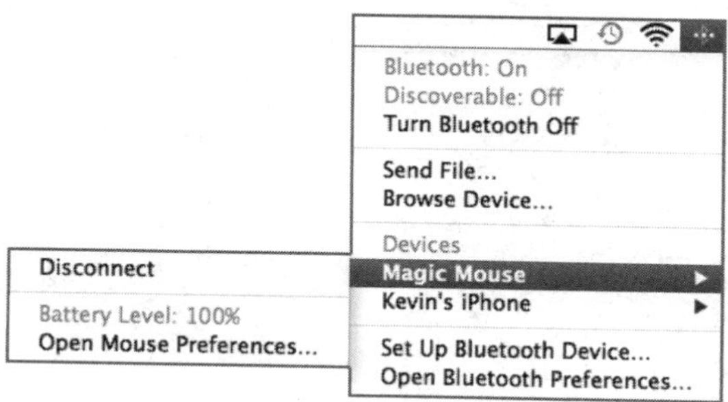

Manage Bluetooth Settings

To access all the Bluetooth management settings, open Bluetooth preferences from either the Apple menu > System Preferences or the Bluetooth status menu > Open Bluetooth Preferences.

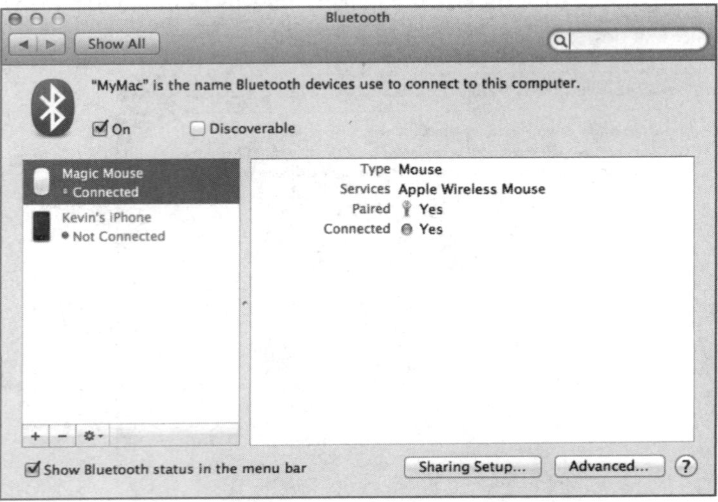

To manage a Bluetooth peripheral, select it from the list, and then click the Action (gear icon) button to reveal a pop-up menu with management choices. You can also use the Add (+) and Delete (–) buttons at the bottom of the Bluetooth devices list to add or delete peripheral pairings. Clicking the Advanced button reveals a dialog allowing you to adjust additional Bluetooth settings. Specifically, the top three settings in the advanced Bluetooth options are extremely important for desktop systems that only use wireless keyboards and mice.

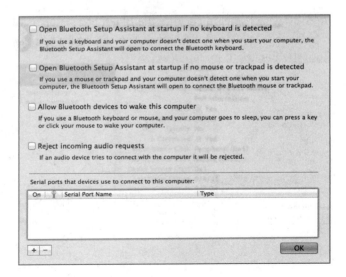

Open Bluetooth Setup Assistant at startup if no keyboard is detected
If you use a keyboard and your computer doesn't detect one when you start your computer, the Bluetooth Setup Assistant will open to connect the Bluetooth keyboard.
Open Bluetooth Setup Assistant at startup if no mouse or trackpad is detected
If you use a mouse or trackpad and your computer doesn't detect one when you start your computer, the Bluetooth Setup Assistant will open to connect the Bluetooth mouse or trackpad.
Allow Bluetooth devices to wake this computer
If you use a Bluetooth keyboard or mouse, and your computer goes to sleep, you can press a key or click your mouse to wake your computer.
Reject incoming audio requests
If an audio device tries to connect with the computer it will be rejected.
Serial ports that devices use to connect to this computer:
On | Serial Port Name | Type
OK

Finally, click the Sharing Setup button to open the Bluetooth pane of the Sharing preferences, which allows you to adjust Bluetooth sharing settings. Like all other sharing services, Bluetooth sharing is disabled by default. Enabling Bluetooth sharing should only be considered as a last resort when traditional file sharing methods aren't possible. Lesson 26, "Host Sharing and Personal Firewall" discusses a variety of alternative file sharing methods, including AirDrop wireless file sharing.

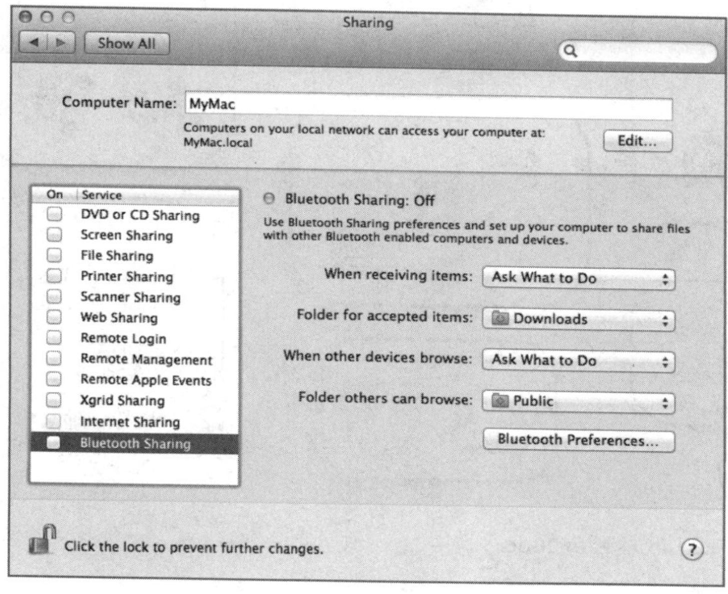

Reference 27.3
Peripheral Troubleshooting

Troubleshooting peripheral issues can be difficult because of the wide variety of devices out there. However, peripheral issues can usually be categorized as either software related or hardware related. The first part of this section looks at how the system software interacts with peripherals and how to identify peripheral issues related to software. As for peripheral hardware issues, replacing or repairing the peripheral or its connections usually resolves the issue. Yet a few general troubleshooting techniques can help you identify and possibly resolve the problem.

Peripheral Device Classes

Peripherals are divided into device classes based on their primary function. OS X includes built-in software drivers that allow your Mac to interact with peripherals from all device classes. While these built-in drivers may provide basic support, many third-party devices require device-specific drivers for full functionality. Detailed information about software drivers is covered in the next section.

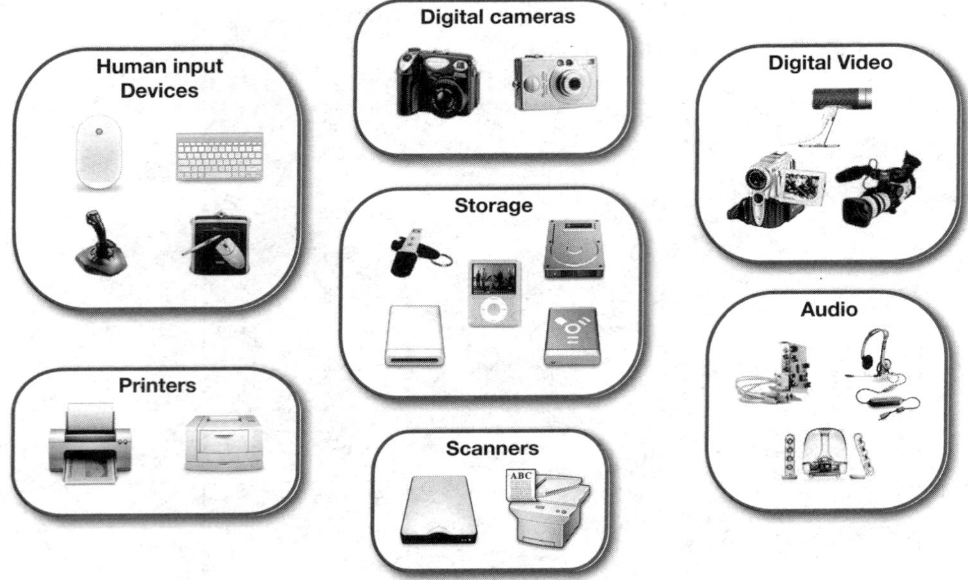

Device classes as defined in OS X include:

- Human input devices (HID)—Peripherals that allow you to directly input information or control the Mac interface. Examples are keyboards, mice, trackpads, game controllers, tablets, and even braille interfaces.
- Storage devices—Internal disks, flash disks, optical drives, and iPods. Storage peripherals are covered in Lesson 10, "File Systems and Storage."
- Printers—Printers of all types, plotters, and fax machines. Printing is covered in Lesson 28, "Print and Scan."
- Scanners—Flatbed, negative, slide, and drum scanners. OS X supports scanners via the Image Capture framework, which allows you to control scanners from /Applications/Image Capture or any other compatible third-party capture application, such as Photoshop. This topic is also covered in Lesson 28.

TIP The Image Capture application supports both locally attached scanners and scanners being shared via the network. Further, the Sharing preferences also allow you to share a locally attached scanner to the network. Network scanner discovery is accomplished using Bonjour, so usually no additional setup is required to locate shared scanning resources.

- Digital cameras—These peripherals include both directly connected cameras and camera storage cards mounted to the Mac computer's file system. Recall that many digital cameras, when connected to a computer, simply extend their internal storage to the computer. In this case, OS X accesses the camera's internal storage, or any directly attached camera storage cards, as it does any other storage device. Applications like iPhoto or Aperture then take over to essentially copy the picture files from the camera storage to the Mac computer's storage. Some cameras support a tethered capture mode in which they are directly controlled by the Mac and send the captured picture data directly to the Mac. OS X supports this type of camera connection via the Image Capture framework, which also allows you to use /Applications/Image Capture or another compatible third-party capture application.
- Video devices—These peripherals include video cameras and video converters connected via USB, FireWire, or an expansion bus. OS X supports these video devices via the QuickTime framework, which allows you to use /Applications/QuickTime Player or any other compatible video application, such as iMovie or Final Cut Pro.
- Audio devices—These peripherals include external audio interfaces connected via USB, FireWire, or an expansion bus. OS X supports these audio devices via the Core Audio framework, so you can use any compatible audio application, such as GarageBand or Logic Pro.

Peripheral Device Drivers

One of the primary responsibilities of the system software is to act as an intermediary between peripherals and applications. If an application supports a general device class, the operating system handles all the technical details of communicating with each model of peripheral in that class.

Here's an example: For an application to receive user input, it needs to receive information from the keyboard, mouse, trackpad, or the like, but it doesn't need to know any details about how to interpret the electrical signals from that device because that's handled by the operating system. This separation of peripherals and applications by the operating system allows you to use nearly any combination of the two with few incompatibilities.

OS X supports peripherals using device drivers, specialized pieces of software that allow peripherals to interoperate with the system. Some peripherals are supported via a generic driver, but many require a device driver created specifically for the peripheral. Although OS X includes a decent selection of common device drivers, you may have to install third-party device drivers to support your peripherals. Nearly all device drivers are installed using an installer utility that places the driver software in the correct resource folder on your Mac. Device drivers are implemented in one of three ways: kernel extensions, framework plug-ins, or applications.

> **NOTE** ▶ OS X only uses a driver if it's already installed. In other words, if you're adding support for a new third-party peripheral that requires custom drivers, install those drivers first before you connect the peripheral to the Mac.

> **NOTE** ▶ It's always best to check the peripheral manufacturer's website to obtain the latest version of the driver software.

Device driver implementations in OS X include:

- Kernel extensions (KEXTs)—This is a special type of software created to add peripheral support at the lowest level of OS X: the system kernel. KEXTs load and unload from the system automatically, so there's no need to manage them aside from making sure they are installed in the correct locations. While some KEXTs are hidden inside application bundles, most are located in the /System/Library/Extensions or /Library/Extensions folders. Remember, in general, nearly all the items in the /System folder are part of the standard OS X install. Examples of peripherals that use KEXTs are human input devices, storage devices, audio and video devices, and other expansion cards.
- Framework plug-ins—This type of device driver adds support for a specific peripheral to an existing system framework. For example, support for additional scanners and digital cameras are facilitated via plug-ins to the Image Capture framework.
- Applications—In some cases a peripheral is best supported by an application written just for that peripheral. Examples are the iPod, iPhone, and iPad, which are managed by the iTunes application.

Inspecting Loaded Extensions

Even though the OS X kernel is designed to manage KEXTs without user interaction, you may still need to verify that a specific KEXT is loaded. You can view currently loaded KEXTs from the System Information application (while holding Option, choose Apple menu > System Information). Once System Information is open, select the Extensions item in the

Contents list; it may take a few moments for the system to scan all currently loaded KEXTs. Once the list appears, you can further inspect individual KEXTs by selecting them from this list.

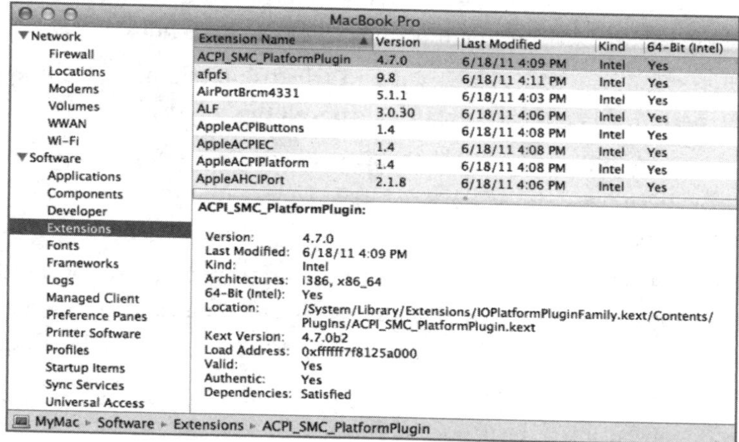

A key feature of OS X is support for a 64-bit kernel, thus necessitating 64-bit KEXTs. OS X Mountain Lion is the first version of OS X that requires the kernel startup in 64-bit mode. From System Information, you can easily verify that all loaded extensions support this mode. However, third-party KEXTs that have not made the transition won't work, as OS X Mountain Lion simply ignores any KEXTs that don't support 64-bit mode.

General Peripheral Troubleshooting

General peripheral troubleshooting techniques include:

- Always check System Information first. If you remember only one peripheral troubleshooting technique, it should be this. Connected peripherals appear in System Information regardless of functioning software drivers. In other words, if a connected peripheral does not show up in System Information, then you are almost certainly experiencing a hardware failure. If a connected peripheral appears as normal in System Information, you are probably experiencing a software driver issue. In that case, use System Information to validate whether the expected extensions are loaded.
- Unplug and then reconnect the peripheral. Doing this reinitializes the peripheral connection and forces OS X to reload any peripheral-specific drivers.
- Plug the peripheral into a different port or use a different cable. This helps you rule out any bad hardware, including host ports, cables, and inoperable hubs.

- Unplug other devices on the same bus. Another device on the shared bus may be causing an issue.
- Resolve potential USB power issues. As covered previously in this lesson, the USB interface can prove problematic if devices are trying to draw too much power. Try plugging the USB device directly into the Mac instead of any USB hubs.
- Shut down and then restart the Mac. This tried-and-true troubleshooting technique reinitializes all the peripheral connections and reloads all the software drivers.
- Try the peripheral with another Mac. This helps you determine whether the issue is with your Mac or the peripheral. If the device doesn't work with other computers, your Mac is not the source of the issue.
- Check for system software and driver software updates. Software bugs are constantly being fixed, so it's always a good time to check for software updates. You can use the OS X built-in Software Update system, but you should also check the peripheral manufacturer's website for the latest driver updates.
- Check for computer and peripheral software updates. Like software updates, firmware updates may also be necessary to resolve your peripheral issue. This possibility is especially likely for more sophisticated devices like iPods, iPhones, and iPads, which have their own internal software as well.

Exercise 27.1
Examine Peripherals via System Information

Prerequisites

- You must have created the Chris Johnson account (Exercise 6.1).

In an earlier exercise you used System Information to view information about your hard disk. Because it is bus-oriented, System Information is extremely useful when troubleshooting peripheral issues. In this exercise, you will use System Information to identify devices on a particular bus. Most Macs have several USB ports and use USB internally for several devices. In a class, your instructor may choose to do this exercise as a demonstration if the equipment in the room doesn't provide USB devices.

Examine Internal Devices

1 If necessary, log in as Chris Johnson.

2 Click the Apple menu.

3 Hold down the Option key. The first item in the Apple menu changes from "About This Mac" to "System Information."

4 With the Option key held down, choose System Information from the Apple menu.

A System Information report opens with the Hardware Overview displayed. The Contents list on the left displays all the report topics that System Information can generate.

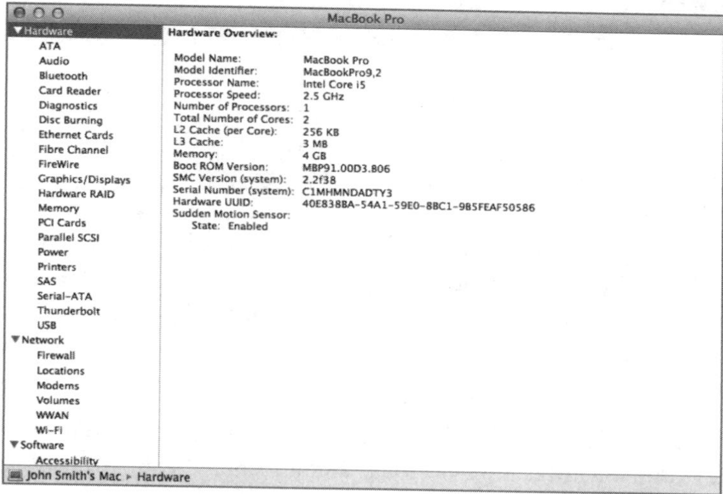

There are several ways of opening System Information. In an earlier exercise, you opened it by choosing Apple menu > About This Mac and then clicking More Info. When you opened it that way, it initially displayed a summary view, and you had to click the System Report button or choose File > Show System Report to get the fully detailed report. This time, because you opened it using a different method, it went straight to the detailed report.

5 In the Hardware list on the left, click Disc Burning.

If your computer has an optical drive, this shows information about the disc formats and writing strategies it supports.

6 Under the Hardware list, click USB to view devices connected to the USB bus.

USB is a very common peripheral bus. It is often used for keyboards, mice, trackpads, printers, scanners, storage devices, and digital cameras.

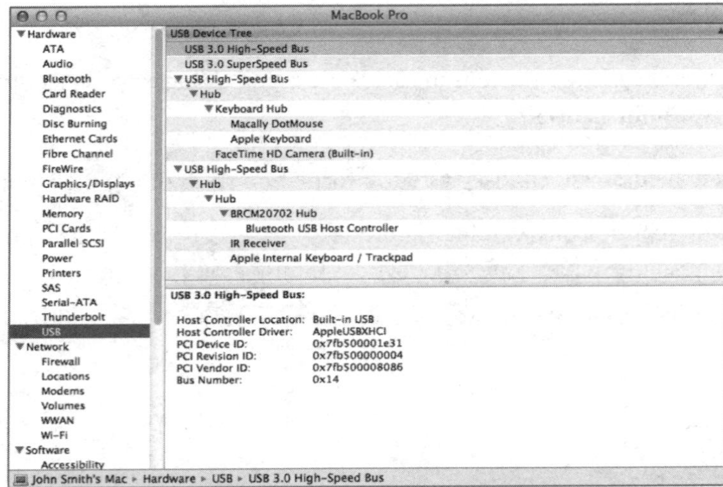

In this example, System Information indicates that there are four USB buses, two of which have devices connected to them. Several of the buses are actually internal to the computer; in this example, the FaceTime HD Camera, Bluetooth USB Host Controller, IR Receiver, and Apple Internal Keyboard / Trackpad are all internal devices connected to internal USB buses.

If a device is connected to a hub, it is listed beneath the hub and indented. This example shows a Keyboard Hub with a Macally DotMouse and an Apple Keyboard connected. While the hub and keyboard are separate devices at the USB level, they are both parts of a single physical device, an Apple USB keyboard. Most USB keyboards contain a built-in hub so you can attach other USB devices to them.

7 Examine the USB report for your computer and determine which devices are internal and which are external.

Examine External USB Devices (optional)

For this section, you will need at least one external USB device connected to your computer. If you are performing these exercises in class, your instructor may be able to provide a device. If there is no suitable USB device available, quit System Information and skip the rest of this exercise.

1 If it isn't already connected, plug in the external USB device and refresh the System Information report by choosing File > Refresh Information (Command-R).

2 Select an external USB device in the USB report for your computer.

   Details about the device are displayed in the lower pane.

3 Examine the Speed listed for the device.

   The speed a USB device can run at depends not only on its own capability, but on the speeds of the port and any intermediate hubs through which it is connected.

4 Examine the Current Available and Current Required figures.

   Your computer can only supply a certain amount of electrical power through each of its USB ports, and if there are too many devices chained off a port there might not be enough for all the devices. To prevent this problem, OS X keeps track of how much electrical power is available at each point in the USB bus, and disables devices if it calculates that there is not enough power available for them.

5 While viewing the USB information, unplug the device from your computer (if it is a storage device, eject it first), plug it into a different USB port, then choose File > Refresh Information (Command-R).

   System Information does not update its display unless you tell it to.

6 Locate the external device in the report to see if it has changed places, or if any of its statistics have changed.

7 If you have an external hub available, try plugging the device in via that.

   Is there enough power available from the hub to run the device? Did its speed decrease because of being connected through a hub?

8 Quit System Information.

Lesson **28**

Print and Scan

Apple and Adobe began the desktop publishing revolution by introducing the first high-quality printing solution for personal computers. Although Adobe created the PostScript printing system, Apple was the first to include it in both the Macintosh operating system and the first PostScript printer, the Apple LaserWriter. Apple has continued to pioneer advancements in printing software with OS X by adopting a printing workflow based on the Adobe Portable Document Format (PDF) and the Common UNIX Printing System (CUPS).

In this lesson you'll learn how OS X supports different print and scan technologies and how to manage and troubleshoot printers and multifunction devices connected to your Mac.

GOALS

- Understand the technologies that allow OS X to print
- Configure OS X for printers and multifunction devices
- Manage and troubleshoot print jobs

Reference 28.1
Print System Architecture

Robust printing has always been an important part of the Mac operating system because of its popularity with graphic design users. OS X continues this tradition with an updated printing system featuring redesigned and simplified printing interfaces.

CUPS

OS X uses the open source Common UNIX Printing System 1.6 (CUPS) to manage local printing. Originally an independent product, CUPS was purchased by Apple and remains an open source project. Architecturally, CUPS uses the Internet Printing Protocol (IPP) standard as the basis for managing printing tasks and uses PostScript Printer Description (PPD) files as the basis for printer drivers. Though still used by CUPS, the PPD name is a bit of a misnomer, as non-PostScript printers can also be described by these files.

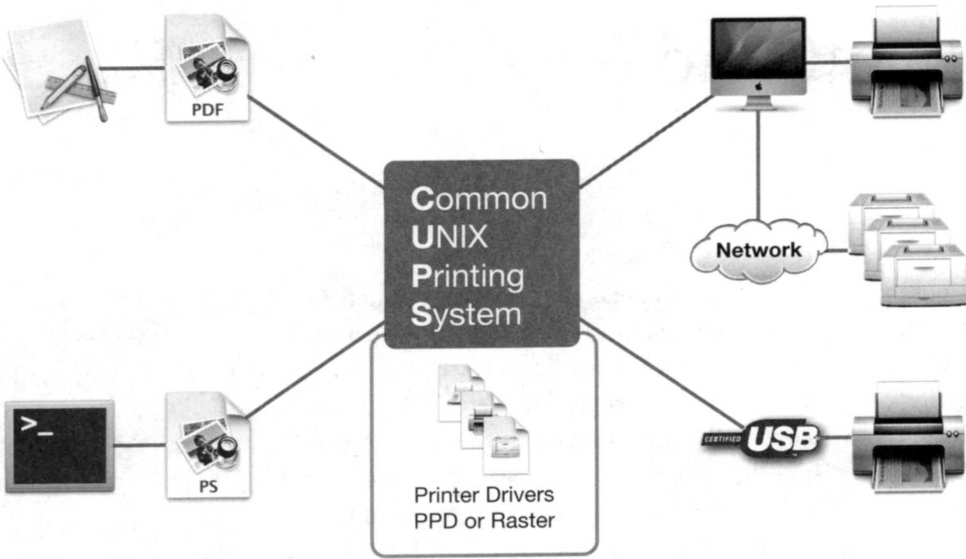

A print job starts when a user prints from either an application in the graphical user interface or the print commands in the Terminal. When you print from an application, the OS X Quartz graphics system generates a Portable Document Format (PDF) file. When you print from the command line, a PostScript (PS) file is generated. In either case, the file created is called a spool file and is placed inside the /var/spool/cups folder.

The CUPS background process, **cupsd**, takes this spool file and passes it through a series of filter processes known as the print chain. These processes convert the spool file to a format that is understood by the destination printer, and then ultimately communicate this information to the printer.

> **MORE INFO ▸** CUPS provides capabilities beyond the scope of this text. To find out more, visit the official CUPS website at www.cups.org.

CUPS Drivers

Before you can print, you must configure printer settings, which includes associating an appropriate printer driver with the printing device. This association happens automatically as you configure a new printing device; however, the system must have the printer driver installed before it can use the printer. Apple supplies printer drivers for most popular models, including Brother, Canon, Epson, Fuji-Xerox, Hewlett-Packard, Lexmark, Ricoh, and Samsung.

MORE INFO ▶ For a complete list of printer and scanner drivers available from Apple for OS X, refer to Knowledge Base document HT3669, "OS X: Printer and scanner software available for download."

The OS X installer is designed to save space on the system volume and to avoid installing unnecessary print drivers. New installations of OS X include only Apple and generic print drivers. OS X upgrade installations only install drivers for printers in use by the Mac. It's expected that additional print drivers will be acquired via the Internet.

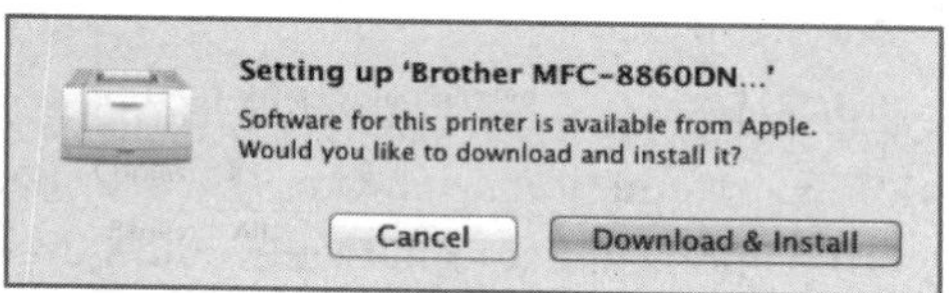

If you attempt to add a printer for which the Mac does not have the driver and you are connected to the Internet, the system prompts you to automatically download and install the driver using the Apple software update service. You can also manually download and install printer drivers from the Apple support website.

NOTE ▶ You should always attempt to use the Apple collection of printer drivers. These drivers provide the most Mac-native experience and automatically update via the software update system.

NOTE ▶ You must log in or authenticate as an administrative user to install printer drivers either manually or via software update.

NOTE ▶ The automatic printer driver installer from software update often installs multiple printer drivers from the same manufacturer simultaneously.

Obviously, if you aren't connected to the Internet, you have to acquire the printer driver manually, though some standard PostScript and PCL printers can use the built-in generic printer drivers. Also, if Apple doesn't provide the printer driver via its software update system, you have to manually acquire the appropriate driver, often directly from the printer's manufacturer.

A few of the built-in Apple printer drivers are installed in /System/Library/Printers, but all the third-party printer drivers are installed to the /Library/Printers folder. The primary folder for drivers is the PPD folder, but you may notice other vendor folders that contain ancillary printer driver resources.

Once you've added a printer configuration, a copy of the PPD with the name of the device is placed in the /etc/cups/ppd folder and two configuration files are modified: /etc/cups/printers.conf and /Library/Preferences/org.cups.printers.plist. Finally, the first time a user prints or accesses a printer queue, the system creates a printer queue application, again with the name of the device, in the ~/Library/Printers folder in the user's home folder.

Reference 28.2
Print and Scan Configuration

How you physically connect to a printer determines how you configure OS X to print to the printer. In many cases, printer configuration is extremely easy and mostly automatic. For example, directly attached and local network printers are automatically configured with little user interaction. However, older printers or nonlocal network printers require a bit more manual configuration.

TIP When adding supported multifunction printers, scanning and faxing services are configured along with general printing services.

Configuring a Directly Attached Printer

If your Mac already has the correct printer driver for a directly attached USB or FireWire printer, the system automatically detects the appropriate settings and configures the new printer for you as soon as you plug it in. If the printer provides faxing and scan support, the system should automatically configure this as well.

You can verify the printer has been added by simply opening the Print dialog from any application (File > Print) or the Print & Scan preferences. In the Print & Scan preferences, you can tell which printers are locally connected if their location is shown as the same name as the local Mac computer's sharing name.

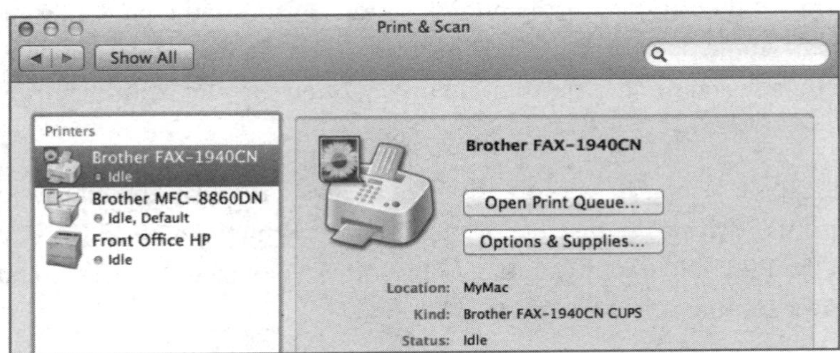

It's important to note, however, that this automatic configuration only occurs if the appropriate printer driver is installed. If the driver isn't installed but is available from Apple, you are prompted with the automatic software update installer when you plug the printer in.

Again, only if an administrative user is logged in will the system be allowed to install the printer driver and then to automatically configure the printer. Thus, if a nonadministrative user attaches a new printer for the first time, there is a good chance the system will not configure the printer because the driver is missing. Also, if a printer driver for a directly attached printer is unavailable from Apple, then nothing happens automatically when you plug it in. An administrative user has to manually acquire and install the printer driver to get it working.

Configuring a Local Network Printer

Network printer configurations must be manually added, but Apple makes this process incredibly easy for locally networked printers. If the printer you wish to add is on the local network, either as a standalone printer advertising via Bonjour or shared via another Mac or AirPort base station, then all you need to do is select it from the Print dialog (File > Print) from any application. Once in the Print dialog, select the Printer pop-up menu, and the system scans the local network for available printers to select.

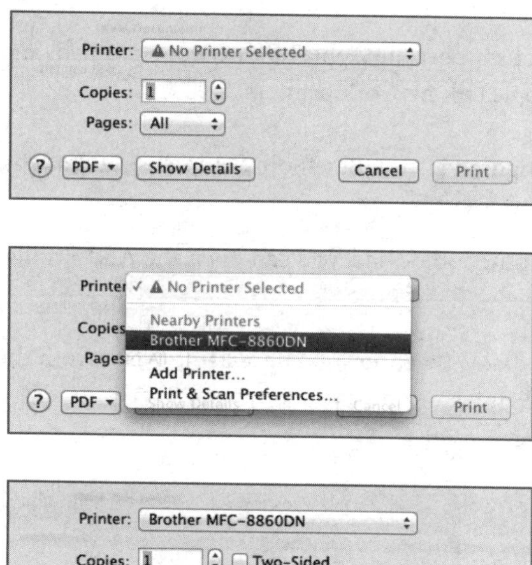

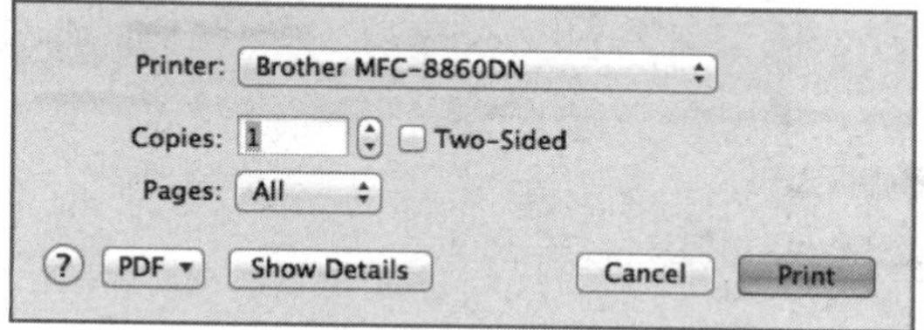

As covered previously, the Mac either configures the printer with a preinstalled driver or prompts to download the driver from the Apple software update service. Again, the system should also automatically configure fax and scan support for multifunction devices. Again note that only administrative users can add printer drivers.

> **NOTE ▶** If a network printer requires authentication, you may be presented with an authentication dialog in order to print to the shared printer.

> **NOTE ▶** Your Mac automatically acquires the appropriate printer drivers from any Mac that is sharing a printer via the network. In other words, the Mac hosting a shared printer automatically sends your Mac the drivers if they aren't preinstalled.

Manually Configuring a Printer

If the network printer doesn't support automatic network discovery via Bonjour, then you must configure it manually via the Add Printer window. Also, if a directly attached printer does not automatically configure, then you can manually add it. You can open the Add Printer window at any time to manually add new printers or multifunction devices. Again, nonadministrative users have to provide administrator authentication to access the Add Printer window.

> **NOTE ▶** OS X v10.6 and later do not support the AppleTalk network protocol and thus do not support printing via AppleTalk network printers.

> **NOTE ▶** Bluetooth printers are configured via the Bluetooth Setup Assistant as covered in Lesson 27, "Peripherals and Drivers."

To manually add a new printer or multifunction device, you can open the Add Printer window via one of the following methods:

- From any application, open a Print dialog by choosing File > Print. Next, from the Printer pop-up menu, choose Add Printer.

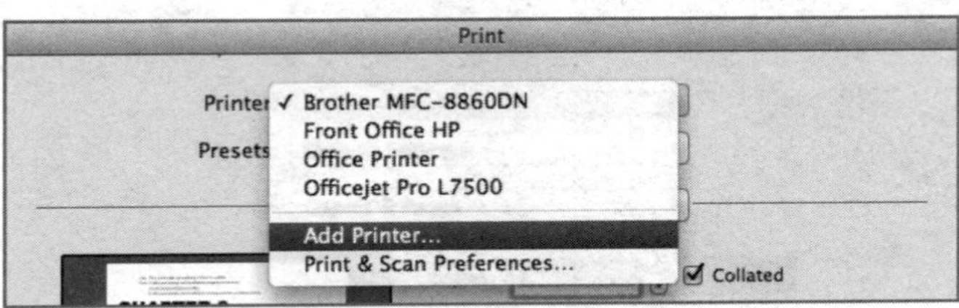

- Open the Print & Scan preferences by choosing Apple menu > System Preferences, then clicking the Print & Scan icon. Click the lock icon in the bottom-left corner and authenticate as an administrative user to unlock the Print & Scan preferences. Finally, click the Add (+) button at the bottom of the Printers list.

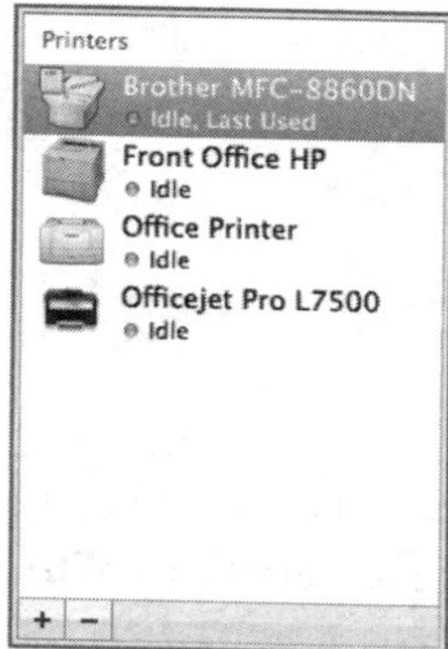

- From the Finder, open the /System/Library/CoreServices/AddPrinter application. This application's icon can also be placed in your Dock.

The Add Printer window features several panes for selecting a printer or multifunction device. These panes are accessed by clicking the following buttons in the toolbar:

- Default—This browser lets you select directly attached USB and FireWire printers and network printers discovered using Bonjour or network directory services.

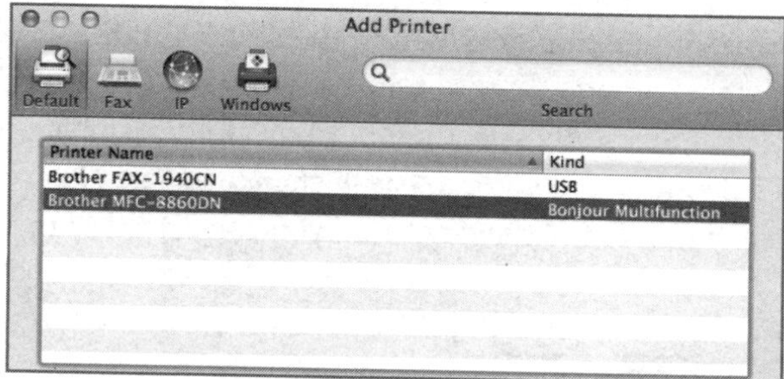

- Fax—This browser allows you to select the specific modem port to use for incoming and outgoing fax transmissions. Configuring your Mac to act as a fax is beyond the scope of this guide.
- IP—This dialog allows you to manually enter the IP address or DNS host name of a Line Printer Daemon (LPD), IPP, or HP JetDirect printer. You must select the appro-

priate protocol from the pop-up menu and enter the printer's address. Entering a printer queue is usually optional.

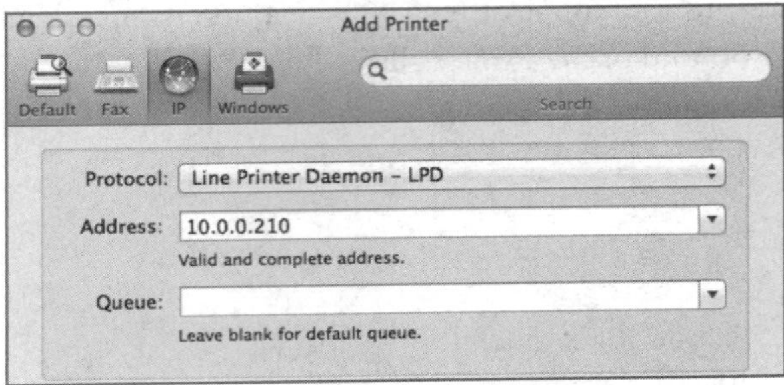

- Windows—This browser lets you select printers shared via the Server Message Block (SMB) printer sharing protocol. Double-click an SMB server and authenticate to access the server's shared printers.

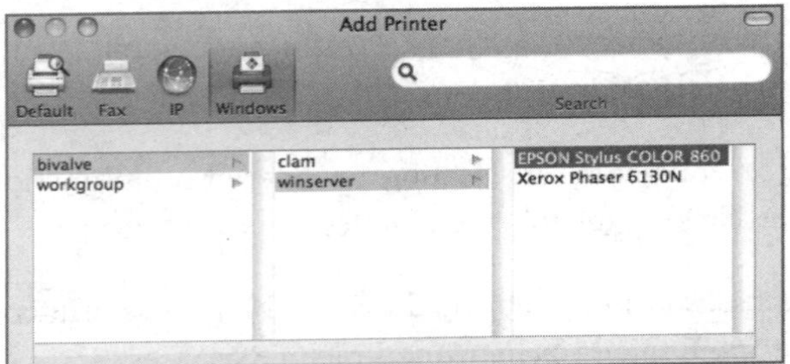

Once you have selected a printer or multifunction device from the top half of the new printer configuration dialog, the system completes the bottom half for you using information it has discovered. This includes automatically selecting the appropriate printer driver if possible. Often this information isn't ideal, and you can easily change it. The Name and Location fields are only there to help you identify the device, so you can set those to anything you like.

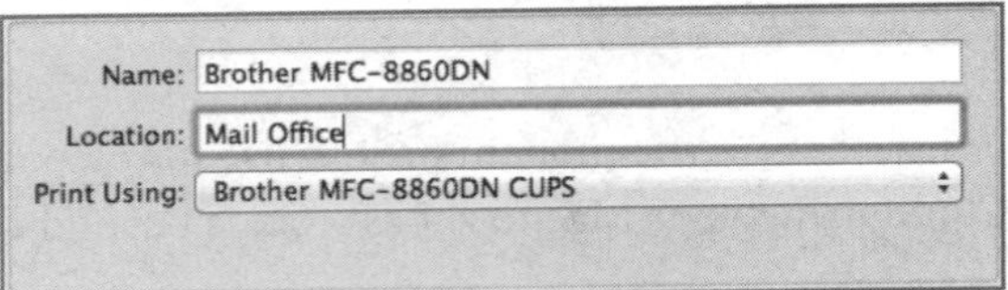

If you're configuring an LPD printer connection, you also have to manually specify the appropriate printer driver. This step can also occur with HP JetDirect and SMB printer connections.

To specify a specific printer driver, choose Select Printer Software from the Print Using pop-up menu. You can manually scroll through the list of installed printer drivers, but using the Spotlight field to narrow the search is much quicker.

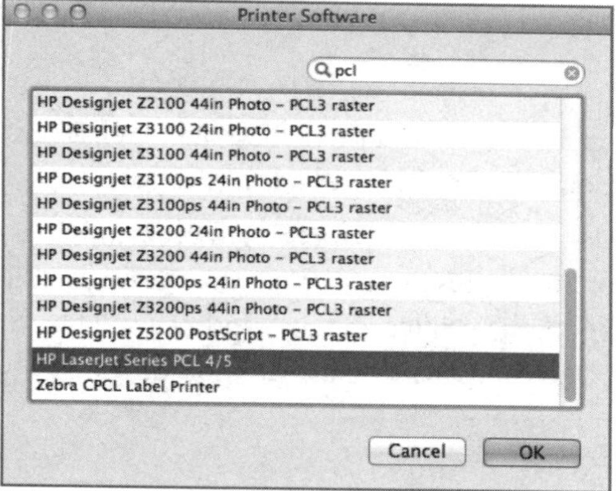

Finally, if you are configuring an IP printer, you may be presented with an additional dialog to select any special options that the printer has. Once the printer configuration is complete, you can verify the printer has been added by simply opening the Print dialog from any application or the Print & Scan preferences. In the Print & Scan preferences, you can tell which printers are connected via network if their location is shown as something different than your local Mac computer's sharing name. Also note that multifunction devices show a Scan tab, indicating the system has also configured the scanning driver software.

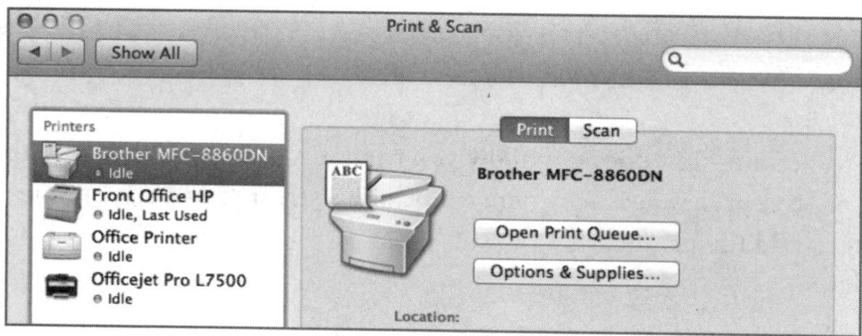

Modify an Existing Printer Configuration

You may find it necessary to edit a printer configuration after you set it up. From the Print & Scan preferences, you can:

- Delete a printer configuration—Select the item you wish to delete from the printer list, and then click the Delete (–) button at the bottom of the list.
- Set printing defaults—From the two pop-up menus at the bottom of the Print & Scan preferences, choose the default printer and paper size. Use caution when setting the default printer for Last Printer Used; because you will effectively have no permanent default printer, the default destination for print jobs may constantly change.

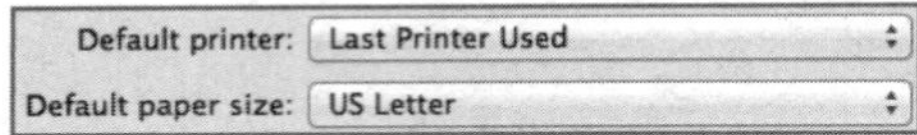

- Open a print queue—Select a printer from the list and then click the Open Print Queue button. Details regarding print queues are covered later in this lesson.
- Edit an existing configuration and check supply levels—Select a printer from the list and then click the Options & Supplies button. In the resulting dialog, you can easily edit the printer's configuration—including changing the printer's name—and, if available, check the printer supply levels and open the printer's hardware configuration utility.

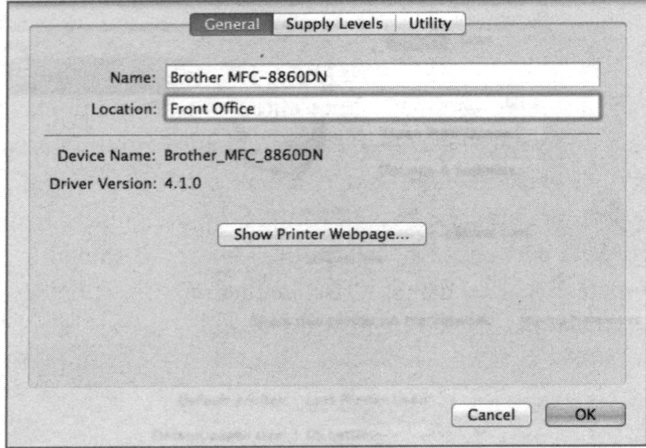

NOTE ▶ OS X Mountain Lion does not allow you to modify the print driver settings from the Print & Scan preferences. To change a printer's selected driver, you must delete and then re-add the printer.

- Manage scanning—Select a multifunction device from the list and then select the Scan tab. From this interface, you can open the scanner image capture interface or enable local network scanner sharing.

Sharing Printers

It's very easy to share printer configurations with OS X. Your Mac computer's shared print service is made available via the IPP printer sharing protocols. While OS X and Windows both support IPP, different versions of Windows may require additional drivers for IPP. Also, the IPP protocol supports automatic printer driver configuration and installation for OS X systems, so when another Mac user connects to your Mac computer's shared print service, her system automatically selects, and downloads if necessary, the appropriate printer drivers.

The CUPS shared print service also allows other network clients to easily locate your shared printer configurations with Bonjour. Again, OS X and Windows support both discovery protocols, but whereas OS X includes support for Bonjour, different versions of Windows may require additional drivers for Bonjour. Alternatively, network clients can manually enter your Mac computer's IP address or DNS host name to access your computer's shared print service. Configuring your Mac computer's identification for providing network services is covered in Lesson 26, "Host Sharing and Personal Firewall."

> **NOTE ▶** Users cannot access shared print services on a Mac in sleep mode. You can disable your Mac computer's automatic sleep activation or enable wake for network access from the Energy Saver preferences.

To share printers from your Mac, open and unlock the Sharing preferences. Select the Printer Sharing checkbox to enable printer sharing. Selecting this checkbox tells the `cupsd` process (which is always running in the background) to listen for IPP print service requests on TCP port 631. By default, only locally connected printers are shared.

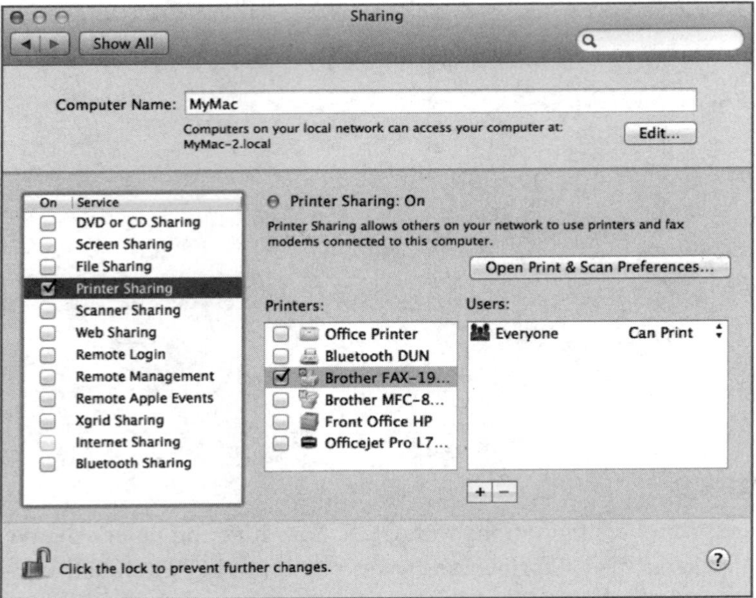

TIP ▶ If your Mac is configured to use a document scanner, you can Enable Scanner Sharing from the Sharing preferences as well. This allows you to share the scanner with other Mac systems on the local network.

To enable sharing for additional printer configurations, simply select the checkboxes next to the printers you wish to share. You can also enable specific printing devices for sharing from the Print & Scan preferences.

NOTE ▶ To avoid confusion, you shouldn't reshare network printers using your Mac computer's shared print services if network printers are already available on your network.

Optionally, you can limit who is allowed to print to your shared printers. By default, all users are allowed access to your shared printing devices. To limit access, select a shared device from the Printers list and then click the Add (+) button at the bottom of the Users list.

A dialog appears, allowing you to select user or group accounts that you wish to grant access to the printing device. When adding accounts, you can also choose to deny access to guest users by selecting No Access to Everyone in the Users list. Also, with limited printing access enabled, all users have to authenticate in order to print to your shared printer.

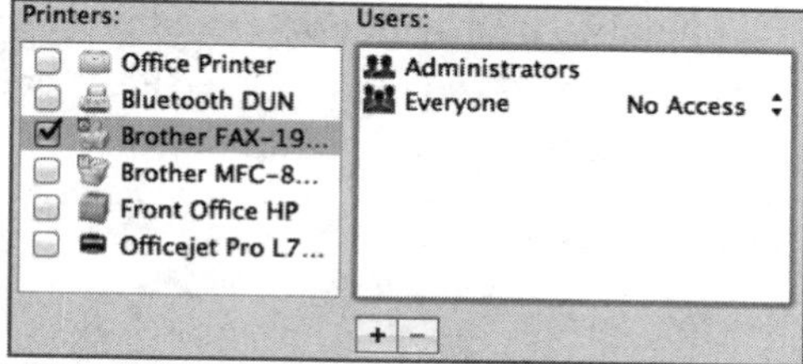

Reference 28.3
Managing Print Jobs

OS X features a unified Print dialog that combines previously separate Page Setup and Print dialogs. The Page Setup dialog typically contains document size, orientation, and scale settings, and the Print dialog includes all other printer settings.

For backward compatibility, OS X allows older applications to continue to use separate Page Setup and Print dialogs, but older apps are still able to use the new unified printing interface when you open a Print dialog. In other words, some older applications have document settings in both the Page Setup and Print dialogs.

This unified Print dialog also features two modes: The basic mode allows you to quickly preview and start a print job based on default settings, and the details mode allows you to specify any page or print option and manage print setting presets.

> **NOTE** ► Some applications, especially graphic design and desktop publishing applications, use custom dialogs for printing that may look different from the standard Print dialog covered in this lesson.

> **NOTE** ► If a network printer requires authentication, you may be presented with an authentication dialog in order to print to the shared printer.

Basic Printing

To start a print job based on default print settings, from an application, choose File > Print or press Command-P.

> **NOTE** ► Some applications bypass the Print dialog and issue a print job to your default printer when you use Command-P.

When the Print dialog appears, in some cases it slides out of the application's window title bar; in other cases it appears as its own dialog window. Most applications show a print preview, but some may just show the basic print options. The default printer and print preset are selected, but you can choose the number of pages, copies, and duplex (two-sided) options if available. Customizing printer presets is covered in the next section of this lesson.

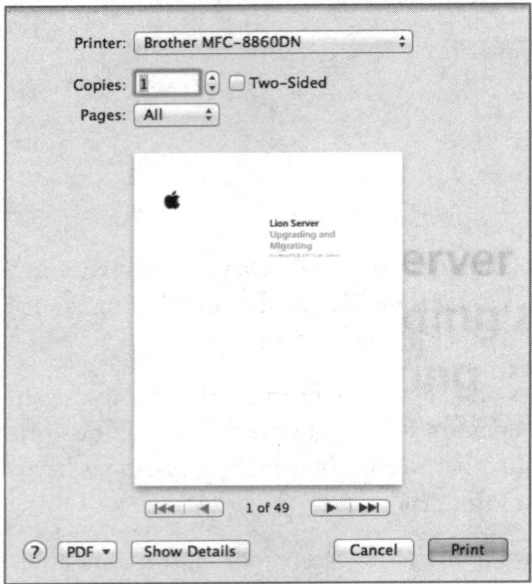

When the print job is started, the system automatically opens the print queue application associated with the destination printer. Though no window opens if the print job is successful, you can click the print queue in the Dock.

Detailed Printing and Print Presets

To start a print job based on custom print settings, from an application, again open the Print dialog. Whenever you open the Print dialog, the default printer and print preset are selected, but you can choose any other configured printer or preset from the associated pop-up menu.

Clicking the Show Details button expands the Print dialog to its full details mode. When in the full details mode, you can click the Hide Details button to return to the basic Print dialog mode. The Print dialog also remembers which mode you were in last for each application. In other words, every application starts with a basic Print dialog the first time you print, but for subsequent print jobs, the Print dialog opens to the mode last used for each individual application.

On the left side of the details Print dialog, you can page through a preview of the print job, similar to the preview in the basic Print dialog. Any changes you make to the page layout settings are instantly reflected in the preview. On the right side of the dialog, you can configure all possible print settings for most applications. The top half features more detailed page setup and print settings.

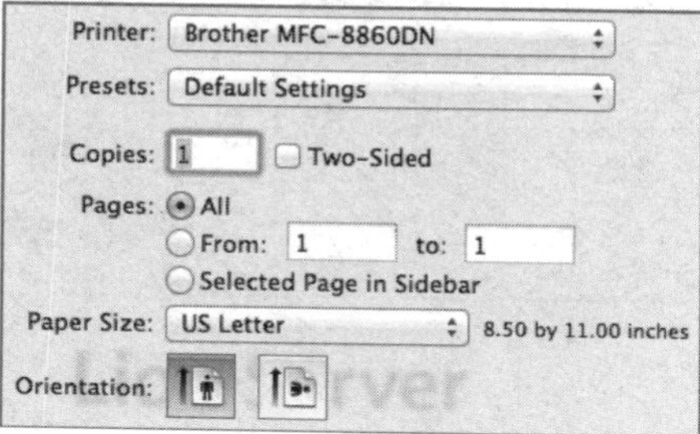

Settings on the bottom half vary based on the application from which you're printing and your selected printer's driver. You can select a category of print settings to modify by choosing it from the pop-up menu that separates the print settings from top to bottom. The settings list and configuration options within vary based on the application, selected printer, and selected printer driver.

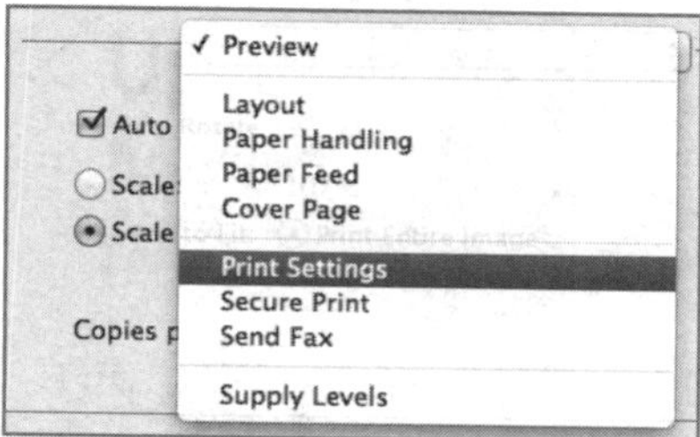

TIP If the selected printer is a multifunction device that provides fax support, one of the items in the Print Settings pop-up menu is Send Fax. From here, you can define fax settings to be used on the multifunction device to send a fax instead of printing a document.

To save the current print settings as a preset, choose "Save Current Settings as Preset" from the Presets pop-up menu. Select if you want this preset to apply to all printers or just the currently selected printer. By saving a preset, you make it accessible from the Presets pop-up menu in the details view of any Print dialog. The print presets are saved to the ~/Library/Preferences/com.apple.print.custompresets.plist file, so each user has her own custom print presets.

NOTE ▶ Print presets do not save application-specific settings.

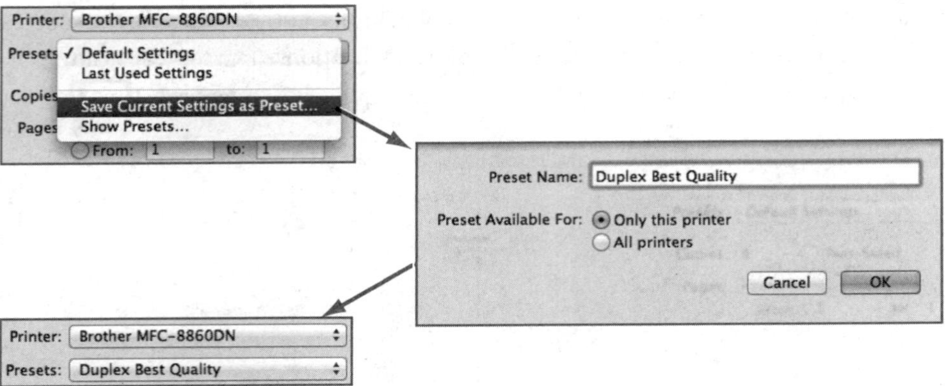

To manage existing print presets, open the print Presets dialog by choosing Show Presets from the Presets pop-up menu. In the print Presets dialog select a preset to see its settings and values, and optionally use the Delete and Duplicate buttons at the bottom of the presets list. Double-clicking a print preset allows you to rename the preset. When you are done managing print presets, click OK to save the changes and return to the Print dialog.

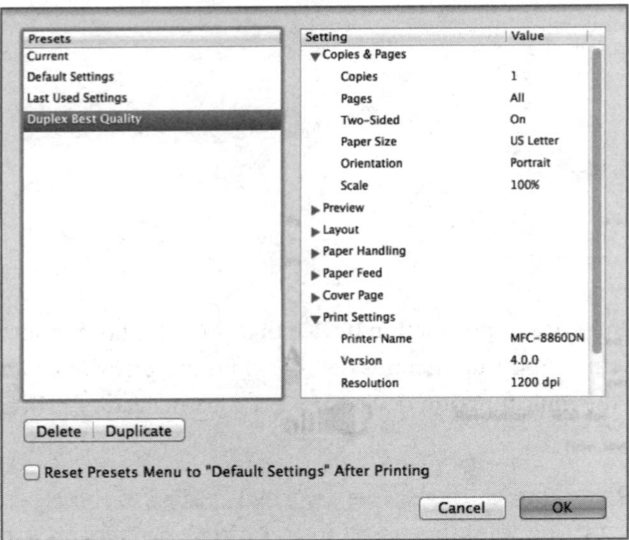

Using PDF Tools

OS X includes a built-in PDF workflow architecture and editing tools. The full Adobe Acrobat suite has more advanced PDF features, but OS X includes all the tools to create PDF documents or perform basic editing. Any application that can print can also use the OS X Quartz imaging system to generate high-quality PDF documents. In any Print dialog, click the PDF button. A pop-up menu appears allowing you to choose a PDF workflow destination, and offering the ability to save a PDF to any location.

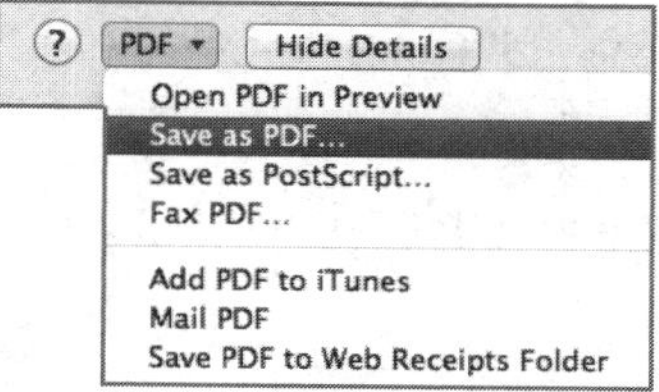

From the PDF pop-up menu, you can also specify a PDF workflow designed to accept and automatically process PDF files. Some preset workflows are built in, but you can add your own PDF workflows by choosing Edit Menu from the PDF pop-up menu. Alternatively, you can manually add PDF workflows to the /Library/PDF Services or the ~/Library/PDF Services folders, depending on who needs access to the PDF workflows. To create custom PDF workflows, you can use either the /Applications/Utilities/AppleScript Editor application or the /Applications/Automator application.

The OS X/Applications/Preview application also offers comprehensive PDF editing functionality—you can edit and adjust individual elements, reorder pages, crop the document, add annotations, fill out form data, and apply digital signatures using an attached video camera. From Preview, you can also convert PDF files to other formats or resave the PDF file using more appropriate settings.

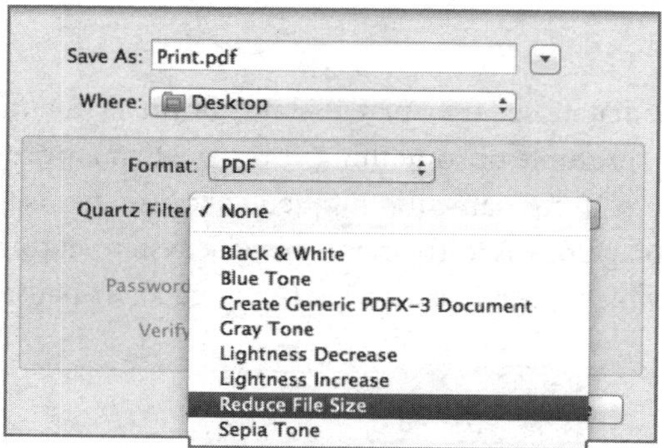

Managing Printer Queues

As stated previously, when a print job is started, the spool file is placed inside the /var/spool/cups folder, and then CUPS takes over to process the file and send it to the printer. When you print from the graphical interface, OS X opens a print queue application to manage the print job. If a job completes quickly, the file is only in the print queue for a few moments, and the print queue application quits when done.

However, printers always seem to be the most problematic of peripherals, so occasionally your Mac will not be able to complete the print job. The printer queue application remains open until the print job finishes or you resolve the print issue. If the system detects an error with the printer, it stops all print jobs to that device. You can still issue print jobs, but they simply fill up in the device's queue.

To manage print job queues, you can access the printer queue application using one of the following methods:

- If a printer queue is already open, simply click its icon in the Dock. In the following example screenshot, the printer queue's Dock icon shows a connection failure badge (horizontal lightning bolt) and a number "2" badge, indicating that printer is not responding and there are currently two jobs in queue.

- You can manually open a printer queue from the Print & Scan preferences by selecting the device from the printer list and then clicking the Open Print Queue button.
- You can manually open a printer queue from the Finder by navigating to the ~/Library/Printers folder.

When the printer queue opens, you immediately see the current status of the printer and any currently queued print jobs. A typical example of something you see when a printer queue is not responding is multiple versions of the same job in queue because the user has incorrectly assumed sending the print job again would fix the issue. The system automatically detects when the printer becomes available again, assuming the queue isn't paused.

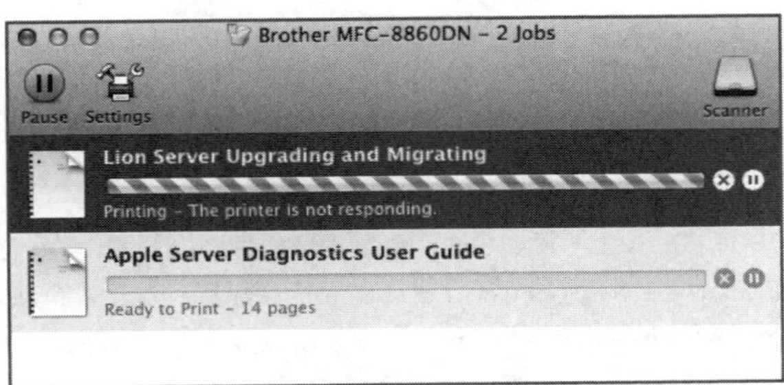

To pause or resume the printer queue, click the Pause Printer or Resume Printer button (the button toggles between the two modes) in the queue application toolbar. To hold or resume a specific print job, select it from the job list and then click the small pause or resume button to the right of the print job progress bar (again, the button toggles between pause and resume). You can also delete a job by selecting it from the job list and then clicking the small X button to the right of the print job progress bar.

TIP Selecting a job in the printer queue list and pressing the Spacebar opens a Quick Look preview window of the print job.

TIP You can reorder print jobs in the printer queue by dragging the job you wish to reorder in the list. You can also drag jobs from one printer queue window to another printer queue window.

Once you are done managing a printer queue, it's acceptable to leave the application running. You may find it useful to leave often-used printer queues in the Dock for direct access. Simply right-click or Control-click the queue application's Dock icon and, from the shortcut menu, choose Options > Keep in Dock.

You can also provide quick access to all your printer queues by dragging the ~/Library/Printers folder from the Finder to your Dock. Clicking this folder in your Dock reveals all configured devices.

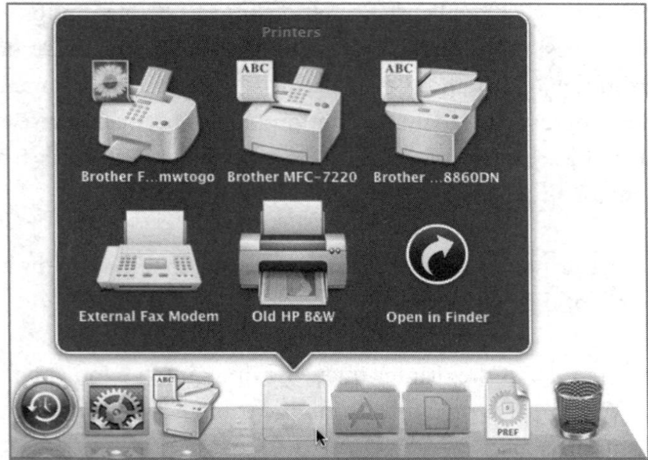

Some other features are also available in the printer queue application's toolbar. For instance, you can reconfigure the printer's settings by clicking the Settings button in the toolbar. Also, if the queue is for a supported multifunction printer, you can click the Scanner button in the toolbar to open the Scanner interface. OS X supports scanning to multifunction devices both locally and via the network.

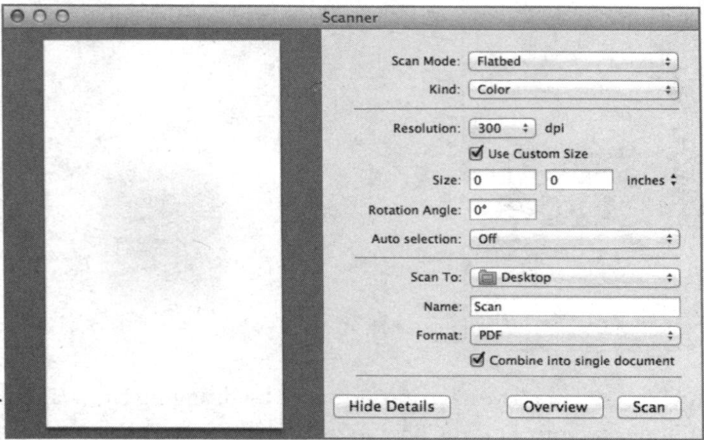

Reference 28.4
Print System Troubleshooting

You will probably experience more printing issues caused by hardware than by software. However, this being a reference about OS X, the following is a series of mostly software-based general print system troubleshooting techniques.

- Always check the printer queue application first. The printer queue application always shows the first symptoms of an issue, and odds are you were made aware of the issue by the queue. The printer queue lets you know if there is a printer connection issue, but you should also check to make sure that the queue is not paused and that none of the jobs are on hold. Sometimes deleting old print jobs from the queue helps clear the problem.
- Double-check page and print settings. If the job is printing but doesn't print correctly, double-check page and print settings using the Print dialog details mode.
- Review the PDF output of the application. Remember that the CUPS workflow is application > PDF > CUPS > printer. Thus, verifying if the PDF looks correct lets you know if the source of the problem is with the application or the printing system.
- Print from another application. If you suspect the application is at the root of the problem, try printing from another application. You can also print a test page while in the printer queue application by choosing Printer > Print Test Page.
- Check the printer hardware. Many modern printers have diagnostic screens or printed reports that can help you identify a hardware issue. Many also have a software utility or a built-in webpage that reports errors. Clicking the Printer Setup button in the printer queue application toolbar accesses these management interfaces. Also, don't forget to double-check cables and connections. Finally, you may be well served by contacting the printer manufacturer to diagnose printer hardware issues.
- For faxing issues, check phone line and phone settings. When sending faxes via a multifunction device, you may encounter issues that are outside your control because you are relying on the phone system and another user's fax hardware. As with any faxing issue, you need to check for fax modem and phone line problems.
- For directly connected printers, use peripheral troubleshooting techniques. For printers connected via USB or FireWire, use the peripheral troubleshooting techniques outlined in Lesson 27.
- For network printers, use network troubleshooting techniques. For printers connected via a network connection, use the network troubleshooting techniques described in Lesson 24, "Network Troubleshooting," and Lesson 25, "Network Services."
- Delete and then reconfigure printers. From the Print & Scan preferences, delete and then reconfigure a troublesome printer using the techniques outlined earlier in this lesson. This resets the device's drivers and queue.
- Reset the entire print system. Sometimes it's necessary to reset the entire printing system. From the Print & Scan preferences, use secondary (or Control) click in the printers list, and choose "Reset printing system" from the shortcut menu. Click OK in the verification dialog. Next you'll have to authenticate as an administrative user. This

clears all configured devices, shared settings, custom presets, and queued print jobs. While this may seem drastic, it's likely to clear up any software-related printing issues.

- Review CUPS log files. Like other system services, CUPS writes all important activity to log files. You can access these logs while in any printer queue application by choosing Printer > Log & History. This opens the Console utility to the CUPS error_log file. While in the Console, you can also check the CUPS access_log and page_log files located in /private/var/log/cups.

NOTE ▶ The CUPS error_log file may not exist if the CUPS service hasn't yet logged any serious print errors.

- Reinstall or update printer drivers. Again, software bugs are always being fixed, so it's good to check for printer driver updates. You can use the OS X built-in software update system to check for system updates and many printer updates. However, be sure to also check the printer manufacturer's website for the latest printer driver updates.
- Repair installed software disk permissions. Third-party installers tend to mess up system software permissions. Use the Disk Utility Repair Permissions feature to resolve permissions issues with printer drivers and other print system files, as covered in Lesson 12, "Permissions and Sharing."

MORE INFO ▶ For advanced print system management and troubleshooting, you can access the Mac CUPS web interface by opening a web browser and entering the following URL: http://localhost:631 and then following the web interface setup instructions.

Exercise 28.1
Configure a Bonjour Printer

Prerequisites

- You must have created the Local Admin (Exercise 3.1 or 3.2) and Chris Johnson (Exercise 6.1) accounts.
- You must have a network printer that supports Bonjour, or a classroom server with the proper server setup, or configured your own server using the Mainserver Setup Instructions.

In this exercise, you will discover and configure a network printer via the Bonjour service discovery protocol. If you are performing these exercises in class, you will use a print queue shared from Mainserver.

1 If necessary, log in as Chris Johnson.

2 Open System Preferences and then click Print & Scan.

3 If necessary, click the lock icon and authenticate as Local Admin.

4 Click the Add (+) button under the printer list.

A pop-up menu appears giving you the option to add a nearby shared printer.

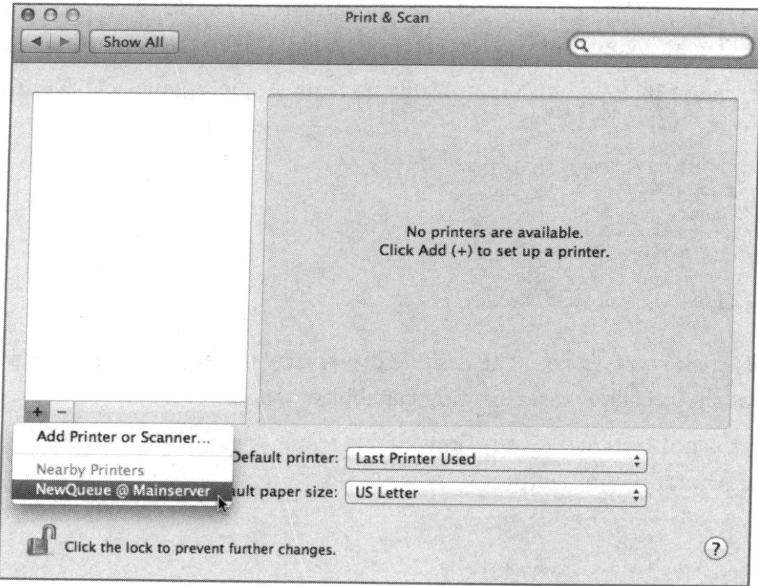

NOTE ▶ What you see on your computer will vary considerably depending on the precise model of printer you are using; the screen shot here and those that follow are intended to illustrate the range of possibilities and will not match what you actually see.

5 Choose the printer you wish to use from the pop-up menu. If you are using the print queue shared from Mainserver, it appears as "NewQueue @ Mainserver."

Depending on the type of printer, one of several things may happen:

- If a driver for the printer is installed on your computer, or available from the computer sharing the printer, it is set up automatically.
- If the driver is not available locally but is available from the Apple software update servers, you are prompted to download and install the update.

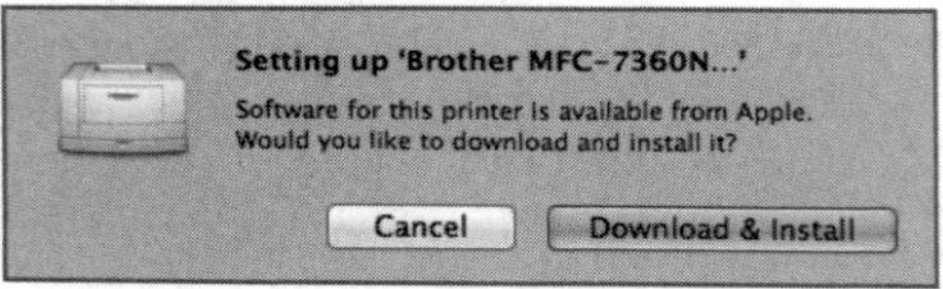

In this case, click "Download & Install," then authenticate as Local Admin when prompted. The appropriate driver package downloads and installs. Depending on the package size and your Internet connection speed, this may take a while.

- If the driver is not installed locally or available from Apple, a generic driver may be sufficient.

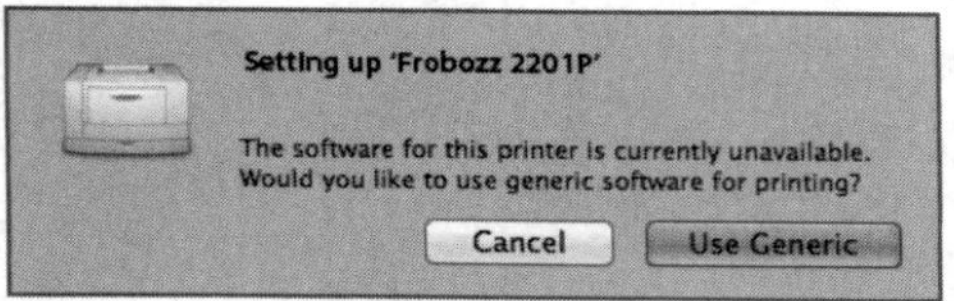

In this case, click Use Generic. The generic driver may not support all the printer's features, but should allow basic printing capability.

- If the driver is not installed locally or available from Apple, you are notified to contact the printer's manufacturer.

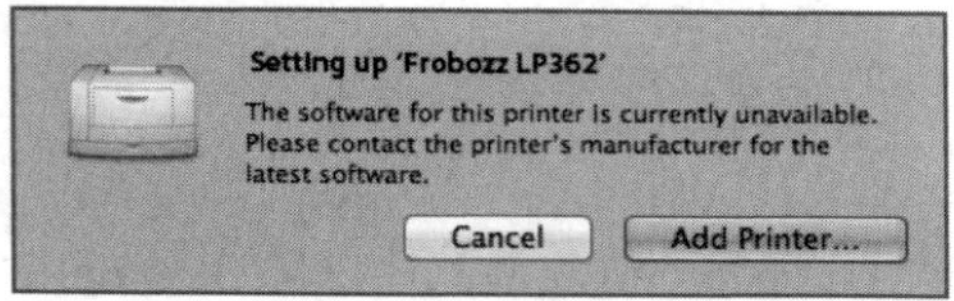

In this case, you need to either find a driver (probably from the printer's manufacturer) or use a generic driver (OS X comes with generic PostScript and PCL drivers) in order to proceed. Click Cancel and try again after finding and installing the appropriate driver.

6 Your computer may fetch information about optional features from the printer itself (or the computer sharing it) and complete the setup process automatically. Your computer is now fully configured to print to this printer.

7 When the new print queue is set up, select it and click the Open Print Queue button.

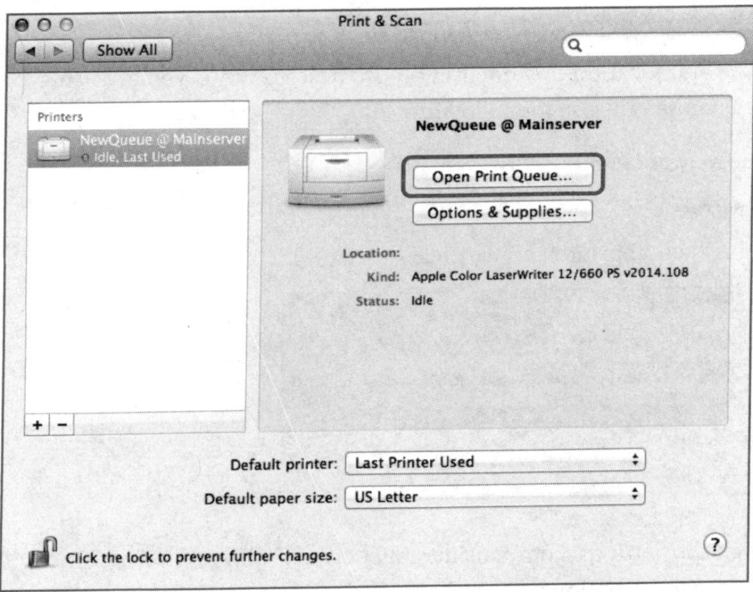

This lets you view and manage print jobs waiting to go to the printer, as well as view and change settings for the print queue itself. Depending on the printer's capabilities, you may see additional options such as a Scanner button.

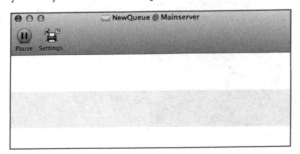

8 Click the Settings button.

The General pane of settings allows you to configure the Name and Location displayed for the printer. It is often useful to name printers that would otherwise only have their model name listed.

You can set more descriptive names for printers by using the Printer Setup button in a queue's window. For supported printers, you also have access to supply-level information from the queue window.

9 Change the name and location to something more descriptive. If you are using "NewQueue @ Mainserver," use the following:

Name: **Pretendco Network Printer**

Location: **Main server**

If you are using an actual printer, enter a real description.

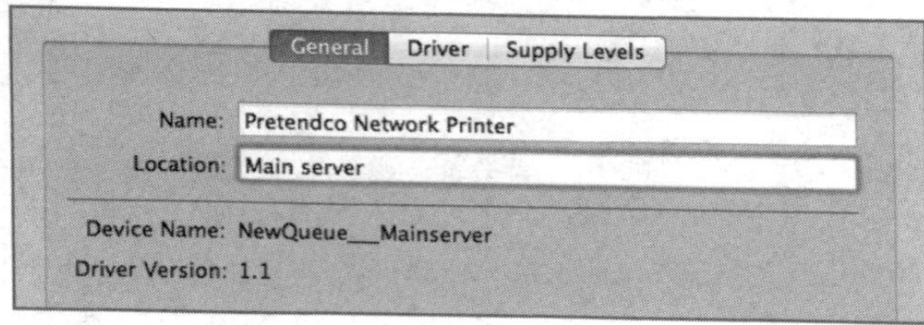

The other tabs in the Settings vary considerably between different printer models; you are unlikely to see all the options shown in the following screen shots.

10 If there is a Driver tab, click it.

If this printer is shared from a Mac, that Mac controls which driver is used for the printer. If you are connecting to the printer directly, you can change the assigned driver if necessary.

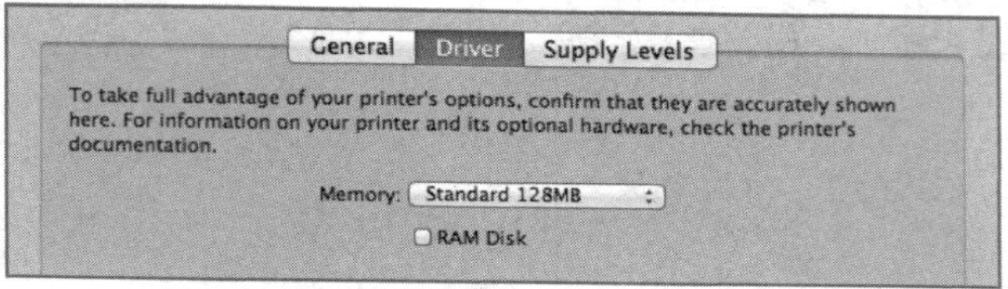

11 If there is a Supply Levels tab, click it.

If you are connecting to the printer directly and the printer supports it, you can view the printer's supply levels here.

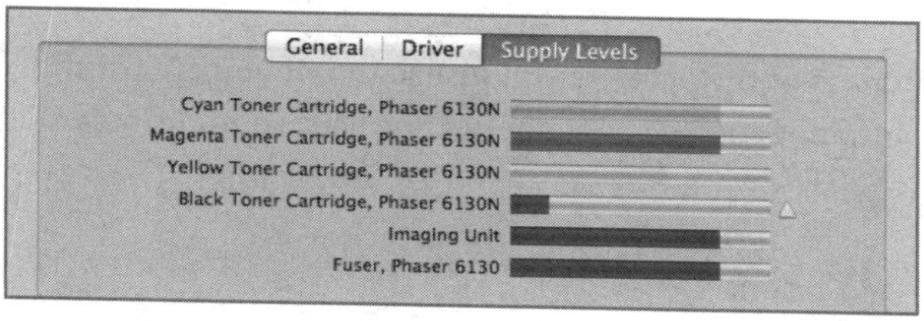

12 If there is a Utility tab, click it.

This tab of the printer setup gives you access to any utilities supplied by this printer's driver. The functions available here vary depending on the printer model you are using.

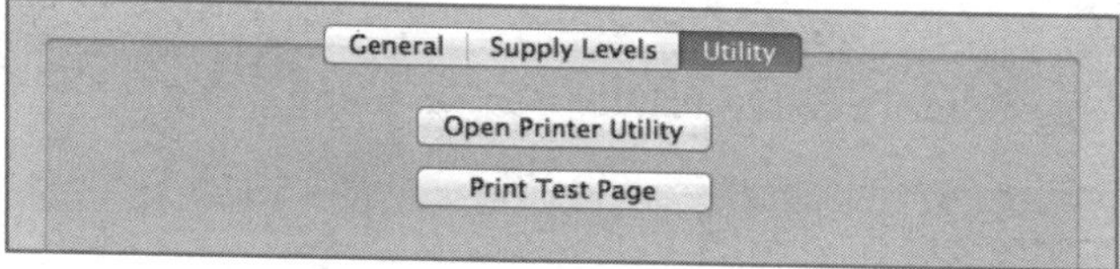

13 Click OK.

14 Quit the printer queue. Note that although it is not really an application, it acts like one, including by offering a Quit option under its "application" menu.

Exercise 28.2
Manage Printing

Prerequisites

- You must have created the Chris Johnson account (Exercise 6.1).
- You must have at least one print queue set up on your computer. You can use Exercise 28.1 to set up a Bonjour-based network printer or set up a different type of printer using the notes in the earlier Reference sections.

This exercise explores both basic and advanced features of the OS X Print dialog, including saving a set of print options as a preset, printing to PDF format, and managing PDF workflows.

Print to a Printer

In this section, you will print to one of the printers you just set up. If you are printing to NewQueue on Mainserver, it does not connect to a physical printer, so no printed output appears.

1 If necessary, log in as Chris Johnson.

2 Open the Student *n*.rtf file from your desktop. If this file does not exist, open TextEdit, type some text into the blank document that opens, and save it to your desktop as "**Student *n***" (where *n* is your student number or 1 if you are working on your own).

3 Choose File > Print (Command-P).

4 In the Print dialog, choose a printer from the Printer pop-up menu.

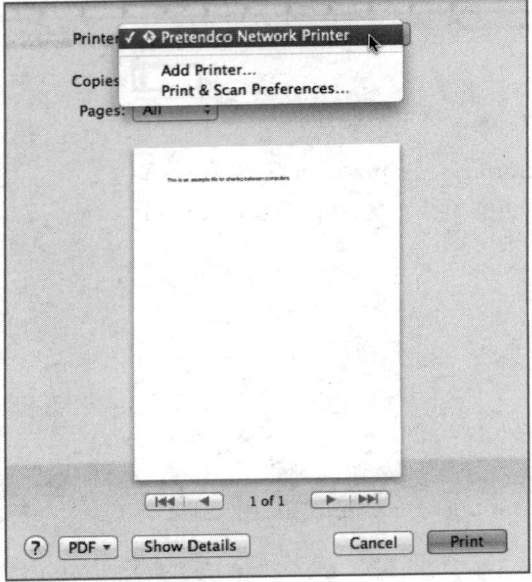

5 Click Show Details.

The Print dialog expands to show additional print settings.

6 Choose Layout from the configuration pop-up menu (initially set to TextEdit).

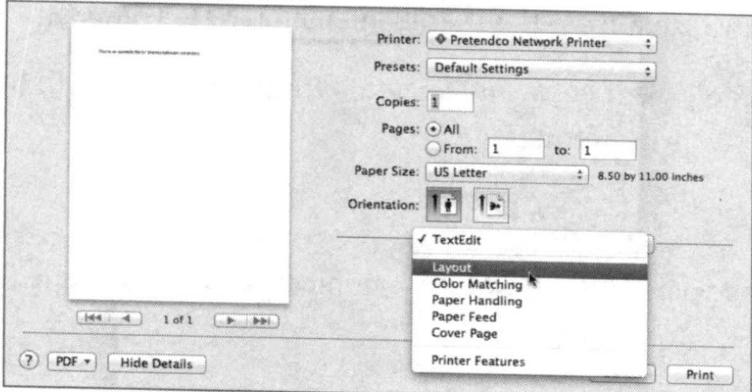

7 From the "Pages per Sheet" pop-up menu, choose 6.

8 From the "Border" pop-up menu, choose "Single Thin Line."

As you change the settings, the preview on the left shows the effects of your changes.

9 From the Presets pop-up menu, choose "Save Current Settings as Preset."

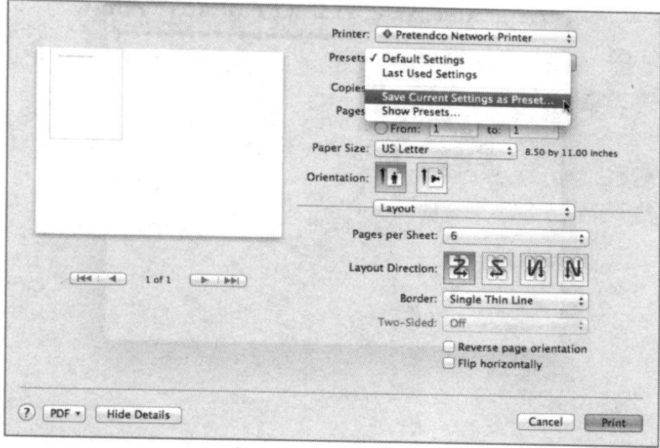

10 Name the preset **6-up with border**, make it available for all printers, and click OK.

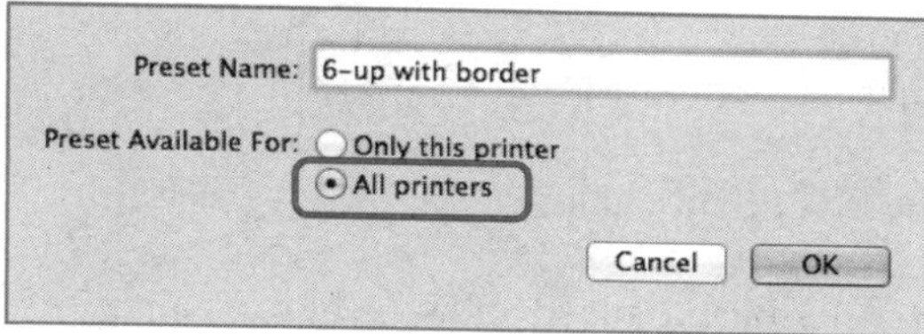

These print settings are now available from the Presets menu anytime you print.

11 Use the Presets pop-up menu to switch between Default Settings and 6-up with border, and watch the effects on the print settings.

12 Click Print.

The print queue icon appears in your Dock, showing the number of jobs in the queue (1).

Manage a Print Queue

1 If you can, click the printer queue in your Dock before it vanishes.

In the queue window, you can watch the job get sent to the printer (or Mainserver) and be removed from the queue.

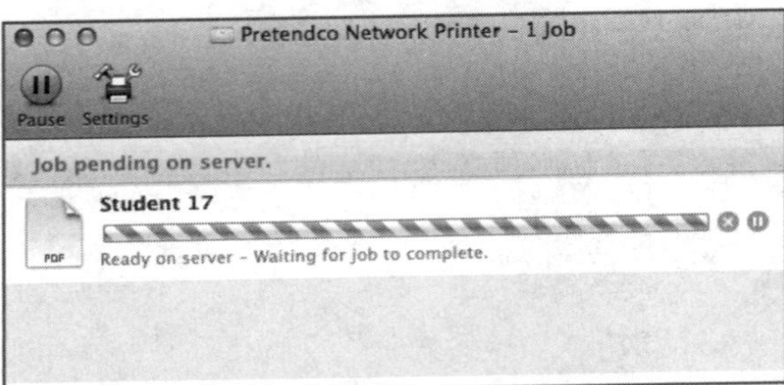

2 If the printer queue icon vanishes from your Dock before you have a chance to click it, open the Print & Scan preferences, select the print queue on the left, and click "Open Print Queue."

3 In the print queue window, click Pause.

4 Switch back to TextEdit and print the document again.

5 When you are warned that the printer has been paused, click "Add to Printer."

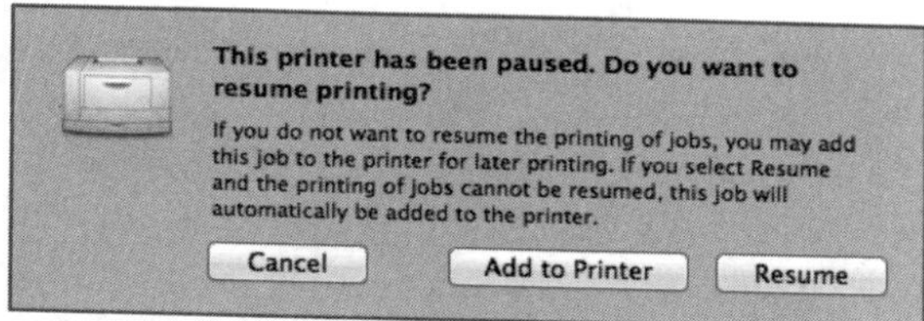

6 Switch to the print queue window. If your document is not shown, quit the print queue and then reopen it from the Print & Scan preferences.

Your document is shown as "Ready to Print."

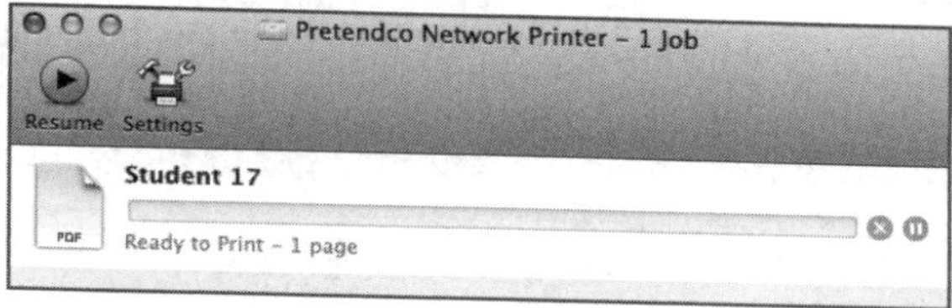

7 Double-click the document in the print queue.

A Quick Look window opens, allowing you to preview the print job.

8 Close the Quick Look window and click the Jobs menu.

This menu has options to hold, resume, or delete individual print jobs. Most of them are also available within the print queue window itself.

9 Click the delete ("X") button to the right of the print job.

The job vanishes from the print queue.

10 Quit the print queue.

Print to PDF

The OS X print architecture can actually do a good deal more than print. In this section, you will use it to produce PDF files.

1 Switch back to TextEdit and press Command-P.

2 Click the PDF button near the bottom left of the Print dialog.

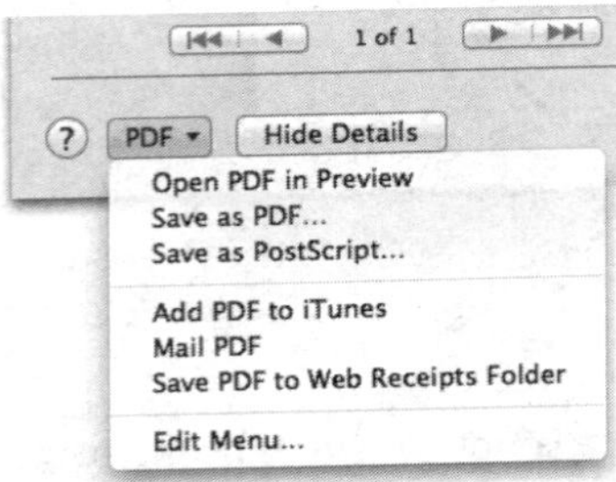

3 Choose Open PDF in Preview.

CUPS produces a PDF version of your document, and it opens in Preview. This feature provides an easy way to do a full-scale preview of documents before printing them. Note that there are Cancel and Print buttons near the bottom right of the window.

4 Click Cancel. This both closes the document and quits the Preview application.

5 In TextEdit, press Command-P again.

6 From the PDF pop-up menu, choose Save as PDF.

7 Save the PDF to your desktop.

Install a PDF Service

You can add choices to the PDF menu by placing items in a Library/PDF Services folder. Supported item types include additional applications to open PDFs, folders in which to save PDFs, scripts and workflows to process PDFs, and aliases to any of these.

1 Open the Lesson28 folder in StudentMaterials.

2 Open "Apply Confidential Watermark.workflow."

This file is a print plug-in created with Automator, one of the easy-to-use Apple automation tools for OS X. Since it is a print plug-in, Automator offers to install it for you.

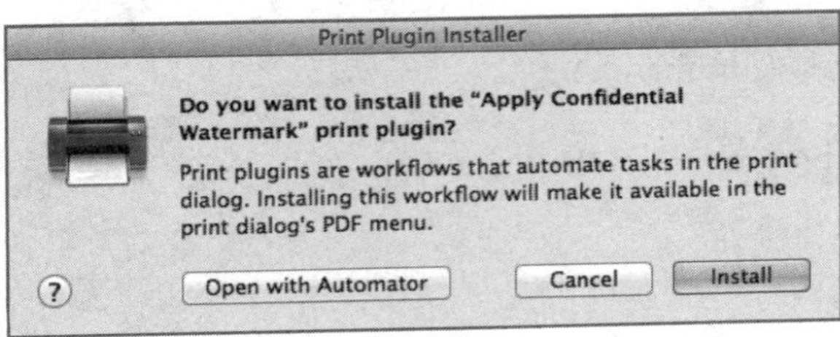

3 Click Install.

4 When you are informed that the installation is complete, click Done.

5 Switch to the Finder, then hold the Option key and choose Go > Library.

6 Inside the user Library, open the PDF Services folder.

When you clicked Install, a copy of the Apply Confidential Services workflow was placed here. You can also create a PDF Services folder in /Library, and any items you place there will be available to all users on this computer.

7 Close the Library folder.

8 Switch back to TextEdit and press Command-P.

9 From the PDF pop-up menu, choose Apply Confidential Watermark.

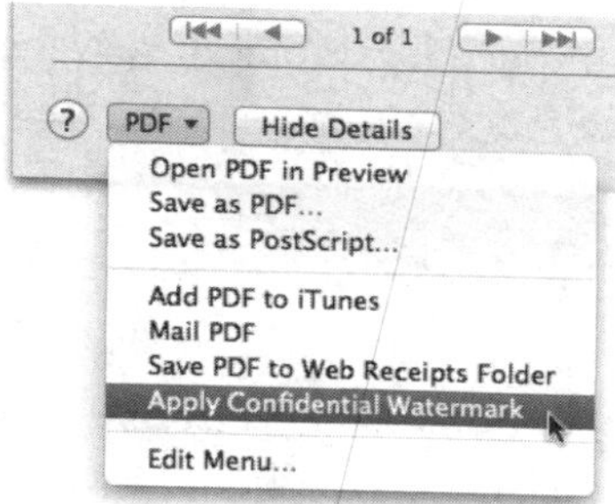

Apply Confidential Watermark is an Automator workflow that takes a PDF (produced by CUPS), overlays a watermark on it (actually the PretendcoConfidential.png image in StudentMaterials/Lesson28), and opens it in Preview.

It may take a few seconds for the workflow to do its work. When it is ready, the PDF document opens in Preview.

10 In Preview, choose File > Duplicate. This opens a copy of the file, which you can save under a different name.

11 Choose File > Save.

12 Save the file to your desktop as **Student *n* watermarked.pdf**.

13 Close all open documents and quit all running applications.

Exercise 28.3
Troubleshoot the Printing System

Prerequisites

- You must have created the Local Admin (Exercise 3.1 or 3.2) and Chris Johnson (Exercise 6.1) accounts.
- You must have at least one print queue set up on your computer.

Troubleshooting printing involves understanding what goes on during the print process. In this exercise, you will examine the logs that are available from the print system as well as how to completely reset the printing configuration if needed.

Examine the CUPS Logs

OS X tracks many different events, including printing, through logs. You can view logs of both system and user events in the Console application. In this exercise, you will use Console to view the available CUPS logs.

1. If necessary, log in as Chris Johnson.
2. Open Console from the Utilities folder. If necessary, click Show Log List in the toolbar to see the list of log locations.
3. Click the disclosure triangle next to /var/log to display the list of logs and then click the disclosure triangle next to cups.

   Because the CUPS logs are located in the hidden folder /var/log in the OS X file system, they are displayed under /var/log in the Console window.
4. Click access_log in the list.

   If you have printed, as you did previously, entries appear in the access log. There are also entries in the page log for each job. The access log shows interactions with the CUPS service while the page log shows actual print jobs. Commands sent to CUPS appear here as well, though not exactly as you entered them at the command line.

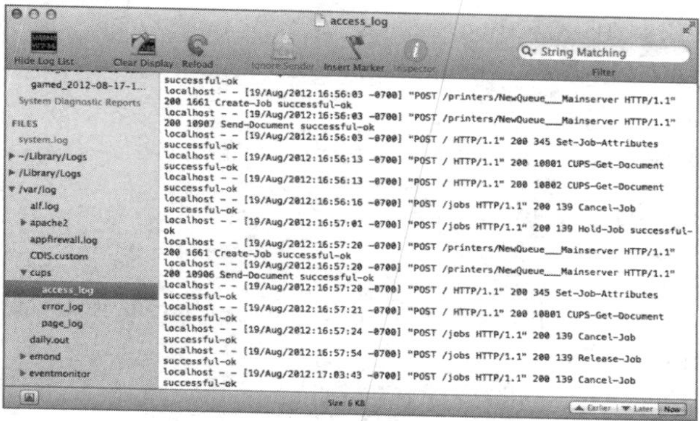

5 View the page_log.

6 If there is an error_log, view it.

7 Quit Console.

Reset the Printing System

If you can't print to your printer and you've tried other solutions, you can restore the printing system to "factory defaults" by resetting it. This process deletes all printers from your printer list, all information about all completed print jobs, and all printer presets. Because this completely resets information, it's likely to be your last option, rather than your first.

1 From the Apple menu, choose System Preferences and click Print & Scan.

2 Hold the Control key and click in the printer list.

3 Choose "Reset printing system" from the menu that appears.

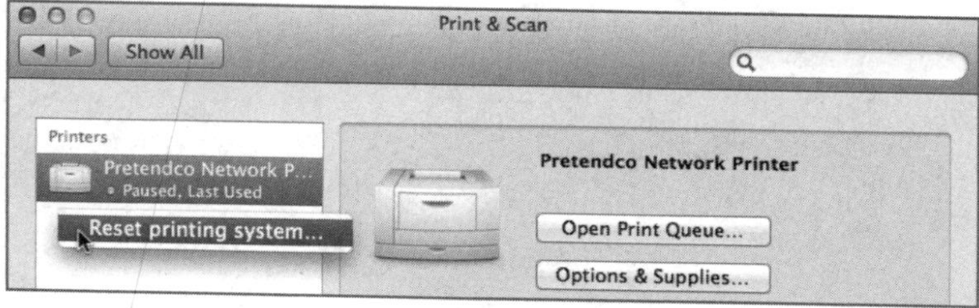

4 Click OK when asked to confirm, then authenticate as Local Admin.

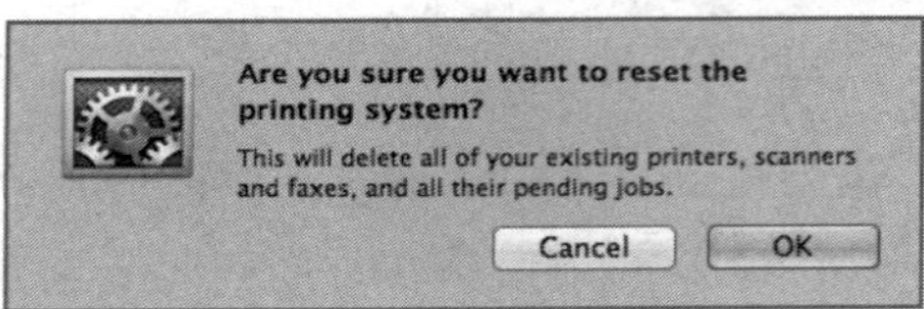

You can re-add your printers when the process is complete, if you like. It is not necessary for the remaining exercises.

5 Quit System Preferences.

System Startup

Lesson **29**

Startup, Shutdown, and Sleep Modes

System startup certainly isn't the most glamorous part of OS X, but it's clearly important and technically quite impressive. Apple has improved startup and runtime processes with every revision of OS X. When things work correctly, the startup process is often under 30 seconds. Obviously, users appreciate a quick startup, but most aren't aware of what goes on during system startup because their Macs usually work properly.

This lesson focuses on the process that your Mac goes through from the moment you press the power button until you ultimately reach the Finder. You will identify the essential files and processes required to successfully start up OS X. The various OS X sleep modes and features are covered as well. Finally, you will explore the steps required to log out and shut down the system.

GOALS

- Understand the OS X startup process
- Identify the various stages of the OS X startup process
- Examine essential files and processes required to successfully start up

Reference 29.1
System Initialization

This section examines the main stages of the OS X system startup procedure. The stages of system startup can be categorized into either *system initiation*, the processes required to start the operating system, or *user session*, the processes required to prepare the user environment. At each stage the Mac presents an audible or visual cue to help you validate startup progress. The startup cues discussed here are what you'll experience during a typical startup. Any deviation will be covered as you learn more about the startup process.

System Initialization

Firmware

Booter

Kernel

System launchd

The four main OS X system initialization stages are, in order:

- Firmware—At this stage the Mac computer's hardware is tested and initialized, and then the booter is located and started. Successfully completing this stage results in an audible startup chime and a bright flash from the power-on light, then all displays show a light gray background.
- Booter—The main job of the booter is to load the system kernel and essential hardware drivers, known as kernel extensions (KEXTs), into main memory and then allow the kernel to take over the system. The booter stage is indicated by a dark gray Apple logo on the main display.
- Kernel—The kernel provides the system's foundation and loads additional drivers and the core BSD UNIX system. It is indicated by a dark gray spinning gear below the Apple logo on the main display.
- System launchd—Once the core operating system is loaded, it starts the first nonkernel process, the system launchd, which is responsible for loading the remainder of the system. This stage is indicated by the disappearance of the dark gray spinning gear and the brief appearance of a white background on all displays. Successful completion of this stage results in either the login screen or the Finder, if the user is set to automatically log in.

System Initialization: Firmware

Your Mac computer's firmware, also called BootROM, resides on flash memory chips built into the main computer board. When you power on your Mac, even before it starts a "real" operating system, the firmware acts as a mini-operating system with just enough software to get things going. Specifically, the firmware tests and initializes the hardware, and then locates and starts the system software booter.

Intel-based Macs feature firmware based on the Intel Extensible Firmware Interface (EFI) technology. Aside from supporting the Intel processor hardware, EFI is what allows your Mac to start up from OS X, Windows, or any other Intel-compatible operating system.

> **MORE INFO ►** EFI is an extremely flexible boot architecture and is now managed by the Unified EFI Forum. In fact, EFI will soon be known as Unified Extensible Firmware Interface (UEFI). You can find out more at www.uefi.org.

Power-On Self-Test

The first thing your Mac firmware does at power on is the Power-On Self-Test (POST). The POST tests built-in hardware components such as processors, system memory, network interfaces, and peripheral interfaces. When your Mac passes the POST, you hear the startup chime and see a light gray background on all displays. After a successful POST, the firmware goes on to locate the booter file.

If your Mac fails the POST, the displays remains blank or off, and you may get hardware error codes. Depending on the age and model of your Mac, these error codes may manifest as audible tones, a series of flashes from the external power-on light, or internal diagnostic lights illuminating. You may even see a combination of these things. Regardless of which error code you experience, it indicates that a hardware problem exists that OS X cannot control. You can visit the Apple support website at www.apple.com/support to identify your specific Mac error code, or you can take your Mac to an Apple Authorized Service Provider.

Booter Selection

By default, the firmware picks the system booter file that was last specified from the Startup Disk preferences in OS X or the Boot Camp control panel in Windows. The booter file's location is saved in your Mac computer's nonvolatile RAM (NVRAM) so that it persists across system restarts. If the booter file is found, EFI starts the booter process and OS X begins to start up. This is indicated by the dark gray Apple logo in the center of the main display.

If the firmware cannot locate a booter file, a flashing folder icon with a question mark appears. Troubleshooting this issue is covered in Lesson 30, "System Troubleshooting."

FileVault 2 Unlock

If the system disk is protected with FileVault 2 encryption, the OS X booter cannot be accessed until the system disk is unlocked by a user. If this is the case, the system instead begins initial startup from the OS X Recovery HD, where a special EFI booter resides that presents the user with an authentication screen much like the login window. The FileVault 2 authentication unlock screen appears just a few seconds after POST and has a much lighter background than the standard OS X login window.

Once the user successfully authenticates and unlocks the encrypted system disk, the EFI firmware is granted access to the system volume containing the OS X booter. Startup then continues as normal, with one exception. Because the user has already authenticated to unlock the disk, he can automatically log into his session without having to authenticate again at the login window. This happens only once per startup and only for the user who unlocked the encrypted system disk.

Startup Shortcuts

Your Mac firmware also supports many keyboard shortcuts, which, when pressed and held down during initial power-on, allow you to modify the startup process. Some of these shortcuts modify the booter selection, while others modify how OS X starts up. Startup shortcuts are detailed in Lesson 30, "System Troubleshooting."

Firmware Updates

Boot read-only memory, or boot ROM, refers to older versions of firmware technology that are not upgradable. Your Mac firmware, however, is upgradable, and on Intel-based Macs it's even replaceable if it becomes damaged.

The OS X Software Update service may automatically update some Mac firmware, but you can also check the Apple Knowledge Base for the latest list of Mac firmware updates. Document HT1237, "EFI and SMC firmware updates for Intel-based Macs," maintains a list of Mac firmware updates. You can replace your Intel-based Mac computer's firmware using a firmware restoration CD as outlined in document HT2213, "About the Firmware Restoration CD (Intel-based Macs)."

> **MORE INFO ▸** You can easily extend your Intel-based Mac computer's EFI capabilities using the open source rEFIt toolkit available at http://refit.sourceforge.net.

System Initialization: Booter

The booter process is launched by your Mac firmware and is responsible for loading the OS X kernel and enough essential kernel extensions, or KEXTs, so the kernel can take over the system and continue the startup process. Your Mac firmware also passes on any special startup mode instructions for the booter to handle, such as entering Safe Mode when the user is holding down the Shift key. The booter process itself resides at /System/Library/CoreServices/boot.efi.

To expedite the startup process, the booter loads cached files whenever possible. These files contain an optimized kernel and KEXTs that load much quicker than if the system had to load them from scratch. These caches are located in the /System/Library/Caches/com.apple.kernel.caches folder. If the system detects a problem or you start OS X in Safe Mode, these caches are discarded and the kernel-loading process takes longer.

As covered previously, the booter process is indicated at startup by the dark gray Apple icon in the center of the main display. If the booter successfully loads the kernel, this is indicated by a small, dark gray spinning gear icon below the Apple icon. Though, some modern Mac systems start up so fast you may not even see the spinning gear before the next stage is indicated.

If your Mac is set to NetBoot and the firmware successfully locates the booter file on the NetBoot server, you again see the dark gray Apple icon. However, in this case the booter and the cached kernel information must be downloaded from the NetBoot server. This process is indicated by a small, dark gray spinning globe icon below the Apple icon. The globe icon is replaced by the standard spinning gear icon once the kernel has been successfully loaded from the NetBoot server.

Finally, if the booter is unable to load the kernel, a dark gray prohibitory icon takes the place of the Apple icon. Again, troubleshooting this issue is covered in Lesson 30, "System Troubleshooting."

System Initialization: Kernel

Once the booter has successfully loaded the kernel and essential KEXTs, the kernel itself takes over the startup process. The kernel has now loaded enough KEXTs to read the entire file system, allowing it to load any additional KEXTs and start the core BSD UNIX system. A spinning gray gear icon below the Apple icon indicates the kernel startup progress.

Finally, the kernel starts the first normal (nonkernel) process, the system launchd, which is ultimately the parent process for every other process. The appearance of anything besides the white startup screen with the Apple logo is an indication that the kernel has fully loaded and the launchd process is starting other items.

Again, in most cases the kernel is loaded by the booter from cached files. However, the kernel is also located on the system volume at /mach_kernel. This file is normally hidden from users in the graphical user interface, because they don't need access to it. Many other hidden files and folders at the root of the system volume are necessary for the BSD UNIX system, and again the average user doesn't need access to these items. As covered in Lesson 27, "Peripherals and Drivers," KEXTs reside in the /System/Library/Extensions and /Library/Extensions folders.

System Initialization: System launchd

Once the kernel is up and running, the Mac is ready to start running processes at the behest of the system and eventually human users. The first normal (nonkernel) process started is the system launchd, located at /sbin/launchd, which runs as root and is given the process identification number of 1. In UNIX terms, the system launchd is the first parent process that spawns all other child processes, and those processes go on to spawn other child processes.

The first task for the system launchd process is to complete the system initialization by starting all other system processes. Previous versions of OS X show the "Welcome to Mac OS X" dialog with a progress bar to indicate system initialization status as the various system processes start up.

However, beginning with OS X v10.5, the launchd process was highly optimized, so the system initialization process takes only a few moments and is difficult to visually discern. The best indication that you have reached this point is that the dark grey Apple logo is replaced by the login window or the user's desktop background. If you have a Mac system with multiple displays you may also notice a brief white flash coming from the secondary displays. This is a result of launchd starting the WindowServer process, which is responsible for drawing the OS X user interface, but it's still a good indication that things are progressing through the system startup process.

The launchd process is designed to expedite system initialization by starting multiple system processes simultaneously whenever possible and starting only essential system processes at startup. After startup, the system launchd process automatically starts and stops additional system processes as needed. By dynamically managing system processes, launchd keeps your Mac responsive and running as efficiently as possible.

> **MORE INFO ▶** launchd is an extremely powerful open source system for managing services. Learn more about launchd by reading its manual page in the Terminal.

System launchd Items

As covered in Lesson 15, "System Resources," launchd manages system processes as described by launchd preference files in the /System/Library/LaunchDaemons folder. Third-party processes can also be managed when described by launchd preference files in the /Library/LaunchDaemons folder.

Apple strongly encourages all developers to adopt the launchd system for all automatically started processes. But the system launchd process also supports legacy startup routines.

This includes support for running the traditional UNIX /etc/rc.local script during system initialization if present, though this script is not included on OS X by default.

The system launchd process also starts the /sbin/SystemStarter process, which manages system processes as described by legacy OS X startup items. OS X does not include any built-in startup items, but SystemStarter still looks in the /System/Library/StartupItems and /Library/StartupItems folders for third-party startup items.

Viewing the launchd Hierarchy

The /Applications/Utilities/Activity Monitor application lists all processes along with their identification numbers and parent/child relationships. In the Activity Monitor, you can sort the process list by clicking the title of the Process ID column, and you can view a process's parent process by double-clicking its name in the list.

You may find it beneficial to open Activity Monitor and examine the process listing as you learn about how OS X starts up the user environment. Detailed information about using Activity Monitor is covered in Lesson 21, "Application Management and Troubleshooting."

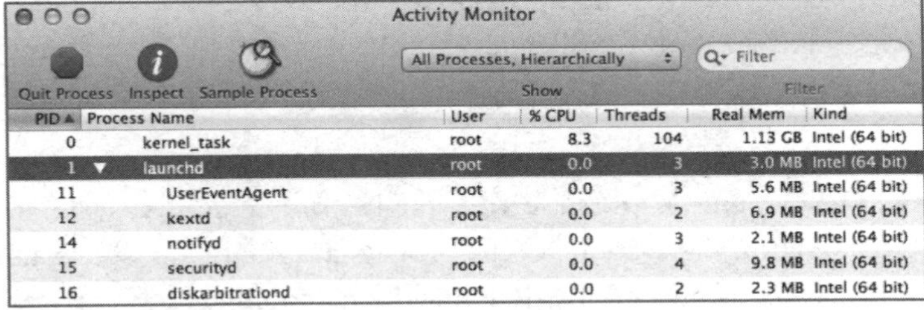

Reference 29.2
User Session

Eventually, after enough system processes have started, the system begins the processes responsible for managing the user session.

The three main OS X user session stages are, in order:

- loginwindow—This is the process responsible for presenting the login screen and eventually logging the user into the system. Successful completion of this stage results in initialization of the user environment, thus allowing user applications to run.
- User launchd—This process works in conjunction with the loginwindow process to initialize the user environment and start any user processes or applications.

- User environment—This is the "space" the user's processes and applications exist in when she is logged into the system. Obviously, the user environment is maintained by the loginwindow and user launchd processes.

User Session

loginwindow

User launchd

User environment

Login Window

A soon as the system has started enough processes to present the login window, the system launchd process starts /System/Library/CoreServices/loginwindow.app. The loginwindow process has the ability to run as both a background process and a graphical interface application. The loginwindow coordinates the login screen and, along with the opendirectoryd process, authenticates the user. After authentication, the loginwindow, in conjunction with the user's launchd, also initializes the graphical interface user environment and continues to run as a background process to maintain the user session.

By default on OS X, the user must authenticate using the login screen, or the loginwindow can be set to automatically authenticate a user at startup. As covered previously, the system also automatically logs in a user if she provided authentication to unlock FileVault 2 during startup. The loginwindow settings are stored in the /Library/Preferences/com.apple.loginwindow.plist preference file. As covered in Lesson 6, "User Accounts," you can configure loginwindow settings from the User & Groups preferences.

If no users are logged into the Mac, the loginwindow process is owned by the root user. Once a user successfully authenticates, the loginwindow process switches ownership to this user and then proceeds to set up the graphical interface user environment with help from the user's launchd.

The User's launchd

The moment a user is authenticated, the system launchd process starts another instance of launchd that is also owned by the authenticated user. All user processes and applications, even those that the user manually opens, are started by the user-specific launchd process. If fast user switching is enabled, the system launchd process starts additional loginwindow and launchd processes to initialize and maintain each user's environment.

The user's loginwindow and launchd processes set up the graphical interface user environment by:

- Retrieving the user account information from opendirectoryd and applying any account settings
- Configuring the mouse, keyboard, and system sound using the user's preferences
- Loading the user's computing environment: preferences, environment variables, devices and file permissions, and keychain access
- Opening the Dock (also responsible for Mission Control and Dashboard), Finder, and SystemUIServer (responsible for user interface elements like menu extras on the right side of the menu bar)
- Automatically opening the user's login items
- By default in OS X, automatically resuming any application that was open before the last logout

It's important to understand the differences between the various autostarting mechanisms in OS X: launch daemons, startup items, launch agents, and login items. Again, launch daemons and startup items are started during system initialization by the system launchd process on behalf of the root user. On the other hand, launch agents and login items are only started on behalf of a specific user. In other words, launch daemons and startup items affect the system as a whole, while launch agents and login items affect individual users.

Specifically, launch agents are started by the user's launchd process on behalf of the user. Launch agents can be started at any time as long as the user's launchd process is running. Most launch agents are started during the initialization of the user environment, but they could also be started afterward or on a regular repeating basis depending on need. Launch agents provided by the system can be found in /System/Library/LaunchAgents, whereas third-party launch agents should be located in either /Library/LaunchAgents or ~/Library/LaunchAgents.

Finally, login items are started only at the very end of the initialization of the user environment. The loginwindow process, again with help from the user's launchd process, is responsible for starting a user's login items. The user's login item list is stored in the ~/Library/Preferences/loginwindow.plist preference file. As covered previously in Lesson 6, "User Accounts," you can configure a user's login item list from the Users & Groups preferences.

Again, from Activity Monitor you can examine the user's launchd process and the resulting user processes. It's especially helpful if the process list is sorted by "All Processes, Hierarchically."

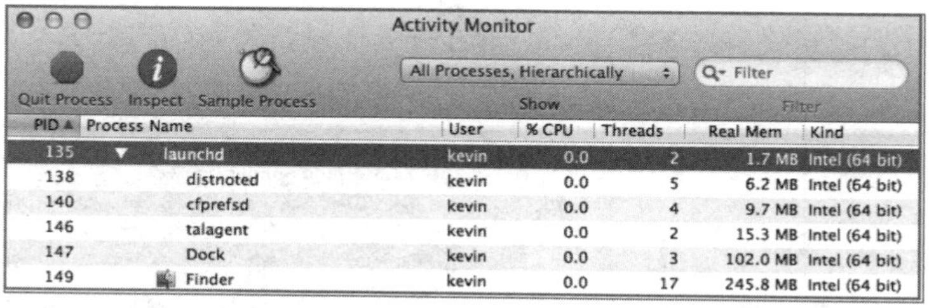

Activity Monitor

Quit Process | Inspect | Sample Process | All Processes, Hierarchically (Show) | Filter

PID ▲	Process Name	User	% CPU	Threads	Real Mem	Kind
135	▼ launchd	kevin	0.0	2	1.7 MB	Intel (64 bit)
138	distnoted	kevin	0.0	5	6.2 MB	Intel (64 bit)
140	cfprefsd	kevin	0.0	4	9.7 MB	Intel (64 bit)
146	talagent	kevin	0.0	2	15.3 MB	Intel (64 bit)
147	Dock	kevin	0.0	3	102.0 MB	Intel (64 bit)
149	Finder	kevin	0.0	17	245.8 MB	Intel (64 bit)

The User Environment

The user-owned launchd and loginwindow processes continue to run as long as the user is logged into the session. The user's launchd process starts all user processes and applications, while the user's loginwindow process monitors and maintains the user session.

The user's loginwindow process monitors the user session by:

- Managing logout, restart, and shutdown procedures
- Managing the Force Quit Applications window, which includes monitoring the currently active applications and responding to user requests to forcibly quit applications
- Writing any standard-error output to the user's console.log file

While the user is logged into the session, the user's launchd process automatically restarts any user application that should remain open, such as the Finder or the Dock. If the user's loginwindow process is ended, whether intentionally or unexpectedly, all the user's applications and processes immediately quit without saving changes. If this happens, the system launchd process then automatically restarts the loginwindow process as if the Mac had just started up. In other words, the loginwindow, depending on configuration, either displays the login screen or automatically logs in the specified user.

Reference 29.3
Sleep Modes, Logout, and Shutdown

At the other end of the spectrum, but still related, are the processes required to pause or end the user session. The main distinction is that your Mac computer's sleep function does not quit any open processes, whereas the user logout and system shutdown functions quit open processes. In most cases, the user manually issues a sleep, logout, or shutdown command from the Apple menu or by pressing the Mac computer's power button.

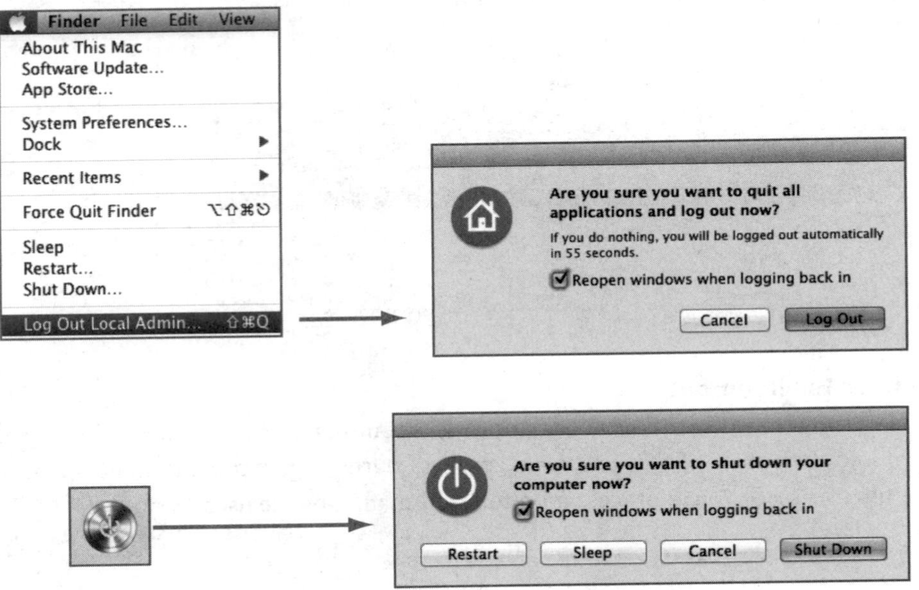

NOTE ▸ OS X features an automatic Resume feature, enabled by default for all users. Upon login the user's items reopen to their previous state. This feature works in conjunction with the application Auto Save as covered in Lesson 20, "Document Management."

However, other processes and applications can also initiate sleep, logout, or shutdown commands. For instance, the Installer and Mac App Store applications can request a restart when the installation of new or updated software requires it.

Further, you can configure the Mac to automatically perform certain commands such as put the system to sleep after a period of inactivity with settings in the Energy Saver preferences; set a schedule to sleep, shut down, or start up the Mac with settings in the Schedule dialog of the Energy Saver preferences; automatically log out users after a period of inactivity with settings in the Security & Privacy preferences; and automatically log out managed users with settings in the Parental Controls preferences. Many of these settings can be managed remotely from Apple Remote Desktop or from a management server.

The Mac sleep function is convenient because it does not quit any active processes or applications. Instead, the system kernel pauses all processes and then essentially shuts down all the hardware. This greatly reduces the amount of power used; as an example, newer portable Macs can remain in sleep mode for up to a month on a single battery charge. Waking your Mac from sleep mode restarts all hardware, and the kernel resumes all processes and applications from the point at which you left them.

Safe Sleep

All OS X Mountain Lion–compatible portable Macs support a safe sleep mode. When these Macs go to sleep, they also copy the entire contents of system memory to an image file on the system volume. This way, if these Macs stay in sleep mode long enough to completely drain the battery, no data is lost when the system has to fully shut down.

When you restart a Mac from safe sleep mode, the booter process reloads the saved memory image from the system volume instead of proceeding with the normal startup process. The booter process indicates that the Mac is restarting from safe sleep mode by showing a light gray version of your Mac screen as it appeared when sleep was initiated and a small progress bar at the bottom of the main display. It should take only a few moments to reload system memory, and the kernel resumes all processes and applications. If FileVault 2 is enabled, the safe sleep-wake process is preceded by the FileVault 2 authentication unlock screen.

Power Nap

Mac systems introduced after mid 2011 that feature all flash storage, like MacBook Air models, gain new sleep functionality in OS X Mountain Lion with Power Nap. This feature allows your Mac to occasionally wake from sleep in a low-power mode, known as "dark wake" because the display does not power up, and perform essential background tasks. Many built-in OS X applications and services support Power Nap including: Mail, Contacts, Calendar, Reminders, Notes, documents in iCloud, Photo Stream, Mac App Store updates, Time Machine backup, Find My Mac updates, VPN on demand, and MDM configuration profile updates.

NOTE ► Power Nap updates only applications that are running when sleep is initiated. Further, if a user logs out of the system prior to sleeping, his items do not update.

For Mac systems that support Power Nap, it is enabled by default for when your Mac is connected to a power adapter. You can verify or adjust this setting from the Energy Saver settings. You can also optionally enable Power Nap for when your Mac is running from battery power, although this obviously reduces the Mac computer's battery faster than normal system sleep.

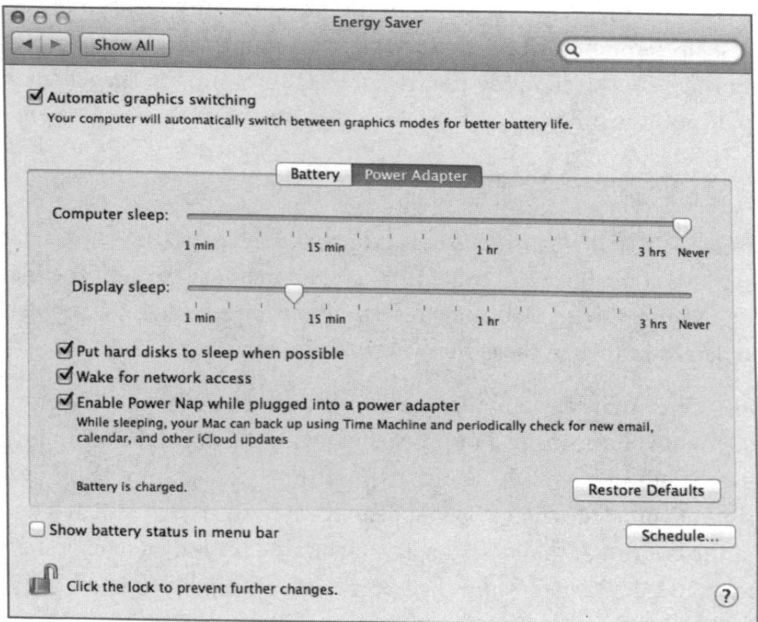

When a Mac is put to sleep with Power Nap enabled, it first waits 30 minutes before dark-waking to check for updates. After that, it dark-wakes every hour to check for updates. You can verify that Power Nap is in effect by checking its log file via Console. The Power Nap log file is located at /var/log/zzz.log.

MORE INFO ▸ Some Macs require firmware updates to support Power Nap. You can find out more about Power Nap and any required updates from Knowledge Base document, HT5394, "Mountain Lion: About Power Nap."

Logout

Users can log out any time they want to end their user session, but they also have to log out to shut down or restart the Mac. When the currently logged-in user chooses to log out, the user's loginwindow process manages all logout functions with help from the user's launchd process.

Once the user authorizes the logout, the user's loginwindow process issues a Quit Application Apple event to all applications. Applications that support the OS X new Auto Save and Resume features immediately save changes to any open documents and quit. Applications that do not support these features still respond to the Quit event, but they are programmed to ask the user if changes should be saved. If the application fails to reply or quit itself after 45 seconds, the logout process is stopped and loginwindow displays an error message.

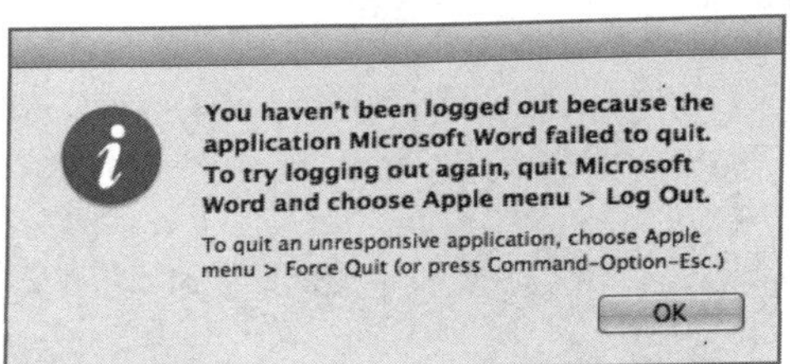

If all the user's applications successfully quit, the user's loginwindow process then forcibly quits any background user processes. Finally, the user's loginwindow process closes the user's graphical interface session, runs any logout scripts, and records the logout to the main system.log file. If the user chooses only to log out, as opposed to shutting down or restarting, the user's loginwindow and launchd processes quit, the system launchd process restarts a new loginwindow process owned by the root user, and the login screen appears.

Shutdown and Restart

When a logged-in user chooses to shut down or restart the Mac, again the user's loginwindow process manages all logout functions with help from the system launchd process. First the user's loginwindow process logs out the current user. If other users are logged in via fast user switching, the loginwindow process asks for administrative user authentication and, if granted, forcibly quits all other users' processes and applications, possibly losing user data.

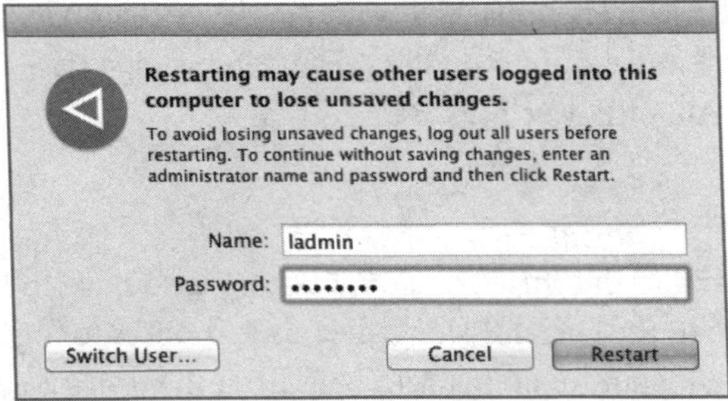

After all user sessions are logged out, the user's loginwindow process tells the kernel to issue the quit command to all remaining system processes. Processes like loginwindow should quit promptly, but the kernel must wait for processes that remain responsive while they are going through the motions of quitting. If system processes don't respond after a few seconds, the kernel forcibly quits those processes. Once all processes are quit, the kernel stops the system launchd process and then shuts down the system. If the user chose to restart the Mac, the computer's firmware begins the system startup process once again.

Exercise 29.1
Examine System Startup

Prerequisites

- You must have created the Chris Johnson account (Exercise 6.1).

As OS X starts up, it gives auditory or visual cues as to which step of the startup process is currently being performed. If the startup process fails to complete, identifying the step where it halted can help illuminate the cause of the issue. In this exercise, you will identify steps in the startup sequence using audible and visible cues. You will then examine the processes that activate automatically when you start up your computer. After completing this exercise, you will be able to identify the sequence of startup events that occur during OS X startup.

Identify Steps in the Startup Process

In this exercise, you will watch the startup process in a standard startup. You will find that the startup process moves through some steps very rapidly, while other steps only flash on the screen, such as an icon that blinks to indicate a component loading. Some steps display onscreen for a significant amount of time only if the underlying process does not start properly.

1 If your computer is on, shut it down. You can use the Apple menu or (if you are not logged in) the buttons on the login screen to shut it down.

2 Start up your computer.

3 As the computer is starting up, use the table below to note the major steps occurring during the startup process (from turning the computer on through the user environment appearing). Keep in mind that certain steps may not apply, since you are not testing hardware issues or situations in which the startup device cannot be found.

   Record the startup process associated with each visible or audible stage of the startup process. Refer to the reference section of this lesson. When you reach the login window, log in as Chris Johnson.

   NOTE ▶ If your computer is encrypted with FileVault 2, there will be an additional startup step for the FileVault unlock screen; note where it occurs in the startup sequence.

Visual or auditory cue	Startup step, or process executing at startup step
Startup chime	
Gray screen with Apple logo	
Gray screen with Apple logo and spinning gear	
Arrow pointer appears	
Login screen	
Desktop and Dock appear	

Examine the Process Hierarchy

The launchd process is an essential part of OS X. It is responsible for starting and managing much of what goes on in the background of OS X. It's important to understand that there is a hierarchy of tasks in the core operating system. The kernel starts launchd, launchd starts a number of other processes, those processes start other processes, and so on. It can be useful, in the event of an issue, to understand this parent-child relationship or hierarchy to identify parent tasks, like launchd, that spawn multiple children to do their work.

1 Ensure you are logged in as Chris Johnson.

2 Open Activity Monitor from the Utilities folder.

3 Choose "All Processes, Hierarchically" from the pop-up menu near the top.

4 Click in the PID (Process ID) column header to display the processes in the order they launched (ascending order by process ID). You want the triangle, indicating the sort order, to be pointing up. If it is not, click the column header again.

5 Click the disclosure triangle next to the launchd process with a process ID of 1 to reduce the view to just kernel_task and launchd.

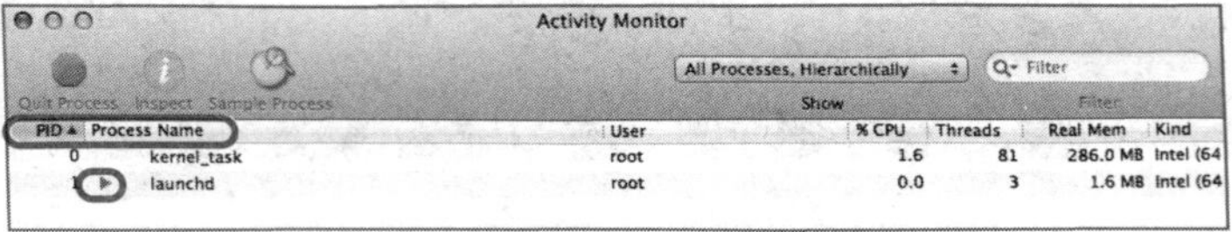

You can see that in the Process ID column, kernel_task is listed as a process. This represents the activity taking place inside the kernel. You can also see that launchd is process 1, meaning that it is the first task that is started by the kernel. This launchd process does not terminate until the system shuts down. All other processes are numbered sequentially after these core tasks. The process ID (PID) is an unsigned 32-bit number with a maximum value somewhere in the neighborhood of 2,147,483,647. Rest assured, however, that should you ever run two billion processes without restarting, the system would not crash when it reaches the maximum PID. It simply starts over again, using currently unused PIDs.

To understand the task hierarchy, you need more information than the task name and ID.

6 Select launchd and click Inspect on the toolbar.

When inspecting a process, the name of the window is the name of the process followed by the process ID in parentheses. The parent process is important when you are trying to evaluate processes during troubleshooting. You can also see various process statistics relating to performance, resource allocation, memory usage, and open files for processes you own. You may also quit a process or sample a process. Sampling involves observing what is happening within the process and can be useful to developers if their application or other process is not responding.

Note that you can click the parent process and open an Inspect window for that task as well. This is very useful when you are working with higher-numbered tasks and tracing the process hierarchy backward.

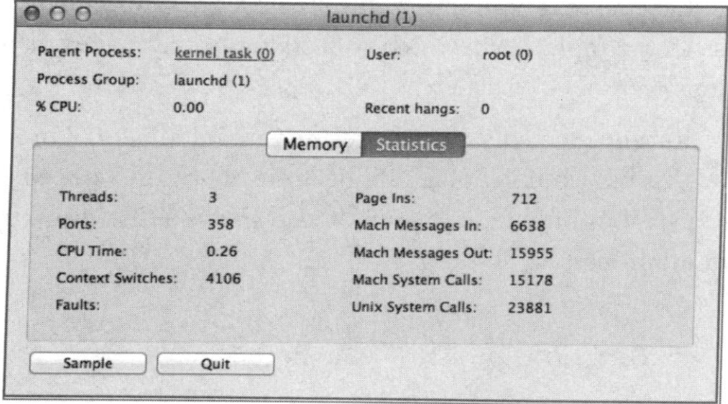

The statistical values in your window will differ from what is shown here.

7 Close the Inspect window.

8 Click the disclosure triangle next to launchd. Open some of the other disclosure triangles, too.

The list of processes running on the computer appears. The low-numbered processes are generally daemons that started before you logged in. *Daemon* is a term for a background process that acts on behalf of the system. *Agents* are background processes that act on behalf of a user. Daemons generally run as root (the System Administrator account) or another system user. Agents run as the users they are acting on behalf of.

A parent-child relationship is indicated by an indent and a disclosure triangle.

9 Look for an instance of launchd owned by you ("chris" in the User column) and click its disclosure triangle to show its child processes.

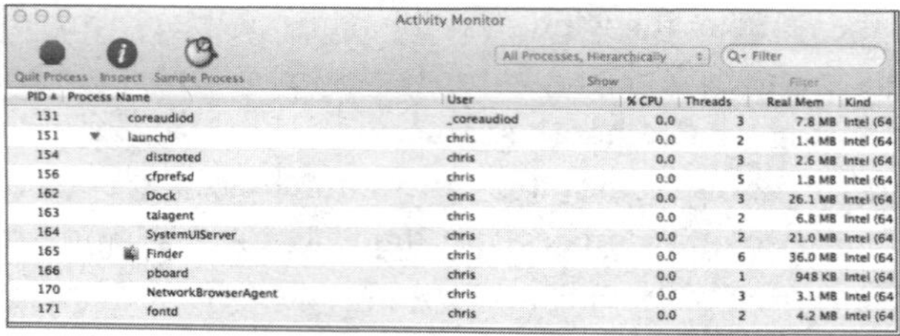

Most of the processes that make up your login session are subprocesses started by this launchd process. This includes applications you started yourself (for example, Activity Monitor), visible agents that were started automatically (for example, Finder and Dock), and also background agents that maintain part of the user environment without any visible indications (for example, fontd, which collects fonts and makes them available to your applications).

Check your launchd process for unexpected subprocesses that might affect the user environment. For example, this list would contain applications that were opened as login items for the current user, but hidden at startup. It also shows a disclosure triangle for processes that have subprocesses.

10 Quit Activity Monitor.

Lesson **30**

System Troubleshooting

As covered by the previous lesson, the OS X system startup routine is often trouble-free and usually completed in under a minute. However, when things do go wrong during system startup, users often fear the worst. Novice users may assume that if their Macs won't start up, they will lose important documents. But the system startup process can fail due to many issues that probably won't result in any user data loss. It's important to properly diagnose startup issues so you can get the Mac up and running, or at least try to recover data.

GOALS

- Learn about the various startup modes used by OS X
- Troubleshoot the processes used at startup and login

This lesson builds on knowledge gained in the previous lesson, but with a specific focus on systemwide and system startup troubleshooting. You will first learn about the various startup shortcuts and diagnostic modes supported by Mac systems and OS X. However, the majority of this lesson focuses on methods that will allow you to effectively troubleshoot system initialization and user session issues.

Reference 30.1
Startup Shortcuts

Your Mac firmware supports many keyboard shortcuts, which, when pressed and held during initial power-on, allow you to modify the startup process. Some of these shortcuts modify the booter selection, while others modify how OS X starts up. These alternate startup and diagnostic modes are often used for troubleshooting system issues.

NOTE ▸ If the Mac has a firmware password set, all startup shortcuts are disabled, save for the Option key (Startup Manager), which prompts for the firmware password. Using a firmware password is covered in Lesson 8, "System Security."

NOTE ► Some hardware does not support startup shortcuts, including some third-party keyboards and keyboards connected via certain USB hubs or a keyboard-video-mouse (KVM) switch. Also, Bluetooth wireless keyboards often do not work either. As such, a Mac administrator should always have a wired USB keyboard and mouse handy for troubleshooting Mac desktop systems.

NOTE ► Startup volumes selected with a shortcut are not saved in NVRAM, so this setting does not persist between system restarts.

Select Alternate Systems

Mac startup shortcuts that allow you to select another system include:

- Option—Starts up into the Startup Manager, which allows you to select any volume containing a valid system to start up from. This includes internal volumes, optical disk volumes, some external volumes, and, on later Macs, Wi-Fi networks and NetBoot images.
- C—Starts up from a bootable CD or DVD in a supported optical disk.
- D—Starts up from the Apple Hardware Test partition on the first restore DVD included with your Intel-based Mac. Later models also include this diagnostic built into the hardware ROM and thus don't require the DVD.
- Command-Option-D—Starts up from the Apple Hardware Test via an Internet connection to the Apple servers. This option is only available to Mac models released after July 19, 2011.
- N—Starts up from the last-used NetBoot server, or the default NetBoot server if none were previously used. The Mac shows a flashing or spinning globe icon in the center of the main display until it locates the NetBoot server, at which point it shows the dark gray Apple logo.
- Option-N—Similar to holding the N key, but this shortcut always starts up from the current default NetBoot server instead of the last-used NetBoot server.
- Command-R—Starts up from the local OS X Recovery, if available. If no local OS X Recovery was found, Mac systems that support OS X Internet Recovery automatically attempt to start up from the Apple recovery servers. Lesson 4, "OS X Recovery," covers this topic in greater detail.
- Command-Option-R—Forces startup to OS X Internet Recovery on supported Mac systems.

Modify OS X Startup

Mac startup shortcuts that modify the OS X default startup:

- Shift—Starts up OS X using Safe Boot, which leaves OS X running in Safe Mode. During Safe Boot, the system clears specific caches, carefully tests startup procedures, and limits automatically launched processes during each stage. While running in Safe Mode, many non-essential system and third-party items are ignored. Details regarding Safe Boot and Safe Mode are covered throughout the troubleshooting sections later in this lesson.
- Command-V—Starts up OS X in Verbose mode. In Verbose mode, the system does not hide the startup progress from you with the light gray screen. Instead, you see a black background with white text showing all details of the startup process.
- Command-S—Starts up OS X in single-user mode. When starting up in single-user mode, the system only starts core kernel and BSD UNIX functionality. You must be familiar with the command-line interface to use single-user mode.

NOTE ▶ Systems with FileVault 2 enabled cannot use OS X diagnostic modes. If you feel the need to access these diagnostic modes you must first disable FileVault 2. For more information see Knowledge Base document, TS4235, "OS X Lion: How to perform a Safe Boot if FileVault 2 is enabled."

Other Startup Utilities

Other useful Mac startup shortcuts:

- T—For Macs with built-in Thunderbolt or FireWire ports, holding this key powers on the Mac in target disk mode, allowing other computers to access your Mac computer's internal drives. Target disk mode details are covered in Lesson 13, "File System Troubleshooting."
- Command-Option-P-R—Resets NVRAM settings and restarts the Mac.
- Eject key, F12 key, mouse or trackpad button—Ejects any removable media, including optical discs.

Reference 30.2
System Initialization Troubleshooting

The most important part of troubleshooting system startup is fully understanding the startup process, as covered in Lesson 29, "Startup, Shutdown, and Sleep Modes." Once you can identify the various stages—and know which processes and files are responsible for each, you are well on your way to diagnosing any startup issue. Case in point, the troubleshooting sections outlined here are organized by each stage of the system initialization process.

Also, throughout the remainder of this section, you will learn how each of the three primary OS X diagnostic startup modes: Verbose mode, Safe mode, and single-user mode, help resolve or identify issues. These three modes are initiated at the firmware stage but affect the remaining system initialization process at each stage. The ramifications of each diagnostic startup mode are covered with each stage throughout this section.

Troubleshooting the Firmware

Issues at the firmware stage are indicated by the inability of your Mac to reach the light gray screen with the dark gray Apple icon. The key to troubleshooting at this point is to determine whether this issue is related to the Mac computer's hardware or system volume.

Serious Hardware Issues

If you don't hear the startup chime or see the power-on light flash, the Mac hardware did not pass the POST. You may also hear a series of diagnostic tones or see a series of power-on flashes. If this is the case, your Mac has a fundamental hardware issue.

You can always check for simple things first. Is the Mac plugged into an electrical outlet? Are the keyboard and mouse working properly? Ultimately, a failure to pass the POST is usually indicative of a serious hardware issue. If this is the case, you'll be best served by taking your Mac to an Apple Store or Apple Authorized Service Provider.

System Volume Issues

If your Mac passes the POST, but you are left with a flashing dark gray question mark folder icon, it means the firmware cannot locate a valid system volume or booter file. The Mac computer's main processor and components are probably working correctly, and you may only have a software issue. Hold down the Option key during startup and use the Startup Manager to locate system volumes.

To troubleshoot system volume issues:

- If the original system volume appears, select it to start up from it. If your Mac starts up from the system on the volume, open the Startup Disk preferences to reset the volume as the startup disk. You can also attempt to define the startup disk when booted from another system volume like an external OS X Recovery disk, as covered in Lesson 4, "OS X Recovery."

- If the original system volume appears, but your Mac still cannot find a valid system or booter, you may need to reinstall OS X on that volume. As always, back up any important data from that volume before you make significant changes.
- If your original system volume does not appear, the issue lies with that storage device. Start up from another system, like an external OS X Recovery disk, and use the storage troubleshooting techniques outlined in Lesson 13, "File System Troubleshooting."

Troubleshooting the Booter

Issues at the booter stage are indicated by a flashing dark gray prohibitory icon—evidence of a failure to load the kernel.

To troubleshoot the booter:

- If you're starting up the Mac from a volume containing a system this Mac has never booted from, the prohibitory icon usually indicates that the version of OS X on the volume is not compatible with your Mac computer's hardware. This is an extremely rare case that usually only occurs when a new Mac is restored using an older system image. The solution as this point is to reinstall OS X, using OS X Recovery, to a version of OS X that is known to support this specific hardware.
- Start up the Mac while holding down the Shift key to initiate a Safe Boot. The booter first attempts to verify and repair the startup volume, indicated by a dark gray progress bar across the bottom of the main display. If repairs are necessary, the Mac automatically restarts before continuing. If this happens, continue to hold down the Shift key. The booter verifies the startup volume again, and if the volume appears to be working properly, the booter attempts to load the kernel and essential KEXTs again. The booter uses the most judicial, and slowest, process to load these items and clears both the KEXT and font caches. If successful, the booter passes off the system to the kernel, which continues to safe-boot.
- If the booter cannot find or load a valid kernel, you may need to reinstall OS X on that volume.

Troubleshooting the Kernel

Issues at the kernel stage are indicated by an inability to reach the login window or automatic login process, as evidence of a failure to load all KEXTs, the core UNIX system, and ultimately the system `launchd` process. If this is the case, your Mac is stuck at the light gray screen with the dark gray spinning gear icon. In these cases, the spinning gear progress indicator may stay visible indefinitely, again signaling a failure to complete the startup process.

To troubleshoot the kernel:

- Start up the Mac while holding down the Shift key to initiate a Safe Boot. In addition to the Safe Boot procedures covered in the "Troubleshooting the Booter" section earlier, this forces the kernel to ignore all third-party KEXTs. If successful, the kernel starts the system launchd process, which continues to safe-boot. Completing the kernel startup stage via a Safe Boot indicates the issue may be a third-party KEXT, and you should start up in Verbose mode to try to identify the problematic KEXT.
- Start up the Mac while holding down Command-V to initiate Verbose mode. The Mac shows you the startup process details as a continuous string of text. If the text stops, the startup process has probably also stopped, and you should examine the end of the text for troubleshooting clues. When you find a suspicious item, move it to a quarantine folder and then restart the Mac without Safe Boot, to see if the problem was resolved. This may be easier said than done, as accessing the Mac computer's disk to locate and remove the item may not be possible if the Mac is crashing during startup. This is an example of where target disk mode really shines. As covered in Lesson 13, "File System Troubleshooting," you can easily modify the contents of a problematic Mac system volume using target disk mode and a second Mac.

  NOTE ▸ If your troublesome Mac successfully starts up in Safe Boot and you're trying to find the issue, do not use Safe Boot and Verbose mode at the same time. If the startup process succeeds, Verbose mode will eventually be replaced by the standard startup interface and you will not have time to identify problematic items.

- If the kernel cannot completely load while safe-booting or you are unable to locate and repair the problematic items, you may need to reinstall OS X on that volume.

Troubleshooting the System launchd

Issues at this stage are indicated by an inability to reach the login screen or log in a user (evidence of a failure by the system launchd process). If the system launchd process is not able to complete the system initialization, the loginwindow process does not start. Your Mac will be either stuck with a black screen or a white screen, depending on how far the system launchd got.

To troubleshoot system launchd issues:

- Start up the Mac while holding down the Shift key to initiate a Safe Boot. In addition to the Safe Boot procedures covered earlier in the "Troubleshooting the Booter" and "Troubleshooting the Kernel" sections of this lesson, this forces the system launchd process to ignore all third-party fonts, launch daemons, and startup items. If successful, the system launchd process starts the loginwindow. At this point the Mac system has fully started up and is now running in Safe Mode. Completing the system initialization process via Safe Boot indicates the issue may be a third-party system initialization item, and you should start up in Verbose mode to try to identify the problematic item.

- Start up the Mac while holding down Command-V to initiate Verbose mode. Again, if the text stops scrolling down the screen, examine the end of the text for troubleshooting clues; if you find a suspicious item, move it to another folder and then restart the Mac normally.
- At this point you may be able to successfully Safe Boot into the Finder. If so, use the Finder interface to quarantine suspicious items.
- While working in Safe Mode, you may also consider removing or renaming system cache and preference files, as they can be corrupted and cause startup issues. Begin by removing /Library/Caches because those files contain easily replaced information. As far as system preferences go, you can remove any setting stored in the /Library/Preferences or /Library/Preferences/SystemConfiguration folders you're comfortable with having to reconfigure. A much safer solution is to simply rename individual system preference files in these folders. Once you have moved or replaced these items, restart the Mac, and the system automatically replaces these items with clean versions.
- If Safe Boot continues to fail or you have located a suspicious system item you need to remove, start up the Mac while holding Command-S to initiate single-user mode. You'll see a minimal command-line interface that allows you to move suspicious files to a quarantine folder. If you want to modify files and folders in single-user mode, you have to prepare the system volume. Start by entering `/sbin/fsck -fy` to verify and repair the startup volume. Repeat this command until you see a message stating that the disk appears to be OK. Only then should you enter `/sbin/mount -uw /` to mount the startup volume as a read-and-write file system. Once you have made your changes, you can exit single-user mode and continue to start up the system by entering the `exit` command, or you can shut down the Mac by entering the `shutdown -h now` command.
- If the system initialization process cannot complete while safe-booting or you are unable to locate and repair the problematic items, you may need to reinstall OS X on that volume.

Reference 30.3
User Session Troubleshooting

If the loginwindow process is not able to initialize the user environment, the user will never be given control of the graphical interface. You may see the user's desktop background picture, but no applications load, including the Dock or the Finder. Or it may appear that the user session starts, but then the login screen reappears.

Safe Mode Login

At this point you should first attempt a Safe Mode login, which is initiated by holding down the Shift key while you click the Log In button at the login screen. You can actually perform a Safe Mode login any time you want to troubleshoot user issues, even if you did not first Safe Boot the system.

With Safe Mode enabled, the loginwindow process does not automatically open any user-defined login items or applications set to resume. Further, the user's launchd process does not start any user-specific LaunchAgents. Obviously, if a Safe Mode login resolves your user session issue, you need to adjust the user's Login Items list from the Users & Groups preferences or any items in the /Library/LaunchAgents or ~/Library/LaunchAgents folders.

If a Safe Mode login doesn't resolve your user session issue, there are other troubleshooting sections in this guide to which you should refer. Primarily, you should follow the troubleshooting steps outlined in Lesson 6, "User Accounts."

Troubleshoot Logout and Shutdown

An inability to log out or shut down is almost always the result of an application or process that refuses to quit. If you're unable to log out, as long as you still maintain control of the graphical interface, you can attempt to forcibly quit stubborn processes using the techniques outlined in Lesson 21, "Application Management and Troubleshooting."

You may find that the loginwindow process has closed your user session but the Mac refuses to shut down. This is indicated by a small spinning gear icon on top of your desktop background or a white screen after all your applications have quit. You should let the system attempt to shut down naturally, but if it takes longer than a few minutes, it means a system process is refusing to quit. You can force your Mac to shut down by holding down the power-on button until the Mac powers off, as indicated by a blank display.

> **NOTE ▸** When you restart the Mac, the firmware does not perform a full POST during the subsequent startup process. Thus, if you're troubleshooting hardware issues, you should always shut down and then start up, never restart.

Exercise 30.1
Use Single-User Mode

> **▶ Prerequisites**
>
> ▸ Your computer must not be encrypted with FileVault 2.

When troubleshooting OS X startup issues that seem to be software-related, you might need to troubleshoot with the operating system started up in single-user mode. Single-user mode is a very primitive state of the operating system. The operating system has loaded only enough services to allow you to interact with it from the command line. It hasn't even mounted the startup disk read/write yet. Single-user mode is a low-level maintenance mode that allows you to bring the system up, look at log files, edit or replace configuration files, and so on. In this exercise, you will start up your computer into single-user mode, then proceed to the user interface and identify various files used during startup.

Use Single-User Mode

In this exercise, you will enter single-user mode, then continue starting up the computer to the login window.

1. Shut down your computer.

2. Start your computer in single-user mode by pressing the power button and then holding down Command-S until you see text appear on the screen.

   Single-user mode looks a lot like verbose mode, except that it never starts the graphical user interface; instead, it gives you a full-screen command-line interface.

   When your computer finishes starting up into single-user mode, OS X displays instructions on how to remount the startup disk read/write and how to continue the startup process to multiuser mode, the usual run mode of OS X or any other UNIX system.

   ```
   Singleuser boot -- fsck not done
   Root device is mounted read-only
   If you want to make modifications to files:
       /sbin/fsck -fy
       /sbin/mount -uw /
   If you wish to boot the system:
       exit
   :/ root#
   ```

   The last line is a prompt for you to enter a command. Note that the user name in the prompt is "root" and the prompt ends with a # instead of the usual $. This tells you that you are logged in as the super user (root, or System Administrator). You have unrestricted access to the startup volume and the rest of the system.

3. To force a check of the file system's integrity, type in the command "`/sbin/fsck -fy`" and press Return.

The computer runs a file system consistency check, correcting any errors that it finds and is able to repair. This is essentially the same as doing a Repair Disk in Disk Utility. On today's large disks, this can take awhile, especially if there are many files and folders in the file system. This is one of the advantages of file-system journaling. Most of the time, a complete fsck does not need to occur, so startup is much faster.

If fsck displays "The volume Macintosh HD appears to be OK", you may proceed to the next step. If its final message is "The filesystem was modified," it found and fixed at least one issue, and you should re-run it to make sure there are no additional issues.

4 To remount the startup disk with write access enabled, type "**/sbin/mount -uw /**" and press Return.

   You are given a new prompt a few seconds later. This command enables you to make changes to the disk.

   This command should not generate any output if all runs correctly. If it generates an alert, double-check your typing. The most common errors with this command are to leave off the trailing /, or to not have spaces where they are needed.

5 Test network connectivity from your computer to itself with the command "**ping -c2 127.0.0.1**". Here, the -c2 means to try twice, and 127.0.0.1 is the address reserved for each computer to talk to itself with. The results look something like this:

```
PING 127.0.0.1 (127.0.0.1): 56 data bytes
ping: sendto: No route to host
ping: sendto: No route to host
Request timeout for icmp_seq 0
Request timeout for icmp_seq 1

--- 127.0.0.1 ping statistics ---
2 packets transmitted, 0 packets received, 100.0% packet loss
```

   Your computer cannot even reach itself via the network because networking has not been started.

   NOTE ▶ If you left off the -c2 option to the ping command, you can tell it to stop pinging by pressing Control-C.

6 Get a process listing with the command "**ps -ax**".

   You see a much shorter list than you previously saw in Activity Monitor. At process ID 1, you see launchd. Process ID 2 is launchctl, which launchd uses in this case to manage the startup process. Process ID 3 is the command shell with which you are interacting. The last process is your ps command. The OS is in a very minimal state.

7 Examine the system log file with the command "less +G /var/log/system.log".

The +G option to less tells it to start at the end of the file (that is, show the most recent log events). Usually, when you need to examine logs in single-user mode, it is because you want to find out what happened just before the system crashed, so starting at the end is more convenient than starting at the beginning. You can scan through the log by pressing "b" to move backward in the file, and pressing the spacebar to move forward.

8 When you are through examining the log, press "q" to exit.

Create a New Administrator Account

If you lose the password to your administrator account, you now know several ways to reset its password; but if the account becomes completely unusable, this will not allow you to regain control of the computer. In this section, you will see how to use single-user mode to create a new administrator account.

1 Move to the /var/db folder with the command "cd /var/db".

Your prompt changes to ":db root#", indicating that you are now in a folder named "db." If it does not match this, the command did not work right and you must try again before proceeding. This section of the exercise involves deleting files, and since you are running as the root user, you are capable of deleting anything (or everything). It is important to be careful when you are running commands as the root user.

2 Start typing the command "rm .AppleSetup" (be sure to capitalize the "A" and "S"), and then press Tab.

If you typed it correctly, it autocompletes to "rm .AppleSetupDone ". If pressing Tab does not make it autocomplete, you have not typed the command correctly and must correct it and try again. Note that you cannot use the mouse to select text to change, although you can use the Left and Right arrow keys to move backward and forward on the command line.

If you cannot get the command to autocomplete, something is still wrong and you should not proceed with the exercise. You can always press Control-C, and then use the command "exit" to exit single-user mode.

The /var/db/.AppleSetupDone file is a placeholder file, which indicates that the Setup Assistant has run on this computer; deleting it makes the computer rerun the Setup Assistant the next time it starts up.

3 If the command autocompleted correctly, press Return to run it.

4 If you see a message starting with "override", type "y" and press Return.

5 If you see the message "rm: .AppleSetupDone: Read-only file system", the mount command in step 4 of the previous exercise did not work; reenter that command, and then try again from step 2 of this section.

6 If the rm command does not display an error, exit single-user mode with the command "exit".

The computer exits single-user mode and continues starting the operating system. With the .AppleSetupDone file gone, it runs the Setup Assistant again just as though this were a new computer.

7 Step through the Setup Assistant screens (see Exercise 3.1 for detailed instructions). When you reach the "Create Your Computer Account" screen, enter the following information:

Full Name: **New Admin**

Account Name: **newadmin**

If you are performing this exercise in a class, enter **newadminpw** in the Password and Verify fields. If you are performing this exercise on your own, you should select a more secure password for the New Admin account.

After you finish the Setup Assistant, you are automatically logged into the New Admin account.

8 Open System Preferences and select the Users & Groups preference pane.

All of your old accounts are still there; New Admin has simply been added to them.

9 Quit System Preferences.

Index

C

O

S

T

X

Y

Z

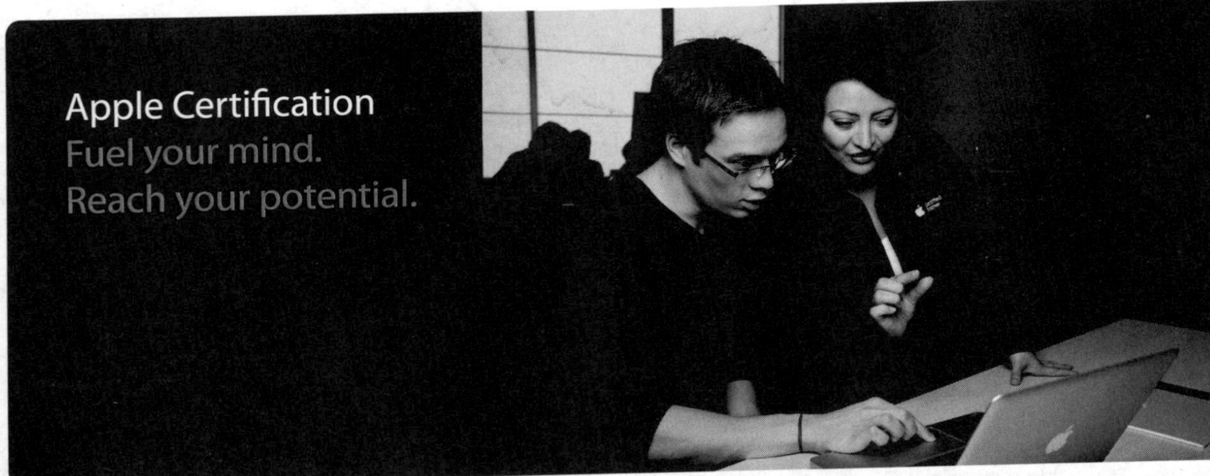

Stand out from the crowd. Differentiate yourself and gain recognition for your expertise by earning Apple Certified Pro status to validate your OS X skills.

This book prepares you to pass the OS X Support Essentials 10.8 Exam and earn Apple Certified Support Professional (ACSP) status. The exam is available at Apple Authorized Training Centers (AATCs) worldwide. ACSP certification is designed for the help desk professional, technical coordinator or power-user who supports OS X users, manages networks, or provides technical support.

Three Steps to Certification

1 Choose your certification path.
More info: training.apple.com/certification.

2 All Apple Authorized Training Centers (AATCs) offer all OS X and Pro Apps exams, even if they don't offer the corresponding course. To find the closest AATC, please visit training.apple.com/locations.

3 Register for and take your exam(s).

"Apple certification places you in a unique class of professionals. It not only shows that you care enough about what you do to go the extra mile to get certified, it also demonstrates that you really know your stuff."

— Brian Sheehan, Multimedia Studio Manager, MFS Investment Management

Reasons to Become an Apple Certified Pro

- Raise your earning potential. Studies show that certified professionals can earn more than their non-certified peers.
- Distinguish yourself from others in your industry. Proven mastery of an application helps you stand out from the crowd.
- **Display your Apple Certification logo.** Each certification provides a logo to display on business cards, resumes and websites.
- **Publicize your Certifications.** Publish your certifications on the Apple Certified Professionals Registry (apple.com//certification/verify) to connect with schools, clients and employers.

Training Options

Apple's comprehensive curriculum addresses your needs, whether you're an IT or creative professional, educator, or student. Hands-on training is available through a worldwide network of Apple Authorized Training Centers (AATCs). Self-paced study is available through the Apple Pro Training Series books, which are also accessible as eBooks via the iBooks app. Video training and video training apps are also available for select titles. Visit training.apple.com to view all your learning options.

Copyright © 2012 Apple Inc. All rights reserve

training.apple.com/certification

The Apple Pro Training Series

Apple offers comprehensive certification programs for creative and IT professionals. The Apple Pro Training Series is the official training curriculum of the Apple Training and Certification program, used by Apple Authorized Training Centers around the world

To find an Authorized Training Center near you, visit: **www.apple.com/software/pro/training**

Apple Pro Training Series: Final Cut Pro X
0321774671 • $54.99
Diana Weynand

Apple Pro Video Series: Final Cut Pro X
0321809629 • $59.99
Steve Martin

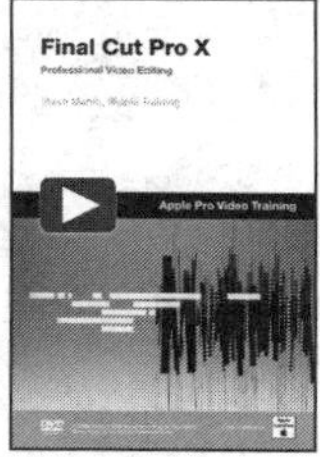

Apple Pro Video Series: Final Cut Pro X (Streaming Only)
0132876302 • $39.99
Steve Martin

Apple Pro Training Series: Final Cut Pro X Quick-Reference Guide (E-book Only)
0132876345 • $19.99
Brendan Boykin

Apple Pro Training Series: Final Cut Pro X Advanced Editing
0321810228 • $59.99
Michael Wohl

Apple Pro Training Series: Motion 5
032177468X • $54.99
Mark Spencer

Apple Pro Training Series: Aperture 3, Second Edition
0321898648 • $54.99
Dion Scoppettuolo

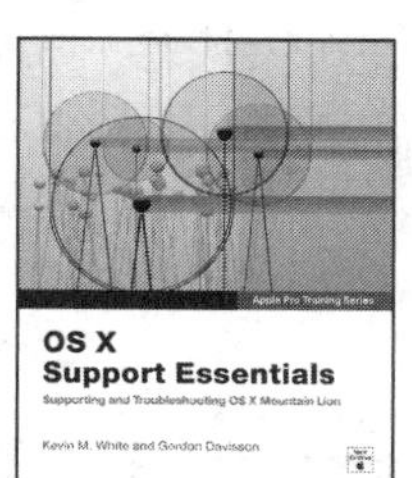

Apple Pro Training Series: OS X Support Essentials
0321887190 • $64.99
Kevin M White,
Gordon Davisson

Apple Pro Training Series: OS X Server Essentials
0321887336 • $69.99
Arek Dreyer, Ben Greisler

Apple Training Series: iLife '11
032170097X • $39.99
Scoppettuolo / Plummer

Apple Training Series: iWork 09
0321618513 • $39.99
Richard Harrington

To see a complete range of Apple Pro Training Series books, videos and apps visit:
www.peachpit.com/appleprotraining

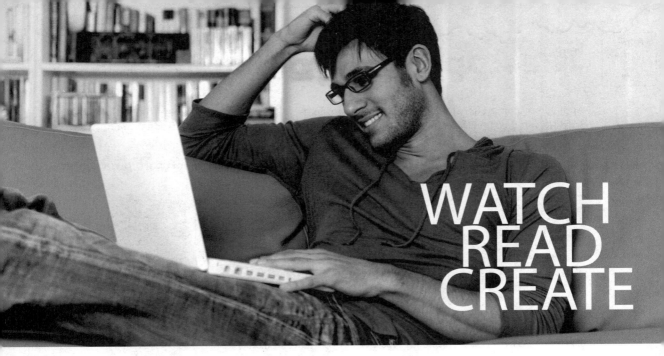

WATCH
READ
CREATE

Meet Creative Edge.

A new resource of unlimited books, videos and tutorials for creatives from the world's leading experts.

Creative Edge is your one stop for inspiration, answers to technical questions and ways to stay at the top of your game so you can focus on what you do best—being creative.

All for only $24.99 per month for access—any day any time you need it.

creativeedge.com